The Annihilation of Hell

Universal Salvation and the Redemption of Time
in the Eschatology of Jürgen Moltmann

The Annihilation of Hell

Universal Salvation and the Redemption of Time in the Eschatology of Jürgen Moltmann

Nicholas Ansell

Foreword by Jürgen Moltmann

CASCADE *Books* • Eugene, Oregon

THE ANNIHILATION OF HELL
Universal Salvation and the Redemption of Time in the Eschatology of Jürgen Moltmann

Copyright © 2013 Nicholas Ansell. All rights reserved. Except for brief quotations in critical publications or reviews, no part of this book may be reproduced in any manner without prior written permission from the publisher. Write: Permissions, Wipf and Stock Publishers, 199 W. 8th Ave., Suite 3, Eugene, OR 97401.

First published in Great Britain in 2013 by Paternoster, 52 Presley Way, Crownhill MK8 0ES. First US edition published by Pickwick Publications under license from Paternoster, 2013.

Cascade Books
An imprint of Wipf and Stock Publishers
199 W. 8th Ave., Suite 3
Eugene, OR 97401

www.wipfandstock.com

ISBN 13: 978-1-62564-357-5

Cataloging-in-Publication data:

Ansell, Nicholas John, 1961–

The annihilation of hell : universal salvation and the redemption of time in the eschatology of Jürgen Moltmann / Nicholas Ansell, with a foreword by Jürgen Moltmann.

xliv + 170 p. ; 23 cm. Includes bibliographical references and index.

ISBN 13: 978-1-62564-357-5

1. Moltmann, Jürgen. 2. Universalism. 3. Hell—Christianity. I. Moltmann, Jürgen. II. Title.

BX4827.M6 A57 2013

Manufactured in the U.S.A.
Typeset by the author

*To David Christopher Ansell and Molly Isobel Ansell,
to Mum and Dad, with love and gratitude*

Contents

Foreword by Jürgen Moltmann	xiii
Preface and Acknowledgements	xv
Abbreviations	xvii

Introduction Inferno e Speranza — 1
0.1 Hope and Hell — 1
0.2 Eschatology — 2
0.3 Hell's Annihilation — 4
0.4 Synopsis — 5
0.5 Contexts and Traditions — 7
0.6 Contradictory/Harmony Monism — 8
0.7 Dialogue — 12
0.8 Some Points of Style — 14
0.9 Hell and Hope — 15

Chapter 1 To Hell and Back — 17
1.1 Until Justice and Mercy Embrace? — 17
1.2 The Annihilation of Hell/The Hell of Annihilation — 21
1.3 The Hell of Freedom — 26
1.4 The Passing of Hell in *The Coming of God* — 34
   1.4.1 The Theology of the Cross — 35
   1.4.2 Freedom — 40
   1.4.3 Justice — 43
   1.4.4 God — 45
   1.4.5 Scripture — 45
1.5 Universalism and Its Critics — 48
1.6 *St Peter's Apocalypse* Revisited — 50

Chapter 2 The Reversal of Time in the Future of God — 54
2.1 The Two Angels of Time — 55
2.2 Augustine as a Point of Departure — 59

2.3 Reversals: Ontic and Epistemological	65
2.4 *Futurum* and *Adventus*	73
2.5 Temporal Diversity and Unity	84
2.6 Time and Eternity; Nature and Grace	96

Chapter 3 The Redemption of Time in the Presence of God — 100
3.1 The Redemption of Time: Fulfilment and Negation	100
3.2 Transience	104
3.3 The Past	110
3.4 Death	120
3.5 Redeemed Time	128
3.5.1 Cyclical Time	130
3.5.2 Presence and the Present (Moment)	133
3.5.3 Eucharist, Sabbath, and the Moment	137
3.6 The Final Coincidence of Opposites	140

Chapter 4 The Triumph of Glory — 145
4.1 (Re-)Placing Hell	146
4.2 Nature, Grace, and Glory	153
4.3 Possible Objections, Possible Answers	172
4.3.1 Universalism of the Cross	180
4.3.2 God's Nature; God's Will	190
4.3.3 The Nature/Promise of Freedom	194
4.4 A Preliminary Response	206

Chapter 5 Between Creation and Eschaton: The Foundational and Transcendental Directions of Time — 210
5.1 Futurity in Bloch, Heidegger, and Beyond	213
5.2 Foundational and Transcendental Time in the Philosophy of Hendrik Hart	228
5.2.1 Modes of Being/Time	231
5.2.2 Founding, Qualifying, Guiding: Past, Present, Future	236
5.2.3 Expression and Reference: Immanence and Transcendence	238
5.2.4 Creation and Eschaton	241
5.2.5 Differentiation and Integration	242
5.3 Comparison with Moltmann	244
5.4 Panentheism?	256

Chapter 6 The Nature of Grace   262
6.1 Creational Grace   263
   6.1.1 *Heaven and Earth: The Covenantal Dynamics of Existence* 268
6.2 The Barth-Brunner Debate   272
6.3 Creational Grace in Moltmann?   282
6.4 Eschatological Grace   293
6.5 God in History?   301
6.6 The Gift of Transience   311

Chapter 7 Doing Justice (According) to Scripture   315
7.1 A Biblical Foundation?   316
7.2 Doing Justice to the Final Judgment   340
7.3 Justice and Mercy: Face to Face   353

Conclusion Grace and *Spes*   360
8.1 A Biblical Universalism?   360
8.2 Final Justice, Final Judgment   362
8.3 From Autonomy to Freedom   368
8.4 *Spes* (within the Economy of Grace)   384

Appendix Birthpangs of the New Creation   391
9.1 Babylon   395
9.2 Birthing   402
9.3 Judgment and Vindication   411
9.4 Fire and Brimstone   414
9.5 Judgment unto Salvation   416

Summary   424

Bibliography   429

Author Index   465

Foreword

A foreword is not an afterword and also not a critical review. A foreword should open the door and point out the worth of a book so that it can be properly read and discussed. Nicholas Ansell's book on *The Annihilation of Hell* and *Universal Salvation* is so far-reaching and profound a theological and philosophical work that a brief foreword really can't do it justice. I'll limit myself here to some biographical references, a few factual observations, and then an attempt to bring the theology of grace and the theology of faith into a theological dialogue.

Any theology of grace will be oriented for God's sake to the universal triumph of grace. Any theology of faith, however, will start from the human decision of faith and will result in the separation of believers from unbelievers. The universalism of salvation, on the one hand, and the particularism of faith and lack of faith, on the other hand, are on two different levels. What is important is to closely connect them.

Since my theology studies in Göttingen, where I wrote my dissertation in 1952 on the "hypothetical universalism" of the Calvinist theologian Moyse Amyraut, who taught at the theological Academy of Saumur in the 17th century, the idea of universalism has not let go of me. Amyraut's idea, that the universal offer of grace is merely hypothetical until faith grasps it, I considered inadequate. Then I read Karl Barth's new doctrine of election which appeared in his *Church Dogmatics* 2/2 and became convinced by his theology of the cross: On the cross of Christ, God took the guilt of sinners upon himself in order to give them his gift of grace. I continued to think through this dialectical universalism of salvation and found in Christ's resurrection from the dead the beginning of the destruction of death and thereby "the annihilation of Hell." Many Easter hymns in the German Lutheran hymnal celebrate the "destruction of Hell" by means of Christ's descent into Hell and resurrection from Hell. In the Orthodox Easter liturgy, the destruction of Hell through Christ is also celebrated. Those who descend into Hell should "abandon all hope" according to Dante. But the Christ who descended into Hell is the "hope of the hopeless" (*spes desperatis*).

I then took up an old desire of Karl Barth and Helmut Gollwitzer, namely to reform the doctrine of the Last Judgment from the perspective of the crucified one who will come to judge the living and the dead. Here I had the Old Testament notion of "divine judging" for help. According to Psalm 96, God will come to judge the earth, and the earth will rejoice and the fields will make merry. In this instance, "judge" means raise up, set straight, heal, and bring to life. How could it be otherwise in the Christian anticipation of God's Final Judgment and coming kingdom! In fact the so-called "Final Judgment" is penultimate; what is truly final is the new, eternal creation in which God becomes "all in all" (1 Cor 15:28).

At this point another thought came to me: With the forgiveness of sins and the overcoming of death, God is concerned primarily with the expulsion of the godless powers of evil, of sin, of death, and of Hell from his beloved creation. Isn't our question as to whether all or only a few will be saved not an anthropocentric and in many cases even a selfish one? For God, it is about God's glorification of all of his creatures. The salvation of the new humanity is only a part of this. If we look to the glory of God, then the universalism and particularism of human salvation are relativised. The "annihilation of Hell" is an action of the cosmic Christ, whose reign is universal. "Universal salvation" is only the human part of the "salvation of the universe."

I must stop here, since I'm only writing a foreword. But you can see how stimulating this study by Nicholas Ansell has been for me. I hope the same holds true for his other readers. There is much to be gained by considering this work and then thinking further on one's own.

Jürgen Moltmann
Tübingen
January 10, 2009

Preface and Acknowledgements

It would, no doubt, be tiring to count the number of times scholars have found themselves quoting Ecclesiastes 12:12: "there is no end to the writing of books" (REB). Ironically enough, no sooner had I penned these words, than I found myself researching how this passage has been largely misinterpreted! Be that as it may, this book on eschatology is finally making its appearance. At long last! It is my pleasure to thank the many people who have supported and thus contributed to its arrival.

As this monograph began as a doctoral thesis defended at the *Vrije Universiteit*, Amsterdam on November 16th, 2005, I will say a little about the revision process. But first, let me start by expressing my gratitude to my supervisors (or *promotoren* as they are known at the VU), prof. dr. H.G. Geertsema and prof. dr. J.H. Olthuis, who, together with copromotor prof. dr. A. van Egmond, all deserve special thanks. Henk's careful attention to the various drafts of the dissertation certainly helped improve it. For his hard work and high standards, I am very grateful. Jim, who was also my mentor during my doctoral (and MPhil) studies at the Institute for Christian Studies in Toronto, has had a profound influence on my thinking, not least through always encouraging me to go my own way. I am very fortunate to have been his student for so many years. I also appreciate Aad van Egmond's input, especially on the penultimate draft of the dissertation version. Special thanks also to the other members of my examining committee for their engagement with this work in its earlier form: prof. dr. Trevor Hart of the University of St. Andrews in Scotland, and prof. dr. Martinus de Boer, prof. dr. Jakob Klapwijk, prof. dr. Kees van der Kooi, and prof. dr. Hendrik Vroom, all of the VU.

It is a particular pleasure to be able to thank Prof. Jürgen Moltmann for the profoundly stimulating nature of his theology and for the privilege of meeting with him in London in 1998 and 2000. The interest that he has shown in this project, including recommending the Paternoster Theological Monographs series to me and writing the foreword, has been humbling and inspiring. It is more than a few years now since the doctoral defence of 2005. But as time passes, my appreciation for his theological insight, sensitivity, and sense of adventure expands and deepens.

Work on the dissertation version began in the UK, while I taught at the University of Bristol, and was finished in Edmonton, Canada, where I spent three happy years at The King's University College. Revisions to the manuscript for this version took place in Toronto, since my return to ICS. The librarians at all three institutions were most helpful. My thanks also goes to

Arlette Zinck, the queen of grammar, and to William Drischler, Carsen Hennings, Hanna Kent, Judith Schulz-Wackerbarth, and Yorick Schulz-Wackerbarth, all of whom have been generous with their command of German. For the many (enjoyable) hours spent penciling in changes to the dissertation version, and talking about the various areas of theology I was attempting to probe, my thanks goes to my ICS Research Assistant, and friend, Jon Stanley. Thanks again to Yvonne Koo, who did the book design for the dissertation version and revised the diagrams at the end of chaps. 3 and 4 for this one. My appreciation too goes to Robin Parry, now at Wipf and Stock, for welcoming this into the PTM series and to Mike Parsons, at Paternoster, for being such a patient and eagle-eyed editor. Any faults that are in the following pages are my own. But for the rest, I could not have produced this without help.

In its present form, this monograph still bears the imprint of the time it was initially written, from just before until a few years after 2000. With the exception of the Appendix, revisions to the main text have almost all been for the sake of improved readability, with updating and new material largely confined to the footnotes. Several pieces I have published elsewhere have been drawn from this manuscript-in-process to find their way back to it in modified form. Special thanks to *Third Way*, the UK Christian social and cultural affairs magazine that deserves an international readership, for allowing me to draw on a different manuscript to write several pieces on the book of Revelation.

The thinking in the following chapters is largely the fruit of many formative years as a student at ICS from 1986–93, a time I consider one of its heydays. Henk Hart has been profoundly influential on far more than chap. 5. I also appreciate the opportunity I had to read *God in Creation* with Brian Walsh and Richard Middleton. I still value the early encouragement from Bill Rowe and the chance to learn from Tom Wright several years before *NTPG*. This was also a time for friendships with many, including Dave Collins and Jeff Dudiak. Further back, and in the UK, I must mention the inspiration of Richard Russell and Mark Roques, and the enthusiasm for Moltmann expressed by Graham Cray at a Greenbelt festival seminar around 1980.

My life and faith have been sustained by family, friends, films, music, and coffee. I am grateful for work done in the Retro café in Bath, England and, more recently, at the Voulez-Vous on Queen Street in Toronto. Friends I have yet to mention must include Rick (Rik), Annette, and Ian. Thanks are not enough for the friend who knows what LOL really means! My son Daniel, now a student of politics and linguistics at U of T, is great company and always knows the best films. Finally, I dedicate this book to my parents.

I know full well that this project on eschatology has often made me too busy. But I now look forward to the future! *Im Ende—der Anfang!*

Nik Ansell
Toronto
June 22, 2013

Abbreviations

The following abbreviations are used for the works of Jürgen Moltmann that are frequently cited in this study.

BP   *A Broad Place: An Autobiography*. Translated by Margaret Kohl. Minneapolis, MN: Fortress Press, 2008.
CoG   *The Coming of God: Christian Eschatology*. Translated by Margaret Kohl. London: SCM Press, 1996.
CPS   *The Church in the Power of the Spirit: A Contribution to Messianic Ecclesiology*. Translated by Margaret Kohl. London: SCM Press, 1977.
CrG   *The Crucified God: The Cross of Christ as the Foundation and Criticism of Christian Theology*. Translated by R.A. Wilson and John Bowden. London: SCM Press, 1974.
DgG   *Der gekreuzigte Gott: Das Kreuz Christi als Grund und Kritik christlicher Theologie*. Munich: Chr. Kaiser Verlag, 1972.
DGL   *Der Geist des Lebens: Eine ganzheitliche Pneumatologie*. Munich: Chr. Kaiser Verlag, 1991.
DKG   *Das Kommen Gottes: Christliche Eschatologie*. Gütersloh: Chr. Kaiser Verlagshaus, 1995.
DWJC   *Der Weg Jesu Christi: Christologie in messianischen Dimensionen*. Munich: Chr. Kaiser Verlag, 1989.
EiT   *Experiences in Theology: Ways and Forms of Christian Theology*. Translated by Margaret Kohl. London: SCM Press, 2000.
EoH   *Ethics of Hope*. Translated by Margaret Kohl. Minneapolis, MN: Fortress Press, 2012.
EtD   *Erfahrungen theologischen Denkens: Wege und Formen christlicher Theologie*. Gütersloh: Chr. Kaiser Verlag/Gütersloher Verlaghaus, 2000.
FC   *The Future of Creation*. Translated by Margaret Kohl. London: SCM Press, 1979.
GC   *God in Creation: An Ecological Doctrine of Creation*. Translated by Margaret Kohl. London: SCM Press, 1985.
GS   *Gott in der Schöpfung: Ökologische Schöpfungslehre*. Munich: Chr. Kaiser Verlag, 1985.
HTG   *History and the Triune God*. Translated by John Bowden. London: SCM Press, 1991.

HP	*Hope and Planning*. Translated by Margaret Clarkson. London: SCM Press, 1971.
IEB	*In the End—the Beginning: The Life of Hope*. Translated by Margaret Kohl. Minneapolis, MN: Fortress Press, 2004.
IGG	*In der Geschichte des dreieinigen Gottes: Beiträge zur trinitarischen Theologie*. Munich: Chr. Kaiser Verlag, 1991.
KKG	*Kirche in der Kraft des Geistes: Ein Beitrag zur messianischen Ekklesiologie*. Munich: Chr. Kaiser Verlag, 1975.
RRF	*Religion, Revolution, and the Future*. Translated by M. Douglas Meeks. New York: Charles Scribner's Sons, 1969.
SL	*The Spirit of Life: A Universal Affirmation*. Translated by Margaret Kohl. London: SCM Press, 1992.
SRA	*Sun of Righteousness, Arise! God's Future for Humanity and the Earth*. Translated by Margaret Kohl. Minneapolis, MN: Fortress Press, 2010.
SW	*Science and Wisdom*. Translated by Margaret Kohl. Minneapolis, MN: Fortress Press, 2003.
TdH	*Theologie der Hoffnung: Untersuchungen zur Begründung und zu den Konsequenzen einer christlichen Eschatologie*. 8th ed. Munich: Chr. Kaiser Verlag, 1969.
TH	*Theology of Hope: On the Ground and the Implications of a Christian Eschatology*. Translated by James Leitch. London: SCM Press, 1967.
TKG	*The Trinity and the Kingdom of God: The Doctrine of God*. Translated by Margaret Kohl. London: SCM Press, 1980.
TRG	*Trinität und Reich Gottes: Zur Gotteslehre*. Munich: Chr. Kaiser Verlag, 1980.
WJC	*The Way of Jesus Christ: Christology in Messianic Dimensions*. Translated by Margaret Kohl. London: SCM Press, 1990.

INTRODUCTION

Inferno e Speranza

Per lor maladizion sì non sì perde,
che non possa tornar, l'etterno amore,
mentre che las speranza has fior del verde.
   Purgatorio, canto 3, lines 133–35

LASCIATE OGNE SPERANZA, VOI CH'INTRATE.
   Inferno, canto 3, line 9[1]

0.1 Hope and Hell

" 'Abandon hope, all ye who enter here'."[2] The presence of these (in)famous words, from the inscription above the entrance to Dante's *Inferno*, in the Introduction to Jürgen Moltmann's *Theologie der Hoffnung* marks a fundamental tension between Hope and Hell, the resolution of which might be said to characterise Moltmann's entire theology.

Descriptively speaking, for Moltmann, Dante is correct: "Hell is hopelessness."[3] We may well reject infernal " 'fairy tales with which one can horrify children'," he was to write a few years later. " 'This hell, with which the

---

[1] The chapter title, which is Italian for 'Hell and Hope', also alludes to esperanza, the Spanish word for hope and expectation. For Dante's Italian text with the following English translation, see *The Divine Comedy of Dante Alighieri: Purgatorio*, trans. Allen Mandelbaum (Berkeley: University of California Press, 1982), 26–27 and *The Divine Comedy of Dante Alighieri: Inferno*, trans. Allen Mandelbaum (Berkeley: University of California Press, 1981), 20–21. Mandelbaum translates as follows:
   Despite the Church's curse, there is no one
   so lost that the eternal love cannot
   return—as long as hope shows something green.

   ABANDON EVERY HOPE, WHO ENTER HERE.
[2] Jürgen Moltmann, *Theology of Hope: On the Ground and the Implications of a Christian Eschatology*, trans. James Leitch (London: SCM Press, 1967), 32, citing *Inferno*, canto 3, line 9. Citations from *Theology of Hope*, hereafter TH, will refer to the pagination of the widely available edition of 1967 and not the (repaginated) SCM Press edition of 2002.
[3] TH, 32. This statement occurs in the same sentence as the Dante quotation.

church makes threats, does not exist'." Yet there are other hells, real hells, and "[w]e know that the history in which we are involved bears out this inscription in manifold ways and places."[4]

But if Hell is the "[a]bandon[ing] [of] hope," "hope," writes Moltmann in the next paragraph, "abandon[s] nothing to annihilation." Hope therefore actively contradicts the way things are.[5] Although Dante's *Inferno* is *closed*,[6] Moltmann insists that the Hell we experience in this world—the Hell that Dante may help us describe—must be "loyally embrace[d] ... in love" by an eschatological hope that "bring[s] to light how *open* all things are to the possibilities in which they *can live* and *shall live*."[7] The difference between Hope and Hell is thus the difference between the future and the present,[8] Life and Death—an opposition that hope looks to be resolved in a "future outlook that embraces all things, even death."[9] This all-embracing, life-anticipating outlook is what Moltmann calls "eschatology."

0.2 Eschatology

Die Eschatologie was a term coined in German in the early 1800s, to appear in English by the middle of the century. In a work published in 1980—the year in which Ronald Reagan and his Republican vice-president came to power across the Atlantic—the British New Testament scholar George Caird was quick to note that *The Oxford English Dictionary* attributed the first written use of "eschatology," in 1845, to an American named "G. Bush." Although the meaning of the term has since been contested, the initial way in which it was understood is still very much alive. As Caird notes,

> In all English dictionaries of the nineteenth century [eschatology] had the clearly defined sense which is still the only one recognised in the *OED* (1891 and

---

[4] Jürgen Moltmann, "Descent into Hell," trans. M. Douglas Meeks, *Duke Divinity School Review* 33, no. 2 (Spring 1968): 115–19. Quotation from p. 115. See also n. 18 below. This rejection of Hell as an instrument of fear (to be distinguished from the hells of history to which he refers) is attributed by Moltmann to the typical 'enlightened' churchgoer (of the late 1960s). But Moltmann seems to concur. Certainly he does not object to this rejection of this kind of Hell.

[5] As Moltmann puts it in TH, 18, "Present and future, experience and hope, stand in contradiction to each other in Christian eschatology, with the result that man is not brought into harmony and agreement with the given situation, but is drawn into the conflict between hope and experience."

[6] On the open nature of the *Purgatorio* in contrast to the *Inferno* without hope and the *Paradiso* without desire, see Jürgen Moltmann, *The Coming of God: Christian Eschatology*, trans. Margaret Kohl (London: SCM Press, 1996), 98. Hereafter CoG.

[7] TH, 32. My emphases.

[8] See n. 5 above. Here the future is open in nature while the present is viewed as being on the way to the closure that is associated with the past. This anticipates the analysis of time offered in chapters 2 and 3 below.

[9] TH, 33.

1933): 'the department of theological science concerned with the four last things, death, judgment, heaven, and hell'.[10]

Moltmann refers to this definition in the opening sentence of his *Theology of Hope* in order to argue that what has become a "loosely attached appendix"[11] should be reconceived as the very 'heart', and thus 'heartbeat', of Christian theology. Echoing the words of Karl Barth—"A Christianity that is not wholly and utterly and irreducibly eschatology has absolutely nothing to do with Christ"[12]—Moltmann writes,

> From first to last, and not merely in the epilogue, Christianity is eschatology, is hope, forward looking and forward moving, and therefore also revolutionizing and transforming the present. The eschatological is not one element *of* Christianity, but it is the medium of Christian faith as such, the key in which everything is set, the glow that suffuses everything here in the dawn of an expected new day.[13]

Traditional "eschatology" (narrowly conceived) had become "barren" and "irrelevan[t]," bearing "no relation to the doctrines of cross and resurrection."[14] But in truth,

> Eschatology is the passionate suffering and passionate longing kindled by the Messiah. Hence eschatology cannot really be only a part of Christian doctrine. Rather, the eschatological outlook is characteristic of all Christian proclamation, of every Christian existence and of the whole Church.[15]

Despite—or because of—this reconception of the heart of theology, Moltmann does not engage in a sustained "eschatological" discussion of the last

---

[10] G.B. Caird, *The Language and Imagery of the Bible*, with a New Introduction by N.T. Wright (1980; repr., Grand Rapids, MI: Eerdmans, 1997), 243. Cf. George Bush, *Anastasis: Or, the Doctrine of the Resurrection of the Body, Rationally and Scripturally Considered* (New York: Wiley and Putnam, 1845), iii, where he refers to "the great scheme of Scriptural Eschatology, or *the doctrine of the last things*." His emphasis. Prior to references to "die Eschatolgie" in German, Abraham Calov used the term "eschatologia" in the same vein to organise the final section of his 12 vol., 1655–77, work, *Systema Locorum Theologicorum*, as noted in Gerhard Sauter, "The Concept and Task of Eschatology—Theological and Philosophical Reflections," *Scottish Journal of Theology* 41, no. 4 (1988): 499–515.
[11] TH, 15. Cf. the first sentence of the preface to CoG, x.
[12] Karl Barth, *Church Dogmatics* 2/1, trans. G.W. Bromiley and T.F. Torrance (Edinburgh: T. and T. Clark, 1957), 634, where Barth is citing the second edition of his own *Der Römerbrief* (1922). Edwyn C. Hoskyns' translation in *The Epistle to the Romans* (London: Oxford University Press, 1933), 314 ("If Christianity be not altogether thoroughgoing eschatology, there remains in it no relationship whatever with Christ") is less clear.
[13] TH, 16. His emphasis.
[14] TH, 15.
[15] TH, 16.

of the four *eschata* for almost 30 years.[16] As the nemesis of hope, however—that is, as a reality that hope must oppose and overcome—'Hell' is ever-resent as an (anti-)eschatological theme in his writings. That Moltmann would eventually explicitly advocate Hell's annihilation—once more citing Dante's inscription[17]—seems inevitable.

0.3 Hell's Annihilation

This study is an engagement with the theme of universal salvation in Moltmann's eschatology, as viewed within the overall structure of his theology. Many of the central themes to be explored are clearly present in the title, *The Annihilation of Hell: Universal Salvation and the Redemption of Time in the Eschatology of Jürgen Moltmann*, while others are more implicit and thus require further clarification.

Taken as an 'objective genitive' (as in 'the annihilation of Hiroshima'), the main title refers to the overcoming of Hell as our eschatological hopes are realised. But "The Annihilation of Hell" can also be read as a 'subjective genitive' (as in 'the annihilation of the Atom Bomb'). In this sense, Hell's annihilation refers to its annihilative power in history—a power with which hope must contend. Both meanings are present in Moltmann's theology and will be explored in the following chapters.

In Moltmann's understanding, Hell's power to bring history to nothing—manifest in, though not reducible to, events such as the Atomic annihilation of Hiroshima—has its origin in the 'nihil' that precedes God's active creating of all things.[18] To speak of the 'an-nihil-ation' of this Hell (objective genitive) has a depth-meaning that is worth noting. Put into more positive language, we may conceive of this redemptive annihilation as God becoming all in all. This leads, in Moltmann's theology, to "universal salvation" and to "the redemption of time."

In the an-nihil-ation of Hell as a possibility (and not just as an actuality), the relationship between God and creation, and thus the structure of reality, is fundamentally transformed. The "redemption" of time in this context alludes to

---

[16] See CoG, 235–55 as explored in 1.4 below. Many elements of this discussion are anticipated in his brief 1968 article "Descent into Hell" cited in n. 4 above.

[17] See CoG, 253–54.

[18] This means that Moltmann opposes the annihilationist interpretation of Hell/Final Judgment. At the beginning of his essay "The Logic of Hell," in *God Will Be All in All: The Eschatology of Jürgen Moltmann*, ed. Richard Bauckham (Edinburgh: T. and T. Clark, 1999), 43–47, he attributes this position to an imagination fired by the bombing of Hiroshima. At the same time, he can say in "The Logic of Hell," 46,
> Our century has produced more infernos than all the centuries before us: The gas ovens of Auschwitz and the atomizing of Hiroshima heralded an age of potential mass annihilation through ABC weapons. So many people have experienced hell! It is pointless to deny hell.

The Hell that is manifest in such hells—which I will spell with a capital H throughout—will be analysed in 4.1 below.

Moltmann's special use of that term to refer not merely to a restoration of something that has become subject to evil but to an eschatological fulfilment. Paying attention to "redemption" in Moltmann's theology allows us, therefore, to examine how salvation takes place within the distinction and relationship that he establishes between creation and eschaton. The redemption of "time" in particular, including the need for its transformation from the very beginning, is taken as a key to the structure of Moltmann's thought. In this way, Moltmann's universalism is examined within the contours and dynamics of what I shall later refer to as his 'theocosmogony'.

Finally, in referring to the "eschatology" of Jürgen Moltmann, I intend to discuss not only his eschatologically oriented theology but also the specific interpretation of 'the four last things' that he offers within his wider theology of hope. Death and to a lesser extent heaven are significant topics in the following chapters, while Final Judgment and the nature of Hell are at the heart of this study.

0.4 Synopsis

Almost all of the central issues of this exploration are introduced in chapter 1 ("To Hell and Back"). This chapter is a microcosm of the study as a whole in that it opens and closes with an exploration of the relationship between judgment and mercy, justice and reconciliation. The 'annihilationist' alternative to the more traditional orthodox view of Hell as a place of everlasting torment is examined with special reference to *The Mystery of Salvation*, a report of the Church of England's Doctrine Commission that appeared in 1995.[19] Moltmann's critical review of this work, its affinity to his theology notwithstanding, serves to introduce Moltmann's own distinctive approach to universal salvation. The important issue of whether universalism necessitates the eclipse of human freedom is brought to the fore in this context, as is the 'Descent into Hell' motif that is central to Moltmann's Christocentric perspective (a motif that is reflected in the chapter title). Moltmann's understanding of authentic freedom, true justice, the nature of God (in particular, the relationship between God's love and God's wrath), and his approach to Scripture—all to be explored in further detail in later chapters—are introduced in order to give a preliminary indication of his overall position. The most widespread objections to universal salvation are also raised to provide a context within which Moltmann's universalism may be evaluated.

Moltmann's enigmatic statement (to be cited in chapter 1) that (a) the divine decision to save and (b) the human decision for or against faith do not exist on the same "level"—a distinction that he relates to the contrast between eternity and time—introduces chapter 2 ("The Reversal of Time in the Future of God"). In this (and the following) chapter, Moltmann's philosophy of time is taken to

---

[19] *The Mystery of Salvation: The Story of God's Gift; A Report by the Doctrine Commission of the General Synod of the Church of England* (London: Church House, 1995).

provide the key to the highly complex and nuanced structure and dynamism of his theology, not least his understanding of the relationship between the human and the divine—or nature and grace—in salvation. Of special interest here are the two 'directions' of time that Moltmann refers to as the historical and the eschatological, the latter being the anticipation within present history of the "redemption of time" mentioned in the title of chapter 3 (and in the overall title to this study).

While chapter 2 focusses on the present, historical opposition between the two directions of time, chapter 3 ("The Redemption of Time in the Presence of God") is concerned with their eschatological reintegration, or with what I call the 'coincidence of opposites' in and through which the God-world relationship is transformed. The way in which this "redemption" constitutes the simultaneous negation and fulfilment of temporal creation is explored with an eye to evaluating whether Moltmann's eschatology in general, and his universalism in particular, lead to an 'eclipse' of creation.

Having thus explored the overall philosophical structure of Moltmann's thought, chapter 4 ("The Triumph of Glory") opens by placing his unique conception of Hell within what I refer to as his 'theocosmogony'. A discussion of the way he understands the nature-grace relationship (the relationship between the human and the divine) is evaluated with reference to the differing emphases and concerns of Arminian and Calvinist views of salvation. Whether Moltmann's universalism might be able to satisfy the requirements of these two different theological paradigms is pursued by means of a description of his universalism of the cross, his discussion of the nature and will of God, and his understanding of freedom. A preliminary response to Moltmann's universalism is offered at the close of this chapter.

Chapters 5, 6, and 7 seek to deepen the analysis of the previous chapters by bringing Moltmann's thought into dialogue with the philosophical and theological proposals of other contemporary thinkers. Chapter 5 ("Between Creation and Eschaton: The Foundational and Transcendental Directions of Time") extends the explorations of chapters 2 and 3 by bringing Moltmann's work into conversation with the philosophy of time proposed by neo-Calvinist philosopher Hendrik Hart. Chapter 6 ("The Nature of Grace") builds on the nature-grace material of chapter 4 by reading Moltmann in the light of the famous Barth-Brunner debate. Chapter 7 ("Doing Justice (According) to Scripture") returns to some concerns first raised in chapter 1 about the biblical foundations of Moltmann's position and the sensitivity (or insensitivity) of universalist theologies to the cry of the oppressed for justice in the Final Judgment. These exegetical and ethical concerns are pursued with the help of proposals that have been made byN.T. Wright and Miroslav Volf.

The concluding chapter will offer some final reflections on whether Moltmann's eschatology can overcome the most common objections to universal salvation. My own central concern, whether it is possible to develop a viable 'covenantal' universalism (to be discussed further below), will also be addressed in relation to Moltmann's proposals. An Appendix deals with some exegetical issues concerning the book of Revelation.

0.5 Contexts and Traditions

Although it goes without saying that all academic monographs are written from within particular contexts, often with the hope that they will be meaningful to those who read them within different contexts, this hope (in my opinion) is most likely to be realised if the context and concerns of the author are openly stated. Ecumenism in theology, to which I am committed, is best served when our theological traditions and assumptions are made explicit.

Although I will beg to differ with Moltmann on a number of important issues in the following pages (explicitly so from the end of chapter 4 onwards), I trust that my own sympathies with Moltmann's universalism will be clearly evident from the outset. Such sympathy is due to the influence of many factors, one of which has been the Anglican tradition's openness to a 'hopeful' (rather than 'dogmatic') universalism,[20] although I would rather connect 'hope' in this context to the conviction and certainty of faith rather than to mere wishful thinking.[21] In addition to the Church of England's report *The Mystery of Salvation*, another document produced within the UK that is also discussed near the beginning of chapter 1 is the Evangelical Alliance's report *The Nature of Hell*. Evangelicalism's concern that biblical authority not be bracketed in theological (and other) discussions is one I continue to share. The report notes, "Today, universalism remains a largely non-evangelical view, although there are signs that it has begun to have some influence on the more radical wing of evangelicalism."[22] It is with that wing that I am most happy to be identified.

This monograph initially took shape initially as a dissertation in the joint doctoral program of the *Vrije Universiteit*, Amsterdam and the Institute for Christian Studies, Toronto, each of which is associated with the neo-Calvinist theologian and statesman Abraham Kuyper (1837–1920). There are a number of references in this study to neo-Kuyperian theologians and their responses to

---

[20] This 'hopeful' universalism is evident in *The Mystery of Salvation*, 198–205. The Church of England's 39 Articles, which took final form in 1571, are indicative of the eschatological openness of this tradition. Although the last of the 42 Articles of 1552 condemned universal restitution as a "dangerouse opinion," Articles 40–42 were withdrawn before 1563 when the 39 Articles were promulgated. Frederic W. Farrar, who cited this Article in his *Eternal Hope: Five Sermons* (London: Macmillan, 1883), 85n2, commented that this omission "leaves even 'Universalism' an open question." Cf. the judgment of D.P. Walker, *The Decline of Hell: Seventeenth-Century Discussions of Eternal Torment* (London: Routledge and Kegan Paul, 1964), 23 (who also cites this Article in full).

[21] I will return to the nature of hope in this context in 5.0 below, where I will articulate my own position in more detail.

[22] David Hilborn, ed., *The Nature of Hell: A Report by the Evangelical Alliance's Commission on Unity and Truth among Evangelicals (ACUTE)* (Carlisle, UK: Acute/Paternoster, 2000), 27. Here *The Nature of Hell* anticipates works such as: Robin A. Parry and Christopher H. Partridge, eds., *Universal Salvation? The Current Debate* (Carlisle, UK: Paternoster, 2003); Gregory MacDonald, *The Evangelical Universalist* (Eugene, OR: Cascade, 2006); and Bradley Jersak, *Her Gates Will Never Be Shut: Hope, Hell, and the New Jerusalem* (Eugene, OR: Wipf and Stock, 2009).

Moltmann's theology, including the suggestion that there are interesting affinities between Moltmann and Kuyper's successor at the VU, Herman Bavinck (1854–1921).[23] Kuyper, the founder of the VU as well as its first Professor of Theology, articulated a Christian cultural vision that inspired scholars in the non-theological disciplines as well, notably via the influence of VU philosophers Herman Dooyeweerd (1894–1977) and D.H.Th. Vollenhoven (1892–1978). Dooyeweerd's philosophy of time, as revised and extended by ICS Professor of Systematic Philosophy emeritus, Hendrik Hart, is given significant attention in chapter 5.

Although my own analysis and suggestions are indebted to this academic and confessional tradition, familiarity with it is not presupposed in the following chapters. But the influence of Vollenhoven's thought on my way of interpreting Moltmann may require special comment at this stage.

0.6 Contradictory/Harmony Monism

Vollenhoven is best known for his "*consequent probleemhistorische methode*" (consistent problem-historical method) which he applied to the history of philosophy in order to develop a typology of positions held historically in relation to certain fundamental, perduring questions (such as the locus of normativity and the relationships between constancy and change, universality and individuality, and unity and diversity).[24] One may, I believe, accept the criticism that Vollenhoven's systematic rather than truly historical concerns easily lead to readings that are somewhat 'aprioristic' and thus insensitive to a given thinker's individuality and singularity,[25] while still recognising the

---

[23] Bavinck was succeeded to the VU theology chair by Valentine Hepp (1879–1950), who was succeeded, in turn, by G.C. Berkouwer (1903–1996) and Jan Veenhof. In sharp contrast to Berkouwer (whose well-known work on Barth is alluded to in the title of chapter 4) and Veenhof, Hepp was hostile to the work of the neo-Kuyperians, Dooyeweerd and Vollenhoven, mentioned below. Veenhof's appreciative dissertation on Bavinck is cited in 6.1n6, where I comment on the affinity that I find between Bavinck and Moltmann. For further details on the VU, see Arie Theodorus van Deursen, *The Distinctive Character of the Free University of Amsterdam, 1880–2005: A Commemorative History*, trans. Herbert Donald Morton (Grand Rapids, MI: Eerdmans, 2008).

[24] For the historical context of this project, see Albert M. Wolters, "On Vollenhoven's Problem-Historical Method," in *Hearing and Doing: Philosophical Essays Dedicated to H. Evan Runner*, ed. John Kraay and Anthony Tol (Toronto: Wedge, 1979), 231–62.

[25] This concern is evident in Wolters, "On Vollenhoven's Problem-Historical Method." Among the numerous works that have been written on Moltmann, Randall E. Otto's published dissertation, *The God of Hope: The Trinitarian Vision of Jürgen Moltmann* (Lanham, MD: University Press of America, 1991) is, in my opinion, the clearest example of an 'aprioristic' (mis-)reading. As Otto does appeal to Vollenhoven's philosophical co-worker Herman Dooyeweerd in his critique of Moltmann, and as his doctoral research for this work was supervised by Robert Knusden, a follower of Dooyeweerd, I should point out that Otto's approach seems to me to be decisively influenced by the presuppositional apologetics of Cornelius Van Til. Dooyeweerd's

heuristic value of highlighting those general structural characteristics that the philosophies of otherwise disparate thinkers may share given their need to take a stand on basic trans-historical (or ever-present) problems.

In the following chapters, I will on occasion refer to Moltmann's 'contradictory/harmony monism', a philosophical stance that James Olthuis, in a lucid presentation of Vollenhoven's method, refers to as "[t]he most complex [form of] genetic monism."[26] After offering some definitions of these terms, I will briefly indicate why I think such a classification is helpful in getting to grips with some of the structural features of Moltmann's theology. I would like to stress that the exposition in the following chapters differs from this rather abstract and necessarily condensed discussion. The unfamiliarity, even within the Kuyperian tradition, of this hermeneutical approach makes some introductory remarks important at this stage. But some readers may wish to treat the rest of this section as an afterword to the present study (or as an extension to n. 11 in chapter 2).

---

clear rejection of Van Til's aprioristic and thus 'transcendent' (rather than 'transcendental') mode of engagement is evident in his contribution to the Van Til *Festschrift*, "Cornelius Van Til and the Transcendental Critique of Theoretical Thought," in *Jerusalem and Athens: Critical Discussions on the Philosophy and Apologetics of Cornelius Van Til*, ed. E.R. Geehan (Phillipsburg, NJ: Presbyterian and Reformed, 1980), 74–89. Cf. Robert D. Knusden, "Progressive and Regressive Tendencies in Christian Apologetics," in *Jerusalem and Athens*, 275–98.

[26] James H. Olthuis, "Models of Humanity in Theology and Psychology" (Toronto: Institute for Christian Studies, 1978), 28. (An earlier printing of this essay, citing James H. Olthuis and Arnold H. De Graaff as co-authors, was entitled "Models of Man in Theology and Psychology".) In addition to D.H.Th. Vollenhoven, *The Problem-Historical Method and the History of Philosophy*, ed. Kornelis A. Bril, trans. John de Kievit et al (Amstelveen: De Zaak Haes, 2005), which incorporates a translation of Vollenhoven's "*De Consequent Probleemhistorische Methode*," *Philosophia Reformata* 26 (1961): 1–34, other presentations of Vollenhoven's method in English include: Kornelis A. Bril, *Vollenhoven's Problem-Historical Method: Introduction and Explorations*, ed. John H. Kok, trans. Ralph W. Vunderink (Sioux Center, IA: Dordt College Press, 2005); Calvin G. Seerveld, "Biblical Wisdom underneath Vollenhoven's Categories for Philosophical Historiography," in *The Idea of a Christian Philosophy: Essays in Honour of D.H.Th. Vollenhoven*, ed. K.A. Bril, H. Hart, and J. Klapwijk, special issue, *Philosophia Reformata* 38 (Toronto: Wedge, 1973), 127–43; and B.J. van de Walt, "Historiography of Philosophy: The Consistent Problem-Historical Method," in *Heartbeat: Taking the Pulse of Our Christian Theological and Philosophical Heritage*, by B.J. van de Walt (Potchefstroom: Potchefstroom University for Christian Higher Education, 1978), 5–29. Cf. 2.1n11 below.

Olthuis's excellent presentation of Vollenhoven's method is, in my view, by far the most compelling and insightful to date, even though he over-simplifies Vollenhoven by reducing his triad of categories concerning the relative presence of structure and process (*louter kosmologische, kosmogono-kosmologische, mythologiserende*) to the contrast between "structuralism" and "geneticism" (on which see below). Seerveld, by contrast (see "Biblical Wisdom," 137), is among those who (rightly) maintain the 'middle' (here the third) category of "mythologizing" philosophy.

Before exploring what 'contradictory/harmony' monism might be, we must distinguish first between "monism" and "dualism" and then between "geneticism" and "structuralism." According to Olthuis,

> Monists are explicitly concerned to explain diversity in terms of tensions between higher and lower diverging dimensions [of the supposed underlying or ultimate unity of life], which can be complementary, contrasting, cooperating, antagonistic, and so on. Dualists [by contrast] are caught up in bridging the distance and effectuating some relation between the primordial twoness [that they posit].[27]

From this it should be clear that monism does not deny diversity anymore than dualism denies unity. Instead monists explain diversity (or duality) *in terms of* unity, while dualists explain unity *in terms of* duality.

The contrast between "geneticism" and "structuralism" works in the same way. Thus a "genetic" position, which may be monistic or dualistic though it is most frequently the former,[28] "emphasizes the provisional, on-going, always changing flow and flux of life." Instead of denying the primary concerns of structuralism, which are "[f]ixed structures, abiding norms, [and] dependency," such realities are "explained solely *in terms of* this indeterminate, genetic flow of the cosmos."[29] Geneticism, in other words, subsumes cosmology within cosmogony, while structuralism subordinates cosmogony to cosmology.

This distinction also finds expression in contrasting approaches to normativity and to evil. Thus while structuralists ('cosmological' thinkers in Vollenhoven's terminology[30]) typically stress "dutiful obedience to a given order," geneticists (or 'cosmogonic' thinkers) celebrate our "responsibility to direct, master and ride the surge of life with its ebb and flow."[31] From this it follows that "structural dualisms inevitably identify evil in some way with the lower reality and perfection with the higher," while in geneticistic monisms, "[e]vil is to get caught at a stage in the process as if it were the final stage."[32]

So what, according to Olthuis, is especially "complex" about the 'contradictory/harmony' form of genetic monism? Some phrases from his characterisation of this position should provide us with a general indication. In this understanding, he writes,

> Simultaneous with the differentiating process with its higher-lower relations is a process in the opposite direction towards unity. Contradictory monism is a unity of opposites, a *coincidentia oppositorum*, as it is often called. . . . Even as the universal cosmic law realizes itself in a process of differentiation, there is the process in the opposite direction of a return to the universal origin and unity.

---

[27] Olthuis, "Models of Humanity," 16.
[28] See Olthuis, "Models of Humanity," 21.
[29] Olthuis, "Models of Humanity," 19. My emphasis.
[30] For Vollenhoven's own terms, see n. 26 above.
[31] Olthuis, "Models of Humanity," 19–20.
[32] Olthuis, "Models of Humanity," 22–23.

Inferno e Speranza

> These two directions in the genetic process are not beside, above or in or under; they take place simultaneously. There are two horizontal currents continually and simultaneously running counter to each other. ...
> For contradictory monism the direction of differentiation is the direction of time, of ... ordinary life. ... But there is also an order of experience which is wholly other, of a different direction, eternal, trans-personal and sacred. ... Salvation or liberation takes place when we are overcome by the transforming awareness that even as we become ourselves, we are absorbed in the whole and the universal. ... Contradictory monism does not call for an ascetic rejection of life, but for an intense struggle to become one with the universal. It does not call for ascent above the ordinary level [or direction] with all its distinctions, but an absorbing of all distinctions into the one. ...
> Contradictory monism calls mankind to a relentless and grim struggle from which there is no deliverance, until suddenly, the light dawns and one .... is able to surrender and see that there is a hidden harmony to what appears contradictory and incongruous. ...
> [T]he eternal, universal direction ... in the end contradicts and invalidates ordinary human experience even as it grounds it. ...
> The call to constant struggle paired with the call to constant surrender is at the heart of contradictory [/harmony] monism.[33]

Clearly, this is a very abstract discussion of the most general structural features and dynamics that a particular position might (or might not) exemplify. To identify such a description, which is at best a skeleton, with the very heartbeat of someone's thought, or to insist that if it could be so typified, a given position must conform to or be contained within such a general philosophical pattern, would run the risk of exegetical violence. But classifications, typologies, and generalisations—which are common in all academic disciplines—may nevertheless be both appropriate and useful. To see Moltmann's theology as conforming to (and diverging from) such a contradictory/harmony monism is, in my opinion, heuristically very valuable.[34]

---

[33] Olthuis, "Models of Humanity," 28–30. His italics.

[34] For such an approach to Moltmann, see J. Matthew Bonzo, *Indwelling the Forsaken Other: The Trinitarian Ethics of Jürgen Moltmann* (Eugene, OR: Pickwick, 2009). For studies that see the theology of Pannenberg as characterised by 'contradictory/harmony monism', see Brian J. Walsh, "Futurity and Creation: Explorations in the Eschatological Theology of Wolfhart Pannenberg" (MPhil thesis, Institute for Christian Studies, 1979); "Pannenberg's Eschatological Ontology," *Christian Scholar's Review* 11, no. 3 (1982): 229–49; "A Critical Review of Pannenberg's *Anthropology in Theological Perspective*," *Christian Scholar's Review* 15, no. 3 (1986): 247–59; and James H. Olthuis, "God as True Infinite: Concerns about Pannenberg's *Systematic Theology*, Vol. 1," *Calvin Theological Journal* 27, no. 2 (November, 1992): 318–25. On Bonhoeffer in this context, see Steven Bouma-Prediger, "Bonhoeffer and Berkouwer on the World, Humans, and Sin: Two Models of Ontology and Anthropology" (MPhil thesis, Institute for Christian Studies, 1984). On Tillich, see Terry Ray Tollefson, "Paul Tillich: His Anthropology as Key to the Structure of his Thought" (MPhil thesis, Institute for Christian Studies, 1977).

The discussion in the following chapters does not offer a description of this typical position and then seek to 'apply' it to Moltmann. Instead, when confronted with particular interpretive puzzles,[35] I suggest that being open to the possibility that Moltmann's thought might display this kind of general structure (though in a way that is unique to Moltmann) may open up fruitful ways of understanding him. One does not need to grasp the general features of this "complex genetic monism" to make sense of the following exposition. But some readers may find it helpful to refer back to Olthuis's characterisation cited above.

0.7 Dialogue

"Every good dissertation," Moltmann has suggested, "does not merely present something, but also initiates a dialogue on the common subject."[36] These words well articulate a central aim of this study. In my brief synopsis above, I have noted that the exposition of chapters 1–4 becomes explicitly 'dialogical' in character in chapters 5–7 (this being a feature that is also anticipated in chapter 1). Part of the dialogue includes some of my own suggestions (on 'creational

---

[35] For example, whatever one might think of Vollenhoven's approach to the structure of a given philosophical conception, the question of whether Moltmann's theology is 'dualistic' or not confronts us even in the Introduction to *Theology of Hope*. What is the relationship, we may ask, between what Moltmann calls the "[p]resent and future, experience and hope [that] stand in contradiction to each other in Christian eschatology" (18)? "Everywhere in the New Testament," he writes with approval, "the Christian hope is directed towards what is not yet visible; it is consequently a 'hoping against hope' and thereby brands the visible realm of present experience as a god-forsaken, transient reality that is to be left behind" (18). Such language, read in isolation, suggests an *otherworldly* eschatology. Yet as we have already seen, Moltmann speaks of a "future outlook that embraces all things, even death" (33) and of a "hope" and "love" that "abandon[] nothing to annihilation" (32). If Moltmann's is a *world-embracing* eschatology, how then do we account for this apparent denigration of "transient reality" and the "visible realm"? If these negative realities of our present experience are not evils that we must hope to escape, are they perhaps better understood as manifestations of a "contradiction" (to use his own term) that must be resolved? Could this 'duality' (rather than dual*ism*) within what might be a 'monistic' conception of reality explain why hope which is "born" out of the contradiction between the "not yet visible" and the "visible," and between "the resurrection" and "the cross" (18), is also said (in what seems to be a rhetorical question) to "reconcile[] [humanity] with what is . . . disharmonious" (31)? Whatever the answer, the question of the general philosophical structure of Moltmann's theology cannot be avoided.

[36] Jürgen Moltmann, foreword to *God's History in the Theology of Jürgen Moltmann*, by Siu-Kwong Tang (Bern: Peter Lang, 1996), 11. Moltmann also deliberately writes in a way that invites dialogue. In the preface to the paperback edition of *The Trinity and the Kingdom* (1981; repr., Minneapolis, MN: Fortress Press, 1993), viii, he speaks of his series of contributions to systematic theology that began with TKG as "*suggestions* [that] are not intended to conclude discussions; they are meant to open new conversations." His emphasis.

grace', for example) that have arisen out of my attempt to closely engage Moltmann's thought and the nature-grace issues with which his work is concerned. My own proposals are often related to the question of whether a 'covenantal' universalism is conceivable. As this is a central issue for this whole project, affecting the way in which I set out to evaluate Moltmann's eschatology, a few words of explanation will be helpful at this stage.

One of the distinctives of the Kuyperian tradition in theology has been its concern that we develop a strong doctrine of creation that affirms the goodness of God's work 'in the beginning' and (despite sin's entry into history) in the here and now.[37] I have already mentioned my interest in exploring whether Moltmann's eschatology leads to an 'eclipse' of creation. In the context of salvation, this is a concern that many have about universalist positions in general. A 'covenantal universalism'—if such a position is possible—would, at least in principle, be able to allay such fears.

By 'covenantal' here I mean a relationship between God and humanity that is not conceived in 'zero-sum' terms nor even as a '50-50' (let alone '80-20') partnership but as a relationship of 'full' mutual participation. Taken together, the two parts of Phil 2:12b–13—"work out your own salvation with fear and trembling; for it is God who is at work in you, enabling you both to will and to work for his good pleasure"[38]—suggest a 'covenantal' understanding of the relationship between God and humanity so beyond heteronomy or autonomy that our current Arminian and Calvinist frameworks should be called into question. And into dialogue.

Universal salvation is a contentious issue. One approach I utilise to defuse this is to explore how, in the context of the polarisation that exists between Arminian and Calvinist theologies, Moltmann's position might need to be modified if it is to enjoy widespread discussion and respect (rather than simply agreement or disagreement). Can Moltmann, in other words, articulate a universalism that can become a part of fruitful conversation within mainstream Protestant theology (and beyond)? A merit of this approach to Moltmann's

---

[37] This is evident in Brian J. Walsh, "Theology of Hope and the Doctrine of Creation: An Appraisal of Jürgen Moltmann," *Evangelical Quarterly* 59, no. 1 (January, 1987): 53–76.

[38] This is the translation offered in the *New Revised Standard Version* (NRSV). The *New International Version* (NIV) emphasises divine agency slightly differently. It reads, "continue to work out your salvation with fear and trembling, for it is God who works in you to will and to act according to his good purpose." Although I will usually cite the NRSV elsewhere in this study as a superior translation in certain respects and contexts, the NIV will be the primary translation cited in 7.1 and in the Appendix because I will be taking issue with its (conservative evangelical) treatment of 'Hell'. Cf. 7.1n8 and 9.0n1 below. Like all translations, the NIV has its strengths and weaknesses. Although it is usually more than adequate for the purpose of citation, I will on occasion side clearly with the NRSV (in, e.g., 7.1n8, where I am especially critical of the NIV, and in 8.3n32) and with the *New Jerusalem Bible* (NJB) (in 7.1n8 and in 7.3n141). Comments on issues of biblical translation in this study are restricted to what is necessary for my 'theological' concerns.

theology is that the way in which he is wrestling with fundamental nature-grace questions—questions with which all theologians must wrestle—may be appreciated regardless of whether we agree that salvation will embrace all people. As the present study is not exclusively concerned with Moltmann's universalism but also with the 'structure' of his theology within which his proposals for Hell's annihilation make sense, I will be seeking to evaluate what I see as the strengths and weaknesses of his eschatology in this more open-ended way (in addition to pursuing my own more particular concerns discussed above). It is hoped that this focus on nature-grace problematics will bring as many readers as possible into this "dialogue on the common subject."

0.8 Some Points of Style

As a matter of style, I will sometimes use the plural 'we' where the singular 'I' might be more common. This is intended to invite the reader into the conversation. It is not intended to mask the fact that my own perspective—about which I have attempted to be open—decisively shapes the discussion.

In order to make this study of use to a wider readership, quotations are given in English. The translations, the majority of which are by highly regarded Moltmann translator Margaret Kohl, are so good that they more than suffice for our present purposes.[39] That said, I have inserted some German phrases where this furthers the discussion and have made comments on the meaning of some terms in the footnotes. On occasion, I have chosen to cite the German text and offer my own translation.

This discussion of Hell and universalism brings us into contact with a great many themes and topics scattered throughout Moltmann's extensive corpus. I have given numerous, often detailed, references in the footnotes to Moltmann's treatment of many issues, in part in the hope that this will be of help to researchers in those areas. Given the presence of a number of partial quotations in the following exposition, for which I have used double quotation marks throughout, I have reserved single, rather than double, quotation marks for those occasions in the discussion where I have simply wanted to emphasise, rather than cite, words or phrases that have an unusual, often technical, meaning. In my citations, and often in my discussion, I have (with exceptions, naturally) tended to concentrate on Moltmann's 'major' works (to be introduced in 1.4 below) as these often incorporate and give more definitive shape to earlier essays.[40]

---

[39] For an indication of just how highly regarded Kohl's work is by both Moltmann and some of his leading interpreters, see the dedication and the comments in Bauckham, ed., *God Will Be All in All*, xv. Kohl has indicated Moltmann's own close involvement with the translation process in, e.g., CoG, xxi and *Experiences in Theology: Ways and Forms of Christian Theology*, trans. Margaret Kohl (London: SCM Press, 2000), xiii. Hereafter EiT.

[40] With respect to Moltmann's doctrine of creation, for example, I give far more attention to his *God in Creation: An Ecological Doctrine of Creation*, trans. Margaret

There are a number of excellent studies of Moltmann's work (both published and unpublished), many of which I have consulted and some of which I have referred to explicitly. There is, however, very little secondary literature that addresses Moltmann's universalism, his interpretation of Hell, or his overall philosophy of time in a detailed way.[41] It is hoped that this study will persuade others just how important these issues are to an understanding of his theology in general.

0.9 Hell and Hope

Moltmann's major work on eschatology, *The Coming of God*, ends with these memorable words:

> The feast of eternal joy is prepared by the fulness of God and the rejoicing of all created being.... The *laughter of the universe* is God's delight. It is the universal Easter laughter.[42]

Kohl (London: SCM Press, 1985), hereafter GC, than to the earlier collection of essays, *The Future of Creation*, by Jürgen Moltmann, trans. Margaret Kohl (London: SCM Press, 1979), hereafter FC, or to his "Creation and Redemption," in *Creation, Christ and Culture: Studies in Honour of T.F. Torrance*, ed. Richard W.A. McKinney (Edinburgh: T. and T. Clark, 1976), 119–34. A study that was especially concerned with the development of Moltmann's theology would naturally differ in focus. Without ignoring developmental issues, I have chosen to focus on the relatively systematic coherence of Moltmann's thought.

[41] The following two works on eschatology, the second of which is dedicated to a discussion of Moltmann's work, remain indicative of the relative lack of detailed attention to the topics of Hell and time in the secondary literature. Thus while the first collection, David Fergusson and Marcel Sarot, eds., *The Future as God's Gift: Explorations in Christian Eschatology* (Edinburgh: T. and T. Clark, 2000), contains some passing references to Moltmann's view of Hell and makes a number of brief (in some cases misleading) references to his view of time (see 3.5.1n207 below), the substantial and helpful essay in that volume, "The Shape of Time" (41–72) by Richard Bauckham and Trevor Hart, two of Moltmann's most reliable interpreters, while clearly indebted to Moltmann, does not specifically discuss his work. In this respect, Richard Bauckham's essay "Time and Eternity," in *God Will Be All in All: The Eschatology of Jürgen Moltmann*, ed. Richard Bauckham (Edinburgh: T. and T. Clark, 1999), 155–226, is the exception that proves the rule as "Time and Eternity," 155–93 provides possibly the only truly extensive, focussed discussion available on Moltmann's view of time *per se*. Yet Bauckham's interest in the "moment" as the point of connection between time and eternity, which is explicit in 187–93, to become a separate discussion of aesthetics in 193–226, seems to be a main concern from the outset. This makes his treatment, though very helpful, narrower than it might have been. This is why in the response piece that follows, "The Bible, The Exegete, and the Theologian," 227–32, Moltmann notes (227–28) that Bauckham "does not enter in detail into my theology of time as found in *God in Creation* ..., 104–39 ... and in *The Coming of God* ..., 279–95." As for the topic of Hell, it is disappointing that Moltmann's own short piece in that volume, "The Logic of Hell," 43–47, does not evoke any comments from the other contributors.

[42] CoG, 328–29. My emphasis.

The penultimate phrase (placed here in italics) closely echoes the language of *The Divine Comedy*[43] as Dante nears the end of the journey that has taken him "To Hell and Back" (to cite the title of an introductory work on the *Commedia*[44] that is echoed, in turn, in the title of the next chapter).

Although Dorothy Sayers insists that Dante's 'Hell' goes back to Mark 9:43–44 and to the final verses of the book of Isaiah (a claim that will be disputed in 7.1 below),[45] Eileen Gardiner, in her *Visions of Heaven and Hell before Dante*, traces this mediaeval tradition back to the second century CE work, *St. Peter's Apocalypse*.[46] As we (in our own way) recapitulate Dante's journey from Hell to Hope, we shall begin with this remarkable Christian text.

LASCIATE OGNE SPERANZA, VOI CH'INTRATE.
  Inferno, canto 3, line 9

Per lor maladizion sì non si perde,
che non possa tornar, l'etterno amore,
mentre che las speranza has fior del verde.
  Purgatorio, canto 3, lines 133–35[47]

---

[43] Moltmann specifically cites *Paradiso*, canto 27, lines 4–5 in *The Trinity and the Kingdom of God: The Doctrine of God*, trans. Margaret Kohl (London: SCM Press, 1980), 128: "This is 'the laughter of the universe'." Hereafter TKG. The Italian ("*un riso de l'universo*") may be better translated as referring to the 'smile' of the universe, but here I am more concerned with Moltmann's appropriation of Dante.
  Interpreted within what I will call Moltmann's 'theocosmogony' (see 2.5 below), the creation here is seen as caught up in the eschatological return movement of God's love—a divine way of be-ing that, in keeping with the analysis of 0.6, has two directions: *kenosis* and *ecstasis*. Once we see the ecstatic homecoming as eschatological fulfilment, the love that God 'is' (see 4.3.2 below) may be seen as a pilgrimage in which we are called to participate. Cf. Joy Ann McDougall, *Pilgrimage of Love: Moltmann on the Trinity and Christian Life* (Oxford: Oxford University Press, 2005).
[44] See Joseph Gallagher, *To Hell and Back with Dante: A Modern Reader's Guide to The Divine Comedy* (Liguori, MO: Triumph, 1996).
[45] See Dorothy L. Sayers, *Introductory Papers on Dante* (New York: Harper and Brothers, 1954), 44–45.
[46] See Eileen Gardiner, ed., *Visions of Heaven and Hell before Dante* (New York: Italica, 1989), vii, 1–12, and 237–38.
[47] For an English translation, see n. 1 above. I have deliberately—and hopefully—reversed the order of the quotations in this citation.

CHAPTER 1

To Hell and Back

1.1 Until Justice and Mercy Embrace?

[T]here is a pit, great and full of fire. In it are those who have denied righteousness, and angels of punishment chastise them there and kindle on them the fire of their torment.

And there are women. They hang them up by their necks and by their hair; they will cast them into the pit. These plaited their hair, not for the sake of beauty but to turn men to fornication, so that they might ensnare their souls to perdition. And the men who laid with them in fornication will be hung by their loins in that place of fire, and they shall say to one another, "We did not know that we would come to everlasting punishment."[1]

These words, which are attributed to Jesus, come from *St. Peter's Apocalypse*, a work that some early Christians accepted as part of their New Testament.[2] Written in the second century CE, probably for a Palestinian Christian community at the time of the Bar Kokhba rebellion against Rome (132–135 CE),[3] this text claims to record a conversation between the risen Jesus and St.

---

[1] "St. Peter's Apocalypse," in *Visions of Heaven and Hell before Dante*, 10. Gardiner reproduces an English translation of the extant Ethiopic text without versification in *Visions of Heaven and Hell before Dante*, 1–12. Although this widely available edition is sufficient for the purposes of this introductory section, any references to specific verses in these footnotes will therefore follow the versification provided in the critical edition of Dennis D. Buchholz, *Your Eyes Will Be Opened: A Study of the Greek (Ethiopic) Apocalypse of Peter*. SBL Dissertation Series 97 (Atlanta, GA: Scholars Press, 1988). For discussion of a crucial Greek fragment—the Rainer fragment—which Gardiner does not utilise but which is vital for an accurate reconstruction and translation of 14:1–5a (especially 14:1), see 1.6 below.

[2] See, e.g., Richard Bauckham, "The Apocalypse of Peter: A Jewish Christian Apocalypse from the Time of Bar Kokhba," in *The Fate of the Dead: Studies on the Jewish and Christian Apocalypses*, by Richard Bauckham (Leiden: Brill, 1998), 160–258, especially 160–61 and F.F. Bruce, *The Canon of Scripture* (Downers Grove, IL: InterVarsity Press, 1988), 164, 190, 191, 218–19, 261 (also 261n21), and 308.

[3] Thus Bauckham, "The Apocalypse of Peter," 160–258, especially 176–94.

Peter prior to the Ascension.[4] The apocalypse unfolds in response to the disciples' request that Jesus "Declare to us what are the signs of your coming and of the end of the world."[5]

In the vision of Hell that the disciples are granted, no fewer than twenty-one categories of sinners are subjected to a Justice whose purpose is clearly retributive. Women who have braided their hair to seduce men (as in the above quotation) now hang from their hair. Their partners hang from their "loins." The breast milk of mothers who have murdered their children will congeal and give rise to flesh-devouring beasts. If they have had abortions, they will stand in a pit up to their necks in excrement or menstrual discharge. Children who have disobeyed their parents will be attacked by flesh-eating birds. The deceitful will have their lips cut off. Sorcerers will burn forever on wheels of fire.[6] An eye for an eye and a tooth for a tooth.

Even before he sees the specific punishments that face the unrighteous, Peter is deeply moved by their suffering and sorrow, exclaiming: "Lord, let me speak your word concerning the sinners. It would be better for them if they had not been created."[7] Indeed, the theme of compassion plays a prominent role in this apocalypse. In the introduction, we are told that "Peter pondered this revelation so that he might understand the mystery of the Son of God, *the merciful one and lover of mercy*."[8] Furthermore, the vision of the affliction of sinners on the Last Day that prompts Peter's exclamation results in the weeping not only of the angels and the righteous, but of Jesus himself.[9]

Nevertheless, despite Christ's own compassion, and despite the fact that Peter's words are carefully chosen, echoing as they do what Jesus had said about Judas in Matt 26:24,[10] he is rebuked. "Peter," Jesus replies, "why do you speak in this way, as if not to have been created would be better for them? You resist God. You would not have more compassion than he does for his image; for he has created them and brought them forth out of nothing. Now because you have seen the lamentation that shall come upon sinners in the last days your heart is troubled; but I will show you the works by which they have sinned against the Most High."[11]

Then follows the graphic description of the Justice—the just deserts—the various kinds of sinners will receive in accordance with the abominations they have committed. While many of the categories of sin are common to a number of Jewish and Christian apocalypses from this period, three kinds of sinners are

---

[4] Gardiner, in her *Visions of Heaven and Hell before Dante*, 237, situates the discourse at the time of the Transfiguration. But see Bauckham, "The Apocalypse of Peter," 165 and 174.
[5] "St. Peter's Apocalypse," in *Visions of Heaven and Hell before Dante*, 1.
[6] For a succinct catalogue, see Bauckham, "The Apocalypse of Peter," 166–67.
[7] "St. Peter's Apocalypse," in *Visions of Heaven and Hell before Dante*, 3.
[8] "St. Peter's Apocalypse," in *Visions of Heaven and Hell before Dante*, 1. My emphasis.
[9] "St. Peter's Apocalypse," in *Visions of Heaven and Hell before Dante*, 3.
[10] See Bauckham, "The Apocalypse of Peter," 233.
[11] "St. Peter's Apocalypse," in *Visions of Heaven and Hell before Dante*, 3.

unparalleled in this kind of literature: "[t]he persecutors and betrayers of my righteous people," "the ones who slander and doubt my righteousness," and "the false witnesses."[12] Richard Bauckham cites the attention shown to such sinners as evidence that the *Sitz im Leben* of this apocalypse is one of persecution and betrayal, faithfulness and martyrdom. The first group are those who have persecuted Christ's followers, the second, those who have apostatised to escape dying for the faith, while the third can be translated as referring to informers "who put to death the martyrs with a lie."[13] Coupled with the fact that many of the punishments are inflicted on the sinners in full sight of their victims, it becomes clear that Justice is at stake, a Justice that honours the innocent suffering of the martyrs.

Bauckham attempts to make this concern intelligible by observing,

> In situations of serious injustice what Max Horkheimer calls 'the longing that the murderer should not triumph over his innocent victim' has an ethical priority and must make first claim on the kind of eschatological theodicy with which the apocalypses are concerned. In such situations an easy universalism which extends benevolent mercy equally to the oppressors and the oppressed would be an affront both to the oppressed and to the divine righteousness for which they long.[14]

This comment not only prevents us from prematurely dismissing *St. Peter's Apocalypse* as a lurid exercise in scare-mongering, but also hints at the possibility that this is a text that can be fruitfully brought into conversation with some of the most searching questions that have arisen in contemporary theological reflection. It is no accident that Bauckham's citation of Horkheimer is taken from Jürgen Moltmann's famous book, *The Crucified God*.[15] Here it occurs in a sympathetic discussion of Horkheimer's "protest atheism" which, in Moltmann's view, takes us close to "the mystery of God and suffering which underlies the dispute between theists and atheists, by going past that dispute." Implicit in Horkheimer's critical theory, claims Moltmann, is the awareness that "If innocent suffering puts the idea of a righteous God in question, so

---

[12] "St. Peter's Apocalypse," in *Visions of Heaven and Hell before Dante*, 7. In the versification suggested by Buchholz, these occur in 9:1–4 (see Buchholz, *Your Eyes Will Be Opened*, 209–11). For the 'traditional' character of many of the other categories and for comment on these three exceptions, see Bauckham, "The Apocalypse of Peter," 183–84.

[13] See Bauckham, "The Apocalypse of Peter," 184. Cf. Buchholz's "literal" and "free" translations in *Your Eyes Will Be Opened*, 211.

[14] See Richard Bauckham, "The Conflict of Justice and Mercy: Attitudes to the Damned in Apocalyptic Literature," in *The Fate of the Dead: Studies on the Jewish and Christian Apocalypses*, by Richard Bauckham (Leiden: Brill, 1998), 132–48. Quotation from p. 136.

[15] See Jürgen Moltmann, *The Crucified God: The Cross of Christ as the Foundation and Criticism of Christian Theology*, trans. R.A. Wilson and John Bowden (London: SCM Press, 1974), 223. Hereafter cited as CrG.

conversely longing for the righteousness of the wholly other puts suffering in question and makes it conscious sorrow."[16]

This reading of Horkheimer's protest atheism as a cry for the righteousness of God leads Moltmann both to embrace and to qualify Horkheimer's "longing that the murderer should not triumph over his innocent victim" in the light of his own theology of the cross. Earlier in *The Crucified God*, Moltmann makes the following observation about the way he sees the cross and resurrection of Jesus bringing about an "eschatological" resolution to the "historically" irresolvable dialectic between the divine justice and innocent suffering that call each other into question. He writes,

> The dispute over the resurrection of Jesus is concerned with the question of righteousness in history. Does it belong to the *nomos* which finally gives each man his deserts, or does it belong to the law of grace as it was manifest by Jesus and in the resurrection of the crucified Christ? The message of the new righteousness which eschatological faith brings into the world says that in fact *the executioners will not finally triumph over their victims. It also says that in the end the victims will not triumph over their executioners.* The one will triumph who first died for the victims and then also for the executioners, and in so doing revealed a new righteousness which breaks through the vicious circles of hate and vengeance and which from the lost victims and executioners creates a new mankind with a new humanity.[17]

Bauckham, who is a highly respected interpreter of Moltmann with a special interest in his approach to theodicy,[18] also explicitly refers to this passage.[19] His point would seem to be that if *St. Peter's Apocalypse* can challenge us not to opt for an "easy universalism"[20] at the expense of justice, then we can ask of this ancient text whether it opts too quickly for an "apocalyptic law of retaliation" (to use one of Moltmann's phrases[21]) that allows victims a triumph that has lost contact with the triumph of the crucified God.

Bauckham's research on the 'Rainer fragment'—a fragment that comes from a Greek version of *St. Peter's Apocalypse* that predates the earliest manuscripts that we possess—indicates that this work, in its original form, wrestled with the relationship between justice and mercy in a very unexpected (and, in my view, promising) way. To this, we shall return at the end of the present chapter.[22] But the answer provided by the extant Ethiopic text of *St. Peter's Apocalypse* to the charge of grace-less retribution is disappointing.

---

[16] CrG, 225.
[17] CrG, 178. In the original, "*nomos*" is italicised. Otherwise, my emphasis.
[18] See Richard Bauckham, *The Theology of Jürgen Moltmann* (Edinburgh: T. and T. Clark, 1995), chap. 4: "Theodicy."
[19] See Bauckham, "The Conflict of Justice and Mercy," 136n18.
[20] Bauckham, "The Conflict of Justice and Mercy," 136 as cited above.
[21] See Jürgen Moltmann, *The Way of Jesus Christ: Christology in Messianic Dimensions*, trans. Margaret Kohl (London: SCM Press, 1990), 335–36. Hereafter cited as WJC.
[22] See 1.6 below.

Once Peter has been shown the cosmic conflagration to come and the punishments to which various kinds of sinners will be subjected, Jesus' rebuke would seem to conclude as follows:

> Afterwards the angels will bring my elect and righteous, who are perfect in all uprightness, and bear them in their hands and clothe them with the garment of heavenly life. They will see justice carried out on those who hated them, when Ezraël punishes them, and the torment of every one will be forever, according to his or her deeds.
>
> All who are tormented will say with one voice, "Have mercy on us, for now we know the judgment of God, which he declared to us before, but which we did not believe." And the angel Tatîrokos will come and punish them with still greater torment, and say to them, "Now you repent, when it is no longer the time for repentance, and nothing of life remains." And they will say, "Righteous is the judgment of God, for we have heard and seen that his judgment is good; for we are paid according to our deeds."[23]

In this passage, "the merciful one and lover of mercy" shows Peter that the fiery torments that these sinners must undergo are, by their own admission, nothing less than what they deserve. God's justice is beyond dispute. Judgment seems to have the final word. When Eileen Gardiner selected this apocalypse to open her collection entitled *Visions of Heaven and Hell before Dante*, she was placing it in an all-too-familiar tradition. That the *Inferno* was directly influenced by *St. Peter's Apocalypse*[24] makes this choice seem all the more appropriate. Here, we are presented with a vision of Final Judgment in which justice and mercy may never embrace. Or so it seems . . . .

1.2 The Annihilation of Hell/The Hell of Annihilation

In portraying Hell as a place of conscious and eternal torment, *St. Peter's Apocalypse* is in line with what is, from a historical perspective, the dominant Christian view of Final Judgment. But while 'traditional orthodoxy' still has many defenders in the world of academic theology, graphic portrayals of the fate of the damned do not feature in their arguments. John Gerstner may claim that "In comparison with the real hell, Stephen King's most frightening tales are amusing."[25] But he is the exception that proves the rule. The apocalyptic imagination that one finds at work in Jonathan Edwards' 1741 sermon "Sinners in the Hands of an Angry God" is far from extinct. But it finds its outlet today in the world of fiction and entertainment. (The reference to Stephen King is most revealing). As the expression of serious theology, Edwards' views, though

---

[23] "St. Peter's Apocalypse," in *Visions of Heaven and Hell before Dante*, 10.
[24] Bruce, *The Canon of Scripture*, 164 notes that "its lurid pictures of the damned . . . in due course exercised some influence on Dante's *Inferno*."
[25] John H. Gerstner, *Repent or Perish: With a Special Reference to the Conservative Attack on Hell* (Ligionier, PA: Soli Deo Gloria, 1990), 15.

much studied and admired by Gerstner (and others), are in this respect widely experienced as belonging to another era.[26]

This is not to claim that what we now call the 'traditional' view of Hell has become outdated and unbelievable in the Modern age. But it would be fair to say that 'traditional orthodoxy' has itself undergone a significant transformation. William Crockett tells the story of a professor in a mainline denominational seminary who often said to his students, "Once we see the glory of Christ, and the hideous nature of sin as God sees it, hell will be understandable. If my own mother were being carried to the mouth of hell, I would stand and applaud."[27] Part of Crockett's point is that he knows his readers will be shocked. It is this reaction that reveals the fact that, despite the very wide theological spectrum that exists among Christians today, we all nevertheless belong to the Modern age.[28] For the idea that the suffering of the damned would increase the joy of the blessed is a constant feature of the theological tradition from the early apocalypses[29] until the seventeenth century.[30]

Remarkably, the idea that the happiness of those in heaven would be ruined rather than enhanced by the misery of the damned does not seem to have occurred to anyone until this was asserted in 1719 by a twenty-two year old Swiss woman named Marie Huber (who would later become a effective

---

[26] Although this is an accurate generalisation in my view, it is still a generalisation. According to the publishers of Jonathan Edwards, *Sinners in the Hands of an Angry God* (Phillipsburg, NJ: Presbyterian and Reformed, 1992), their reprinting marked the 250th anniversary of a "message" that "is desperately required in our day of great ungodliness" (6). In the last twenty years, a multitude of versions have appeared, some in modernised English. For John H. Gerstner's appreciation of Edwards, see his *Heaven and Hell: Jonathan Edwards on the Afterlife* (Ligonier Ministries and Grand Rapids, MI: Baker, 1991). For a very different appropriation of Edwards, see Miroslav Volf, "The Final Reconciliation: Reflections on a Social Dimension of the Eschatological Transition," *Modern Theology* 16, no. 1 (January, 2000): 91–113, especially 103 and 112n67. This important essay will be discussed in 7.2 below.

[27] William Crockett, "The Metaphorical View," in *Four Views on Hell,* ed. William Crockett (Grand Rapids, MI: Zondervan, 1992), 48.

[28] If our age can be described as Postmodern, then in this respect (at least), the Postmodern is built upon the Modern.

[29] For a list of relevant apocalyptic texts (including *St. Peter's Apocalypse* 13:2), see Bauckham, "The Conflict of Justice and Mercy," 135. On p. 136, just prior to his reference to Horkeimer (cited above), Bauckham expresses the rationale of this theme in the apocalypses by noting that "If hell is a triumph for God's justice, setting to rights the injustice of this world, then the righteous *ought* to rejoice to see it." His emphasis.

[30] Crockett, "The Metaphorical View," 47n14, cites Augustine's *City of God*, 20.22 and Aquinas' *Summa Theologica*, supp. to pt. 3, q. 94, art. 1, 3. Aquinas would claim to be celebrating God's justice. But see the comments on this latter passage in Friedrich Nietzsche, *On the Genealogy of Morals*, First essay, sec. 15, in *Basic Writing of Nietzsche*, ed. and trans. Walter Kaufmann (New York: The Modern Library, 2000), 484–88. Other exponents of this tradition are listed in Walker, *The Decline of Hell*, 29.

proponent of universal salvation).[31] The same point was to be argued forcefully just over 100 years later by the 'Father of Modern Theology', Friedrich Schleiermacher.[32] The judgment of Bauckham is to the point: "the modern Christian's sympathy with [this] view, [which] is typically modern in its appeal . . . . places him on Schleiermacher's side of a great transition in the history of attitudes to suffering."[33] He underlines this observation by noting that while C.S. Lewis countered Schleiermacher's argument (in the middle of last century) by denying that heaven and Hell co-exist in unilinear time, "He does *not* argue, as earlier theologians would have done, that pity for the justly punished would be misplaced."[34]

By 1877, Dean Farrar, in a much debated series of sermons on eternal punishment preached in Westminster Abbey, could refer to the time-honoured idea that "the bliss of the saved may be all the more keen because they are permitted to gaze on the punishment of the wicked" as "the abominable fancy."[35] While he was happy to note that "the thoughts and hearts of men are often far gentler and nobler than the formulae of their creeds,"[36] he also observed that "It is only when these topics fall into vulgar handling, —it is only when they reek like acrid fumes from the poisoned crucible of mean and loveless conceptions,—that we see them in all their intolerable ghastliness." "Many true and loving Christians [who] have ... held these views," Farrar observed, "have mourned with aching hearts over what seemed to them the fatal necessity for believing them."[37]

Today's defenders of the traditional view of Hell rarely entertain "the abominable fancy." Robert Morey speaks for almost all of his fellow traditionalists when he writes, "We wish there was no suffering or pain in this world or in the next. We do not delight in these things. To do so would be a moral sickness." If Morey and his colleagues have the "aching hearts" of Farrar's contemporaries, then, like them, they also experience the traditional view of Hell as a "fatal necessity." Again speaking for many, Morey declares,

---

[31] This is the judgment of Walker, *The Decline of Hell*, 261. He notes the influence of Huber's novel assertion on Rousseau.

[32] See Friedrich Schleiermacher, *The Christian Faith*, ed. H.R. Mackintosh and J.S. Stewart (Edinburgh: T. and T. Clark, 1928), sec. 163, "Appendix: on Eternal Damnation," especially 721. This English translation is from the second German edition published in 1830, four years before his death. The first edition appeared in 1821–22.

[33] Richard J. Bauckham, "Universalism: A Historical Survey," *Themelios* 4, no. 2 (January 1979): 51.

[34] Bauckham, "Universalism," 51n25. His emphasis.

[35] Farrar, *Eternal Hope*, 66. On the "abominable fancy," see Philip C. Almond, *Heaven and Hell in Enlightenment England* (Cambridge: Cambridge University Press, 1994), 97–100. On the widespread debate which Farrar provoked and to which he contributed, see Geoffrey Rowell, *Hell and the Victorians: A Study of the Nineteenth Century Theological Controversies Concerning Eternal Punishment and the Future Life* (Oxford: Clarendon, 1974), chap. 7.

[36] Farrar, *Eternal Hope*, 63.

[37] Farrar, *Eternal Hope*, 64.

"The issue is not what we feel or think, but what God has revealed in His Word."[38]

Because we all live on "Schleiermacher's side of a great transition," as even Morey's response to the suffering of the damned illustrates, we can postulate that without belief in the authority of the Bible, the traditional view of Hell might virtually disappear. On the other hand, biblical authority, to which millions of Christians today are committed, exerts an influence that Modernity and Postmodernity are most unlikely to displace.[39] Once the Bible is taken into account, it may look as if traditional hellfire is here to stay, whether we like it or not.

But even this is not guaranteed. For those who would be happy to be known as 'Bible believing' Christians, the greatest challenge to time-honoured views of Final Judgment comes from an increasing number of their own leaders who are proclaiming that "what God has revealed in His Word" is something very different. The 'annihilation of Hell' is a phenomenon that is taking place *within* the world of conservative theology itself.

In this respect, the publication of *Essentials: A Liberal-Evangelical Dialogue* by David Edwards and John Stott in 1988 was especially significant, for it was here at the probing of Edwards (the "Liberal" of the dialogue), that Stott, who was sometimes referred to as 'the Pope of evangelicals', first committed his beliefs about the Final Judgment to print.[40] Despite expressing his concern for evangelical unity and his respect for "longstanding tradition that claims to be a true interpretation of Scripture,"[41] and while refusing to "dogmatise" about his "tentatively"-held position,[42] Stott did not pull his punches. "I want," he wrote, "to repudiate with all the vehemence of which I am capable the glibness, what almost appears to be the glee, the *Schadenfreude* [malicious pleasure], with which some evangelicals speak about Hell. It is a horrible sickness of mind or spirit."[43] Thus far he was echoing the sentiments of most evangelical leaders. But he went further. Commenting on the Hell of 'traditional orthodoxy' in which sinners are subjected to "eternal conscious torment," he wrote, "I find the concept intolerable and do not understand how people can live with it without either cauterising their feelings or cracking

---

[38] Robert A. Morey, *Death and the Afterlife* (Minneapolis, MN: Bethany, 1984), 100.

[39] The way in which biblical authority is conceived and thus functions is, of course, influenced by Modernity and Postmodernity. But I am simply stating that the basic trust in the Bible is unlikely to be displaced.

[40] David L. Edwards with John Stott, *Essentials: A Liberal-Evangelical Dialogue* (London: Hodder and Stoughton, 1988). For more documentation, see my "Hell: The Nemesis of Hope?," in *Her Gates Will Never Be Shut: Hope, Hell, and the New Jerusalem*, by Bradley Jersak (Eugene, OR: Wipf and Stock, 2009), 191–210, especially 192–195. A more recent work that has sparked a comparable debate within evangelical circles (and beyond) is Rob Bell, *Love Wins: A Book About Heaven, Hell, and the Fate of Every Person Who Ever Lived* (New York: HarperOne, 2011).

[41] Edwards with Stott, *Essentials*, 319.

[42] Edwards with Stott, *Essentials*, 320.

[43] Edwards with Stott, *Essentials*, 312. His emphasis.

under the strain."[44] He then proceeded to argue that the Bible points to a Final Judgment in which the impenitent are to be subjected not to ongoing suffering but to *annihilation*.

To reduce his argument to its basic elements, Stott begins by highlighting the frequent use of the language of destruction in the Bible's portrayal of the Last Judgment, language which he believes we can fully appreciate once we realise that the immortality of the soul, which coheres so naturally with the traditional idea of everlasting punishment, is a Greek rather than biblical notion. He then suggests that the imagery of (hell)fire is also best (re-)interpreted along such lines. In raising the question of Justice with respect to Hell's eternity, he suggests that the ongoing punishment that traditional orthodoxy envisions is only conceivable if there is to be ongoing rebellion against God. Having raised this possibility, he then declares that it is untenable because of the biblical promise that God will ultimately be "all in all."[45]

Stott's plea that there be "frank dialogue among evangelicals on the basis of Scripture" has certainly been fulfilled. Numerous publications have appeared, almost all since 1988, to defend, modify, and challenge the position that he has suggested. There have been books (some arranged as dialogues between traditionalists and annihilationists), symposia, magazine and journal articles, and technical doctoral dissertations.[46] While controversial to some, and unpersuasive to many, 'annihilationism' has emerged as an evangelical option with many articulate and highly respected advocates. That it is now firmly established is evidenced by an important publication by ACUTE (the UK's Evangelical Alliance Commission on Unity and Truth among Evangelicals)

---

[44] Edwards with Stott, *Essentials*, 314.

[45] The preceding summary is drawn from Edwards with Stott, *Essentials*, 314–19. On Stott's belief in 'conditional immortality' (that is not shared by all annihilationists), see my "Hell: The Nemesis of Hope?," 192n6. In this view, God does not actively annihilate the unrepentant, but allows them, in their natural mortality, to pass out of existence.

[46] Important publications that highlight the debate include: William Crockett, ed., *Four Views on Hell* (Grand Rapids, MI: Zondervan, 1992); Edward William Fudge and Robert A. Peterson, *Two Views of Hell: A Biblical and Theological Dialogue* (Downers Grove, IL: InterVarsity Press, 2000); Nigel M. de S. Cameron, ed., *Universalism and the Doctrine of Hell: Papers Presented at the Fourth Edinburgh Conference in Christian Dogmatics* (Carlisle, UK: Paternoster; Grand Rapids, MI: Baker, 1992), especially John W. Wenham, "The Case for Conditional Immortality," in *Universalism and the Doctrine of Hell*, 161–91 and Kendall S. Harmon, "The Case against Conditionalism: A Response to Edward William Fudge," in *Universalism and the Doctrine of Hell*, 193–224; K.E. Brower and M.W. Elliott, eds., *'The Reader Must Understand': Eschatology in Bible and Theology* (Leicester, UK: Apollos, 1997), especially E. Earle Ellis, "New Testament Teaching on Hell," in *'The Reader Must Understand'*, 199–219; Peter M. Head, "The Duration of Divine Judgment in the New Testament," in *'The Reader Must Understand'*, 221–27; and Tony Gray, "The Nature of Hell: Reflections on the Debate between Conditionalism and the Traditional View of Hell," in *'The Reader Must Understand'*, 231–41. An important doctoral study is David J. Powys, *'Hell': A Hard Look at a Hard Question; The Fate of the Unrighteous in New Testament Thought*. Paternoster Theological Monographs (Carlisle, UK: Paternoster, 1998).

entitled *The Nature of Hell*. Refusing to side 'officially' with either traditional orthodoxy or with annihilationism, it concludes that both positions can be described as "evangelical," the differences between them being "secondary" rather than "essential in respect of Christian doctrine."[47]

This annihilationism, which the report recognises as "a significant minority evangelical view,"[48] brings evangelical theology into contact with more 'mainstream' approaches to Final Judgment. Of special significance in this regard is another report that also appeared in the UK five years before *The Nature of Hell*: the Doctrine Commission of the Church of England's publication *The Mystery of Salvation*.[49] While the latter drew on the input of evangelicals, its perspective is far broader (the theological differences within the Anglican communion and between some of its contributors being detectable in its pages, though 'arguably' not at the expense of its basic coherence). It also sets out to cover the wider theme of salvation rather than the specific topic of Final Judgment. However, when it does address this subject, it suggests that "Annihilation might be a truer picture of damnation than any of the traditional images of the hell of eternal torment. If God has created us with the freedom to choose, then those who make such a final choice choose against the only source of life, and they have their reward."[50]

Historically, the other alternative to traditional hellfire has been belief in universal salvation. For *The Nature of Hell*, universalism (despite the attention given to some of the evangelicals who hold to this position) is judged to be unacceptable because of its lack of biblical support and because it "violate[s] the facility God has given his creatures, to reject or to accept his gospel in faith."[51] For *The Mystery of Salvation*, "Dogmatic universalism" is rejected because God's love "cannot compel" the surrender of our hearts. "Final judgment, therefore, remains a reality."[52] Thus in both reports, it is annihilationism that is presented as the only truly viable alternative to seeing conscious eternal torment as a "fatal necessity" of Christian belief.[53]

1.3 The Hell of Freedom

The Mystery of Salvation has a number of points of contact with important themes in the theology of Jürgen Moltmann. More specifically, it provides us with a helpful entrée into his approach to the topic of Final Judgment. Soon after the publication of this report, Moltmann wrote a brief review article for the German periodical *Evangelische Kommentare* under the title "Am Ende ist

---

[47] Hilborn, ed., *The Nature of Hell*, 134.
[48] *The Nature of Hell*, 134.
[49] See 0.4n19 and 0.5n20 above.
[50] *The Mystery of Salvation*, 199.
[51] *The Nature of Hell*, 31.
[52] *The Mystery of Salvation*, 198–99.
[53] As noted below, *The Mystery of Salvation* is open to an open form of universalism. But it does not put this forward as a position in the same way.

alles Gottes: Hat der Glaube an die Hölle ausgedient?" ('In the End Everything Is God's: Has belief in Hell Had Its day?').[54] A version of this piece with some important additions (and with little of significance edited out) appeared in English as "The Logic of Hell" a few years later.[55]

Before we examine these articles, it will be helpful if we situate his response to the report by noting some of the general ways in which *The Mystery of Salvation* has been influenced by Moltmann's theology.[56] These points of contact extend well beyond the two direct references to Moltmann's interpretation of God's suffering and Christ's sacrifice.[57] It is his understanding of creation and eschatology—both of which are also central themes in this present study—that is most pervasive.

Also very striking are the numerous references in the report to the transience of the present creation. With reference to the "big crunch" postulated by contemporary cosmologists, we are told:

> The final futility of the universe puts in question any ultimate recourse to evolutionary optimism. The unfolding of the present process will end either in collapse or decay, so that those who trust in a true and everlasting hope will have to look elsewhere for its ground and guarantee. Only God could release the universe from its "bondage to decay" (Rom. 8.21).[58]

This point is later reiterated by the claim that Christians live by hope "in a world of injustice, flawed by sin, and marked by an ultimate futility."[59]

But if our hope cannot be grounded *in* creation, it is still a hope *for* creation as "God promises to take creation beyond transience and mortality into

---

[54] Jürgen Moltmann, "Am Ende ist alles Gottes: Hat der Glaube an die Hölle ausgedient?," *Evangelische Kommentare* 29 (September 1996): 542–43. The translation in brackets here and below is my own. For an English translation of this essay, see "The End of Everything Is God: Has Belief in Hell Had Its Day?," trans. John Bowden, *Expository Times* 108 (June 1997): 263–64 or "In the End, All Is God's: Is Belief in Hell Obsolete?," trans. Paul F.M. Zahl, *Sewanee Theological Review* 40 (Easter 1997): 232–34. We might also translate "ausgedient" (from ausdienen) as 'worn out' or as 'no longer serving a purpose'. The phrase 'es hat ausgedient' suggests that something has 'come to the end of, or has actually exceeded, its useful life'. The title (but not the subtitle) to this article comes from a quotation from Christoph Blumhardt which also appears in the concluding paragraph of the revised English version entitled "The Logic of Hell" referred to in the next note. See also CoG, 254.
[55] See Moltmann, "The Logic of Hell," 43–47.
[56] Although Moltmann's commentator Richard Bauckham was a member of the Doctrine Commission from the beginning, we need not attribute all this influence to him! Other contributors included Geoffrey Rowell, whose important work on the Victorian debate about Hell is referred to in n. 35 above, and N.T. Wright, whose views on NT apocalyptic will be explored in 7.1 below.
[57] See *The Mystery of Salvation*, 112 and 114.
[58] *The Mystery of Salvation*, 13.
[59] *The Mystery of Salvation*, 186.

permanent union with God's own everlasting aliveness."[60] The transience of the world is not only evidence of the futility of the world considered apart from the mystery of salvation; it is also a sign of hope:

> Evening and morning, built into the present creation, witness to its impermanence. This is not simply a matter of the fallenness of humankind or the world. The creation was made, it seems, to point beyond itself. Birth, growth, decay and death all indicate that, even apart from sin, the present creation was not intended to be the creator's last word.[61]

In this light, the report asserts that "the world, and history, are the good creation of the good God, though not in themselves complete. They are made for the further purposes of the creator, and he will one day be 'all in all' in relation to them."[62] The new creation cannot "simply be a re-run of the old creation" as "presumably [this] would recapitulate the latter's transience and death."[63] Nevertheless, "The value of the old creation is implied by its redemptive transformation being the raw material of the new creation."[64]

The old and new creations are therefore intimately related but also significantly different. Even apart from the presence of evil (which the report insists is "not inherent in the nature of things"[65]), the former is "a world allowed to exist as something 'other', given by God the freedom to be itself" (which, it is suggested, may provide a "clue to answering the problem of physical suffering").[66] The new creation, by contrast, "will be a world freely reconciled to God in Christ (Col. 1.20), a transfigured universe completely suffused with the divine presence.... It will be a *cosmos pneumatikos*—a universe animated by God's Spirit, in the most intimate connection with its creator."[67] In bringing the present world into existence, therefore, "God has 'made way' for it as an entity other than himself."[68] But "ultimate salvation is *theosis*, participation in the life of God himself."[69]

The similarity between this line of thought and Moltmann's theology (for which the rest of this study will provide ample documentation) is unmistakable. Even the ambiguities provide some instructive parallels. What, for example, are we to make of the claim that "Creation may be transitory, *but* it was and

---

[60] *The Mystery of Salvation*, 55.
[61] *The Mystery of Salvation*, 72.
[62] *The Mystery of Salvation*, 74.
[63] *The Mystery of Salvation*, 191.
[64] *The Mystery of Salvation*, 195.
[65] *The Mystery of Salvation*, 52.
[66] *The Mystery of Salvation*, 194.
[67] *The Mystery of Salvation*, 194–95. Their italics.
[68] *The Mystery of Salvation*, 188. In 4.1 below, I will connect this with Moltmann's *zimzum* doctrine of creation.
[69] *The Mystery of Salvation*, 189. Their italics.

remains good"?[70] As we move to the specific topic of Final Judgment, the relationship is far less striking. But the connections are still real.

Not only does Moltmann exist on "Schleiermacher's side of [the] great transition," as we all do, with respect to the "abominable fancy"; he also sides with Schleiermacher in a more specific way by advocating universal salvation. As we have seen, *The Mystery of Salvation* suggests an annihilationist interpretation of the Final Judgment. However it still remains open to universal salvation, provided it is not at the expense of human freedom. Love may not be able to force the surrender of those who resist. But there remains "an unconquerable hope" for their salvation.[71] Because of human freedom, Final Judgment must "remain a reality." And any who "choose against the only source of life" will in so doing "have their reward." Nevertheless, the report adds, "Whether there be any who do so choose, only God knows."[72] (By contrast, the *Nature of Hell*, while "emphasis[ing] that God's mercy might extend further than we can legitimately contemplate,"[73] nevertheless states: "Hell does exist, and ... it is occupied to some degree."[74]) In this way a 'hopeful' rather than 'dogmatic' universalism is affirmed as deeply Christian. It is in this light that we should understand the title chosen for the concluding section to the report: "That nothing be lost," for this does not only express the "universal range" or scope "of salvation" offered by a God who "continues to pursue the completion and perfection of the whole of creation";[75] it also to articulates the conviction that in the cross, we see "God's willingness to risk all to save all."[76]

Given the affinity of this report to Moltmann's overall theology, and given its openness to at least some form of universalism, we might expect that his response would be favourable. As annihilationism is often perceived a lying between 'traditional orthodoxy' and 'universalism' (especially by those who see it as succumbing to the slippery slope that leads from 'Biblical Christianity' to theological liberalism), some might anticipate that if he were to be critical at all, it would be because *The Mystery of Salvation* does not go far enough. In actual fact, Moltmann's *rejection* of the report's approach to Hell is as uncompromising as we might expect from any conservative theologian. Asking why his response is so critical will help us gain insight into his distinctive understanding of the eschatological and soteriological issues surrounding the Final Judgment.

---

[70] *The Mystery of Salvation*, 72. My emphasis. In context, the "but" can be read as 'contrary to what dualistic theologies might make of this transience ... '. But read in the light of the whole report, the 'goodness' of transience is far from clear!
[71] *The Mystery of Salvation*, 198.
[72] *The Mystery of Salvation*, 199. Cf. 179: "We can never say that someone is not saved."
[73] *The Nature of Hell*, 34.
[74] *The Nature of Hell*, 32.
[75] *The Mystery of Salvation*, 201, 204.
[76] *The Mystery of Salvation*, 205.

Not only does Moltmann reject the report's interpretation of Hell as decisively as any advocate of traditional orthodoxy, but, perhaps more surprisingly, he does so for the same fundamental reason: in his judgment, this interpretation of Hell as total non-being is far more "modern" than "Christian."[77]

Firstly, Moltmann claims that since the nuclear bombing of Hiroshima in August 1945, "the imagination of modern men and women has been fascinated no longer by burning but by annihilation." " 'Fire' and 'annihilation',," he observes, "are merely metaphors for an inescapable remoteness from God, or a God-forsakenness from which there is no way out." Thus, in *The Mystery of Salvation*, the "hell fire of old" has simply been replaced "by the annihilation of modern times."[78]

The second (and more significant) way in which the report betrays a modern outlook is in its focus on "freedom of choice." He cites the report as saying:

> It is our conviction that the reality of hell (and indeed of heaven) is the ultimate affirmation of the reality of human freedom.[79]

"It is here," says Moltmann, "that the real theological problem about this modern explanation of hell lies."[80]

At this point, Moltmann demonstrates that far from setting out to advocate a form of universalism that emancipates itself from past Christian thought, he actually wants to situate his approach firmly within the mainstream theological tradition. Thus he notes that in *The Mystery of Salvation*, it is Erasmus rather than Luther or Calvin who has become "the saint of modern times." Similarly, "It is apparently not Augustine who is the Father of Anglo-Saxon Christianity; the Church Father who secretly presides over it is Pelagius." It is thus with an

---

[77] Moltmann, "The Logic of Hell," 44 ("the annihilation of modern times" and "it is Erasmus who is the saint of modern times, not Luther or Calvin") and 46 ("The Christian doctrine of hell is to be found in the gospel of Christ's descent into hell, not in a modernization of hell into total non-being"). For the conservative claim that annihilationism is a capitulation to a modern mindset, see, e.g., Larry Dixon, *The Other Side of the Good News: Confronting the Contemporary Challenges to Jesus' Teaching on Hell* (Wheaton: IL: Bridgepoint, 1992), 182–83.

[78] Moltmann, "The Logic of Hell," 43–44. The comments about Hiroshima are missing from "Am Ende ist alles Gottes." However in personal correspondence to this author (dated October 3rd, 1996) soon after its publication, Moltmann commented with reference to this article and to *The Mystery of Salvation*, "Before Hiroshima it was 'brimstone and fire', after it is just 'annihilation'. I don't like [either], having seen more of hell on earth than I could stand."

[79] This is taken from *The Mystery of Salvation*, 199.

[80] Moltmann, "The Logic of Hell," 44. Two works which attempt to defend belief in Hell by appealing to (a libertarian understanding of) human freedom, and which would evoke a similar critique from Moltmann here, are Jonathan L. Kvanvig, *The Problem of Hell* (Oxford: Oxford University Press, 1993) and Jerry L. Walls, *Hell: The Logic of Damnation* (Notre Dame, IN: University of Notre Dame Press, 1992). (Moltmann refers to the latter work in CoG, 373n232, but does not specifically engage its argument.)

implicit appeal to Luther, Calvin, and Augustine that he raises his first challenge to "the logic of hell" by asking:

> Does God's love preserve our free will, or does it free our enslaved will, which has become un-free th[r]ough the power of sin? Does God love free men and women, or does he seek the men and women who have become lost?[81]

Moltmann then asks how children who die early, the severely disabled, those suffering from geriatric diseases, and those who have never been faced with the choice of the Gospel will all fare if 'free choice' determines our eternal fate. He also raises questions about the place of Israel ("God's chosen people"), the adherents of other religions, and non-human creatures in God's future.[82] There are, of course, standard answers to this line of questioning. *The Mystery of Salvation* spends an important chapter defending a non-exclusivist approach to non-Christian faiths[83] and is adamant about the creation-wide scope of redemption. Similarly, *The Nature of Hell* (a report that also emphasises the importance of free choice in relation to salvation) pays special attention to the plight of infants and the mentally handicapped.[84] Moltmann's point however would seem to be that one needs to supplement a 'free choice' approach to salvation in such cases. If God's purposes can be fulfilled in other ways, so Moltmann's (implicit) argument goes, why do we have to make "choice" a *sine qua non* in relation to salvation at all?

There is also a more 'pastoral' point to be made. If salvation "all depends on the human being's free will," Moltmann points out, then we are being asked to "base the assurance of our salvation on the shaky ground of our own decisions." Does this not "expect too much" of us? Will this not abandon us to "a state of uncertainty"?[85]

Moltmann's next argument against the "logic of hell" goes beyond claiming it is "inhumane" to observing that it is "also extremely atheistic." Here Moltmann is thinking of a 'practical' atheism in which human choice is viewed as so sovereign and so autonomous that God is reduced to an "accessory who puts that will into effect." Not only do we "dispose over our own lives here; [we] decide on our eternal destinies as well." In effect, we "have no need of God at all." As Moltmann puts it,

> After a God has perhaps created us free as we are, he leaves us to our fate. Carried to this ultimate conclusion, the logic of hell is secular humanism, as Feuerbach, Marx and Nietzsche already perceived a long time ago.[86]

---

[81] Moltmann, "The Logic of Hell," 44.
[82] Moltmann, "The Logic of Hell," 44–45. The comments about non-human creatures are missing in "Am Ende ist alles Gottes."
[83] See *The Mystery of Salvation*, chap. 7.
[84] See *The Nature of Hell*, 93–95.
[85] Moltmann, "The Logic of Hell," 45.
[86] Moltmann, "The Logic of Hell," 45.

That no author of *The Mystery of Salvation* would wish to defend such a position is beside the point. Moltmann is not simply examining their conclusions. He is analysing the "logic" of their position.

Finally, Moltmann introduces his own perspective by stating that "The Christian doctrine of hell is to be found in the gospel of Christ's descent into hell, not in a modernization of hell into total non-being."[87] Replacing the image of "annihilation" is not the issue, for Moltmann admits that it is a genuine metaphor for a "God-forsakenness from which there is no way out."[88] (This is why we will see him using the language of annihilation and even hell-fire below.) The real problem is that in *The Mystery of Salvation*, this "God-forsakenness" is not explicitly related to and understood in the light of the cross. It is this that his reflections on Christ's descent into Hell are intended to address.

"Hell," writes Moltmann, following Luther, "is not a place in the next world, the underworld; it is an experience of God." Similarly, Christ's descent is not his journey to the Grave in which he preached to the spirits of the dead (as we find in the Apostles' Creed); it is "his experience of God-forsakenness from Gethsemane to Golgotha."[89]

It is this "experience of God," this "God-forsakenness," that provides the connection between Christ and contemporary experience. "Our century," Moltmann says (writing in 1999), "has produced more *infernos* than all the centuries before us: The gas ovens of Auschwitz and the atomising of Hiroshima heralded an age of potential mass *annihilation* through ABC [Atomic, Biological, and Chemical] weapons. . . . It is pointless to deny hell." But in relating to Christ in our hells, we may speak of "*the gospel* of Christ's descent into hell." A Christian view of hell requires us, contrary to Dante and the dominant theological tradition, to declare to the whole creation, 'Do *not* abandon hope, all who enter here!' "Christ suffered the 'God-forsakenness' that knows no way out," writes Moltmann, "so that he could bring God to the God-forsaken." It is only "[i]n the crucified Christ [that] we see what hell is, because through him it has been overcome."[90]

"The universality of God's grace" (which *The Mystery of Salvation* also wishes to affirm) cannot, Moltmann insists, be grounded in "free will," a grounding which inevitably—logically—leads to a double outcome of heaven and hell. Instead it is to be grounded in "the theology of the cross" which leads (as Karl Barth and Christoph Blumhardt realised) to "universal reconciliation."[91] And because salvation is not based on "the shaky ground of our decisions,"[92] if we seek ourselves in Christ rather than in ourselves, as

---

[87] Moltmann, "The Logic of Hell," 46.
[88] Moltmann, "The Logic of Hell," 44.
[89] Moltmann, "The Logic of Hell," 46.
[90] Moltmann, "The Logic of Hell," 46. My emphases throughout.
[91] Moltmann, "The Logic of Hell," 46–47.
[92] Moltmann, "The Logic of Hell," 45.

Luther advised, then what we experience as our "uncertain election" is "made sure."[93]

The fact that there is no double outcome does not mean, in Moltmann's understanding, that there is no judgment. Admittedly, judgment is not "God's last word." That will be " 'Behold, I make *all things* new' (Rev 21:5)." But it is a vital, penultimate word that "establishes in the world the divine righteousness on which the new creation is to be built." From the making new of "*all things*" (Moltmann's italics), "no one is excepted." In the earlier German version of this piece, this is emphasised by the addition of the phrase: "auch nich die Massenmörden der Weltgeschichte, die wir zur Hölle wünschen" (not even the mass murderers of world history whom we wish to damn to Hell). The German then brings the article to a close by saying "Liebe ist Gottes Erbarmen mit den Verlorenen." While the English version also has this statement ("Love is God's compassion with the lost"), it follows it with the additional concluding comments:

> Transforming grace is God's punishment for sinners. It is not the right to choose that defines the reality of human freedom. It is the doing of the good.[94]

It is these additional statements that are perhaps the most provocative of all as they address the two most common objections to universal salvation: that it entails an overriding of human freedom and that it ignores issues of justice. Here Moltmann does no more than hint at how he might respond. But he clearly has a kind of freedom in mind that he wants to affirm, a freedom that is distinct from the idea of autonomy.[95] It sounds as though he is advocating the biblical notion that freedom is found (or consists) in embodying the will of God.[96] Perhaps, he might say that, in God's grace, we are all saved from our autonomy for true freedom. Such a perspective does not immediately solve every problem. Questions remain. (We might ask, for example, whether "*doing* the good," to use Moltmann's language, does not itself presuppose '*choosing* the good'?) But enough has been said to suggest that Moltmann's position is sufficiently nuanced in this respect to resist being quickly dismissed.

His statement "Transforming grace is God's punishment for sinners" is even more suggestive. It should be read as making two simultaneous assertions: "*Transforming grace* is God's punishment for sinners" and "Transforming grace is *God's punishment for sinners.*" God's compassion and God's judgment

---

[93] Moltmann, "The Logic of Hell," 46, citing Luther.
[94] Moltmann, "The Logic of Hell," 47. His emphasis. German quotations in this paragraph are from "Am Ende ist alles Gottes," 543.
[95] In this light, his earlier claim in "The Logic of Hell," 44, that "The logic of hell is nothing other than the logic of human *free will*, in so far as this is identical with *freedom of choice*" (my emphases) bears re-inspection as it may suggest not only a notion of freedom that is distinct from autonomy ("freedom of choice") but also a non-autonomous and thus acceptable notion of "free will." I explore this possibility in the Conclusion in 8.3 below.
[96] See Jas 1:25.

are envisioned as two sides of the same coin. This is particularly borne out in the German version of the essay which, immediately prior to its reference to "mass murderers," states that from God's making new of all things, "Davon ist niemand ausgenommen oder freigestellt" ('no one is excluded or exempt'). This reference to 'exclusion' means that we will not be able to damn murderers to Hell. The reference to 'exemption' suggests that transforming grace is far from permissive.

This double-edged notion of transforming grace must be interpreted in the light of the victory of the cross, which is a victory for all, over all. To cite part of the passage from *The Crucified God* discussed above, "The message of the new righteousness which eschatological faith brings into the world says that in fact the executioners will not finally triumph over their victims. It also says that in the end the victims will not triumph over their executioners."[97] This "new righteousness" that faith anticipates in the present age, should be connected to what Moltmann here (over 25 years later) refers to as "the divine righteousness" that God's "Judgment establishes in the world."[98]

"The Logic of Hell" (and its German counterpart) is a provocative piece (due in part to the fact that it is barely four pages in length). It raises many questions. Clearly it is no substitute for the more detailed exposition that Moltmann provides elsewhere. But it does provide us with a most suggestive introduction. Here, we are presented with a view of universal salvation in which Final Judgment is central to Christian hope. Here is a vision for the salvation of all people in which true human freedom is affirmed. Here is a universalism in which the cry for Justice is to not to be silenced. Moltmann's eschatology, rooted in the theology of the cross, holds out the promise that in the end justice and mercy will embrace.

1.4 The Passing of Hell in *The Coming of God*

Moltmann's nine major works can be subdivided into his early trilogy (*Theology of Hope*,[99] *The Crucified God*, and *The Church in the Power of the Spirit*[100]) and his more recent "systematic contributions to theology" series (*The Trinity and the Kingdom of God*,[101] *God in Creation*,[102] *The Way of Jesus*

---

[97] CrG, 178 as cited in 1.1 above.
[98] Moltmann, "The Logic of Hell," 47 as cited above.
[99] Jürgen Moltmann, *Theology of Hope: On the Ground and the Implications of a Christian Eschatology*, trans. James Leitch (London: SCM Press, 1967). Hereafter TH.
[100] Jürgen Moltmann, *The Church in the Power of the Spirit: A Contribution to Messianic Ecclesiology*, trans. Margaret Kohl (London: SCM Press, 1977). Hereafter CPS.
[101] Jürgen Moltmann, *The Trinity and the Kingdom of God: The Doctrine of God*, trans. Margaret Kohl (London: SCM Press, 1980). Hereafter TKG.
[102] Jürgen Moltmann, *God in Creation: An Ecological Doctrine of Creation*, trans. Margaret Kohl (London: SCM Press, 1985). Hereafter GC.

Christ, The Spirit of Life,[103] *The Coming of God*,[104] and *Experiences in Theology*[105]). If we view the final volume (*Experiences in Theology*) as a kind of appendix (or belated prologue) on theological method, then we may recognise the way in which *Theology of Hope* and *The Coming of God* form an important *inclusio*. While the former attempts to re-centre the entire theological enterprise in eschatological expectation, thus setting the tone for Moltmann's theologising for more than 30 years, it is in *The Coming of God* that Moltmann finally gives sustained attention to eschatology as a theological topic in its own right. *Theology of Hope* is an exercise in theology *as* eschatology. *The Coming of God* concerns the theology *of* eschatology. With the possible exception of a short section on Christ as the Judge of the living and the dead at the end of *The Way of Jesus Christ* (to which we shall refer briefly below), it is here that we find Moltmann's only relatively detailed discussion of Final Judgment.[106] And it is to this discussion that we should now turn.

1.4.1 The Theology of the Cross

After surveying a number of universalist and non-universalist arguments, both biblical and theological, Moltmann sets out his own position on the outcome of the Final Judgment in a final section entitled "Christ's Descent into Hell and the Restoration of All Things." Parallels with "The Logic of Hell" are numerous, not the least of which is his commitment to developing a theology of the cross in this context. He writes,

> If we follow the method of providing christological answers to eschatological questions, then in trying to measure the breadth of the Christian hope we must not wander off into far-off realms, but must submerge ourselves in the depths of Christ's death on the cross at Golgotha.[107]

In attempting to ground "the restoration of all things" in "Christ's descent into Hell," Moltmann is distinguishing his approach from that of the four positions that he has surveyed in the previous section, as all of these (at least in his analysis) approach the question of whether the Final Judgment has a double

---

[103] Jürgen Moltmann, *The Spirit of Life: A Universal Affirmation*, trans. Margaret Kohl (London: SCM Press, 1992). Hereafter SL.

[104] Jürgen Moltmann, *The Coming of God: Christian Eschatology*, trans. Margaret Kohl (London: SCM Press, 1996). Hereafter CoG.

[105] Jürgen Moltmann, *Experiences in Theology: Ways and Forms of Christian Theology*, trans. Margaret Kohl (London: SCM Press, 2000). Hereafter EiT.

[106] References in other works will be discussed in 7.2 below.

[107] CoG, 250. Cf. CoG, 237: " 'Universalism', '*apokatastasis panton*', 'universal salvation' or 'the restoration of all things' are all terms for the most disputed question in Christian eschatology. It is an eschatological question. But theologically it can be decided only in the framework of christology."

or single outcome in terms of the doctrine of predestination, thus attempting to "answer questions about the end with the presuppositions of the beginning."[108]

Two of these positions—the "true universalism" of Schleiermacher and the "open universalism" of Barth and Christoph Blumhardt—actually reach conclusions very similar to Moltmann's. It is in his analysis of "true particularism" as worked out in the supralapsarian approach to predestination (a position associated with Calvin), that the implications of Moltmann's theological method are most clear. Moltmann does not "wander . . . into far-off realms" in criticising this position.[109] In keeping with his "christological" focus, he simply observes that "According to this supralapsarian doctrine of predestination, God's decision about the salvation and damnation of human beings *is not already revealed in Christ, nor is it revealed in the gospel*. It is revealed provisionally in history, in faith and disbelief, but finally only at the Last Judgment."[110] Although he goes on to observe that its "universalism of God's glorification" by the eternal existence of heaven and hell is shaped by an Aristotelian aesthetic in which beauty is enhanced by contrasting antitheses[111]—a view of God's glory radically different from his own[112]—, it is the fact that this position is not grounded in the theology of the cross that constitutes the decisive reason for its rejection.

It is important to stress that this is an issue of fundamental theological method. One might well observe that Moltmann's position is not simply 'grounded' in the cross but rests on a particular *interpretation*—perhaps a *misinterpretation*—of the cross. One might also point out that the 'Calvinist' position that Moltmann rejects can connect its eschatological conclusions to its own interpretation of the cross via its doctrine of the atonement. But this is beside the point. Moltmann's analysis aims to show that its interpretation of the outcome of the Final Judgment is not *centred* in the theology of the cross. It would not be an exaggeration to say that from Moltmann's point of view, it is for this reason not really a 'Christian' position at all.[113]

---

[108] CoG, 246.

[109] In this, he is also eschewing the 'speculative' theology often associated with universalism (as noted in CoG, 240).

[110] CoG, 246. My emphasis.

[111] See CoG, 247.

[112] On which, see CoG, 323–39: "Glory: Divine Eschatology."

[113] Presumably, the same judgment would apply to infralapsarianism. In his four-fold typology, Moltmann also analyses the "hypothetical universalism" associated with Moyse Amyraut (on whom he wrote his doctoral dissertation). In this position, God's universal salvific intent is not realised because the Gospel can only save under the condition of faith. In postulating that it is only at the Last Judgment that "the eternal particularism of the divine election and rejection will . . . be manifest" (CoG, 247–48), this viewpoint would be vulnerable to the same criticism with respect to the decisive revelation of God's purposes in the cross. But Moltmann makes no critical comments in his very brief description. The fact that at least God's salvific intent is expressed in the cross in this view brings it closer to the Christocentric approach that Moltmann advocates. The same might be said for the similar perspective of *The Mystery of*

As a result of his own methodological choice to "provid[e] *christological* answers to eschatological questions,"[114] Moltmann develops the view that it is only in the light of the cross that we may discern the true nature of Hell. "The *Christian* doctrine about the restoration of all things," he writes, "denies neither damnation nor hell. On the contrary: it assumes that in his suffering and dying Christ suffered the true and total hell of God-forsakenness for the reconciliation of the world, and experienced for us the true and total damnation of sin."[115]

He then proceeds to connect the two halves of his chosen title—"Christ's Descent into Hell and the Restoration of All Things"—by declaring,

> It is precisely here that the divine reason for the reconciliation of the universe is to be found. It is not the optimistic dream of a purified humanity, it is Christ's descent into hell that is the ground for the confidence that nothing be lost but that everything will be brought back again and gathered into the eternal kingdom of God. *The true Christian foundation for the hope of universal salvation is the theology of the cross, and the realistic consequence of the theology of the cross can only be the restoration of all things.*[116]

The connection between this "existential"[117] Hell and salvation for all is developed by the following three-fold claim:

> *Christ's descent into hell* therefore means: even in the experience of hell you are there (Ps. 139.8).
> *Christ's descent into hell* means: you have suffered the experience of hell for us, so as to be beside us in our experience of hell.
> *Christ's descent into hell* means, finally: hell and death have been gathered up and ended in God.[118]

Moltmann's train of thought in the three assertions should be interpreted as follows:

Salvation (which only differs significantly from Amyrautism in not stressing a doctrine of election). But for Moltmann, the cross (understood as Christ's descent into Hell) reveals far more than God's *intent* to save all people, as the following discussion will show.

[114] CoG, 250 as cited above. My emphasis.
[115] CoG, 251. His emphasis. Cf. CoG, 252, where he echoes Luther's conviction that when Christ was dying, he experienced not only "God's present anger over the godless world" but also his "future wrath" and "future hell."
[116] CoG, 251. His emphasis.
[117] CoG, 252. He finds the idea of Hell as an "existential experience" in Luther, Calvin, Barth, and Pannenberg. He also cites here his own early work, CrG, 246: "Only if disaster, forsakenness by God, absolute death, the infinite curse of damnation and sinking into nothingness is gathered into God himself, is community with this God eternal salvation, infinite joy, indestructible election and divine life."
[118] CoG, 252. His emphases.

1. Because Christ descended into Hell, he (and thus God) is there in the Hell we experience today (a point made with an allusion to the language of Ps 139:8).
2. Through suffering Hell for us, Christ (or God in Christ) is beside us in our hells.
3. Through Christ's death and resurrection, God entered the "God-forsaken space" of Hell *for the first time*, thus taking it up into his omnipresence and overcoming its deadly power.[119]

The nuances and full implications of this last point are best appreciated when this passage is read in the light of Moltmann's overall theological position—a reading to which we shall return in the following chapters of this study.[120] But the basic thrust is accessible if we follow the way Moltmann develops his argument.

To this end, Moltmann refers sympathetically to a line of thought developed by Urs von Balthasar that sought to mediate "in the spirit of Origen" between the Eastern Fathers' concern for the assurance of salvation and Western theology's "emotional emphasis on freedom." Thus the godless are seen as

---

[119] For Moltmann's description of Hell as "God-forsaken space," see 4.1 below. The important point that God enters Hell for the first time through Christ's descent is somewhat obscured by an ambiguity in the way Moltmann expresses himself in the above quotation. Should we (a) take the "you" being addressed in the first two assertions as *Christ*, perhaps interpreting the confessional second person form in line with Luther's advice (a discussion of which frames this passage) that we look on Hell not in ourselves but in him, or should we (b) take the reference to Ps 139:8 ("if I make my bed in Sheol, you are there") as evidence that the "you" is *God*? If we opt for the latter, this raises the question of whether (c) Moltmann, in saying "you are there" with reference to this verse, means that God has been in "hell" all along, as the psalmist recognised in his own time, Christ's descent simply revealing this fact in a decisive way. If that is so, then God does not enter Hell for the first time in Christ.

In my opinion, (a) is probably correct, (b) is possible, and (c) is false. At least in part, the "you" being addressed in the first two assertions is Christ, the switch to "God" occurring only in the third assertion. Moltmann is simply alluding to (not exegeting) the language of Ps 139:8 for his own purposes and applying it to Christ who has descended into Hell. But (b) is certainly plausible, *if* Moltmann is understood as referring not simply to God but to *God in the crucified Christ*. This way of phrasing things brings the two interpretations together. It also coheres with GC, 91 which cites Ps 139:8 also. There is, in fact, very little at stake unless we move from (b) to (c). It is here that the ambiguity threatens to lead to a reading that is precisely the opposite of the one Moltmann intends. For evidence that God, in Moltmann's understanding, enters Hell in Christ, see below, especially with reference to the quotation from CoG, 253. Cf. 4.1 below. For a clear statement in a more recent essay that rules out (c), cf. Jürgen Moltmann, "The Presence of God's Future: The Risen Christ," *Anglican Theological Review* 89, no. 4 (Fall 2007): 577–88, especially 582, where he writes: "*Since* Christ's descent into hell there is hope where all prospects vanish: Even in hell you are there (Ps. 139:8)." My emphasis.

[120] Moltmann's *zimzum* doctrine of creation, explored in 4.1 below, is important in this context. That God enters Hell for the first time in Christ's descent is clear in GC, 91—a passage cited and discussed there.

experiencing the Hell, or state of God-forsakenness, that they have chosen for themselves (a view also expressed in *The Mystery of Salvation*.[121]) Nevertheless, because Christ has descended into Hell, he is their companion. Those who wish to escape God find God in their solitariness, a God who "in the absolute powerlessness of love ... [is] on the side of the one who damns himself."[122]

Having thus covered points one and two of his understanding of Christ's descent into Hell (as outlined above), Moltmann's summary of von Balthasar's position proceeds to the final point by noting that,

> [I]n his forsakenness by the Father [Christ] experiences hell, because in pure obedience he seeks the Father *where he is not to be found*, and through his descent into hell takes hell and all those who are in it into his trinitarian fellowship with the Father.[123]

This substantiates my claim that God becomes present in Hell for the first time through Christ descent. It is only through him, that the gates of Hell, which hitherto are closed tight in the self-enclosure of sin (as Moltmann likes to put it[124]), are finally blown open. It is this that grounds our certain hope in the restoration of all things.

This '*certain* hope', as I have referred to it, and the "confession of hope" with which he brings his discussion to a close,[125] need to be carefully distinguished from the 'hopeful' universalism that finds approval in *The Mystery of Salvation*. In the latter, the universal salvation we 'hope' for is something that we desire, without knowing for sure what God will finally be able to achieve in the face of human freedom. Because there is no way that we can be certain, in this understanding, the best we can do is 'hope' for the best. 'Dogmatic' universalism is thus inappropriate. Moltmann's 'theology of hope' is very different. While he would certainly agree that God's eschatological Judgment is still to come, and is thus not something we can describe, at the same time, he insists that because the revelation of God's purposes in the Christ event has already taken place, a hope that is rooted in the cross is not simply an expression of what we would like to happen. Given God's decisive action in

---

[121] Although *The Mystery of Salvation*, 199 also applies this to the *post-mortem* state of the unrepentant.

[122] CoG, 253.

[123] CoG, 253. My emphasis. For a succinct statement of Hans Urs von Balthasar's position, which has many affinities to Moltmann's perspective, see his *Dare We Hope "That All Men Be Saved"? With a Short Discourse on Hell*, trans. David Kipp and Lothar Krauth (San Francisco: Ignatius, 1988). For the charge that this "forsakenness by the Father" in Moltmann's thought is abusive, see Jürgen Moltmann, *A Broad Place: An Autobiography*, trans. Margaret Kohl (Minneapolis, MN: Fortress Press, 2008), hereafter BP, 198–200. For my response to this misreading, see 4.1n38 below.

[124] For example, in TKG, 213, he writes of God's "liberation of men and women ... from their deadly withdrawal into themselves, their closed-in-ness."

[125] See CoG, 254, with reference to Blumhardt's "confession of hope."

Christ, we can be confident of the outcome: "What Christ *accomplished* in his dying and rising is *proclaimed* to all human beings through his gospel and will be *revealed* to everyone and everything at his appearance."[126] The "confession of hope," as articulated by Christoph Blumhardt, can and should be preached with conviction. This has nothing to do with merely 'hoping for the best'. For hope, in Moltmann theology, provides the way to certainty. And the cross provides the way to hope. In "submerg[ing] ourselves in the depths of Christ's death on the cross," Moltmann writes, "... we find the *certainty* of reconciliation without limits."[127]

Finally we should note that Moltmann's emphasis on the theology of the cross allows him to respond to the charge that universalism advocates (what Dietrich Bonhoeffer called) "cheap grace." To this Moltmann replies that God's "all-reconciling love" cannot be considered "cheap" firstly because it is "free" as grace always is, and secondly because it is so "costly." Thus he writes,

> [I]t is born out of the profound suffering of God and is the costliest thing that God can give: himself in his Son, who has become our brother, and who draws us through our hells.[128]

1.4.2 Freedom

Moltmann's sympathy for von Balthasar's position is of special interest because it hints once more at Moltmann's understanding of salvation as an overcoming of our autonomy that at the same time avoids (and even resists)

---

[126] CoG, 254. His emphases. This emphasis on what Christ has accomplished means that Tim Chester's claim, in *Mission and the Coming of God: Eschatology, the Trinity and Mission in the Theology of Jürgen Moltmann and Contemporary Evangelicalism* (Milton Keynes, UK: Paternoster, 2006), 75, that Christ, for Moltmann, is "the revealer of salvation rather than the means of salvation" in what is ultimately "an un-christological soteriology," is unfounded, not least because it ignores the descent into Hell motif, which could hardly be more central or more Christocentric. As T. David Beck notes in *The Holy Spirit and the Renewal of All Things: Pneumatology in Paul and Jürgen Moltmann*. Princeton Theological Monograph Series 67 (Eugene, OR: Pickwick, 2007), 105, Moltmann's theological creativity, coupled with his desire to engage the biblical witness, transcends the evangelical-liberal divide in Protestant theology—a divide that would appear to lie behind Chester's critique. In this context, Moltmann also escapes the limits of Protestant and Catholic soteriology as he is closer to Eastern Orthodox concerns. On the latter, see Hilarion Alfeyev, *Christ the Conqueror of Hell: The Descent into Hades from an Orthodox Perspective* (Crestwood, NY: St. Vladimir's Seminary Press, 2009). Moltmann's affinity with Eastern theology more generally is explored in Nicholas Constas, "Eschatology and Christology: Moltmann and the Greek Fathers," in *God's Life in Trinity*, ed. Miroslav Volf and Michael Welker (Minneapolis, MN: Fortress Press, 2006), 191–99. This affinity is worthy of further study.

[127] CoG, 250. My emphasis. My sympathy with this approach to certainty is explored in 5.0 below.

[128] CoG, 254.

saying that God overrides our 'freedom'. Thus, the Christ who meets us in Hell is the God of "powerless[] ... love."

It would be a mistake, I suggest, to claim that Moltmann does not in any sense share von Balthasar's openness to what Moltmann (admittedly somewhat disparagingly) calls "the emotional emphasis on freedom of Western theology."[129] This point bears illustration. Moltmann ends his brief summary of "true" (as opposed to "hypothetical" and "open") universalism with a footnote to John A.T. Robinson's book *In the End, God*, noting that Robinson sees "the problem of universalism in the encounter between human freedom and divine love." How is this "encounter" to be resolved? Although Robinson suggests that those who resist God's will come to the point where, in the words of one of Charles Wesley's hymns, they can say:

> I yield, I yield,
> I can hold out no more;
> I sink by dying love compelled
> To own thee conqueror!,

Moltmann notes with what I suggest is considerable approval:

> *But what he really finds convincing* is Origen's legendary saying that Christ hangs on the cross as long as there is a sinner in hell. God will in the end be all in all, *not because God's love overcomes the very last believer*, but because the shadows of Christ's cross dissolve hell.[130]

There is every indication that when Moltmann refers to the widespread fear that universalism treats God's grace as "a force of destiny" or "compulsive power which disposes over people without asking them,"[131] he does not believe that his own position can be described in this way.

What is perhaps most intriguing about Moltmann's position is that he resists the notion that our salvation is in any way dependent on whether we choose to accept or reject it[132] *while at the same time* avoiding the idea that salvation is forced upon us. So how does he understand the relation between God's will and the human will in salvation?

Moltmann is adamant that it is *God* and *God alone* who decides for a person's salvation, making that decision at Golgotha where the "great turning

---

[129] CoG, 253.
[130] CoG, 372n221. My emphases. Cf. John A.T. Robinson, *In the End, God: A Study of the Christian Doctrine of the Last Things*, 2nd ed. (London: Fontana, 1968), 133. The verse from Wesley is cited on p. 123. (There is a new edition of this work, edited by Robin Parry, with an Introduction by Trevor Hart (Eugene, OR: Cascade, 2011), but like Moltmann, I cite the pagination of the older edition.)
[131] CoG, 244.
[132] The section under discussion in *The Coming of God* contains a number of comments that are reminiscent of the critique he mounted against our all-too-modern notions of freedom in "The Logic of Hell." See, e.g., CoG, 245.

point from disaster to salvation" took place and the whole cosmos was reconciled with God (2 Cor 5:19). "Faith," he writes, "means experiencing and receiving this turning point personally, but faith is not the turning point itself. It is not my faith that creates salvation for me; salvation creates faith for me." Having established this point, however, his thinking begins to hint—albeit briefly—at a position that could transcend the disagreements between standard 'Reformed' and 'Arminian' theologies if it were developed further. For he says,

> It is only if a qualitative difference is made between God and human beings that God's decision and human decision can be valued and respected. God's decision 'for us', and our decisions for faith or disbelief no more belong on the same level than do eternity and time. We should be measuring God and the human being by the same yardstick if we were to ask: what, and how much, does God do for the salvation of human beings, and what, and how much, must human beings do?[133]

From this it is clear that to attribute 100% of our salvation to God and 0% to ourselves would be mistaken. By the same token, salvation cannot be seen as a 50%-50% divine-human partnership. (Moltmann is particularly scathing about views that speak of salvation as a divine "offer" that we, for our part, are called to "accept," saying that such formulations turn God "into the purveyor of a

---

[133] CoG, 245. This important passage will be discussed in 2.0, 2.6, 4.3.1, and 8.3 below.

In saying that Moltmann's thinking here might 'transcend' the differences between standard Reformed and Arminian theologies, I mean, in part, that although Moltmann's rejection of a libertarian conception of freedom has thus far been in line with mainstream Reformed theology (cf. the clear discussion of Richard A. Muller, "Freedom," in *The Westminster Handbook to Reformed Theology*, ed. Donald K. McKim (Louisville, KY: Westminster John Knox, 2001), 87–89 and of James I. Packer, "Free Will," in *The Westminster Handbook to Reformed Theology*, 86–87), he seems intent on giving a place to human decision (in relation to God) that is far more defined and forthright in nature than that allowed for by the fundamentally mysterious divine-human *concursus* (concurrence) that Reformed thinkers tend to invoke when responding to Arminian theology. For a contemporary example of the latter, see any of the essays in John Piper, Justin Taylor, and Paul Kjoss Helseth, eds., *Beyond the Bounds: Open Theism and the Undermining of Biblical Christianity* (Wheaton, IL: Crossway, 2003). This response volume to the neo-Arminianism of Open Theism frequently asserts the reality of (non-libertarian) human freedom but never spells out or even explores its nature. As this work may not demonstrate Reformed theology at its most constructive, it is worth observing that even the most nuanced Reformed discussions of freedom tend to be highly circumspect. See for example Paul K. Jewett, *Election and Predestination* (Grand Rapids, MI: Eerdmans, 1985), 73–76. In this respect, I suggest, Karl Barth (on whom see 6.1 and 6.2 below) is an exception that proves the rule. For the most general characteristics of Reformed (specifically Calvinist) and Arminian theologies, see 4.3 below. For the generally Reformed (not exclusively Calvinist) orientation of Moltmann's theology, see Jürgen Moltmann, "*Theologia Reformata et Semper Reformanda*," in *Toward the Future of Reformed Theology: Tasks, Topics, Traditions*, ed. David Willis and Michael Welker (Grand Rapids, MI: Eerdmans, 1999), 120–35. For Moltmann's view of freedom, see 4.3.3 below.

cheap offer in the religious supermarket of [our] society."[134]) Moltmann seems to be suggesting that salvation involves the (re-)establishment of a covenant between God and humanity in which our freedom and God's will are not placed in a competitive, zero-sum relationship. What remains unclear is whether all people eventually come to faith (and if so, how) or whether the fact that God and unbelief do not exist on the same "level" in the end renders faith (and repentance) unnecessary.[135] As noted in the Introduction, whether Moltmann's theology offers a truly covenantal understanding of universal salvation is a central question in this present study.

1.4.3 Justice

The discussion of the restoration of all things in *The Coming of God* is framed by important statements about the nature and importance of justice. Near the beginning of his discussion, Moltmann writes, with a clear allusion to Horkheimer,

> Originally, hope for the Last Judgment was a hope cherished by the victims of world history, a hope that the divine justice would triumph over their oppressors and murderers.[136]

Close to the end, he states,

> 'The Last Judgment' is not a terror. In the truth of Christ it is the most wonderful thing that can be proclaimed to men and women. It is a source of endlessly consoling joy to know, not just that the murderers will finally fail to triumph over their victims, but that they cannot remain the murderers of their victims.[137]

The continuity between these two statements and the difference between them lies in Moltmann's understanding of the nature of the justice by which God's judgment is to be passed. After the time of Constantine, he argues, the Last Judgment, which was originally so relevant for the victims of evil, became oriented to the question of what should happen to the perpetrators, its Judge thus becoming "the prototype of imperial judicial power."[138] Against this worldly view of justice, Moltmann insists on a Christocentric vision. Once more, the theology of the cross is cruc-ial: "No expiatory penal code will be

---

[134] CoG, 246.
[135] With respect to these different "level[s]," we might also ask, What does the difference and relationship between the divine and human will have to do with the difference and relationship between time and eternity? But this is to anticipate the topic of our next chapter. Moltmann's understanding of repentance in this context is addressed in the Conclusion, in 8.3 below, building on the discussion of freedom in 4.3.3.
[136] CoG, 235. Cf. WJC, 334.
[137] CoG, 255.
[138] CoG, 235.

applied in the court of the crucified Christ."[139] If Jesus, who was condemned for the benefit of sinners, is to be the Judge, if he is to judge according to the law he revealed and embodied—"the law of love for our enemies and the acceptance of the poor, the sick and sinners"—, if the righteousness that this Judgment serves is God's righteousness that *creates* justice, then this Judgment is not a *Last* Judgment in the sense of a "final reckoning" but can be seen to serve and pave the way for the restoration of all things.[140]

This justice "will restore this ruined world and put everything to rights again." But it does not serve "the final restoration of a divine world order that has been infringed." It is thus restorative justice rather than retributive justice. It is "creative" not "retaliatory."[141] In this light, Moltmann introduces his entire discussion by saying, "it is high time to discover *the gospel of God's judgment* and to awaken *joy in God's coming righteousness and justice*."[142] Later he writes, "What we call the Last Judgment is nothing other than the universal revelation of Jesus Christ, and the consummation of his redemptive work."[143]

There are two sides to the restoration of all things: God's kingdom "which awakens to new life" and God's judgment "which puts things to rights." Judgment is thus "the side of the eternal kingdom that is turned towards history."

> In that Judgment all sins, every wickedness and every act of violence, the whole injustice of this murderous and suffering world, will be condemned and annihilated, because God's verdict effects what it pronounces. In the divine Judgment all sinners, the wicked and the violent, the murderers and the children of Satan, the Devil and the fallen angels will be liberated and saved from their deadly perdition through transformation into their true, created being, because God remains true to himself, and does not give up what he has once created and affirmed, or allow it to be lost.[144]

The Final Judgment is not only 'for' the wicked and/or impenitent. The condemnation and annihilation of injustice and the liberation, salvation, and transformation of the unjust are two sides of a Justice that comes to pass for both the oppressors and for their victims.

---

[139] CoG, 250 as cited more fully in 7.2 below.
[140] CoG, 236–37. Cf. CoG, 250–51.
[141] CoG, 250. In linking the ideas of world order, retribution, and retaliation, I am making a connection that is not explicit in the text. A careful reading, I suggest (especially in the light of Moltmann's wider corpus), will show that this is certainly implicit in what he actually says.
[142] CoG, 235. His emphases.
[143] CoG, 250.
[144] CoG, 255. This passage is discussed further in the Conclusion in 8.3 and in 9.3n61 below.

1.4.4 God

In his introductory section, Moltmann notes that behind the debate about the outcome of the Final Judgment stands "the question about God." This breaks down into two questions. *Firstly*, "Does God, as their creator, go with all his created beings into life, death and resurrection—or does God as judge stand over against those he has created, detached and uninvolved, to pardon or condemn?" and *secondly*, "How can the God who loves what he has created condemn not just what is evil, destructive and godless in created beings but these beings themselves?"[145]

The first question is answered emphatically in terms of the God who "goes with" his creatures in Christ and who judges them through Christ in accordance with the righteousness that creates justice, as summarised in 1.4.3 above. The second question seems as if it is only asked of the "God" who judges by standing "over against" his creatures. But it re-emerges in a discussion of the relation between God's love and wrath where Moltmann speaks of God's judgment separating the sin he hates from the person he loves, condemning it, and giving "the person of the sinner" a free pardon. The relation between God's love and wrath is then addressed in the statement, "The anger with which the righteous God condemns the unrighteousness which makes people cast themselves and this world into misery is nothing other than an expression of his passionate love." Love emerges not simply as the strongest attribute of God, eventually overcoming his anger, but as the central attribute of the divine. As Moltmann puts it earlier, "In God himself love outbalances wrath, for God is angered by human sin not *although* he loves human beings but *because* he loves them."[146]

From the centrality of love in God, Moltmann concludes that the election and rejection that occurs in history "must serve the universalism of salvation." Similarly, God's Last Judgment has no double outcome of salvation and damnation, but "serves . . . the new creation of all things." "The preponderance of God's grace over his anger, which is experienced in faith, means that Judgment and the reconciliation of the universe are not antitheses."[147] God does not stand over against us, but stands with us and goes with us. To Hell and back.

1.4.5 Scripture

The same pattern—in which particularism ends up serving the restoration of all things—emerges in the section on the Bible. Here the initial "antitheses" are, on the one hand, those texts that seem to support universal salvation (Eph 1:10; Col 1:20; Phil 2:10; I Cor 15; Rom 5:18; 11:32) and, on the other hand, those passages or sayings that seem to support a double outcome of judgment (Matt

---

[145] CoG, 236.
[146] CoG, 243. His emphases.
[147] CoG, 243. The relationship between God's wrath and God's love is explored in 4.3.2, 4.4, and in the Conclusion, 8.2 below.

7:13–27; 12:32; 25:31–46; Mark 9:45–48; 16:16; Luke 16:23; John 3:16; 3:36; Phil 3:19; 1 Cor 1:18; 2 Cor 2:15, etc.).[148]

As both positions are "well attested biblically," one cannot decide one way or the other simply by appealing to Scripture. "If one presupposes that scripture does not contradict itself, because the word of God to which it testifies is inerrant," however, "one can then try to resolve the contradiction in the sense of the one side or the other."[149] This Moltmann does, first resolving in favour of universalism and then in favour of particularism. In the latter case, it is interesting to note that the position he puts forward is basically that of *The Nature of Hell*, the universal texts being understood as expressing God's salvific intention, while the particularist texts are seen as describing the actual outcome of his judgment.[150]

The argument that resolves the antitheses in favour of universalism draws on the testimony of the book of Revelation that in the end there will be no more death, "neither 'natural' death, nor 'the death of sin' nor 'everlasting death'." In fact, this is all we know from the Bible about "the ultimate goal of God's salvific plan." Everything else is "penultimate." This is consistent with the fact that Paul and John speak of being "lost" as a present but not a future state. Similarly, there is a telling asymmetry in Matt 25 as the kingdom promised for the blessed, unlike the fire that awaits the damned, has been prepared "from the foundation of the world." This implies that "the fire does not have to last until the end of the world either." Indeed, this fire according to Mark 9:49 is purifying. Its description as *aiōnios* means (like the Hebrew *'ôlām*), "time without a fixed end, a long time, but not time that is 'eternal' in the absolute, timeless sense of Greek metaphysics." "Only God himself is 'eternal' in the absolute sense, and 'unending' in the qualitative sense."[151]

One could easily read Moltmann's discussion as deliberately presenting us with an 'exegetical' stalemate which then has to be resolved by the 'theological' arguments of the next section. When he prefaces his arguments for resolving the contradiction between universalist and particularist texts by saying that such an attempt "presupposes that scripture does not contradict itself, because the word of God to which it testifies is inerrant," we might wonder if this is simply stated 'for the sake of argument'. Perhaps Moltmann thinks the contradiction is real, forcing both sides in the debate to stop simply appealing to the Bible and begin engaging the wider theological issues.

From what Moltmann says elsewhere, however, we can conclude that he is sincere about the arguments he puts forward here for interpreting the particularist texts within a wider universalist understanding of God's revelation

---

[148] See CoG, 240–41.
[149] CoG, 241.
[150] Here one might compare CoG, 242–43 with *The Nature of Hell*, 28–31.
[151] CoG, 242. I have summarised Moltmann's arguments in reverse order to highlight what I suspect is his starting point.

in Scripture.¹⁵² At the same time, his other writings illustrate the way in which he can envision a considerable gap—indeed a contradiction—not only between individual texts but between the "inerrant . . . word of God" and the scriptures which "testif[y]" to it.¹⁵³

This is especially evident in his treatment of Final Judgment in *The Way of Jesus Christ*, a work that Moltmann brings to a close by anticipating the subject matter of *The Coming of God*, at that time planned as the next book in the series.¹⁵⁴ Here he writes critically of "the apocalyptic law of retaliation" in which "the divine righteousness which *creates* justice recedes in favour of the righteousness which merely *establishes facts* and reacts accordingly."¹⁵⁵ This is to be sharply contrasted with "the law" Jesus will use to judge the world and establish his kingdom. For while the former is a "penal law of retaliation," the latter is, in Moltmann's judgment, a "law whose purpose is rehabilitation [Resozialisierungsstrafrechtes]."¹⁵⁶ The problem here is that Moltmann finds both perspectives attributed to Jesus himself in Matthew's Gospel. With reference to Matt 25:31–46, he writes,

> It is impossible to overlook the contradiction between the divine righteousness which Jesus proclaims to the poor and to sinners according to Matthew's Gospel itself, and the punitive law of retaliation which the universal Judge apocalyptically enforces.¹⁵⁷

Moltmann may go on to say that "The final judgment is at all events no more than the beginning of the new creation of all things, and must be viewed in this provisional character."¹⁵⁸ But it seems highly unlikely that he thinks that this apocalyptic text (and others like it) can be "rehabilitat[ed]"—subsumed under the law whose purpose is rehabilitation—simply by postulating a *penultimate* law of retaliation. It is clear from elsewhere that Moltmann believes biblical material must itself be critically subjected to the "[W]ord of God."¹⁵⁹ If the New Testament portrayal of the Final Judgment is itself judged

---

¹⁵² See Jürgen Moltmann et al., "Talk-back Session with Dr. Jürgen Moltmann," *Asbury Theological Journal* 48, no. 1 (Spring 1993): 41.

¹⁵³ These words are from CoG, 241, as cited about but in a different order. For the subjection of certain biblical texts/words to the Word, see the references from EiT cited in n. 159 below.

¹⁵⁴ See WJC, 382n33: "This ["the statements about judgment in the New Testament"] will be the subject of full discussion in the fourth volume of these contributions, which will be devoted to eschatology." CoG ended up as the fifth volume, preceded by SL.

¹⁵⁵ WJC, 335–36. His emphases.

¹⁵⁶ WJC, 337–38 [*DWJC*, 363]. I discuss this "Resozialisierungsstrafrechtes" further in 7.2 below.

¹⁵⁷ WJC, 336.

¹⁵⁸ WJC, 338.

¹⁵⁹ CoG, 241 as cited above. See EiT, 124–25 and 129 in the light of, e.g., 136 and 281. This raises the question of how one might distinguish subjecting biblical texts/words to the Word (a hermeneutical practice that, arguably, all who accept biblical authority engage in, one way or another) from according the final say to the judgment of the

in this way, then it seems inevitable that this will lead to a 'double outcome' in that some texts will be refused entry into what is, in effect, Moltmann's 'canon within the canon'.

1.5 Universalism and Its Critics

The foregoing discussion has sought to introduce Moltmann's approach to the Final Judgment by highlighting certain topics—such as justice, freedom, and Scripture—that are central to most of the objections that have been made against universal salvation as a tenable position.[160] We will thus revisit these topics in later chapters.[161] One other question that is often raised—Does the belief that all will be saved in the end undermine our motivation to spread the Gospel?—is touched on but not directly addressed in the material discussed.[162] But the fact that Moltmann cites Blumhardt's utter determination to have his "confession of hope" "preached . . . as far as the lowest circles of hell"[163] gives some indication of his probable response.[164]

A universalist position that does not *undermine* commitment to justice, freedom, Scripture, and the spreading of the Gospel (in word and action) is the only kind of universalism that can hope to be widely respected in the Christian community. A universalist position that could be recognised as actively

---

professional theologian and thus to Theology rather than to God speaking to God's people through Scripture). In a "Postscript about the Universal Theology of Grace and the Particularist Theology of Faith and the Universal Glorification of God" which constitutes the final page of his essay, "Sun of Righteousness: The Gospel about Judgment and the New Creation of All Things," in *Sun of Righteousness, Arise!: God's Future for Humanity and the Earth*, by Jürgen Moltmann, trans. Margaret Kohl (Minneapolis, MN: Fortress Press, 2010), 127–48, hereafter SRA, Moltmann writes,
> I recognize that Matthew, the Synoptic Little Apocalypse [Matt 24–25; M[ark] 13], and the book of Revelation talk about an anthropocentric dualism rather than about a theocentric universalism. For me, the casting vote was given by the Old Testament concept of divine justice for victims and the all-rectifying judgment of God. The different biblical traditions about judgment cannot be harmonized. A decision has to be made *on the foundation of theological arguments*.

My emphasis. I comment on this further in 9.5n82.

[160] For the most common objections, see, *inter alia*, *The Nature of Hell*, 31; Stephen H. Travis, *Christian Hope and the Future of Man* (Leicester, UK: Inter-Varsity Press, 1980), 129–33; and Trevor Hart, "Universalism: Two Distinct Types," in *Universalism and the Doctrine of Hell: Papers Presented at the Fourth Edinburgh Conference in Christian Dogmatics*, ed. Nigel M. de S. Cameron (Carlisle, UK: Paternoster; Grand Rapids, MI: Baker, 1992), 1–34.

[161] Divine and human freedom will be examined in 4.3, 4.3.1, 4.3.2, 4.3.3, 4.4, 6.3, 6.4, and 8.3 below. Scripture is discussed in 7.1 below. Justice is discussed in 7.2 and 8.2 below.

[162] See CoG, 239.

[163] CoG, 255.

[164] I will return to this issue explicitly in the Conclusion, in 8.2 below.

expressing and *promoting* such commitments could gain considerable support. Whether Moltmann has developed such a position, or whether his theology provides the resources for so doing, are (as I have stressed in the Introduction) central questions in the following study.

The concerns of the critics of universal salvation will therefore be echoed in the following chapters. But my questions will not be dictated by the standard objections to universalism. This study is first and foremost an engagement with Moltmann's theology. It is thus important to note that the concerns listed above are ones that Moltmann himself shares. This should already be clear with respect to the call to justice. The foregoing discussion should also suffice to show that freedom is a theme that is not alien to his concerns. Its central role in his theology can be easily documented from his writings that we have yet to examine.[165] When I return to the topic of biblical interpretation in 7.1 below, therefore, I will do so not to subject Moltmann's position to 'extraneous' criteria, but in the awareness that he himself has cited having "a biblical foundation" as one of the three main characteristics of the theology he is attempting to develop.[166]

The material that I have summarised from "The Logic of Hell" and from *The Coming of God* raises many questions: What exactly is the 'freedom' that Moltmann wants to affirm in the context of universal salvation? If it is not defined by "the right to choose" but by "the doing of the good," do we not still have to *choose* the good? Is the transformation of murderers at the Final Judgment, such that they no longer remain the murderers of their victims, a miracle in which the victims have no say and play no part? What is the relationship between this *transformation* and what Moltmann's calls Christ's "law of *rehabilitation* [Resozialisierungsstrafrechtes]"? Can the claim that God's anger is 'really' an *expression* of his Love do justice to the biblical notion of God's compassion *overcoming* his anger? How can such a thoroughly *Christocentric* vision of universal salvation have a *Christ* who in the synoptic gospels speaks of the judgment to come in a way that provides the strongest biblical argument *against* such a vision?[167]

To see how Moltmann would address these and other possible objections to his position, we would not only need to look at what he says about Hell, universal salvation, and Final Judgment (and related topics) in the rest of his

---

[165] See n. 161 above.

[166] See Jürgen Moltmann, "My Theological Career," in *History and the Triune God: Contributions to Trinitarian Theology*, by Jürgen Moltmann, trans. John Bowden (London: SCM Press, 1991), 165–82, hereafter HTG. On p. 182, he concludes by saying, "If I were to sum up the outline of my theology in a few key phrases, I would have at the least to say that I am attempting to reflect on a theology which has:
– a biblical foundation,
– an eschatological orientation,
– a political responsibility."

[167] Many of these questions will be discussed in 7.1 and 7.2 below. On the question of freedom, see 4.3, 4.3.1, 4.3.2, 4.3.3, 4.4, 6.3, 6.4, and 8.3 below. On whether God's wrath is really an expression of Love, see 8.2 below.

corpus,[168] but, more importantly, we would need to examine his understanding of broader questions such as the nature of the relationship between nature and grace, creation and eschaton. Moltmann's conception of Hell, for example, is 'original' in a double sense as we shall see. Despite the strong emphasis that he places on the theology of the cross as the way to discern its true nature, it can only be fully understood with reference to Moltmann's doctrine of creation which itself is intimately related to his conception not only of divine action but also divine passion.[169] Placing his ideas about Final Judgment within the wider context of his overall theological vision will thus be central to chapters 2, 3, and 4, providing us with a context within which to revisit questions about, and objections to, the material surveyed in this chapter (including those questions specifically listed above).

As mentioned in the Introduction, chapters 5, 6, and 7 of this study further examine Moltmann's thought by bringing it into dialogue with some other voices. This too is in line with Moltmann's own priorities. In reflecting on his theological career, he writes, "I have tried to seek the truth in dialogue, and to avoid monologistic conversations with myself."[170] It is in that spirit that I will also bring this introductory survey of Moltmann's approach to Final Judgment to a close by returning to the text with which I opened this chapter: *St. Peter's Apocalypse*. Our initial investigations suggested a text committed to promulgating the "apocalyptic law of retaliation." What on earth might such a text have to say to us about developing a viable vision of universal salvation today?

1.6 *St. Peter's Apocalypse* Revisited

We left *St. Peter's Apocalypse* at the point where those faced with eternal conscious torment in Hell confess, "Righteous is the judgment of God, for we have heard and seen that his judgment is good; for we are paid according to our deeds." The Ethiopic text then reads:

> Then I will give my elect and righteous the baptism and the salvation that they sought from me in the field of Acherousia that is called Elysium. They will adorn the group of the righteous with flowers, and I will go and rejoice with them.[171]

---

[168] There is virtually no sustained discussion of these topics prior to CoG and WJC, but there are numerous brief yet suggestive references and comments scattered throughout his major writings. For further references to Hell, see the discussion in 4.1 below. For references to Final Judgment, see 7.2 below. For universal salvation in his corpus, see 4.3.1 below.

[169] On Hell in this context, see 4.1 in particular.

[170] EiT, xvii.

[171] "St. Peter's Apocalypse," in *Visions of Heaven and Hell before Dante*, 10.

However, the Rainer fragment, which was first published in the 1920s, reveals a Greek text that is strikingly different (and undoubtedly far closer to the original) at precisely this point. It reads:

> Then I will grant to my called and elect ones whomsoever they request from me, out of the punishment. And I will give them [i.e., those for whom the elect pray] a fine . . . baptism in salvation from the Acherousian lake (which is, they say, in the Elysian field), a portion of righteousness with my holy ones.[172]

This changes everything. Now the request of the sinners in Hell—"Have mercy on us, for now we know the judgment of God, which he declared to us before, but which we did not believe"[173]—can be seen as addressed to the righteous. Peter's original request for mercy is rejected because the issue of justice must first be understood. This is why he witnesses the punishments of the sinners which not only fit their crimes, but take place in the sight of those they have sinned against and persecuted for their faith. Retributive justice is imposed for their sake. No one else has the right to pray for these sinners to be released from their torments except their victims. This is why St. Peter's plea is denied. But if the victims have mercy, God will hear their prayers. Then those in Hell will be released and enter the Acherousian lake.[174]

It is significant that in the Greek tradition, this lake is a place of purificatory punishment located in Hades. Thus in Plato's *Phaedo*, there is a group of sinners, deemed curable, who enter this lake after a year in Tartarus. Most significant is the fact that without the forgiveness of their victims they cannot leave it, but must return to their previous torment. In the Rainer fragment, much of this thought world can be detected, except that the lake, while still purifying, is no longer a form of punishment. Hence its new location in the Elysian fields.[175]

This reading not only removes a number of incongruities present in the Ethiopic text at this point (such as why the righteous appear to be promised the

---

[172] This translation is from Bauckham, "The Conflict of Justice and Mercy," 145 and Bauckham, "The Apocalypse of Peter," 232. The gloss in the square brackets is his. I have omitted a Greek word he adds in parentheses. This text is 14:1 in Buchholz's versification, the entire Rainer fragment running from 14:1 to 14:5a. For the Greek text and for Buchholz's translation, see his *Your Eyes Will Be Opened*, 228 and 344–45. For his account of the discovery and early scholarly discussion of this fragment—so called because it is in the Rainer collection in Vienna—see 346–62, where he uses it to reconstruct what is, in his judgment, the "most corrupt portion" (342) of the Ethiopic text. Both Buchholz and Bauckham are convinced that the Rainer fragment represents the lost original text (which was also Greek according to Buchholz, *Your Eyes Will Be Opened*, 426) far better than the Ethiopic.

[173] "St. Peter's Apocalypse," in *Visions of Heaven and Hell before Dante*, 10 as cited in 1.1 above.

[174] See Bauckham, "The Conflict of Justice and Mercy," 145–46 and Bauckham, "The Apocalypse of Peter," 233–34.

[175] See Bauckham, "The Apocalypse of Peter," 234–35. The Plato reference is to *Phaedo* 114 A-B. We will return to Plato's 'eschatological myth' in 7.2 below.

Acherousian lake, given its associations with the wicked); it also coheres well with the rest of the apocalypse. Finally we can make sense of why it is introduced with the words "Peter pondered this revelation so that he might understand the mystery of the Son of God, the merciful one and lover of mercy." Far from being a vindictive sub-Christian work committed to the "apocalyptic law of retaliation,"[176] *St. Peter's Apocalypse* reveals a Final Judgment in which Justice and Mercy embrace.

With reference to this last point, Richard Bauckham comments that "One obstacle to universal salvation—that of which the apocalyptic tradition, because of its origins in situations of injustice and persecution, was most aware—is effectively removed by the compassion and forgiveness of the saints."[177] This is far from being an anachronistic observation as the theme of the intercession of the righteous, which is widespread in Christian apocalyptic writings of this kind, gives the whole tradition a definite tendency towards *apokatastasis* that is actually realised in *at least* one text (a recension of the Armenian version of *The Apocalypse of Paul*).[178]

Dennis Buchholz is convinced that "a form of universal salvation" was originally taught in *St. Peter's Apocalypse* itself, this being visible once again in the Rainer fragment. "[T]here can be no doubt," he writes, "that the references to it were removed from our [Ethiopic] text [tradition] because someone had theological objections to it."[179] If an anti-universalist agenda can indeed be plausibly ascribed to whoever translated the text from Greek,[180] it is probably an overstatement to claim that the universalism of the original is "clearly" taught rather than "implied."[181] Nevertheless, Bauckham (who is far more cautious here than Buchholz) argues that a very good case can be made for saying that this apocalypse did inspire thinking along these lines, the fruit of which is probably present in one of the universalist positions—distinct from that of Origen—that Augustine seeks to reject in Book 21 of *The City of God*.[182] That there is what we might call a universalist *Tendenz* in such an early

---

[176] *Contra*, e.g., Alice K. Turner, *The History of Hell* (New York: Harcourt Brace, 1993), 83–86.
[177] Bauckham, "The Conflict of Justice and Mercy," 146.
[178] See Bauckham, "The Conflict of Justice and Mercy," 141–42.
[179] Buchholz, *Your Eyes Will Be Opened*, 348. See his reference to other early texts, Sibylline Oracles 2:330–38, the Coptic Apocalypse of Elias, and the Epistula Apostolorum 40, in this context. He also finds support in the opinion of the early twentieth century *Apocalypse of St. Peter* scholar M.R. James. He reiterates this judgment in *Your Eyes Will Be Opened*, 425–26.
[180] As Bauckham, in "The Conflict of Justice and Mercy," 145n42, writes more cautiously: "The reference to the salvation of sinners from hell has perhaps been deliberately suppressed in the Ethiopic version."
[181] Buchholz, in *Your Eyes Will Be Opened*, 348, uses both terms. His overall argument suggests an *implicit* universalism.
[182] See Richard Bauckham, "Augustine, the 'Compassionate' Christians, and the Apocalypse of Peter," in *The Fate of the Dead: Studies on the Jewish and Christian Apocalypses*, by Richard Bauckham (Leiden: Brill, 1998), 149–59.

text—one that is suggestive of a form of universalism that the dominant theological tradition has yet to seriously engage—is very significant.

What might be gained by bringing this ancient text into conversation with Jürgen Moltmann's concerns? There are certainly significant points of contact: in this vision, murderers do not triumph over their victims, but neither do the victims triumph over their oppressors. Furthermore, the fate of the wicked is determined by Christ's "law of love for our enemies." Unlike Moltmann's understanding, however, this is integrated with a retributive view of justice and punishment. God's wrath does not seem to be viewed as an expression of his love, there being a far more fundamental tension between his anger and mercy. We may also note that in portraying the wicked as fully repentant before they benefit from the compassion of the righteous, human freedom is affirmed unambiguously.

All of these points will be raised again in dialogue with Moltmann's suggestions. Perhaps the most striking and challenging difference from Moltmann's position (as it has been exposited so far) lies in the way this ancient apocalypse does not attribute the Final Judgment to God or to Christ alone but also involves those who have been brutalised by human evil. In this light, universal salvation—if it is to be a viable theological position—needs to be envisioned not only as a divine gift and promise, but also as a human calling. "Injustice cries out to high heaven.... The innocent victims must not be forgotten," writes Jürgen Moltmann.[183] "Without forgiveness," writes Archbishop Desmond Tutu of South Africa, "there really is no future."[184] In *St. Peter's Apocalypse*, there is to be Truth *and* Reconciliation.[185] In this ancient text, God's forgiveness and human forgiveness are integrated. Such an eschatology clearly has relevance for us not only today, but in the here and now.

---

[183] WJC, 334.

[184] Desmond Tutu, *No Future without Forgiveness* (London: Rider, 1999), chap. 11.

[185] I allude, of course, to South Africa's Truth and Reconciliation Commission and to Desmond Tutu's moving account cited above. A number of other important works on justice and mercy appeared about the same time, including L. Gregory Jones, *Embodying Forgiveness: A Theological Analysis* (Grand Rapids, MI: Eerdmans, 1995); Timothy Gorringe, *God's Just Vengeance: Crime, Violence and the Rhetoric of Salvation* (Cambridge: Cambridge University Press, 1996); and Christopher D. Marshall, *Beyond Retribution: A New Testament Vision for Justice, Crime, and Punishment* (Grand Rapids, MI: Eerdmans, 2001). The latter work is especially relevant to the present study as it pays significant attention to Hell and Final Judgment.

CHAPTER 2

The Reversal of Time in the Future of God

> It is only if a qualitative difference is made between God and human beings that God's decision and human decision can be valued and respected. God's decision 'for us', and our decisions for faith or disbelief no more belong on the same level [auf einer Ebene] than do eternity and time. We should be measuring God and the human being by the same yardstick if we were to ask: what, and how much, does God do for the salvation of human beings, and what, and how much, must human beings do?[1]

In this most enigmatic passage, Moltmann draws a parallel between the nature-grace distinction—to use the main categories within which theologians interpret the relationship between human and divine desire, action, responsibility, power, and freedom—and the even more mysterious distinction between time and eternity. In making this connection, he thereby touches on a central concern of this present study: the relationship between universal salvation and the redemption of time.

If "God's decision and human decision" are to be "valued and respected," says Moltmann, they must not be seen as belonging "on the same level." There is a "qualitative difference" between them that may be compared—and perhaps associated—with the distinction between eternity and time and the different "level[s]" to which they, too, belong. If this parallel seems to do little more than compound the mystery, it nevertheless strongly suggests that in order to understand Moltmann's way of distinguishing and relating nature and grace—which is crucial if we are to understand his universalism—we might be well advised to first explore his philosophy of time. This is the subject of this and the following chapter.

---

[1] CoG, 245 [*DKG*, 273] as cited in 1.4.2 above and in 4.3.1 and 8.3 below. For further discussion, see also 2.6 below. Moltmann continues (CoG, 245–46 [*DKG*, 273]), "To see God and a human being on the same level [auf der gleichen Ebene] means humanizing God and deifying the human being. 'Offer and acceptance' is a frequently used formula which brings divine grace and human decision on to the same level in just this way [auf eine solche gleiche Ebene]." "Ebene" means a 'plain' in geography and a 'plane' in mathematics. The phrase "auf der gleichen Ebene" would often be translated as 'on a par'. The same term appears in relation to time in CoG, 26 [*DKG*, 43] as cited in 2.4 below.

Indeed, Moltmann's philosophy of time provides us with an excellent entrée into the overall contours and dynamics of his thought, in the light of which his interpretation of the much contested relationship between nature and grace—or as he prefers: nature, grace, and glory—is best understood. This relationship will be examined in chapter 4. In chapter 5, I will explore a different model of time from which will flow an alternative understanding of nature and grace to be discussed in chapter 6. As these explorations will be carried out in close conversation with Moltmann's writings, they will enable us to examine his universalism in greater depth. In chapter 7, we shall return to issues concerning the Final Judgment introduced in the previous chapter. Throughout this study, questions raised in chapter 1 will never be far from the surface.

The present investigation into Moltmann's philosophy of time will continue in chapter 3, where we shall examine his vision for the redemption of time. These two chapters are foundational to the rest of this study as they will enable us to place 'Hell' and its 'annihilation' within the overall structure of Moltmann's cosmology/cosmogony and to understand how he might respond to those who do not, or who cannot, believe that all will be saved.

After some introductory observations that will explore connections between Moltmann's thought and the (related) concerns of Walter Benjamin (2.1) and Augustine (2.2), we shall examine the 'reversal' of time central to the contrast and correlation that Moltmann posits between time's historical and eschatological directions (2.3). The two directions of time will also be seen as the key to understanding the distinction he makes between the future as *futurum* and as *adventus* (2.4). The penultimate section (2.5) will explore the way in which his conception of historical diversity and eschatological unity—or temporal differentiation and (re-)integration—shapes his understanding of the creation/eschaton relationship. The chapter ends (2.6) by looking at how an appreciation of Moltmann's philosophy of time can shed light on the vital soteriological question of the relationship between the divine and human will.

2.1 The Two Angels of Time

Having begun with the enigmatic parallel(s) that Moltmann makes between nature and grace, time and eternity, we shall now turn our attention to the evocative contrast he draws between the two angels who introduce *The Coming of God*. Commenting on the fourteenth century portrayal of Luke 1:28 that had inspired him during the writing process, he notes,

> The angel [of the Annunciation] is not looking back to the wreckage of history, as does Paul Klee's 'Angelus Novus', which Walter Benjamin called the Angel of History. The angel of the future is gazing with great eyes towards the messianic Child of the coming God, and with green branches in his hair and in Mary's hand proclaims the Child's birth. The tempest of the divine Spirit is

blowing in the angel's garments and wings, as if it had blown him into history. And its meaning is the birth of the future from the Spirit of promise.[2]

Two angels: the angel who looks back and the angel who looks forward; the angel of history and the angel who has been blown into history; *Angelus Novus* and the angel of the future; the wreckage of history and the messianic promise for history. Separated in time by just over 600 years, these two angels—Paul Klee's *Angelus Novus* from 1920 and Simone Martini's *Angel of the Annunciation* from 1315 — represent two perspectives on time, two visions of (and for) the past, present, and future.

This description of the *Angel of the Annunciation* was written, appropriately enough, during Advent in 1994.[3] Walter Benjamin's interpretation of *Angelus Novus*, mentioned here briefly as a point of comparison, had also received Moltmann's attention twenty-two years earlier in *The Crucified God*. There what comes to light in Klee's painting is contrasted with Benjamin's own messianic vision. "Since for [Benjamin], history is fundamentally a history of suffering," Moltmann notes, "it cannot become pregnant with a messianic future. The messianic history of life runs counter to the history of suffering of the world which leads to death, and approaches it from the future. But in this counter-course it has a redemptive relationship to the whole history of death and the dead."[4]

It is precisely this "reversed 'eschatological reading of history'," as Moltmann calls it in *The Crucified God*, that he finds in Martini's *Angel of the Annunciation*. The "wreckage of history"/"history of suffering" cannot give birth to the Christ. So "the tempest of the ... Spirit blow[s] ... into history"/ "from the future." The redemption of history runs "counter" to history. This is the "birth of the future" "from the future."

In a more recent essay entitled "Progress and Abyss: Remembering the Future of the Modern World," Moltmann reflects once again on Benjamin's interpretation of Klee's painting in order to highlight the contrast between these two different temporal directions. Of *Angelus Novus* who is looking to the past, paralysed by a storm from paradise that is blowing him backwards into the future, Moltmann asks,

> What ... does this angel want to do? Why was he sent? He wants to remain to awaken the dead and to make whole what has been smashed. As long as the storm has caught his wings, he cannot do it. This "storm" is what we call

---

[2] CoG, xvii. This passage occurs at the end of the preface and thus just before the opening chapter. Cf. n. 5 below. On the "Angel of History" in Benjamin, see Stéphane Mosès, *The Angel of History: Rosenzweig, Benjamin, Scholem*, trans. Barbara Harshav (Stanford, CA: Stanford University Press, 2009), the 1992 French original of which Bauckham, in "Time and Eternity," 161n14, notes has influenced Moltmann considerably.
[3] See CoG, xvii. The connection between the *coming* of God and *Advent*—the future understood as *adventus* rather than as *futurum*—will be explored in 2.4 below.
[4] CrG, 165.

progress, as Benjamin states it. Said in an alternative way: If we could turn this storm around and be released from the winds of progress, then the angel could awaken the dead, and make whole what has been smashed.[5]

Moltmann finds the answer to the angel's desire for the redemption of history in Ezekiel 37. This resurrection vision, which comes to the prophet after he has looked back at the dry bones of Israel's history, is not for a "historical future," a "future *in* history," but "a future *for* history."[6] To "turn this storm around" will require the transformation of time itself. "If we compare Benjamin and Ezekiel," writes Moltmann, "the storm that we call "progress" and the storm that brought life to the dry bones blow in *opposite directions*."[7]

The two "directions" of time, which Moltmann refers to as the "historical" and the "eschatological,"[8] thus appear to be in contradiction. In the one, an

---

[5] Jürgen Moltmann, "Progress and Abyss: Remembering the Future of the Modern World," *Review and Expositor* 97, no. 3 (Summer 2000): 301–14. Quotation from p. 309. This 'dawn of the new millennium' essay, which he presented on Saturday 9th September, 2000 at St. John's (Anglican) Church, London (and elsewhere), is reprinted in *2000 Years and Beyond: Faith, Identity and the 'Common Era'*, ed. Paul Gifford (London: Routledge, 2003), 16–34. A revised version, entitled "Progress and Abyss: Remembrances of the Future of the Modern World," appears in *The Future of Hope: Christian Tradition amid Modernity and Postmodernity*, ed. Miroslav Volf and William Katerberg (Grand Rapids, MI: Eerdmans, 2004), 3–26, the cover of which reproduces Klee's *Angelus Novus*. In what follows, I will be referring to the earlier version.
Moltmann is commenting here on thesis 9 of Walter Benjamin's "Theses on History," as found in his *Illuminations*. (The passage cited in "Progress and Abyss," 306 is undoubtedly the basis of Moltmann's comments in CoG, xvii also.) The publication details provided in "Progress and Abyss," 314n2—(New York: Schocken, 1978), 257–58—refer to a reprint of the translation by Harry Zohn, edited with an introduction by Hannah Arendt.
[6] Moltmann, "Progress and Abyss," 309–10. His emphases (capitalised in the original).
[7] Moltmann, "Progress and Abyss," 310. My emphasis. It is instructive to compare Moltmann's juxtaposing of Ezekiel and Benjamin's reflections on Klee's angel with the strategy of Gillian Rose, who in "Walter Benjamin—Out of the Sources of Modern Judaism," in *The Actuality of Walter Benjamin*, ed. Laura Marcus and Lynda Nead (London: Lawrence and Wishart, 1998), 85–117, contrasts *Angelus Novus* (which is reproduced on p. 107) with another of Klee's angels, *Angelus Dubiosus* (see 108–10). There can be no doubt that in recommending the latter to us as an answer to the former, Rose presents us with a very different vision from that found in Martini's *Angel of the Annunciation*, Ezekiel and Moltmann.
[8] See, e.g., CrG, 113 [*DgG*, 106] as cited in 2.3 below. "[D]irection," conveyed in the German text by the phrase "auf der Linie . . . ," also occurs in this passage. Although 'eine Linie' commonly refers to a 'line', it may also refer to a 'direction', as in the phrase 'keine klare Linie erkennen lassen' ('to show no clear direction'). It may also be a synonym for 'Ebene' ('level' cf. n. 1 above and n. 165 below), as in 'er stellt X auf die gleiche Linie mit Y' ('he puts X on a level with Y'). Cf. WJC, 206 [*DWJC*, 229] as cited in 2.4 below and cf. n. 165 below. In CPS, 60 [*DKG*, 76], cited in 2.5 below, there is an explicit, unambiguous reference to the "two directions" (in German "die beiden Richtungen").

angel looks to the past while a storm blows humanity out of paradise into the future, wreaking havoc in the name of progress. In the other, an angel welcomes a resurrection storm that blows from the future over the killing fields of history, bringing the dead back to life. The one consigns us to a future in history that leaves the past behind and thus tempts us to forget the dead. The other offers "a future for all of history" which it can deliver because it has "a transcendent foundation."[9] The eschatological, redemptive, and transcendent thus seem to be opposed to the creational, fallen, and immanent.

This opposition, though real, is not absolute. Having declared that the storms witnessed by Benjamin and Ezekiel blow in opposite directions, Moltmann can still ask,

> In what ways do both of these storms, "progress" and "resurrection," *belong together*? How are the transcendent hopes in God bound up with the immanent hopes of people? I believe that they are *contrary* to each other. Because and insofar as the resurrection hopes are seen as future for those who have gone before, then those living in the present gain courage for the future. Because of this great hope in the overcoming of death and past time, our small hopes of better times in the future gain power and will not fall into resignation and cynicism. In the middle of the "Age of Anxiety," we hope 'in spite of' and do not give up. We gain courage to "be" in the face of non-being, as Paul Tillich strikingly formulated it. *Our limited hopes* for the future thus become a reaction [that is, response] to *the divine future* for the vanquished.[10]

Although the eschatological and the historical are "contrary" to each other, Moltmann is saying, they "belong together" because their respective futures—the future for history and the future of history—may be integrated, the eschatological providing the ultimate direction for the historical. History must become responsive to, subject to, an orientation or direction that is eschatological in character. In this way, the opposites may be harmonised, even if they may never be fully resolved—or become 'one'—in the present age. To anticipate the discussion (and terminology) of 2.4 and 2.6 below, our *phenomenal* past, present, and future (nature) must become oriented to, and oriented by, the *transcendental* future of the coming of God (grace).

It is this simultaneous opposition and integration of the two directions of time that characterises Moltmann's overall theology, in my opinion. Moltmann's cosmology—or better his cosmogony—does not present us with a historical-eschatological dualism but with what we might describe as a 'contradictory/harmony monism'.[11] When he is addressing the evils of history

---

[9] Moltmann, "Progress and Abyss," 309.
[10] Moltmann, "Progress and Abyss," 310. My emphases.
[11] The identification of contradictory/harmony monism as cosmological framework evident in various thinkers throughout the history of Western thought is set out very helpfully by Calvin G. Seerveld, "The Pedagogical Strength of a Christian Methodology in Philosophical Historiography," in *Social Theory and Practice: Philosophical Essays in Honour of Prof. J.A.L. Taljaard*, ed. H. Conradie et al. Special issue, *Koers* 40, nos.

which are so at odds with God's promises and when he is confronted by the inherent limits of historical time which cannot contain the God who will be all in all, Moltmann's analysis may be described as a '*contradictory* (harmony) monism', a position that comes extremely close to a dualistic perspective. The two angels are unable to see eye to eye. By contrast, his panentheistic vision for the consummation of history represents a '(contradictory) *harmony* monism' in which the opposites of time and eternity, God and creation, interpenetrate and coincide. Meanwhile, in the present age, in as much as God's promised future finds a response in our hopes and thus in our lives, the unity and difference between the historical and eschatological, the old age and the new age, must each (and must both) be given their due.

Such a cosmogony can, I suggest, be seen throughout Moltmann's corpus. If the contradiction between the historical and the eschatological is emphasised in his earlier more "apocalyptic" works,[12] the harmonising impulse becomes more evident as Moltmann pays increasing attention to the doctrine of creation and becomes more explicit about his vision of the future of creation in God.[13] In what might be called the 'creation mysticism' that develops in his more recent writings, this eschatological harmony may even be experienced in a limited way in what he calls the depth of the present "moment" (to be examined in 3.5.2 and 3.5.3). Tracing the contours and dynamics of Moltmann's 'contradictory/harmony monism' is a central concern of this and the following two chapters.

2.2 Augustine as a Point of Departure

The fact that the opposing storms do not, in the end, constitute a *dualism* but a *duality* within an all-embracing redemptive-monistic movement of time 'back to the future' can be seen in the way in which Moltmann takes his bearings from Augustine's view of time, only to depart from it as he develops his own distinctive perspective. Augustine thus functions as a 'point of departure' in a double sense.

In *The Church in the Power of the Spirit*, Moltmann draws on a contrast that he finds in the *Confessions* in the context of developing a "theological

---

4–6 (1975): 269–313. Seerveld explicitly acknowledges his debt to D.H.Th. Vollenhoven. For a more wide-ranging appropriation of Vollenhoven's "problem-historical" method, see also Olthuis, "Models of Humanity in Theology and Psychology." "Contradictory monism" is briefly discussed on pp. 28–30. In addition to my comments in 0.6 above, see also 3.6 below.

[12] This is Moltmann's own language. See the discussion of his own early work in Jürgen Moltmann, "Hope and Reality: Contradiction and Correspondence; Response to Trevor Hart," in *God Will Be All in All: The Eschatology of Jürgen Moltmann*, ed. Richard Bauckham (Edinburgh: T. and T. Clark, 1999), 77–85, especially 84 as cited in 3.3 below.

[13] Jürgen Moltmann, preface to the paperback edition of *God in Creation: An Ecological Doctrine of Creation* (1985; repr., Minneapolis, MN: Fortress Press, 1993), xi–xii, is instructive in this respect. This new preface is dated May 1990.

understanding of time" that corresponds to the Christian experience of the Lord's Supper.[14] With reference to Augustine's distinction between the three modes of temporal experience (expectation, direct experience, and memory), Moltmann notes that "In this *general experience* time runs from the future through the present into the past. . . . Life is [thus] dispersed in the stream of transience."[15] But he then observes that, for Augustine,

> The *specifically Christian experience* of time, on the other hand, is different; this is the experience which faith has when it forgets what lies behind and strains forward to what lies ahead (Phil. 3. 12ff.). In intense concentration it looks towards coming eternity. . . .[16]

"It is this particular experience of the eschatological era," concludes Moltmann, "which the soul has in the presence of the risen Christ in the Lord's Supper."[17] In this contrast between what lies behind and what lies ahead, the transience of the present age and the eschatological era to come, we may again detect the presence of the two angels and their two contrasting angles of vision. For Moltmann, Augustine's stream of transience and Benjamin's winds of progress each reveal a history that, in being subject to the forces of death, is opposed to and opposed by the Life of the age to come.

This sympathetic summary of Augustine's "Christian experience of time" also suggests that the Angel of History is to be associated, in Moltmann's understanding, with *diversity* while the eschatological angel brings the promise of *unity*. The passage on which this summary is based (*Confessions* 11. 29. 39), begins with Augustine's complaint that his life "is a distension in several directions," and progresses, via a quotation from Paul's Letter to the Philippians (to which Moltmann refers above), to speak of "leaving behind the old days" and being "gathered to follow the One, 'forgetting the past' and moving not towards those future things which are transitory but to 'the things which are before' me, not stretched out in distraction but extended in reach, not by being pulled apart but by concentration."[18] In this light, the "concentration" to which Moltmann refers is the answer to the way in which "life is dispersed in the stream of transience" (as Moltmann puts it). That this contrast is present in his sympathetic summary (and not merely in Augustine) is evidence of a similar distinction in Moltmann's own view of time. There is, I suggest, a

---

[14] CPS, 243.
[15] CPS, 391n75. My emphasis. Here Moltmann refers to *Confessions* 11. 21. 27. As Moltmann speaks this way himself, it is worth noting that his summary is very close to Augustine's own language. Cf. Saint Augustine, *Confessions*, ed. and trans. Henry Chadwick (Oxford: Oxford University Press, 1991), 236: "[Time] must come out of the future, pass by the present, and go into the past."
[16] CPS, 391n75. My emphasis. Here Moltmann refers to *Confessions* 11. 29. 39, a passage I will discuss below. Moltmann also cites Phil 3:13 in CoG, 139, as noted in 3.3 below.
[17] CPS, 391n75.
[18] *Confessions*, 243–44.

relationship between Moltmann's frequent references to God's "gather[ing] together" of what has been "fan[ned] out" in history (to be discussed in 2.5 below) and Augustine's language of existence being "gathered" in relation to "the One."

This passage from the *Confessions* is brought to a close with the words,

> The storms of incoherent events tear to pieces my thoughts, the inmost entrails of my soul, until that day when, purified and molten by the fire of your love, I flow together to merge into you.[19]

Commenting on the language of this final phrase, Henry Chadwick writes,

> Augustine's image of the historical process is that of a flowing river or rivers, with many stormy cataracts. Underlying this passage is the language of Plotinus ([*Enneads*] 6. 6. 1. 5) about the fall away from the One as a scattering and an extending. Temporal successiveness is an experience of disintegration; the ascent to divine eternity is a recovery of unity.[20]

This raises the question as to whether there is a relationship between these storms of incoherence that will be overcome in eternity and Moltmann's storm of progress that must somehow be turned around in the redemption of history. The extent to which Moltmann's affinity to Augustine's position extends to the latter's *Neoplatonic* understanding of unity and diversity is an issue to which I shall return at the end of this section,[21] as the way in which Augustine's position functions here as a point of departure (in a double sense) is a key to understanding the contours and dynamics of Moltmann's thought.

However Moltmann may differ from Augustine in the final analysis, his agreement with Augustine's distinction between the "general" and the "Christian" experiences of time is very clear. At the same time, there is one fundamental disagreement that is somewhat neutralised by Moltmann's sympathetic summary. When Augustine "look[ed] towards coming eternity" (in Moltmann's language), it is important to realise that he was hoping to be

---

[19] *Confessions*, 244.

[20] *Confessions*, 244n31. Commenting on Augustine's complaint at the beginning of this passage that his life "is a distension in several directions," Chadwick, in 243n30 (which refers back to 240n27), writes,

> Plotinus 3. 7. 11. 41 ... speaks of time as 'a spreading out (*distasis*) of life ... the life of the soul in a movement of passage from one way of life to another'. This text may have influenced Augustine's coining of the term *distentio*. But in Augustine this psychological experience of the spreading out of the soul in successiveness and in diverse directions is a painful and anxious experience, so that he can speak of salvation as a deliverance from time .... The theme is developed ... where St. Paul's language of 'being stretched' (Phil. 3: 13) becomes linked with the thought of Plotinus (6. 6. 1. 5) that multiplicity is a falling from the One and is 'extended in a scattering'.

His italics.

[21] In addition to comments at the end of this section, see 3.6 below.

delivered from time.[22] In this respect, the Church Father is looking for a very different "experience of the eschatological era" than Moltmann. Rather than hoping to escape in dualistic fashion from history into eternity, Moltmann is looking for the Angel of the Annunciation in history and for history. With Ezekiel, Moltmann looks to God's coming future not to "forget what lies behind" (to cite Augustine's [mis]appropriation of St. Paul) but to find a "future hope for the past."[23] With Benjamin, he believes the "counter-course" of "the messianic history of life . . . [has] a redemptive relationship to the whole history of death."[24]

In his more recent work *God in Creation*, Moltmann continues to agree with Augustine that "our lifetime flows from the future into the past," referring to this as "the vector of transience."[25] Moltmann often speaks of the 'flow' of time in precisely this way, equating the movement from the future to the present as an "irreversible" movement from potentiality to reality, thus equating this future with the "source" of time.[26] A "vector" implies direction; in the case of transience, the direction of the Angel of History. Time moves into the past. Even the storm of progress, though it may move us to leave the dead in the past, cannot overcome this movement, for "what will be[,] passes away; what is born[,] dies; and what is not yet[,] will once again no longer be."[27] On the all-pervasive nature of transience, Moltmann admits, Augustine is correct.

Nevertheless, Moltmann criticises Augustine for simply "*identif*[*ing*] time with transience,"[28] thus ignoring the way in which time may also display an eschatological direction. Where Moltmann clearly wants to speak of the "ontological" "precedence" of the future in this context[29]—a future that, as we shall see, differs from the projections of progress—Augustine (on Moltmann's reading) always gives "ontological precedence" to the past, thus effectively seeing death as the end of all things. This results in a desire to escape from time into eternity. For Moltmann, who is here attempting to develop a doctrine of creation in the face of the current environmental crisis, the world-negating implications of such a view are not attractive. He writes,

---

[22] See n. 20 above.
[23] Moltmann, "Progress and Abyss," 309.
[24] CrG, 165 as cited in 2.1 above.
[25] GC, 117. Thus he often cites Augustine with approval when referring to the nature of our existence as "restless." Cf. 3.2n68 below.
[26] See CoG, 26, where all of these ideas are present. Other passages that equate the future with potentiality and the present with reality include CoG, 289 and EiT, 32. In CoG, 286 he equates the future with potentiality, the present with reality, and the past with necessity. On the "irreversible" flow of time, see n. 50 below.
[27] Moltmann, "Progress and Abyss," 309.
[28] GC, 118. My emphasis.
[29] This is clear in a parallelism in CoG, 287 where Moltmann writes, "If reality is realized potentiality, then potentiality must be *higher ontologically* than reality. If out of future there is past, but out of past never again future, then the future must have *pre-eminence* among the modes of time." My emphases. Cf. GC, 120: "it is the future that has *precedence* in the different modes of time." My emphasis.

[I]f this is the character of time, are we then to suppose that God made his creation for death? Is the time of creation the time of death? Surely created time belongs within God's time, the time of its Creator? What meaning can the creation of transience have? If death is already the destiny of creation itself, not only the destiny of sin, then created existence is not anything we can possibly affirm. All that remains for the soul is the yearning, searching glance for its home beyond, in the eternity of God. The inescapable transitoriness of all things in the flux of time can only be countered by a religious flight from the world into the divine eternity.[30]

In developing an alternative position, Moltmann expands on his conviction (expressed above) that "created time belongs within God's time" by exploring various "experiences of time in the history of God."[31] Because time is never empty but always " 'ful(l)-filled'," Moltmann contends that it cannot be treated as a formal category. Biblical concepts of time are therefore "determined by whatever is fundamentally experienced in time—that is to say, experienced about God."[32] In this light, "[t]he inescapable transitoriness of all things in the flux of time," which Moltmann does not deny, may be "countered" without abandoning time for an eternity beyond.

Moltmann characterises God in the biblical traditions as the God of promise in relation to whom the covenant people became oriented to the future in hope. Because God is faithful to his promises, time is experienced as "the coming time" that "fulfils the earlier time and gathers it into itself." "Looking back," therefore, "we can also say that what was earlier points to what comes afterwards." This coming/anticipatory character—to look at time's movement and our response to that movement—is evidence that time "in the history of God" is "determined by what happens from God's side." Its promise-fulfilment structure, its eschatological nature, cannot be understood as a movement in the vector of transience even though it is experienced in history. As Moltmann puts it,

> Whatever happens from God's side has a certain direction, pointing from creation at the beginning to the eternal kingdom. For God did not create the world for transience and death. He created it for his own glory, and therefore for its own eternal life. Augustine evidently did not take this dimension of time into account.[33]

In this light, Moltmann's understanding of the two *dimensions* or *directions* of time—the movement towards non-being and the movement towards the

---

[30] GC, 117. Whether Moltmann does full justice to Augustine's theology here (and elsewhere) is beyond the scope of the present study.
[31] GC, 118. This is the title to GC, chap. 5, sec. 4. Cf. GC, 118–24.
[32] GC, 118. What Moltmann calls "experiences of time in the history of God" are thus also what we might call 'experiences of God in the history of time'. What this means for the time of the Age to Come will be explored in 3.5 below.
[33] GC, 124. For Moltmann's appreciation of the related theme of 'restlessness' in Augustine's world-picture, see 3.2n68 below.

eschatological fulfilment of creation—leads him to interpret the two different *experiences* of time that he finds in the *Confessions* quite differently from Augustine. This can already be seen in *The Church in the Power of the Spirit*, in the same section in which this reference to Augustine's "specifically Christian experience of time" is to be found. For in speaking of the crucified Jesus being present in the Eucharist "in the temporal sense ... as the One who is to come in the Spirit of the new creation and final redemption," Moltmann interprets the Lord's Supper as "the real anticipation" not of Augustine's eternity beyond time but "of the *coming fullness* of time." Time is thus not *negated*. Rather, the feast is "a sacrament of time" in which "the experience of time is itself *transformed*."[34]

In this eschatological context, writes Moltmann,

> [Time] no longer flows, as a stream of *transience, from the future through the present into the past*; on the contrary, through the Christ event it is opened up once and for all, in order to be consummated in his parousia. Time has become *eschatological time* and flows, as it were—to keep the image—*out of his past through his presence into his future*. The images of evanescence are evening and parting. The image of eschatologically transformed time is morning and the greeting of hope.[35]

This suggests that if there are Neoplatonic tendencies in Moltmann's thought,[36] they have become thoroughly temporalised.[37] For Moltmann, Augustine's "coming eternity" has become the "coming fullness of time."[38] The contrasting Neoplatonic movements of ascent and descent, out of time and into time, 'up' to an original unity and 'down' into a diversity increasingly alienated from the divine, have become the two directions of (for) time itself. Rather than recovering the unity of existence by ascending to divine eternity, all of creation finds its (re-)integration in turning to greet the new dawn of God's coming future.[39]

---

[34] CPS, 254. My emphases.
[35] CPS, 254. My emphases. Cf. CPS, 83–84, where Moltmann describes "the exodus of the last days in which the church finds itself" as "an eschatological movement away from the past and out of death, towards the future and into life."
[36] On Moltmann's Neoplatonism, see further 3.6 (and also 4.2, 6.3, and 6.4) below.
[37] By "temporalised," I mean simultaneously historicised and eschatologised.
[38] For Moltmann's description of Augustine's "coming eternity" see CPS, 243 as cited in 2.2 above. For Moltmann's reference to the "coming fullness of time," see CPS, 254, cited above. As I suggest in 2.6 below, taken in parallel, these phrases (which occur in the same section on "The Lord's Supper") suggest that Moltmann understands "eternity" as "the fullness of time" of the eschaton. Cf. his own reference to "coming eternity" in WJC, 206 as cited in 2.4 below.
[39] The basic idea that Moltmann's thought represents a temporalised (and in that sense horizontalised) Neoplatonism has been recognised by other interpreters. See, for example, H.G. Geertsema's *Vrije Universiteit* doctoral dissertation, *Van boven naar voren: Wijsgerige achtergronden en problem van het theologische denken over geschiedenis bij Jürgen Moltmann* (Kampen: J.H. Kok, 1980) where this is even evident

2.3 Reversals: Ontic and Epistemological

In the preceding passage, the vector of transience in which time flows from future to past is countered by an eschatological movement from past to future.[40] We might represent this as follows:

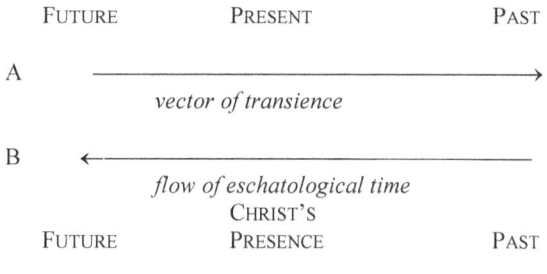

figure 1

This basic schema will prove most helpful in understanding the contours and dynamics of Moltmann's theology. But it is vulnerable to misunderstanding without some important clarifications. This will be the concern of the present section.

To focus on the vector of transience first, time in the historical sense (A)—that is, interpreted without reference to its redemptive, eschatological reintegration (B)—moves *out of the future* which is viewed as the *origin* of time as it is the future that is associated with the potentiality from which all the actualities of present and past are birthed.[41] In order to emphasise its primordial, 'originary' significance in Moltmann's thinking, I have placed the future on the left in the above diagram. As this might be widely experienced as counter-intuitive, it will be helpful to explore how this portrayal relates to the more common understanding of time's flow (also usually pictured from left to right) as a movement not *out of* but *towards the future*.

Clarification is vital here as in Moltmann's own discussion of the two orders of time, the language of moving *from future to past* (associated with the vector of transience in figure 1) is sometimes used to characterise eschatological time in which the ultimate overcoming of transience is

---

in the main title, taken from Ernst Bloch, which we could translate as 'From Above to What Is Ahead'. Cf. Bloch's comment "The forward-look has replaced the upward-look," in his *Atheism in Christianity: The Religion of the Exodus and the Kingdom*, trans. J.T. Swann (New York: Herder and Herder, 1972), 265. Cf. n. 66 below and 5.1n20 below.

[40] Cf. EiT, 32: "The future becomes past, but the past never again becomes future. The time-arrow of the divine promise points from the past into the future."

[41] See CoG, 287 and CoG, 26 as cited in 2.4 below. In 2.4 below, I will explore how for Moltmann, this (transcendental) future is the origin not only of the past and present but also of the future as a mode of time.

anticipated! Similarly the movement *from past to future* (associated in figure 1 with the eschatological direction) may be attributed to the unredeemed time of ordinary human experience. Thus, for example, Moltmann writes in his previous work, *The Crucified God,*

> In the *historical* account [auf der Linie der historischen Darlstellung], birth precedes life, and life precedes death. The past can be narrated, and every narration, like enumeration, begins at the beginning and proceeds to the end. But in the direction of *eschatological* anticipation [Auf der Linie der eschatologischen Vorwegnahme], the last must come first, the future precedes the past, the end reveals the beginning and objective time-relationships are reversed.[42]

How is this apparent contradiction to be understood? And how does figure 1 relate to the common linear portrayal of time as beginning in the past?

Although Moltmann does not directly address the inconsistency of his terminology,[43] he does provide the solution. In commenting on why Karl Barth speaks of the movement of time as being "from the past through the present, and into the future" while Augustine's vector of transience seemingly points the opposite way (into the past), Moltmann observes that while "[a]ccording to our everyday feelings, our lifetime flows from the future into the past . . . [y]et at the same time we count the years in the reverse direction, from a temporal beginning or centre of time in the direction of an endless future."[44] This distinction can be applied to the passage cited above. "[N]arration" and "enumeration," do not (in Moltmann's view) describe—except very indirectly—how time (including our "lifetime") actually flows in the present age (that is, from potentiality to actuality). When he refers to past preceding future in this passage, he is simply offering a description in accordance with the way we (re)count time, a perspective exemplified by Barth and evident in the well-known linear conception.

If we are used to thinking of time as flowing towards rather than from the future, we may not be persuaded that our portrayal is due simply to the way we measure temporality. 'Is this not time's actual movement?', we may ask. 'Surely the past precedes the present!' But this is not as inconsistent with figure

---

[42] CrG, 113 [*DgG*, 106]. My emphases.
[43] Moltmann could not be said to agonise in his writings over (laying bare) the systematic coherence of his corpus. See Jürgen Moltmann, "The World in God or God in the World: Response to Richard Bauckham," in *God Will Be All in All: The Eschatology of Jürgen Moltmann*, ed. Richard Bauckham (Edinburgh: T. and T. Clark, 1999), 35–41, where, on p. 35, he writes with reference to Bauckham (whose books he honours as "far and away the best accounts of my theology"): "[W]hereas when I come to the end of one book I have to concentrate on the subject of the next, he has the advantage of being able to survey the whole path I have taken, with its deviations, deflections and detours. So if I want to arrive at an overall view of my theological pilgrimage I have to depend on him."
[44] GC, 117.

1 as it may first appear, provided that we see the 'past' in this (linear) context as what Moltmann would call a "past *future*," that is: as a potentiality that, from a present point of view, has given rise to past reality, and to see the 'future' in our linear portrayal as a "future *past*," that is: as a future that will 'in time' itself pass away.[45]

In this sense, the familiar movement from 'past' to 'future', from yesterday to tomorrow, is included in what Moltmann means by the flow of time from future to past, especially as this 'past' may still contain much potential – in as much as it is a "past *future*" in distinction from what he calls the "past past"[46]— that we may wish to actualise. I will continue to portray historical time in Moltmann's thought by means of figure 1's vector of transience, however, and will thus resist translating this into the more common linear model that begins with the past, as I wish to highlight Moltmann's own emphasis on *passing* (and coming) time which is somewhat bracketed in our past-to-future measurements, predictions, and extrapolations. Seeing time's origin as (in) the past and *its* movement as future-bound, Moltmann would say, is vulnerable to a reductionism in which we focus on *our* movements, plans, and actions *in* time at the expense of (our fuller experience of) the movement *of* time beyond our control. In the popular linear conception, we focus on what Moltmann calls the future as "*futurum*," thus ignoring the future as "*adventus*" and failing to see how the future that may emerge—or that we may bring about—out of past and present possibilities has its origin in a fuller "transcendental future."[47] If the left-to-right vector of figure 1 (A) strikes us as counter-intuitive, this may be a strength of this kind of portrayal as to fully appreciate Moltmann's view, our intuitions may indeed need to be countered.

Once this basic point about the fundamental movement of time is established, we are in a better position to grasp the fact that within the terms and parameters of Moltmann's portrayal, the 'reversal' of time's flow *towards* the past (A in figure 1 above) into a narrated or predicted movement *out of* the past (A' in figure 2 below) is not to be confused with the eschatological "reversal" of time/history (B in figure 1) that Moltmann appropriates from Walter Benjamin. The former is an example of the way in which the "order of knowing" works in the opposite direction from the "order of being" as Moltmann observes in a number of places in his corpus,[48] while the latter is, ultimately (i.e., echatologically), a reversal in the order of be(com)ing itself.

This ontic reversal as portrayed in figure 1 (as B) also requires clarification as the return to the origin that it represents—which is a return to God (who is both the source and end/goal of time)—is not a return to a "past future" or even

---

[45] To speak of the "past-future," "future-past," and "past past" is to utilise (the terminology of) Moltmann's (and others') 'modalised' view of time, which is touched on in n. 57 and explored in 3.3 below.
[46] See the previous note.
[47] This terminology will be explored further in 2.4 below.
[48] See, e.g., CrG, 91; TKG, 152–53; WJC, 49 and 77 (both with reference to Aristotle, cf. CoG, 247); and CoG, xvi.

to a "future past" but to a different future that will not pass away, a future—God's future—that comes to us even as we (re)turn to it. Eschatological time is not historical time reversed in the sense of being somehow played backwards (like a video that we might watch whilst it is being rewound).[49] Central to eschatological time, as we shall see in 2.5 below, is the reintegration of what has been diversified in (and as) the transience and finitude of history. The 'reversal' signified by B in figure 1 is thus ontic rather than historical in nature.

The crucial difference between the aforementioned epistemological and ontic reversals—the epistemological contrast between A and A' or B and B' and the ontic contrast between A and B—is illustrated in figure 2 below:

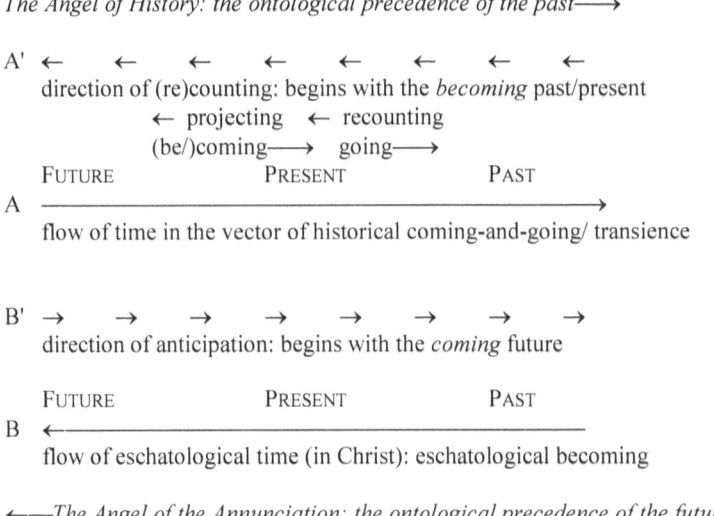

figure 2

---

[49] This eschatological reversal is *ontic* rather than *epistemological* and *eschatological* rather than *historical*. As discussed in 2.1 above, we must not imagine a historical reversal of time here, such as the highly unredemptive, historical reversal of time that is brilliantly explored by Martin Amis in his novel *Time's Arrow: Or the Nature of the Offence* (London: Penguin, 1991). Bauckham, "Time and Eternity," 163, captures the meaning of Moltmann's eschatological reversal well. He writes,

> It is not, of course, the movement from potentiality to actuality which will be reversed, but the movement in which reality passes into the past and is no longer present reality. In other words, not time's creativity, but time's transience will be reversed. Whereas in time everything passes away and is lost, in eternity everything that has passed away will be recovered so that nothing is lost.

In the present age, ordinary, unredeemed time, for Moltmann, flows "irreversibly" from future to past (A),[50] but is counted from past to present and predicted by extrapolating from (or via) present to future (A'). While such calculating activity turns its back on the movement into non-being and focusses on the phenomenon of *becoming*—on what, for example, may come out of present possibilities—nevertheless, whatever future may be accurately planned for (and thus brought about) in this way, though it may not yet have taken place, will in time 'come to pass' and thus 'pass away'. Historical becoming and passing-away thus belong on the same time-line. In this direction, transience has the last word.

When Moltmann speaks in the passage from *The Crucified God* cited above of a historical movement from past to future, therefore, he is not describing the *experienced*, ontic direction of the "time-arrow" of history (A) to which we are subject, but is focussing on a specific epistemological response to the flow of time geared to narrating or planning human *action* (A').[51] This concern with the actualising of given possibilities highlights the fact that there is a future (that is, an as yet unrealised potentiality) in the past. But this account takes place, and highlights a temporal development that takes place, within a more all-encompassing movement from primordial future to inexorable past. Thus in figure 2 above, the recounting of time (and thus our ability to extrapolate into the future and shape what will be) is associated exclusively with the transient nature of time as we know it. It is strictly confined to and thus takes place within—or as—*history*.

---

[50] On the "irreversibility" of time in the present age, see for example CPS, 60; and CoG, 26 and 287 (relevant extracts from all of which are cited in 2.4 and 2.5 below). Cf. Jürgen Moltmann, *Science and Wisdom*, trans. Margaret Kohl (London: SCM Press, 2003), 89–90. Hereafter SW. Alan J. Torrance in "Response to Jürgen Moltmann," in *Christ and Context: The Confrontation between Gospel and Culture*, ed. H.D. Regan and A.J. Torrance (Edinburgh: T. and T. Clark, 1993), 192–200 (a response to Moltmann's essay "Christ in Cosmic Context" on pp. 180–91) and in "*Creatio ex Nihilo* and the Spatio-Temporal Dimensions, with Special Reference to Jürgen Moltmann and D.C. Williams," in *The Doctrine of Creation: Essays in Dogmatics, History and Philosophy*, ed. Colin E. Gunton (Edinburgh: T. and T. Clark, 1997), 83–103, has criticised Moltmann for assuming that time moves (irreversibly or otherwise). For Moltmann's brief defence of irreversibility, see his "Replying to Alan J. Torrance and Gustavo Gutiérrez," in *Christ and Context: The Confrontation between Gospel and Culture*, ed. H.D. Regan and A.J. Torrance (Edinburgh: T. and T. Clark, 1993), 207–208. My own view, explored in 5.2 below, is that motion is a dimension of our temporal experience as it is a mode of time. 'Time' should not be reified. But metaphors for 'time' that draw on our experience of movement need not (and cannot) be avoided.

[51] See CrG, 113 cited above. Cf. GC, 117 cited above. The language of the "time-arrow" is used in EiT, 32. Just as there is so much more to the reality of time/*chronos* than we can capture in our *chronologies*, so the 'experience' of (being subject to) time to which I am referring here is a far more all-encompassing category than the more specific experience/knowledge we may gain when we negotiate time by strategies of 'counting' or 'narrating'. Cf. n. 73 below.

Anticipation, by contrast, is placed in the middle of the diagram where it stands in relation both to the time-arrow of history (above it) and to the ontic reversal of time (placed below it) associated with the eschaton to come. I will deal with these two relationships (B' to A; B' to B) by discussing the nature of first, 'historical' anticipation and then, 'eschatological' anticipation — thus making explicit a distinction that is, somewhat confusingly, only implicit in Moltmann's writings.[52]

Anticipation (whether historical or eschatological) represents a *receptive* epistemological response to the flow of time associated with *hope* rather than with forward *planning*.[53] Healthy anticipation involves openness rather than passivity in the sense of resignation. All anticipation, whether motivated by trust in God or fear of the unknown, looks to the future not as the outcome of present possibilities, not as what *will be*, but as what is *to come*. The historical time-arrow is thereby seen in a different light. The direction of anticipation (B' in figure 2) is thus in line with the historical direction of time (A) viewed (in a

---

[52] Due to Moltmann's lack of terminological precision, what I have termed 'historical' anticipation is itself referred to as "eschatological" in one passage. As Moltmann puts it in GC, 135,

> The content of the future we hope for and consider desirable, or the future we dread and wish to avoid, always has to do with our fundamental concerns, the things towards which our whole existence is aligned and on which it depends. These are the symbols of the eschatological future.

This description would seem to classify as "eschatological" both the future envisioned by adherents to the secular myth of progress, which Moltmann judges to be a dangerous illusion (see GC, 125; WJC, 24; and CoG, 30, 45), and the way faithful Christians have chosen to symbolise God's coming Kingdom. In *true* eschatological anticipation in its fullest sense, however—and Moltmann only uses the explicit language of 'eschatological anticipation' in relation to authentic hope—we look to the future as the Age to Come. Dreams of progress and fears of ultimate destruction are thus not truly eschatological. As Moltmann writes (approvingly) of the biblical apocalypticists in *Creating a Just Future: The Politics of Peace and the Ethics of Creation in a Threatened World*, trans. John Bowden (London: SCM Press, 1989), 31, "They establish hope in danger since they see through the horizon of the end of the world into the coming new world of God." In a section entitled "Hope against Danger," in *Creating a Just Future*, 37, he goes on to note that the Indonesian word for hope means "to 'see through the horizon'." In *Jesus Christ for Today's World*, trans. Margaret Kohl (London: SCM Press, 1994), 52 Moltmann refers to "anxiety" as "the inescapable and self-evident sister of hope." Such anxiety can help make us wise, he says. But he also states, "Hope can lead to anxiety, but anxiety can never lead to hope." In a characteristically nuanced discussion that seeks to bring together the respective insights of Kierkegaard and Bloch (50–57), he argues that fear can be taken up into hope. But 'in itself' it separates us from God's future.

[53] The distinction and connection between the two is reflected in Jürgen Moltmann, "Hope and Planning," in *Hope and Planning*, by Jürgen Moltmann, trans. Margaret Clarkson (London: SCM Press, 1971), 178–99. Hereafter HP. Our hopes and our plans, our anticipating and our extrapolating, though distinguishable, are always combined, as GC, 135 makes clear.

focussed or selective way) as a *coming* into being rather than as a *passing* out of existence.

What we may call '*historical*' anticipation (B' in relation to A) responds to the time-arrow by focussing on the Future as the source of time as we know it. In this context, we may anticipate death as well as life and thus experience fear as well as hope.[54] What we anticipate as yet to come will one day come to pass. Nevertheless, if our hope is in God, there is a "surplus" of meaning to the promises we trust that is not subject to the historical power of non-being.[55] This surplus is the key to *historical* anticipation becoming *eschatological* in character. God's future, though truly experienced in the here and now, is never exhausted in (or by) history. We know that when time is determined by what happens from God's side, then creation's ultimate destiny is glory and eternal life and not transience and death.[56] The future that comes into view via this '*eschatological*' anticipation is thus a "paradigm of transcendence."[57]

If *historical* anticipation looks at the flow of time as a coming (into being) *rather than* as a passing (out of existence), *eschatological* anticipation focuses on a coming that is *at odds with* the passing of time, a coming that *contradicts* and makes penultimate the otherwise ultimate transience of history. In such anticipation, we do not even look to the future as the source of time as we know it (as in historical anticipation), but to the future as the *Age to Come*, a *New* (kind of) *Age* (/time), in the hope that God's promises will be fully realised. In terms of figure 2, anticipation in this eschatological sense (B') must also be viewed in relation to the ontic reversal of history (B) symbolised below it. As an order of knowing, it is now the reverse—and hence the correlate—of eschatological time.

---

[54] See GC, 134–35.
[55] On promise as containing a "surplus" beyond historical fulfilment, see CPS, 24; GC, 286; WJC, 238; SL, 152; and EiT, 91, 105, and 126.
[56] See GC, 124 as cited in 2.2 above. On the contrast between life and death, see n. 57 below.
[57] See Jürgen Moltmann, "The Future as a New Paradigm of Transcendence," in *The Future of Creation*, by Jürgen Moltmann, trans. Margaret Kohl (London: SCM Press, 1979), hereafter FC, 1–17. (This essay appeared in an earlier translation as "The Future as New Paradigm of Transcendence," in *Religion, Revolution, and the Future*, by Jürgen Moltmann, trans. M. Douglas Meeks (New York: Charles Scribner's Sons, 1969), hereafter RRF, 177–99). This future is the "transcendental future," on which see 2.4 below. In SW, 95 this is "*the future of history* [which] determines the times" and thus (in the language of Moltmann's 'modalised' view of time to be explored in 3.3 below) "makes of the past past-future, of the present present-future, and of future times future-future." His emphasis. Cf. CoG, 26 as cited in 2.4 below. In SW, 101, this is the "[e]schatological future [which] determines and ensouls all three modes of time." To 'ensoul' is to bring to life. The death that we anticipate in fear is not "the future of history." Neither is it the "future-future" or "present-future" but merely a 'future present'.

This "eschatological time" (B) is not the "eternal time"[58] of the eschaton, but a temporal movement that anticipates (in hope and in action) the time of the Age to Come here and now. This "eschatological time," which unlike transient history might be said to be on the way to God's Future, can be seen most clearly in the risen Christ whose life is no longer an existence unto death. Thus in the preface to *The Way of Jesus Christ*, Moltmann explains that he wants to develop a *christologia viae*, "a christology of the way . . . which points beyond itself and draws people towards the future of Christ, so that they remain on Christ's path, and move forward along that path."[59] In the language of the passage from *The Church in the Power of the Spirit* with which I introduced figure 1 above, "Time has become eschatological time and flows . . . out of [Christ's] past through his presence into his future."[60]

The permanent eschatological *transformation* of time's present structure, which is not represented in figure 2 but which gives rise (as we shall see) to the ontic *reversal* of time (B) that we may now see in the risen Christ, will be brought about by God's coming future which is ultimately nothing less than God's own coming presence. Commenting on Jesus' words in Rev 1:4, "Peace to you from him who *is*, and who *was* and who *is to come*," Moltmann remarks that the absence in the third term of the future of the verb ("*will be*") breaks through the linear conception of time. "God's being," he notes, "is in his coming, not in his becoming. If it were in his becoming, then it would also be in his passing away. . . . The coming of God means the coming of a being that no longer dies and a time that no longer passes away."[61] Elaborating on this last point, he goes on to say,

> When God comes in his glory, he will fill the universe with his radiance, everyone will see him, and he will swallow up death for ever. This future is God's mode of being in history. The power of the future is his power in time. His eternity is not timeless simultaneity; it is the power of the future over every historical time.[62]

The coming of God's future does not mean the coming of an atemporal eternity but the "coming of . . . a time . . . ." Yet for all that, God, transience, and death cannot co-exist. Consequently, "[t]he eschaton means a change in the transcendental conditions of time."[63] As a result, the historical direction of time, as we shall see in chapter 3 (especially 3.1 and 3.5.1), will not only be countered and contradicted—as it is by "eschatological time" in the present

---

[58] For "eschatological time," see CPS, 254 as cited in 2.2 above and as cited below. For "eternal time," see CoG, 26. The latter is explored briefly in 2.4 below and at length in chapter 3 (especially 3.1 and 3.5.1).
[59] WJC, xiv.
[60] CPS, 254 as cited in 2.2 above.
[61] CoG, 23. His emphases.
[62] CoG, 24.
[63] CoG, 26.

age—but will also be transformed by being brought into harmony with the eternal. There will be a coincidence of opposites. "[E]ternal time" will begin.

Clearly, this coming future differs from the future that is the origin of present historical time (though these futures are related as we shall see in 2.4 below). Furthermore while the God of this future is coming and not becoming—is coming *to* history rather than emerging *from* or (merely) journeying *with* history—God's future gives rise to a kind of eschatological becoming in the here and now (represented by B in figure 2). "[E]schatological time" is not the (eternal) time of the eschaton. But it may be described as the beginning of the New Creation. "The eschatology of the coming God," Moltmann writes, "calls to life the history of new human becoming, which is becoming without any passing away, a becoming into lasting being in the coming presence of God."[64]

There are thus two (correlative) 'sides' to eschatological time (as there are to historical time): (i) the *coming* to which we are subject and (ii) the *becoming* of human (and non-human) action and experience. Just as there is (i) a (divine) Future that is the source of history (A) and that gives rise to—or that finds a response in—(ii) our historical becoming (A) (thus providing the context in which we know the future through prediction [A' in relation to A] and historical anticipation [B' in relation to A]), so there is (i) a Future—God's coming Future—that is the source of eschatological time (B) and that gives rise to—or that finds a response in—(ii) an eschatological becoming (B) (thus providing the context in which we know the future by eschatological anticipation [B' in relation to B]).

We see this latter response to—and thus manifestation of—the coming eschaton supremely in Christ who is on a path that leads "from his resurrection to his parousia." The risen Christ is on the way to his (our) future, a way "he takes in the Spirit to Israel, to the nations, and into the breadth and depth of the cosmos." Theology's centre and ultimate horizons are thus intimately connected for Moltmann as "christology is no more than the beginning of eschatology; and eschatology . . . is always the consummation of christology."[65]

2.4 *Futurum* and *Adventus*

As God, in Moltmann's theology, is seen both as the future potentiality from which all actualities spring in the present creation and as the coming future that calls the New Creation into be(com)ing, we may say that, cosmologically speaking, the eschatological direction of time (B) 'back to the future' (or forward to the future in the language of Christ's eschatological becoming) represents a return to the Origin.[66] But this future trajectory is not a return to a

---

[64] CoG, 24.
[65] WJC, xiv.
[66] A return to the Origin is characteristic of contradictory/harmony monism. See n. 11 above and the comment in the Introduction (0.6). I have capitalised "Origin" here as Moltmann, in my reading, virtually equates God with the ultimate transcendental source

(future-to-past) movement into non-being. If it were, then Moltmann would be advocating an eschatology committed to the myth of the eternal return of the same; a way of thinking that he has always opposed.[67] God is the one Origin of creation/new creation. But the eschatological 'Future' and the 'Future' as the origin of the time of the present age must be distinguished.

Another kind of future—the "future" that we speak about in the context of "count[ing] the years ... in the direction of an endless future"[68]—must also be distinguished from the 'eschatological future' in Moltmann's understanding, as this is simply the future towards which the Angel of History is being blown (while facing the past). If the movement towards the eschatological future (B) is a (re)turn to the (divine) origin of time that contradicts the vector of transience, this is not the case with this historical future, as we have seen.[69] To seek God's kingdom is, in the language of Augustine's *Confessions* (which Moltmann would certainly endorse here), to seek " 'the things which are before' me" rather than "those future things which are transitory."[70] In Moltmann's terminology, the historical "becoming" of creation—the temporal movement highlighted by counting the years into the future—must not be confused with the "coming" of God.[71]

These three futures—the future as origin of what presently comes into being, the future we may plan/predict, and the eschatological future are (linguistically) distinguished by Moltmann as (i) the "transcendental" future, (ii) the future as "*futurum*," and (iii) the future as "*adventus*." Whether this is reducible to a two-fold distinction (or expandable to a four-fold distinction) is a question to which we shall return.

In addressing the future in this first (transcendental) sense, Moltmann writes,

> If reality is real-ized potentiality, then potentiality must be higher ontologically than reality. If out of future there is past, but out of past never again future, then the future must have pre-eminence among the modes of time.
>
> If time is irreversible, then *the source from which time springs* must lie in the future. But it cannot be identical with future time, for every future passes

---

of time, the transcendental Future (or Future 'for' rather than 'of' time), as argued towards the end of this section. This 'blurring' of God and creation fits with what I will later describe as Moltmann's 'horizontalised Neoplatonism' which involves a historicising/eschatologising of the 'great chain of being'. Cf. n. 39 above, 6.4n153 below, and the discussion in 3.6 and 6.4 below. Also relevant is the brief discussion of privileged metaphors for God (such as King, Love, and Future) to be found in 8.3 below.

[67] See the discussion in 3.5.1 below. For a clear statement, see, e.g., SW, 81.
[68] GC, 117 as cited in 2.3 above.
[69] Thus the future we may calculate, A' in figure 2, though it may seem to point in this direction, is represented by a broken, not a solid, line.
[70] *Confessions*, 243–44 as cited in 2.2 above.
[71] This is certainly the case with historical becoming. Yet as CoG, 24 indicates (as cited at the end of 2.3 above), there is an eschatological becoming that may be called to life in us. This human becoming is the correlate, rather than the opposite, of the coming of God.

away. Here we can follow [Georg] Picht in distinguishing the future as mode of time, and the future as source of time. As a mode of time, future belongs to phenomenal time, as the source of time, future is the transcendental possibility of time in general. In the transcendental sense, future is present to every time—to future, present and past time. In this respect it is also the unity of time. The future offers in a certain sense 'the whole, of which the past is merely a part'.[72]

This notion of the transcendental future as temporal source, wholeness, and unity is pivotal in Moltmann's overall cosmogony. Closely related to God as the source of all things (cf. my opening paragraph to this section), this is not the future *of* existence but *for* existence.

Phenomenal time in this description is time as an experienced reality or phenomenon rather than time as a (transcendental) condition for experience.[73] Within "phenomenal" time in this sense, Moltmann distinguishes between our experience of the future as *futurum* and our experience of the future as *adventus*. Reflecting on the Lord's Supper in *The Way of Jesus Christ*, Moltmann writes,

> In the eucharistic experience of time, past and future do not lie on a single temporal line [liegen . . . nicht auf einer Zeitlinie]. These are two different world times: the passion history of death on the one hand—the resurrection history of life on the other. 'The future of Christ' does not lie on the line [liegt nicht auf der Linie] of future time (*futurum*). It belongs to the coming eternity which will end time (*adventus*).[74]

For Moltmann, therefore, the future as *futurum* is not an eschatological category at all.[75] Probably the clearest explanation Moltmann offers for this conclusion occurs in a section entitled "Future or Advent?" to be found in the opening chapter of *The Coming of God*. Here Moltmann asserts,

---

[72] CoG, 287. His emphasis. Cf. CoG, 26 and the very similar passage in SW, 91 where Moltmann adds: "The future of time is a reservoir of inexhaustible energy." The short quotation in CoG, 287 (also in SW, 91) is from Kierkegaard. Cf. the slightly different translation in *Kierkegaard's The Concept of Dread*, ed. and trans. Walter Lowrie (1944; repr., Princeton: Princeton University Press, 1957), 80. Kierkegaard's approach to time, though different from Moltmann's in important respects, provides another point of contact in his notion of the "moment" as an atom of eternity, to be discussed in 3.5.2–3.5.3 below.

[73] The transcendental/phenomenal distinction is clearly borrowed from Kant's discussion of time, as GC, 111 indicates. But Moltmann does not adopt Kant's subjectivist view of the transcendental or apriori conditions for existence. To relate the transcendental/phenomenal distinction to the discussion of 2.3 above, phenomenal experience embraces both sides of the ontic/epistemological contrast. Similarly, time in the ontic sense and as it is known in narration and calculation is subject to transcendental conditions (even though those conditions may be more consciously experienced in the ontic time to which we are subject than in the phenomenal future, the *futurum*, of our more self-confident and grandiose plans). Cf. n. 51 above.

[74] WJC, 206 [*DWJC*, 229]. Italics from the ET.

[75] See CoG, 26.

Future in the sense of *futurum* develops out of the past and present, inasmuch as these hold within themselves the potentiality of becoming and are 'pregnant with future' (Leibniz's phrase). Only that can become which is already implicit or dormant in being, and is heralded in the trends and latencies of the historical process. In the Greek myth, Physis is the eternally fruitful womb of Being. Physis is Being that brings forth. But that is only one side of her: if future (*futurum*) is her eternal process of becoming, past is her eternal process of dying. Matter is both matrix and moloch, the mother who bears and devours, like the Indian goddess Kali in Calcutta. In the process of ever-recurring 'die and become', the times are equal. The future offers no special reason for hope, for the past predominates, inasmuch as that which is not yet, will one day no longer be. Because what is future is already latent in the tendencies of process, these tendencies cannot, either, bring anything astonishingly new. In this concept of time, the future enjoys no primacy, there is no category *novum*, and really no 'principle of hope' either.[76]

This is the future that is known by extrapolation and calculation rather than by (eschatological or historical) anticipation and hope (although what I have

---

[76] CoG, 25. His italics. Cf. GC, 133. The reference to a "principle of hope" alludes, of course, to Ernst Bloch's *magnum opus*, *Das Prinzip Hoffnung* (Frankfurt am Main: Suhrkamp Verlag, 1959), ET: *The Principle of Hope*, 3 vols., trans. Neville Plaice, Stephen Plaice, and Paul Knight (Cambridge, MA: The MIT Press, 1986). In CoG, 344n58, (a footnote to the passage just cited), Moltmann points out that Bloch's ontology cannot take him beyond teleology. There is no room in his system for the *novum ultimum* that he so desired. Moltmann pushed Bloch on this point in a 1965 discussion with Bloch and Wolf-Dieter Marsch that was later published as "Gespräch über die Kategorie Novum," in *Im Gespräch mit Ernst Bloch: Eine theologische Wegbegleitung*, by Jürgen Moltmann, Kaiser Traktate 18 (Munich: Chr. Kaiser Verlag, 1976), 55–62. In this light and in this respect at least, Karl Barth's famous claim that Moltmann simply gave Bloch's philosophy a Christian baptism in his *Theology of Hope*—for which, see Karl Barth, *Letters 1961–1968*, ed. Jürgen Fangmeier and Hinrich Stoevesandt, trans. G.W. Bromiley (Grand Rapids, MI: Eerdmans, 1981), 175—is both simplistic and false. For Moltmann's response, see EiT, 92. Cf. n. 80 below and 3.4n135 below. In his foreword to *Time Invades the Cathedral: Tensions in the School of Hope*, by Walter H. Capps (Philadelphia: Fortress Press, 1972), xiv, Moltmann writes,

> Ernst Bloch's *Das Prinzip Hoffnung* has, of course, made a deep impression on me and I am greatly indebted to its author for many insights. But the theology of hope was in my thoughts—and writings—long before that. After all, studying under Hans-Joachim Iwand, Ernst Käsemann, and Arnold van Ruler was bound to have an effect on me. One cannot judge a theologian exclusively in terms of his mentors, but neither should one judge him wholly in terms of his philosophical expression. While that is important too, it is a relatively incidental matter.

His italics. Moltmann writes with some justification here. For a discussion of characteristic features of Moltmann's thought that *predate* his exposure to Bloch, see Geiko Müller-Fahrenholz, *The Kingdom and The Power: The Theology of Jürgen Moltmann*, trans. John Bowden (London: SCM Press, 2000), 26–39. See also the discussion of Bloch's more-than-incidental yet epistemological rather than ontological influence on Moltmann in 5.1 below.

termed 'historical anticipation' in 2.3 above could include the expectation or dread of what we predict will happen). As such, the *futurum* is a future related to human power rather than to God's promised redemption, to our potent-ial mastery over or shaping of history rather than to our openness to a future that lies beyond our control. If our plans for the future in this sense are not combined with (and thus shaped by) a hope for God's future,[77] then the *futurum* is profoundly suspect, potentially dangerous, and inherently anti-eschatological. As Moltmann puts it,

> There are trends and lines of development in past and present which we can extrapolate into the future. But these extrapolations turn the future into a prolongation of the present. These prolongations of the present are always used to stabilize present conditions of ownership and power; for only the person who has the power to implement his purposes can plan, and has any interest in extrapolation. But the prolongations and extensions of present conditions do not create a real future. On the contrary, they suppress the alternative possibilities the future holds. Extrapolations do not treat the future as an open field of the possible; they see it as a reality already determined by past and present. But this is illusory: it leads to a dangerous blindness to the apocalypse among men and women in the modern system.[78]

This perspective is also evident in a sympathetic summary of Walter Benjamin's "Theses on the Philosophy of History" in which Moltmann conveys the observation that,

> The victors desire the historical prolongation of their power, and develop a corresponding temporal continuum. But the oppressed desire redemption from the advance and temporal continuum of their victors, and wait for the break-in of a wholly different future.[79]

This "wholly different future" in Moltmann's understanding is the future as *adventus*. In the first explicit reference to the *adventus/futurum* distinction in his major works, which is to be found in *The Church in the Power of the Spirit*,[80] Moltmann writes,

---

[77] As can be seen in GC, 135 and also in Moltmann's "Progress and Abyss," 310 as cited in 2.1 above. Cf. n. 53 above.

[78] GC, 134. In a footnote to this passage (GC, 339–40n54), he takes issue with the would-be eschatologies of Karl Rahner and Hendrikus Berkhof, finding support in Heidegger's opposition between "the true historical past" and "the coming of what is destined." On the possible influence of Heidegger on Moltmann, see 5.1 below.

[79] CoG, 39.

[80] The fact that Moltmann referred to the future in two different senses without recourse to this terminological distinction caused considerable misunderstanding of his first major work, *Theology of Hope*. In the response volume, Wolf-Dieter Marsh, ed. *Diskussion über die »Theologie der Hoffnung« von Jürgen Moltmann* (Munich: Chr. Kaiser Verlag, 1967), to which Moltmann contributed an "Antwort auf die Kritik der »Theologie der Hoffnung«" (201–38), he therefore explained how (the natural

> The three temporal modes speak fundamentally not about a future [*Zukunft*], but only about the *futurum* of being. There is what was, what is and what will be. 'What is to come' [*adventus*] is, it is true, close to what will be, but is not totally absorbed by that; it stands in relationship both to the future and to the present and past. For what is to come does not emerge out of the forces and trends of growth and decay but comes in liberation to meet what is becoming, what has become, and what has passed away. To this extent, what is to come also contains the end of growth and decay.[81]

In this light, the future as *adventus* is to be identified with what I have previously referred to as the eschatological rather than the historical future. It is only this kind of future that can ground human hope and bring the truly new—the *novum*—into history. When Moltmann speaks of time being eschatologically transformed so that it is opened up to its consummation and no longer subject to transience, and thus speaks of time moving in Christ towards his future, it is the kind of temporal movement that is made possible by the future as *adventus* that he has in mind.[82]

So far, my exposition could be read as suggesting that Moltmann's transcendental future as the source of time (which we could picture at, or to, the far left of A in figure 2 above) should be distinguished from the phenomenal futures (plural), experienced as *futurum* and *adventus* (A' and B respectively). Moltmann, however, would seem to identify the future as *adventus* with the transcendental future in some passages, thus contrasting the latter with the phenomenal future (singular). Although this is a complex matter that requires us to make explicit what is merely implicit in Moltmann's philosophy of time (in contrast to the more systematically articulated material we will examine in

---

connotations of) the German word for the future—*Zukunft*—should, in his eschatology, be understood as referring to *adventus* rather than to *futurum* (see 210-11). In this context (see 211), he also takes issue with Bloch, on whom he had been accused of being over-dependent, for his inability to get beyond the future in the latter immanent, history-bound sense. Cf. n. 76 above, 3.4n135 below, and 5.1 below. The first reference to the *futurum*/*adventus* distinction in Moltmann's corpus is to be found in his 1966 essay translated as "Trends In Eschatology," in *The Future of Creation*, by Jürgen Moltmann, trans. Margaret Kohl (London: SCM Press, 1979), 18–40, especially 29–31. In a note (180n52), he refers to what he takes to be the first use of this distinction to be found in the 1953 German original of Emil Brunner, *Eternal Hope*, trans. Harold Knight (London: Lutterworth Press, 1954), 25.

[81] CPS, 130 [*KKG*, 150]. His italics. "Zukunft" is italicised in the German text. For its significance, see the previous note. I have added "*adventus*" for the sake of clarity. It occurs just before this citation in CPS, 130 [*KKG*, 149]. Cf. GC, 133 and WJC, 317. See also the previous note.

[82] On time in Christ, see CPS, 254 as cited in 2.2 above; WJC, xiv as cited in part in 2.3 above; and the reference to "the future of Christ" in WJC, 206 cited earlier in this section. In the light of the distinction I make, at the end of 2.3 above, between the two 'sides' to each of the two directions of time, we might say that (for Moltmann) the future as *adventus* represents the *coming* eschatological future while the movement of time in Christ towards his future represents the *becoming* eschatological future. I will suggest this later in this section.

2.5), it will be instructive to explore how and why both the two-fold and three-fold formulations are faithful to the structure of Moltmann's thought.

First, we should examine how Moltmann articulates his position in a way that would seem to support a two-fold distinction in this context. In the opening chapter of *The Coming of God*, he writes,

> The eschatology put forward here accords with the *Theology of Hope* in that it starts from a concept of the future which neither allows the history 'which continues to run its course' to swallow up every eschatology, nor permits the eternity that is always present to put an end to every history. The eschaton is neither the future of time [*futurum*] nor timeless eternity. It is God's coming and his arrival. In order to express this we shall take an *Advent-like* concept of the future that springs from the history of God, from the experiences and expectations of God as these are developed in the biblical writings.

Thus far, Moltmann's comments are compatible with the three-fold distinction suggested above. However, Moltmann continues as follows:

> We shall develop this [*Advent-like*] concept philosophically, in an understanding of time which sees the future as the origin and source of time in general—of time *per se*. We shall take the category of the *novum*—the new thing—as the historical category which characterizes the eschatological event in history.[83]

Here the identification of the transcendental future with the future as *adventus*—that is, the equation of what was earlier described as "the source from which time springs"[84] and what is here identified as "the origin and source of time in general"—seems very clear. Moltmann would thus appear to reject the proposed distinction between three futures—the transcendental, *adventus*, and *futurum*—in favour of a two-fold distinction between a transcendental *adventus* and a phenomenal *futurum*.

This impression is reinforced a few pages later when Moltmann writes,

> What happens when we carry this concept of the future [as *adventus*] into the usual linear notions of time? We then find that we are dealing with two different concepts of the future: on the phenomenal level [Auf der phänomenalen Ebene]—the level of everyday experience—we are conscious of past time – present time – future time [*futurum*]. But on the transcendental level [auf der transzendentalen Ebene] we then presuppose the future as the necessary condition if time is to be a possibility at all [*adventus*]. The future as God's power in time must then be understood as the source of time. It then defines the past as the past-future and the present as present-future and future time as future-future. Historical time is irreversible: the future becomes the past, but the past never becomes future. That is because reality emerges from potentiality, all past and present realities being realized potentialities; but reality never again turns into potentiality. Just as potentiality surpasses reality, so the future exceeds the

---

[83] CoG, 22. His italics and emphases.
[84] CoG, 287 as cited above.

present and the past. Of course this is true only of the transcendental future of time, not future time in the phenomenal sense. If transcendental future is the source of time, then it does not abolish time as does timeless-simultaneous eternity, nor does it lose itself in the maelstrom of the general transience of all temporal being. It rather throws open the time of history, qualifying historical time as time determined by the future."[85]

Here "phenomenal" time, or time "on the phenomenal level," is not simply the time of experience, but the time of "everyday" (or we might say 'ordinary') experience. This corresponds to the way we know time when we recount the past and project the future—the future that Moltmann elsewhere refers to as *futurum* (and that he here calls "the phenomenal future"). In this context, time is commonly thought of as a linear continuum. It remains on this "phenomenal" level as long as we pay no attention to its transcendental conditions, which transcend (and make possible) our "everyday" temporal experience. In our "everyday" experience of time, we may often pay attention to present possibilities but not to what makes possible "time *per se*."

Apparently incompatible with the idea that the future as *adventus* is a transcendental rather than phenomenal future is the fact that this future is also known in experience. According to Moltmann, the "*Advent-like* concept of the future ... springs from ... [certain] *experiences* and expectations of God."[86] He also speaks of Christ's advent future in the context of "the eucharistic *experience* of time."[87] Nevertheless, from Moltmann's point of view, although this future could be subjected to a *phenomenological* analysis—which is one reason why I have referred to it as a *phenomenal* future above—such an analysis would only highlight the fact that this is not an "everyday" experience "on the *phenomenal* level" as Moltmann uses that phrase. Just as potentiality "surpasses" reality, so the transcendental future "exceeds" the present. In this sense, unlike the immanent *futurum* of "phenomenal" or everyday experience, it is (experienced as) a future that transcends us.

That said, Moltmann's identification of the future as *adventus* with the transcendental future raises questions about the internal coherence of his thought. While it may make sense to see the transcendental source of time as the 'future' potentiality from which all temporal reality comes forth, it is not immediately apparent why this source should be so closely identified with the *eschatological* future. In other words, why should the future as *adventus* be associated with the way all things 'come' into existence, with the (source of) movement from potentiality to actuality? Is this not (from Moltmann's own point of view) to confuse the eschaton with (the source of) the present creation? Even if we grant that like the transcendental future, the future as *adventus* is not on the "phenomenal level" (even though it may be experienced), why should these two futures be equated?

---

[85] CoG, 26 [*DKG*, 43]. On "Ebene," see CoG, 245 [*DKG*, 273], cited at the beginning of this chapter, together with n. 1 above.
[86] CoG, 22 as cited above. Second emphasis mine.
[87] WJC, 206 as cited above. My emphasis.

Moltmann's position (and terminology), I suggest, needs to be clarified along the following lines. If the "future as what is to come," for Moltmann, "corresponds to ... anticipation,"[88] then it follows that just as there is a distinction to be drawn between 'historical' and 'eschatological' anticipation (as argued in 2.3 above, though this too is not made explicit by Moltmann), so we must speak of the advent, or coming, (of the) future in both an eschatological and non-eschatological sense. This is evident in at least one passage where Moltmann writes,

> [I]f we understand future as *adventus*, it means what is coming—what is on the way towards the present. What we describe as a 'coming' event is not something that develops out of the present. It confronts the present with something new, *whether it be good or evil.*[89]

Here it is apparent that the coming of evil into history can be seen in terms of the movement from potentiality to actuality—and can thus be related to the transcendental source of time—because the very conditions of possibility of/for the present age are caught up in evil.[90] At the same time, it is clear that Moltmann would never speak of an eschatological coming in a "whether it be good or evil" way. The coming of God signifies the decisive overcoming of all that is opposed to his kingdom. Thus, while it makes sense to associate *adventus* in a historical sense with the transcendental source of historical time, this is highly problematic in the case of *adventus* as eschatological coming, which is what the term signifies in the two extended passages cited above from *The Coming of God*.

The correct way to resolve this apparent contradiction, I propose, is to see the *eschatological adventus* in terms of the way the ultimate transcendental source of time—God the Creator—finally *enters* time when he becomes all in all.[91] The focus in these two passages is therefore not on the way historical time *comes from* its transcendental source (the future as 'historical *adventus*' in my suggested terminology), but on the way the transcendental future *comes into*

---

[88] GC, 134.
[89] GC, 133. In the original, "*adventus*" is italicised. The remaining emphasis is mine.
[90] See GC, 169 where Moltmann states that,
> There are apparently also perversions ... in the sphere of the potencies which are intended to make the life processes possible. These then hinder and destroy those life processes. Because these are potencies which do not belong to the human sphere but which yet have a destructive effect on that sphere, we talk about demonic or satanic forces.

See 4.2 below.
[91] This is clear in CoG, 280 as discussed at the beginning of 3.1 below. Cf. n. 131 below. With this interpretive suggestion in mind, we can read Moltmann's question "What happens when we carry this concept of the future [as *adventus*] into the usual linear notions of time?" raised at the beginning of the above quotation from CoG, 26 as 'What happens when God enters "linear" historical time?' It also sheds new light on why Moltmann states in the next paragraph that the "eschaton" that works with his concept of God and the future as *adventus* may "*enter* time." His emphasis.

time both in the eschaton and, in a qualified, 'anticipatory' sense, in the here and now.

In the eschaton, this *coming of God*, this divine *adventus*, does not signify an escape from history into eternity but is the coming of eternity into time itself. Time as we know it will come to an end,[92] though it simultaneously finds its true 'end' or goal. The historical movement of time into non-being will be *reversed* (as indicated by the eschatological direction of time in figures 1 and 2 above) and then *transformed* into its glorified state (to be explored in 3.5–3.6 below). "Evolution," writes Moltmann of historical becoming, becomes "re-volution" as "*linear* time" is "carried into a unique and then final eschatological *cycle*."[93] The vector of becoming and passing away is thus transformed into the cyclical, regenerating, temporal rhythms of the New Creation.[94] When God is all in all, God will be in creation and creation will be in God. Eternity and time will thus interpenetrate. In Moltmann's words, "With the coming of God's glory, future time [*futurum*] ends and eternal time begins."[95]

Within history, for those who find their orientation in time by looking beyond experience on the phenomenal level to the promises of the coming God, this *advent* future (in its eschatological sense) becomes the transcendental source of time that comes into history through lives of eschatological anticipation. Therefore, in the way we shape the future that is within our control (*futurum*) and respond to the coming future that includes the possibility of a full-scale environmental catastrophe (historical *adventus*), we may anticipate the coming—the eschatological *adventus*—of God's future kingdom. As "men and women ... [who] anticipate this future in knowledge and in deed," says Moltmann, we "participate in the eschatological, liberating history of God."[96]

Although such anticipation "does not take the place of consummation," it may still be described as "the 'now already' in the 'not yet'."[97] Beyond merely disrupting and stirring up the otherwise "homogeneous temporality of 'the river of time'," our participation in God's coming actually changes the course of history. Writes Moltmann,

> Conversion and the rebirth to a new life change time and the experience of time, for they make-present the ultimate in the penultimate, and the future of time in the midst of time. From this, surprising partings of the way emerge, and new

---

[92] See WJC, 206 as cited more fully above, where Moltmann says, " 'The future of Christ' does not lie on the line of future time (*futurum*). It belongs to the coming eternity which will end time (*adventus*)." His italics.

[93] WJC, 303 as cited more fully in 2.5 below. My emphases.

[94] The redeemed time of the new creation will be explored in detail in our next chapter (especially in 3.5 and 3.6). Here our focus is on the anticipation of what is to come in the here and now.

[95] CoG, 26.

[96] Jürgen Moltmann, "Methods in Eschatology," in *The Future of Creation*, by Jürgen Moltmann, trans. Margaret Kohl (London: SCM Press, 1979), 41–48. Quotation from p. 47.

[97] Moltmann, "Methods in Eschatology," in FC, 47.

ramifications of time, as the historical narratives of the Old Testament show. The future-made-present creates new conditions for possibilities in history. Mere interruption just disturbs; conversion creates new life.[98]

This discussion highlights the fact that it is indeed meaningful to speak of there being three futures in Moltmann's cosmogony. The key to appreciating this is found in the way reality (or time) for Moltmann can and must be viewed in two different 'directions' or perspectives simultaneously (although we must look at time from each of these two perspectives in turn before we can hold them together in our minds). *In the historical direction of time*, we must distinguish between (1) the *transcendental* future as the source of all that comes into being (the future at, or to, the far left of A in figure 2) and (2) the *futurum* as that phenomenal future we may predict and plan for on the basis of present possibilities (the future of A'). *In the eschatological (re-)direction of time*, the transcendental future (A) *becomes* (3) the future as *adventus* (B) or, we might say, historical *adventus* (A) becomes eschatological *adventus* (B). This transcendental, eschatological future, unlike the transcendental future in the historical direction of time, does not supply the formal conditions that make history possible in all its ambiguity. By contrast, as "God's power in time," this transcendental, advent future has an unambiguous, redemptive-eschatological character that makes possible and gives rise to the *novum*, which must be understood as a counterpart to the future as *futurum* in that it "does not emerge from the old."[99]

In the eschaton, (i) the *novum* that is experienced in history makes way for the new creation and (ii) the "new conditions for possibilities in history" (created by the presence of God's future, without which the *novum* would be impossible) make way for a thorough-going "change in the transcendental conditions of time" in which the "resurrection of the dead and the life of the world to come" are fully realised.[100] In the eschatological direction of time that we experience in faith and hope here and now, we anticipate the time of the eschatological future. In the eschaton itself, the "time of futurity" makes way for "eternal time."[101]

Although a *three-fold* distinction between the futures of A, A', and B is required for the sake of clarity, the eschatological transformation of the transcendental future from A to B—in which God the Creator here and now becomes historically revealed in/as the eschatological end and fulfilment of history, thus anticipating an Age in which the futures of A and B will coincide[102]—explains why Moltmann presents the difference between

---

[98] CoG, 22.
[99] CoG, 27.
[100] CoG, 26.
[101] CoG, 294: "Once death is no more, there will be no more time either, neither the time of transience nor the time of futurity." On the beginning of "eternal time" and the ending of "future time," see CoG, 26 as cited above. On whether there is future as *adventus* or *futurum* in the eschaton for Moltmann, see 3.6 below.
[102] This will be explored in the next chapter, especially 3.6.

eschatological *adventus* and historical *futurum* as a *two-fold* distinction between a transcendental and a phenomenal future.

For maximum clarity, I suggest, we should actually distinguish between *four* futures in Moltmann's conception of time. Building on the discussion at the end of 2.3 above, I suggest that there are two (correlative) 'sides' to time in each of its two directions: (i) the *coming* to which we are subject and (ii) the *becoming* of human (and non-human) action and experience. If we explore this correlation in the historical direction, therefore, we may speak of (i) the transcendental Future (future-H1) as the source of history that in its coming gives rise to—or finds a response in—(ii) our historical becoming, thus providing the context in which we know the phenomenal future as *futurum* (future-H2). Similarly, in the eschatological direction we may speak of (i) the transcendental Future, or (eschatological) *adventus* (future-E1), as the source of coming, eschatological time that gives rise to—or finds a response in—(ii) an eschatological becoming in which we must situate the *novum*. This becoming may be described as the movement of time in Christ towards his future (future-E2).

If we focus on the two 'sides' of temporal existence, therefore, we may distinguish 'future-H1' and 'future-E1' as the 'future(s) *for* existence' from 'future-H2' and 'future-E2' as the 'future(s) *of* existence'.[103] If, on the other hand, we focus on the two 'directions' of time, we may distinguish 'future-H1' and 'future-H2' as the two sides of historical time from 'future-E1' and 'future-E2' as the two sides of eschatological time.

Viewed in this light, Moltmann's *adventus-futurum* distinction is a distinction between transcendental eschatological coming and phenomenal historical becoming, or between 'future-E1' and 'future-H2'. It thus contrasts the *eschatological* direction *for* time with the *historical* direction *of* time.

Although this two-fold distinction is very important in Moltmann's thinking, it is not ultimate. The eschaton is not to be understood dualistically as the rejection of *futurum* and the embrace of *adventus*. In God's future, these two futures are to be brought together and thus transformed. There is to be a *coincidentia oppositorum*, a coincidence of opposites. It is the message of the Angel of the Annunciation and it is the hope and prayer of the Angel of History that one day, the phenomenal future of the present age will be subject to the coming transcendental future of the Age to Come. In the "eternal time" of the Age to Come (which we shall explore in 3.5 and 3.6 below), the two shall become 'one'. And this, as we shall see in 2.6 below, and in more detail in chapter 4, is the key to the unity of nature and grace.

2.5 Temporal Diversity and Unity

Thus far, I have argued that in Moltmann's cosmogony, the two angels of time represent two temporal orders or directions, both of which are real 'at the same

---

[103] The distinction between the two 'sides' of temporal reality is also explored by Moltmann by means of the heaven-earth distinction/correlation, on which see 4.2 below.

time'. In the *historical* direction, in which we may experience the storm of progress and the wreckage of history, time is oriented to the future as *futurum*. In the *eschatological* direction, in which we may anticipate the storm of the resurrection and the life of the Age to Come, time is oriented to the future as *adventus*. In the final coming of God, all time will be caught up in this resurrection storm, this raising of the dead. For the time being, those who place their trust in God are called to shape the future as *futurum* in the light of the *advent* future of the kingdom of God, and thus give *historical* expression to their *eschatological* hope.

In the previous section, I cited Moltmann as saying that "as the source of time, ... the transcendental ... future is present to every time—to future, present and past time" and is "[i]n this respect ... also the unity of time." Moltmann also notes that this "future offers in a certain sense 'the whole, of which the past is merely a part'."[104] This indicates that temporal unity and diversity are understood in terms of Moltmann's distinction between the eschatological and historical orders of time.[105]

It would be a mistake, however, to see 'unity' here as an exclusively eschatological reality in Moltmann's cosmogony. As argued in the previous section, the transcendental future, which he identifies as the source and unity of time, can be understood in each of the two temporal directions. If that is the case, it follows that the transcendental unity of existence may be viewed from a historical as well as from an eschatological perspective. *In the historical direction*, this unity is diversified in (and indeed *as*) time. *In the eschatological direction*, by contrast, we may speak of a movement of (re-)unification. The movement in the direction of *time* represents the *differentiation* of a transcendental unity. The eschatological movement, which may be described as in the direction of coming *eternity*,[106] represents the *integration* of phenomenal diversity.

Moltmann speaks of this historical differentiation as a "fan[ning] out" or "unfurl[ing]" in time that is to be 'reversed' in the eschaton when all created diversity is to be "gathered [up]" into the presence of God. This is clearly evident in *The Way of Jesus Christ* where Moltmann states that in "the primordial moment," "all the potentialities are gathered together and prepared which God then unfurls in the time of creation." "The primordial moment," Moltmann continues, "contains within itself eternity's readiness for time, while in the moment of inception [which proceeds from the primordial moment] time issues from eternity and, in the wake of the creation process, fans out as created

---

[104] CoG, 287 as cited in 2.4 above.

[105] To reiterate an important point, the eschatological direction of time is not itself the eschaton. Consequently, the eschaton itself (as we shall explore below in 3.5 and 3.6) will not herald the eradication of diversity but will be a 'time' in which unity and diversity 'coincide' in a way that is not possible in the present age.

[106] On Moltmann's understanding of eternity, see 3.5 (including 3.5.1, 3.5.2, and 3.5.3) below. Cf. n. 38 above. "[C]oming eternity," for Moltmann, is not the same as the full presence of eternity, as discussed in 2.6 below.

time into before and after, future, present and past."¹⁰⁷ Conversely, in the eschaton, when "[c]reated beings emerge out of time into the aeon of the divine glory. . . [t]hen all things will be brought back again from time, and will be gathered together."¹⁰⁸

Key to the ongoing and increasing diversification of life for Moltmann is the evolutionary process in which the emergence of greater complexity leads to increased communication, transformation, and freedom. The goal of evolution is community not uniformity. "[A]s ever more complex life systems develop and fan out," Moltmann explains, "the communicative relationships grow and the warp and weft of the diverse life systems densifies into whole new organisms. The more the organization of information and the exchange of energy becomes possible, the richer life will become in the diversity of living things in their relationships."¹⁰⁹ It is God's "creative Spirit [who] is the dynamic of the universe and the power that creates community in the widening, differentiating network of the living."¹¹⁰ At the end of this section from *The Spirit of Life*, which is entitled "Fellowship as Process," he illustrates his vision of the diversification of creation in time by stating,

> The evolution process is not a linear progression. It would be better to compare it with a tree, whose branches fan out in the air in which it lives, or a forest which spreads out into its environment. The goal is neither unity nor difference, but the differentiated community which liberates the individual members belonging to it.¹¹¹

The process of differentiation, however, needs to be complemented or countered by a process of (re-)integration that goes beyond the communal interrelationships that develop in history. In answer to the question of whether God's ultimate future for the world "will be *teleologically* achieved by way of evolution," Moltmann replies that this is "not conceivable, because the process of creation takes place in time, and 'becoming' inevitably involves transience."¹¹² "The perfecting of the whole creation, extended over time in the creation process, is only conceivable *eschatologically*," he writes. In other words, "The teleology of creation is not its eschatology." "What is eschatological," he continues, "is the bringing back of all things out of their past, and the gathering of them into the kingdom of glory." This he describes as "the movement of *redemption*, which runs counter to evolution" and

---

¹⁰⁷ WJC, 329. Cf. CoG, 282.
¹⁰⁸ WJC, 329.
¹⁰⁹ SL, 226–27.
¹¹⁰ SL, 227. Cf. SL, 289, where Moltmann writes, "*The personhood of God the Holy Spirit is the loving, self-communicating, out-fanning and out-pouring presence of the eternal divine life of the triune God.*" His emphasis.
¹¹¹ SL, 228. For a comment on evolution, the two directions of time, evolutionary naturalism, and the 'Intelligent Design' movement, which is also concerned with the "organization of information" (SL, 226–27 as cited above), see 5.2.1n77 below.
¹¹² WJC, 302. His emphasis.

"comprehends the redemption of evolution itself, with all its ambiguities." In language that graphically expresses his conception of the two orders or directions of time, he continues,

> In this redemption, evolution turns and becomes re-volution, in the original sense of the word. The linear time of evolution will be carried into a unique and then final eschatological cycle: into the return of all the pasts in the eternal aeon of the new creation of all things.[113]

The contrast between historical differentiation and eschatological integration—the movements of temporal diversity and temporal unity—can also be observed in Moltmann's early works. In *Theology of Hope*, for example, Moltmann speaks of the "wholeness" and "unity" of reality as an eschatological "new reality, which does not put the finishing touch to the reality of history up to then, but so to speak *rolls it up*."[114]

This pattern of thought is also very clearly evident in the following reflections on the Trinity to be found in *The Church in the Power of the Spirit* where Moltmann writes,

> If we compare the *two directions* [die bieden Richtungen] in which the history of Christ and the Spirit can be understood in the history of God's dealings with the world, we find correspondences, additions and one irreversible direction [eine unumkehrbare Richtung]. The trinity in the *sending* is, from its *eternal origin*, open to the world and to men. For with this the history of God's *seeking love* is begun. The Trinity in the *glorification* is, from its *eschatological goal*, open for the *gathering* and *uniting* of men and the whole creation with God and in God. In it the history of the *gathering love of God* is completed. Through the *sending* of the Son and the Spirit the history of the Trinity is opened for the history of the *gathering, uniting and glorifying* of the world in God and of God in the world. The opening and the completion correspond to one another in the openness of the triune God.[115]

A few pages later, Moltmann elaborates further by speaking of the "two sides" of the "divine experience of history" as follows,

> If we trace the thought of the *sending* of the Son consistently to the end, we are bound to talk about God's vulnerability, suffering and pain, in view of Christ's passion, his death on the cross and his descent into hell. God experiences suffering, death and hell. *This is the way he experiences history*.
>
> If we think in the direction of the *glorification*, then—in view of the resurrection, exaltation and perfection of Christ, and remembering the history of

---

[113] WJC, 303 as cited in part in 2.4 above. His emphases. On the specific meaning(s) of "redemption" for Moltmann, see 5.3 (including 5.3n128) below.

[114] TH, 278. My emphasis. Mention might also be made here of the role of the cross in "*gather*[*ing*] all that is and all that is no more into the new creation" in CrG, 219. My emphasis.

[115] CPS, 60 [*KKG*, 76]. My emphases.

the Spirit—we must talk about God's joy .... *This is the way God creates history.*

God *experiences* history in order to *effect* history. He *goes out of himself* in order to *gather into himself.*[116]

In passages such as these, Moltmann can be seen to go beyond philosophising about (created) time to developing what we might call a 'theocosmogony'.[117]

Given its focus on the Trinity, the previous passage sees Moltmann in the last volume of his early trilogy anticipating the first volume of his "contributions to messianic theology" series, *The Trinity and the Kingdom of God*. In that work, having spoken of "the *outpouring* of the Spirit" in which "the Spirit comes *from the Father through the Son*," he goes on to describe how "we find the order of the Trinity reversed" in the "*glorification*" through the Spirit" in the wake of which "the song of praise and the unity proceed *from the Spirit through the Son to the Father*."[118] Moltmann distinguishes the "two orders of the Trinity" in the now familiar contrast of sending and gathering, here identified respectively as a work "outwards" and a work "inwards." In the latter, "All people and things" will "partake of the 'inner-trinitarian life' of God.... join[ing] in the responding love of the Son and ... thereby becom[ing] the joy of the Father's blissful love."[119] Towards the end of this work he elaborates further by speaking of "the eschatological kingdom of glory in which people will finally, wholly and completely be gathered into the eternal life of the triune God and—as the early church put it—be 'deified' (*theosis*)."[120]

The deification of all people and of the entire cosmos is a theme that occurs frequently in Moltmann's discussion of eschatological glory.[121] In this context, he often refers to the understanding of *theosis* to be found in the Church Fathers or in the Eastern Orthodox tradition.[122] With respect to the glorification of human beings, the following passage from *God in Creation* is typical. Building on a discussion of Paul's distinction in 1 Cor 13:12 between seeing in a mirror and seeing face-to-face, he comments,

---

[116] CPS, 63–64. My emphases.

[117] I have adapted this term from Rosemary Radford Ruether, who refers to her own position in her *Gaia and God: An Ecofeminist Theology of Earth Healing* (San Francisco: HarperCollins, 1992), 247 as a "theocosmology." In this work, Ruether's view of God and the world has a similar structure to that of Moltmann. See the analysis in my *The Woman Will Overcome the Warrior: A Dialogue with the Christian/Feminist Theology of Rosemary Radford Ruether* (Lanham, MD: University Press of America, 1994), 264–68.

[118] TKG, 126–27. Emphasis added to "outpouring." Otherwise emphases in the original.

[119] TKG, 127–28.

[120] TKG, 213. I have transliterated *theosis* from his Greek original.

[121] On the divinization of "all being," CrG, 277 is an important early text, the trinitarian panentheism of which is evidence of a fundamental continuity between Moltmann's trilogy and his later writings. Later references to the *theosis* of the cosmos include WJC, 302; CoG, 92, 272–75; and EiT, 323.

[122] Patristic support is invoked in WJC, 47–48 and SL, 208. The Orthodox tradition is referred to in SL, 343n26 and CoG, 268. The two are connected in CoG, 272.

> The eschatological becoming-one-with-God of human beings (*theosis*) is inherent in the concept of 'seeing', for the seeing face to face and the seeing him as he is transforms the seer into the One seen and allows him to participate in the divine life and beauty. Participation in the divine nature and conformity to God, flowering into perfect resemblance, are the marks of the promised glorification of human beings.[123]

Moltmann continues by speaking of a three-stage development from creation to salvation and finally to glorification that repeats a distinction he has just made between conforming to the presence of the Creator, conforming to the presence of God's grace, and finally becoming like God.[124] He writes,

> The God-likeness that belongs to creation in the beginning becomes God-sonship and daughterhood in the messianic fellowship with the Son, and out of the two springs the transfiguration of human beings in the glory of the new creation.[125]

If we bear in mind the strong connection between the Spirit and the new creation for Moltmann,[126] then a trinitarian pattern is clearly discernible here, as is what he elsewhere identifies as a progression from the kingdom of *nature* to the kingdom of *grace* that comes to rest in the kingdom of *glory*.[127]

This eschatological development 'beyond' creation stands in correlation with the way in which we are, by virtue of creation, already 'more' than creatures. Earlier in this work in a discussion of 2 Pet 1:4, which is commonly thought to promise us that we shall partake of the divine nature,[128] Moltmann relates this text to our creation out of God's overflowing love and claims that the fact that we are "his offspring," to use the language of Acts 17:28, "suggests a fellowship with God which really does go *beyond mere creatureliness*." Elaborating on this point, he writes, "To be God's creature and his image means being *more than merely a work of his hands*. It means being actually 'rooted' in the creative ground of the divine life."[129]

There is thus a creational 'beyond' and an eschatological 'beyond', the former being related to God as the Origin, the latter to God as the Goal of all things. The Origin and Goal of the world and its history are thus related in (as) God. Consequently, our being " 'rooted' in the creative ground of the divine life" is seen as a source from which our eschatological transfiguration will

---

[123] GC, 229. His italics. For a comment on 1 Cor 13:12 in relation to Final Judgment, see 7.3n141.
[124] See GC, 228–29.
[125] GC, 229.
[126] See CPS, 34, 105, 191, 205, 247, 257, 295, 298; TKG, 89, 104; GC, 67, 96, 162; SL, 66, 162; CoG, 196; and EiT, 158.
[127] The three kingdoms will be the subject of 4.2 below.
[128] For a different—and in my judgment better—interpretation, see Albert M. Wolters, " 'Partners of the Deity': A Covenantal Reading of 2 Peter 1:4," *Calvin Theological Journal* 25 (April 1990): 28–44.
[129] GC, 85. My emphases.

spring.[130] In the eschaton, at one and the same time, creation is taken up into God's trinitarian life thus to participate in its divine goal and destiny, while God as the origin of all things enters the creation to dwell therein.[131] In biblical language, God will be "all in all."[132]

If *theosis* is a term closely related to the eschatological movement of the fulfilment and ingathering of the diversity of creation, *kenosis* is a term used of God's presence in the historical movement of differentiation. "According to Christian theology," writes Moltmann with approval, "incarnation and indwelling are grounded in the kenosis of God. By virtue of this lowering of himself, the infinite God is able to indwell the finite being of creation."[133] While many theologians are willing to explore this idea with reference to

---

[130] See GC, 229 as cited above.

[131] For the two movements together prior to the eschaton, see GC, 258. In an eschatological context, the connection between gathering up and indwelling is evident in EiT, 40–41, where Moltmann speaks of the way in which Moses' "face to face" encounter with God in Deut 34:10–12 gives rise to "the hope that God's presence will not be mediated solely out of remembrance of the history of promise, but will be experienced directly." When this hope is fulfilled, writes Moltmann, we may expect to encounter:

> a divine presence which is eschatological, no longer historical, a divine presence in which history will be abolished or gathered up, in the double sense of the German word *aufheben*. On the foundation of the discernment of God in history, this is what is expected of the kingdom of glory and the new creation, which God's glory will indwell.

His italics. Taking these two sentences together, this means that the eschatological abolishing/gathering up of history *into God's presence* is simultaneously the *presence*, or dwelling, *of God in* (the new) creation.

When Moltmann claims that what "we can call ... 'the deification of the cosmos' finds its ground in the *cosmic incarnation* of God," in WJC, 302, he wants us to be clear that "creation does not return home to God in order to be absorbed into the divine eternity from which it has come. On the contrary, God enters the world, making it the dwelling place that corresponds utterly to him." His emphasis. This is not a denial of the simultaneity highlighted above, even though it does draw our attention to its theocentric character. Furthermore, given Moltmann's stress on the eschatological nature of God's cosmic incarnation, it would be important to speak of creation *finding*—rather than "return[ing] to"—its home in God in this context. Cf. the mutual indwelling of God and world that Moltmann envisions in CoG, 307 as cited in 4.2n113 below.

One reason we can be confident that Moltmann would affirm some notion of homeward movement for creation, albeit one that does not involve divine absorption, is that this allows for a parallel between the "deification of the cosmos" and the way in which time will be "gathered up, fulfilled and transformed through the eternity of the new creation" when God's "eternity appears *in* the time of creation," according to CoG, 280. His emphasis. This gathering/fulfilling/transforming of time complements the gathering/abolishing of history in EiT, 40–41 cited above.

[132] For Moltmann's appropriation of Paul's language, see TH, 88, 224, 278, 282; CrG, 101, 255, 277, 335; CPS, 100; TKG, 105, 110; GC, 288; WJC, 174, 329; SL, 162, 212; and CoG, 238, 278, 294, 306, and 335.

[133] EiT, 316.

Christology and to biblical texts such as Phil 2:5–8, Moltmann attempts to trace its meaning back to the origin of time by speaking of the incarnation as fulfilling a "divine kenosis" and "self-humiliation" that began with (or before) the creation of the world.[134] Beyond the incarnation of the Son, in which the triune God "accepts and adopts ... the limited, finite ... state of being man [thus] making it part of his own, eternal life,"[135] this kenotic self-humiliation is completed and perfected in the cross. For here, God enters into, accepts, and adopts "our sin and God-forsakenness as well."[136]

At the end of a discussion that links the indwelling and *kenosis* of God with the sufferings of the Shekinah,[137] Moltmann indicates that divine historical diversification has only a penultimate status relative to eschatological re-integration when he writes, "Ultimately, in the redemption, God and his Shekinah will be indistinguishably one. God's 'self-differentiation' will end."[138] This suggests that time and eternity, diversity and unity are not equally ultimate, but that *kenosis* comes to its 'end' in *theosis*.[139]

Although, as I will explore in 3.6 below, it may be the case that the eschaton effectively marks the termination of historical differentiation for Moltmann (at least in its present form), it does not signal the eradication or absorption of diversity. Admittedly, Moltmann does speak of an "eschatological glorifying and unifying of God"[140] and of a "glorifying of the world in God and God in the world."[141] It is also the case that he defends his claim that divine self-differentiation will end by noting that, "According to the Christian idea, Christ will hand over the kingdom to the Father, so that God may be 'all in all'." Nevertheless he is quick to add, "but the Son does not therefore make himself superfluous, and there is no self-dissolution of the Son in the Father. In glory too, God is still the triune God."[142] Created diversity, we may conclude by extension, also has a future.[143]

Similarly, there is clearly an asymmetrical relation in Moltmann's cosmogony between the diversifying way in which God goes out of himself in history and the unifying way he gathers the world into himself in glory. But this is nevertheless coupled with a clear affirmation of the ongoing significance of *kenosis* in/for the new creation. This is evident in the following passage from *The Church in the Power of the Spirit* where Moltmann states,

> The history of God's suffering in the passion of the Son and the sighings of the Spirit serves the history of God's joy in the Spirit and his completed felicity at

---

[134] TKG, 118.
[135] TKG, 118
[136] TKG, 119.
[137] See CoG, 302–305.
[138] CoG, 306.
[139] On whether there is a future for *kenosis* in the eschaton, see 3.6 below.
[140] CPS, 62.
[141] CPS, 60.
[142] CoG, 306.
[143] See 3.6 below.

the end. That is the ultimate goal of God's history of suffering in the world. But once the joy of *union* [Vereinigung] is complete[,] the history of suffering does not become obsolete and a thing of the past. As suffering that has been endured, and which has brought about liberation, eternal life and *union* [Vereinigung], it remains the ground of eternal joy in the salvation of God and his new creation.[144]

This passage indicates that divine suffering is the key to the transition from historical differentiation, in which it takes place, to eschatological re-integration. That God experiences the suffering of the cross, Moltmann claims on the previous page, "means that he has absorbed this death into eternal life, that he suffers it in order to give the forsaken world his life."[145]

This eternal life is closely associated with "union" (which I have italicised in the above quotation). In the preceding section upon which this passage builds, Moltmann distinguishes between (a) "the divine *unity* [Einheit Gottes]" that we arrive at by "historical" reflection on what he calls "[t]he Trinity in the sending" and (b) the unity—or as he prefers, "the '*union*' of God [Vereinigung Gottes]"—that can be discerned eschatologically as we consider "[t]he Trinity in the glorification." While the former is identified either with the Father as "source of the Godhead," or with the "one nature behind the three persons," the latter gives priority to the Holy Spirit as "the force that glorifies" and "the power of unification."[146] Elaborating on these two unities or, to be more precise: the divine unity as viewed in the two directions (the historical and the eschatological respectively), he writes,

> [T]he unity of God is viewed as that which is ontologically the foundation of the sendings of Son and Spirit (or even as the foundation of the Trinity itself). In the eschatological anticipation of history, however, the unity of God contains within itself the whole union of creation with God and in God. Eschatologically, the unity of God is therefore linked with the salvation of creation, just as his glory is linked with his glorification through everything that lives and rejoices.[147]

---

[144] CPS, 64 [*KKG*, 80–81]. My emphases.

[145] CPS, 63. On the cross as the transition from nature to glory, see 4.2 below.

[146] CPS, 60–61 [*KKG*, 77]. My emphases. Cf. his discussion of Franz Rosenzweig's "Becoming Unity" in CPS, 61. In particular, pt. 2, bk. 3 of Rosenzweig's *The Star of Redemption*, trans. William W. Hallo (Notre Dame, IN: Notre Dame Press, 1985), entitled "Redemption or the Eternal Future of the Kingdom," has been influential for Moltmann's view of the eschatological direction of time. See 5.1 below. With respect to "Einheit" and "Vereinigung," John J. O'Donnell, in his *Trinity and Temporality: The Christian Doctrine of God in the Light of Process Theology and the Theology of Hope* (Oxford: Oxford University Press, 1983), 196, notes that the latter term "[o]n strictly linguistic terms has a more active connotation." From this he claims that Moltmann "does not have so much a theory of the divine unity as a doctrine of the divine uniting."

[147] CPS, 61.

As Moltmann puts it a couple of pages later, "God does not desire to be united with himself without the uniting of all things with him."[148]

The transition from the historical to the eschatological direction of time may thus be understood as follows. The out-pouring of God's love in creation leads to the God/world *distinction* and, even apart from sin, to an "*isolation*" of creation from God.[149] This creative act of *kenosis*[150] is followed by God's "*separation* from himself" as his Shekinah-Spirit suffers with his people in history and as the Father and Son endure total separation on the cross. Yet it is here that the process of *kenosis* is reversed. In the cross, God "suffer[s] with the Godforsakenness of the godless and so vicariously abolish[es] it."[151] This out-pouring of God's love leads to a oneness, a "union," between God and creation. In the light of the cross, history, differentiation, finitude, and suffering are thus revealed as, and enabled to be, a *means* to an eschatological *end* both for the world and for God. Put most strikingly, "in the craving of his love [God] want[ed] his creation to be necessary to his own perfection."[152]

The language of 'means' and 'ends', however, although almost unavoidable is misleading unless we emphasise that creation is not a historical means to a *historical* end, but a historical means to an *eschatological* end. Consequently, the 'means' is not discarded when the 'end' is reached. Though suffering will be no more, for example, it will for all eternity be "the ground of . . . joy."[153] By extension, the process of differentiation remains foundational to—and in—the new creation, even though—or even as—it comes to an end (at least in its present form). Creation has a future in, and in a qualified sense as, the new creation.

The claim that for Moltmann the creation is merely a 'means' that will eventually be done away with when it has served its purpose can be found in a probing essay by neo-Kuyperian theologian, Steven Bouma-Prediger. He writes,

> In the new creation, according the Moltmann, the old creation will be "caught up and absorbed in its fulfilment (*wird aufgehoben*)"; when the kingdom is fully consummated, creation will be "discarded (*abgetan*)." In short, the new creation is not the renewal but the annihilation of creation.[154]

---

[148] CPS, 63.
[149] CoG, 306. My emphasis.
[150] The *kenosis* that gives rise to creation is explored by Moltmann with reference to the kabbalistic notion of the *zimzum*. This will be examined in 4.1 below.
[151] CPS, 61. My emphasis.
[152] CPS, 62.
[153] CPS, 64 as cited above.
[154] Steven Bouma-Prediger, "Creation as the Home of God: The Doctrine of Creation in the Theology of Jürgen Moltmann," *Calvin Theological Journal* 32 (1997): 72–90. Quotation from p. 89. His italics. This passage is also found in his *The Greening of Theology: The Ecological Models of Rosemary Radford Ruether, Joseph Sittler, and Jürgen Moltmann* (Atlanta, GA: Scholar's Press, 1995), 246.

While it is certainly true that *aufheben* can mean 'abolish', and does so in this passage, it may also be translated as 'preserve'. Bouma-Prediger's analysis is at best one-sided and thus misleading precisely because both meanings are present here at the same time.[155] This becomes clear if we look at the phrases he cites from Moltmann in context. In the relevant passage from *God in Creation*, Moltmann writes,

> It is theologically necessary to view created things as real promises of the kingdom; and it is equally necessary, conversely, to understand the kingdom of God as the fulfilment, not merely of the historical promises of the world, but of its natural promises as well. There is more than merely a parable here. A parable points to something different, and presents the other thing by way of 'the pointer', the image. But a promise points towards its own fulfilment and anticipates a future still to come. The promise is *caught up and absorbed in its fulfilment* [In der Erfüllung wird die Verheißung aufgehoben]: when what has been promised is *realised*, the promise is *discarded* [Das Verheißene wird verwirklich, die Verheißung abgetan]. If the world as creation is the real promise of the kingdom of God, it then belongs to the history of the kingdom and is not merely its 'stage and backcloth'; for at the end of this history it is destined to be revealed in its eternal transfiguration [denn sie soll am Ende dieser Geschichte in ihrer ewigen Verklärung offenbar werden].[156]

This final sentence concerning the world's eschatological destiny is itself most revealing. Although creation-as-promise may indeed come to an end, creation-as-fulfilment remains.

That creation, and thus the diversity that has come into being in history, has an eschatological future is rooted, for Moltmann, in the fact that "God forgets nothing that he has created. Nothing is lost to him. He will restore it all."[157] The eschatologically new, Moltmann says explicitly, does not "annihilate" the old creation (contrary to Bouma-Prediger's claim) but creates continuity with it by "gather[ing] it up and creat[ing] it anew." The perishable and mortal nature of

---

[155] Moltmann is certainly not adverse to exploiting this double-meaning elsewhere. For an explicit example, see EiT, 40. This is cited in n. 131 above. On Barth's use of this term, see 6.5 below. Hegel is famous for exploiting the double-meaning. See, e.g., G.W.F. Hegel, *Lectures on the Philosophy of Religion: The Lectures of 1827*, ed. Peter C. Hodgson, trans. R.F. Brown, P.C. Hodgson, and J.M. Stewart with H.S. Harris (Berkeley: University of California Press, 1988). The glossary (on p. 528) translates "aufheben" with "sublate," a term it further renders as "transcend, supersede, annul."

[156] GC, 63 [*GS*, 76–77]. My emphases. For further discussion of GC, 63, see 6.5 below. Moltmann's claim that there is "more than a parable here" (in which, as in his reference to creation as no mere "stage and backcloth," he is distinguishing himself from Karl Barth, cf. 60–62) also negates Bouma-Prediger's claim, in "Creation as the Home of God," 89; *The Greening of Theology*, 246, that "In fact, creation is a parable of the coming glory since, Moltmann rhetorically asks, "Does not everything passing remain merely a parable of what is immortal?" This sentence, from GC, 62, is taken out of its context. Here Moltmann is attempting to reorient Barth's discussion.

[157] WJC, 303. On nothing being lost for God, cf. CoG, 294–95 and CoG, 251. The latter text grounds our confidence for the restoration of all things in Christ's descent into Hell.

this present creation, Moltmann notes with reference to 1 Cor 15:53, must put on immortality and the imperishable. We must say that the risen Christ is both "the crucified Christ and no other" and also "the crucified Christ in transfigured form." By the same token, the transfigured creation or "*creatio nova* is . . . the new creation of this one, the creation that is perishing from its sin and its injustice."[158]

But if "nothing will be lost" that came into being in time, time as we know is not among the "all" that God restores. On the one hand we will be raised with our "whole life history." On the other hand we will be "simultaneous in all [our] temporal Gestalts," earlier listed as including our childhood, adolescence, and adulthood.[159] As Moltmann explains,

> What is spread out and split up into its component parts in a person's lifetime comes together and coincides in eternity, and becomes one. If what is mortal puts on immortality, its mortality is ended and everything past becomes present.[160]

The "spread[ing] out," "split[ting] up," "fan[ning] out," and "unfurl[ing]" of history will no longer characterise the new creation. In Moltmann's understanding, this seems to be because such diversifying is a feature of the mortality and thus the death that can be no more. While death "is the power of separation" not only in the sense of biological disintegration and social isolation but also "in time as the stream of transience," the "raising to eternal life, conversely, is the power to unite." Thus, Moltmann implies, the power of death is evident in the life of a forty-year-old man (for example) not only because he will die in the future but also because he was a child in the past. When this power is overcome in the unifying power of the resurrection, "all [his and our] temporal moments" will be gathered "into the eternal present."[161]

Temporal differentiation seems to be valued because it allows an ever greater richness of our personhood and of the natural world to come into existence. "The kingdom of God," writes Moltmann, "is as brilliantly variegated as the creation we know now. [It] is not an impoverishment of creation. It is creation in a still greater wealth."[162] At the same time, temporal differentiation is viewed as something from which we must ultimately be liberated. Under present conditions, the variety as it is spread out in time cannot be 'presently' experienced by us. The "still greater wealth" eludes us. "Eternal life," he says "is the final healing of this life into the completed wholeness for which it is destined."[163] How do we make sense of this simultaneous

---

[158] CoG, 29. His italics.
[159] WJC, 267.
[160] WJC, 268.
[161] CoG, 71. The eternal present will be explored in 3.5 (including 3.5.1–3.5.3) below.
[162] SL, 194.
[163] CoG, 71. On the theme of wholeness, cf. Moltmann's reference to the transcendental future as offering "in a certain sense 'the whole, of which the past is merely a part' " in CoG, 287 as cited at the beginning of this section and in 2.4 above.

celebration and denigration of differentiation? For Moltmann, I suggest, the *diversity* will be fully present (and present to us) in the new creation while the *diversification* associated with the transience of history will end. It is in this light that Moltmann's *aufheben* as both fulfilment and negation (cf. 3.1 below) must be read.

2.6 Time and Eternity; Nature and Grace

I began this chapter by noting the enigmatic way in which Moltmann associates the qualitative difference between our decision and God's decision with respect to salvation, on the one hand, and the distinction between time and eternity, on the other hand. This, I argued, suggests that there is a certain parallel between his understanding of the nature-grace relationship and his philosophy of time. Although I shall present a more detailed analysis of this connection in chapter 4 (in 4.3.1), it will be worthwhile, in bringing this chapter to a close, to offer some comments based on what we have discovered so far.

Much of this chapter has been concerned with exploring the historical and eschatological directions of time that constitute Moltmann's 'theocosmogony', as reality, both created and divine, must be viewed in each—and in both—of these perspectives if we are to fully appreciate the contours and dynamics of his position. The contrasts and correlations discussed in the preceding sections include the following:

HISTORICAL DIRECTION	ESCHATOLOGICAL DIRECTION	SECTION
creational	eschatological	2.1
fallen	redemptive	
immanence	transcendence	
transience	coming eternity/ coming fullness of time	2.2
narration	anticipation	2.3
planning	hope	
futurum	*adventus*	2.4
differentiation	re-integration	2.5
sending	gathering	
kenosis	*theosis*	

figure 3

These distinctions require that we expand figures 1 and 2 (in 2.3 above) into the far more complex figure 4 to be found at the end of the next chapter.

In the previous section, it was also suggested that Moltmann sees temporality as the differentiation of the eternal fullness of time. In 2.2, I suggested that Augustine's eucharistic experience of "coming eternity" becomes for Moltmann an eschatological vision of the "coming fullness of time."[164] Taken together, these points suggest that the relationship between time and eternity is related to the contrast we find in Moltmann between historical differentiation and eschatological (re)integration.

This raises the question of whether Moltmann's insistence, in the passage cited at the beginning of this chapter, that eternity and time—and by the same token, the divine will and the human will—do not "belong on the same level [auf einer Ebene]" is his way of referring to these two directions. This interpretation, which coheres with Moltmann's language elsewhere,[165] is certainly partially correct in my view. But it requires qualification.

Although there is a relationship between eternity and the eschatological direction in Moltmann's thought, they cannot be simply identified as *eternity* is not a direction of *time*. The eschatological direction, as the *anticipation* of the Age to Come, is the direction of *coming* eternity not the full *presence* of eternity *per se*. In the present age, eternity in distinction from time is a *transcendental* reality.[166] It is the fullness of time that we find in the transcendental future, both as origin of history and as origin of the New Creation. Although still a temporal category, "eternity" transcends the modes of phenomenal time. Indeed, the transcendental-phenomenal distinction undoubtedly plays an important role in Moltmann's claim that eternity and time do not inhabit the same "level" of being.[167]

This, however, does not mean that the two directions of time are irrelevant in this context. As I have argued in 2.4 above, in Moltmann's view of the eschatological reorientation of history, the transcendental-phenomenal distinction can be combined with the eschatological-historical distinction to form the contrast (and correlation) between transcendental-eschatological *adventus* and phenomenal-historical *futurum*. This, I suggest, provides us with the kind of distinction that is at work in Moltmann's analysis of the irreducible "level[s]" to which the divine will and human will belong in the event of salvation.

The differentiation, *kenosis*, and 'alienation' of phenomenal time from its transcendental source—the differentiation of time from eternity—*in history*, on the one hand, and the subjection of phenomenal *futurum* to transcendental

---

[164] See n. 38 above.

[165] See the similar language used in EiT, 108 [*EtD*, 105] where Moltmann writes, "Christ's *historical* death and his *eschatological* resurrection certainly do not belong *qualitatively on the same, single line* [auf einer Linie], so that we could add them together." My emphases. Read in context, we should, I think, contrast the clearer reference to 'levels' rather than 'lines' in n. 167 below. Although in everyday German, 'eine Linie' can refer to 'a level' as well as to 'a direction' (as noted in n. 8 above), for Moltmann "Linie" tends to refer to a 'time-line'. Cf. the close association between "Zeitlinie" and "Linie" in *DWJC*, 229 (WJC 206) as cited in 2.3 above.

[166] On the "transcendental," see 2.4 above. On "eternity" see n. 38 above, the various references cited in 2.5 above, and the discussion in 3.5 (including 3.5.1–3.5.3) below.

[167] See the reference, in the context of a discussion of time, to the transcendental "level [Ebene]" and the phenomenal "level [Ebene]" in CoG, 26 [*DKG*, 43] as cited in 2.4 above.

adventus—the subjection of passing time to the coming fullness of (and for) time—*in the eschatological redirection of history*, on the other hand, do provide us, therefore, with parallels to Moltmann's understanding of the divergence and convergence of the human will and divine will. This is crucial to his view of (universal) salvation.

As the transcendental/phenomenal contrast refers to the distinction and correlation between the conditions for existence and the response of existence to those conditions, the subjection of the phenomenal *futurum* to the transcendental *adventus* may be seen as the way in which what humans do on the "level" of nature becomes subject to what God does on the "level" of grace. In order to briefly sketch how this comes about (a topic to be explored in some detail in chapter 4), we must elaborate on some points that have been made in previous sections of the present chapter concerning the relationship between God's 'action' and God's 'passion'.

In 2.4 above, I noted that in the historical direction, the transcendental future provides the formal conditions of possibility for history in all its ambiguity. In this direction, the divine will and the human will 'in time' become opposed to each other. Yet God does not seek to overcome evil by (re-) subjecting the world to an original creation order but enters into the history of our sin and alienation in order to open up a new future, a new creation, to be brought into existence through divine suffering. "God," as we have observed in 2.5 above, "*experiences* history" in this way "in order to *effect* history."[168] Divine *vulnerability* thus paves the way for divine *power*.

The vital role that divine suffering plays means that "God's decision 'for us' " (and thus what happens on the divine "level")[169] must be understood in the historical-kenotic direction and not only in the eschatological direction. Nevertheless, it is divine action in the latter direction that is 'decisive' even as divine passion, which marks the transition to the Age to Come, is 'crucial'.[170] In Moltmann's words, the coming, eschatological future is "God's mode of being in history." Consequently, the "power of [this] future [transcendental *adventus*] is his power in time. . . . over every historical time [phenomenal past, present and future/*futurum*]."[171] The new history that God "creates"[172] in the eschatological redirection of time, therefore, results in the transformation of the transcendental-phenomenal relationship as we know it in history such that the human will becomes subject to the divine will in hope. Moltmann's understanding of the distinction and correlation of nature and grace, I will suggest in 4.3.1 below, may be fruitfully understood along the same lines.

---

[168] CPS, 64 as cited in 2.5 above. My emphases
[169] CoG, 245 as cited at the beginning of this chapter.
[170] On the role of divine suffering as the transition between the two directions of time for God, see 4.2 below.
[171] CoG, 24 as cited in 2.3 above.
[172] CPS, 64 as cited in 2.5 above. In SW, 80–81, Moltmann prefers to speak of this "universal transformation" as a "mak[ing] all things new" (to use the language of Rev 21:4) rather than as a "creat[ing]."

The eschatological direction (in which our hopes and actions become attuned to God's will for the fulfilment of history) is the *anticipation* of the fullness of time and in that sense the anticipation of "eternity." The actual *recovery/realisation* of that fullness, however, takes place in the eschaton. This is a central topic in the next chapter. In the Age to Come, the contrast between the historical and eschatological directions is replaced by (or finds fulfilment as) "eternal time" in which the opposites of time and eternity coincide (see 3.5–3.6 below). Here the divine and human wills are so 'at one' in Moltmann's vision (as noted at the end of 2.4 above) that to refer to them as not "belong[ing] on the same level" may no longer be appropriate.[173] We may still speak of a divine-human or eternal-temporal distinction. But, for Moltmann, there will be no dichotomies when God is all in all. The mutual indwelling of God and creation (on which see 4.3.3, 4.4, and 5.4 below) will ensure that the harmonious distinctions and connections of the eschaton are not the hierarchies and oppositions of present history. Thus the language of our 'subjection' to (the will of) God, as we shall see in 4.3.3 below, makes way for the language of friendship, participation, and 'freedom'.

In the eschaton itself, we move, in Moltmann's terminology, beyond nature and grace to "glory." This we shall explore in chapter 4. In the next chapter, we shall anticipate and set the stage for this discussion by moving beyond the eschatological redirection of history—beyond "the *reversal* of time in the *future* of God," beyond what we might call 'the *salvation* of time in the *coming* of God'—to examine "the *redemption* of time in the *presence* of God."[174]

---

[173] The quotation from CoG, 245 with which this chapter begins continues with the words, "To see God and a human being on the same level means humanizing God and deifying the human being." (cf. n. 1 above). This resistance to divinization and thus to the confusion of "level[s]" must be relativised by Moltmann's enthusiasm for the theme of *theosis*, which is explored in 2.5 above.

[174] On the contrast between salvation and "redemption" in Moltmann's terminology, see 5.3 (especially 5.3n128) below. On the importance of "presence" see 3.5.2 below.

CHAPTER 3

The Redemption of Time in the Presence of God

In the previous chapter, it was suggested that Moltmann's philosophy of time expresses and reveals the contours and dynamics of his overall 'theocosmogony'. The present chapter continues this exploration into the structure of Moltmann's theology in the conviction that his understanding of universal salvation and the redemption of time are interrelated.

In what follows, we shall deepen our analysis of Moltmann's vision of time by examining his vision *for* time. It is in this eschatological context that his understanding of the 'perichoretic' relationship between eternity and time—and thus between God and creation—comes most clearly into view. This ultimate horizon sheds light on the complex, nuanced way he relates nature and grace in the universalism that he proposes.

The redemption of time for Moltmann comes about through the simultaneous fulfilment and negation of time as we know it. After briefly examining the two-sided nature of Moltmann's *Aufhebung* in this context,[1] we shall proceed, via a discussion of his apparent denigration not only of death but also of transience and the past, to explore what he thinks redeemed time will look like.

3.1 The Redemption of Time: Fulfilment and Negation

As I have already pointed out in 2.4 above,[2] the eschatological consummation may be viewed not only as the gathering up of creation into God, but as God's entry into the creation in which he will now dwell, even as it will now dwell in him. In this context, the coming of God into creation is not a movement of *kenosis* but of *theosis*. For Moltmann, the indwelling of all things in God, which he refers to as "the deification of the cosmos," is grounded in "cosmic incarnation."[3]

On the one hand, this would seem to imply an eschatological 'deification of time' (even though he nowhere uses this phrase). As Moltmann puts it,

---

[1] Cf. 2.5 above.
[2] See also the discussion in 2.5 above, including 2.5n130.
[3] WJC, 302.

> If God himself appears *in* his creation, then his eternity appears *in* the time of creation, and his omnipresence *in* creation's space. Consequently temporal creation will be transformed into eternal creation, and spatial creation into omnipresent creation.[4]

On the other hand, the idea of temporal *theosis* seems incompatible with what he says elsewhere in the same passage. Through God's "real presence," we are told, death will be swallowed up and what is corruptible "in time" will perish. "Consequently," says Moltmann in the language of Rev 10:6, " 'time shall be no more'."

This does not signify time's annihilation, however, for Moltmann immediately adds:[5]

> it will be gathered up, fulfilled and transformed through the eternity of the new creation.

This "eternity," he continues, is, to follow mediaeval terminology, *aeonic*, as it is a "relative" eternity that must be distinguished from the absolute eternity of God in which it participates. This will "transform" *chronos* into what Moltmann calls "aeonic *time*."[6] The redemption of time thus involves its simultaneous negation and fulfilment: *chronos* will be no more; aeonic time, or what we might fairly call 'deified time', will never end.

When he explores these themes again later in the same work, Moltmann once more initially seems to speak only of the eradication of time. "Creation's departure from time into the aeon of glory," he writes, "comes about through the annihilation of death and the raising of the dead. Once death is no more, there will be no more time either, neither the time of transience nor the time of futurity."[7] Because it seems absolutely clear throughout Moltmann's corpus that death has no future in any sense,[8] we might be forgiven for reading him here as saying that the *death of death* leads to the *death of time*.

But this is true only of the *time of death*. There is thus a (characteristic) twist in Moltmann's argument. Time, unlike death, may be subjected in a positive way to the power of the resurrection. Thus with the raising of the dead,

---

[4] CoG, 280. His emphases.
[5] There is actually a semi-colon joining these two sentences.
[6] CoG, 280. My emphasis. Surveys of the various ways in which time and eternity have been related in Christian thought that give some attention to Moltmann's approach include: Michael Plathow, "Zeit und Ewigkeit: Ein Thema der christlichen Vorsehungslehre heute," *Neue Zeitschrift für systematische Theologie und Religionsphilosophie* 26, no. 2 (1984): 95–115 and Charles Stinson, "On the Time and Eternity 'Link'," *Religious Studies* 13 (March 1977): 49–62. On Moltmann in particular, see Bauckham, "Time and Eternity," 155–226.
[7] CoG, 294.
[8] See, for example, WJC, 286 as cited in 3.4 below. On the future of death, in addition to 3.4, see 3.6 below.

there is "a *reversion* of the time that is here *irreversible*."⁹ It is precisely because the vector of *transience* is *contradicted*, that past *time* has a future in the eschaton.¹⁰ In the context of predicting that "all the times which in God's creative resolve were fanned out will also be gathered together" and suggesting that the imagery of Rev 5 intimates that "[t]he unfurled times of history will be rolled up like a scroll,"¹¹ he claims that,

> In 'the restoration of all things', all times will return and—transformed and transfigured—will be taken up into the aeon of the new creation.¹²

Furthermore, not only will past *times* be present but *time* itself will be an eschatological reality: the "time of eternal life . . . of eternal livingness."¹³ But while this precludes the annihilation of time, it necessitates its transformation. "[W]ith the parousia of Christ and his kingdom," writes Moltmann, "not only will everything in time be different; time itself will be different."¹⁴ The eschatological transformation of time, we might say, goes 'all the way down' as even its "transcendental conditions" will change.¹⁵

In the present age, "eternity" and "time"—as reflected in the coming/eschatological and passing/historical directions of reality¹⁶—are opposites. In the eschaton, however, Moltmann's cosmogony moves from being a '*contradictory*/harmony monism' to being a 'contradictory/*harmony* monism'.¹⁷ Moltmann refers to this important shift explicitly and succinctly

---

⁹ CoG, 294. His emphases.
¹⁰ Cf. WJC, 35 in which he argues that a truly universal-historical resurrection is impossible in a linear-teleological view of temporality but requires a "cutting right through the times of history." Cf. also WJC, 239, where he says that the resurrection of the dead "talks about a future for those who belong to the past, and in so doing reverses time's direction" and WJC, 303, which in the context of speaking of "the movement of redemption" as "run[ning] counter to evolution," states, "the linear time of evolution will be carried into a unique and then final eschatological cycle: into the return of all the pasts in the eternal aeon of the new creation of all things."
¹¹ CoG, 294–95. In Jürgen Moltmann, "The Bible, the Exegete and the Theologian: Response to Richard Bauckham," in *God Will Be All in All: The Eschatology of Jürgen Moltmann*, ed. Richard Bauckham (Edinburgh: T. and T. Clark, 1999), 227–32, Moltmann makes it clear (on p. 232) that he is adopting an image and not making an "exegetical claim."
¹² CoG, 294. Cf. WJC, 24, "the future redemption will liberate the whole past, and will make it present, freeing it from its suppression, and its repression. . . . [R]edemption . . . redeems the past, making it the eternal present."
¹³ CoG, 295.
¹⁴ CoG, 199.
¹⁵ See CoG, 26 as cited in n. 19 below.
¹⁶ I say 'reflected in' because eternity and time are not to be simply equated with the eschatological and historical directions of time. See 2.6 above.
¹⁷ For this terminology, see my comments in 0.6 and 2.1 (including 2.1n11) above, and 3.6 below.

when he writes, "The Creator no longer remains over against [gegenüber] his creation."[18] Given the mutual indwelling of God and the world,

> In that new aeon a mutual perichoresis between eternity and time also comes into existence, so that on the one hand we can talk about 'eternal time' and on the other about 'eternity filled with time'.[19]

It is in this light that we should understand the unqualified, and in that sense misleading, claim that we find in *Experiences in Theology*, where he writes,

> [W]ith the raising of Christ, the revelation of God's glory begins, the glory which overcomes the force of time, together with the power of death, and which will bring about the eternal creation.[20]

Passages like this one must not be read in terms of a time-eternity dualism. Moltmann's position is subtle. On the one hand, the "force of time" that will be overcome is *chronos*, "the power of transience."[21] On the other hand, the "eternal creation" will include "aeonic time."[22]

The difference that Moltmann posits between the transient time of the present age and the redeemed time of the Age to Come is thus not dualistically conceived. But there is a decisive distinction to be made, nevertheless. This is spelt out most clearly in *God in Creation*, where Moltmann states,

> It is ... even permissible to assume that in the kingdom of glory there will be time and history, future and possibility, and these to an unimpeded degree, and in a way that is no longer ambivalent. Instead of timeless eternity it would therefore be better to talk about 'eternal time'; and instead of 'the end of history'

---

[18] CoG, 295 [*DKG*, 325]. In the context of discussing the eschatological end of space in CoG, 307 [*DKG*, 337], Moltmann calls this "opposition" that is to be overcome a "distanced contraposition [distanzierten Gegenüber]."

[19] CoG, 295. Cf. the vision of this mutual indwelling in CoG, 307–308, in which "[c]reated beings participate in the divine attribute[] of eternity, just as the indwelling God has participated in their limited time ... taking [it] upon himself." Consequently, "for those God has created, the time (*chronos*) of remoteness from God and of transience ceases" while "God's indwelling eternity gives to created beings eternal time." Cf. also CoG, 26, "The 'eschaton' of an eschatology which works with the concept of God suggested here, and with the advent understanding of the future, is not an eternity which can neither *enter* time, nor remain *outside* time. This eschaton means a change in the transcendental conditions of time. With the coming of God's glory, future time ends and eternal time begins." His emphases. For a wide-ranging discussion of the notion of *perichoresis*, in conversation with Moltmann's thinking *inter alia*, see Graham Buxton, *The Trinity, Creation and Pastoral Ministry: Imaging the Perichoretic God*. Paternoster Theological Monographs (Milton Keynes, UK: Paternoster, 2005), a work to which Moltmann supplies an appreciative foreword.

[20] EiT, 63.

[21] CoG, 13. Cf. CoG, 284 which speaks of " 'a new *time*' ... in which *chronos* will enjoy no more efficacy." My emphases.

[22] CoG, 280.

we should talk about the end of pre-history and the beginning of the 'eternal history' of God, human beings and nature. This of course means thinking of *change without transience, time without the past, and life without death* [Veränderung ohne Vergehen, Zeit ohne Vergangenheit und Leben ohne Tod].[23]

Moltmann's final sentence suggests that before we can further explore his positive vision of time in the new creation—a time characterised by "life" and including "change"—we must first examine his view of transience, the past, and death, as it is the negation of these realities that makes redeemed time thinkable.

3.2 Transience

When Moltmann writes in his most recent major work, "The enslavement under which created being suffers is transience" and contrasts "[f]uturity" as "the time of life" with "[t]ransience" as "the time of death,"[24] he expresses sentiments that can be found throughout his corpus.

Of the hundreds of references to transience in his writings, only a very few could in any sense be construed as positive. Transience is identified, or closely associated, with: Godforsakenness,[25] remoteness from God,[26] the "godless" nature of time in the present age,[27] annihilation,[28] destruction,[29] vanity,[30] futility,[31] tragedy,[32] bondage and slavery,[33] torment,[34] suffering,[35] sickness,[36] wretchedness,[37] degeneration,[38] growing old (viewed in a negative light),[39] death and separation in time,[40] isolation,[41] sin,[42] injustice,[43] and God's wrath.[44] The power of transience is compared with "Chronos, who devours his own

---

[23] GC, 213 [*GS*, 220]. My emphases.
[24] EiT, 111–12.
[25] See TH, 18.
[26] See CoG, 308.
[27] CoG, 310.
[28] See TH, 26.
[29] See CoG, 284.
[30] See TH, 94 and 214.
[31] See GC, 68.
[32] See GC, 68.
[33] See GC, 39 and WJC, 251.
[34] See CrG, 93.
[35] See GC, 102.
[36] See SL, 88 as cited below.
[37] See WJC, 48, cf. WJC, 45.
[38] See GC, 105.
[39] See SL, 195.
[40] See CoG, 71.
[41] See GC, 69.
[42] See CrG, 179; CPS, 23; and CoG, 273.
[43] See CoG, 136.
[44] See CoG, 80.

children."[45] That transience is a "curse" is a point he makes by appeal to Rom 8,[46] a chapter that he cites frequently in this context.[47] The following passage from *The Spirit of Life* is representative:

> [I]n the coming of the Spirit of the resurrection of the dead and in the power of the new creation of all things, the world is revealed as a world of death which has failed to find God and itself. Transitory time and the mortality of all the living was hitherto held to be the 'natural' condition of all created things, because there was no alternative; but the condition now emerges as sick. In the daybreak colours of their new creation, all things are revealed in their 'sickness unto death'. Once there is reason to hope for the world's redemption, that world ceases to be seen as natural and finite. It can now be perceived as an unredeemed world. Out of the general transience of things, unredeemed creation can be heard 'sighing and groaning' for its liberation.[48]

The subtitle of the work from which this passage comes is "A Universal Affirmation,"[49] an affirmation that, for all its universality, does not include, but is presumably made in the face of, transience. That said, it is important to reiterate that the "liberation" Moltmann anticipates must not be understood as an exodus out of the temporal flux into a higher realm characterised by timeless eternity. Throughout his corpus, Moltmann consistently distinguishes his view of transience from that of the dominant tradition of Greek metaphysics that has so influenced Western thought.[50]

That we should not be satisfied with the present, passing nature of the world is a point that Moltmann seems happy to concede to dualistic thinkers. "The question of human existence," he observes, "is the question of all earthly being:

---

[45] CoG, 24.
[46] GC, 189.
[47] See TH, 161; CrG, 218 (cited below); GC, 68 and 39; CoG, 70 and 276; and EiT, 111–12.
[48] SL, 88. Here Moltmann uses the language of Kierkegaard as he does on other occasions. See the discussion in 3.5.2 below.
[49] While *The Spirit of Life: A Universal Affirmation* is the English title found in the UK and North American editions, the German original is actually *Der Geist des Lebens: Eine ganzheitlich Pneumatologie* ['A Holistic Pneumatology']. But this work, like all of his recent works, was translated in full consultation with Moltmann (see SL, xv). So the significance of this difference should probably not be over-emphasised.
[50] See TH, 28, 140, 141, 159, 301; CrG, 68; TKG, 21; GC, 247; and SL, 90. He also distances himself from the denigration of transience found in transcendental eschatology in TH, 74 and in existentialism in TH, 150. In SL, 91, Moltmann writes, "If the seeking soul thinks that what is transitory is God, then it begins to be afraid that these transitory things will not live up to what it expects of them, and this fear in its turn evokes hate of the things and hate of the self—that is to say aggression." Here Moltmann is giving an account of Augustine's thought. Read carefully in context, however, he is sympathetic at this point. Moltmann clearly rejects this hatred of and hostility towards the transience of creation. It is highly probable that he would understand the origin of the negative posture of Greek metaphysics, and its dualistic, modern counterparts, in the light of these dynamics.

how can finite being . . . acquire a continuance that will resist transience in time and decay in death?" The answer, however, is not to be found in the soul's escape to another world but in the participation of "the whole cosmos" in "the glory of the divine being."[51]

This perspective allows Moltmann to maintain significant sympathy for mainstream Greek philosophical thought, even as he 'eschatologises' its metaphysical longings, thus advocating a very different theology of hope in the light of the crucified God. He writes,

> *Like* the metaphysics of finite being, the theology of the cross sees all creatures subject to transitoriness and nothingness. *But* because it does not arise in this context, but sees nothingness itself done away with in the being of God, who in the death of Jesus has revealed himself and constituted himself in nothingness, it changes the general impression of the transitoriness of all things into the prospect of the hope and liberation of all things. 'For the creation was subjected to nothingness, not of its own will but by the will of him who subjected it in hope' (Rom. 8.20). *Thus the metaphysical longing of all that is transitory for intransitoriness and of all that is finite for infinity undergoes an eschatological transformation and is taken up into the hope of the freedom of the sons of God and the freedom of the new creation that does not pass away.*[52]

This perspective can help us appreciate the fact that when Moltmann in a much later work states, "Transience is the time of death. Futurity is the time of life,"[53] he is positing a cosmo*gonic* dual*ity* rather than a cosmo*logical* dual*ism*.[54] Given the presence of God in the cross, given Christ's descent into Hell, the world's "underlying irreversible time-structure"[55] that prior to the experience of redemption we know only as transience, becomes the context of hope. Transience, we might say, becomes (even as it is contradicted by) futurity. Time may now be experienced in the eschatological direction. We may turn our attention, in the midst of a world in which all is passing away, to what is coming. The groaning of a creation subject to futility may be heard as the cry of hope.[56] Thus Moltmann says that Christ's resurrection "shines as messianic

---

[51] WJC, 47.
[52] CrG, 218. "Like" is italicised in the original, the subsequent emphases being mine. Although his reference to "the metaphysics of being" is to the outlook of classical theism, his sympathetic critique and critical sympathy can be fairly said to extend to the Greek metaphysical tradition that is re-presented here.
[53] EiT, 112.
[54] On the tendency for cosmogonic, "geneticistic," or process-oriented world-pictures to be monistic and for cosmological, "structuralistic" world-pictures to be dualistic, see Olthuis, "Models of Humanity in Theology and Psychology," 18–23. Cf. 0.6 and 2.1n11 above.
[55] EiT, 112.
[56] Thus in WJC, 252, Moltmann writes, "If we look at nature from the perspective of Christ's resurrection, then the sphere in which nature is experienced moves into the horizon of expectation of its new creation. The experiences of life's transience and the unceasing suffering of all living things no longer end only in grief, but also already lead

light on the whole sighing creation, giving it, *in* [not despite] *its transience* [in ihrer Vergänglichkeit], an eternal hope that it will be created anew as the 'world without end'."[57]

If there is hope *in* transience, is there any hope *for* transience? In 2.2 above, I observed that Moltmann took exception to Augustine's portrayal of the time of creation as the time of death. In the context of making the damning observation that in the Church Father's perspective "created existence is not anything we can possibly affirm," Moltmann raises the question, "What meaning can the creation of transience have?"[58] The implication seems clear enough: for God the Creator, and thus for us, the transience of the world must have a positive significance in relation to the Age to Come.

How transience is "affirm[ed]" as part of "created existence" in Moltmann's eschatological vision, however, is anything but straightforward. Moltmann concludes his alternative to Augustine's position with the words, "God did not create the world for transience and death. He created it for his own glory, and therefore for its own eternal life."[59] From this it would seem to follow that the "meaning," purpose, and fulfilment of the world's *transience* is to be found in *its own* passing.[60] This sounds thoroughly negative: the fulfilment of history necessitates the *transience of transience*.

If Moltmann is distancing himself from Augustine, however, it is unlikely that he intends to be read as implying that transience "is not anything we can possibly affirm." That it is not the ultimate destiny of the world is clearly stated. But as itself part of a "world .... created ... for [God's] glory," transience (presumably) must be related to the eternal life of the eschaton in a way that affirms its nature within God's creative purposes. Moltmann's position seems to be that if the very fulfilment of history, including the fulfilment of transience, lies in the transience of transience, then the "meaning" that transience has as a pervasive feature of the original creation is that it— positively—*makes way for* the Age to Come. Although there is no hope *for* transience, there is no hope *without* it.

In other words: there is no hope (but) for transience. We hope for a world without transience; yet without transience, life would be hope-less. This paradoxical affirmation is a consistent feature of Moltmann's vision for the future. Thus in *Theology of Hope*, he writes,

> In the eyes of Christian hope[,] the epithet 'transient' belongs not only to the things which we generally feel are destined to pass away, but it sees as transient those very things which are generally felt to be always there and to cause the transience of all life, namely, evil and death. Death becomes transient in the

---

to hope. Creation is 'subjected' but 'in hope' (Rom. 8.20)." Moltmann calls this an "eschatological reinterpretation of transience."
[57] GC, 7 [GS, 21]. My emphases.
[58] GC, 117 as cited in 2.2 above.
[59] GC, 124 as cited in 2.2 above.
[60] Cf. CoG, x, "the time of transience must sometime pass away."

promised resurrection. Sin becomes transient in the justification of the sinner and the righteousness for which we have to hope.[61]

Similarly, in *The Coming of God*, Moltmann claims that although "[t]here can be no *telling* [Erzählungen] of the ultimate future," we can nevertheless speak of the "past in the future" and " '*tell*' [erzählen] of the passing away of the powers of injustice and death."[62] This apocalyptic "*negation of the negative*," he insists, must be constantly related to the messianic "*position of the positive* [[d]ie *Position des Positiven*]" (and vice versa).[63] Thus in both works, transience, though a 'negative' phenomenon in Moltmann's cosmogony, plays an integral, redemptive role not only towards sin and injustice, which were not part of God's creative purpose, but also towards death which, in Moltmann's understanding, was an original feature of God's "good" creation.[64] To those with hope, transience thus not only speaks of the passing away of present evils; it also signifies the movement of creation towards its eschatological fulfilment.

Evidence for this relatively positive reading of the "meaning" of "the creation of transience"—a reading that goes beyond the "negation of the negative"—is not at all widespread in Moltmann's writings. But there is one passage, in the immediate vicinity of the text from *Theology of Hope* cited above, that points us in this more 'promising' direction. Having claimed that " 'history' ['Geschichte'] arises in the light of its end, in the things which happen because of, and become perceptible through, the promise that lights up the way ahead," Moltmann writes,

> The impression of general transience that comes of looking back sorrowfully upon the things that cannot endure, has in actual fact as such nothing to do with history. Rather, that transience is historic [[g]eschichtlich] which comes of hope, of exodus, of setting out towards the promised, not yet visible future.[65]

Here "transience" refers to the provisional nature of the present age in a way that is suggestive of, and that thus directs us towards, a better future. In this light, Moltmann's statement, "God did not create the world for transience . . . [but] for his own glory," can be read as implying that the transience of God's creation can be accepted gratefully as evidence that history is on the move

---

[61] TH, 165. Cf. TH, 268 on "mak[ing] death . . . a passing thing."
[62] CoG, 140 [*DKG*, 160–61]. My emphases. In CoG, 141, he calls this "an anticipation in the mode of the narrated past of what must pass away."
[63] CoG, 141 [*DKG*, 161]. His emphases.
[64] On death as part of God's "good" creation, see 3.4 below. In speaking here of the "redemption" not only of something fallen (sin) but also created (death), I am following Moltmann's own use of the term in distinction from my own. See n. 271 below and the discussion in 5.3, especially 5.3n128, below.
[65] TH, 165 [*TdH*, 149]. Although 'geschichtlich' and 'historisch' both mean 'historical', the former term may also refer to what is judged to be of 'historic' significance.

towards the glory of the eschaton. In the words of *The Mystery of Salvation*, which have probably been consciously influenced by Moltmann at this point,[66]

> Evening and morning, built into the present creation, witness to its impermanence. This is not simply a matter of the fallenness of humankind or the world. The creation was made, it seems, to point beyond itself. Birth, growth, decay and death all indicate that, even apart from sin, the present creation was not intended to be the creator's last word.[67]

While the idea that history for the eschatologically oriented Christian is a dynamic, restless, forward-looking, and, in that sense, 'transient', pilgrimage is certainly present in all Moltmann's writings,[68] the way he here equates "historic ... transience" with what he elsewhere calls futurity is possibly unique to this one passage.[69] "Transience," in his usual terminology, is a 'passing away' rather than a 'passing through'. It is what we might call the 'flip-side' (or 'down-side') of futurity just as passing away is the correlate of coming into being. Moltmann can say that "In the present kairos of faith, the impression of time is transformed, metaphorically speaking, from transience into futurity,"[70] because futurity and transience name the two directions of the one temporal process.[71] Hope, therefore, does not take flight from transience, but makes it

---

[66] As suggested in 1.3 above.

[67] *The Mystery of Salvation*, 72 as cited in 1.3 above.

[68] On the "restless" nature of present existence, Moltmann finds another point of contact with Augustine (cf. 2.2 above), although he understands the origin of this restlessness differently. Thus in TH, 88 he says that "[i]t is the *promissio inquieta* that is the true source of Augustine's *cor inquietum*." Cf. TH, 196, 276, and 285. Moltmann cites Augustine's famous dictum, "Our hearts are restless until they find rest in thee," favourably in the final paragraph of TKG (see TKG, 222), although in GC, 282, he observes that this restlessness extends beyond the heart to the whole creation. Other explicit references to Augustine in this context include GC, 151 and SL, 198–99. Other texts in which an affinity with Augustine is evident include GC, 69 and 205. Yet in his qualified sympathy for the restless, experimental, American life-style in CoG, 176 and in his references to *God's* unrest in CoG, 266 and 319, Moltmann could not be said to be Augustinian.

[69] Given the very extensive nature of Moltmann's corpus, with many items still being published, claims to find "unique" examples in his work are risky. That this is a departure from Moltmann's usual terminology, however, can be seen earlier in TH, 110, where he notes that when salvation history is no longer viewed in the light of God's promise and mission, "provisional events that point to the future of promise," come to be seen as "events [that] belong within the sphere of transience" and that at best "reflect the eternal intransience of the Deity."

[70] CoG, 294.

[71] This is why at one and the same time, "the future of Christ," in WJC, 317, "brings the end of becoming and the end of passing away." Cf. CoG, 294, where Moltmann states, "Once death is no more, there will be no more time either, neither the time of transience nor the time of futurity."

bearable.[72] The affirmation is thus paradoxical: transience makes hope possible; but it also makes it necessary.

The one other way in which Moltmann advocates what we might call a positive transience occurs in a discussion of the closely related idea of death. Although the term itself does not appear, it is fair to say that an active rather than passive 'transience' is in view, here understood as a *kenotic* dying to self that Moltmann believes is central to the love of others. Thus Moltmann writes,

> The body of love integrates dying into the affirmation of life, and does not suppress death. In the life of love, dying is experienced daily and a resurrection [is experienced] every morning. Every act of love is experienced by the man as 'a little death' [la petite mort] and every birth is experienced by the woman as a surrender of life. So loving and dying are not antitheses. They are correspondences. For loving and dying are simply the immanent sides of the resurrection and eternal life. Dying and death can be integrated into the loving affirmation of life if there is hope for 'the resurrection of the body'. It is only this hope which makes a person prepared to live and love in the body, here and now, wholly and without reserve, and in love to die. . . .[73]

In hope, therefore, we trust that transience will itself prove to be transient, and in lives of "historic . . . transience," we give (of) ourselves in love, knowing that (in the words of Matt 10:39) "Whoever seeks to gain his life will lose it, but whoever loses his life will preserve it."[74] It is in such *kenosis* that Moltmann's own question, "What meaning can the creation of transience have?" may find its most positive answer.

3.3 The Past

For the most part, the past is also portrayed in a negative light in Moltmann's writings. In particular it is associated with the power and burden of sin[75] and with the bondage of guilt.[76] In this context, the past is often contrasted unfavourably with the future. Thus "the *communio peccatorum* [that the church] acknowledges is its past," while "the *communio sanctorum* that it believes when it believes in the forgiveness of sin is its future."[77] When

---

[72] Cf. CoG, 133, "Only the idea of history's ultimate goal makes the experience of the transitoriness of all things endurable." Here Moltmann is summarising post-Hegelian German theology of history. Although he finds it ultimately one-sided, he is—in my judgment—sympathetic at this point.

[73] WJC, 260–61.

[74] CrG, 15. Here the translators have followed Moltmann's German text rather than citing this text in a standard English version. Matthew 10:39 (as Moltmann reads it) is also alluded to in, e.g., GC, 269; CoG, 67 and 119. See n. 172 below.

[75] See CPS, 22 and CoG, 175.

[76] See EiT, 147. Cf. EiT, 168 where Moltmann notes that to form a judgment is to pin someone down to their past. "Judgment" here can be read in both a neutral and a negative way.

[77] CPS, 354–55. His italics.

Moltmann comments on how the church's prophetic mission "evokes conflicts between the powers of the past and the forces of the future," this is described as a conflict between powers of "oppression and liberation," respectively.[78] Similarly, "[t]he future is the kingdom of not yet defined potentialities, whereas the past represents the limited kingdom of reality."[79] Put more starkly, the " 'compulsive' . . . laws and forces of the past" are to be sharply contrasted with the liberating impact of "God's messianic future."[80]

These distinctions all reflect what Moltmann calls *"the qualitative differentiation between past and future."* For those who have an "eschatological experience of time,"

> 'Past' becomes the scheme of this old world, which will pass away because it has no permanence. 'Future' [by contrast] is filled with the image of the new creation, which will remain eternally. Those affected will therefore no longer conform to the pattern of the old world but will renew themselves in the in-streaming energies of the world that is new, saying with Paul: 'I forget what lies behind and strain forward to what is ahead' (Phil. 3.13, following Isa. 43.18f.). Past and future are then like night and day, and the chance of the present lies in that fact: 'Let us cast off the works of darkness and put on the armour of light' (Rom. 13.12).[81]

While past and future are as far apart as night and day here, this is not the black and white distinction it may first appear to be, for Moltmann also acknowledges that there is 'future in the past' and 'past in the future'. In the complex "modalisation" of time that he proposes, these are referred to, respectively, as the "past future" and "future past."[82]

The positive way in which he views the "past future" can be seen in the following passage from *The Church in the Power of the Spirit*. Here (as elsewhere in Moltmann's corpus) memory is affirmed, but only if our looking back is a way of nurturing our hope.[83] Thus in discerning the difference

---

[78] CPS, 83.
[79] TKG, 217.
[80] CoG, 45.
[81] CoG, 138–39. His emphases. Paul's words in Phil 3:13 are also used by Augustine to articulate what Moltmann judges to be his "specifically Christian experience of time," as noted in 2.2 above.
[82] On the modalisation of time, see GC, 124–35 especially 128–130, (an earlier presentation of this material being *"Verschränkte Zeiten der Geschichte: Notwendige Differenzierungen und Begrenzungen des Geschichtsbegriffs," Evangelische Theologie* 44 (1984): 213–27); CoG, 284–91, especially 286–90; and the briefer comments in GC, 117; WJC, 240; and CoG, 26.
[83] On hope-ful, eschatological memory, see CrG, 5 (on J.B. Metz's "dangerous remembrance," also discussed in CoG, 234) and 165 (on the "general structural connection of recollection and hope"); CPS, 75 (as cited below), 219 (on "remembrance in the mode of hope"), 243 (on the "coincidence of remembrance and hope" in the Lord's Supper), and 281 ("The power of continuity won through memory is directed towards the rebirth of the whole . . . creation"); GC, 120 ("The [OT] story . . . awakes

between the "eternal" and the "temporally conditioned" in the Bible, he suggests that we distinguish "the future in its past" from what simply "belongs to the past."[84] The past is thus eschatologically significant when it is characterised by what Moltmann elsewhere calls the "ontological" "precedence" of the future.[85] Thus he writes,

> In the light of the eschatological person of Christ, the church does not live from the past; it exists as a factor of present liberation, between remembrance of his history and hope of his kingdom. Its remembrance of Jesus, his mission, his self-giving and his resurrection is past made present and can be termed 'remembrance in the mode of hope'. Its hope of his parousia is future made present and can be termed 'hope in the mode of remembrance'. If the eschatological orientation is lost, then remembrance decays into a powerless historical recollection of a founder at the beginning of things. The church can then itself take the place of hope, setting itself up as the prolongation of his former incarnation, and the aim of its growth as being his parousia.[86]

These comments about an anti-eschatological attempt to prolong the past are closely echoed in *God in Creation* when Moltmann speaks of extrapolation, in distinction from anticipation, as the attempt to secure a future that "stabilize[s] present conditions of ownership and power."[87] This kind of future is not the *adventus* of the new creation but the *futurum* of the old world order. It is the "future past," a future (*futurum*) that "offers no special reason for hope, *for the past predominates*, inasmuch as that which is not yet, will one day no longer be."[88]

---

remembrance in order to justify hope") and 132 (on the inscription at Yad Vashem, Jerusalem: "Forgetfulness leads to exile, while remembrance is the secret of redemption"—redemption being an eschatological category for Moltmann [see 5.3, and especially 5.3n128, below]); WJC, 8 ("hope must always be preceded by some positive remembrance"), 10 (on non-nostalgic memory aroused and transformed by new beginnings), and 210 (citing Metz on "anticipatory memory"); CoG, 28 (on how "remembrance" of the Exodus, for example, in relation to the New Exodus "now only has the significance of being the advance radiance of what is new, or its prototype"), and 234 (on how the "*memoria resurrectionis Christi* lets us look . . . beyond the horizon of this world's end into God's new world"). His italics. In his essay, "The Beginning of Time in God's Presence," in *The End of Time? The Provocation of Talking about God*, by Joseph Cardinal Ratzinger, Johann Baptist Metz, Jürgen Moltmann, and Eveline Goodman-Thau, ed. Tiemo Rainer Peters and Claus Urban, trans. J. Matthew Ashley (New York: Paulist Press, 2004), 54–64, Moltmann notes, on p. 63: "Without memory there is no hope; without hope no memory." That he is stressing *hope-ful* memory, and not merely 'balancing' past and future, despite his recognition of their interwovenness, is evident in his related claim, made earlier on the same page, that "There is so much future in the past that will not let the past be past."

[84] EiT, 279–80.
[85] See CoG, 287 and GC, 120 as cited in 2.2n29 above.
[86] CPS, 75.
[87] GC, 134 as cited fully in 2.4 above. Cf. CoG, 45.
[88] CoG, 25 as cited fully in 2.4 above. My emphasis.

The notion of the "future in the past," or the "past future," by contrast, accounts for many of Moltmann's positive comments about "tradition." Thus he writes approvingly with reference to the Old Testament,

> In this ["eschatologizing"] conception of tradition the future which is announced and promised increasingly dominates the present. This tradition of promise turns our eyes not towards some primaeval, original event, but towards the future and finally towards an *eschaton* of fulfilment. We do not drift through history with our backs to the future and our gaze returning ever and again to the origin, but we strive confidently towards the promised future. It is not the primaeval ancients who are near the truth and dwell nearer to the gods, but it is to future generations that the promises are given, in order that they may see the fulfilment.[89]

From this it follows that "Christian tradition is . . . not to be understood as a handing on of something that has to be preserved, but as an event which summons the dead and the godless to life."[90] If in ancient non-Israelite religion, the "prerogative of tradition is expressed in the phrase 'from of old',"[91] for the Christian, "Tradition is forward-moving mission."[92] If in line with modern romanticism, we expect the gospel of the risen Christ to "provide anti-revolutionary, Western continuity . . . in the history of transience," he writes, then we "put [it] to the service of foreign gods and ideologies."[93] "[T]he day that we speak 'conservatively' of tradition, we no longer have it."[94]

The quotations in the above paragraph, which all come from *Theology of Hope*, illustrate well how Moltmann's early work tends to posit a fairly rigid antithesis between cross and resurrection, night and day, old and new, that may be contrasted with the more flexible, trinitarian dialectic that characterises his "systematic contributions of theology" series. In a discussion that explicitly acknowledges this development, Moltmann points out that the "apocalyptic contradiction . . . of the kingdom of God to the conditions of this world" that is highlighted in his early work is complemented in his more recent writings by the "messianic correspondence" of world and kingdom.[95]

Because there appears to be a profound suspicion towards this idea in *Theology of Hope*, it is instructive that Moltmann clarifies his understanding of the *continuity* that he now sees as existing between the two aeons of God's world by pointing out that while flesh and blood do not inherit the kingdom (as

---

[89] TH, 298. His emphasis. My insertion of "eschatologizing" is taken from Moltmann's own discussion earlier on the same page. Cf. TH, 291–303, a sub-section entitled, "The Tradition of the Eschatological Hope."
[90] TH, 302.
[91] TH, 296.
[92] TH, 301. Cf. TH, 284.
[93] TH, 301. The phrase "in the history of transience" comes from earlier in the paragraph.
[94] TH, 292.
[95] Moltmann, "Hope and Reality," 84.

noted in *Theology of Hope*), the mortal must nevertheless put on immortality. The New Creation, present now in the Spirit, embraces and transforms the old, he says, thus establishing the continuity between the two ages, which runs from new to old, but not vice versa.[96]

It is, I suggest, better to speak here of a change of emphasis than a fundamental departure.[97] In his later works, Moltmann continues to speak most positively of the past only when its eschatological potential is in view.[98] Furthermore, even this new focus on continuity between the two ages is not incompatible with what we might find in his early writings.[99]

What is more novel is that there are times when Moltmann does seem to affirm the importance of a continuity that moves from past to future and thus in the historical rather than eschatological direction of time. In his most recent major work, *Experiences in Theology*, for example, Moltmann writes,

> The religions which are called 'historical' have . . . become scriptural religions. The point of the long genealogies in these writings is, read backwards, *continuity in the origins*; read forward it is their content as promise. In relation to the people's remembrance of God's promises, the reading that points forwards takes precedence—*in relation to God's remembrance of the sufferings of his people, the reading that points backwards.*[100]

---

[96] See Moltmann, "Hope and Reality," 82–84.

[97] This is best seen as a shift of emphasis as the basic framework of Moltmann's thought has not changed. In the terminology of my earlier discussion (see 2.1 above), his *contradictory* (harmony) monism is in his later works more evidently a contradictory *harmony* monism.

[98] This is implicit, of course, in the language of "*messianic* correspondence." My emphasis. In CoG, 289, Moltmann writes, "True tradition is always at the same time *remembered hope*. In our uncertainty about our own future we seek for future in the past, and find it in the unfulfilled hopes of past generations." His emphasis. Other references to the past in which it is the future of that past that is the focus of attention include CPS, 25 (on the "wealth of past experience" viewed as "the wealth of untried possibilities"), 212 (in which he claims, "The proclamation and the history of Christ which opens up faith is not a past history in the historical sense; but in the eschatological sense it is an event of the past which opens up the divine future"), and 254 (where very similar language is used of the cross); GC, 120 ("The [OT] story makes the past present, in order to proclaim the future. It awakens remembrance in order to justify hope. The story tells of the divine faithfulness which has been experienced, in order to awaken new trust in God in the future. The promise that has gone forth, and the divine faithfulness that has been experienced, point to the future; and it is the future that has precedence in the different modes of time."); WJC, 77 (in which he states that " 'In the light of the resurrection' [Christ's] past history is not merely made present and retrospectively interpreted; he himself is manifested in this past history in the light of his present future"); and EiT, 104 which (via EiT, 357n41) traces the idea of the "future in the past" or "past future" back to Ernst Bloch.

[99] In TH, 300, for example, he states "the gospel which reveals the presence of the coming Lord requires a continuity with the earthly Jesus which has constantly to be discovered anew . . . ."

[100] EiT, 33. My emphases. In the original passage, "scriptural religions" is italicised.

In contrast to this more balanced appreciation of the historical and the eschatological, the disparaging of those whose "gaze return[s] ever and again to the origin"[101] that we find in *Theology of Hope* appears unnuanced.

Nevertheless, even in this passage, the continuity from past to future is deemed necessary lest we forget a past still in need of *redemption*.[102] Thus the past is not being affirmed as foundational to the present in a positive, 'creational'[103] sense. Moltmann prefaces his discussion with the claim that "It is memory alone which preserves continuity in time,"[104] which does suggest a perspective that is more historical than eschatological, but this soon develops into a discussion of the function of the story remembered by religions of exile (such as Judaism) in which,

> The past is remembered because the future it hides is to awaken the hopes of the next generation. So what is told is not really something past, which has had its time. It is something which has gone forth but which still has its time ahead of it. The story of the divine promises is told and passed on in the form of the remembered hopes of the people. This is remembrance in which one can live and which is essential to living.[105]

Once again, it seems that it is the past *future*—the advent future in the past, the divine promise of redemption—that is valued.[106]

---

[101] TH, 298 as cited above.

[102] See also WJC, 207–208, 211; and SL, 27.

[103] By 'creational' I mean time and history viewed as a good gift of God from the beginning, a gift that can be received and brought to fruition as we make history in covenant with God. See the discussion of 'originary' below. 'Eschatological', by contrast, relates to the promise of the future. The creational future is, to use Moltmann's terminology, *futurum*, which (contrary to Moltmann) I would wish to view as in principle as positive a reality as the eschatological *adventus*. In 5.2.1–5.2.4 below, I refer to this as the 'foundational' future in contrast to the eschatological 'transcendental' future. (In this context, 'transcendental' does not refer to conditions for 'phenomenal' reality but to the eschatological direction of time.)

[104] EiT, 32.

[105] EiT, 33. For a very similar, ultimately hope-oriented, approach to the importance of memory for continuity in Moltmann's early work, see CPS, 281. When compared with EiT, 33, there is little evidence of fundamental development (still less change) on this topic.

[106] Cf. Moltmann's discussion in SW, 95:
> Genuine traditions are always also remembered and passed-on hopes. In our own orientation towards the future we search for the hopes of the past and find them in the unfulfilled hopes and the still unpaid debts of the past generations that went before us. If we view our political histories, our cultural histories, and the history of humanity as still unfinished, unfulfilled processes, then we shall take up the histories of hope which are bound up with them. 'The American dream' has still not been fulfilled. The vision of human rights and of democracy has not yet been realized. The hope for 'eternal peace' in the family of the nations which Kant voiced still beckons us after three hundred years. In this respect *the future*

The affirmation of the past as a foundational, empowering reality in our lives does however receive attention in an important passage in *The Spirit of Life*. With reference to the "limit situations" of life, love, and death that we all encounter, Moltmann writes,

> There are events in the past which never become 'past', but are constantly present to us. We repress them, we work on them, we puzzle over them and interpret them, for we have to live with them. Our biographies are moulded by experiences like this, experiences which affect us in this elemental way.[107]

Later in this discussion, which stays remarkably free from Moltmann's characteristic tendency to resort to eschatological categories in order to find true value in human existence,[108] he reflects on what we might call the 'originary' power of the past by observing,

> Out of its fathomless source, life thrusts forward to expression, expression through living. This is why the deeper experiences of life remain uncompleted. We discover ourselves in them again and again, each time in a different way. This is the charm of re-membrance. We experience life with these experiences, and they travel with us.[109]

To anticipate the terminology I will explore in 5.2.4, the past is here seen to have 'creational' or historical rather than simply eschatological significance. Here we see intimations of a vibrant theology of creation that readers of his early work will search for in vain.

Even here, however, we must not posit a *rupture* with his earlier writings. The foundational role of the past as a *sine qua non* for healthy existence in the present and as more than simply a resource for our hopes is evident as early as *The Crucified God*. In a critical conversation with Freud, Moltmann pursues a discussion of what in his later modalisation of time would be called the "present past."[110] Here he justifies his claim that periods of "regression" may be both useful and enriching by noting that,

---

of history [his emphasis] determines the times, and makes of the past *past-future* [my emphasis], of the present present-future, and of future times future-future. Cf. SW, 101.
[107] SL, 20–21.
[108] Contrast, for example, the affirmation of traditions and "roots" in CPS, xiv and also the claim made in CPS, 28–29 that "Hope must return to remembrance if it is not to lose its real foundation." Despite this affirmation of 'origins', the "roots" and "foundation," respectively, are understood Christologically, with Christ being viewed in terms of his eschatological future. The origin in question is thus not that of creation but of the New Creation.
[109] SL, 22.
[110] On this notion (also referred to as "the past-made-present") and on the "past present," see CoG, 288; GC, 128, 132, and in particular, 131 as discussed in n. 113 below.

> They once again open up the present to the past and make the past present. Then man does not run the course of his life in a series of punctiliar presents which then disappear, but collects himself for the full present of his past and present life. The surrender of the infantile phase and the overcoming of the pleasure principle can easily lead the mature man to apathy in respect of his youth. But that would not make him richer, but poorer.[111]

In developing the claim that " '[t]he infantile' is not a morally derogatory category," he writes,

> Dream regressions into the world of infantile wishes can ... enrich the sense of present reality in that they bring to consciousness not only the man of the moment but the whole man with all his life history. There is no present identity of a man without continuity with his past. Only then is a man present with all the strata of his life, for his childhood is a part of his present form.[112]

Continuity, it would seem, is not simply established with the past but consists in keeping the past alive within us.

These passages notwithstanding, the foundational or 'creational' role of the past is a relatively minor theme in Moltmann's thought compared with his eschatological emphasis on the (advent) future in the past. That he seems to understand the (arguably) rather different role of the past in each of these perspectives solely in terms of the "past future" or "future in the past"[113] also suggests that the peculiar dynamics of the historical or 'creational' direction of time (and thus the nature of what I shall call the foundational future in distinction from the transcendental future[114]) do not receive his theoretical attention, even if they are not wholly absent from his discussions.

---

[111] CrG, 310. In CrG, 311, he follows this with the suggestion that if we were to examine the dreams of healthy people "at the climatic experiences of their lives"—a phrase that calls to mind the "limit" experiences that are in view in SL, 20–21 (as cited above)—we "would probably come across [a] double presence of past and future."

[112] CrG, 311–12.

[113] GC, 131, for example, seems to me to contain a helpful discussion of what I would specify as the *creational-foundational future* in and of the past (cf. n. 103 above). Here in opposition to historicism's "imperialism on the part of the present present towards earlier presents," and in contrast to its inability to recognise that "[t]he past is more than merely a prologue to the present," Moltmann suggests that the "present past," which he identifies with "tradition, both conscious and unconscious" (in distinction from the "past present" understood as the "things as they really were" that historians try and reconstruct), be "compared with its own future and its own possibility, which were already implicit or in germ in that past present. ... Then the possibilities of the past present which were cut short or suppressed or merely neglected, can be picked up once more and integrated into the future of the present present." Moltmann continues: "*The future in the past* brings a prospective into the historical retrospective." My emphasis. The discussion is indeed insightful, but the terminology lacks the precise (creational/eschatological) distinction I am looking for.

[114] See n. 103 above.

Having examined the "future past," the "past future," the "present past," and the "past present,"[115] we should finally turn our attention to the 'past past'. Although Moltmann does not actually discuss this form of the past by name,[116] it is clearly presupposed in his modalisation of time. Once we remind ourselves that he identifies the future with possibility and the past with reality,[117] it becomes evident that the 'past past' is that dimension of what has taken place that can never be made present in the present order of time. We may remember the dead. They may be present to us. They may be with us. "The past is past," writes Moltmann in this context, "and at the same time is still in its own way *present*, so that it becomes intransient."[118] But we may put this the other way round: the past may be present and thus alive but at the same time 'the past is *past*'. The dead we remember (to—literally—say nothing of those we forget) are also absent. The 'past past' refers to what has been and gone.

In stressing "the *interlaced* times of history"[119] and the "perichoretic" nature of the modes of time,[120] much of Moltmann's discussion of the past deliberately directs our attention away from its pastness.[121] Thus he observes that "it is . . . not only present things but the things of the past too which are in a state of flux." Past history, in other words, is far from over. Nevertheless, the past cannot be exhaustively understood within the ongoing stream of life. In cautioning historians that "There is a *rebus sic stantibus* only at the end of history," he adds ": only then will things stay as they are."[122]

When read in context, these words have an ominous ring to them. In discussing the dangers of the "modernity" project in the previous paragraph of the same work, he comments, "we shall have to introduce our misgivings into the expectations of 'the modern world' . . . [i]f we do not want our future to

---

[115] The "future past," "past future," and the "present past" have all been explored in the text above. But the "past present" has only been discussed in n. 113. Cf. n. 106 above on the "past-future" "present-future" and "future-future."

[116] He does however refer to it with the abbreviation "P P" in his summary of the "Matrix of the times (tenses)" in the diagram in GC, 129.

[117] See TKG, 217 as cited above and also CoG, 286.

[118] CoG, 124. My emphasis.

[119] The title to GC, chap. 5, sec. 5. My emphasis.

[120] GC, 125.

[121] And thus away from the 'past past'. See, e.g., n. 106 above.

[122] CoG, 290. His italics. The phrase *rebus sic stantibus*, often used in international law, means 'while things remain as they now stand' or 'so long as conditions remain the same'. In this context, it conveys *stasis*. Moltmann continues, "As long as history continues and its future is open, historical judgments can be made under the proviso *rebus sic fluentibus*, as Ernst Bloch said—that things are still in a state of flux." His italics. We should read this in the light of Jürgen Moltmann, *Ethics of Hope*, trans. Margaret Kohl (Minneapolis, MN: Fortress Press, 2012), hereafter EoH, 3, where he observes that in the experience of hope, "[w]e perceive things not only *sic stantibus* but also *sic fluentibus* [his italics], as *fluid* not *static* [my emphases], and try to realize their potentialities for change in a positive direction." The distinction between stasis and the (fluid) abiding of the Age to Come is explored below.

become in a few decades *nothing but the past*."[123] The spectre of environmental catastrophe looms large here. We can bring about the past past of all our futures.

Given the vector of transience, we must reckon with the pastness of the past even now. We cannot keep the dead alive. Thus in *Theology of Hope*, Moltmann writes, "It is ... ultimately *death* that makes the past irretrievably past. What was, does not return. What is dead, is dead."[124] This coheres with a passage in *The Coming of God* in which Moltmann contrasts "the direction of hope" with earthly time viewed "[i]n its destructive possibilities" and equated with "the time of transience." He writes,

> *Chronos* then becomes the power of futility, the futility of everything that happens or is done in time. Chronos devours all the children whom he bears. Everything that is, will one day no longer be.... In the end everything that could be, and that was, is past, and at the end of the past stands universal death, the total non-being of all temporal things and happenings. The exit from time is not an entrance into eternity; it is the entry into Being-that-is-no-longer. Here time turns from being a form of futurity into a form of transience, and from a form of life into a form of death. The temporality of earthly creation does not reflect the presence of God—it reflects his absence.... It is not just what happens in time that changes; time itself changes too: primordial futurity becomes inexorable past.[125]

Here, "in the end," what "was, is past." The past past. Nothingness. The end of life. The absence of God. In this context, Moltmann links the experience of time as a form of death with the apocalyptic idea of "the time of 'this passing aeon' ... the world-time of evanescence, not of any abiding."[126] This sounds as if it is in conflict with the ominous claim (cited above) that at the end of time, history would no longer be in flux as things would finally stay as they are. But the contradiction is more apparent than real as the *stasis* of the 'past past' is not a form of abiding for Moltmann. The "permanence" that the "past" lacks[127] is the dynamic ability to *per-manere*: the capacity to remain through time and thus remain in existence. In Moltmann's model, the past only has this in relation to the other modes of time. In itself—and we might define the "past past" as 'the past in itself'—it has no staying power.[128] Abiding is not 'staying put'—the stasis or death of the past past—but staying alive. Hope thus looks to the renewal of time itself and to " 'the abiding aeon' of an 'everlasting life' ...

---

[123] CoG, 290. My emphasis. The two halves of this sentence have been reversed. Here the 'past past' can be seen as the 'apocalyptic past' in Moltmann's thinking.

[124] TH, 267. His emphasis. Cf. TH, 265, where in opposition to Nietzsche, he speaks of "the 'death' that has made past history irretrievably past."

[125] CoG, 284. His emphasis.

[126] CoG, 284.

[127] See CoG, 139 as cited at the beginning of this section.

[128] For Moltmann, anything that is "in itself" excludes itself from the Age to Come. See 3.4 (and 3.4nn153 and 178), 3.6 (including 3.6n270), 4.2, and 5.3n129 below.

in which chronos will enjoy no more efficacy."[129] The apocalyptic contrast between the present age and the Age to Come, so striking in his early works, is still alive and well. The contrast between the power of the future and the power of the past over the three modes of time is the difference between life and death.

3.4 Death

It should come as no surprise, therefore, that death is also a predominantly negative reality in Moltmann's theology. This is especially evident in his theology of the cross. Although the willing sacrifice of Christ is, for Moltmann, a "unique, historical and eschatological event,"[130] his death, which is "experienced and proclaimed" as nothing less than "god-forsakenness, as judgment, as curse, as exclusion from the promised life, [and] as reprobation and damnation,"[131] reveals the true nature of the death to which we are all subject.

While Christ alone "suffered on the cross the hell of forsakenness and absolute death,"[132] we too, even in the midst of life, experience death as an annihilative power.[133] We are thus subject to something more than mere mortality. There is a "deadly cohesion to which all life belongs."[134] Citing Ernst Bloch, Moltmann writes,

> 'The jaws of death grind everything to dust, and the maw of putrefaction eats away every teleology.' Death is not just a reality on which utopias of the better life break, like waves on a shore. It is true 'anti-utopia'.[135]

---

[129] CoG, 284, citing I John 1:2 and Rev 10:6. This is clearly a fluid (not static) abiding. See n. 122 above. Moltmann's eschatological vision for a world of "change without transience, time without the past, and life without death (GC, 213, cited at the end of 3.1 above) might therefore be characterised as a world of 'flux without evanescence'.

[130] CrG, 43.

[131] TH, 210–11. Christ's resurrection in this context is described as "a conquest of all that is dead in death" and as "a negation of the negation of God."

[132] WJC, 191. Cf. CrG, 149: "Just as there was a unique fellowship with God in his life ... so in his death there was a unique abandonment by God." For Moltmann, when we suffer our hells, God is with us in Christ. When Christ descended into Hell, however, he was radically alone. The important discussion of CrG, 149–53 must thus be read together with CoG, 250–55 (especially 251–53) discussed in 1.4.1 above. Cf. 4.3.1 below.

[133] See, for example, TH, 201, 214, 224; CrG, 24, 170; CPS, 98, 110, 273; GC, 66; WJC, 108, 191, 257, 264, 286; and SL, 112.

[134] CPS, 195.

[135] CoG, 63. Moltmann uses Bloch's observation about the opposition between death and teleology, or the future as *futurum*, to highlight the acute problem of Bloch's own lack of a genuine eschatology in CoG, 25 and 344n58. Cf. Jürgen Moltmann, "Ernst Bloch and Hope without Faith," in *The Experiment Hope*, by Jürgen Moltmann, trans. M. Douglas Meeks (Philadelphia: Fortress Press, 1975), 30–43. Cf. 2.4nn76 and 80 above.

Not only is death the enemy of a better future; right here and now, it "is the power of separation, both in time as the stream of transience, materially as the disintegration of the person's living Gestalt or configuration, and socially as isolation and loneliness."[136]

Death is thus a hope-defying, divisive, destructive, evil power. Lest we conclude from this that death is *inherently* evil for Moltmann, we must be careful to read these words alongside his claim, made later in the same work, that it is "[s]eparation from God, the wellspring of life, [that] leads us through isolation to experience temporality as transience, and to see death as its universal end."[137] Although in the words of *Theology of Hope*, death, together with evil, is "generally felt . . . to cause the transience of all life,"[138] according to Moltmann's mature thought, this is true of human experience only because of our alienation from God.[139] Time and death, Moltmann implies, could (have) be(en) experienced very differently. Consequently, it is possible to glimpse what we might (almost) call a 'good' death in Moltmann's theology. I will pay particular attention to this at the end of the present section.

For the most part, however, his attitude to death can 'at (its) best' be described as ambivalent. The fact that death is not simply viewed as an evil, annihilative power[140] is borne out by an investigation of its relationship to sin and evil within Moltmann's web of theological beliefs. Although Moltmann's position is (as usual) both nuanced and complex, it is clear that he does not attribute the origin of mortality to human sin but to the way God has made the world.[141] As such it is "a characteristic of frail, temporal creation which will be overcome through the new creation of all things for eternal life."[142] Read in context,[143] this means that even apart from sin, creation always needed to undergo an eschatological transformation. "It is true," Moltmann concedes, "that God judged the first creation to be 'very good', but the new creation for glory is more."[144]

While Moltmann may infer from this statement that "If we turn back from the end to the beginning, then the death of all the living is a sign of the first, temporal and imperfect creation,"[145] these same words, read in context from a different angle, would also seem to suggest that, by virtue of its place in God's

---

[136] CoG, 71.
[137] CoG, 292.
[138] TH, 165.
[139] He may well still agree with *Theology of Hope* about what is "generally felt" to be the case.
[140] Despite CrG, 51 where he states, "[Christ's] death is the death of the one who redeems men from death, which is evil." See also GC, 169.
[141] This complex matter will be discussed in some detail in 4.2 below.
[142] CoG, 78.
[143] See CoG, 77–95.
[144] CoG, 91.
[145] CoG, 91.

world, death in the beginning was (in some sense) "good."[146] If this inference seems unavoidable (given what Moltmann has actually written), it is not one for which Moltmann shows much enthusiasm. Instead, he prefers to assert that "The death of all the living is neither due to sin *nor is it natural.*"[147] Elsewhere he even claims that "although the death of all the living is a destiny to which all life is subject, it is not an intrinsic part of life. All life is intended to live and not to die."[148]

So how does this fit with the idea that death is a part of God's " 'very good' " creation and is not simply a manifestation of evil? If we are not to misinterpret him at this point, it is important to realise that what is "intrinsic" or "natural" is being viewed here in accordance with eschatological rather than creational criteria. As he puts it,

> Even if death is part of temporal creation, it does not have to be called 'natural' in the sense of being self-evident or a matter of course; and if it is called natural, this 'nature' by no means has to be taken as final.[149]

To introduce a little more clarity into Moltmann's terminology, we might say that he views death as creationally "natural" but eschatologically (and thus ultimately) 'unnatural'. Its presence in the beginning does not mean that it was ever intended to be there at the end, to be "final" as he puts it. Its thoroughly temporal and thus temporary nature is revealed by the new creation that we see coming into existence through the cross and resurrection. In hope, we may know—as presumably humans would always have known if they had not become alienated from the source of life[150]—that "Death will die."[151]

Moltmann's simultaneous refusal to trace death back to sin or allow it any place in the new creation accounts for his proposal, in *The Way of Jesus Christ*, that for those who hope in the resurrection, "death needs neither to be accepted nor repressed." In the light of hope, "life and death" in the here and now can

---

[146] Here, my argument is that Moltmann's words should be read in the context of his comment about God's "very good" (though not-yet glorified) creation cited above from the same page. Despite his eschatological qualifier, his claim does begin with the words, "It is true that . . . ."

[147] CoG, 92. My emphasis.

[148] WJC, 253.

[149] CoG, 91. Cf. SL, 88 as cited in 3.2 above: "Transitory time and the mortality of all the living was hitherto held to be the 'natural' condition of all created things, because there was no alternative; but the condition now emerges as sick. In the daybreak colours of their new creation, all things are revealed in their 'sickness unto death'. Once there is reason to hope for the world's redemption, that world ceases to be seen as natural and finite. It can now be perceived as an unredeemed world."

[150] See SL, 87 in which Moltmann says that in losing God, we lose touch with the very source of our own lives and thus find death.

[151] CoG, 84. That we would always have known this if we had not lost our connection with God/Life is an inference that I believe to be well grounded in Moltmann's thought. I was also able to speak with Professor Moltmann about this matter in London on September 9th, 2000.

thus "be brought into harmony."[152] In his following major work, *The Spirit of Life*, Moltmann makes it clear that this is not a balancing act. Priority is clearly given to the love of life, from which flows the acceptance of "life's natural frailty and mortality." While repression remains unhealthy, and while what we might call 'death *in itself*'[153] remains unacceptable, nevertheless in what he calls "*the harmonies and accords* of life," death is accorded its place. Thus Moltmann writes,

> To resist the death-drive does not mean suppressing death. On the contrary, it means accepting it, and making it a part of life. In the love that is 'strong as death' the death-drive is extinguished.[154]

Towards the end of this section, we will explore how this "accept[ance]" may actually entail a recognition of the way death is connected in a positive sense to the life of the Age to Come. For the most part, however, what Moltmann seems to have in mind is best understood as a hopeful form of endurance. In this sense, resisting the death-drive requires that we recognise death's relative, temporary place in history. To "accept[]" death in hope is to relativise it, thus refusing to allow it to function as an evil power and thus bring the movement of and towards life to a halt. Hope enables us to resist the "[a]pathy and cynicism [which as] ... forms of spiritual petrification and creeping death ... go ahead of the end of the world, anticipate it, and in their own way bring it about."[155] "[P]etrified ... closed systems ... condemn ... themselves to death."[156] But in "making [death] a part of life," we resist such closure, remaining radically open to God and neighbour and thus open to the future of this groaning creation. We thus do not flee from its mortality but embrace it in love. In his active suffering with his creatures, God calls us to participate in a love of life that endures and thus overcomes the death of a self-enclosed world.[157]

In this form of spirituality, death is not to be overcome by the eradication of certain so-called 'lower' dimensions of existence. Moltmann rejects such a "structural dualism" in favour of a "genetic monism"[158] in which the defeat of

---

[152] WJC, 266.
[153] Cf. n. 128 above.
[154] SL, 173–74. His emphasis.
[155] CoG, 230. On the link between petrification and death, see also GC, 266 and SL, 56.
[156] GC, 211.
[157] Here I am connecting SL, 173–74 with GC, 210–11.
[158] For this terminology (which is ultimately dependent of D.H.Th. Vollenhoven, on whom see 2.1n11 and 0.6 above), see Brian J. Walsh, "Theology of Hope and the Doctrine of Creation: An Appraisal of Jürgen Moltmann," 55–56.

Moltmann's rejection of dualism is clearly expressed in SL, 87 where in commenting on "the sphere of the flesh as the sphere of sinning, and the sphere too of death because of sin," he writes, "It is not a question of an ontologically lower rung on the ladder of being, compared with the higher rung of the soul or spirit. What is meant [by Paul—and here Moltmann is clearly sympathetic] is sin and death as a field of force

death is understood as the result of an eschatological process. Moltmann's position would have us assert two things simultaneously: the fact that death is creationally natural does not make it ultimately—that is eschatologically—acceptable. At the same time, the fact that death is eschatologically unnatural does not mean that it is in itself penultimately or creationally unacceptable. In this light, we may make sense of how in clearly looking forward to death's eschatological annihilation,[159] he nevertheless believes that "the *new creation* of all things" is anticipated by a hope that "*embraces* all things, including also death."[160]

Central to this process is the cross through which God "absorbed [Christ's] death into eternal life."[161] Consequently, "the unfestive, dark side of life—defeat, guilt, fear and death—all belong to [the crucified Christ's] feast of freedom."[162] This does not mean that death has a future—far from it! The "gathering together of all things in Christ" must be viewed in the light of his resurrection which signifies "the conquest of the power of death." What we might call the 'eschatological embrace' of all things marks the triumphant omnipresence of life and thus the end of evil. Death, precisely in being taken up into eternal life, is overcome. Moltmann states categorically that, "the powers of death which are hostile to God and life are not going to be reconciled and will not be integrated even into Christ's rule of peace. His rule means they will be eliminated from creation."[163]

But is Moltmann's theology of mortality as straightforward as it looks here? Given Moltmann's claim (noted above) that death was originally part of God's "very good" albeit "imperfect" creation, we may ask whether his thought allows us to view these "powers of death that are hostile to God" as, in words that appear on the previous page of the same work, "powers of creation that are good [and] which will be put right in Christ's rule of peace"?[164] While the

---

into which the whole person has entered, body and soul, together with his whole social world."

[159] See TH, 163, 172; CrG, 170; GC, 189; WJC, 108, 252, 284; CoG, 65, 68, 90–91, 110, and 196.

[160] TH, 33 as cited in 0.1 above. My emphases.

[161] CPS, 63.

[162] CPS, 114. Moltmann's monism is also evident in the next two sentences: "Then everything really does 'work for good' (Rom. 8. 28, RSV marg.). Nothing excludes us from the feast, not even 'my sins' (Augustine)." The monism I am referring to lies neither in Paul nor in Augustine, but in Moltmann's appropriation of them.

[163] WJC, 286. Cf. CrG, 169–70 and CoG, 26.

[164] (Cf. 9.3n61 below.) This language appears in WJC, 285, where Moltmann contrasts the eschatological outlook of Ephesians and Colossians (which he does not attribute to Paul) with that of the apostle. When, on WJC, 286, he states, "It is not possible to harmonize the two viewpoints and there is no point trying to do so," he could be read as contrasting the view that the powers were created good (in Ephesians and Colossians) and the view that the powers are hostile to God (which he attributes to Paul). As I think Moltmann's theology is quite capable of bringing these two perspectives together, I think that the harmonising Moltmann rejects is between what he sees as the partially realised eschatology of the former and the more future-oriented eschatology of the latter.

language of "put[ting] right" is consistent with the view that even creational (in distinction from 'fallen') death has no future in the new creation,[165] as it was always intended to be temporary, the description of the powers as "good" encourages us to ask whether there are intimations of a less ambivalent, more positive assessment of death yet to be found in Moltmann's work. I believe that this is indeed the case.

There are, I suggest, two other ways in which Moltmann indicates that viewing death as "god-forsakenness, ... judgment, ... curse, ... exclusion from the promised life, ... reprobation and damnation"[166] does not represent the full picture. Firstly, given faith in the resurrection,[167] we can be thankful that "the life that has already been lived has been saved from annihilation and is kept safe in eternity from the perils of time."[168] Secondly, in trusting that it is not the end, we may see death itself as "a transition to a different kind of being, and a metamorphosis into a different Gestalt."[169]

If the first point speaks only of a death in which death's annihilating power is broken, the second suggests that death actually plays a necessary role in our being raised to the life of the new creation. This calls for further comment as it suggests that the "accept[ance]" of death that Moltmann advocates goes beyond hopeful endurance. "The human being," he says, "is made for transformation" not *despite* but "*through* and beyond [durch ... hindurch] death."[170]

This idea is explored in relation to two biblical texts, 1 Cor 15:36 and John 12:24: " 'What you sow does not come to life unless it dies' .... 'Unless a grain of wheat falls into the earth and dies, it remains alone; but if it dies, it bears much fruit.' " In what are probably Moltmann's most positive reflections on mortality, he comments,

---

As for the "no point" comment, it may be the case that Moltmann finds harmonising the two different views of the powers unnecessary because death will in no sense exist in the new creation.

[165] On whether there might be another kind of 'creational death' for Moltmann—a form of *kenosis* that is other than a passing into non-being—that might have a future in the eschaton, see 3.6 below.

[166] TH, 210–11 as cited above.

[167] This resurrection hope is vital for what follows. As Moltmann states in WJC, 264, "Christian faith starts from the assumption that it is impossible to reconcile life and death without the future of God."

[168] GC, 139. Here Moltmann is taking up and modifying Whitehead's notion of the "objective immortality of the dead."

[169] GC, 275. The original is in italics. This also affects how we may experience the death of others. In CoG, 125, Moltmann writes, "If death is the side of the transformation to eternal life that is turned towards us, then our grief is transformed from mere lamentation over the loss into a new community with the dead."

[170] GC, 275 [*GS*, 278]. My emphasis. The original is in italics throughout. Cf. WJC, 250, "Dying and coming to life are two elements in the transformation process of the new creation of all things."

[I]n actual fact the grain of wheat only undergoes a transformation: out of the seed comes the plant, and out of the plant the fruit. One form decays so that another may come into being. In the metaphor of the grain of wheat, death and life are not contrasted as radically as they are in the metaphor of death and raising. Here we are shown a transition, not a total breach and a new beginning. That is why Christ is called 'the first fruits' of the dead (1 Cor. 15.20).[171]

Elsewhere, Moltmann connects John 12:24 (cited above) to the kenotic process of *dying* to self that he finds in the next verse of this gospel.[172] In what begins as a paraphrase and soon becomes an extended midrash, Moltmann writes,

[A]nyone who lives his life and commits it and surrenders it, will gain that life; he already gains it by coming alive. . . . Surrendering one's life means going out of oneself, exposing oneself, committing oneself and loving. In this affirmation life becomes alive in the truly human sense. . . . [L]ife that is truly and fully affirmed can die. Dying belongs to the lived life and is part of it.

If we talk about the Spirit of life in this affirmation of happiness and pain, life and death, we are saying that in this life there is already a life that is in fact immortal, eternal. . . . In the New Testament [this] Spirit is described as the power of the resurrection. This life-giving Spirit is experienced in this life in unconditioned and unconditional love. . . . There is [therefore] an eternal life before death.

A life lived in the divine power of the resurrection does not die. It is transformed *through death* into eternal life after death. For the eternal life of God revealed in the death and the resurrection of Christ is manifest here in the surrender of love, and there in the resurrection of the dead.[173]

As usual, a close examination of Moltmann's writings reveals a nuanced, complex, and almost paradoxical position. Death is viewed both as an "*exclusion* from the promised life"[174] and as the *transition* to the life of the Age to Come. *On the one hand*, loving and dying are opposites, for if we accept death as a natural part of life, "[t]hen we must renounce love, which desires the life of the beloved and not his death."[175] *On the other hand*, "loving and dying are not antitheses. They are correspondences,"[176] for "[i]n the image of the grain of wheat" in which we see "the power of surrender . . . . [,] [t]he love

---

[171] WJC, 248–49. In WJC, 249–50, he goes on to explore the idea of transition in terms of death throes/birth pangs and transformation/transfiguration.

[172] This is one of the most frequently cited sayings of Jesus in Moltmann's corpus. For references to his use of this saying, which, in addition to John 12:25, also occurs in Matt 10:39; 16:25; Mark 8:35; Luke 9:24; and 17:33 (which is the specific text he links to John 12:24 in GC, 269, although he clearly has John 12:25 in mind), see the n. 74 above.

[173] GC, 269–70. My emphasis.

[174] TH, 211 as cited above in relation to Christ's death. My emphasis.

[175] WJC, 264. Cf. CoG, 93 in which Moltmann states that love brings us into solidarity with the whole groaning creation, while our hope for it and for ourselves "means that we cannot come to terms with dying at all, or with any death whatsoever, but remain inconsolable until redemption comes."

[176] WJC, 260.

which is the power of the 'sowing' here and the resurrection which is the power of the 'harvest' there are two sides of the same coin."[177]

The contrast between (a) love's *opposition* to death and (b) love's *harmony* with death is rooted in a contrast between (a) the (highly negative) death of the (loved) *other* (in which we too experience death *ourselves*) and (b) the (positively viewed) death of the *self* (for the sake of the *other*). This in turn may be related to a contrast between (a) death as *creational* (in which death is viewed 'in itself'[178]) and (b) death as *eschatological* (in which death is viewed in relation to what lies beyond itself). (To these we may perhaps also relate another contrast between death as *fallen* and death as *redemptive*[179]). Moltmann's positive assessment of mortality, in other words, relates death to other-directed, eschatologically-open love.

Given his at least tacit acceptance of death as part of God's "very good" creation (as noted above), we should bring this discussion to a close by asking whether death plays any positive 'creational' role in Moltmann's thought. Death may well function as a "transition" from the life of this age to the life of the Age to Come, from "the first creation" to "the new creation of glory,"[180] but does it play a positive role in history or from the beginning?

In response, I can only offer a hypothesis as Moltmann does not directly address this issue. At the end of the discussion of temporal unity and diversity in 2.5 above, I suggested that Moltmann values temporal differentiation (only) because it allows an ever-greater richness of our personhood and of the natural world to come into existence. This richness is then gathered up into the kingdom of glory even as the differentiating that has generated this wealth and variety comes to an end. Death, I suggest, for Moltmann, can also be seen as having a positive role within this process as it gives rise to numerous, successive generations each of which add to the richness of life that will be gathered into the presence of God in the eschaton. "Without dying and being born," Moltmann observes, "there can be no sequence of generations."[181] Elsewhere he asserts, "The created life of created beings in the succession of the generations and times will *as such* be redeemed from guilt and grief and transformed into eternal joy."[182] Diversity, including the temporal diversity of succession, will thus have an eternal future in glory. Death and differentiation—that is, differentiation as we know it, the differentiation

---

[177] WJC, 262–63.
[178] On the qualification "in itself," which (in Moltmann's outlook) is related to evil if it absolutised, cf. nn. 128 and 153 above. See also 3.6 (including 3.6n270), 4.2, and 5.3n129 below.
[179] This latter correlation is strengthened by the fact that redemption, for Moltmann, has an eschatological character. See 5.3 (including 5.3n128) below.
[180] Here I am connecting the "transition" of GC, 275, as cited above, and the language of CoG, 91.
[181] CoG, 90. Although Moltmann is commenting on Gen 1, read in context it is clear that this argument for mortality 'from the beginning' is one he also endorses.
[182] WJC, 262. His emphasis.

connected with death—are "good" and "accept[able]"[183] (if only as a means to an end that itself marks the end of the means.

3.5 Redeemed Time

In the kingdom of glory, as we have already noted, Moltmann believes the structure of time will thus be transformed giving rise to "change without transience, time without the past, and life without death."[184] This 'X without Y' structure appears elsewhere when Moltmann approaches this subject. Relatively early in his corpus, for example, he speaks of "the life of the risen, transfigured and transformed Christ" as "life without death, time without transience, and participation in the glory of God without hindrance."[185] More recently he has written of the Age to Come as "a 'world without end',"[186] "a 'beginning without end',"[187] "duration without transience,"[188] "continuance without transience"[189] and even as "a 'time without time' ['Zeit ohne Zeit']."[190]

Does it make any sense whatsoever to speak of a time of change that is not 'at the same time' a time of transience? Is Moltmann simply playing with words when he speaks of a "timeless form of time [zeitlose Form der Zeit]"?[191]

---

[183] For this language in relation to death, see CoG, 91 and SL, 173–74 as discussed above. Here I am commenting on historical differentiation. For the possibility of differentiation and *kenosis* in the Age to Come, for Moltmann, see 3.6 below. Eschatological *kenosis* opens up the possibility that just as there is "an eternal life before death" for Moltmann (see WJC, 260 as cited as discussed in 3.2 above), so there is a kind of death within eternal life. In the context of the eschaton itself, I am confident (given his terminology elsewhere) that Moltmann would speak here of 'love' not death. But if "loving and dying are not antitheses" in the present age (WJC, 260 as cited and discussed in 3.2 above), is there not a sense—albeit a carefully qualified one—in which they will not be antitheses in the Age to Come? See my exploration of the gift and future of transience (and thus death) in 6.6 below.

[184] GC, 213 as cited at the end of 3.1 above.

[185] CPS, 113. Cf. CoG, 32 where "life without death" language occurs in Moltmann's discussion of Bloch's position.

[186] GC, 184.

[187] WJC, 158.

[188] GC, 270. Here Moltmann writes, "Wherever the divine Spirit of the resurrection becomes alive in us and we perceive him, duration without transience already begins, and eternity is experienced in the present moment." It is clear that in speaking of something that already begins, Moltmann sees "duration without transience" as characteristic of the Age to Come and not only of our present anticipation of it in the Spirit.

[189] CoG, 84.

[190] WJC, 158 [*DWJC*, 179]. Cf. Jürgen Moltmann, "Der 'eschatologische Augenblick': Gedanken zu Zeit und Ewigkeit in eschatologischer Hinsicht," in *Vernunft des Glaubens: wissenschaftliche Theologie und kirchliche Lehre. Festschrift zum 60. Geburtstag von Wolfhart Pannenberg,* ed. John Rohls and Gunther Wenz (Gottingen: Vandenhoeck and Ruprecht, 1988), 588, where he cites a hymn by Johann Rist that begins "O Ewigkeit, Zeit ohne Zeit . . . ."

[191] CoG, 282 [*DKG*, 311].

Moltmann readily admits that whatever it is that he is talking about is barely imaginable because "all reflections about time here and now are determined by the *memento mori*, the remembrance of death."[192] Nevertheless, the attempt to think about such "timeless . . . time," Moltmann would insist, is not, or need not be, mere speculation. The resurrection of Christ from the dead reveals an eschaton in which there will be "a change in the transcendental conditions of time."[193] What is now impossible—change without transience, "time" without "time"—is thus thinkable and profoundly meaningful in the light of the resurrection.

The fact that the present transcendental conditions do not allow for such a time, on Moltmann's own account, might lead us to expect him to characterise the 'Age' to Come by means of a *via negativa*. To some extent, this is what we find. Moltmann thus speaks of "what is to come" as "contain[ing] the end of growth and decay."[194] "[D]eath," we are told, "and therefore transitory time as well, will be no more."[195] Temporal negation would seem to extend to the positive phenomenon of hope, for "Once death is no more, there will be no more time either, neither the time of transience nor the time of futurity."[196] Even some of Moltmann's more positive statements about the time to come are fairly traditional double negatives.[197]

There are, however, two main ways in which Moltmann does attempt to describe redeemed time in more positive terms. One of these utilises the temporal image of the present "moment" which we shall explore below (3.5.2), and, via the related idea of "presence," shall connect to his understanding of the Eucharist and the sabbath (3.5.3). The other approach, which we shall explore first, and which will also return in our discussion of the sabbath, describes redeemed time by using the apparently spatial image of the circle.

---

[192] CoG, 26. His italics. Cf. GC, 213 where, immediately after he speaks of "thinking of change without transience," he adds, "this is difficult in the history of life and death, becoming and passing away, because all our concepts are moulded by these experiences of transitoriness." Cf. also CoG, 295 where, in the context of describing ancient ideas of aeonic, cyclical time, Moltmann notes "The preferred images for eternal life are therefore dance and music, as ways of describing what is as yet *hardly imaginable in this impaired life*." My emphasis. Moltmann is extremely sympathetic to the tradition he is describing here (as I will discuss below). Included in the "impaired" nature of life for Moltmann are mortality and transience, I suggest, even though these are created by God in the beginning.

[193] CoG, 26.

[194] CPS, 113.

[195] WJC, 158.

[196] CoG, 294. But see GC, 213 as discussed in 3.5.1 below.

[197] He thus speaks in GC, 184 of "a life that is 'eternal', and a joy in existence 'which *does not pass away*' " and in CoG, 84 of an existence rooted in the "divine life" that is "eternal, *intransient* and *immortal*." My emphases.

3.5.1 Cyclical Time

Perhaps the first point that should be made is that the new age is, he would insist, truly temporal, even though—or better, precisely because—its time is not "transitory" but "aeonic." As Moltmann explains,

> Aeonic time can be thought of as a time corresponding to the eternity of God: a time without beginning and end, without before and after. The figure, or configuration, of time that corresponds to the one, unending eternity is *cyclical* time, which has no end. It represents the reversible, symmetrical, unending and hence timeless form of time.[198]

If, despite calling this aeonic *time*, the image of the circle suggests an ahistorical, ultimately static reality, Moltmann's comments elsewhere make it clear that the spatial image is intended to convey its peculiar *dynamic*. To say that aeonic time is "timeless," he would insist, means that it is 'end-less' not 'motion-less'. Its circular nature means that it literally will not stop. Thus he writes,

> One essential difference between time and aeon is to be found in the *movement* of the two. It is part of the nature of created time to be experienced by way of irreversible changes. In the 'before' and the 'after', future and past become distinguishable. Experiences of this kind make it possible to talk about linear courses of time, and enable us to project lines of time teleologically. But the *movement* from which aeonic time, or relative eternity, is perceived is circular. . . . [C]reated time, which is aligned towards the future, will be transformed into the circular movements of the aeonic time of the new creation. In the presence of God's absolute eternity, created time becomes the relative eternity of the new creation that corresponds to him. Cyclical and full of repetition are the hymns and dances in which created beings express their wondering love of God and their joy in their own existence.[199]

It is the "timeless"—that is to say, deathless—nature of this time that makes it so dynamic and so alive. This is "the 'fulfilled time', the aeonic time, the time filled with eternity, the eternal time[,]. . . the time of eternal life . . . of eternal livingness."[200] The circle, it turns out, is less a spatial metaphor than an image of motion.

The transformation from the irreversible time of history to the reversible time of the aeon and the process of constant, "cyclical" regeneration that characterises the life of the Age to Come[201] is brought about by a change in the relationship between God and the world. "The temporality of earthly creation,"

---

[198] CoG, 282. His emphasis.
[199] WJC, 330–31. My emphases. We should understand Moltmann's circle image in the light of his championing of the fluid over the static, which gives rise to (and which reflects) his dynamic understanding of permanence and abiding, as explored in 3.3 (including 3.3nn122 and 129) above.
[200] CoG, 295.
[201] See WJC, 331.

writes Moltmann in one of his most transience-denigrating statements, "does not reflect the presence of God—it reflects his absence."[202] By contrast, in the Age to Come "The Creator no longer remains over against his creation" but dwells within it as it dwells in him.[203] As we noted in 2.2 above, time must not be treated as a formal category because it is "determined by whatever is fundamentally experienced in [it]."[204] In the Age to Come, the God who actually enters time makes all the difference in the world. The resultant "*perichoresis* of divine and cosmic attributes" leads to a mutual indwelling of eternity and time that gives the life of the Age to Come the following temporal rhythm:

> In the aeonic cycles of time, creaturely life unremittingly regenerates itself from the omnipresent source of life, from God. An analogy is provided by the regenerating cycles of nature, and the rhythms of the body, which already sustain life here. The purposeful time of history is fulfilled in the cyclical movements of life's eternal joy in the unceasing praise of the omnipresent God. The preferred images for eternal life are therefore dance and music, as ways of describing what is as yet hardly imaginable in this impaired life.[205]

This dance of eternal life must, in Moltmann's understanding, be carefully distinguished from the " 'cosmic rounds' of birth and death" associated with Shiva Nataraja, the Hindu Lord of the Dancers and "creator and destroyer of worlds." In this respect, "[t]he cyclical element in the Indian concept is broken through."[206] The time of the new creation is not a 'vicious' circle.

Similarly, the imagery of repetition should not be understood as an example—certainly not a straightforward example—of the 'myth of the eternal return' over against which Moltmann has sought to posit a truly biblical eschatology throughout his career.[207] Given the fact that the circular nature of

---

[202] CoG, 284.
[203] CoG, 295 as cited in 3.1 above. Cf. the reference to CoG, 307 as cited in n. 18 above.
[204] GC, 118 as cited in 2.2 above.
[205] CoG, 295. His italics. This appeal to the images of dance and music has the potential of combining dynamic repetition and open-ended improvisation. Moltmann might convey this more clearly by speaking of a spiral rather than a circle, however.
[206] GC, 307 and 304.
[207] See, for example, his critical summaries and evaluations of this pattern of thought in both its ancient and contemporary forms in TH, 95–102; CrG, 43–44; CPS, 265–72; GC, 104–12, 163; CoG, 19 (in the context of 13–22), 41–44, 223 (in the context of 218–26), 263 (in the context of 261–67); and EiT, 41–42. Luco J. Van den Brom's negative (mis)interpretation of Moltmann's view of cyclical time in his "Eschatology and Time: Reversal of Time Direction?," in *The Future as God's Gift: Explorations in Christian Eschatology*, ed. David Fergusson and Marcel Sarot (Edinburgh: T. and T. Clark, 2000), 163n11, does not take this into account. Unfortunately, Van den Brom is followed too closely here by John Polkinghorne, *The God of Hope and the End of The World* (New Haven, CT: Yale University Press, 2002), 118–20. Contrast the more recent, clear statement in SW, 81: "The eschatological moment will end the linear time which we have here called the irreversible time of this world, and take into itself an element of

the time of the Age to Come is most fully and enthusiastically explored in *The Way of Jesus Christ* and *The Coming of God* (as illustrated in the above quotations), it is most significant that the latter work also contains a number of critical references to the 'myth of eternal return'.[208] As there is not the slightest hint that Moltmann believes that its proponents have simply ascribed to the fundamental structure of present history what is in actual fact the time of the eschaton, we can be confident that he would not see himself as eschatologising this mythological thought-pattern in his own theology.

The differences between these two 'cyclical' positions are instructive. In *God in Creation,* Moltmann describes "the structure of [the] archaic awareness of time" as follows:

> The archaic human being lives in the eternal presence of particular divine archetypes, which pre-form his ideas and experiences, and his perception of reality. He lives in particular divine rituals, which mould all his actions. He experiences time as the continual repetition of what is identical with itself. It is only this repetition that gives life permanence. He exists in an *eternal present* which we have to call *timeless.* Through the continually recurring suspension of time in the feast, he is able to annul time's irreversibility, which he very well perceives. For him, time acquires a *cyclical structure.* His life runs its course *within time's circular flow.* So *no event is unique,* and no past is final. Everything comes round again. Every moment, everything begins again from the beginning. So *nothing new ever happens in this world,* and nothing in the world can ever really pass away either. It is true that things appear and pass away in time. But because time is conceived of in terms of the eternal return, everything really abides. The eternal return keeps the universe alive, quickening it anew out of its eternal origins. To experience time like this is *not to experience the individuality of events* and the irreversibility of their happening. The very opposite is true. The experience of time is the experience of repetition. But the experience of repetition is nothing other than the experience of eternity.[209]

In the above passage, I have italicised certain phrases in order to pinpoint some key differences. I have also drawn attention to certain similarities at the level of language in order to clarify how these are, on close examination, superficial.

---

cyclical time. What will come about is *not an eternal return of the same thing* [my emphasis] but a *unique* return [his emphasis] of everything." In his later essay "Eschatology and Time: Which Relationship?," in *Christian Hope in Context 1*. Studies in Reformed Theology 4, ed. A. van Egmond and D. van Keulen (Zoetermeer: Uitgeverij Meinema, 2001), 144–62, Van den Brom, noting that "the whole idea of repetition neglects the infinite divine creativity and suggests that nothing new can happen," claims that Moltmann's eschatological dance cannot avoid being characterised as *"taedium vitae"* (156–157n14). The material that I discuss for the rest of this section suggests otherwise. See also n. 205 above.

[208] See the references to CoG in the previous note.

[209] GC, 108. My emphases. In GC, 107, Moltmann states that while this "archaic" person is generally thought to belong to prehistoric cultures, this is also a description of "post-historic man." On the relation to "post-modern" times, see EiT, 41–42.

For the most part, these observations will be illustrated by citing what Moltmann says elsewhere in the same work.

The fact that later in *God in Creation*, Moltmann rejects "timeless eternity" in favour of "eternal time"[210] illustrates that, as I have already pointed out earlier in this section, "timeless" for him means *without death*. Archaic timelessness, by contrast, really amounts to an existence *without life* as he would understand it.

This has much to do with what he calls the mythical "abolition of history."[211] While in the eternal return of the same, ideas are "pre-form[ed]" and "no event is unique" or is experienced as having any "individuality," Moltmann states that "in the kingdom of glory, there will be time and history, future and possibility, and these to an unimpeded degree."[212] Possibility is the key word here. The time of futurity may be no more,[213] but only because long-suffering hope is no longer necessary. This hardly means that there will be nothing new under the sun—quite the opposite. "[T]he kingdom of God is the *eschatological springtime* of the whole creation."[214]

The character of the *new* creation in this respect is anticipated in/by the "open systems" of our world. Because with increasing complexity, the systems of nature display an ever "greater openness to time and a growing wealth of possibility" and because human beings "display the greatest degree of indeterminacy in their behaviour, and the most extensive degree of openness to time and the future[,] . . . it is impossible to conceive of the kingdom of glory, which completes the process of creation through the indwelling of God, as a system that has finally been brought to completion and is therefore itself now closed."[215] The eschatological dance of life, we might say, unlike the attempted enclosure of time that occurs in archaic myth, takes place within a moving, ever-widening, open circle.

3.5.2 Presence and the Present (Moment)

The second main image that Moltmann uses for the time of the Age to Come is the more explicitly temporal image of the "present," this being another instance of a linguistic similarity—again more superficial than substantial—between his theology and the structure of archaic time-consciousness. Just as "Death is the power of separation [that] in time [is manifest] as the stream of transience. . . . [,] [t]he raising to eternal life, conversely, is the power to unite—in time, as the

---

[210] GC, 213.
[211] GC, 107.
[212] GC, 213. See also SW, 81 as cited in n. 207 above.
[213] See CoG, 294 as cited in 3.5 above.
[214] SL, 194. My emphasis. Cf. WJC, 327: "The time that was created in the alteration between the evening and the morning will come to an end, and will be consummated in the morning glory of eternity and in the eternal *spring* of the new creation." My emphasis. Cf. CoG, 29: "with time, life only becomes old, never young and never new" in the light of WJC, 331: "Time makes things old. Only eternity remains young."
[215] GC, 214.

gathering of all temporal moments into the *eternal present*."²¹⁶ "With eternal life," says Moltmann, "continuance without transience begins, and *enduring present* [bleibende Gegenwart] in the *eternal presence* [ewigen Gegenwart] of God."²¹⁷ The intimate relationship between "present" and "presence" is clearly significant. That God will be "present" in the time of the New Creation for Moltmann²¹⁸ signifies a radical rejection of the supra-temporal divinity of mythological consciousness.

We can gain further insight into the "present" and "cyclical" nature of the redeemed time of the Age to Come by looking at the ways in which Moltmann believes it is anticipated in time as we know it. In this context, it is helpful to note that the present experience of the 'present/presence' to come is often described with reference to what Moltmann calls "the moment." In a few places, this language is also used of eschatological time itself. Speaking of the future that "bears the impress, no longer of Christ's struggle but of his kingdom," Moltmann says that "This time is determined no longer by transience, but by a tarrying and abiding in the felicitous moment."²¹⁹ Moltmann also notes with considerable sympathy that,

> When the word *adventus* was translated into German by *Zukunft*, the German word acquired a messianic, advent note. What is meant is something that is coming and which will never go or pass away; something which remains. It is the moment to which we can say, with Goethe's Faust, 'Tarry awhile, thou art so fair'. This is the new, enduring world of the Jewish and Christian hope."²²⁰

Later in the same work, Moltmann states that "The open system of the world . . . thrusts beyond itself because, by virtue of its imbalance, it cannot

---

[216] CoG, 71 as cited at the end of 2.5. My emphasis. Cf. WJC, 49 where Jesus' raising "is simultaneous to all moments of his life." Cf. also WJC, 24: "[T]he future redemption will liberate the whole past, and will make it present, freeing it from its suppression, and its repression. Just as the catastrophe ends history, condemning it to be something past, so, conversely, redemption gives history a new beginning, and redeems the past, making it the eternal present. Where the catastrophe represses memories, redemption will bring them back again."

[217] CoG, 84 [*DKG*, 102]. My emphases.

[218] See, for example, CoG, 23 where he writes: "In the eschatological coming, God and time are linked in such a way that God's being in the world has to be thought eschatologically, and the future of time has to be understood theologically."

[219] CoG, 200.

[220] GC, 133. His italics. Cf. CoG, 291. We might contrast Moltmann's sympathy for Goethe here with e.g., TH, 27. On Bloch's appropriation of Goethe here, see Bauckham, "Time And Eternity," 190–91. Bauckham discussion of the "moment" in Moltmann (187–93) is also very helpful. Cf. the discussion of the "eschatological moment" in Medard Kehl, " 'Bis du kommst in Herrlichkeit . . .': Neurre theologische Deutungen der 'Parousie Jesu'," in *Hoffnung über den Tod hinaus: Antworten auf Fragen der Eschatologie*, ed. Joseph Pfammater and Eduard Christen (Zürich: Benziger Verlag, 1990), 95–137.

apparently 'tarry' in any given condition."²²¹ This is only true, however, when we look at life in its 'historical' direction alone, for Moltmann can also say, again in the same work, "Wherever the divine Spirit of the resurrection becomes alive in us and we perceive him, duration without transience begins, and eternity is experienced in the present moment."²²²

In this experience, Moltmann continues, "Human life is then so *intensely* alive that death disappears."²²³ Similar language appears in *The Spirit of Life* when he describes "the perception of *the eternal moment*" as,

> an awareness of the present which is so intense that it interrupts the flow of time and does away with transience. We call the moment in which life is as intensively experienced as this, *ecstasy*. It is a momentary awareness of eternity, not a permanent one. Although every moment in life can be ecstatically lived in just this way, it is only the crowning ecstasies which interrupt everyday life; and we feel that these belong to a different category that our everyday standards cannot grasp or judge them."²²⁴

In this light, we can make sense of the otherwise surprising fact that Moltmann, the theologian of hope, accords the present a privileged status among the modes of time.²²⁵ The *hic et nunc* of the present establishes the "unity of time" by "constitut[ing], distinguish[ing] and link[ing] past and future." The present alone is a "category of Being" "between [the] Being-that-is-not-yet" of the future and the "Being-that-is-no-longer" of the past. In not requiring the mediation of remembrance or expectation, "Only present can be experienced as immediate existence." "*Present*," Moltmann declares emphatically, "is the real secret of the times."²²⁶

---

²²¹ GC, 205.
²²² GC, 270.
²²³ GC, 270. My emphasis. Moltmann makes it clear in this passage that this does not cancel out "the pains of death." Cf. the reference to "lament and grief" in SL, 303 discussed below.
²²⁴ SL, 303. His emphases. (I comment on the last line of this passage in 8.4n69 below.) This passage also demonstrates the connection between the moment and the circular as two ways to speak of the presence of the eschaton. The perception of the eternal moment is said to correspond in life to the "trinitarian doxology in the divine liturgy" in which (according to the following paragraph) "the *circular* movements begin." His emphasis.
  On "the moment" in SL, see Bauckham, *The Theology of Jürgen Moltmann*, chap. 11 ("Mysticism"), especially 238–42. In his helpful essay "Time and Eternity," 187–93, Bauckham has extended this earlier discussion to cover material in CoG.
²²⁵ We should remember, though, that the advent future is not a mode of phenomenal time and so is not made secondary "among the modes of time" by the present. See CPS, 130 as cited and discussed in 2.4 above.
²²⁶ CoG, 285. His emphasis. The future "Being-that-is-not-yet" in this context refers to more than the *futurum* as Moltmann speaks here of the way we "grasp the future, which *is* not yet, only by virtue of the *expectation* [rather than planning] that makes-present." Second emphasis mine. Although the eschatological horizon is not necessarily in view

The present not only links the future and the past; it constitutes an ontological connection or 'overlap' between God and creation. As Moltmann puts it, "Present is the category of eternity in time: the moment is 'an atom of eternity'."[227] Its role in Moltmann's theocosmogony is a central one.

As the final phrase in this important two-part statement is taken from Kierkegaard who, together with Barth and Bultmann, is repeatedly criticised in *Theology of Hope* for his correlation of time and eternity,[228] it might be argued that here we have evidence of a *volte-face*. But, as is often the case with Moltmann's writings, what at first appears to be a contradiction is in fact evidence of development. Thus, not only do we find the same misgivings about Kierkegaard in *The Coming of God* (the work in which his "atom of eternity" phrase is utilised),[229] but we also find a far more nuanced critique. The problem with Kierkegaard, it emerges, is that he "equate[s] the historical and the eschatological moment" or what Moltmann calls "the moment" and "the fulness of time." This doesn't negate his claim that "time and eternity 'touch' in the moment";[230] it simply means that this present is an anticipation of eschatological presence. Of "the fulness of the times," Moltmann observes, "the 'fulfilled moment'—the moment full-filled entirely and wholly with life—gives only a foretaste."[231]

This anticipation, however, grounds analogy: "there is a historical similarity, in spite of all eschatological dissimilarity; and to this the imaginative power of hope can cling."[232] The present moment may thus reveal much about the aeonic time to come. Beyond the relative simultaneity of past and future, beyond the present as *kairos* or unique opportunity, there is the "moment . . . [that is] a mystical 'depth-dimension' of time: *nunc aeternum*." Here Kierkegaard's language if not his framework becomes appropriate:

> As 'an atom of eternity', the fulfilled moment drops out of the sequence of time, interrupts time's flow, abolishes the distinction of the times in past and future, is an ecstasy that translates out of this temporal life into the life that is eternal.[233]

---

here, this expectation would seem to include our orientation to what I have termed the historical *adventus* in 2.4 above.

[227] CoG, 285. He also writes: "The Now is 'the event of eternity in Being' as the mystical experience of the Deity present in the moment has always said: *nunc aeternum*, eternity in the Now." Cf. his comments on "the mystical moment" in SL, 205. The connection of the latter with an "immediate" experience of God in SL, 205–208 also has connections with the passage under discussion. The "atom of eternity" phrase comes from Kierkegaard. See *Kierkegaard's The Concept of Dread*, 79.

[228] On Kierkegaard, see TH, 29 (together with Moltmann's comments in TH, 31) and 164. On Barth, see TH, 1. On Bultmann, see TH, 66.

[229] See CoG, 292–93. This section also registers Moltmann's disagreement with Barth and Bultmann. Cf. CoG, 14, 18, 19, 21, 22, and 29.

[230] CoG, 292.

[231] CoG, 295.

[232] CoG, 294.

[233] CoG, 291. His italics.

Moltmann goes on to connect the experience with the "*intensive* life," the "*wholeness* of the lived life," "*undivided* presence in the present," and "*absolute presentness*."[234] Here, I suggest, we have the (experienced) presence of that "transcendental future" that he elsewhere refers to as "the *unity* of time" and (again in the words of Kierkegaard) as " 'the *whole* of which the past is merely a part'."[235] With characteristic verbal dexterity, he writes, "Out of this experience of *present eternity* arises the longing for an *eternal present*."[236] This still historical moment is thus not the 'eschatological (more-than-a-) moment' we are all waiting for. It is only momentary. But it enables us to recognise that in the present age, "Eternity is one of life's dimensions: it is life in depth."[237]

3.5.3 Eucharist, Sabbath, and the Moment

There are two other temporal contexts in which the theme of eschatological 'presence' comes to the fore in a special way. The first, which I have also explored above,[238] is the Eucharist that, following his Göttingen teacher Otto Weber, Moltmann is happy to describe as "the first gleaming of the Eschaton."[239] This is linked to a discussion of the "simultaneity" of remembered suffering and anticipated glory and the "simultaneous presence of the Christ who has come and the Christ who will come."[240] The connection with the "present" is thus clear. But we should also remember that "the moment," as noted in 3.5.2 above, gives us access to a present that is 'beyond' simultaneity.[241] In its depth, we find eternity. In the Eucharist, by contrast, we find an "exemplary and definitive" experience of life "between the times."[242] This is characterised as much by the opposition of eternity and time as it is by God's presence.[243]

---

[234] CoG, 291. "Intensive" and "absolute presentness" are italicised in the original. The other emphases are mine.

[235] CoG, 287 as cited in 2.4 above. My emphases.

[236] CoG, 291. My emphases.

[237] WJC, 331. Cf. SL, 40: "Eternity is found in the depths of the experienced moment, not in the extension of time."

[238] See 2.2 above.

[239] EiT, 90. Here, this occurs as a sympathetic quotation. In EiT, 347n33, it appears in explicit connection with Moltmann's own position articulated in EiT, 37.

[240] EiT, 37.

[241] See CoG, 291 as discussed in 3.5.2 above. Thus in SL, 302, Moltmann speaks of "the *eucharistic Trinity* chang[ing] into the *trinitarian doxology*." My emphasis. It is the latter that, in the words of SL, 303, "directs the senses to *the eternal present* in which we no longer remember the past and no longer wait for any other future." His emphasis. On the context, see n. 243 below.

[242] EiT, 37.

[243] Thus in SL, 302, Moltmann says that "in the human eucharistic counter-movement we experience the infinite difference between men and women as *historical* beings, and the *eternal* God." My emphases. This claim (like the comments cited in n. 241 above) is made with reference to a discussion of two directions within the Trinity. In SL, 300, he writes, "whereas in the monarchical 'sending' Trinity the foundation is *an experience of*

The other temporal context in which the eschaton is emphasised is the sabbath, which "is itself the presence of eternity in time, and a foretaste of the world to come."[244] It is also said to be "the one unambivalent anticipation of the messianic era in the midst of the eras of history."[245] The sabbath thus appears to escape the tension of cross and resurrection that is characteristic of the Eucharist.

In our discussion of "the moment," we noted that it was related to the intensive life rather than to life in the extension of time. We also noted that it was related to (though not equated with) an immediate rather than mediated experience of God. Similar distinctions surface in Moltmann's view of the sabbath. Thus he writes,

> The works of creation show God exoterically and indirectly, as it were, as the Creator. But the sabbath, in its peace and silence, manifests the eternal God at once esoterically and directly as the God who rests in his glory. Creation can be seen as God's revelation of his works; but it is only the sabbath that is the revelation of God's self.[246]

A few pages later, he says that "In the resting, and hence direct, unmediated presence of God" found in the sabbath "all created beings find their dwelling."[247]

The exact relationship between the "moment" and the sabbath is nowhere explicitly addressed by Moltmann.[248] As presences of eternity, their similarities outweigh their differences. But the complementary ways in which they are described are intriguing. The sabbath experience, for example, is nowhere said to be "intensive." By the same token, the "moment" is nowhere described in the

---

identity which tells us that God is present *in* his revelation, in the eucharistic Trinity of glorification we discover *an experience of differentiation*." His emphases. Here "differentiation" does not refer to the differentiating direction of time, but to the way God may be known to differ 'in himself' from his historical manifestations. The eucharistic direction is thus one of deeper knowledge. If this is more a discussion of the Trinity than the Eucharist *per se*, Moltmann's choice of the term "eucharistic" is still significant.

[244] GC, 276.

[245] WJC, 27. In "The Bible, the Exegete and the Theologian," 228, Moltmann compares and contrasts the sabbath as a "messianic interruption of transitory working time" with Sunday as an "eschatological interruption."

[246] GC, 280.

[247] GC, 282.

[248] A parallel to the question of the sabbth-moment relationship would be: How does Moltmann understand the relationship between the "anticipations" of "absolute time" to be found in Rosenzweig's sabbath presence and Bloch's "darkness of the lived God" as discussed in CoG, 38, the latter being related (as CoG, 32 makes clear) to Bloch's notion of "the darkness of the lived moment" and the "inexhaustible depths of the immediately experienced moment"?

language of movement. Thus only the sabbath is said to be "the *dynamic* presence of eternity in time."²⁴⁹

If the "moment" speaks of the eschatological "present," the sabbath reveals something of the "circular" time of the Age to Come. In a discussion of what he calls the "*rhythmicization of the times* of history" in which the eschaton is foreshadowed, Moltmann observes,

> Rhythm and ecstasy condition each other mutually, analogously to the eschatological finale and the times which vibrate in it. Life-time is ordered, not in a linear sense but rhythmically. Only working-time and mechanical-time are linearly directed towards goal and purpose. But every living organism experiences the time in which it lives in the rhythm of its inward and outward movements, in tension and relaxation.

This Moltmann connects to Israel's experience of the weekly sabbath and Jubilee. Similarly, with reference to the Christian Sunday, he notes that "the expectation of the final future of the world induces, not a linearization of lived time but its rhythmicization. In the expectation, time vibrates and dances."²⁵⁰

The connection between these vibrations and the "messianic dance of eternal life"²⁵¹ and thus the circular nature of aeonic time to come is unmistakable.²⁵² Revisiting this theme later in the same work, Moltmann writes,

> Rhythm is at once repetition and progress. In the rhythm of the sabbath interruptions of 'time's flow', earthly creation—human beings, animals and the earth—vibrate in the cosmic liturgy of eternity. The ever-flowing stream of time regenerates itself from the presence of eternity in the sabbath rhythm of the days, the years, and the seventh year, thus preparing for the messianic sabbath of the End-time creation and, through that, for the eschatological sabbath of the eternal creation.²⁵³

---

²⁴⁹ CoG, 266. My emphasis. This can be related to its anticipatory character. It is a "foretaste" of the endless sabbath" in CPS, 269 and in GC, 6, "the prefiguration of the world to come" and a "sacred anticipation of the world's redemption." In GC, 288, despite its "tranquillizing character," it is said to "conceal[] an unheard-of promise for the future." In CoG, 264, it is "the promise of future consummation built into the initial creation." In CoG, 267, therefore, "the sabbath in time thrusts forward to God's End-time Shekinah."

²⁵⁰ CoG, 138. His emphasis. Although I am suggesting that the "moment" speaks of the eschatological "present" while the sabbath speaks of the "circular" nature of eschatological time, the "moment" and "circular" time are also related. See n. 224 above.

²⁵¹ GC, 307.

²⁵² There is no contradiction between this and the fact that the sabbath may, in the words of GC, 286, "break through the cyclical rebirth of natural time by prefiguring the messianic time." In Moltmann's understanding, the circular time to come is dynamic and open in a way that the present cycles of nature are not.

²⁵³ CoG, 283–84. Cf. the theme of regeneration associated with the "aeonic cycles of time" in CoG, 295 as cited in 3.5.1 above.

Given that Moltmann begins by speaking of "[r]hythm and ecstasy," it is interesting that he only develops the idea of rhythm in relation to the sabbath. Because of the close connection between "ecstasy" and the "moment" (which we have noted above[254]), it is an intriguing possibility that the way rhythm and ecstasy mutually condition each other provides us with Moltmann's implicit way of understanding the interrelationship between these two manifestations of the Age to Come. In "the moment" and the sabbath (in both their historical and eternal forms), we have the "tension" and "relaxation" that make up—and that will make up—the dance of eternal life. The moment and the sabbath, I suggest, represent respectively: the outward and the inward, activity and rest, and 'eternity in time' and 'time in (or open to) eternity'.[255] They are two sides of the one mo(ve)ment.

3.6 The Final Coincidence of Opposites

As we draw this discussion of Moltmann's philosophy of time to a close, it will be helpful to focus the concluding summary by asking how Moltmann can assert that in the kingdom of glory "there will be time and history, future and possibility . . . to an unimpeded degree" if in that " 'eternal history' " there will be "change *without transience*, time *without the past*, and life *without death*"?[256] Does this mean that the two directions of time—the historical and the eschatological—will become 'one' in the sense that the historical direction is jettisoned in favour of eternity, or 'one' in the sense that the two directions are in some way harmonised? In other words, is Moltmann's theology dualistic or monistic? And how (on either account) can there be history without transience?

In figure 4 below, I have attempted to summarise the preceding discussion by setting out the contours and dynamics of Moltmann's 'contradictory/ harmony monism'.[257] In what we might call his 'horizontalised Neoplatonism',[258] in which the themes of emanation and return predominate, existence is not separated into two realms but moves simultaneously in two

---

[254] See SL, 303 and CoG, 291 as cited and discussed in 3.5.2 above.

[255] If this suggested reading is correct, then the fact that Moltmann refers to the sabbath as the "presence of eternity in time" rather than as an example of 'time in eternity' in GC, 276 and CoG, 266 (as cited above) shows that he is not presenting his position in a detailed, systematic way. I would only claim that the systematic distinctions I am highlighting here are at least *implicit* in his theology. Furthermore, for Moltmann eternity in time and time in eternity are distinguishable but very intimately related. Eschatologically speaking, when God is in creation, creation is in God and vice versa.

[256] GC, 213 as cited at the end of 3.1 above. My emphases.

[257] See 0.6 and 2.1n11 above.

[258] See the end of 2.2 above (including 2.2n39). For Moltmann's undeniable affinity with Neoplatonism, see GC, 306, where he refers sympathetically to Plotinus as he develops the image of the "world as dance" and, most importantly, SL, 212 and 283, where he explicitly engages in a pneumatological appropriation of the Neoplatonic motifs of emanation and return. See also the discussion in 4.2, 6.3, and 6.4 below.

directions. In the *direction of history* (which in the diagram is the vision from left to right), the transcendental future makes possible, and thus fans out into, the phenomenal modes of time leading to differentiation and transience, while in the *eschatological direction* (a vision from right to left), we may discern *theosis* and integration as created diversity is gathered together in the coming of God.

For those without hope, there is, experientially, only futility: the movement into non-being. All things must pass. Even those who exert their power by trying to make history cannot escape history, which ends in death. For those with faith, however, life is experienced as consisting of two directions that are opposed to one another. But, for Moltmann, this opposition—in which hope contradicts the way things are—is not the solution. Somehow, it must be resolved.

In 'dualistic' cosmologies and cosmogonies, to recall the discussion of 0.6 above, the solution to our present futility is to be found in the separation—in that sense, the 'dis-integration'—of what can be saved from those dimensions of existence that are considered inherently (and thus irredeemably) evil. For 'monistic' positions, however, resolution is to be found in the re-integration of all that has become alienated from the true Origin. Although Moltmann's *description* of the futility that hope must oppose may sound dualistic, his *prescription* is ultimately monistic.

Key to the reintegration of all things is the "turning point" of history that takes place in the Christ event.[259] The crucified and risen Jesus is the *coincidentia oppositorum*. In and through the cross, the oppositions of history become the harmonies of the eschaton. (In the following diagram, this central transformation—the transition between the present age and the Age to Come— is represented by the 'loop' which, for the sake of visual clarity, has been separated from the 'point' at which, in the historical direction, the present bifurcates into *futurum* and past and at which, in the eschatological direction, the reintegration of the Age to Come is experienced under the conditions of the here and now).

In the "turning point" of the "cross of Christ," everything re-turns to the God who "took evil, sin and rejection on himself, and in the sacrifice of his infinite love transformed it into goodness, grace and election."[260] The dream of *Angelus Novus* that the "storm" of "progress" might be "turn[ed] around"[261] will become a reality through Christ who is on the way to glory.[262] The arrow of time, the annihilating power of transience, will be reversed. The "tempest of

---

[259] For the language of the "turning point" see CoG, 245 as cited in 1.4.2 above and discussed in 4.1 (including 4.1n11), 4.2 (including 4.2n110), 4.3.1, 4.3.3, and 8.2. This turning point includes Christ's descent into Hell as discussed in 1.3 and 1.4.1 above. This will be explored further in 4.1 and 4.3.1 below.
[260] SL, 212 as cited and discussed in 4.3.1 below.
[261] Moltmann, "Progress and Abyss," 309 as cited in 2.1 above.
[262] For the emphasis on Christ in his eschatological "becoming," see WJC, xiii. The title of this work should, in part, be read in this light.

the divine Spirit" that blows the Angel of the Annunciation "into history"[263] becomes the "resurrection storm" that "blow[s] . . . from the future into the past and brings back the irretrievable . . . and heals the unhealable."[264] This is "the divine tempest of the new creation, which sweeps out of God's future over history's fields of the dead, waking and gathering every last created being."[265] The scope of redemption is as long as history and as wide as creation. As God enters time in the eschaton, history is taken up into the circular rhythms and ecstasies of the divine life of the Trinity. What were opposites—time and eternity—become harmonised as God becomes all in all.

But if history is taken up into God's eschatological presence, will the Age to Come be historical? If what has become differentiated over time has a future in what Moltmann calls "the new creation of this creation,"[266] will 'differentiation itself', which is a facet of "this creation," come to an end? Is the redemption of history a redemption from history? The answer, to what might be understood here as variant forms of a single question, seems to be both Yes and No.

On the one hand, Moltmann's eschatological vision seems to be as negative as any dualistic position could hope to be. "Redemption," writes Moltmann, "is the final new creation of all things out of their sin, transitoriness and mortality, for everlasting life, enduring continuance and eternal glory."[267] In the "daybreak colours of their new creation," he says, "[t]ransitory time and the mortality of all the living . . . emerge[] as sick."[268] As this "sickness unto death"[269] on Moltmann's own account is inherent to the historical direction of time from the beginning, this history must end.

Nevertheless, and for this reason, history has a future. Although in Moltmann's contradictory/harmony monism, the unifying direction is of supreme, redemptive significance, the two directions remain eternally. What is overcome is not 'differentiation *itself*' but what we might call 'differentiation *in itself*' as nothing may exist in (and for) itself if it is to be open to God rather than enclosed—self-enclosed—in evil.[270] In the new creation, it would seem, there can be a kind of history as any differentiation that takes place will be simultaneously-immediately (re)integrated. We can even imagine a kind of *kenosis* if we also realise that this will only take place within the ongoing regeneration of all existence from a future that will never pass. Because this

---

[263] CoG, xvii as cited in 2.1 above.
[264] Moltmann, "Progress and Abyss," 310.
[265] WJC, 303.
[266] WJC, 262. This occurs in a passage in which Moltmann argues that creation will not be replaced or denatured in the eschaton.
[267] SL, 9.
[268] SL, 88 as cited more fully in 3.2 above. I have reversed the order of these phrases.
[269] Moltmann cites this famous phrase of Kierkegaard in the same passage in SL, 88. This is cited more fully in 3.2 above.
[270] Thus the historical direction is not *inherently* evil, though it may be seen as evil *in itself*. On the relation between evil and self-enclosure, see the discussion in 4.2 below and see TKG, 209–210 and WJC, 283 cited there. On the significance of something 'in itself' for Moltmann, see also nn. 128, 153, and 178 above and 5.3n129 below.

The Redemption of Time in the Presence of God 143

movement into time will no longer occur outside ongoing redemption,[271] because we will differ *in* God rather than *from* God, there will be change without transience and life without death.

In the presence of God, in "the triumph of glory" (to cite the title and subject matter of the next chapter), non-being is impossible. The redemption of time in the presence of God means the transience of transience, the death of death, the annihilation of Hell. As God will be all in all, all will be saved.

---

[271] In Moltmann's framework and terminology, "redemption" means re-integration as eschatological fulfilment. As an eschatological concept, it means more than (though not less than) the healing of the world from the effects of our sin. See the discussion in 5.3 (especially 5.3n128) below. This gives added significance to the title of this chapter and to the subtitle of this study.

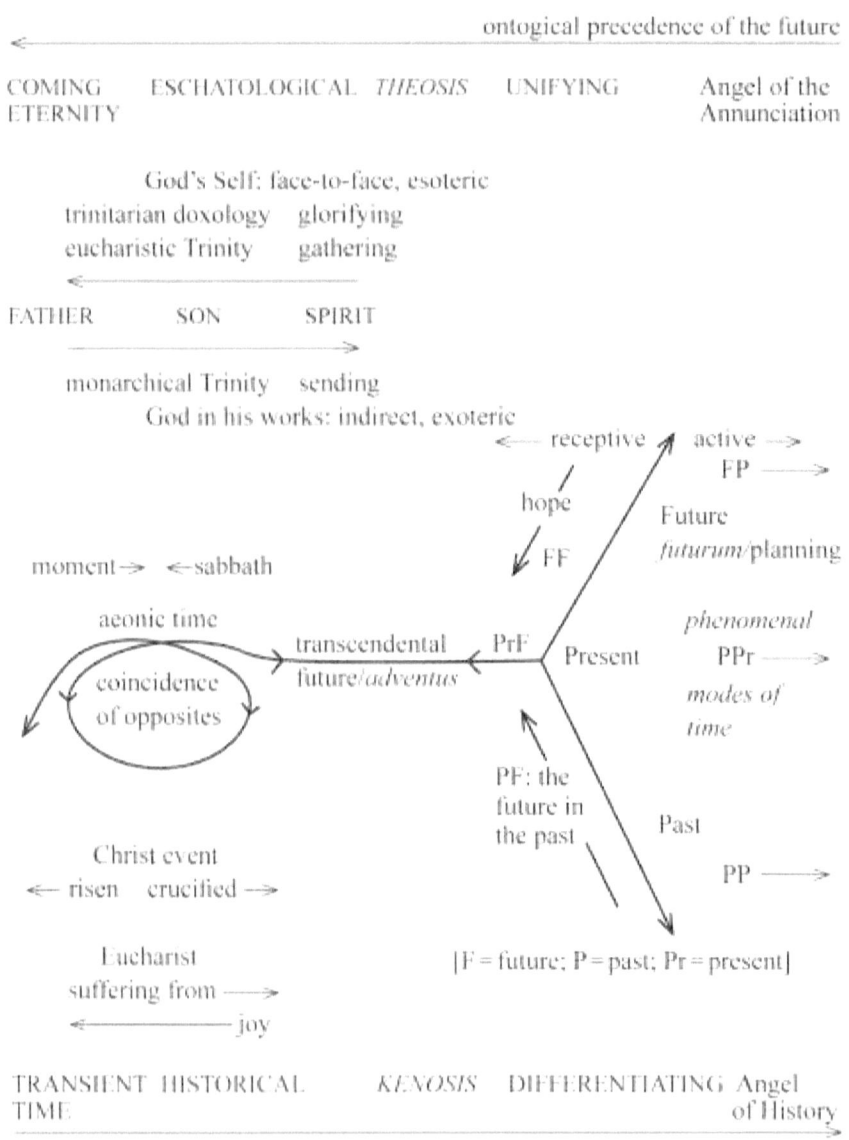

figure 4

NOTE: the 'coincidence of opposites' illustrated by the 'loop' should be 'located' at the point of bifurcation/convergence of past and future, as explained above, but has been separated for visual clarity.

CHAPTER 4

The Triumph of Glory

The present chapter aims to place 'Hell' (as Moltmann understands it) within the theocosmogony we have been exploring in the previous two chapters. In asking questions such as: What kind of reality is it?, Where is it located?, and How can its annihilation be secured?, we shall be taking up the central concerns of chapter 1 and relating them to the ontological analysis of chapters 2 and 3.

Moltmann's strikingly original ontology, or ontotheology,[1] of Hell, read in the light of his characteristically eschatological vision of/for history, will also help us understand the 'Annihilation of Hell' as a motif in his theology. Both forms of annihilation—Hell's *annihilating* power in history and the way Hell will be *annihilated* by, and thus excluded from, the coming reality of God's future—will be examined in this chapter.

In referring to this eschatological overcoming of Hell as "the triumph of glory" in the title to the present discussion, I am alluding to G.C. Berkouwer's famous study, *The Triumph of Grace in the Theology of Karl Barth*.[2] Whatever parallels may exist with Barth's theology in general and with his universalism in particular,[3] Moltmann attempts to transcend the category of grace and resolve the duality of the nature and grace relationship by introducing the eschatological category of *glory*. This theological proposal, to be explored in 4.2 below, clearly flows out of the philosophical foundations of Moltmann's thought analysed in the last two chapters.

---

[1] 'Ontotheology', understood as a pattern of thought in which both God and creation are placed within the category of being/Being, seems a more appropriate term for Moltmann's 'theocosmogony' than 'ontology' as 'ontotheology' and 'theocosmology' both suggest a blurring of any putative distinction (certainly separation) between the Divine nature and created being. As I note in 4.1 below, primordial Hell for Moltmann is really an 'a/theological' reality as it involves the negation of the Divine. Perhaps we should speak of an 'onto-a/theology'.

[2] See G.C. Berkouwer, *The Triumph of Grace in the Theology of Karl Barth* (Grand: Rapids, MI: Eerdmans, 1956). Moltmann refers to the "triumph of grace" in "Sun of Righteousness: The Gospel about Judgment and the New Creation of All Things," 148 and in the foreword to the present study.

[3] We shall briefly explore some of these parallels in 6.2–6.5 below. See also 4.3.1 (especially 4.3.1nn147–48) below.

While the previous chapters engaged the philosophical structure of Moltmann's thought, this one returns to the more theological concerns of chapter 1. After setting out some typical 'Arminian' and 'Calvinist' concerns that many theologians might have about Moltmann's universalism (4.3), we shall anticipate how Moltmann might respond by examining what I am calling his 'universalism of the cross' (4.3.1). This section, appropriately, stands at the centre of this the central chapter of the present study. In 4.3.2 and 4.3.3, respectively, we shall be concerned with the important question of the nature of freedom, both divine and human.

This chapter will continue the 'expository' approach of previous chapters, but will move towards some more explicitly critical comments at the end. Some of my concerns, in retrospect at least, may be visible in my exposition. One of these is implicit in the title of the present chapter. If "glory" replaces 'grace' for Moltmann, my reference to its "triumph" hints at what I see as an eschatological 'eclipse' of 'nature', here understood as creation and history. I will comment on this problematic feature of Moltmann's thought more directly in 4.4 and extensively in the following chapters.

To that end, the material examined here is indispensable. In particular, the need to replace the primordial Godforsaken space that Moltmann proposes (to be examined in 4.1) would seem to make this eschatological 'eclipse' of creation unavoidable. Furthermore, the relationship between this 'space' and the (ambivalent) nature of freedom, to be examined in 4.3.3 below, is also telling. It is thus to Moltmann's original and 'originary' conception of Hell, and to the central space that it occupies in the structure of his theology, that we must now turn.

4.1 (Re-)Placing Hell

According to Paul Fiddes, "dogmatic" (rather than "hopeful") universalists—and here he includes Jürgen Moltmann—have three options if they want to give "full weight" to the "biblical witness." Faced with those texts that speak of "a destiny of separation from God," they will understand this strand of the New Testament "as referring to [1] an experience of 'hell' in this life before death, or to [2] the experience of forsakenness which Christ suffered vicariously on the cross, or to [3] a fate which *would* have befallen humanity but for the work of Christ."[4]

---

[4] Paul S. Fiddes, *The Promised End: Eschatology in Theology and Literature* (Oxford: Blackwell, 2000), 194. His emphasis. My enumeration. He refers to Moltmann in 194n24. The biblical texts he cites are Matt 7:13–14; 25:31–46; Mark 9:45–8; Luke 16:23; and John 3:36.

The widespread distinction between "dogmatic" and "hopeful" universalism is, I suggest, inadequate and misleading, not least because it is usually made by those who wish to advocate the latter over against the former ("dogmatic" being a pejorative designation; it is not a term that any universalist uses to define her own position). Furthermore, those who are what we might call 'convinced' universalists hold to a number of different positions. Rather than speaking about universal*ism*, it would be

The Triumph of Glory 147

Leaving aside for the time being Moltmann's exegetical and hermeneutical strategy for dealing with the texts in question,[5] we may note that all three descriptions that Fiddes offers correspond to Moltmann's understanding of the nature of Hell as explored in chapter 1.[6] But as we now turn to examine this question in more detail, we should also note that there is a fourth dimension to his position also briefly alluded to in our earlier discussion.[7] Hell, for Moltmann, is a reality that exists—perhaps we should say 'un-exists'—before the creation of the world. His "existential"[8] understanding, therefore, is grounded in a primordial reality that 'precedes' the hells of human history and human experience.

In the previous chapters, I explored the way in which the two directions of passing time and coming eternity, *kenosis* and *theosis*, activity and receptivity, the outgoing and incoming, not only hold for creation but also for God.[9] Moltmann's doctrine of creation, therefore, does not begin with the "outward" action of God. Prior to the *actio Dei* is the *passio Dei*,[10] which he describes as the "transition from eternity to time."[11] The 'Let there be!' of Genesis 1, on this

---

more accurate to speak of universal*isms* (cf. Moltmann's distinction between his own position, the "open" universalism of Barth, the "real" universalism of Schleiermacher, and the "hypothetical" universalism of Amyraut in CoG, 247–49). Although Fiddes does exploit this twofold distinction for rhetorical purposes, his observations about the different considerations on which "dogmatic" universalism—convinced universalisms—may be based are helpful and will be cited in 4.3 below.
[5] On this subject, see 1.4.5 above and 7.1 below.
[6] See 1.3 and 1.4.1 above.
[7] In my brief discussion of Moltmannian themes in *The Mystery of Salvation* in 1.3, I mentioned that in bringing the present world into existence, God is described as having "*made way* for it as an entity other than himself" (*The Mystery of Salvation*, 188, my emphasis). In 1.3n68, I note the connection with Moltmann's *zimzum* doctrine of creation.
[8] This is his terminology. See 1.4.1 above and the discussion below.
[9] See, for example, the discussion of the Trinity in the two directions in 2.5 above.
[10] See TKG, 59 and (for the terminology of *passio Dei* and *actio Dei*) TKG, 109–10.
[11] In GC, 114, Moltmann writes, "The unique transition from eternity to time is to be found in [God's] self-determination ... [in which] God withdrew his eternity into himself in order to take time for his creation and to leave his creation its particular time." In terms of figure 4 at the end of the previous chapter and, especially, figure 5 at the end of the present chapter, I see the *passio Dei* as the change, transition, reversal, 'flip', or "turning point" (cf. CoG, 245, cited and discussed in 1.4.2 and 3.6 above and 4.2, including 4.2n110, 4.3.1, 4.3.3, and 8.2 below) from the unifying direction to the differentiating direction of time. It is mirrored by the cross-centred transition from the historical to the eschatological in the 'passion', explored in 4.3.1 below. For God, being open to otherness involves an opening of Godself to the historical. This occurs out of (even as it goes beyond) God's inner-trinitarian yet other-directed love for the Son (on which see TKG, 112 as cited in 4.3.3 below and also TKG, 58–59). Conversely, for humans to be open to otherness, we must surrender historical control in hope for what is to come. In hope lies the transition from the historical to the eschatological. On the latter, see 4.2 and 4.3.1 below. See also nn. 27 and 167 below. See also the note below figure 5.

account, involves not simply the outward command '*Be!*' but the inward decision '*Let* . . . be!' The "feminine" movement precedes the "masculine."[12]

This feminine, inward movement is one of self-restriction, giving way, withdrawal, making room for a finitude within. In Moltmann's words, "The *nihil* for his *creatio ex nihilo* only comes into being because—and in so far as—the omnipotent and omnipresent God withdraws his presence and restricts his power."[13] Prior to creating outwards, God gives or concedes to the world "time *in* his eternity, finitude *in* his infinity, space *in* his omnipresence and freedom *in* his selfless love."[14] "Eternity breathes itself in, so as to breathe out the Spirit of life."[15]

While Moltmann draws explicitly on the kabbalistic tradition, saying of Isaac Luria's doctrine of the *zimzum* (contraction) that it "is the only serious attempt ever made to think through the idea of 'creation out of nothing' in a truly theological way,"[16] he rejects the kabbalistic idea that God's self-restriction leaves behind a "vacuum."[17] Even if this is not seen as a negative image, it is evidently too neutral to capture the way God makes space *for* the world. "By withdrawing himself and giving his creation space," Moltmann prefers to say, "God makes himself the *living space* of those he has created."[18]

As Moltmann describes the inward movement as "motherly,"[19] and refers to the primordial living space as a "feminine metaphor,"[20] it seems natural to see creation as a birthing process. Certainly he intends the "feminine" movement within and the living space that this concedes to be viewed in a positive light. God's *nihil* becomes pregnant with possibilities. This "*living space in God*" is described by using the German term "*Geborgenheit*," a "safekeeping"

---

[12] For this use of "masculine" and "feminine," and the theme of 'Let there be'/letting-be, see TKG, 109 and GC, 88.

[13] GC, 86–87. His italics. This 'surrender' of power mirrors the receptivity of hope referred to in n. 11 above.

[14] TKG, 109. His emphases.

[15] TKG, 111.

[16] TKG, 110. On Isaac Luria, see Gershom Scholem, *Kabbalah* (New York: Times, 1974), 420–28. On the *zimzum*, see Scholem, *Kabbalah*, 128–52 (which includes Scholem's discussion of "The Doctrine of Creation in Lurianic Kabbalah" on pp. 128–44). On "Isaac Luria and His School," see also Gershom Scholem, *Major Trends in Jewish Mysticism*, 3rd rev. ed. (New York: Schocken, 1961), 244–86. For a helpful overview that highlights the selective nature of Moltmann's engagement with this tradition, see Celia Deane-Drummond, "Towards a Green Theology through Analysis of the Ecological Motif in Jürgen Moltmann's Doctrine of Creation" (PhD diss., University of Manchester, 1992), 241–45. "*Zimzum*" is often spelt "*zimsum*" in Moltmann's writings. Scholem has "*tsimtsum.*" I have adopted the *zimzum* spelling, which is also found throughout WJC.

[17] CoG, 298.

[18] CoG, 299. My emphasis.

[19] GC, 88.

[20] CoG, 299.

associated with "the mother's womb."[21] This is a 'pre-space space',[22] a space for Life.

This womb, however, will experience severe birth-pains ('*contractions*'). When Moltmann says that God's "action is grounded in his passion,"[23] that passion involves *suffering*. Even of the primal withdrawing and making way, Moltmann uses the language of endurance and self-humiliation,[24] and does not

---

[21] CoG, 299 read together with CoG, 300. His italics and emphasis. "Geborgenheit" appears in the English translation. (Mother's) womb in German is 'Gebärmutter'. Although Moltmann uses "Mutterschoß" instead in *DKG*, 330, he does use terms with the geb- prefix here such as "geboren" (born) and "Geburt" (birth). On Moltmann's sympathy for womb imagery, see also TKG, 165; SL, 274; and CoG, 279.

[22] The idea of a primordial 'spacing' of this kind has interesting affinities to Derrida's discussion of the *Khôra* or receptacle of Plato's *Timaeus* (48e–53c). See Jacques Derrida, "*Khôra*," trans. Ian McLeod in Jacques Derrida, *On the Name*, ed. Thomas Dutoit (Stanford, CA: Stanford University Press, 1995), 87–127 and his earlier essay "How to Avoid Speaking: Denials," trans. Ken Frieden in *Derrida and Negative Theology*, ed. Harold Coward and Toby Foshay (Albany, NY: State University of New York Press, 1992), 73–142. See also the discussion in John D. Caputo, *Deconstruction in a Nutshell: A Conversation with Jacques Derrida* (New York: Fordham University Press, 1997), chap. 3. For an analysis of Derrida and Caputo, see James H. Olthuis, "The Test of *Khôra*: *Grâce à Dieu*," in *Religion With/out Religion: The Prayers and Tears of John D. Caputo*, ed. James H. Olthuis (London: Routledge, 2002), 110–19, and the more recent interchange: James H. Olthuis, "Testing the Heart of *Khôra*: Anonymous or Amorous?," and John D. Caputo "The Chance of Love: A Response to Olthuis," in *Cross and* Khôra: *Deconstruction and Christianity in the Work of John D. Caputo*, ed. Marko Zlomislić and Neal DeRoo (Eugene, OR: Pickwick, 2010), 174–86 and 187–96. Moltmann would seem to eschew the neutral character of this primordial 'space' that Olthuis detects in Derrida and Caputo in favour of a positive opening for life that Olthuis supports. Yet for Moltmann this 'space' also has a character that is altogether more abysmal.

Reference should also be made to Barth's understanding of "Nothingness" (*das Nichtige*) in the context of his doctrine of creation in *Church Dogmatics* 3/3 (sec. 50), on which see the fine exposition by Jeffrey Dudiak, "Barth's Doctrine of Nothingness: Creational and Theological Reflections" (Toronto: Institute for Christian Studies, 1986). Cf. S.U. Zuidema, "The Structure of Karl Barth's Doctrine of Creation," trans. Art Helleman, in his *Communication and Confrontation: A Philosophical Appraisal and Critique of Modern Society and Contemporary Thought* (Assen: Van Gorcum; Kampen: J.H. Kok, 1972), 309–28, especially 320–22. In GC, 334–35n29, Moltmann contrasts his own position (set out in GC, 87) with that of Barth by stating: "In his doctrine of creation Barth does not go beyond the Platonic definition of nothingness. However, in his doctrine of election (CD II/2) he develops insights into the annihilating nothingness drawn from the theology of the cross which lend theological depth to the Platonic Non-being." From this (as well as from GC, 87), it is clear that "Non-Being" does not capture the 'Hellish' character of Moltmann's *nihil*, on which see below. The latter is not simply a space or opening for Life.

[23] TKG, 110.

[24] See TKG, 59.

hesitate to connect this with the cross.[25] If the world is to exist, God must 'bear' it.

If Moltmann would no doubt wish to honour this kind of suffering as a divine compassion, a suffering-with and -for rather than an involuntary suffering-from,[26] the threatening character that the primordial space assumes cannot be played down. In his own words,

> Creation is ... threatened, not merely by its own non-being, but also by the non-being of God its Creator—that is to say, by Nothingness itself. The character of the negative that threatens it goes beyond creation itself. This is what constitutes its demonic power. Nothingness contradicts, not merely creation but God too, since he is creation's Creator. Its negations lead into that primordial space which God freed within himself before the creation.[27]

This argument, however, has its twists and turns. The *nihil* that is opened up by the divine self-negation is not (simply) identical to this demonic *Nothingness*. In some of his comments, Moltmann seems to resist ascribing to it any inherently destructive characteristics. "[T]he *nihil*," he writes, "only acquires [a] menacing character through the self-isolation of created beings to which we give the name of sin and godlessness.... As a self-limitation that makes creation possible, the *nihil* does not yet have this annihilating character; for it was conceded in order to make an independent creation 'outside' God possible." Taken in isolation, this sounds as if the *nihil* as space for creation only becomes a 'danger zone' through our evil. Moltmann, however, immediately continues, "But this implies the *possibility* of the annihilating Nothingness."[28] In relation to the demonic negative, the *nihil* thus emerges as what we might call a *sine qua non*.

If this could be passed off as something more neutral than ominous, a mere formal possibility, Moltmann's next comments suggest otherwise for he explicitly states that the Nothingness signifies the "non-being" not of the creation but "of God."[29] This "Nothingness emerges" not with human sin, but in the *zimzum*.[30] The danger it represents for the world lies in the fact that it is the primordial absence of God. As Moltmann explains,

---

[25] See GC, 87 in the light of his comments in GC, 88.

[26] The suffering that is the opposite of joy in figure 4 of the previous chapter is a suffering *from* that is in the direction of *kenosis*. The *passio Dei* reveals a suffering to which the self is not merely subjected but which it embraces: a suffering *with*. In Moltmann's terminology in TKG, 81, this is a "*passio activa.*" His italics. It enacts a transition from divine unity towards the diversity, *kenosis*, and otherness of creation/history in the case of the *passio Dei* and a transition from *kenosis* and alienation to glory in the case of the passion of the cross. Cf. n. 11 above, n. 167 below, and figure 5 at the end of this chapter.

[27] GC, 88.

[28] GC, 88. The *nihil* is in italics in the original. Additional emphasis mine.

[29] GC, 88. In this way, he departs from the Platonic position of Karl Barth. See GC, 334–35n29 (which relates to the discussion in GC, 87). Cf. n. 22 above.

[30] GC, 87, citing Gershom Scholem sympathetically.

God makes room for his creation by withdrawing his presence. What comes into being is a *nihil* which does not contain the negation of creaturely being (since creation is not yet existent), but which represents the partial negation of the divine Being, inasmuch as God is not yet Creator. The space which comes into being, and is set free by God's self-limitation is *literally God-forsaken space*. The *nihil* in which God creates his creation is *God-forsakenness, hell, absolute death*; and it is against the threat of this that he maintains his creation in life.[31]

Its nature thus appears far more abhorrent than a mere vacuum. To be fair to the nuances of Moltmann's position, the *nihil* may only *become* "menacing" and "annihilating" in relation to creation in the context of sin. But Godforsakenness and absolute death, by his own account, preexist creation. And so too does Hell.

Moltmann may sympathise with the view that "hell is not some remote place, but an existential experience."[32] He may use "existential" language himself when he speaks of the "hells of Auschwitz, Hiroshima and Vietnam"[33] or states that "Hell is hopelessness."[34] But when we say that "we are making the world hell," Moltmann is convinced that in the various "economic, political, cultural and industrial vicious circles" in which we are caught, there is "a deeper, more embracing drive [at work]: *the vicious circle of senselessness and godforsakenness.*"[35] In Moltmann's mature thought, that godforsakenness is related to the primordial *nihil*. This is not existentialism. Hell is not confined to human experience, or even to the general drift of creation into non-being. As primal godforsakenness, Hell is the power (or to borrow Moltmann's language: "a more embracing drive") that may be discerned in transience, death, and the past.[36]

When it is used of Christ's experience on the cross, therefore, this term has its full onto/theological, a/theological weight.[37] Its central place in Moltmann's theology is revealed in his theology's central event: Christ's descent into Hell.

[B]y yielding up the Son to death in Godforsakenness on the cross, and by surrendering him to hell, the eternal God *enters the Nothingness out of which he created the world*. God *enters that 'primordial space' which he himself*

---

[31] GC, 87–88. The *nihil* is italicised in the original. Additional emphases mine.
[32] CoG, 252.
[33] CrG, 220.
[34] TH, 32. Cf. his reference to the "hell of our lostness" in CoG, 127.
[35] CrG, 331. His emphasis.
[36] For the connection between Hell and the "powers of this world," see EiT, 26. For the Godforsaken characteristics of transience, the past, and death see 3.2, 3.3, and 3.4 above.
[37] In addition to the discussion of Christ's descent into Hell in 1.4.1 above (and the discussion of this descent in CrG, 158n70; CPS, 64, 95; TKG, 81; WJC, 189–91; CoG, 106, and 250–55), see CrG, 175 ("a hellish death"), 255 ("the hells of the negative"), 263 (Christ uniquely "experiences death and hell in solitude. His followers experience it in his company"); TKG, 77; WJC, 167 ("a sinking into nothingness"), 174; SL, 136; and Jürgen Moltmann, *In the End—the Beginning: The Life of Hope*, trans. Margaret Kohl (Minneapolis, MN: Fortress Press, 2004), hereafter IEB, 147–48.

conceded through his initial self-limitation. He pervades the space of Godforsakenness with his presence. It is the presence of his self-humiliating, suffering love for his creation, in which he experiences death itself. That is why God's presence in the crucified Christ gives creation eternal life, and does not annihilate it. In the path of the Son into self-emptying and bondage, to the point of the death he died, and in the path of his exaltation and glorification by the whole creation, God becomes omnipresent. By entering into the God-forsakenness of sin and death (which is Nothingness), God overcomes it and makes it part of his eternal life: 'If I make my bed in hell, thou art there' (Ps. 139.8).[38]

Thus God, who is omnipresent before the creation of the world yet who surrenders a space within himself for life other than his own, historically enters that space for the first time through his concentrated presence in/as the Christ.[39] "This is the beginning of the language of the kingdom of God," says Moltmann, "where 'God will be all in all'."[40]

But it is only the beginning. If "hell" is to finally "go to hell,"[41] the primordial *zimzum* must be countered by an eschatological de-restriction.[42] If the *passio Dei* was an "act" that "veil[ed]" his presence from creation,[43] God will finally "appear[] in his creation in the splendour of his *unveiled* glory."[44] If God originally made way for "time *in* his eternity ... [and] space *in* his omnipresence,"[45] in the eschaton, his "eternity appears *in* the time of creation, and his omnipresence *in* creation's space."[46] If in order to create the world, God

---

[38] GC, 91. My emphases. Cf. his earlier statement in TH, 198: "The experience of the cross of Jesus means for [his disciples] the experience of the god-forsakenness of God's ambassador—that is, an absolute *nihil* embracing also God." His italics. I read this passage as saying that God entered the *nihil* for the first time in Christ's descent. Cf. the argument in 1.4.1 above.

This is also evident in EoH, 181, where Moltmann writes, "If God goes wherever Jesus goes, he brings God to the victims.... He himself [i.e., Jesus] entered into Godforsakenness on the cross in order to bring God to the forsaken." That God follows Jesus is intimately connected to God "yielding up" and "surrendering" Jesus (GC, 91 as cited above). This "yielding up" occurs because Jesus truly goes beyond the presence of the Father, though he brings God with him. If the "surrendering" is not interpreted in this context, it will be misread as abuse—a charge brought against Moltmann by Dorothee Sölle, and a cause of much distress to him as is clear in BP, 198–200. Cf. the account and analysis of feminist theologian, Elisabeth Moltmann-Wendel, *Autobiography*, trans. John Bowden (London: SCM Press, 1997), 177–80.

[39] On the 'concentration' of the kingdom of God in Christ and on the claim that "Through his death, the mercy of God which he presented and represented is realized *in history*," see WJC, 205. My emphasis.

[40] WJC, 174.

[41] CoG, 84.

[42] See WJC, 328–30 and CoG, 294–95.

[43] TKG, 110.

[44] CoG, 295. My emphasis.

[45] TKG, 109 as cited above. His emphases.

[46] CoG, 280. His emphases.

conceded a *nihil* as a space for life, now there is to be a "redeeming *annihilatio nihili*."[47]

In its positive potentiality, the *nihil* is no longer necessary as "[o]nce God finds his dwelling space in creation, creation loses its space outside God and attains to its place in God."[48] In its negative potentiality, "the distance and space of [God's] creation," which is said to have "*resulted* in isolation from God, and sin," is closed forever. God's cosmic incarnation thus not only does away with the God-forsakenness of sinners, but also with this "potentiality for sin."[49] The filling of the primordial space with the glory of God (and with the "omnipresent" creation[50]) thus not only overcomes the godless self-isolation that he elsewhere says allows the *nihil* to *become* an annihilating power;[51] it also eradicates a "potentiality for sin" that appears to issue forth from the *nihil* itself.[52]

The end is thus unlike the beginning. Redemption, if it is to be "final,"[53] cannot be conceived of as a *restitutio in integrum*.[54] God's primordial self-negation is itself negated through the self-negation of the cross. God takes back the God-forsaken/ness through Christ's descent into the "abyss,"[55] so that his eschatological embrace of the creation may leave no space for Hell.[56]

4.2 Nature, Grace, and Glory

Hell is thus the abysmal, Godforsaken space that is opened up in the *passio Dei* prior to the creation of the world. In Moltmann's *zimzum*, Hell is the Creator-creation distinction, 'negatively conceived'. At the same time, this opening,

---

[47] GC, 90. His italics. Cf. his earlier statement in TH, 198 (which follows on from the citation in n. 38 above): "The experience of the appearance of the crucified one as the living Lord therefore means for them the experience of the nearness of God in the god-forsaken one, of the divineness of God in the crucified and dead Christ—that is, a new totality which annihilates the total *nihil*." His italics.
[48] CoG, 307.
[49] CoG, 306–307 as cited more fully in n. 241 below. My emphasis.
[50] CoG, 280.
[51] See GC, 88 as cited above.
[52] I will elaborate on and further document this important point in 4.2 and 4.4 below.
[53] CoG, 307.
[54] For Moltmann's consistent rejection of this view of redemption, see TH, 136; CrG, 261, 264; CPS, 266; GC, 207–208; WJC, 188, 281, 286; CoG, 91, 262–65; and EiT, 90.
[55] WJC, 167.
[56] Hell is not placed cosmologically as the *anus mundi* (which is where Hell was located in the Great World Mother of ancient religion as discussed in GC, 299), but a/theologically as *uterus Dei* (reading his reference to the human foetus in the uterus in CoG, 300 in the light of CoG, 299). If the "*annihilatio nihili*" (GC, 90 as cited above) signals a divine hysterectomy, it also means that God becomes the womb of the world while also regaining his omnipresence and thus dwelling within it. This theme calls out for the analysis of feminist theologians. It is surprisingly absent at crucial points (such as pp. 234 and 250) in Elizabeth A. Johnson's important work, *She Who Is: The Mystery of God in Feminist Theological Discourse* (New York: Crossroad, 1997).

rooted in God's desire to make way for what is other than himself, is also a 'space' for Life. In the consummation of history, when the distinction between Creator and creation is transformed forever, when the distance this entails is gone 'for good', this promising yet threatening space comes to an 'end' in the double sense of fulfilment/negation. The space that makes life and freedom possible comes to fruition as the Godforsaken space makes way for the God who is finally all in all. God and creation have arrived home in one another.

If this account explains why Hell, for Moltmann, cannot be an eternal reality, this is not yet a convincing argument for universal salvation. One might still wonder, for example, why the *annihilatio nihili* should not include the impenitent who give themselves to the Nothingness of sin.[57] To understand further why Moltmann believes that no one will be finally subjected to the annihilation of Hell, we must explore his thought in terms of the dynamics of 'nature' and 'grace', the categories in which theologians typically attempt to relate divine and human action, responsibility, power, and freedom. This will set the stage for an examination of his 'universalism of the cross' in 4.3.1 below.

Briefly formulated, 'nature', as a theological category, might be said to correspond to what is within our power while 'grace', by contrast, could be said to refer to what we need that is beyond our control (or beyond the power of creation). If 'nature' could thus be said to be our responsibility (in some sense), 'grace' would thus point to God's gifts and promises, to God's action rather than to our own.

While 'nature' is normally a term used of *creation*, viewed in terms of its 'natural' (God-given) capacities or in relation to God's work of preservation in the face of evil,[58] 'grace' is almost always related to *redemption*. This is understandable given its strong associations with 'forgiveness' in many

---

[57] Moltmann's conviction that we are set free from our compulsion to damn ourselves is examined in 4.3.3 below.

[58] On the latter, see for example Michael Cromartie, ed., *A Preserving Grace: Protestants, Catholics, and Natural Law* (Washington, DC: Ethics and Public Policy Center; Grand Rapids, MI: Eerdmans, 1997). While the title shows that there is a kind of grace related to nature, this is a 'common' rather than 'special' form of grace that is not salvific. For the creation-/history-/culture-affirming potential of common grace, see Abraham Kuyper, *De Gemeene Gratie*, 3 vols. (Amsterdam: Hoveker and Wormster, 1902–1905), the selections (translated by John Vriend) in the section entitled "Common Grace," in *Abraham Kuyper: A Centennial Reader*, ed. James D. Bratt (Grand Rapids, MI: Eerdmans, 1998), 165–201 and the constructive criticism and appreciation of Kuyper to be found in Jacob Klapwijk, "Antithesis and Common Grace," in *Bringing into Captivity Every Thought: Capita Selecta in the History of Christian Evaluations of Non-Christian Philosophy,* ed. Jacob Klapwijk, Sander Griffioen, and Gerben Groenwoud (Lanham, MD: University Press of America, 1991), 169–90 and S.U. Zuidema, "Common Grace and Christian Action in Abraham Kuyper," trans. Harry Van Dyke, in his *Communication and Confrontation: A Philosophical Appraisal and Critique of Modern Society and Contemporary Thought* (Assen: VanGorcum; Kampen: J.H. Kok, 1972), 52–105.

languages. The Dutch term *Genade*, for example, also means 'mercy', while in German, *Gnadentod* means euthanasia in the literal sense of 'mercy killing'. Although there would be nothing to stop someone using 'nature' and 'grace', at least in English, to refer to different facets of the covenant relationship between God and humanity in a creational context,[59] this is unusual.[60] The rich terminology that has developed to distinguish grace in its "actual," "cooperating," "efficacious," "elevating," "habitual," "irresistible," "sufficient," and "uncreated" forms witnesses to its strong connections with God's salvation.[61]

---

[59] I will explore this possibility in 6.1–6.3 below.

[60] Certainly this is unusual in Protestant theology. Yet in a Roman Catholic contribution to the otherwise evangelical Protestant discussion, Zachary J. Hayes, in "The Purgatorial View," in *Four Views on Hell*, ed. William Crockett (Grand Rapids, MI: Zondervan, 1992), 114, states:

> One of the crucial convictions of Christianity, whether in its Protestant or Roman Catholic form, is the mystery of God's limitless love, forgiveness, and acceptance. For Christian theology, it is the creative power of God's love that brought forth the created universe, conferring on it the very gift of existence. It is the same mystery of God's creative love that brings the potential of created being to fulfillment in eschatological completion. And it is that forgiving, merciful love that reaches to us through the historical mediation of Jesus Christ. *For Roman Catholic theology, this has long meant that the language of grace does not begin with the doctrine of redemption. It begins already, at least in an analogous way, with the doctrine of creation.* For existence itself is a free and unmerited gift from the creative love of God.

My emphasis. Moltmann's comment in GC, 335n31 is also instructive: "Grace is really already to be found in the divine *preservation* of the creature who closes himself against God. . . . But if there is grace in the preservation of the world, then there must also be grace in the creation of the world, from the beginning." His emphasis. Moltmann's 'creational' grace here, read in context (see GC, 89), would seem to refer (at least in part) to a divine preservation of creation from the annihilating forces of the primordial *nihil*. What is most pertinent in this context, however, is the fact that Moltmann, in speaking of a 'creational' grace, clearly sees himself suggesting a connection that is not usually made.

[61] The terminology is drawn from Van A. Harvey, "Grace," in *A Handbook of Theological Terms*, by Van A. Harvey (New York: Macmillan, 1964), 108–112 and E.J. Yarnold, "Grace," in *A New Dictionary of Christian Theology*, ed. Alan Richardson and John Bowden (London: SCM Press, 1983), 244–55. On preserving grace, which is an exception that proves the rule, see n. 58 and Moltmann's comment in n. 60, above. On the nature-grace relationship, see Leonardo Boff, *Liberating Grace*, trans. John Dury (Maryknoll, NY: Orbis, 1979), 40–46; Stephen J. Duffy, *The Graced Horizon: Nature and Grace in Modern Catholic Thought* (Collegeville, MN: Liturgical Press, 1992); Thomas C. Oden, *The Transforming Power of Grace* (Nashville, TN: Abingdon, 1993), 95–107; and Philip S. Watson, *The Concept of Grace: Essays on the Way of Divine Love in Human Life* (London: Epworth, 1959), 77–83. The classic debate of the last century is undoubtedly to be found in Karl Barth and Emil Brunner, *Natural Theology: Comprising "Nature and Grace" by Professor Dr. Emil Brunner and the Reply "No!" by Dr. Karl Barth*, trans. Peter Fraenkel (London: Geoffrey Bles, Centenary Press, 1946), on which see 6.2 below.

So how is the 'grace' of salvation to be related to the 'nature' of our humanity? If (for the sake of argument) all people will be saved, does this mean that we all have a 'natural' desire for God? If not, does God's sovereign grace necessarily eclipse human freedom? Do God and human beings need to 'co-operate' in salvation such that those who are lost have literally only themselves to blame? Or is our rejection of God something from which we are saved (by definition, against our will)? Can we come to a saving knowledge of God via a natural theology or through general revelation? Or must God's grace (and our response) be mediated by the Church or a community of faith? If others must be involved in our salvation, does this mean that God saves entire communities—perhaps humanity as a whole—and not only individuals? If there is to be a final distinction between the saved and the lost, is this distinction to be traced back to the will of God or only to our unbelief? Is having faith in God itself a gift of God or is it (also) our responsibility? If our faith comes from God, does this mean that unbelief comes from ourselves? If we are involved in the response of faith, is God also involved in our lack of faith? What is the relationship (if any) between God's forgiveness of our sins and the forgiveness we may or may not receive from those against whom we have sinned? In all these questions, the nature-grace relationship is central. Whether we are sympathetic to or apprehensive about a salvation that includes all people, the specific way we relate grace and nature will determine how we articulate our own position and will give rise to certain objections that we feel must be met if we are to consider changing our mind.[62]

---

[62] The following observation of Albert M. Wolters, "Christianity and the Classics: A Typology of Attitudes," in *Christianity and the Classics: The Acceptance of a Heritage*, ed. Wendy E. Helleman (Lanham, MD: University Press of America, 1990), 192–93, is to the point:

> The problem of the relationship of nature to grace is fundamental to all Christian thought and experience. It is a confessional problem (in its developed intellectual form we might call it a theological problem) which is unavoidable. At bottom, it deals with two fundamental realities: . . . All Christians have to deal with the primacy of the realities of new life in Jesus Christ [grace] and old life outside Christ [nature]. This is a basic issue which all Christians cannot help but confront, to which they cannot help but give some basic answer, whether or not the answer is explicit.

Wolters' development of a five-fold typology based on H. Richard Niebuhr's *Christ and Culture* (New York: Harper and Row, 1951) lets us distinguish the following basic postures: I, grace equals nature, II, grace perfects nature, III, grace flanks nature, IV, grace opposes nature, and V, grace restores nature. James H. Olthuis, "Must the Church Become Secular?," in *Out of Concern for the Church: Five Essays*, by John A. Olthuis et al (Toronto: Wedge, 1970), 120, also adapts Niebuhr's typology. Favouring the grace restores nature position with Wolters, he distinguishes the remaining four ways of relating nature and grace (presented here in the same order as above) as follows:

I   Nature = Creation [sin] — Grace = our calling [God's gift]
II   Nature = Creation (sin) —— Grace = our calling (God's gift)
III   Nature = Sin (creation) ——— Grace = God's gift (our calling)
IV   Nature = Sin [creation] ——— Grace = God's gift [our calling]

Of the many typical ways in which grace and nature are related in different theological systems, one well-known dualistic perspective, associated with the Lutheran doctrine of the 'two kingdoms', separates them in accordance with the respective spheres of church and state.⁶³ It is against this background⁶⁴ that we can appreciate Moltmann's desire to speak of *three* kingdoms and to open up standard theological categories by speaking of them as the kingdoms of nature, grace, *and glory*. This approach also coheres extremely well with the structural contours of Moltmann's cosmogony. In the following analysis, I will suggest that 'nature' in Moltmann's system refers to the historical direction of differentiation, 'glory' to the eschatological redirection in which all things find their integration, and 'grace' to the way in which the "storm of history" (to use an image from 2.1 and 3.6) is "turned around" to face and embrace God's future.

The present section will focus primarily on the category of 'nature', in the context of which Moltmann's understanding of creation and fall comes to the fore. We shall also look at the theme of 'glory' in which his vision of the 'universal' reintegration of all things is clearly related to his universalism. The

---

In this schema (see "Must the Church Become Secular?,"125n18), "[]" enclose minimised/neglected factors, "( )" enclose factors that are taken into consideration but not given their rightful place (from a 'Christ transforms culture' perspective), and "—" indicates increasing tension between nature and grace." (Where Olthuis speaks of "man's task," I have substituted "our calling." The relationship between "gift" and "calling" will be explored in chap. 6, especially 6.1.1, below).

⁶³ Olthuis, in "Must the Church Become Secular?,"121, sees "the classic Lutheran two-realm theory" as belonging to type III of the schema set out in the previous note.

⁶⁴ See Moltmann's essay, "Luther's Doctrine of the Two Kingdoms and its Use Today," in *On Human Dignity: Political Theology and Ethics*, by Jürgen Moltmann, trans. M. Douglas Meeks (Philadelphia: Fortress Press, 1984), 61–77, which is also available in a different translation as "The Lutheran Doctrine of the Two Kingdoms and its Use Today," in *The Politics of Discipleship and Discipleship in Politics: Jürgen Moltmann Lectures in Dialogue with Mennonite Scholars*, by Jürgen Moltmann et al, ed. Willard M. Swartley (Eugene, OR: Cascade, 2006), 3–18, and his recent analysis of the same theme in EoH, 9–13, together with his appreciative comments about Bonhoeffer's Christocentric overcoming of dualism in this context in "The Lordship of Christ and Human Society," in *Two Studies in the Theology of Bonhoeffer*, by Jürgen Moltmann and Jürgen Weissbach, trans. Reginald H. Fuller and Ilse Fuller (New York: Charles Scribner's Sons, 1967), 61–62. In his reflections on the history of this way of thinking in TKG, 206–208, Moltmann notes that orthodox Protestantism has generally held to a *two kingdom*, nature and grace, position thus departing from the earlier *threefold* distinction, made with reference to Christ's kingly office, between the *regnum naturae*, the *regnum gratia*, and the *regnum gloriae*. He also notes Joachim of Fiore's *fourfold* distinction between the respective kingdoms of the Father, the Son, and the Spirit, which precede the final kingdom of glory.

In his perceptive comments about how the mediaeval nature-grace position became the antinomy-ridden dialectic of necessity and freedom in the Enlightenment, his analysis bears an uncanny similarity to that of Herman Dooyeweerd, *Roots of Western Culture: Pagan, Secular, and Christian Options*, ed. Mark Vander Vennen and Bernard Zylstra, trans. John Kraay (Toronto: Wedge, 1979), chap. 6.

transition from nature to glory, which is touched on at the end of this section, raises the question of how God's universal salvation is related to our humanity (including our faith and repentance). This will be the focus of 4.3.1 below.

So how does Moltmann articulate an alternative to the nature-grace dualism of the 'two kingdoms'? Appropriately enough, he first develops what he calls his "trinitarian" doctrine of the kingdoms in *The Trinity and the Kingdom of God* where, following the example of Joachim of Fiore, it actually takes a four-fold form.[65] The kingdom of the *Father* (the "*regnum naturae*"), says Moltmann, "consists of the creation of a world open to the future." Providence, he suggests, must be understood as the way God "keeps the world's true future open for it through the gift of time, which works against all the world's tendencies to close in on itself, to shut itself off." This is evidence not of God's "power" but of his "patience," a patience Moltmann here connects with the self-limitation of the *zimzum*. In this kingdom, "the liberty of created beings is given space and allowed time, even in the slavery they impose on themselves."[66] This giving "space," I suggest, should be related to the primordial *nihil* as viewed in its positive potentiality. It is the freedom we have been given by virtue of the initial distinction between God and creation.

The kingdom of the *Son* is the "lordship of the crucified one" in which he "liberates men and women from servitude to sin through his own servitude." In this he "consummates the Father's patience"—a comment that reveals the implicit way Moltmann sees the *zimzum* (again in its life-affirming capacity) as a prelude to the cross. If the kingdom of the Father is not "simply" a kingdom of "power," the kingdom of the Son takes on an even more explicit servant form. Liberation *from* the self-enclosure of sin, liberation *for* "primal openness," can only "come about . . . through vicarious suffering and the call to that liberty which vicarious suffering alone throws open."[67]

The kingdom of the *Spirit* is associated with the energies of the new creation that are experienced in *history*—a fact that shows it is not the kingdom of glory towards which it points. In this scheme, therefore, it appears that the kingdoms of the Son and the Spirit are both forms of the "*regnum gratia.*" The kingdom of glory ("*regnum gloriae*"), by contrast, is "the consummation of the Father's creation, . . . the universal establishment of the Son's liberation, and the fulfilment of the Spirit's indwelling." It is thus the "goal—enduring and uninterrupted—for all God's works and ways in history."[68]

In Moltmann's next major work, *God in Creation*, he once again expresses his dissatisfaction with "two-term, dual dogmatics"[69] by claiming that we must see "nature and grace, and the relationship between nature and grace, in a forward perspective, in the light of the coming glory, which will complete both

---

[65] See TKG, 207–208 and the previous note. Joachim of Fiore's fourfold distinction is further discussed in 4.3.3 below in relation to Moltmann view of freedom.
[66] TKG, 209–10. His italics.
[67] TKG, 210.
[68] TKG, 211–12. His italics.
[69] GC, 7.

nature and grace, and [which] hence already determines the relationship between the two here and now."⁷⁰ In Moltmann's eschatologically oriented thinking, therefore, "two-term . . . dogmatics" typically makes way for three-term dynamics.

This can be seen later in *God in Creation*, when Moltmann correlates the nature-grace-glory distinction with a proposal for a single theology that is determined by different modes of God's presence. This theology may thus be viewed as a *"theologia naturalis"* (understood as theology under the conditions both of creation-in-the-beginning and of sin and corruption) that is taken up into a *"theologia revelata"* (in which God's revelation under the conditions of a history now determined by sin and death is centred in the cross). These, in turn, are fulfilled and perfected in—or as—a *"theologia gloriae"* (which "subsists in the enraptured gaze upon the unveiled glory of God, face to face").⁷¹ In the following work in his "systematic contributions to theology" series, *The Way of Jesus Christ*, the same threefold distinction is worked out as a "cosmic christology" in which Christ's mediation in creation is interpreted in the following "movements":

> 1. Christ as the ground of the creation of all things (*creatio originalis*); 2. Christ as the moving power in the evolution of all things (*creatio continua*); and 3. Christ as the redeemer of the whole creation process (*creatio nova*).⁷²

While nature is thus distinguished from grace (and in the first example becomes quickly associated with sin), grace is, in turn, distinguished from glory.⁷³ This latter distinction is an especially important feature of Moltmann's thought. In the second passage, the *regnum gloriae* (rather than the *regnum gratia*) is explicitly connected to Christ as *"redeemer,"* suggesting an understanding of (at least a dimension to) *redemption* that cannot be reduced to *salvation*, even though glory and grace are intimately related. This bears clarification. On the one hand, the *eschaton* is not simply a historical outworking of (and in that sense completion of) '*redemption*'—in the sense of *salvation*—as Moltmann tells us that "*glory* . . . will complete *nature* and [not

---

⁷⁰ GC, 8.
⁷¹ GC, 59. His italics.
⁷² WJC, 286. His italics. On the connection between *creatio continua*, evolution, and the *regnum gratia*, see n. 170 below. In WJC, 286–87, he immediately continues, "By preceding in this way we are really taking up the old Protestant doctrine of Christ's threefold office (*officium regium Christi*), developing it in the context of today's recognitions: Christ rules in the kingdom of nature (*regnum naturae*), in the kingdom of grace (*regnum gratiae*) and in the kingdom of glory (*regnum gloriae*)." His italics.
⁷³ On the connection between nature and fallenness, see the discussion of the *theologia naturalis* in GC, 59 (briefly referred to above). Cf. CoG, 91: "Theologically, we call 'nature' the state of creation which is no longer creation's original condition, and is not yet its final one." Almost identical wording appears in GC, 59. For the grace/glory distinction, see also CoG, 71. The threefold distinction also appears in CoG, 200.

only] grace," thus bringing to full fruition the process of *creation*.[74] On the other hand, this *redemption-as-fulfilment*,[75] while clearly transcending 'redemption' in a soteriological sense, is nevertheless (and therefore) the eschatological consummation not only of creation/history but also of *salvation* (being the completion of "nature *and grace*"). In this respect it is, if we choose to exploit the terminological ambiguity, the redemption of redemption. As an eschatological-redemptive power for salvation-redemption, glory is—to use and transcend traditional terminology—truly a redemptive power in history. The specific form of universal salvation that Moltmann advocates needs to be understood against this horizon.[76]

One reason why there are a variety of universalist eschatologies is that the category of 'nature' can be understood in different ways. Where one theologian may argue for the salvation of all people on the basis of what s/he trusts is a 'natural' desire for God deep within the human spirit, another may emphasise salvation as "the triumph of grace" over nature to echo the title of Berkouwer's famous study of the (universalist) theology of Karl Barth.[77] Moltmann's most revealing comments about this theological category occur in *God in Creation* when he relates nature, grace, and glory to the "dual world"[78] of heaven and earth (in Latin, *caelum/coelum* and *terra*) thus developing another threefold distinction: the *coelum naturae*, the *coelum gratiae*, and the *coelum gloriae*.

Heaven, in Moltmann's understanding, is to be understood as "the kingdom of God's energies, his potentiality (*possibilitas*) and his efficacious power (*potentia*)." God's "potentiality *for* the earth [Möglichkeit *für* die Erde] . . . [as] indefinable but defining" is thus not to be reduced to "the potentiality *of* the earth [Möglichkeit der Erde]."[79] The active potentialities of heaven *out of which,* and the passive potencies *in which* God creates have "ontological priority" over all earthly powers, belonging as they do to a "non-transient" (yet "finite") kingdom. They are thus not exhausted in their realisations. "Heaven," writes Moltmann, "is the first world . . . which God created so that from there he might *form* the earth, *encompass* it, and finally *redeem* it."[80] God's forming is thus mediated by the energies of the heaven of nature, while his encompassing and redeeming of the earth are related to the heavens of grace and glory respectively.

---

[74] GC, 8 as cited above. My emphases. Cf. TKG, 116 (as cited towards the end of 4.3.3), where Moltmann speaks of "the power of the new creation which consummates creation-in-the-beginning."
[75] As noted in 5.3n128 below, "redemption" is frequently a category of eschatological fulfilment (and not just healing) for Moltmann.
[76] Cf. 6.4 below.
[77] See Berkouwer, *The Triumph of Grace in the Theology of Karl Barth*, cited in n. 2 above. The belief of some universalists in a 'natural' inclination of the soul for God is briefly discussed in 4.3 below.
[78] GC. 158.
[79] GC, 165 [*GS*, 174]. The italicisation of "of" is mine. The other emphases are in the originals.
[80] GC, 166. My emphases.

The "heaven of nature," therefore, is specifically identified as "the kingdom of *the Creator's* potentialities" and is said to include the "archetypes for all created realities." We may see these "created Ideas" as "closer" to God's Being than their realisations on earth provided that we also recognise that their realisations are closer to the concerns of God's love than the archetypes. "According to the biblical traditions," notes Moltmann, "God's especial concern is men and women, not the angels."[81]

If these transcendental conditions for life are "closer" to God's Being than what occurs on earth, the ontological distance between them and the Creator is still such that Moltmann (in continuing to use biblical language for these realities) can speak of "the *fall* of the angels."[82] The fact that evil only occurs in the *coelum naturae* (and not in the *coelum gratiae* or *coelum gloriae*),[83] coupled with the way in which it comes into being, reveals some of Moltmann's deepest assumptions about "nature" as a theological category.

"Evil," writes Moltmann, "is the perversion of good, the annihilation of what exists, the negation of the affirmation of life." God the Creator, having no "dark side," decided on only creative potentialities for the world. Yet not only are there perversions "on the human level" (such as separation and isolation, sin and death) and "on the level of the life processes" (such that constructive potentialities become destructive); evil extends beyond the potentialities of earth into heaven itself, or more specifically into the heaven of nature. Thus Moltmann writes,

> There are apparently also perversions of the same kind in the sphere of the potencies which are intended to make the life processes possible. These then hinder and destroy those life processes. Because these are potencies which do not belong to the human sphere but which yet have a destructive effect on that sphere, we talk about demonic or satanic forces. They make the life processes impossible instead of possible. It is these dimensions of evil, transcending human beings and the earth, that are meant by the symbols of 'the fall of the angels' and 'the rule of Satan'. Deliverance from evil therefore also means the restoration of the good in earthly potentialities for living *and* in the heavenly potencies which make these potentialities possible. The very powers which have been perverted into what is destructive will themselves be redeemed; for their power is created power, and is as such good. It is only their power of destruction that was evil.[84]

For Moltmann, the perversion of these powers is an example of what he calls "*the 'sin' of the whole creation*, which has *isolated itself* from the foundation of its existence and the wellspring of its life, and has fallen victim to

---

[81] GC, 167. His emphasis. This passage is cited more fully in n. 91 below.
[82] GC, 169 as cited below. My emphasis.
[83] Compare GC, 169 (as cited below) with sec. 3, "The heaven of Jesus Christ" and sec. 5, "God's glory 'in heaven as it is on earth' " in GC, 169–75 and 181–84.
[84] GC, 169. His emphasis.

universal death."[85] "If angels are God's potencies of good in heaven," Moltmann reasons, "then 'fallen angels' are *self-isolating* and thus perverted potencies, which when they are cut off from God fall, pulling other creatures down with them into the abyss of annihilation."[86]

This cosmic tendency towards the self-enclosure of sin in the present age seems to be grounded in the ontological 'space' between God and the world that (despite God's good intentions) opens up in the act of creation. In the previous section, I suggested that the way Moltmann speaks of "the distance and space of [God's] creation" as "*result*[*ing*] *in* isolation from God, and sin" suggests a "potentiality for sin" beyond ourselves that appears to issue forth from the *nihil*—and thus from Hell itself.[87] Moltmann's talk of heavenly potencies "pulling other creatures down with them" gives considerable weight to this claim. If 'nature' is to be identified with the differentiating direction of Moltmann's cosmogony as suggested above, the self-isolating movement or "fall" that takes place specifically in the "heaven of nature" raises the question of the relation of evil to the very fabric and structure of history in both its heavenly and earthly dimensions.

If, as Moltmann says, the "word of creation is the continuum joining the Creator to his creation,"[88] the movement into diversity (and thus increased vulnerability to self-isolation) would seem to occur at least as early as the transition from the *creative Word* to the *forming* of the world which begins with the division of light from darkness, heaven from earth, day from night.[89] In heaven (which is itself the result of differentiation), this diversifying movement is expressed in the distinction between the creative Word and the creative "archetypes" and potentialities. Between heaven and earth, differentiation is further evident in the movement from a given archetype, which exists in aeonic time,[90] to its multiple realisations in historical time.

---

[85] WJC, 283. My emphases. The "whole creation" here includes what he calls, in GC, 158, "the dual world" of heaven and earth. Thus in WJC, 284, Moltmann goes on to speak of the reconciliation of "cosmic powers."

[86] WJC, 106. My emphasis. Cf. his comments about demonic forces "arous[ing] the death-wish in human beings." Although he is here summarising (and interpreting) biblical material, he is clearly appropriating it.

[87] CoG, 306–307 as cited in 4.1 above and most fully in n. 241 below. My emphasis.

[88] GC, 76. "Word" begins with a capital letter in the previous sentence of the ET and perhaps should here also. (As a noun, it is, of course, capitalised in the German original).

[89] See GC, 76–77, where, having stated that "at decisive points God 'makes' his creation through the Word he utters," Moltmann goes on to say, "This separation is not identical with the divine 'making', but is the concrete form which the making takes. Even less can it be called the divine creative activity; for it is the result of that activity." There is, prior to this, a movement towards diversity within the Trinity as discussed in 2.5 above. But this does not involve a vulnerability to becoming self-isolated. It thus follows that it is the unity and diversity of the life of the Trinity in which creation must live in the eschaton if the danger of another Fall is to be removed.

[90] That the time of heaven is "aeonic" is evident in GC, 184 although the term is not used. This is explicit however in CoG, 282.

The whole creative process of differentiation would seem to be one in which God's distance from creation is emphasised, for (as we have seen) the archetypes are said to be "closer" to God than their earthly realisations.[91] Furthermore, "[t]he temporality of earthly creation," writes Moltmann with reference to transience, "does not reflect the presence of God—it reflects his absence."[92] If the movement of differentiation away from the divine Origin is one of increasing ontological distance from God's Being, does this not mean that the *coelum naturae* is, by its very 'nature', prone to becoming alienated from God? If the potentialities of heaven became destructive quite apart from human rejection of the Word of life, does this not mean a fall in heaven was inevitable? If the latter is the case, does this not mean that the fallen nature of human history was thereby unavoidable?

These are important questions. If creation and fall are necessarily and not just contingently related, this will inevitably affect Moltmann's view of grace and glory.[93] If this is the case, grace and glory are unlikely to seen as restoring or completing nature but would have to oppose and/or perfect it. This opposition to or perfection of our (human) 'nature' could easily undermine the attempt to develop a covenantal universalism (as discussed in 0.7 and 1.4.2 above).

The *vulnerability* of the heavenly potentialities to self-isolation in the ontological movement into differentiation seems undeniable in Moltmann's framework. His own comments about cosmic "sin" would also suggest that he accepts this. That this "fall" in *heaven* was *unavoidable* would also seem to follow,[94] although there is nothing in Moltmann's writings that can be read as a clear recognition of this fact. However he might respond to this conclusion, the suggestion that *human* sin was thereby inevitable is one that Moltmann would

---

[91] In GC, 167, Moltmann writes: "If, like Plato and the Fathers of the church, we start from the assumption that the Ideas have a stronger and more intense degree of existence than sense phenomena, it is then quite understandable that they should be 'in heaven', and that they should be closer to the eternal Being of God than their realizations and correspondences on earth." This movement from heaven to earth is the movement into differentiation away from the divine presence. When Moltmann continues, "But it then also becomes obvious that the realization of these Ideas on earth are [*sic*] closer to the concerns of God's love, and therefore to his joy as Creator, than the archetypes or Ideas themselves," I take it that this movement of response from earth to heaven is viewed here in the integrating direction of glory in which distance is overcome. Differentiation calls for the response of love that ensures the creation does not become alienated from God. That is one reason why Moltmann says in TKG, 99 that God "expects and *needs* love." My emphasis.

[92] CoG, 284 as cited in 3.3 above.

[93] The rest of this section will support the claim that in Moltmann's theology, the creation-fall distinction is indeed blurred. The correlative conflation of redemption and eschaton will be noted in 5.3 below.

[94] If the "angels" of heaven were personal beings as in traditional theologies, then this would not follow. But for Moltmann, these heavenly realities are "forces," as will be documented later in this section with reference to WJC, 106.

certainly resist.[95] Whether in the final analysis his theological framework is in conflict with his own best intentions here is a question to which I shall return. But first we will examine how he might argue against identifying any historical fall into sin with the differentiating structure of time.

At first glance, we might think that the self-isolations that have occurred in heaven suggest that historical sin is, from the beginning, a foregone conclusion as earthly time represents an even more extreme falling away from the presence of God into non-being. But this does not follow. Transience in the sense of a passing into non-being, we should remind ourselves, only becomes problematic for Moltmann when it becomes absolutised in our experience.[96] Passing away is the correlate of coming into being or futurity. As such, it may be accepted. It is only in sin that we strive in our own strength to get beyond our finitude, building a future (*futurum*) on the basis of our would-be autonomy such that it becomes cut off from God's coming future (*adventus*). In faith, by contrast, we may hope in God's promised new creation in which we shall find fulfilment beyond the present age. In the light of hope, finitude and thus transience may be seen to point to their own negation (and fulfilment) in the eschaton. In accepting the finitude of finitude and the transience of transience in hope, we make a covenant with the life of the age to come and thus with life in the here and now. In looking to the future as *adventus*, we keep transience in perspective.

But if we lose that eschatological horizon, we may succumb to the temptation to try and negate temporal finitude here and now. Rather than relativising the present age by being oriented to God's future, we become immersed in it. Rather than finding genuine freedom, we become slaves to the present order. In (autonomously) taking on *God's task* of eschatologically overcoming transience, we ironically yet tragically become closed to our true destiny, which is for a glory beyond transience. In trying to escape from, or control, our mortal limits, we make a "covenant with death."[97]

The movement into non-being is not responsible for this deadly rejection of life. Creaturely non-being is not the primordial Nothingness.[98] The demonic is a category used of heavenly rather than earthly realities. Transience is potentially dangerous but not inherently so. If experienced in hope, futurity would have remained at the forefront of our awareness and the "destructive possibilities" of earthly time in which "*Chronos* . . . becomes the power of futility"[99] need never have become a dominant force in history.

---

[95] I am confident of this in large part due to a (recorded) conversation with Professor Moltmann in London on September 9th, 2000. What I present as his probable line of argument in the following three paragraphs is the result of reflecting on his writings in the light of that conversation.
[96] See 3.2 above.
[97] This phrase comes from CoG, 94, a passage to which I shall soon return.
[98] Cf. 4.1 above.
[99] CoG, 284. His italics.

The Triumph of Glory 165

Although I am confident that the interpretation offered in the three preceding paragraphs is faithful to Moltmann's own creation-affirming intentions, it is persuasive only if we look at phenomenal time apart from its actual transcendental conditions. But earthly history does not exist in isolation from the *coelum naturae*. In the final analysis, there seems to be a demonic 'power' at work in and through the movement into non-being that cannot be explained in terms of our lack of faith. It is this rather than transience that, for all intents and purposes, makes human sin inevitable within Moltmann's cosmogony. To bring this to light, we must explore the relationship that exists, for Moltmann, between sin and Death.

Reflecting his conviction that mortality does not come into existence through original sin as Augustine assumed,[100] Moltmann states that "If death *in general* is part of creation in time, then the *particular* 'death of the sinner' has come into the world through sin. There is no causal connection between the two." He does however speak of there being a "correlation" between them. Thus he suggests,

> The frailty of the temporal creation of human beings is like a detonator for the sin of wanting to be equal to God and to overcome this frailty. Death is only the consequence of sin inasmuch as sin exists because of death: we cannot endure mortality, and by killing we can make other people die. The vulnerability of creation-in-the-beginning makes the act of violence against life possible.[101]

Thus far, one might easily conclude that the deadly nature of sin comes into history through sin itself, death or mortality being merely the 'occasion' for our evil. Death may be a detonator, but (to stay with a related image) we load the gun and pull the trigger. There is nothing in this account to suggest that mortality or even the experience of frailty are inherently or inevitably destructive.

Moltmann's comments are more revealing, however, when he goes on to explore the correlation from a different angle. In considering whether "sin" might not be "the wages of death"—a reversal of the Pauline text (Rom 6:23) appropriated by Augustine—he writes,

> That would mean: sin presupposes the awareness of death .... It is the awareness of death which first *creates* fear for life, the fear of not getting one's fair share, of not having enough from life, the fear that life will be cut short. This leads to a craving for life, and to greed. The person who senses death in the midst of life wants to live, and if not to be already immortal, at least to be invulnerable while living. People ... break away from their poor, frail, vulnerable and mortal human nature and want to be like God. ... That is the *origin* of the sin that destroys life: not being willing to be what one is, but having to be something different. ... [This] is the *source* of all inhumanities against other people and oneself. ... Sin is the usurpation of life which *springs*

---

[100] See CoG, 90.
[101] CoG, 91. My emphases.

from the awareness of death. Sin is the violence against life which *springs from* knowledge of mortality.[102]

Rather than the covenant with death originating in our sin, "sin . . . originates in the covenant with death."[103] Given the emphasis on mortality as itself a creative (i.e., destructive) source and origin, we might better reflect its agency by speaking of sin having its beginning in the covenant Death makes with us. Moltmann's language suggests that nothing less than the annihilating potentialities of the *nihil*—of Hell—are at work in the transience and mortality of history.

'Nature', in Moltmann's scheme, would thus seem to refer to both creation and fall simultaneously. Although it would be going beyond the evidence to say that the differentiating direction of time is a power of *evil*, it is certainly more than plausible to see it as the power of *temptation*.[104] In reflecting once more on his comment that "the distance . . . of . . . creation" from God "*resulted in* isolation from God, and sin"[105] in the light of the foregoing discussion, we are surely justified in asking whether the creation process itself (as Moltmann conceives of it) was not a 'fall into finitude' that made a Fall in the religious sense virtually inevitable.[106] Given the "fall of the angels," the human task of orienting history to the eschaton in hope becomes, in effect, a task of redemption (in the sense of healing) from the very beginning. This (at least partial) blurring of the creation/fall distinction at the level of heavenly potencies or transcendental conditions is compounded by the fact that the primordial Nothingness at work in the power of Death so undermines the call to hope that would empower and guide our reorientation of creation that this call is, for all intents and purposes, beyond us, creationally speaking. The fall into temptation thus appears unavoidable. Creation may have its origins in God's best intentions. But the process of creation—the way in which Moltmann envisions creation taking place—would seem to pave the way for a road that leads straight from the Hell of the *zimzum* to the hells of human history.

If this is indeed the (implicit) 'logic' of Moltmann's cosmogony, this provides an additional reason why Moltmann rejects the idea of redemption as a *restitutio in integrum*. Given the ontological vulnerability of creation-in-the-beginning to estrangement from God, it is no wonder that he sympathises with

---

[102] CoG, 93–94. My emphases.
[103] CoG, 94.
[104] To my knowledge, Moltmann does not make this identification. I can only stress therefore that it seems implicit in the structure of his thought. Cf. Ron Highfield's comment on Moltmann's appropriation of the Reformed doctrine of the eternal resolve, which parallels the *zimzum*, in his "Divine Self-Limitation in the Theology of Jürgen Moltmann: A Critical Appraisal," *Christian Scholar's Review* 32, no. 1 (Fall, 2002): 49–71, especially his observation, on p. 64, that for Moltmann, "God's absence . . . creates the *temptation* for creatures to project imaginary gods into the vacuum as idolatrous justifications for lives of vanity and nothingness." My emphasis.
[105] CoG, 306, first cited in 4.1 above and cited most fully in n. 241 below. My emphasis.
[106] Mortality, for example, now seems less like a detonator than a 'time' bomb.

the view that "grace must end, not just actual sin, but even the possibility of sinning" as this "excludes the next Fall after the restoration of creation."[107] For Moltmann, an eternal return of the same would be Hell indeed![108] Given a whole creation that is prone to the "sin" of self-isolation, a *"renovatio omnium"*[109] is required so that in the circular rhythms of the age to come there is no linear time that can lure us away from the God in whom we must live and move and have our being.

If the monism of Moltmann's system is reflected in the way he appears to see evil as less a religious choice between Life and Death than an ontological tendency in the direction of non-being opened up by the Creator-creation distinction, corresponding dynamics can be detected in his view of grace which, as I have suggested above, should be understood as the way in which all creation is enabled to return to its true (divine) Origin—from which it has been separated by primal Godforsakenness—in the glorification of all things. Given the analysis of Moltmann's view of time in the previous two chapters in which the historical and the eschatological move in opposites directions, it is interesting that Moltmann refers to what "took place on Golgotha" as "The great *turning point* [Die große *Wende*] from disaster to salvation [vom Unheil zum Heil]."[110]

In a thorough-going monism, even the disaster would somehow be taken up into the reintegrating movement of redemption. This Moltmann would seem to resist. Thus in a sustained critique of Hegel's philosophy of reconciliation, he writes,

> [T]here is something in the cross of Christ which resists every attempt to *absorb* [sich gegen jede Aufhebung . . . sperrt] it into its theological concept: and that is the pain of Christ and his death cry: 'My God, why . . . ?' No theology of the cross can answer this cry, because it is not adequately answered by any explanation of his death, but only through his resurrection from death and the Easter jubilation of the raised. In the cross of Christ elements of the fortuitous

---

[107] CoG, 263–64. I have rearranged the order of these phrases. The reference to Augustine on CoG, 264 connects the discussion with CoG, 86 and with Moltmann's sympathy with the Augustinian idea that "Grace . . . abolishes sin and perfects nature," although we should read this in the light of Moltmann's preferred formulation, in GC, 8: "*gratia non perfectit, sed praeparat naturam ad gloriam aeternam; gratia non est perfectio naturae; sed preparatio messianica mundi ad regnum Dei.*" His italics. Cf. 6.4 below.

[108] It is interesting that, as Fiddes notes in *The Promised End*, 198, "images of circularity in the religious and literary imagination have been most frequently applied to the experience of the damned in hell."

[109] CoG, 265. His italics.

[110] CoG, 245 [*DKG*, 273]. My emphases. On the "turning point," see CoG, 245, cited in 1.4.2 above and discussed in 3.6 and 4.1 (including n. 11) above and in 4.3.1, 4.3.3, and 8.2 below. 'Eine Wendejacke' is a reversible jacket (that can be turned inside out). Furthermore, 'wenden', the verbal form of "Wende," can be used of 'turning' and in that sense 'flipping' an omelet. Cf. my reference to 'reversal' and to the 'flip' in Moltmann's cosmogony in n. 11 above.

character of history and its inner contradictions remain, elements which cannot be *absorbed* [aufgehoben] into any theory and thereby ended.[111]

Nevertheless, while true eschatological unification transcends our conceptual grasp, and is thus not to be equated with "the optimistic total claim of historical reason which Hegel propounded," even in this passage Moltmann can be read as saying that the contradictions of history are to be overcome in an ontological sense in the "jubilation" that follows the eschatological event of the resurrection. Thus five pages later, he writes, "the difference between cross and raising is *absorbed* into the reciprocal glorification of the Son and the Father [die Differenz zwischen Kreuz und Auferwekung in der wechselseitigen Verherrlichung des Sohnes und des Vaters aufgeht]."[112]

The harmonising character of Moltmann's eschatology in which all is finally 'one'[113] is deliberately absent from his portrayal of the present age. To say that 'in reality' all things are already reconciled such that the future will simply disclose what is already the case—even if that reconciliation is said to have been brought about through the cross—is to adopt a position Moltmann

---

[111] CoG, 329 [*DKG*, 357]. My emphases.

[112] CoG, 334 [*DKG*, 363]. My emphasis. 'Aufgehen', used in this last passage, is not a cognate of aufheben/Aufhebung. Beyond its literal meaning of to 'go up', it can mean to 'evaporate' or to 'dissolve'. 'Aufgehen in etwas' means 'to be completely absorbed in something'. To translate "in ... aufgeht" as "absorb[] into" in this context is entirely appropriate. On the jubilation in which all is resolved, cf. Moltmann's reference to "jubilation" in CoG, 329 as cited above, and to "the universal Easter laughter" in the final words of the book on CoG, 339. Moltmann's closing comments in his article, "Theodicy," in *A New Dictionary of Christian Theology*, ed. Alan Richardson and John Bowden (London: SCM Press, 1983), 564–66, seems to go in the same direction with respect to resolution. On p. 565, he writes, "The question of theodicy remains open until a new creation, in which God's righteousness dwells, gives the answer." Furthermore, there is a comment in Jürgen Moltmann, "Can Christian Eschatology Become Post-Modern? Response to Miroslav Volf," in *God Will Be All in All: The Eschatology of Jürgen Moltmann*, ed. Richard Bauckham (Edinburgh: T. and T. Clark, 1999), 259–64, that sounds as if it goes beyond an eschatological resolution to an eschatological legitimation of evil. On p. 263, Moltmann claims that "[i]n so far [as] redemption serves the consummation," this may be "turn[ed] round dialectically" to say that "even the Fall serves creation's consummation." Moltmann then goes on to cite, and ascribe universal meaning to, Joseph's words in Gen 50:20, " 'You meant evil against me, but God meant it for good.' " (Cf. 8.3n31 and 8.3n35 below, where I refer to Moltmann's apparent ontologising of evil and suffering.)

[113] This unity by no means precludes diversity and distinction. Thus in CoG, 307, Moltmann writes: "it is neither necessary for the world to dissolve into God, as pantheism says, nor for God to be dissolved in the world, as atheism maintains. God remains God, and the world remains creation. Through their mutual indwellings, they remain *unmingled and undivided*, for God lives in creation in a God-like way, and the world lives in God in a world-like way." My emphases. This concept of *perichoresis* would, no doubt, be extended to the relation between humans and other creatures.

explicitly rejects.[114] Glory cannot be reduced to the hidden grace of history. In this he differs from Hegel. But in terms of the *structure* of their thought, the difference may not be so decisive.[115] Earlier in the same book, Moltmann's own philosophy of reconciliation—albeit an eschatological reconciliation—is evident when he writes,

---

[114] See CoG, 329 where he finds this "Hegelian" notion also in the theology of Karl Barth's "theology of reconciliation." 'Contradictory/harmony' monism (see 0.6 above) is certainly a typical position that can be exemplified in a non-eschatological way. John Valk's study of Eliade's work, cited in n. 161 below, is a case in point. For Moltmann, the 'hidden harmony' that now exists is at best a momentary presence (see 3.5.1–3.5.3) of what is to come when God is all in all.

[115] Cf. Calvin Seerveld's comments on the structural similarity between the thought of Hegel and Ernst Cassirer in "The Pedagogical Strength of a Christian Methodology in Philosophical Historiography," 298–99. Cf. 2.1n11 above. It may be that the dominant reading of Hegel errs in being too teleological (or too quick to assume Hegel's *telos* is closed) with the result that he appears more totalising that he really is. If Hegel is read in a more eschatological vein (see, e.g., John F. Hoffmeyer, *The Advent of Freedom: The Presence of the Future in Hegel's Logic* (Cranbury, NJ: Associated University Presses, 1994), commented on in 5.1n45 below), the affinity between Moltmann and Hegel with respect to the structure of their thought is naturally accentuated. But this kind of reading is not a prerequisite. On Moltmann's 'Hegelianism', see Anne V. Primavesi, "The Cross and the Rose: The Interaction of Lutheran Paradox and Hegelian Dialectic Exemplified in the Theology of Jürgen Moltmann" (PhD diss., Heythrop College, University of London, 1987), especially 268–89, a title inspired by the sympathetic engagement with Hegel (and Luther) found in Jürgen Moltmann, "The 'Rose in the Cross of the Present': Towards an Understanding of the Church in Modern Society," in *Hope and Planning*, by Jürgen Moltmann, trans. Margaret Clarkson (London: SCM Press, 1971), 130–54. See also William J. Hill, *The Trinity as a Mystery of Salvation* (Washington, DC: Catholic University of America Press, 1982), 166–75. The decisive and pervasive influence on Moltmann of his neo-Hegelian teacher Hans Joachim Iwand is discussed in M. Douglas Meeks, *Origins of the Theology of Hope* (Philadelphia: Fortress Press, 1974), 30–41. Hegel himself is also explicitly discussed in this context and is referred to frequently in this important study. It is certainly possible to argue, against some of his critics, that Moltmann differs significantly from Hegel. See, for example, Siu-Kwong Tang, *God's History in the Theology of Jürgen Moltmann* (Bern: Peter Lang, 1996). I only wish to point to a similarity at the level of the structure of their theo-cosmologies/cosmogonies. Richard J. Bauckham (the supervisor of Tang's 1994 PhD dissertation at the University of St. Andrews) in his *Moltmann: Messianic Theology in the Making* (Basingstoke, UK: Marshall, Morgan, and Scott, 1987), 107 makes an observation about Moltmann's view of the Trinity that holds, I suggest, for his thought more generally, when he writes, "His trinitarian dialectic is certainly Hegelian in *structure* [he cites CrG, 246 and CrG, 253–54 *inter alia*], but not necessarily in *content*." My emphases. I have also commented on Moltmann's historicised Neoplatonism in 2.2 and 3.6 above. Cf. 6.3 and 6.4 below. On the connection between Hegel and Neoplatonic thinking, see Hans-Georg Gadamer, *Hegel's Dialectic: Five Hermeneutical Studies*, trans. P. Christopher (New Haven, CT: Yale University Press, 1976), 21.

In the end all things will have worked together for good (Rom. 8.29), even things which have made us inconsolable, and which we shall never understand.[116]

In relation to the eschaton as 'opposed' to history, therefore, there appears to be no ultimate antithesis between good and evil.[117] Redemption amounts to the eschatological re-direction of reality, the reintegration of diversity and the overcoming of self-isolation in the openness of God. Nothing is excluded. Thus in another remarkable passage, Moltmann writes,

> [I]f hate is really love-gone-wrong, if superstition is distorted faith, and if sin is a perverted relationship to God, then—odd though it may sound—it is not only human beings who must be redeemed from sin; the energies of sin themselves have to be redeemed too: hate must be changed into love, superstition into faith and despair into hope. Although it is always only sinners who are justified, never their sins, yet it is not only sinners who are redeemed. In this sense sins themselves are also redeemed and put right.[118]

The monistic character of this claim is perhaps best appreciated if we compare it to an alternative (non-monistic) understanding.[119] What if we were to affirm the cosmic scope of redemption and eschatological transformation (with Moltmann) while still insisting that evil *per se* cannot be redeemed? In other words, what if we were to claim that we are *redeemed from* evil and set free *from* sin, thus experiencing a liberation that (given the profound effect humanity has, and is called to have, on history in the widest sense) has universal, cosmic significance?

This vision of being finally 'separated' from evil, it could be claimed, honours the genuine insight of dualistic theologies, whilst avoiding the serious mistake—the dualistic error—of reading the evil that is destined for destruction into the very fabric, the very possibility and actuality, of (some aspects of) reality. To hope for a future for God's good creation as a whole and in all its dimensions is ultimately incompatible with dualism. To admit the full reality of evil as that which ought not to be while denying that evil a future of any kind in God's future for the world is ultimately incompatible with monism. Contrary to

---

[116] CoG, 85.
[117] Cf. the discussion of the eschatological resolution of what is historically irresolvable in CrG, 178 in 1.1 above.
[118] GC, 234.
[119] What follows in this and the next paragraph is a view that would represent my own thinking. In the next (i.e., third) paragraph, I anticipate questions that could be put to that position by Moltmann. I would reject Moltmann's monism but I appreciate the way his thought can help us move beyond dualism. The kind of (covenantal) universalism that I (re-)articulate in 5.0 below, and develop in the chapters that follow is non-monistic in the way it seeks to honour the freedom of the will. But with Moltmann, I resist equating 'freedom' (and the 'freedom' or 'duality' of the will) with 'autonomy'. This is explored in 6.1 below. I comment further on the monism discussed here in 8.2 below.

Moltmann, one might claim, it is precisely because our sins and our evils are to be "put right" that sin and evil cannot and will not be "redeemed."

How might Moltmann reply to this line of thought? I think it is highly likely that he would reject this view of evil and its future as too centred in human sin. The logic of his system, I suggest, would invite us to probe the link between the "energies" of sin and those heavenly potencies that the biblical tradition symbolises in personal terms. As should be clear from Moltmann's comments on the fall of the angels in the *coelum naturae*, to claim that demonic powers come into being only as creation is pulled into the vortex of *human* evil would be dismissed by Moltmann as "negative hubris."[120] Furthermore, if these are actually impersonal "forces," as Moltmann seems to suggest,[121] his position raises the question of whether seeing the duality of the *will* as the focus of redemption is ultimately too anthropocentric? Can insisting on a redemption *from* sin do justice to the cosmic nature of reconciliation? Instead of (or in addition to) a (conscious) turning *from* evil to good, must we not (also) speak of a turning *of* evil *to*, and in that sense *into*, good?

The implications are significant. If we focus on the human choice between good and evil, the possibility that a Final Judgment might have a dual outcome comes to the fore. If we place (relativise) the human will within a cosmic reconciliation, then 'universal' salvation (in both senses of the term) becomes more plausible.

If there are monistic, Neoplatonic, and Hegelian tendencies in the structure of Moltmann's thought that would lend themselves to a universalistic position—and by now I trust that this is clear enough—it is important to stress that there is absolutely nothing to suggest the reconciliation of all things to God is an automatic and in that sense necessary or inevitable process in his understanding. Creation has no 'natural' impetus towards "glory": quite the opposite! The forgiveness of sins, even if that includes an overcoming of primordial energies incapable of repentance, only occurs because of the cross and Christ's descent into Hell. It cannot even come about by divine fiat but requires God's action—and passion—in history. In Moltmann's words,

> If, now, God's 'other', the world, becomes estranged from God and contradicts him instead of corresponding to him, while God, notwithstanding, desires to remain true to his creation and hence to himself, then God must empty himself into the estrangement of this world and take upon himself the absolute pain of

---

[120] I argue at length for this deliberately anthropocentric claim in my "The Call of Wisdom/The Voice of the Serpent: Towards a Canonical Approach to the Tree of Knowledge," *Christian Scholar's Review* 31, no. 1 (Fall 2001): 31–57. For the language of "negative hubris," see CoG, 90.

[121] This seems to be the case in WJC, 106: "These demons are apparently forces, conceived of in personal terms . . . . Even if we do not imagine these forces of destruction in personal terms, to accept them permits us to interpret phenomena . . . ."

dichotomy in order to bring about the reconciliation of what is separated from him.[122]

Moltmann's universalism is thus a 'universalism of the cross' (as discussed in 1.4.1 above and to be explored further in 4.3.1 below). Just as the Creator God makes way, in the *passio Dei*, for all that is to happen in history, so the crucified Christ, in/as the *passion of God*, descends into Hell that God and creation may be all in all. Divine suffering marks the 'turn-return' from eternity to time and from history to eschaton. In Moltmann's theology, the 'crucial' transition from 'nature' to 'glory' may only take place in 'grace'.

4.3 Possible Objections, Possible Answers

If grace is central to most theologies seeking to be faithful to the Christian gospel, the claim that this grace savingly embraces all people is widely seen as problematic or even unacceptable. One way to appreciate the specific form of universalism that Moltmann advocates is to analyse how well he might be able to respond to some of the typical objections that are brought against the idea that all people will experience God's salvation. Before proceeding with our examination of the transition from nature to glory in Moltmann's position, therefore, we shall pause to look at those objections. This will provide a useful context within which to assess the strengths and weaknesses of his proposals. It will also help us determine whether his position might earn widespread respect as a serious Christian option.

Universalists who wish their views to be taken seriously within what we might call 'mainstream' Protestant theology[123] have to contend with the fact that there is no theological theory (theology) of salvation that is not itself prone to significant criticism from within that mainstream. Among the numerous soteriologies on offer, there are two main approaches that need to be distinguished if we are to set the stage for the present discussion. These we can label as 'Calvinist' and 'Arminian' (with John Calvin and Jacobus Arminius

---

[122] CoG, 327. On the importance for Moltmann of realisation in history, see also WJC, 205 as cited in n. 39 above.

[123] By "mainstream," I mean little more than all those views that their advocates would wish to be recognised as 'mainstream'. For some, the preferred term is 'historic Christianity' or 'theological orthodoxy'. Recognising this as clearly definable or normative or both is irrelevant to my purpose here. Whether this stream is wide or narrow, there are a number of positions within it. None of these positions are regarded, even by their advocates, as providing the banks for that stream (by which I mean the limits of what is acceptable if a theology is to be judged as belonging to 'historic Christianity' or the like). I specifically refer to Protestantism not only because Moltmann and I are Protestants but in order to reject the far narrower, neo-patristic, and (arguably) ahistorically 'ecumenical' understanding of the 'mainstream' exemplified, for example, in Oden, *The Transforming Power of Grace*.

seen as merely exemplifying certain general tendencies).[124] One of the biggest challenges that universalists face is that it is extremely difficult to engage with

---

[124] In what follows, I will (for the sake of the present discussion) run the risk of discussing two 'typical' positions largely in abstraction from the claims and counter-claims of actual theologians (trusting that abstraction per se need not distort). For an account that captures many of the nuances and complexities that my 'high altitude' view cannot bring into focus, see the lucid discussion of Jewett, *Election and Predestination*. For a brief, helpful overview, see also Gregory A. Boyd and Paul R. Eddy, *Across the Spectrum: Understanding Issues in Evangelical Theology* (Grand Rapids, MI: Baker, 2002), chap. 9.

Considerable evidence in favour of the view that a great deal of the history of theology prior to (and to some extent at least, subsequent to) the Reformation has been characterised by a 'synergism' that can be located 'between' these two Protestant 'extremes', even as Arminian and Calvinist theologies can be seen to have their precursors down the ages, can be gleaned from Oden, *The Transforming Power of Grace*. For Oden's explicit endorsement of "synergy" as a grace-empowered working or co-operating with God, see *The Transforming Power of Grace*, 52.

Oden's position here is very close to Zachary J. Hayes's portrayal of Roman Catholic theology, in "The Purgatorial View," 113–17. Leonardo Boff's important study (which is so different in tone from Oden's) also sees contemporary Catholic theology as mediating between two extremes. In *Liberating Grace*, 15, Boff states that "The chief problem in discussions about grace lies in the effort to maintain the proper balance between the two poles involved: God and human beings. Grace is essentially encounter and relationship. It is God communicating himself and human beings opening themselves up. When we maintain this polarity then we can properly ponder and talk about grace." In his diagram on the following page (16), Boff suggests that, in contrast to the polarisation between God-centred Greek theology and human-centred Latin theology, the correct polarity is maintained by de Lubac, Rahner, Guardini, and Segundo.

In this context, Boff identifies "synergism" with Molina, an exemplar of Latin theology. We should note, however, that this term may be used in different ways. Van Harvey's discussion in "Synergism," in *A Handbook of Theological Terms*, 233, notes that this comes in various forms "ranging from Pelagianism to the more subtle formulations characteristic of Roman Catholicism." Boff's own position, like that of Hayes, might be described as 'synergistic' in this light. It is just such a "subtle" form that Oden sees as representing Christian theology at its ecumenical-traditional best.

Although a good case could be made, with the help of the many works cited favourably by Oden (and Boff), for seeing a grace-empowered "synergy" (for want of a better term) as at least approximating (however inadequately) to a 'covenantal' *alternative* to both Arminianism and Calvinism in their classic forms, it should be noted that Oden himself (*The Transforming Power of Grace*, 152) sees the classic Arminian theologians of the Remonstrance as in line with an ancient ecumenical consensus that avoids the extremes (explored in chaps. 6–8) of Pelagius and the late Augustine (and their respective followers). This very different case for what exemplifies an authentic 'third way' illustrates how difficult it is to make generalizations in this area as the various positions are at odds about how one should describe the lie of the land. Thus while many Calvinists would gladly acknowledge the links between Calvinism and Augustine's mature thought, it is also fair to say that they would see far less difference between Pelagius (Pelagianism) and Arminius (Arminianism) than Oden. Thus Michael

and respond to 'Calvinist' and 'Arminian' concerns and priorities at the same time.[125]

Historically, the five points of Calvinism—known by the acronym TULIP, which stands for: total depravity, unconditional election, limited atonement, irresistible grace, and the perseverance of the saints—were crystallised at the Synod of Dort in 1618 as a reply to and refutation of a five-point manifesto called the 'Remonstrance', which was put forward by the followers of Arminius.

James Packer claims that the theology of this manifesto stemmed from two basic principles: "first, that divine sovereignty is not compatible with human freedom, nor therefore with human responsibility; second, that ability limits obligation." From these principles, Packer continues, two deductions were drawn: "first, that since the Bible regards faith as a free and responsible human act, it cannot be caused by God, but is exercised independently of him; second,

---

Horton, in his *For Calvinism* (Grand Rapids, MI: Zondervan, 2011), 33–34 suggests that in the final analysis, despite its non-Pelagian emphasis on "prevenient" grace (as both enabling and preceding any human response to God), Arminianism's endorsement of "synergism" makes it fundamentally indistinguishable from "Semi-Pelagianism," even though he also notes (198n10) Roger E. Olson's claim, in his *Arminian Theology: Myths and Realities* (Downers Grove, IL: InterVarsity Press, 2006), 18, that "Contrary to confused critics, classical Arminianism is neither Pelagian nor semi-Pelagian! But it is *synergistic*." Horton's emphasis. (Olson's original reads: "But it *is* synergistic.")

Clearly, generalisations about the Arminian-Calvinist debate (including my own) inevitably reflect the position one takes on and in that debate. (Boff, for example, as a Catholic theologian, virtually ignores it, even though he is grappling with issues that are central to it.) That said, generalisations—especially if we pay attention to the way in which they are so often contested—do serve to draw our attention to key issues.

[125] I trust that the dangers of generalisation in the following discussion will be outweighed by the way these considerations help us evaluate perceived strengths and weaknesses in Moltmann's position. Calvinist works that exemplify the tendencies I identify whilst engaging Arminian objections, include: Horton, *For Calvinism*, Jewett, *Election and Predestination* (both mentioned in the previous note), and two works by G.C. Berkouwer, *Divine Election* (Grand Rapids, MI: Eerdmans, 1960) and *Faith and Justification* (Grand Rapids, MI: Eerdmans, 1954). For comparable Arminian engagement, see: Roger E. Olson, *Against Calvinism* (Grand Rapids, MI: Zondervan, 2011), John A. Sanders, *No Other Name: An Investigation into the Destiny of the Unevangelized* (Grand Rapids, MI: Eerdmans, 1992), and two works edited by Clark H. Pinnock, *Grace Unlimited* (Minneapolis, MN: Bethany, 1975) and *The Grace of God and the Will of Man* (1989; repr., Minneapolis, MN: Bethany, 1995). Historical studies of Calvinist and Arminian soteriologies in their classic forms, include: Olson, *Arminian Theology* (cited in the previous note) and two works by Richard A. Muller, *Christ and the Decree: Christology and Predestination in Reformed Theology from Calvin to Perkins* (Grand Rapids, MI: Baker, 1988) and *God, Creation, and Providence in the Thought of Jacob Arminius: Sources and Directions of Scholastic Protestantism in the Era of Early Orthodoxy* (Grand Rapids, MI: Baker, 1991).

that since the Bible regards faith as obligatory on the part of all who hear the gospel, ability to believe must be universal."[126]

Packer summarises the five points of the Arminian manifesto and the corresponding five points of the Calvinist response as follows:[127]

Arminianism's Declarations:
1. Man is never so completely corrupted by sin that he cannot savingly believe the gospel when it is put before him.
2. Man is never so completely controlled by God that he cannot reject the gospel.
3. God's election of those who will be saved is prompted by His foreseeing that they will of their own accord believe.
4. Christ's death did not ensure the salvation of anyone, for it did not secure the gift of faith; rather it created the possibility of salvation for everyone if they believe.
5. It rests with believers to keep themselves in a state of grace by keeping up their faith; those who fall here fall away and are lost.

Calvinism's Responses:
1. Fallen man in his natural state lacks all power to believe the gospel and the law despite all external inducements.
2. God's election is a free, sovereign, unconditional choice of sinners, [who are] to be redeemed by Christ, given faith, and brought to glory.
3. The redeeming work of Christ had as its end and goal the salvation of the elect.
4. The work of the Holy Spirit in bringing men to faith never fails to achieve its object.
5. Believers are kept in faith and grace by the unconquerable power of God until they come to glory.

As this summary (fair though it is in my judgment) comes from someone who sympathises with the Calvinist position, it will be helpful to briefly examine the control beliefs listed in an important work in the area of soteriology by John Sanders, as these exemplify an 'Arminian' perspective in the broad (heuristic) way in which I am using that term.[128] Sanders writes,

---

[126] James I. Packer, "Introductory Essay," in John Owen, *The Death of Death in the Death of Christ* (1648; repr., Edinburgh: The Banner of Truth, 1959), 3.

[127] For the following, see Packer, "Introductory Essay," 3–4. I have adopted the minor changes in Neal Punt, *Unconditional Good News: Towards an Understanding of Biblical Universalism* (Grand Rapids, MI: Eerdmans, 1980), 66–67. Because I am primarily interested in how Arminian and Calvinist theologies shape contemporary concerns, I have not referred to the original seventeenth century formulations in what follows.

[128] In what follows, for example, there is nothing to correspond to the third Arminian declaration. 'Arminians' in the broad sense would disagree amongst themselves on the topic of election and foreknowledge. On this point, Arminius can be seen to be re-formulating certain 'Calvinist' concerns that are of lesser importance to many 'Arminians' in the broad sense. Sanders notes his own departure from classic

My treatment of the materials in this work is . . . influenced by [1] my belief in the substitutionary atonement of Jesus for the sins of every human being, [2] my understanding of sin as rebellion against God that affects every area of our lives, [3] my belief that God desires to redeem every human being who has ever lived, and [4] my belief that an "act of faith" is necessary for appropriating salvation into our lives.[129]

If we compare these affirmations to the 'five points' of Calvinism, then the second might be seen as corresponding to belief in total depravity, though many Calvinists would find the latter to be incompatible with Sanders' fourth affirmation and might therefore question what is meant here by sin (merely) "affect[ing]" our natural capacities. Sanders' final affirmation might also be seen to conflict with belief in unconditional election and irresistible grace. Certainly this charge would be made if he had spoken of 'attaining' and not just "appropriating" salvation here. The clearest point of disagreement, however, is evident in Sanders' first and third affirmations as these unambiguously rule out belief in a Calvinism's third point: limited atonement.

It is probably fair to say that to critics of five-point Calvinism, limited atonement—the idea that the cross atones for the sins of the elect and not the sins of humanity as a whole—would be considered to be its weakest element.[130] On this point, non-Calvinists tend to be extremely confident that the Bible is on their side. Conversely, critics of the Arminian system would probably cite its

---

Arminianism in Christopher A. Hall and John Sanders, "Does God Know Your Next Move? Pt. 1," *Christianity Today* 45, no. 7 (May 21, 2001): 38–45, especially 43 and "Does God Know Your Next Move? Pt. 2," *Christianity Today* 45, no. 8 (June 11, 2001): 50–56, especially 55. (Cf. Christopher A. Hall and John Sanders, *Does God Have a Future? A Debate on Divine Providence* (Grand Rapids, MI: Baker, 2003), 19 and 34–35. This work reproduces and extends the initial debate. The comparison between "classical theism," "freewill theism" (Arminianism), and "open theism" set out in the chart in *Does God Have a Future?*, 142–43 is a welcome addition.) In referring to this departure, Sanders speaks for fellow advocates of "openness theism" (a modification of "free will theism") as articulated in Clark H. Pinnock et al., *The Openness of God: A Biblical Challenge to the Traditional Understanding of God* (Downers Grove, IL: InterVarsity Press, 1994). Three of that work's five authors, Clark H. Pinnock, Richard Rice, and Sanders himself, contributed to the 'Arminian' collection, *The Grace of God and the Will of Man*, ed. Clark H. Pinnock. For a work that (in effect) makes much of the third Arminian declaration as a vital expression of an ancient ecumenical consensus, see Oden, *The Transforming Power of Grace*, chap. 7 et passim.

[129] Sanders, *No Other Name*, 32. My enumeration.

[130] See for example, Donald M. Lake, "He Died for All: The Universal Dimensions of the Atonement," in *Grace Unlimited*, ed. Clark H. Pinnock (Minneapolis, MN: Bethany, 1975), 31–50, I. Howard Marshall, "Universal Grace and Atonement in the Pastoral Epistles," in *The Grace of God and the Will of Man*, ed. Clark H. Pinnock (1989; repr., Minneapolis, MN: Bethany, 1995), 51–69, and Terry L. Miethe, "The Universal Power of the Atonement," in *The Grace of God and the Will of Man* (1989; repr., Minneapolis, MN: Bethany, 1995), 71–96.

belief that the cross merely makes salvation *possible* as its weakest and most biblically untenable assertion.[131]

While a universalist position can avoid both of these perceived weaknesses, this is not enough to gain it a hearing in the Protestant mainstream. Because the Calvinist and Arminian positions are so firmly established, universalism (of whatever form) must not only defend itself in the face of its *own* perceived weaknesses (including its *prime facie* conflict with certain biblical texts); it must also be seen as capable of avoiding the pitfalls of each of these (generally) non-universalist theological systems at the same time.

Universalists who do not wish their views to be dismissed without serious engagement, therefore, face the challenge of developing and articulating a position that cannot be accused of *either* subordinating the will of God to a human 'freedom' that is actually autonomy *or* subjecting the human will to a divine 'freedom' that is actually heteronomy. Theological proposals that sound to Calvinist ears as if we can figure out how God 'must' behave will be highly suspect no matter how 'loving' God is said to be. Accounts of salvation that sound to Arminian ears as though creaturely existence is being overpowered will be unacceptable no matter how much this is said to be liberating or 'for our own good'. A soteriology is required that is neither humanistic nor dehumanising, that simultaneously honours both nature and grace. Theologically speaking, universalists must reconcile God and creation!

The issue here is not how a universalist position can be formulated that could command universal assent—that would be an impossible ideal—but how universalists might gain widespread respect and interest. To see how the crossfire of Arminian and Calvinist claims and counter-claims makes this so difficult, let us consider the following. Paul Fiddes has made the helpful observation that what I am calling 'convinced' universalist positions "may be based on one or more of the following considerations:"

> [1] that the soul, being created from God, has a natural inclination to return to its origin; [2] that for any created beings to remain in rebellion against their creator would be a defeat of the power of God's love; [3] that for created persons to have the power of choosing or declining their own salvation would be to make them into God themselves; and [4] that the representative nature of Christ's atonement means that all humanity must be included within it (unless one were to take Calvin's view of an atonement limited to an elect few).[132]

How might these proposals fare in the Protestant 'mainstream'? And how do they relate to the specific form of universalism that Moltmann wishes to advocate?

---

[131] See, for example, Horton, *For Calvinism*, 90–98; Packer, "Introductory Essay," 9–10; and Loraine Boettner, *The Reformed Doctrine of Predestination* (1932; repr., Phillipsburg, NJ: Presbyterian and Reformed, 1980), 172–76. Horton, in *For Calvinism*, 80, notes that this amounts to a "limited" view of atonement, admitting that with respect to both extent and efficacy, this is a charge that only universalists can avoid.

[132] Fiddes, *The Promised End*, 194. My enumeration.

To begin with, we may confidently conclude that the first line of argument would be rejected by both Arminian and Calvinist theologians as incompatible with the universal sinfulness of humanity (whether or not the language of total depravity is used). In this respect, it is outside the 'mainstream' altogether.[133] It is also significant that it is not present in Moltmann's theology. Whatever "return to [the] [O]rigin" may occur in 'glory' is not "natural."

The second assertion would receive a mixed reaction. To the Arminian, the possibility of "defeat" or lack of success is inherent to the nature of love, divine or human. Fiddes (himself a "hopeful" universalist) fairly represents this kind of response. Not only must we "tak[e] seriously the freedom God has granted to creation," but we must also allow "to God the humility of being willing to be rejected." This, he says, is a dimension of "the tragedy within the victory of love."[134]

For the Calvinist, this second universalist assertion is basically acceptable if it is applied to the elect. For them, God's grace is irresistible. For the non-elect or reprobate to "remain in rebellion," however, is not a defeat of God's love. It is either a victory for his justice or its meaning (like its origin) remains shrouded in the inscrutability of the divine will.[135]

The second assertion, in as much as it advocates a heteronomic view of divine Love, is also not representative of Moltmann's thinking. Fiddes finds this claim in the position advocated by John A.T. Robinson.[136] In 1.4.2 above, I noted that what Moltmann finds attractive in Robinson's universalism is his rather different claim (inspired by Origen) that so long as one sinner remains in Hell, Christ remains on the cross. In response, Moltmann comments, "God will be all in all, not because God's love *overcomes* the very last believer, but because the shadows of Christ's cross dissolve hell."[137] This distinction is related to Moltmann's antipathy towards seeing salvation as a force of destiny. His opposition to autonomy (also discussed in 1.4.2) is in the name of freedom.

The problem with the third assertion is that it is really a *general* criticism of non-Calvinist soteriologies and so cannot function as a *specific* argument for universal salvation. For the Calvinist, nothing is being said that is not already self-evident. For the Arminian, by contrast, what is being asserted clashes so uncompromisingly with a central conviction that it will seem patently false: the power to choose is not the power to play *God*; it is inherent to being *human*.

---

[133] Fiddes, in *The Promised End*, 194n22, cites as his exemplar here John Hick, *Death and Eternal Life* (London: Collins, 1976), 250–59.

[134] Fiddes, *The Promised End*, 195.

[135] On the former, see, e.g., Boettner, *The Reformed Doctrine of Predestination*, 269–73. On the latter, see, e.g., Jewett, *Election And Predestination*, 133–39.

[136] Fiddes, in *The Promised End*, 194n23, cites Robinson, *In The End, God*, chaps. 10–11.

[137] CoG, 372n221 as cited in 1.4.2 above. My emphases. Here he does not sympathise with Robinson's claim that the divine love "must win."

It is significant that Moltmann is cited as exemplifying this position.[138] In my discussion of the relevant passage in 1.3 above, I noted the way Moltmann consciously sides with Augustine rather than Pelagius, and with Luther and Calvin rather than Erasmus in this context. There is no doubting the basically 'Reformed' character of his thought. But Moltmann is not defending God's prerogatives in the face of an all-too-human hubris, as Fiddes' formulation may seem to suggest. The issue is the human danger of practical atheism and the pastoral observation that assurance of salvation cannot be rooted in our own power and freedom. Even if Moltmann's perspective reflects Reformed sensitivities here, the ways in which he also pushes beyond the Calvinist-Arminian polarity (as discussed in 1.4.2) must not thereby be forgotten.

Finally we come to the issue of the atonement. To persuade the five-point Calvinist that the atonement is unlimited (or that all human beings are elect in Christ), is (at the level of logic) all that is required to make a compelling case for universal salvation.[139] For the Arminian (in the heuristic sense in which I am using the term), the atonement is, in contrast to the third point of Calvinism, already 'unlimited': Christ has died for the sins of the whole world (whatever may be believed about the connection between election and salvation). But because the grace that is made available through the cross is not irresistible, the atonement may (in effect) be limited by our lack of faith. The non-universalist Calvinist needs to be persuaded to change his/her view of God's sovereign purposes as these are revealed in and enacted through the cross. The non-universalist Arminian needs to be persuaded that our lack of faith will not thwart God's desire—so evident in Christ's crucifixion—to save all people from their sins.

Alone of all the possible bases for universalism that Fiddes cites, the idea of an unlimited atonement in which all people are represented in Christ's death and resurrection emerges as indispensable to Moltmann's position. We shall therefore now turn our attention to the way this is presented in Moltmann's theology of the cross. But if an unlimited atonement is necessary if one is to construct a viable universalist soteriology, it is insufficient for a universalism that wishes to command widespread respect. In what follows, therefore, we shall also pay significant attention to the nature of human and divine freedom to

---

[138] The reference, in Fiddes, *The Promised End*, 194n24, is to Moltmann, "The Logic of Hell,"45.

[139] Thus Boettner, in *The Reformed Doctrine of Predestination*, 174 writes, "Evangelicalism with a universal atonement leads to universal salvation." An important work by a universalist Calvinist is Jan Bonda, *The One Purpose of God: An Answer to the Doctrine of Eternal Punishment*, trans. Reinder Bruinsma (Grand Rapids, MI: Eerdmans, 1998). Bonda, in his preface (xxiv–xxv), notes the encouragement he received from Reformed theologians Hendrikus Berkhof and Jan Veenhof. Cf. the near-universalism of Punt, *Unconditional Good News*, evident in his subtitle: *Towards an Understanding of Biblical Universalism.*

see if Moltmann's theology might be able to address fundamental Arminian and Calvinist concerns.[140]

4.3.1 Universalism of the Cross

"[T]he theology of the cross," writes Moltmann in his early work *The Crucified God*, "is the true Christian universalism. There is no distinction here, and there cannot be any more distinctions. All are sinners without distinction, and all will be made righteous without any merit on their part by his grace which has come to pass in Christ Jesus (Rom. 3.24)." Christ's atonement for our sins is truly unlimited. That "God's Son has died for all," says Moltmann, "must undermine, remove and destroy the things which mark men out as elect and non-elect."[141]

If the theological systems that distinguish between elect and reprobate are among those "things" the cross "must undermine," some may wonder, what about God's sovereign right to choose those whom he will save? In traditional Calvinist theology, election (which in other theologies may refer simply to God's choice to make certain people his agents in history[142]) is closely related

---

[140] In 4.3.1–4.3.3 below on the theology of the cross, the nature of God, and the nature of human freedom, I am taking up the topics of 1.4.1, 1.4.2, and 1.4.4 above. The topics addressed in 1.4.3 and 1.4.5, which relate to universalism's own perceived weaknesses (rather than those allegedly shared with non-universalist Arminian or Calvinist theologies), will be taken up in 7.1 and 7.2 below, where we will consider the strength of universalism's biblical foundations and examine whether it necessarily undermines the cry for justice.

[141] CrG, 194–95. In the light of the full discussion of CoG, 235–55, the 'universalist' significance of Moltmann's earlier writings can now be easily grasped. But for earlier commentators, such as Stephen N. Williams, in his *Jürgen Moltmann: A Critical Introduction* (Leicester, UK: Religious and Theological Studies Fellowship, 1987), 24–26, the nature and even the reality of Moltmann's universalism was a real question. (This study is reprinted with some updating as "Jürgen Moltmann: A Critical Introduction," in *Getting Your Bearings: Engaging with Contemporary Theologians*, ed. Philip Duce and Daniel Strange (Leicester, UK: Apollos, 2003), 75–124. For comments on Moltmann's universalism, see pp. 102–103.)

[142] Van A. Harvey's article "election," in *A Handbook of Theological Terms*, 76–77 though brief, is characteristically lucid and insightful, capturing this breadth far better than treatments that subsume "election" under 'predestination' and 'salvation'.

Walter Vogels in *God's Universal Covenant: A Biblical Study* (1979; repr., Ottawa: University of Ottawa Press, 1986), 8, writes, "[T]he election of Israel implies that other nations, other peoples, are called. . . . [E]lection is not a privilege to profit from, but a privilege which implies service to be rendered." This allows us to see election not as 'election to salvation' such that the non-elect are not (to be) saved but as 'election to embody and mediate salvation' and thus be a light to the Gentiles. In the process the elect will hopefully experience the salvation that is on offer to all people. (In 8.3n32 below, I indicate that this is the view of election that I would advocate and suggest a connection with a particular reading of the primordial "let there be light" of Gen 1:3 that is discussed in 6.4, including 6.4n124, below.)

to predestination, understood as the eternal decree of God that results in the salvation of some (the 'elect') and that directly or indirectly results in the damnation of others.[143] As we have seen in 1.4.1 above, Moltmann sees all attempts to deduce whether there is a double or single outcome to the Final Judgment from a doctrine of predestination as falling into the error of "answer[ing] questions about the end with the presuppositions of the beginning." "[T]o eschatological questions," Moltmann is convinced, we must provide "christological answers."[144] The doctrine of predestination too must be brought before the cross of Christ.

None of this is meant to deny God's sovereign choice. The issue, for Moltmann, is how that choice may be discerned. In response to the doctrine of predestination in its supralapsarian form, for example, Moltmann notes that in this position, "God's decision ... is not already revealed in Christ, nor is it revealed in the gospel. It is revealed provisionally in history, in faith and disobedience, but finally only at the Last Judgment."[145] For Moltmann, however, the Christ event is the very locus of revelation.[146] It is here that God's

---

[143] There are debates within traditional Calvinist theology about whether God's choice or decree is a response to the Fall (infralapsarianism) or not (supralapsarianism). 'Double predestination' is the view that election is unto salvation and damnation. 'Single predestination' is the view that the damned are simply not elected unto salvation and are thus merely passed over. I have used the terms 'direct' and 'indirect' to refer to this latter distinction. For the nuances and internal diversity of Reformed theology, one might consult Donald K. McKim, ed., *The Westminster Handbook to Reformed Theology* (Louisville, KY: Westminster John Knox Press, 2001), especially the articles on "Decree(s) of God" by Philip C. Holtrop (54–56), "Infralapsarianism" by John M. Frame (121–22), "Predestination" by Dewey D. Wallace Jr. (180–82), and "Supralapsarianism" by William Klempa (214–15).

[144] CoG, 246 as cited in 1.4.1 above.

[145] CoG, 246 as cited in 1.4.1 above.

[146] Thus in TH, 84, Moltmann writes, "Christian theology speaks of 'revelation', when on the ground of the Easter appearances of the risen Lord it perceives and proclaims the identity of the risen one with the crucified one." That cross and resurrection are held together in the Christ event means that its revelation has a promissory, open-ended character, on which see TH, 84–94. But the cross remains a touchstone for our hope. This is closely related to the idea that revelation must not be identified with the Greek notion of epiphany; God is revealed in his opposite. On this epistemological principle, which runs throughout Moltmann's corpus, see TH, 57 and, with specific reference to the theology of the cross: CrG, 25–28, the sympathetic reference to Luther's notion that God is known *sub contrario* in EiT, 88 and especially EiT, 173 (in the light of his extended discussion of dialectical knowing in EiT, 169–73). See also n. 161 below on the "alchemy" of the cross.

Sympathising with Luther, Moltmann writes in EiT, 173, "The place where God encounters us, the *locus theologicus*, is the God-forsaken misery of the cross." His italics. In EiT, 62–63, Moltmann speaks of an eschatological revelation of God's total self that "in the history of the non-divine world would destroy that world." Thus in history God "reveals himself through the consonance of promise and fulfilment, for in that consonance his faithfulness is revealed, and faithfulness is his essential nature. . . . According to the New Testament, the raising of the crucified Christ is the final and

sovereign will (and true nature) have been revealed. To look elsewhere, this side of the kingdom of glory, is to fail to practice Christian theology.

Although Moltmann's christocentrism gives him a strong affinity with Karl Barth's view of election[147]—in which it is Christ who is the elect and reprobate One in whom God's intention to elect all people is revealed—his arguments focus less on a christo-*logical* reworking of abstract doctrinal positions than on directing our attention to what is historically revealed in the sheer Hell of the cross.[148] In a passage from *The Crucified God* that Moltmann himself cites over twenty years later in *The Coming of God*, he writes,

---

eschatological proof of God's essential faithfulness, since this act overcomes the power of death. So with the raising of Christ, the revelation of God's glory begins . . . ." Even this revelation, which in its full eschatological form of face-to-face knowing will presumably be analogous to epiphany, is in the here and now intimately related to Christ. Whether it is the cross that is the *locus theologicus* in Moltmann's theology, or whether it is the resurrection, revelation is Christologically conceived. Cf. Jürgen Moltmann's article, "Cross, Theology of the," in *A New Dictionary of Christian Theology*, ed. Alan Richardson and John Bowden (London: SCM Press, 1983), 135–37.

Moltmann's interest in the theology of creation in his more recent works (especially GC) has not displaced this Christocentric focus, but has been an impetus behind his development of a "cosmic christology" (on which see WJC, chap. 6). In GC, 59, Moltmann refers to "*Theologia revelata*" (cf. 4.2 above) as "the one, single theology in the *regnum gratiae*. It presupposes the self-revelation of God in the history which is determined by human sin and death. Consequently the full concentration and expression of this theology is the *theologia crucis*: in the cross of Christ God reveals himself to the godless." His italics. He continues in GC, 60, "We have defined the theology which is given and possible at the present time as revealed theology; and we have called revealed theology, in the Christian sense, messianic theology. Messianic theology is theology under the presupposition of the presence of the Messiah and the beginning of the messianic era. On this presupposition, the messianic understanding of the world is the true natural theology."

[147] For Moltmann's affinity with Barth's view of election, see CoG, 248–49 for a summary that is sympathetic in tone. For more explicit evidence, see CPS, 374n48 (following the discussion of CPS, 93) where he suggests a supplement to Barth's position and GC, 81 where he says that Barth "picked up" the Reformed doctrine of decrees and "emended [the tradition] brilliantly in his christological doctrine of election."

[148] The difference in theological style between Moltmann and Barth is not absolute. On the one hand, there are features of Barth's argument, such as his appeal to the story of Israel, that need not be regarded as abstract (or doctrinal). For a good overview (which also captures how Christ is both electing and elected), see Jewett, *Election and Predestination*, 48–54. On the other hand, Moltmann has engaged in detailed investigations at the doctrinal level, especially in his early work *Prädestination und Perseveranz: Geschichte und Bedeutung der reformierten Lehre 'de perseverantia sanctorum'* (Neukirchen: Neuchirchener Verlag, 1961). In a more recent article, "Perseverance," in *A New Dictionary of Christian Theology*, ed. Alan Richardson and John Bowden (London: SCM Press, 1983), 441–42, which draws in part on this research, Moltmann notes that "The doctrine of perseverance is the other side of the doctrine of election."

Only if all disaster, forsakenness by God, absolute death, the infinite curse of damnation and sinking into nothingness is in ["is gathered into"] God himself, is community with this God eternal salvation, infinite joy, *indestructible election and divine life*.[149]

It is in focussing on this Christ that we become sure of our election.[150] "It is in christology that the final eschatological questions are decided with the certainty of faith."[151] It is in encountering the revelation of this crucified God that we come to the realisation that "the realistic consequence of the theology of the cross *can only be* the restoration of all things."[152]

While this is an appeal to what Moltmann himself takes to be the very heart of a Christian *experience* of Christ crucified,[153] it is also intended as an *argument* (for those open to this kind of experience). At the theo-logical level, it may be persuasive to the Calvinist given the intimate relationship that is believed to exist between election and salvation. To the Arminian, however, the question remains as to how the gap is to be bridged between God's desire to save that is so powerfully revealed in the cross (which is indeed a descent into Hell) and those of us who remain unmoved (and who—apparently at least—wish to remain in the hells of our own making). In other words, how does this salvation which, in extending from the cross to the entire creation, embraces all people result in all people embracing it?

In answer to this question, Moltmann makes one of his most enigmatic statements (as we have seen in the introduction to chapter 2):

> It is only if a qualitative difference is made between God and human beings that God's decision and human decision can be valued and respected. God's decision 'for us', and our decisions for faith or disbelief no more belong on the same level than do eternity and time. We should be measuring God and the human being by the same yardstick if we were to ask: what, and how much, does God

---

For some of Moltmann's other thoughts on election, see WJC, 16, 35, 339 (on perseverance); CoG, 174; EiT, 97 (on Exod 19:5, correctly translated, *contra* the NIV and NRSV); and, with reference to universal salvation, CoG, 238 and 243–49.

[149] CrG, 246. My emphasis. The phrasing in square brackets comes from the translation in CoG, 252 [cf. *DKG*, 281]. The first edition of *DgG*, 233 has the phrase "in Gott selbst ist" at this point. This is translated in CrG, 246 as "is in God himself," following the second German edition, which is identical at this point. The translation in CoG, 252 follows *DKG*, 281 which cites an unspecified later edition of *DgG*. Here the German phrase is "in Gott selbst *aufgehoben* ist." My emphasis.

[150] On this point, see the appropriation of Luther in "The Logic of Hell," 46 as cited briefly in 1.3 above.

[151] Jürgen Moltmann, "Theology in the Project of the Modern World," in *A Passion for God's Reign: Theology, Christian Learning, and the Christian Self*, by Jürgen Moltmann, Nicholas Wolterstorff, and Ellen T. Charry, ed. Miroslav Volf (Grand Rapids, MI: Eerdmans, 1998), 1–21. Quotation from p. 17.

[152] CoG, 251 as cited in 1.4.1. My emphasis. (In the original, the entire phrase is italicised.)

[153] Cf. his personal reflections in EiT, 3–4.

do for the salvation of human beings, and what, and how much, must human beings do?[154]

This reference to the time-eternity relationship at a crucial point confirms my suggestion that Moltmann's philosophy of time is extremely important for understanding the dynamics of his theology. As I suggested in 2.6 above, the fact that God's decision and our decision do not belong "on the same level" should be understood with reference to a particular correlation between (i) the transcendental-phenomenal distinction and (ii) the distinction between the historical and eschatological directions of time (also the directions of *kenosis* and *theosis*, nature and glory). More specifically, the eternity-time and 'grace-nature'[155] distinction/relationship that Moltmann posits can be interpreted as the contrast/correlation between *transcendental adventus* and *phenomenal futurum*. It is within that context that Moltmann would address Arminian concerns about the eclipse of human freedom in the Calvinist conception of God's salvation.

If Moltmann's statement is read with our previous two chapters in mind, it raises a series of questions: How do God's will and the human will (eternity and time) interrelate in present history? Are they structurally opposed or may they become 'one', thus forming an analogy with aeonic time (cf. 3.5.1)? Is there a "moment" as when eternity is present in time in the here and now when God's will and our will coincide (cf. 3.5.2)? Can our desires, like the sabbath, remain structurally open to what lies beyond (cf. 3.5.3)? Does the human will, like time in its transience, have an inbuilt tendency in the absence of the eschaton to become self-enclosed? Instead of the human will being open to God, must it be opened and thus redeemed before it can respond to him? Will the human decision for salvation only come about when the will, like the storms of history, is "turned around" and taken up into the divine will?

If we examine Moltmann's writings with these questions in mind, we find two important, apparently contrasting, motifs. Firstly, the transition from sin to salvation that Moltmann sees taking place in and through the cross would, on a first reading at least, seem to occur quite apart from any human response of faith. Secondly, however, we encounter a (related) emphasis in Moltmann's writings on what we might call the divine and human 'Let there be' which will be far more attractive to theologians who wish to safeguard human freedom. In our exposition, we shall begin with the mysterious transition that Moltmann associates with the cross. Then we shall examine the role of human participation in "the great turning point from disaster to salvation."[156]

---

[154] CoG, 245 as cited in 2.0 and 1.4.2 above and 8.3 below.
[155] The general 'nature-grace' (human-divine) distinction I am referring to here is not Moltmann's 'nature-grace-glory' distinction at work in the two directions of time. In the latter, 'nature' refers to the historical direction, 'glory' refers to the eschatological direction (and to what that direction anticipates), and 'grace' refers to the transition made possible through the cross. See the discussion in 4.2 above and chap. 6 below.
[156] CoG, 245 as cited in 1.4.2, and discussed in 3.6, 4.1 (including 4.2n11), and 4.2 (including 4.2n110) above and in 4.3.3 and 8.2 below.

Close to the heart of Moltmann's soteriology are a number of passages which indicate that in the event of grace, a given reality may 'turn into its opposite'. Thus in *The Crucified God*, we are told, "In the one who became a servant for our sake, we are grasped by God's freedom. In the one who became sin for us, sinners become the righteousness in the world."[157] In *The Church in the Power of the Spirit*, we learn that "even though Jesus' dying cry reveals his total abandonment by the Father, he is at the same time entirely one with the Father, and the Father with him, in this event of self-surrender, which sunders the two so far from one another that heaven and hell are included in its grasp, and all men can live in it." This "surrender" at the very heart of salvation/history literally changes everything. "The whole history of [the] passion stands under the sign of [Christ's] self-surrender, which is *on the one hand* to be seen as abandonment by God and *on the other* as the consummation of God's love."[158] In *The Spirit of Life*, God even "moulds and *alchemizes* [verarbeitet...] the pain of his love into [... zur] atonement for the sinner."[159]

---

[157] CrG, 186–87. Cf. the quotation from Zinzendorf, cited below, which occurs here in CrG, 187.

[158] CPS, 95 and 94. My emphases. On the abandonment, see n. 38 above.

[159] SL, 136 [*DGL*, 149–50]. My emphasis. Jürgen Moltmann, "Justice for Victims and Perpetrators," in *History and the Triune God: Contributions to Trinitarian Theology*, by Jürgen Moltmann, trans. John Bowden (London: SCM Press, 1991), 44–56 is for the most part identical to SL, 124–41, although the latter is a later discussion that is more developed in places.) Margaret Kohl's expanded translation of 'verarbeiten' as to "mould[] and alchemize[]" in SL, 136 is, in my judgment, perceptive. Here we may contrast John Bowden's translation in the equivalent, here identical, part of "Justice for Victims and Perpetrators," in HTG, 52 [*IGG*, 84], which reads "He turns the pain of his love into atonement for sinners"). 'Verarbeiten' normally means to 'process'. In a psychological sense, this 'processing' often has negative or even painful connotations. In an industrial context, 'verarbeiten' may refer to the processing of raw materials. Moreover, in connection with 'zu[r]' it may mean 'to make something into something else'. Moltmann would seem to have both psychological and industrial (or chemical) 'processing' in mind. If one wanted to translate the English 'alchemize' (back) into German without resorting to a neologism (such as 'alchimieren'), 'verarbeiten zu[r]' would be an obvious choice if one wanted to stress that the transmutation was painful to the 'Alchemist' in question (here God). That is certainly the point here. Cf. n. 160 below. Admittedly translation possibilities between two languages are not automatically 'reversible'. 'Verarbeiten zu' is hardly specific to alchemy or even to the world of chemistry. But read in context (see the sustained discussion of suffering, contradiction, transformation, and atonement in SL, 135–37 [*DGL*, 148–51]) and bearing in mind that 'context' includes sensitivity to the structure of Moltmann's thought, I do think that *clear connotations* of alchemy can be detected here. Furthermore, "verarbeitet" in the equivalent sentence in *IGG*, 84 is placed within quotation marks. The sentence is otherwise identical to *DGL*, 149. This indicates that Moltmann is using this verb in a somewhat special way, consonant (I suggest) with the above discussion. On alchemy and suffering, see n. 161 below. On Moltmann's undoubted awareness of Bloch's substantial discussion of alchemy, see 5.1n20 below. Given the discussion of 4.1 above (including 4.1n16), it is interesting that there are significant connections between the

Perhaps the most striking claim, however, occurs later in the same work where Moltmann writes, "In the cross of Christ God took evil, sin and rejection on himself, and in the sacrifice of his infinite love transformed it into goodness, grace and election."[160]

In these passages, Christ becomes sin, sinners become righteousness, abandonment becomes embrace and the consummation of love, evil becomes goodness, sin becomes grace, and rejection becomes election. And there is *alchemy*—a term full of mysterious and even occultic associations![161] How is

---

kabbalistic tradition and alchemy, as noted by, e.g., Gershom Scholem, *Alchemy and Kabbalah*, trans. Klaus Ottmann (Putnam, CT: Spring, 2006).

[160] SL, 212 as cited in 3.6 above. Cf. SL, 135 in which "God's 'wrath' becomes his compassion." (In the German original [*DGL*, 149], the terms "wrath" and "compassion" ["Zorn" and "Erbarmen"] are both in quotation marks.) Although the transformation of SL, 212 might be read in the light of what I refer to as Moltmann's 'Alchemy of the Cross' (cf. figure 5 below), the German verb translated as "transformed" here, 'verwandeln' (*DGL*, 226), does not convey the idea of deliberately, actively, and painfully processing something into something else as strongly as 'verarbeiten (zu)' on which see n. 159 above.

[161] It is most interesting to read the reference to, or connotations of, alchemy in SL, 136 (on which see n. 159 above) in the light of Mircea Eliade's claim, in *From Gautama Buddha to the Triumph of Christianity*, vol. 2 of *A History of Religious Ideas*, trans. Willard R. Trask (Chicago: University of Chicago Press, 1982), 304–305, that,

> [T]he great innovation of the [Hellenistic] alchemists [was that] *they projected on matter the initiatory function of suffering*. By virtue of alchemical operations, homologized with the "tortures," "death," and "resurrection" of the mystes, substance is transmuted, that is, obtains a transcendental mode of being: it becomes "Gold." Gold, we know, is the symbol of immortality. So alchemical transmutation is equivalent to perfecting matter.

His emphasis. Cf. Mircea Eliade, *The Forge and the Crucible: The Origins and Structures of Alchemy*, trans. Stephen Corrin, 2nd ed. (Chicago: University of Chicago Press, 1978). Chapter 15 of this work ("Alchemy and Temporality"), which addresses the theme of the overcoming of time, is especially suggestive for reflections on Moltmann's possible sympathy to this way of thinking.

The fact that alchemical transmutation was connected eschatologically to the *apocatastasis* of the cosmos and that alchemy was given a Christological significance in sixteenth century Europe, point us even more clearly to a religious tradition with which Moltmann may have some affinity at the level of cosmogony. On *apocatastasis*, see Eliade, *From Gautama Buddha to the Triumph of Christianity*, 305n58. On the Christological interpretation, see Mircea Eliade, *From Muhammad to the Age of Reforms*, vol. 3 of *A History of Religious Ideas*, trans. Alf Hiltebeitel and Diane Apostolos-Cappadona (Chicago: University of Chicago Press, 1985), 257. It is interesting that Eliade's own thought can be characterised as non-eschatological 'contradictory/harmony monism'. See John Valk, "The Concept of *Coincidentia Oppositorum* in the Thought of Mircea Eliade" (MPhil thesis, Toronto: Institute for Christian Studies, 1979), which is distilled as an essay by the same title in *Mircea Eliade: A Critical Reader*, ed. Bryan Rennie (London: Equinox, 2006), 176–85.

The alchemy of the cross in and through which realities may turn into their opposite is probably relevant to a full understanding of Moltmann's conception of the revelation of God in God's opposite, as briefly discussed in n. 146 above. Bauckham's suggestion,

this transformation from evil into good possible?, we may ask. In the words of Zinzendorf whom Moltmann cites in the first of these passages, " 'The cross is his method, and lasts until his future'."

The cross is thus (at) the heart of salvation/history and (at) the heart of God. "The cross is at the centre of the Trinity,"[162] says Moltmann. "In the light of creation, the cross of Christ is the consolidation of the universe [die wahre Befestigung des Alles]."[163] In the suffering of the cross lies the transition from the history of the present age to the joy of the age to come, the transition from nature to glory. God "*experiences* history" in the sending of the Son that ends in his descent into Hell, says Moltmann. But he "*creates* history" in "the resurrection, exaltation and perfection of Christ" and in "the history of the Spirit." "God experiences history in order to effect history. He goes out of himself [in the historical direction of time] in order to gather into himself [in the eschatological (re)direction of time]."[164]

The transition from crucifixion to resurrection (and by extension from rejection to election and from sin to grace) lies in God's passion not in his

---

in *Moltmann: Messianic Theology in the Making*, 68, that God's revelation 'in' his opposite "must mean ... *in the context of*" the opposite (his emphasis) though helpful, may over-identify Moltmann's position with that of Luther here, as William J. Hill notes in his *The Trinity as a Mystery of Salvation*, 169, before exploring Moltmann's neo-Hegelian view of the Trinity in this context (see 169–75). In my view, Bauckham may miss the transformational and thus (for Moltmann) revelatory nature of the overcoming of the negative—and thus the revelatory nature of the negative that is overcome; a negative (supremely in the case of Christ's Hellish suffering/annihilation unto death) in which God becomes present in a deeply mysterious, transmutational, and thus non-epiphanous way. As discussed in the text above, God becomes *present* in his opposite—death—when the Father *experiences* (the Son's) death for himself. He is revealed as *The Crucified God*. From this experiencing flows the power of the resurrection.

[162] TKG, 83. This is clearly not meant by Moltmann in only a soteriological sense. Commenting on Rev 5:12 (cited as "the Lamb who was slain before the foundation of the world"—he presumably means Rev 13:8), Moltmann continues, "Before the world was, the sacrifice was already in God. No Trinity is conceivable without the Lamb, without the sacrifice of love, without the crucified Son. For he is the slaughtered Lamb glorified in eternity." James P. Mackey, in his *The Christian Experience of God as Trinity* (London: SCM Press, 1983), 208, raises the pertinent question here when he writes,

> Is it really the case that one cannot have Moltmann's major insight that the cross of Jesus is the most radical critique of all human ideas about God and the one, true index to the being and action of God, without the duplication involved in having a kind of pre-existent Calvary taking place between three divine persons in some (non-temporal) sense 'before the world'?

This duplication is related to the structure of Moltmann's theocosmogony. See 8.3n31 below for further discussion.

[163] GC, 91 [*GS*, 104]. More literally, this phrase means 'the true reinforcement of all things'. In a military context, 'Befestigung' can refer to a fortification. "[C]onsolidation" is a good translation here provided that we don't overlook the implicit reference to the 'weakness' of creation from the beginning in Moltmann's thinking.

[164] CPS, 64 as cited more fully in 2.5 above. My emphases.

action. Because to experience is to be alive, death is not something we can experience for ourselves. The Father however—and this is absolutely central to Moltmann's understanding of salvation—in experiencing the death of the Son, *the death of his own*, actually experiences—we might say 'lives through'—*his 'own' death*.[165] In this, Hell and godforsakenness are embraced by God and are overcome forever. God dies (participates in human death) that we might live (participate in his eternal life).

In the Christ event, suffering precedes power. *Zimzum* and cross thus correspond even as they contradict. The making way of the primordial *nihil* is countered even as it is paralleled in/by the descent into Hell. Just as the transition from God to creation lies first in the *passio Dei* and only then in the *actio Dei*, so the movement from creation back to its true Origin comes about in the grace, passion, and the 'Let there be' of God's pain.[166]

---

[165] On this point, see Jürgen Moltmann, "The Passion of Christ and the Suffering of God," *Asbury Theological Journal* 48, no. 1 (Spring 1993): 19–28, especially 23, where Moltmann refers to the way God "*delivers* Christ to a godforsaken death and yet at the same time is also the one who *exists* "in Christ" and is present there" (his emphases) as a mysterious, paradoxical truth. Thus Moltmann writes in CrG, 192: "In the passion of the Son, the Father himself suffers the pains of abandonment. In the death of the Son, *death comes upon God himself*, and the Father suffers the death of his Son in his love for forsaken man." My emphasis. My paraphrase of Moltmann at this point—that (trinitarian qualifications and nuances notwithstanding) God really experiences his 'own' death, that God is *The Crucified God*—does not mean that I read Moltmann as simplistically referring to the cross as constituting the "death of God." While noting that this phrase "has an element of truth in it," Moltmann, in CrG, 207, prefers to speak of the crucifixion of Jesus as "death *in* God." His emphasis. His concern for the "trinitarian dimension" of this event (evident in this passage and in his later reflections) may explain why God's experience (the Father's experience) of his 'own' death, though central to Moltmann's understanding of salvation, is not easy to grasp in, e.g., TKG, 80–83 and WJC, 172–78 (the latter being a nuanced response to some rather unnunaced critiques). Even in these passages, the Father's experience of *the Son's* death is clearly stated, thus implying the Father's *experience of* (the Son's) *death*. If, as in WJC, 177, "Jesus's sufferings are divine sufferings," if, as in WJC, 180–81, " 'the sufferings of Christ' are God's sufferings," then Jesus's death is suffered and experienced, and undergone by the Father and the Spirit as their own, yet in their own way.

The citation from CrG, 192 should be read in the light of the important discussion of CrG, 190–96 (at the beginning of which we find a reference to the two directions of time). It is also significant that just after the above quotation, Moltmann elaborates on the transition from God's 'internal' to "external" work by stating, in CrG, 192–93, "*Creation*, new creation and resurrection are external works of God against chaos, *nothingness* and death." My emphases. This clearly anticipates the *zimzum* doctrine of his later work.

[166] In GC, 114, Moltmann writes, "The *unique transition* from eternity to time is to be found in [God's] self-determination . . . [in which] God withdrew his eternity into himself in order to take time for his creation and to leave his creation its particular time." My emphasis. It follows that the transition from time to eternity (more specifically, to aeonic time) is to be found in a redemptive self-determination that parallels (though it also overcomes) the *zimzum*. Cf. nn. 11 and 26 above.

From this it follows that our access to the life-giving energies of the new creation lies not in action but in a 'Let there be' on the human level. "It is not," writes Moltmann, "in our dominion that the coming God is present through his life-giving Spirit; it is in our hope. It is not in our power that the grace that raises us up is made perfect; it is in our weakness."[167] For human beings, hope is the way in which nature is open (or is opened) to grace. It is this kind of response—this openness—that God in his suffering love wishes to evoke. It is in this context that Moltmann abandons the language of human beings being "grasped"[168] by God's salvation in favour of a vocabulary far more amenable to Arminian concerns. In opening history, God is looking to create the space for his creation to willingly embrace his future.

In this context, 'guidance' becomes a central theme. In the *coelum gratiae*, therefore, heavenly potentialities "will cease to terrify human beings and the earth, but will minister to them.... [W]hen 'heaven opens', this means that God's energies and potentialities appear in the visible world, in order to open the life systems which are closed in on themselves and to *guide them* into their new, richer future."[169] At "the root of [God's] creative activity in history" is his "inexhaustible patience and his active capacity for suffering" through which he "maintains communication" with all "petrified" closed systems which have "condemn[ed] themselves to death" and, in enduring this "breach of communication," keeps their future with its "possibilities for conversion" open for his creatures, creating for them "quite specific chances for liberation from isolation." "It is not through supernatural interventions that God *guides history* to its goal," writes Moltmann. "Because it is a fundamentally suffering and enduring creating, the activity of God in history is also a silent and a secret one."[170]

If this language of non-coercion suggests that God's strives to re-open "communication" with his creatures, we may ask, is this communication two-way? If this is not the heteronomic Deity that the Arminian fears, then is there a

---

[167] Moltmann, "Theology in the Project of the Modern World," 16. That our access to the New Creation is not through power (which ties us to the historical direction of time) but through the surrender of power, for Moltmann, explains the negative view of power and the apparently simplistic contrast between power and love that Bauckham observes in *Moltmann: Messianic Theology in the Making*, 135. Cf. the contrast between power and hope and the antipathy to divine power and hierarchy that A.J. Conyers detects (and resists) in his *God, Hope, and History: Jürgen Moltmann and the Christian Concept of History* (Macon, GA: Mercer Press, 1988), 15 et passim. As these oppositions reflect the complex structure of Moltmann's cosmogony, they are not simplistic—even if they may well be judged erroneous and unwarranted, given a different cosmology/cosmogony.

[168] CrG, 187. Cf. the "grasp" of CPS, 95. Both of these texts are cited above.

[169] GC, 172. My emphasis.

[170] GC, 210–11. My emphasis. I have reversed the order of these sentences. The "specific chances" offered include those "for the evolution of the various open life systems." Thus *creatio continua* and Moltmann's description of Christ as "the moving power in the evolution of all things" in WJC, 286 occur within the *regnum gratiae*.

real space given in this opening-process to human freedom? On this subject, the answer appears to be unambiguously positive:

> Love that communicates itself requires response if it is to find bliss. But from his image in the world [in distinction from other creatures] the Father can only expect the love that is a free response; and in order to make this free response possible, love must concede freedom and offer freedom to the beloved. In order to experience the free response it desires, love must wait patiently. It cannot compel a response by violence. For the sake of freedom, and the love responded to in freedom, God limits and empties himself. He withdraws his omnipotence because he has confidence in the free response of men and women.[171]

If, for the Arminian, this emphasis on human freedom, coming from a 'Reformed' theologian, is a welcome surprise, the last sentence will surely provoke the question: How much "confidence" can we have (or can God have) that all will freely and willingly respond to the salvation they have been offered in Christ? There may be a suspicion that this confidence is grounded in the fact that the freedom that is founded on the withdrawal of omnipotence that creates the *nihil* as space for otherness will not survive the *annihilatio nihili*. We will not be free to resist forever. Perhaps, some may wonder, all those who do not freely respond to God's future in history will, in the eschatological transformation of all things, be subject to the divine alchemy of the cross in which evil becomes good. Perhaps in being taken to another "level,"[172] those who reject God will find that—against their will—they now have faith. For the Arminian, this is not an attractive possibility.

4.3.2 *God's Nature; God's Will*

In his description of "dogmatic" universalism as the belief that "all created persons will *inevitably* be brought into the salvation of life with God in eternity,"[173] Fiddes touches on what many consider to be universalism's most troubling feature: If all people 'must' be saved, how do they have a choice? And if this is something that God 'must' do, how is he truly sovereign? To deal with both sides of this objection is a challenge. If Moltmann has yet to satisfy the typical Arminian on the subject of *human freedom* (and to this we shall return in 4.3.3 below), the Calvinist may raise questions about *God's* freedom. In this section, therefore, we shall explore Moltmann's attempt to relate God's will and nature (and thus his freedom and necessity), and shall examine the relationship he sees between God's love and God's wrath.

This first issue is addressed in most detail in *The Trinity and the Kingdom of God* and in Moltmann's subsequent major work, *God in Creation*. In the following passage from the earlier of these two works, Moltmann's attempt to bring our notions of God's will and nature together is articulated as follows:

---

[171] TKG, 119.
[172] See CoG, 245 as cited above. I will return to this concern explicitly in 8.3 below.
[173] Fiddes, *The Promised End*, 194. His emphasis.

The eternal origin of God's creative and suffering love must have these two sides. It is God's free self-determination, and at the same time the overflowing of his goodness, which belongs to his essential nature. His *decision* is a *disclosure* of himself. It is only when we see both sides that God's self-determination ceases to be something arbitrary, and the overflowing of his goodness ceases to be a natural event. That is why the continual polemic against the (originally neo-Platonic) doctrine of emanation—a polemic carried on in the name of God's presumptive liberty—is out of place. If God's self-determination is not an essential emanation of his goodness, it is not self-determination at all. Neither *the fact* of God's self-determination nor *what* he determines himself to be can be viewed as arbitrary, in the sense that it need not have been. God makes nothing out of himself which he was not already from eternity.[174]

If God is here seen as "beyond every kind of polarity between freedom and necessity which human beings experience,"[175] at the same time his essential goodness, from which his self-determination flows, seems to have a certain priority.

This impression—of a will that is rooted in and expressive of a nature—is reinforced in another passage in the same work, which also does much to clarify what freedom and necessity (will and nature) must mean when applied to God. Here Moltmann writes,

One way of reconciling the elements of truth in Christian theism and Christian pantheism emerges when we cease to interpret God's liberty as arbitrariness, and the nature of God as a divine natural law. The naturalistic images of an eternally productive divine substance (*natura naturans*) are just as inappropriate as the images of the absolutist monarch in heaven. If God's nature is goodness, then the freedom of his will lies in his will to goodness.... If we lift the concept of necessity out of the context of compulsive necessity and determination by something external, then in God *necessity* and *freedom* coincide; they are what is for him axiomatic, self-evident. For God it is axiomatic to love, for he cannot deny himself. For God it is axiomatic to love freely, for he is God. There is consequently no reason why we should not understand God as being from eternity self-communicating love. This does not make him 'his own prisoner'. It means that he remains true to himself.[176]

I take this to mean that necessity and freedom coincide within God's (loving) nature. That is why for God to love and to love freely is "axiomatic." Self-communicating love is what (who) God is.

In *God in Creation*, we find the same ideas. God's "nature [as] goodness," present in the passage above, emerges as even more basic than his loving, which is, in turn, more basic than his freedom. Thus if we say that "God created the world 'out of freedom'," writes Moltmann, "we must immediately add 'out of love'.... God's freedom ... is love, which means the self-communication

---

[174] TKG, 54. His emphases.
[175] CoG, 329. This is originally framed as a rhetorical question.
[176] TKG, 107–108. His italics and emphases.

of the good. . . . In his love God can choose; but he chooses only that which corresponds to his goodness."[177]

Moltmann continues to try and articulate a view of God beyond the polarity of will and nature elsewhere in this work, yet his very language points to a nature that grounds the will or implies a 'being' that is expressed in a 'doing'. "The unity of will and nature in God can be appropriately grasped through the concept of love," he writes. "God loves the world with the very same love which he eternally *is*."[178]

Let us try and pull together some of the ideas from the four passages from *The Trinity and the Kingdom of God* and *God in Creation* that have been cited in the four previous paragraphs.[179] The love that God "is" in this final passage, I suggest, is his "goodness" (passages one, two, and three) which "belongs to his essential nature" (passage one). The love that God *shows* to the world—"God loves . . ." (passage four)—is his "*self*-communicating love" (passage two, my emphasis); what we might call his '*goodness*-communicating' love/loving. That is why Moltmann says (in passage three) that "love [loving] . . . means the self-communication of the good."

This leads Moltmann to assert in a number of passages not simply that God '*loves*' but God "*is* love."[180] This has definite consequences for the way in which Moltmann relates the themes of God's love and his wrath, and this (not surprisingly) has a bearing on his understanding of the Final Judgment. "It is not just that God loves, in the same way that he is angry," says Moltmann. "He *is* love. His very existence is love. He constitutes himself as love."[181]

As love is the very heart of God's being in this conception, God's wrath is relativised—which is to say, related—to love also. "Love" therefore "is the source and basis of the possibility of the wrath of God. . . . As injured love, the wrath of God is not something that is inflicted, but a divine suffering of evil."[182] Similarly,

> God's wrath . . . is not the antithesis of his love. It is nothing other than his love itself, repulsed and wounded. It is not that the passionate love for the life of what he has created, and for his human children, is now transformed into deadly

---

[177] GC, 75–76.
[178] GC, 85. His emphasis. Here "eternally is" is dynamic. Cf. 0.9n43 above.
[179] The four passages in order are: (1) TKG, 54 ("The eternal origin . . ."); (2) TKG, 107–108 ("one way of reconciling . . ."); (3) GC, 75–76 (". . . God created the world . . ."); and (4) GC, 85 ("God loves the world . . .").
[180] The "is" is frequently italicised by Moltmann as in: CrG, 193 (which occurs just after the important passage cited in n. 165 above), 244, 247; TKG, 53, 57, 82, 151, 197; GC, 83, 85; and WJC, 175. Cf. also CrG, 205, 230; TKG, 57–59, 117; and EiT, 309–10. Cf. the discussion in Jürgen Moltmann, "The Christian Doctrine of the Trinity," in *Jewish Monotheism and Christian Trinitarian Doctrine*, by Pinchas Lapide and Jürgen Moltmann, trans. Leonard Swidler (Philadelphia: Fortress Press, 1981), 45–57, especially 54–55. This "is" should be understood dynamically. Cf. 0.9n43 above.
[181] TKG, 82. His emphasis.
[182] CrG, 272.

anger. On the contrary, this love assumes the form of such anger so that it may remain love. Only the withdrawal of God from his creation would be deadly. But his anger contains within itself the persevering and enduring love, and in his judgment is his grace. That is why in 'the devouring fire' of his anger [Deut. 4.24, Ps. 18.8] the ardour of his love is manifested and experienced.[183]

If love and wrath appear to be opposites, deep down they are not. It is the cross, with its power to harmonise realities that contradict one another, that reveals the truth. "The love of God wounded by human injustice and violence becomes the love of God which endures pain," writes Moltmann. "God's 'wrath' becomes his compassion."[184] Reading this statement in the light of the present discussion, it is evident that " 'wrath' " is placed in inverted commas here because it has no ontological weight in its own right. In comparison with Love, it would seem, it is (relatively speaking) not really real.

The same approach is used when Moltmann considers whether the Final Judgment might have a double outcome. Thus Moltmann argues,

> In God himself love outbalances wrath, for God is angered by human sin not *although* he loves human beings but *because* he loves them. He says No to sin *because* he says Yes to the sinner. He says a *temporal No* because in *eternity* he has said *Yes* to human beings, as the beings he has created, and his image. He judges the sins of the world so as to save the world. . . . The anger with which the righteous God condemns the unrighteous which makes people cast themselves and this world into misery is nothing other than an expression of his passionate love.[185]

In the light of Moltmann's philosophy of time analysed in the previous chapters, it is significant that wrath and love, the penultimate and the ultimate, the subsequent and the original are (like the human and divine wills discussed in 4.3.1 above) related to the distinction (and relation) between (passing) time

---

[183] SL, 280. References in square brackets are taken from SL, 279–80.
[184] SL, 135.
[185] CoG, 243. I have emphasised "temporal No" and "eternity . . . Yes." The other emphases are his. Other references to God's love winning out over his wrath include: TH, 131, to be cited in 4.4 below, a passage that is atypical in that it speaks of "the *overcoming* . . . of the wrath of God by his goodness" (my emphasis) thus implying a more basic conflict described there as "the overcoming of God by God"; TKG, 69, where John the Baptist's proclamation of "wrathful judgment" is succeeded by Jesus' proclamation of the "kingdom of God's coming grace and mercy"; and the ultimately positive SL, 178, where "the Spirit . . . sanctifies life . . . with the Creator's wrath against all the forces that want to destroy it." Other apparently unqualified references to wrath in Moltmann's corpus, such as CPS, 49, 222; and WJC, 185 should ultimately be read in this context.

and (coming) eternity. God's wrath is, we might say, 'merely' temporal and thus temporary. God's love, however, is eternal and therefore 'Final'.[186]

As to the question raised at the beginning of this section, it now appears that God's wrath is an expression of his love, which is, in turn, the communication of his goodness. As the temporal No must serve, and is really an expression/anticipation of, an eternal Yes, universal salvation seems certain, and in that sense 'inevitable'. Whether this leads to an eclipse of the human will is the subject we shall consider next. But as for God, this salvation is an expression of his freedom, for it is in his freedom that he freely communicates his love and it is in—and out of—his freedom and his love that he expresses his wrath and judgment.[187] Universal salvation is not the 'inevitable' outworking of a Law to which God is subject. It is rooted in the grace of the divine nature.

4.3.3 The Nature/Promise of Freedom

Of the numerous positive references to "freedom" throughout Moltmann's corpus, the majority refer to the freedom of liberation, or to a promised freedom that does not yet (fully) exist.[188] Unlike eschatological freedom, the freedom of/for the original creation is ambivalent as it makes space for evil.[189] The many passages that speak of the present age as being unfree or in bondage[190] reflect the conviction that through our abuse of that space, this freedom (as space for Life) has been lost. As Moltmann puts it,

---

[186] We shall return to the importance of this time/eternity distinction in 7.1 and in 8.2 below, where its significance for the 'Final' Judgment (which should already be apparent) will be explored further.

[187] For other references to God's freedom, see: TH, 127; CrG, 4, 128, 187, 195, 229, 297; TKG, 39, 52–56, 107, 151; GC, 82–83; CoG, 13, 72, 115–16, 281, and 329.

[188] A less detailed version of the present section forms the greater part of my essay, "The Annihilation of Hell and the Perfection of Freedom: Universal Salvation in the Theology of Jürgen Moltmann (1926–)," in *"All Shall Be Well": Explorations in Universal Salvation and Christian Theology from Origen to Moltmann*, ed. Gregory MacDonald (Eugene, OR: Cascade, 2011), 417–39.

For freedom as liberation, as freedom *from*, a freedom that is not yet fulfilled, see: TH, 206, 291; CrG, 1, 4, 19–20, 40, 72–73, 104, 106, 114, 142, 168, 187, 191, 216, 218, 248, 249, 263, 266, chap. 7 (291–316), chap. 8 (317–40); CPS, 10, 19, 49, 59, 65, 74, 80–108, 112, 163, 178–80, 190, 191, 193, 195, 218–19, 220, 223–24, 240, 243, 255, 261, 262, 267, 288, 297; TKG, 57, 60, 111, 113, chap. 6 (191–222, especially 211, 213, 222); GC, 17, 69, 172, 292; WJC, 7, 96, 257; SL, 88, and 114–22.

[189] See TKG, 59, 109–11; CoG, 282, 306–307, and 332–33. The connection between ambivalent, 'creational' freedom and the *zimzum* is explicit in all of these passages, which should thus be read in the light of the discussion of the *zimzum* in 4.1 above and in the light of the discussion of CoG, 306–307 (which is cited most fully in n. 241 below) in 4.2 above. For an early reference to 'creational' freedom as ambivalent prior to Moltmann's development of a *zimzum* model of creation, see CrG, 261. For the ambivalence of freedom in the face of God's promise, see TH, 104.

[190] See CrG, 173; CPS, 14, 18, 36, 87, 98, 99, 104, 111, 180, 191, 194, 273, 274, 361; TKG, 111; SL, 88, 103, 138–39; and EiT, 158.

The first sin is committed out of free choice, the second out of habit and the third out of an inward compulsion. The result is what Augustine accurately described as *non posse non peccare*—I am unable not to sin.[191]

This loss of freedom is reflected in Moltmann's view of salvation. For the Arminian theologians of the "Remonstrance," "Man is never so completely corrupted by sin that he cannot savingly believe the gospel when it is put before him."[192] For Moltmann,

> Sin turns the human being's relationship to God upside down: correspondence becomes contradiction. With the human being's contradiction, his capacity for obedience (the *potentia oboedientialis*) ceases in his particular case, for his free will then becomes an 'unfree will', as Luther rightly said.... Out of his relationship to the human being, and through an act of grace, God can restore the human being's *potentia oboedientialis*, and make what was for him impossible, once more possible: it becomes possible for him to correspond to his Creator and the source of his life. The *potentia oboedientialis* is a divine reality before it becomes a human possibility.[193]

This human "correspondence" to God involves a genuine, uncoerced response.[194] Furthermore, in the movement from impossibility to possibility, Moltmann emphasises not only the freedom with which we respond, but also the freedom in which we *act*. "Even though [the] liberation of the captives is made possible through the message 'God is king'," Moltmann writes, "yet it is equally the act of men who 'free themselves'."[195] "The imminence of the kingdom, as it is preached and believed, makes men free [. . .] to *repent*."[196]

---

[191] SL, 138. His italics.
[192] This is Packer's formulation in his "Introductory Essay," 3 as cited in 4.3 above.
[193] EiT, 158. His italics.
[194] See CPS, 119 ("God ... gives man an irreplaceable dignity, respects him in his freedom and responds to him."); TKG, 30 ("Love seeks a counterpart who freely responds and independently gives love for love."), 59 ("Creation .... exists because the eternal love seeks fellowship and desires response in freedom."), 60 ("[God's] creative love ... desires free fellowship with the world and free response in the world."), 99 ("[God's] hope for a free response to his own goodness and love"), 113 ("The purpose of creation, and God's desire for self-communication, is fulfilled in the free joy of existence ..."), 117 ("[God] desires to find bliss through this other's responsive love. But this responsive love is a free response."), 119 (cited near the end of 4.3.1 above); SL, 196 (" 'In the Spirit' we come to know ... the *freedom* which makes us our own individual, separate selves." [his emphasis]); and CoG, 323 ("Free human self-expression is an echo of the Creator's good pleasure in the creations of his love.").
[195] CPS, 78. Cf. the discussion of repentance and freedom in Moltmann's early essay "The First Liberated Men in Creation," in *Theology and Joy*, by Jürgen Moltmann (London: SCM Press, 1973), 26–90, especially 63–64.
[196] CPS, 80. My emphasis. I have inserted the break ("[. . .]") to stress the two sides: being set free ... to act. That action is itself referred to in this passage as a "turning to freedom."

That we thereby turn "from this world of oppression, death and evil to the future of life, righteousness and freedom"[197] reveals not only a freedom in which we act, but a freedom towards which we move. We shall examine this freedom associated with "the future of life" presently. As for the freedom in which are now to act, our faith plays a key role. "It cannot be forgotten," writes Moltmann, "that the universal call to the decision of faith, by virtue of this decision, itself brings about the separation between believers and non-believers."[198] The "*assent* of faith ... says 'amen' to its messianic liberation."[199] But if "it is only through justifying faith that the liberating power of Christ's resurrection *is experienced*,"[200] we must remember that "[i]t is not faith that makes Jesus the Christ: it is Jesus as the Christ who creates faith."[201] As Moltmann puts it, with reference to the transition from disaster to salvation that is the cross, "Faith means experiencing and receiving this turning point personally, but faith is not the turning point itself. It is not my faith that creates salvation for me; salvation creates faith for me."[202]

This point is central to Moltmann's argument for universal salvation and for his rebuttal to certain objections, as we have seen in 1.4.2 above. Salvation (and thus the assurance of it) is not "dependent on the will of human beings."[203] If Moltmann's acknowledgment of the "amen" of faith may sound promising to Arminian ears, salvation is not be construed as a matter of " 'Offer and acceptance' " as this "brings divine grace and human decision on to the same level."[204] Faith is not a way of deciding to let God save us; it is the way we experience God's salvation in the here and now.

This has important pastoral implications. Fiddes, as we have seen, notes that universal salvation in Moltmann's case is based on the observation that "for created persons to have the power of choosing or declining their own salvation would be to make them into God themselves."[205] It is true that Moltmann says

---

[197] CPS, 80.
[198] CPS, 48–49.
[199] CPS, 223. My emphases. Cf. CPS, 230, "The justification of the sinner and prevenient grace come about when a person believes, not directly at baptism."
[200] WJC, 184. My emphasis.
[201] CPS, 197.
[202] CoG, 245 as cited in 1.4.2, 4.2, and 4.3.1 above, and in 8.2 below. On the relationship between grace and faith in salvation, see especially the important, yet playful, discussion in Jürgen Moltmann, "Will All Be Saved, or Only a Few? A Dialogue between Faith and Grace," trans. Margaret Kohl, in *Theology as Conversation: The Significance of Dialogue in Historical and Contemporary Theology; A Festscrift for Daniel L. Migliore*, ed. Bruce L. McCormack and Kimlyn J. Bender (Grand Rapids, MI: Eerdmans, 2009), 235–40 and his "Postscript about the Universal Theology of Grace and the Particularist Theology of Faith and the Universal Glorification of God" at the end of "Sun of Righteousness: The Gospel about Judgment and the New Creation of All Things," in SRA, 148. In these two pieces, Moltmann develops precisely the line of thought that is expressed in the foreword to the present work.
[203] CoG, 240.
[204] CoG, 245–46.
[205] Fiddes, *The Promised End*, 194 as cited in 4.3 above.

that to place grace and nature (God's salvation and human decision) on the "same level" means "humanising God and deifying the human being."[206] It is as if we assume that "the customer is king" (to echo a popular German saying) and then turn the customer of a "religious supermarket" into "God's king too."[207] But Moltmann makes these observations not to reassert that God is the supreme Monarch of the universe;[208] his concern is with a view of human decision that is de-humanising and that undermines the certainty of faith that we need.[209] It is with these pastoral concerns uppermost that he claims, in Calvinist style,

> *God* decides for a person and for his or her salvation, for otherwise there is no assurance of salvation at all. 'If God is for us, who can be against us . . .' (Rom. 8.31f.)—we may add: not even we ourselves! God *is* 'for us': that has been decided once and for all in the self-surrender and the raising of Christ.

That Moltmann is not a traditional Calvinist is clear when he adds:

> It is not just a few of the elect who have been reconciled with God, but the whole cosmos (II Cor. 5.19).[210]

The 'Reformed' (or Calvinist) rather than Arminian shape of Moltmann's theology is also evident in his understanding of the 'freedom' for which we have been set free. Although it involves being liberated from a condition in which we are unable not to sin (Augustine's *non posse non peccare*), the restoration of our creational free 'choice' is not the goal. The freedom of glory, freedom's "highest stage," is beyond the freedom of nature. In Moltmann's words,

---

[206] CoG, 245.

[207] CoG, 246 as cited, in part, in 1.4.2 above. The meaning of "the customer is king" for the head chef and for the owner of a gourmet restaurant in Hamburg is explored in the charming German film *Bella Martha* (ET, *Mostly Martha*), written and directed by Sandra Nettelbeck (Cologne: Pandora Film, 2001).

[208] Cf. his comments about God as "absolutist monarch" in TKG, 107–108 as cited in 4.3.2 above. Moltmann's comments in TKG, 218 about developing a view that "overcomes monarchical dependency" are also instructive:
> An immovable and apathetic God cannot be understood as the foundation of human freedom. An absolutist sovereign in heaven does not inspire liberty on earth. Only the passionate God, the God who suffers by virtue of his passion for people, calls the freedom of men and women to life. He gives human freedom its divine room for living. The triune God, who realizes the kingdom of his glory in a history of creation, liberation and glorification, *wants human freedom, justifies human freedom and unceasingly makes men and women free for freedom.*

My emphasis.

[209] Cf. "The Logic of Hell," 45.

[210] CoG, 245. His emphases.

> The freedom of having to choose between good and evil is less than the freedom of desiring the good and performing it. Man does not already participate in God's eternal freedom in the *posse non peccare* of his primordial condition; he only partakes of it in the *non posse peccare* of grace and glory. This is therefore *freedom for the good*. The person who is truly free no longer has to choose. A German proverb tells us that 'wer die Wahl hat, hat die Qual'—the person who chooses has the torment of choice. Anyone who has to choose is continually threatened by evil, by the enemy, by injustice, because these things are always present as potentialities. True freedom is not 'the torment of choice', with its doubts and threats; it is simple, undivided joy in the good.

True human freedom thus images the divine freedom we have analysed in 4.3.2. It is "the self-communication of the good."[211] In contrast to the duality of the will, which was considered in 4.2 above, this reference to "simple, *undivided*" joy (my emphasis) is further evidence of the monistic tendency of Moltmann's theology.

Moltmann's most sustained discussion of freedom occurs in the closing chapter of *The Trinity and the Kingdom of God*. Here his ideas about the kingdoms of nature, grace, and glory, as expressed in the four-fold scheme that he finds in Joachim of Fiore, are developed into a "trinitarian doctrine of freedom." As he introduces the final major section of this work, he summarises the preceding analysis (which we examined in 4.2 above) as follows:

> We said that the kingdom of the *Father* is determined by the creation of the world and its preservation through God's *patience*. This *constitutes* the freedom of created things and preserves for them the *necessary space* in which to live.
>
> The kingdom of the *Son* is determined by the *liberation* of men and women, through *suffering love*, from their deadly withdrawal into themselves, their closed-in-ness. This *restores* the freedom of created beings and *redeems* them from self-destruction.
>
> The kingdom of the *Spirit*, finally is determined by the powers and energies of the *new creation*. Through these powers and energies people become God's dwelling and his home. They participate in the new creation. This *gives liberty its bearings* and fills it with infinite hope.
>
> These three determinations of the history of God's kingdom point towards the eschatological kingdom of *glory* in which people will *finally, wholly and completely* be gathered into the eternal life of the triune God and—as the early church put it—be 'deified' (*theosis*).[212]

In the discussion that follows, the first form of freedom that Moltmann considers begins with our gaining control over nature, viewed as a liberation from the realm of necessity. The mere possession of power, however, does not determine how it will be used. The answer to the "torment of choice" to which

---

[211] TKG, 55. I have italicised "freedom for the good." The other italics are his. Here Moltmann is referring to human freedom. He uses exactly the same phrase to describe God's freedom in GC, 75 as cited in 4.3.2 above.

[212] TKG, 212–13. My emphases. Paragraphs have been added for clarity. *Theosis* has been transliterated.

this gives rise lies in our relation to "the realm of the Good, beyond necessity and freedom" as its "values ... transcend the realm of freedom in quality." Freedom thus has two "sides": "the liberation from compulsion and necessity, and the striving for the realization of the Good."[213]

This reference to compulsion calls to mind the "inward compulsion" Moltmann associates with the condition Augustine described as *non posse non peccare*.[214] This suggests that an important dimension of sin (in Moltmann's position) is that we become enslaved to the realm of necessity from which we must be set free.[215] True liberation, however, must be more than a freedom 'from'; it must be a freedom 'for' the Good.[216]

The "realm of the Good" for which we are liberated, says Moltmann, is not the "ambiguous world" of choice but "that unequivocal world in which freedom consists of joy in the Good and in doing what is right simply as a matter of course." We "always live in the transition from necessity to freedom ... from freedom of choice to the practice of what is good." In this movement, the three realms are not separate ages but "strata in the concept of freedom generally." Our striving beyond the "realm" of freedom requires that this "realm" must be seen in terms of history, struggle, and process. If we do not live in the "unequivocal world" of the Good, Moltmann clearly implies, it is in living *towards* it that our world becomes open to God's coming kingdom.[217]

In the course of history, the more we are freed from necessity, "the more urgent the orientation towards the realm of the Good" becomes. In finding our fundamental direction in life beyond the realm of freedom, our power—including the power of choice—is not thereby lost but deepened, enriched, and transformed. We "acquire power over ... [our] power" and may now "make free use of ... [our] liberty."[218]

From this vantage point, Moltmann then proceeds to evaluate the different conceptions of freedom that have emerged in the history of the West, first as the *subject-object* relationship of "master-y" and "lord-ship" (the patriarchal connotations of which Moltmann notes) and secondly as the *subject-subject* relationship of community in which freedom is found in love. In this latter context, the divide and rule of conquest makes way for solidarity as the individual discovers that the other person does not limit her/his freedom but expands it.[219] To these conceptions, Moltmann adds a future-oriented "freedom

---

[213] TKG, 213–14.
[214] SL, 138 as cited above.
[215] Hence the heading to sec. 3 (i) in CPS, 87: "Liberation from the Compulsion of Sin."
[216] Cf. SL, 114, where Moltmann notes: "In political history, nations have often enough been 'freed' from one slavery by another. But in faith we experience *liberation for freedom*." His emphasis. Cf. also SL, 120.
[217] TKG, 214.
[218] TKG, 214.
[219] See TKG, 214–16. (The references to "master-y" and "lord-ship" can be found on TKG, 215.) This discussion is paralleled in SL, 114–19. In SL, 114–15, Moltmann prefaces a discussion of these two forms of freedom with a reference to the Greek idea of freedom as harmony with the divine *nomos* and *logos*. When Marx defines freedom

in the relationship of *subjects* to a *project*."[220] Moltmann distinguishes these three "dimensions" as follows:

> Freedom as the lordship of man over objects and subjects is a function of property. Freedom as community between people is a social function. Freedom as a passion for the future is a creative function. We might sum it up by saying that the first means having, the second being, and the third becoming.[221]

In the light of this discussion, Moltmann make critical use once again of Joachim of Fiore's four-fold view of the trinitarian stages of history (also reconceived as "strata in the concept of freedom"[222]) in order to explore the trend or growth in the theological experience of freedom that may occur over time.

In the kingdom of the Father, therefore, we are the "property" of the Creator on whom we are utterly dependent. In *serving* God, however, we "experience the extraordinary freedom of having to have 'no other gods' beside him."[223] In the kingdom of the Son, the "*servants* of the Lord become the *children* of the Father" as the "inward quality" of our service changes. No longer God's "property," we are his "heirs."[224] As the inward quality of this already intimate form of freedom changes in the kingdom of the Spirit, we "become God's

---

as "insight into ["the historical"] necessity ["of the given situation"]," he notes, we meet this notion again. In SL, 115–16, his discussion of the idea of freedom as subjectivity includes reference to the Reformers' emphasis on the freedom of personal faith. In his discussion of the social form of freedom, Moltmann observes, in SL, 119, that this is reflected in the German word for hospitable, *gastfrei*, as this literally means 'guest free', i.e., free for (not from!) guests.

[220] TKG, 215–16. Emphasis to "subjects" added. Otherwise his emphasis. Cf. SL, 119–20 and GC, 129.

[221] TKG, 217.

[222] TKG, 221. In the original, this whole phrase is italicised. For helpful discussions of Moltmann's use of Joachim of Fiore, see Conyers, *God, Hope, and History*, chap. 6: "The Call of Freedom: Moltmann and the Joachimite Tradition"; Richard Bauckham, *The Theology of Jürgen Moltmann* (Edinburgh: T. and T. Clark, 1995), chap. 8: "The Trinity and Human Freedom," (especially 179–81); and Richard Bauckham, *God and the Crisis of Freedom: Biblical and Contemporary Perspectives* (Louisville, KY: Westminster John Knox, 2002), 205–209.

[223] TKG, 219. Here, there is less emphasis than before on the "space" we have been given in the creation of the world (to cite the language of TKG, 212–13 as cited above) as this examination of the kingdom of the Father (*regnum naturae*) would now seem to echo the subsequent discussion of the freedom associated with our liberation *from* the realm of necessity, a freedom here restored by means of a theologically transformed subject-object relationship.

[224] TKG, 220. My emphases. As brothers and sisters, their "liberty . . . lies not least in the free access to each other which [they] find in the love that binds them." Here, freedom as "community" is coming to the fore. That this freedom does not evolve out of the previous form but "only becomes possible where the Son appears" implicitly indicates a transition has taken place to the *regnum gratiae*.

friends." The "distance enjoined by sovereignty ceases to exist" as we are given "the chance to influence God and participate in his rule."[225]

This development (from servant to child to friend) does not come to rest in history as it anticipates an eschatological or "total" freedom yet to come. Moltmann thus brings *The Trinity and the Kingdom of God* to a close with the following words:

> The thirst for freedom cannot be quenched by any partial satisfaction. It knows no limits. That is why even the freedom of God's friends is not yet complete freedom. In history it is the best of all possible freedoms in our relationship to God. But even this points beyond itself to the freedom that only achieves its complete and perfect bliss in God in the kingdom of glory. When God is known face to face, the freedom of God's servants, his children and his friends finally finds its fulfilment in God himself. Then freedom means the unhindered participation [der ungehinderten Teilnahme] in the eternal life of the triune God himself, and in his inexhaustible fullness and glory. 'Our hearts are restless until they find rest in thee', said Augustine. And when we think of freedom we may surely say: 'Our hearts are captive until they become free in the glory of the triune God.'[226]

If this has by now left the "torment" of "free choice" far behind, there should be no doubting Moltmann's commitment to freedom as a major theological theme. How might these proposals sound to someone with Arminian concerns (concerns which, in this context, I share)?

One question that could be raised concerns Moltmann's own admission that the liberation of the kingdom of the Son "*restores* the freedom of created beings and redeems them from self-destruction."[227] If this entails what Moltmann calls the "restor[ation] [of] the human being's *potentia oboedientialis*,"[228] and if this obedience includes what he calls the " 'amen' " of

---

[225] TKG, 220–21. My emphasis. That "[t]his friendship too is born out of Christ's giving of himself for his friends" (TKG, 220) would seem to connect this kingdom of the Spirit to the *regnum gratiae*, just as suggestions of a subject-subject relationship with God (and not just among his "subjects") point to a theological expression of the second communal dimension of freedom. At the same time, the fact that the indwelling of the Spirit enables us to "enter into [a] new 'direct' relationship with God" (TKG, 220) would seem to anticipate the *regnum gloriae*. In sharing God's rule, the creativity associated with the third dimension of freedom (expressed in SL, 119 as "participation in God's creative acts") is present. Previously (in TKG, 217), this third dimension was very specifically related to our experience of the Spirit. The rather unsystematic nature of Moltmann's explorations here is partly due to the numerous transitions that may be anticipated in a developmental model. Ambiguities seem to cluster around the *regnum gratiae*, as its mediating role between nature and glory make it especially complex. But some of the lack of systematic coherence is the result of his attempt to combine a threefold (nature-grace-glory) schema with a fourfold (Father-Son-Spirit-Glory) schema.
[226] TKG, 222 [*TRG*, 239].
[227] TKG, 213 as cited above. My emphasis.
[228] EiT, 158. His italics.

faith,[229] how is this potential actualised if not by free will? And how, on Moltmann's own account—for what happens in the kingdom of the Son occurs long before eschatological freedom becomes a fully experienced reality—can we be sure that a given person will not abuse (or simply fail to use) that freedom? If we grant Moltmann that in this liberation we are "redeem[ed] from self-destruction" (as the above quotation puts it) and that our being set free from "the compulsion to sin" includes our determination to damn ourselves,[230] that still does not give us the will to assent to our salvation. Surely this must be an uncoerced human response. Why in their "restor[ed] freedom" may some not begin once more down a path in which the *potentia oboedientialis* is lost again (and again)?

If we conclude that some who encounter God's grace in the here and now do not choose to move into the deeper freedom of love and hope, why should we assume that this will be any different at the 'end' of history? Or does Moltmann assume that those whose potential for obedience is not restored until the eschaton (for he, presumably, must imagine this for all who do not "experienc[e]"[231] salvation in their present lives) will somehow escape this (so called) "torment" of choice? If that is the case, does this not amount to an eclipse of their very humanity?

The question about the pre-eschatological actualisation of the *potentia oboedientialis* is, to the best of my knowledge, nowhere addressed in Moltmann's writings. But this is of limited significance as it is its eschatological—and in that context universal—realisation that is the central issue. As for the suspicion of eschatological 'coercion', there are, in my judgment, only a small number of passages where this suspicion could be raised with some justification.[232] On their own, they are probably inconclusive.

So if universal salvation does involve a universal response to the freedom of Life for Moltmann, how does his theology envision that coming about? To obtain an answer, I suggest, we have to 'read between the lines' in a way that is sensitive to the contours of his overall cosmology/cosmogony.

---

[229] CPS, 223 as cited more fully above.

[230] The phrase is from CPS, 87 although the idea is from "The Logic of Hell," 45.

[231] By speaking of "experiencing" salvation here, I refer to Moltmann's claim in CoG, 245 (as cited above and in 1.4.2 above) that our faith does not create salvation, but salvation creates faith, the latter allowing us to experience that salvation in the here and now.

[232] What might we make of Moltmann's claim in TKG, 168 that "Creation ... is destined to join in the Son's obedience and in his responsive love to the Father, and so to give God delight and bliss"? What about the following line of thought in CPS, 297 [*KKG*, 324]: "Our [Christian] dealings with the particular social, biological, cultural and religious conditions into which we are called are therefore to be free, determined [bestimmt] by the eschatological freedom which overcomes [überwindet] this world and *makes* the new creation *obedient* [gehorsam macht]"? My emphases. Moltmann may not be specifically advocating a coercive view of salvation here, but his language could be said to be revealing. Cf. his reference to "people becom[ing] co-opted [kooptierten] sons and daughters of the Father" in TKG, 121 [*TRG*, 137].

The Triumph of Glory 203

One place to begin is with his statement (already cited in 4.3.1) that "[F]rom his image in the world, the Father can only expect the love that is a free response."[233] Earlier in the same chapter from *The Trinity and the Kingdom of God*, Moltmann explains why this expectation can be a confident one. In outlining the inner-trinitarian dynamics of the creation of the world, Moltmann states,

> It is because he loves the Son that [the Father] becomes the Creator. His self-communicating love for the one like himself [i.e., the Son] opens itself to the Other [i.e., the creation] and becomes creative, which means anticipating every possible response. Because he creates the world by virtue of his eternal love for the Son, the world is, through his eternal will, destined for good, and is nothing other than an expression of his love. The world is good, just as God is himself goodness. That is why God has pleasure in it. *That is why he can expect his image, man, to respond to his creative love*, so that he may not only enjoy bliss with his Son, in eternity, but may also find bliss in man, in time.[234]

On what grounds can God be so confident? The fact that "the world is good" does not mean that "the soul, being created from God, has a natural inclination to return to its origin."[235] Moltmann's claim is probably best taken as a reference both to the world's origin in God's goodness and to its eschatological destiny (hence the earlier reference to it being "destined for good") rather than to its actual nature in history. That human beings would possibly, probably, or actually fall into the bondage of sin would seem to have been included in the "every possible response" that God anticipates.[236] God's

---

[233] TKG, 119 as cited more fully at the end of 4.3.1 above.

[234] TKG, 112. My emphasis.

[235] Fiddes, *The Promised End*, 194 as cited and discussed in 4.3 above.

[236] Moltmann's corpus contains very few references to God's foreknowledge—a topic that is prevalent in discussions of salvation (universal or otherwise) in much contemporary analytic philosophy of religion. (Cf. Lindsay Hall, *Swinburne's Hell and Hick's Universalism: Are We Free to Reject God?* (Aldershot, UK: Ashgate, 2003), including her helpful bibliographies on "Foreknowledge" (232–33) and "Middle Knowledge" (239–40).) This topic is not addressed in relation to Moltmann's writings in Ron Highfield's otherwise helpful article, "Divine Self-Limitation in the Theology of Jürgen Moltmann." The brief discussions in GC, 165 (which touches on "potential worlds" and thus perhaps 'middle knowledge'); CoG, 13 (where Moltmann rejects the view of God as "the watchmaker of world history and the author of a master blueprint of foreknowledge"), and, most significantly, CoG, 282 (where he suggests that in the *zimzum*, "God restricts his omniscience in order to give what he has created freedom") suggest that, for Moltmann, God's knowledge of the future is more limited than it is in Classical Theism or Classical Arminianism. In Moltmann et al., "Talk-back Session with Dr. Jürgen Moltmann," 45, he is recorded as saying, "The foreseeing of God is, I think, a question which must be rethought. To say that God knows everything in the future and has no expectation and there can be no surprises to God is a bit abstract. I think God is waiting and God is making his experiences too, and perhaps also his disappointments with people."

confidence, even in the face of this possibility, would seem to lie not in the creation itself but in the fact that its being and future are grounded in (the Father's love for) the Son.

The centrality of the Son becomes even more evident as Moltmann's discussion develops into an exploration of the incarnation. It is in this context that we find Moltmann claiming, "Ultimately, love cannot be content simply to overcome sin. It only arrives at its goal when it has also overcome the conditions that make sin possible." The justification of sinners is therefore "*more than* merely the forgiveness of sins"[237] as the cross, in Moltmann's understanding, addresses and overcomes these conditions of possibility (which in the light of our discussion in 4.2 above would include the Hellish potentialities of the *coelum naturae*).

This future response of creation must therefore be understood in the context of the relationships between nature, grace, and glory. Expanding on the "more than" of justification, Moltmann writes,

> This surplus of grace over and above the forgiveness of sins and the reconciliation of sinners, represents the power of the new creation which consummates creation-in-the-beginning. It follows from this that the Son of God did not become man simply because of the sin of men and women, but rather for the sake of perfecting creation.[238]

Highfield alludes to some parallels between Moltmann and the contemporary evangelical theology known as 'Open Theism', though he only discusses divine omniscience in relation to the latter. One way in which Moltmann's view of providence would differ from that of Open Theists is that he would resist "presentism" (cf. Hall and Sanders, *Does God Have a Future?*, 220), the view that God's knowledge of the future, and thus God's hopes and plans for the future, is largely dependent on, and thus limited to, God's knowledge of the past and present and what can be predicted on that basis. Moltmann would place a far greater emphasis on the way in which God's *promises* (not just God's plans) open up and thus guide history. Cf. 6.3 (including 6.3nn88 and 94) below.

As for Open Theism's response to Moltmann, a representative evaluation may be found in John Sanders, "Historical Considerations," in *The Openness of God: A Biblical Challenge to the Traditional Understanding of God*, by Clark H. Pinnock et al. (Downers Grove, IL: InterVarsity Press, 1994), 59–100. Here Sanders, having found a point of contact with the "relational" view of God advocated by Moltmann and by Wolfhart Pannenberg (98), adds, in 190n164, after a reference to TH and CrG: "A caution must be given, however, since these two theologians are heavily influenced by Hegel and utilize the dialectical method. Hence certain passages suggest the open God while others seem to take it back, intimating that God is not genuinely involved in the temporal process, only in the dialectical (logical) process."

[237] TKG, 116. My emphasis. In light of the analysis of the relation between sin and mortality in 4.2 above, it is significant that Moltmann's discussion moves seamlessly into a reference to the latter in the very next sentence.

[238] TKG, 116. Cf. n. 74 above. He continues, "So 'the Son of God would have become man even if the human race had remained without sin'. This is how we should have to answer the question, if we wanted to embark on empty speculation." Such (non-) speculation is actually revealing. Is it "empty" for Moltmann because the distinction

What this implies is that in the eschatological perfection of creation, the conditions of possibility will be transformed. This means that sin will no longer be an 'option'. If I am correct in seeing the historical direction of time that flows out of the (fallen) potentialities of the *coelum naturae* as (in effect) the power of *temptation*,[239] then this sheds light on why Moltmann speaks of the redemption of time in the presence of God as "the full 'day of God' . . . 'the day of liberty' " in which "everyone does what is good just because it *is* good."[240] With the *annihilatio nihili*, which is the annihilation of Hell (objective genitive), the annihilation of Hell (subjective genitive)—the annihilating God-forsakenness that finds expression in our present tendency to forsake the good and annihilate ourselves in sin—comes to an end.

The ambivalent nature of freedom—which corresponds to the ambivalent pre-space space opened up in the *zimzum*—is eschatologically resolved as Hell—which is the Creator-creation distinction negatively conceived—is overcome.[241] The dangerous space, distance, and distinction that exists between God and creation is closed for all time. Alienation, distance, and the temptation to opt for self-enclosure and *autonomy* make way for the *true freedom* of the

---

between creation and fall though theoretically (or in principle) meaningful was always going to be historically (or practically) meaningless? The "surplus" of grace will be explored further in 6.4 below.

[239] See 4.2 above.

[240] TKG, 205. His emphasis. Although Moltmann is summarising the views of Joachim of Fiore here, read in the context of the whole chapter (as discussed in this section), this represents Moltmann's own position as well.

[241] This ambivalence towards freedom (which in figure 5 below corresponds to freedom viewed as positive in the eschatological direction and as potentially negative in the historical direction—negative, that is, if the historical direction is not fulfilled in/countered by the eschatological direction) is most evident in the following passage from CoG, 306–307 [*DKG*, 336] (from which I have quoted briefly at certain key points in the discussion of 4.1 and 4.2 above):

> Through the space conceded by God, creation is given detachment [Abstand] from God and freedom of movement [Bewegungsfreiheit] over against [gegenüber] him. If God were omnipresent in the absolute sense, and manifested in his glory, there would be no earthly creation. In order to make himself endurable for his earthly creatures, God has to veil his glory, since 'he who looks upon God must die'. Remoteness from God and spatial distance from God result in the withdrawal of God's omnipresence and 'the veiling of his face'. They are part of the grace of creation, because they are conditions for the liberty of created beings. It is only for sinners, who cut themselves off from God, that they become the expression of God's anger towards them in their God-forsakenness. If God himself enters into his creation through his Christ and his Spirit, in order to live in it and to arrive in his rest, he will then overcome not only the God-forsakenness of sinners, but also the distance [der Abstand] and space of his creation itself, which resulted in isolation from God, and sin; for redemption can only mean that with sin itself the potentiality for sin has also been surmounted; otherwise redemption would not be final.

I will return to this passage and to this topic in 8.3 below. For further references to the ambivalence of freedom, see n. 189 above.

"perichoretic space of reciprocal in-existence" which "corresponds on the creaturely level to the concept of the eternal inner-trinitarian indwellings of the divine Persons." Space no longer 'comes between us'. Mutual indwelling, which in the eschaton comes to characterise the relationship not just between creatures but also between God and creation, forms what Moltmann calls "the wide spaces in which [we] can move freely."[242]

Freedom will thus outlast autonomy as mutuality overcomes separation. As all of life will be taken up into the eschatological direction in which we find true life together, there will (presumably) be free will *within* the Good rather than an autonomy that places the choice of good and evil before us, thus leaving us *outside* the God in whose nature we are called to participate. In this divine, eschatological context, there will thus be free choice without the "torment." Universal salvation is rooted in the sure promise that in the kingdom of glory, we shall all be(come) truly and finally free.

4.4 A Preliminary Response

In the following chapters, I will highlight what I personally take to be the strengths and weaknesses of Moltmann's eschatology. Here our focus has been examining his theology in the light of certain 'typical' Arminian and Calvinist concerns about the notion of universal salvation. The aim has not been to see if he anticipates and defends himself against every possible objection but to find out if his position has the necessary scope, flexibility, and sensitivity to command serious consideration. On this fundamental level, the answer is, in my judgment, in the affirmative.

Against the charge that universalist theologians inevitably subject God to a necessity of their own making, Moltmann can reply that in saving all people, God is expressing his own nature, freedom, and goodness and is thus being who he is. In the face of other views of who God 'is', the strength of Moltmann's position is that he can point to what God *does*, specifically and definitively to what God has done *in Christ*. In taking the cross and descent into Hell as so central to God's revelation to us, Moltmann's challenge to other positions is clear: 'Do not tell me that some people may or must go to Hell on the basis of some theological system (indeed some theological 'necessity'); say that (if you can) in the light of the cross, in the face of the crucified God.' I personally find this to be a very powerful argument.

Moltmann's case is weakened, however, when he constantly tells us that 'God *is* Love', as this sounds as if universal salvation can be deduced from this 'central' attribute without God's wrath being taken fully seriously. If God's wrath is *really* (that is: only) wounded love, his judgment is *really* (only) a

---

[242] CoG, 301, which should be read in the light of CoG, 296–319. The "in-" of "in-existence" refers to existing in or within (perhaps we should say 'with/in'). See the translator's note in CoG, 298 and the discussion of Heidegger's *inextensia* in CoG, 300. The "wide spaces" theme, echoing Ps 31:8, is present in the title and autobiographical hopes and reflections of BP.

means to salvation. (Apparently) 'Final' Judgment must then make way for (truly) 'Final' Forgiveness. This sounds suspiciously easy. Can we really maintain this in the face of Christ crucified and in the face of innocent suffering?

The problem here is not with God's forgiveness outlasting his anger or with his love *overcoming* his wrath; it is that there can be no real overcoming if God simply is Love. In the Conclusion to the present study (see 8.2 below), I will side with the Moltmann of *Theology of Hope* in suggesting that we speak of "the overcoming of God by God—of the judging, annihilating God by the saving, life-giving God, of the wrath of God by his goodness."[243] This view of a God who is 'beside himself' and who is driven to extreme inner duality in the face of evil does better justice to a theology of the cross and to the reality of evil, in my opinion, than the rather bland (monistic) picture of God sometimes suggested in Moltmann's later writings.

As for Arminian concerns about preserving the freedom of the will, Moltmann's position is sufficiently well argued to merit serious attention, in my view. That we cannot be enamoured with an alleged divine right to *autonomy* is a point Moltmann makes well. It also seems clear enough that any viable eschatology must posit a progression from creation-in-the-beginning to creation-in-the-eschaton that is at least roughly equivalent to Augustine's movement from *posse non peccare* to *non posse peccare*. If all can come to share in that final state, universal salvation would seem to follow. That the kingdom of glory in Moltmann's position is one of true freedom (and therefore not autonomy) makes it hard to simply dismiss his theology as championing a heterononomic Sovereign Will to which we must all submit, whether we want to damn ourselves to Hell or not.

A great strength of Moltmann's vision of the mutual indwelling of God and humanity (and indeed creation as a whole) is that he clearly intends to transcend the limitations of both the Calvinist and Arminian positions. Thus towards the end of the "cosmic eschatology" section of *The Coming of God*, having described "God's *rule over* [the peoples of the new creation]" as a rule that "is *simultaneously their participation in that rule*," he writes:

> That can be regarded as the reconciliation of the sovereignty of God and human freedom.[244]

Here, as elsewhere, Moltmann seems to want what we might call a 'covenantal' universalism.[245] Whether he achieves this will be a central question in the following chapters.

---

[243] TH, 131.

[244] CoG, 319. My emphases. Moltmann's understanding of the mutual, participatory character of eschatological rule here appeals to Rev 22:3, 5.

[245] Cf. 0.7 above on what I mean by 'covenantal' here. Certainly Moltmann sees himself as a 'universalist' and as a 'covenantal' theologian, influenced by Reformed, federalist theology. In his foreword to *God, Hope, and History: Jürgen Moltmann and the*

My main misgivings (to be explored in the next chapter in particular) lie in the structure of Moltmann's cosmology/cosmogony. In figure 5 below, I have represented the preceding discussion of the dynamics of nature, grace, and glory in a model that supplements (and can thus be superimposed on or correlated with) figure 4 of the previous chapter.[246]

My concern is that *at best*, the historical movement of time is in its own right *structurally neutral* with respect to God. Thus the religious direction that we require to be truly free is provided by the eschatological movement. I certainly appreciate Moltmann's understanding of eschatological freedom as our "unhindered *participation*"[247] in God's freedom. Nevertheless, in his understanding, if we are to be free, we cannot move 'out of' but must move 'beyond' our creational origins. This is not the kind of creation-affirming position that I believe a truly covenantal universalism requires. *At worst*, the historical movement of time represents the power of temptation, which must be permanently, structurally, ontologically, overcome in the eschaton if God and the world are to move beyond suffering to joy. For Moltmann's vision of freedom as "the *unhindered* participation in the eternal life of the triune God"[248] to come about, time (in its pre-aeonic form) must not be allowed to get in the way. In the 'triumph of glory',[249] creation is (literally) de-natured.

Christian Concept of History, by A.J. Conyers (Macon, GA: Mercer Press, 1988), viii, he writes with approval,

> Federalist theology presupposed that, according to the Bible, the relationship between God and humans is not one of domination and submission, but rather one of covenant. The covenant is given by God and entails mutual loyalty and commitment.

[246] To give one example, if one correlates figure 5 with figure 4, it is easy to see the link between (i) freedom as a relationship between subjects and a project and (ii) our orientation to the future as *futurum*, which may or may not be reoriented in hope to the future as *adventus*.

[247] TKG, 222 as cited above. My emphasis. In my view, this stress on *participation* takes us fruitfully beyond the rather limited options of the 'libertarian' and 'compatibilist' views of freedom that can dominate discussions between philosophers of religion (and theologians). Cf. Hall, *Swinburne's Hell and Hick's Universalism*, 24–28 (and her helpful bibliography on "Freedom" on pp. 233–34). If one insisted on using these two categories, then one would have to say that Moltmann's eschatological view of time, in taking us "From autonomy to freedom" (the title of 8.3 below), takes us from 'libertarian' freedom to 'compatibilist' freedom. But this would be misleading, I suggest, as the soft determinism associated with 'compatibilism' is not present in Moltmann's view of eschatological grace in this context (on which see 6.4 and my reference to "willing participation" near the end of 8.3 below). Cf. 8.3n35 below.

[248] TKG, 222 as cited above. My emphasis.

[249] Here I allude to the title of (and some of the discussion in) Berkouwer's well-known work, *The Triumph of Grace in the Theology of Karl Barth* as referred to in n. 2 and in 4.2 above.

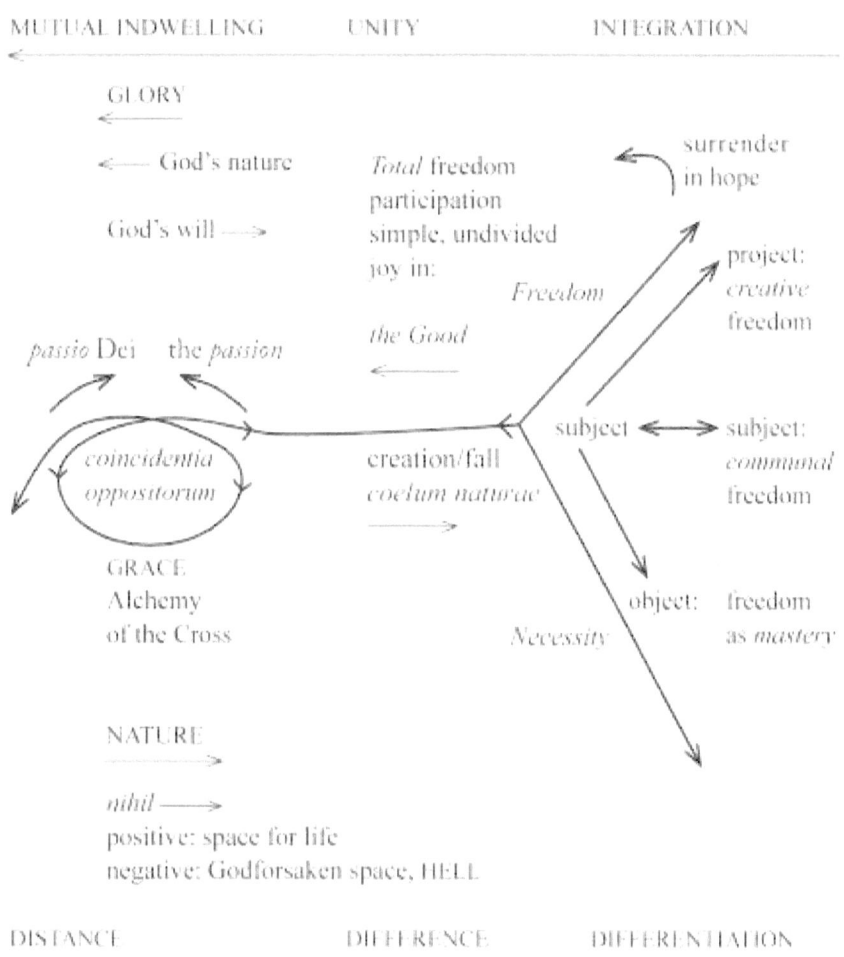

figure 5

NOTE: As with figure 4, this needs to be interpreted by 'reading' reality (as Moltmann's conceives of it) in the *historical* direction, from left to right, and in the *eschatological* direction, from right to left. The transition from (historical) nature to (eschatological) glory occurs in the transition of grace, represented as before by the 'loop'. Although this has been separated from the bifurcation of freedom and necessity, subject and object, it should ideally be 'located' at that point where freedom and necessity diverge/converge (i.e., *diverge* in the course of history/*converge* on the way to glory). The curved arrows represent the role of the *passio Dei* in the transition to history in creation and the role of the 'passion' and surrender/hope in the transition to the eschatological. These transitions are discussed in 4.1nn11 and 26, and at the end of 4.2 above. Finally, the subject-object distinction should, ideally, visually parallel the freedom-necessity distinction.

CHAPTER 5

Between Creation and Eschaton: The Foundational and Transcendental Directions of Time

In the preceding chapters, I have made the claim that Moltmann's theological argument for universal salvation (chapter 1) is rooted in a particular way of relating the themes of nature, grace, and glory (chapter 4) that is, in turn, an outworking of the contours and dynamics of his philosophy of time (chapters 2 and 3).[1] In this chapter, I will seek to deepen my analysis of Moltmann's concerns and proposals by bringing his thinking into dialogue with an alternative philosophy of time that (as I shall explore further in chapter 6) is suggestive of a different way of construing the nature-grace relationship.

From this emerge a number of possibilities for a vision of salvation that is potentially as universal as Moltmann's, but that differs from it in crucial ways, even as it maintains significant points of contact. The development of this alternative approach is offered in the conviction that the best way to become truly *conversant* with Moltmann's theology is to bring it into *conversation* with other voices.[2] Listening carefully to Moltmann in this way, I suggest, may bring to light certain features of his thinking that an 'interrogation' of his writings is unlikely to reveal. A 'dialogical' investigation of Moltmann's thought (anticipated in 1.6 above) will thus characterise this and the following two chapters.

One way in which I hope to avoid my own voice controlling this dialogue is by openly (re-)stating my own position. I trust that, as a consequence, my own views can be relativised with respect to the wider conversation I wish to open up. My own sympathy with Moltmann's belief in universal salvation was made clear in the Introduction, where I expressed appreciation for the 'hopeful universalism' of the Anglican tradition, while also proposing that this 'hope'

---

[1] One can of course rightly argue that his view of nature, grace, and glory has shaped—and has thus not only been shaped by—his philosophy of time. I am simply following the order of my exposition here.
[2] As this fits with Moltmann's understanding of the true nature of theological creativity, it seems especially appropriate for a study of this kind. I refer to Moltmann's "conviction that, humanly speaking, truth is to be found in unhindered dialogue" and his eloquently stated vision for communal ways of theologising to be found in TKG, xiii.

should be connected to the confidence or certainty of faith rather than identified with either 'wishful thinking', in which a biblical view of hope is lost, or with the dogmatism that results from our attempts to invest our theological formulations with a certainty that is misplaced. A universalism of hope, I was thereby suggesting, is neither a dogma nor a 'nice idea'. Those who, in looking forward to God's final victory over evil, find themselves looking forward in hope and confidence to a 'universal' salvation are convinced of something that others cannot be convinced of unless—or until—they come to share in that hope. In my view, a conviction of this kind, which is pre-theological and pre-doctrinal in character, is legitimate—at least in principle—even if those who hold to it cannot justify it theologically. Moltmann himself captures this pre-theoretical confidence well when he describes his own position as "a universalism of hope which is not a doctrine ... but is a presupposition."[3] This is a hope I share and a 'universalism' I accept.

Although it is important to distinguish our hopes from our theological beliefs and doctrinal systems, they cannot be separated. Although we may (typically) argue *from* rather than *to* our hopes, this is not a one-way relationship as arguments (may) also affect what we trust in and hope for. The many dimensions of our experience, though irreducible, interpenetrate. Thus our hopes may be evaluated in terms of the theologies to which they give rise (just as they may be evaluated by the other, non-academic dimensions of the lives in which they are expressed). To justify Moltmann's hope is something that exceeds the scope of an academic investigation. To evaluate the theological articulation of that hope in a study such as this, however, is both conceivable and appropriate.[4] Moltmann's *pre-theological* 'universalism of hope' animates

---

[3] Moltmann et al, "Talk-back Session with Dr. Jürgen Moltmann," 41. I have left out the words "or a certainty" which I take to mean a doctrinal certainty not the certainty of faith or hope. Moltmann's reference to "certainty" in the context of hope and universal salvation in CoG, 250 supports this claim. The 'certainty of faith' that I am referring to (here and in 5.2.1 and 5.2.3) is not, first and foremost, the kind of certainty that we might have about our beliefs or theologies. (Authentic) 'faith certainty' is the fruit of (authentic) trust in what is truly Ultimate and trustworthy, namely God. Faith and belief(s) can thus be distinguished (and related). In this sense, I believe that we may distinguish a 'certainty' that invites encounter from the antithetical dogmatism that Hendrik Vroom, in "From Antithesis to Encounter and Dialogue: Changes in Reformational Epistemology," in *Philosophy as Responsibility: A Celebration of Hendrik Hart's Contribution to the Discipline*, ed. Ronald A. Kuipers and Janet Catherina Wesselius (Lanham, MD: University Press of America, 2002), 27–41, sees as a danger in Abraham Kuyper. On the *distinction* between faith and belief, Wilfred Cantwell Smith's *Faith and Belief* (Princeton, NJ: Princeton University Press, 1979) is still very valuable, although it needs to be supplemented by serious reflection on the *relationship* between faith and belief.

[4] Universal salvation as a theological position may thus be judged for its coherence with other basic theological and confessional claims and its ability to open up further theological exploration. It may also be evaluated in the light of its implications for an authentically Christian way of life. In all this, a pre-theological "universalism of hope"

a theological position. This *theological* 'universalism' is one with which I sympathise. Yet it is a 'universalism' about which I have misgivings.

As I have indicated in the Introduction, a viable universalist position must: (a) propose a salvation that offers justice for the victims of our evil; (b) be able to demonstrate that it is biblically authorised; and (c) posit an understanding of salvation that is 'covenantal' in nature, thus affirming rather than negating authentic human freedom. Any theology that succeeds in these three respects would more than merit being taken seriously in the Protestant 'mainstream'— the concern of the previous chapter. To fail in any of these areas, however, renders the form of universalism in question untenable, in my opinion.

The first two concerns—the question of justice and of Scripture—will be central to the explorations of chapter 7. It is the third concern—whether there can be a freedom-affirming universalism—that will occupy us for this and the following chapter. Although I will be offering what is, in the final analysis, a *sympathetic* critique of Moltmann's theological position, it is a *critique* nonetheless—one that I trust will connect with the concerns of many whose stance towards the idea of universal salvation is more reserved or critical than my own.

To substantiate the claim, made at the end of 4.4, that Moltmann's eschatology may represent the de-naturing of creation, a position that would undermine the 'covenantal' view of salvation his theology would otherwise seem to support, we will return to the topic of the nature of time. After briefly looking at parallels between Moltmann's understanding and the 'messianic' view of time that is advocated by Rosenzweig and Benjamin, and noting that to view the future as a 'coming' reality is more characteristic of Heidegger's phenomenology of existence than Bloch's philosophy of hope (5.1), we shall examine the way in which both sides of the *futurum-adventus* distinction are evident in the philosophy of time proposed by neo-Calvinist philosopher Hendrik Hart (5.2). From Hart's interpretation of the two directions of time, which differs from Moltmann's in that it maintains a correlation between historical differentiation and eschatological integration where Moltmann posits a contradiction (a difference that is examined in 5.3), we shall be able to detail the way in which Moltmann's theology represents an 'eclipse' of creation. At the same time, the final section (5.4) explores how the 'panentheism' that he advocates might take a creation-affirming form.

Out of the dialogue between Hart and Moltmann's respective positions, we shall also develop the category of 'creational grace', to be explored in detail in chapter 6. In that chapter, I will argue that this form of grace is vital if, in the context of salvation, we wish to affirm authentic human freedom while rejecting both the divine heteronomy that Arminians fear and the human autonomy to which Calvinists object. The present chapter thus begins to explore the extent to which Moltmann's (pre-theological) "universalism of

---

may also be indirectly evaluated. But the arena for evaluating hope is nothing less than life and history. An adequate evaluation cannot be merely theological or academic.

hope" is translated into a theological position that is truly covenantal in nature (and in grace).

5.1 Futurity in Bloch, Heidegger, and Beyond

More than anything else, it is Moltmann's detailed and nuanced investigation into the ontological priority of the future that sets his thought apart from most philosophies of time. By contrast, even a cursory glance at the contents pages and indexes of contemporary works in this area reveals that if the 'future' is discussed in any depth, it is the *futurum* that is in view, the crucial category of *adventus* (or its equivalent) being almost entirely absent.[5]

---

[5] Moltmann's position represents a greatly expanded understanding of what philosophers call the A-series view of time (as 'past, present, future') in distinction from the B-series view of time (as merely 'before and after'). For an account of these two models, see Philip Turetzky, *Time* (London: Routledge, 1998), 117–55. From Moltmann's point of view even the A-series view of time in general and the future in particular is very reductionistic. The advent future is largely overlooked.

Works that contain (surprisingly) little sustained discussion of the future per se include: Barry Dainton, *Time and Space* (Montreal: McGill-Queen's University Press, 2001); J.T. Fraser, ed., *The Voices of Time: A Cooperative Survey of Man's Views of Time as Expressed by the Sciences and by the Humanities*, 2nd ed. (Amherst, MA: University of Massachusetts Press, 1981); Gregory E. Ganssle, ed., *God and Time: Four Views* (Downers Grove, IL: InterVarsity Press, 2001); Alfred Gell, *The Anthropology of Time: Cultural Construction of Temporal Maps and Images* (Oxford: Berg, 1992); William Hasker, *God, Time, and Knowledge* (Ithaca, NY: Cornell University Press, 1989); Robin Le Poidevin and Murray MacBeth, eds., *The Philosophy of Time* (Oxford: Oxford University Press, 1993); Stuart McCready, ed., *The Discovery of Time* (Naperville, IL: Sourcebooks, 2001); Quentin Smith and L. Nathan Oaklander, *Time, Change and Freedom: An Introduction to Metaphysics* (London: Routledge, 1995); G.J. Whitrow, *The Natural Philosophy of Time*, 2nd ed. (Oxford: Clarendon Press, 1980); and G.J. Whitrow, *Time in History: Views of Time from Prehistory to the Present Day* (Oxford: Oxford University Press, 1989).

Works that pay far more attention to the future but without providing significant points of connection with Moltmann's advent future include: J.T. Fraser, *Of Time, Passion, and Knowledge: Reflections on the Strategy of Existence*, 2nd ed. (Princeton, NJ: Princeton University Press, 1990); Richard M. Gale, ed., *The Philosophy of Time: A Collection of Essays* (1968; repr., New Jersey: Humanities Press, 1978) (though cf. n. 37 below); J. Alexander Gunn, *The Problem of Time: An Historical and Critical Study* (London: George Allen and Unwin, 1929); Errol E. Harris, *The Reality of Time* (Albany, NY: State University of New York Press, 1988); Stephen Kern, *The Culture of Time and Space 1880–1918* (Cambridge, MA: Harvard University Press, 1983); Irwin C. Lieb, *Past, Present, and Future: A Philosophical Essay about Time* (Urbana, IL: University of Illinois Press, 1991); J.R. Lucas, *The Future: An Essay on God, Temporality and Truth* (Oxford: Blackwell, 1981); Peter K. McInerney, *Time and Experience* (Philadelphia: Temple University Press, 1991); D.H. Mellor, *Real Time 2* (London: Routledge, 1998); Robert Cummings Neville, *Eternity and Time's Flow* (Albany, NY: State University of New York Press, 1993); Paul Ricoeur, *Time and Narrative*, 3 vols., trans. Kathleen

Where in the philosophical tradition might we find an appreciation for—or even a recognition of—Moltmann's central concerns? Moltmann's own discussion in *The Coming of God* suggests that he finds most affinity with those Jewish scholars who were involved in the twentieth century "Rebirth of Messianic Thinking."[6] Of the six writers that he discusses, however, only two—Franz Rosenzweig and Walter Benjamin—appear to have clearly developed an 'advent' understanding of the future. Rosenzweig's anti-

---

McLaughlin/Blamey and David Pellauer (Chicago: University of Chicago Press, 1984–1988); and Turetzky, *Time*.

Although the lack of attention to the future as *adventus* is also borne out in Charles M. Sherover, ed., *The Human Experience of Time: The Development of its Philosophic Meaning* (New York: New York University Press, 1975), this important work, which contains extracts from Genesis and Heraclitus to twentieth century thought, together with introductory commentary, not only contains a helpful section (455–65) on Heidegger (on whom see below) but also refers to Eugène Minkowski's highly relevant distinction between pushing towards and expecting the future (see p. 453). This will be discussed briefly in n. 47 below. Generally speaking, however, one has to consult works that draw on the Jewish and Christian eschatological traditions to find a view of the future with significant affinities to Moltmann's outlook. Special mention should be made of Wolfgang Achtner, Stefan Kunz, and Thomas Walter, *Dimensions of Time: The Structures of the Time of God, of the World, and of Humans*, trans. Arthur H. Williams, Jr. (Grand Rapids, MI: Eerdmans, 2002) as this work not only (briefly) engages the future as advent but also discusses the modalisation of time with reference to Moltmann's main interlocutors.

On Jewish thought, primary sources would naturally include the works of Ernst Bloch, Franz Rosenzweig, Gershom Scholem, Walter Benjamin, and Jacob Taubes, whose work (together with that of Karl Löwith) Moltmann discusses in CoG, 29–46 in a section entitled "The Rebirth of Messianic Thinking in Judaism." Some important secondary resources include, Andrew Benjamin, *Present Hope: Philosophy, Architecture, Judaism* (London: Routledge, 1997) and Marjorie Reeves, *Joachim of Fiore and the Prophetic Future: A Medieval Study in Historical Thinking*, rev. ed. (Stroud, UK: Sutton, 1999). The extent to which Jewish messianic/eschatological thinking affects certain contemporary 'postmodern' philosophers (such as Derrida and Levinas) is worthy of discussion. Cf. 8.4n65 below. On philosophy of time in this context, see David Wood, *The Deconstruction of Time*, with a new preface by the author (1989; repr., Evanston, IL: Northwestern University Press, 2001), especially pt. 4, chap. 6, "The Philosophy of the Future." Cf. Richard Rand, ed., *Futures of Jacques Derrida* (Stanford, CA: Stanford University Press, 2001). On "messianic time" in Derrida, see John D. Caputo, *The Prayers and Tears of Jacques Derrida: Religion without Religion* (Bloomington, IN: Indiana University Press, 1997), 77–88 et passim. Cf. Caputo's own distinction between the "absolute future" and the "future present" in his *On Religion* (London: Routledge, 2001), 7–17. On Levinas, see Tina Chanter, *Time, Death, and the Feminine: Levinas with Heidegger* (Stanford, CA: Stanford University Press, 2001).

[6] CoG, 29. See the final paragraph of the previous note. Although my discussion below suggests that Moltmann's understanding of the two directions of time owes only a moderate debt to Rosenzweig and Benjamin, owes little to Bloch, and nothing to Scholem, Taubes, and Löwith, there are other aspects of these thinkers' understanding of time, such as the nature of the "moment" and the need for an apocalyptic understanding of history, that Moltmann appropriates.

historicist "reversal" of past, present, and future in the face of an eternity that "without ever ceasing to be future, is yet present"[7] and Benjamin's comparable understanding of the two "contradictory orders of time: the secular order, with its striving for happiness within history, and the messianic order of redemption, which runs counter to that"[8] have certainly influenced Moltmann's philosophy of time. Yet although this messianic "contradict[ion]" of history is clearly very present in Moltmann's thought, the *correlation*, or *quasi-correlation*, that he establishes between these two orders, in which passing time 'makes way' for coming eternity,[9] would seem to have no comparable precursor here.

Moltmann's discussion of the thought of Ernst Bloch is revealing in this "messianic" context as the Jewish neo-Marxist atheist whose work is often taken to have decisively shaped Moltmann's theology is read here—as elsewhere—as holding to a view of the future that falls entirely within the confines of Moltmann's *futurum*.[10]

The distance between Bloch and Moltmann in this respect is worth underlining. In an early essay entitled "Ernst Bloch and 'the Pull of the Future'," Harvey Cox noted that the philosopher drew "on the same 'left-wing Aristotelianism' that nourished Marx" by postulating that there is an inherent "restlessness of matter [attributable to] its longing for form." Despite the 'evocative' title of his piece, therefore, Cox observed that Bloch "seems closer to the [evolutionary] vision of Teilhard de Chardin than he does to those theologians who posit a God who beckons to the cosmos from a radically other future."[11] For those open to the coming of God, to what Moltmann would call a truly *eschatological* perspective, Bloch's "principle of hope"[12] will surely appear all-too-*historical* and thus far from 'promising'.[13]

---

[7] CoG, 35–36. Cf. 2.5n146 above.

[8] CoG, 40. Cf. the references to Benjamin in 2.1, 2.3, and 2.4 above.

[9] See the discussion of the positively conceived idea of 'making way' in 2.4, 3.2, and 4.1 above. See also Moltmann's simultaneous emphasis on "contradiction" and "correspondence" as discussed in 6.5 below.

[10] See CoG, 30–33. Note the contrast with Rosenzweig concerning "redemption from history" at the end of this section. For some of Moltmann's other comments on the limitations of Bloch's advent-less ontology, see 2.4nn76 and 80, and 3.4n135 above, together with the references cited there.

[11] Harvey Cox, "Ernst Bloch and 'The Pull of the Future'," in *New Theology No. 5*, ed. Martin E. Marty and Dean G. Peerman (New York: Macmillan, 1968), 198 (= Harvey Cox, foreword in *Man on His Own: Essays in the Philosophy of Religion*, by Ernst Bloch, trans. E.B. Ashton (New York: Herder and Herder, 1971), 14). For Cox's title, cf. Walter H. Capps, *Time Invades the Cathedral: Tensions in the School of Hope* (Philadelphia: Fortress Press, 1972), 18: "[Bloch] prides himself on being able to view the world as though it were being pulled ahead by the future." For Cox's earlier comparison between Teilhard de Chardin and Bloch, see his afterword in *The Secular City Debate*, ed. Daniel Callahan (New York: Macmillan, 1966), 197–99. He refers to Bloch's "historicism" as being at odds with a truly open view of the future on p. 202.

[12] I refer, naturally, to Bloch *magnum opus*, *Das Prinzip Hoffnung* (Frankfurt am Main: Suhrkamp Verlag, 1959)—in English: *The Principle of Hope*, 3 vols., trans. Neville Plaice, Stephen Plaice, and Paul Knight (Cambridge, MA: MIT Press, 1986)—which so

So how can Bloch justify belief in the "[p]ull of" rather than mere 'push towards' the future? Wolfhart Pannenberg's exposition of Aristotelian futurism is helpful in this context. He writes,

> In the Aristotelian connection of *eidos* and *telos*, the Socratic striving for the good (and the futuristic element implied therein) finds a new ontological formulation. The essence of a thing, its *eidos*, is the goal of its movement—at least of its unforced movement. Thus, the yet unattained goal is present in an anticipatory way in the moved as entelechy, and this indwelling of the goal effects the movement towards the goal. For Aristotle, this was explicitly connected with the Socratic question about the good: "According to our doctrine, then," he says in the first book of the *Physics*, "there is, on the one side, the opposite (privation, formlessness); and in between, something which by nature strives for the good."

Although Pannenberg does not refer to Bloch, he makes a telling comment that, in the final analysis, parallels Moltmann's evaluation of the latter's entelechy: "[I]f [for Aristotle,] the movement brings forth nothing except what is already actual somewhere else, then nothing new can arise."[14] Nature, Moltmann might say, cannot give birth to glory.

---

captivated Moltmann in 1960, as detailed in EiT, 92 and BP, 78–81. Among the best discussions of Bloch's influence on Moltmann are Bauckham, *Moltmann: Messianic Theology in the Making*, chap. 1 ("The Emergence of the Theology of Hope in Dialogue with Ernst Bloch") and Meeks, *Origins of the Theology of Hope*, 80–92. For an extensive listing of secondary literature on Bloch, see Bauckham, *Moltmann*, 146–47n18. For Moltmann's response to Bloch and *The Principle of Hope*, see EiT, 92. Cf. n. 80 below and 3.4n135 above. For a discussion of characteristic features of Moltmann's thought that *predate* his exposure to Bloch, see Müller-Fahrenholz, *The Kingdom and the Power: The Theology of Jürgen Moltmann*, 26–39.

[13] In an appendix to *Theologie der Hoffnung*, which was excluded from TH, but which was translated by James W. Leitch (the translator of TH) to appear as "Hope And Confidence: A Conversation with Ernst Bloch," in *Religion, Revolution and the Future*, by Jürgen Moltmann, trans. M. Douglas Meeks (New York: Charles Scribner's Sons, 1969), 149–76, Moltmann's observes, on pp. 157–58, that Bloch's "All" or "Nothing" prognosis, his demythologised "heaven" and "hell"—on which see *The Principle of Hope*, 1:313 in the light of 1:306–12. Cf. 3:1311 for the correlation between the "miraculous" and the "In Vain"—is "apocalyptic" rather than eschatological in character.

[14] Wolfhart Pannenberg, "Appearance as the Arrival of the Future," in *New Theology No. 5*, ed. Martin E. Marty and Dean G. Peerman (New York: Macmillan, 1968), 125. His italics. For Moltmann's evaluation of Bloch as unable to justify the *novum* for which he longs, see 2.4nn76 and 80 and 3.4n135 above. That Pannenberg would extend his comment on entelechy to Bloch and would find Moltmann's contrast between hope and mere extrapolation on target is evident in his *Systematic Theology*, vol. 3, trans. Geoffrey Bromiley (Grand Rapids, MI: Eerdmans; Edinburgh: T. and T. Clark, 1998), 175–76 (including 175–76n223).

Of course Bloch's ontology of the "not-yet" goes well beyond Aristotle, but arguably not beyond Aristotelianism. With reference to Bloch's *Avicenna und die*

In this light, Moltmann's enthusiastic citation of Bloch's description of Yahweh (YHWH) as "a God 'with the future as his essential nature' "[15] on the second page of his *Theology of Hope* can be seen as very misleading. Bloch's German text speaks here not of the coming God who transforms the very nature of history but of God "mit *futurum* als Seinsbeschaffenheit."[16] That Moltmann, soon after the publication of *Theology of Hope*, chooses Bloch's Latin term to specify the non-eschatological future is very significant.[17]

M. Douglas Meeks' observation, which is made in the context of a lucid and thoroughly researched discussion of the relationship between the philosopher and theologian of hope, seems apt:

Aristotelische Linke (Frankfurt am Main: Suhrkamp, 1963), Meeks, in his *Origins of the Theology of Hope*, 92n68, notes that to define "the 'objective real possible' Bloch appropriates and deepens the matter and nature concepts of the 'Aristotelian left' as well as 'all panvital images of nature' in the philosophical and mystical traditions." In "Hope and Confidence," 155, Moltmann identifies Bloch's "pantheistic, left-wing Aristotelianism," noting that for his thinking to be consistent, "The ground of matter's longing must then lie in form-creating matter itself, the ground of the *eidos* must then lie in the *eros* itself, the ground of hope in hope itself." His italics. The rest of Moltmann's discussion indicates that what Cox, in his "Ernst Bloch and 'The Pull of the Future'," 199, calls "the magnetic pull" of the "vacuum" that Bloch postulates in a valiant attempt to solve this dilemma, is a 'pull' that can only be successfully grounded in the *coming* God (cf. "Hope and Confidence," 175). "[I]t is natural," writes Cox in "Ernst Bloch and 'The Pull of the Future'," 196, "that we should be impressed by a man whose life has been spent examining the '*futurum*', the idea of the new, the '*Impuls der Erwartung*' and the 'principle of hope'." His italics. From a Moltmannian perspective, however, to spend a lifetime searching for the answer to one's hopes in the 'not-yet' of the *futurum* (rather than in the 'not-yet' of *adventus*) is as tragic as it is heroic.

[15] TH, 16.

[16] Moltmann does not give the reference here, but it comes from *Das Prinzip Hoffnung*, 2:1458. Often this phrase is translated as referring to God with the future as the "mode of his being." See, for example, Jürgen Moltmann, "Introduction to the 'Theology of Hope'," in *The Experiment Hope*, by Jürgen Moltmann, trans. M. Douglas Meeks (Philadelphia: Fortress Press, 1975), 44–59, especially 48, and Conyers, *God, Hope, and History*, 6. One can also contrast the older translation of *Das Prinzip Hoffnung* here as "one whose being was the quality of the future" (in Bloch, *Man on His Own*, 173) with the more recent translation by Neville Plaice, Stephen Plaice, and Paul Knight, where we find "with futurum as an attribute of Being" (in *The Principle of Hope*, 3:1236). Unless we wish to emphasise that the future rather than the present is God's mode of time, the "mode" translation is a misleadingly weak. "*-beschaffenheit*" *intensifies* rather than qualifies "*Sein*." The future is God's 'very being'. CoG, 23 renders Bloch's same phrase by "future as the essence of his Being." In Moltmann, "Trends in Eschatology," in FC, 180n53 (which discusses the ambiguity of "future" in Bloch in the light of Moltmann's distinction between *Futur* and *Zukunft* [and *Adventus*, cf. "Tends in Eschatology," in FC, 29–30]), the phrase is translated as "with the future tense as his constitutive character."

[17] On Moltmann's unintended ambiguity in TH in this respect, see 2.4n80 above.

Generally speaking, the subjective anthropological, and *epistemological* elements of Bloch's thought were formally and materially more influential on Moltmann's theology than the objective, natural, and *ontological* elements.[18]

The numerous points of contact between Moltmann and Bloch, which even include the latter's substantial discussion of alchemy and his passing reference to Isaac Luria's *zimzum* doctrine of creation, are undeniable. But Bloch's thinking is a point of departure for Moltmann in a double sense,[19] his wide-ranging, visionary, epistemological exploration into the nature of hope and "anticipatory consciousness" functioning as a vital catalyst for Moltmann's very different ontology of time.[20]

Given the theological climate of the 1960s, it is perhaps understandable that the earliest responses to Moltmann's *Theologie der Hoffnung* in North America did not fully appreciate this difference. "I believe," wrote Harvey Cox in 1966, "that Bloch's massive *Prinzip Hoffnung*, first published in 1954, a difficult, often unclear but epochal book, supplies the only serious alternative to Martin Heidegger's even more opaque *Sein und Zeit* (1927) as a philosophical partner for theology." In Cox's judgment, Heidegger's "enormous" influence on modern theology had been "almost wholly deleterious."[21] But there was hope. "[I]f theology can leave behind the God who *is* and begin its work with the God who *will be*, or, in biblical parlance, '*He who cometh*'," Cox continued, "an

---

[18] Meeks, *Origins of the Theology of Hope*, 92n70. My emphases.

[19] Cf. the discussion of Augustine in 2.2 above.

[20] It is important to note that vol. 1, pt. 2 of *The Principle of Hope*, entitled "Anticipatory Consciousness" (1:45–339), is foundational to Bloch's whole project. For his discussion of alchemy, see *The Principle of Hope*, 2:634–46 (and cf. 4.3.1 above). For his reference to the *zimzum*, see *The Principle of Hope*, 3:1237 (and cf. 4.2 above).

Other points of contact include: the *novum*, on which see *The Principle of Hope*, 1:198–205; the "moment" (or "Now"), on which see *The Principle of Hope*, 1:287–300; the "*nihil*" (or "Nothing"), on which see *The Principle of Hope*, 1:306–13 (cf. n. 13 above); and the interest in Joachim of Fiore, on whom see *The Principle of Hope*, 2:509–15. The numerous entries under "Bloch" in the index of, for example, CoG (see CoG, 386) testify to his status as an ongoing dialogue partner for Moltmann.

"The forward-look has replaced the upward-look," writes Bloch in his *Atheism in Christianity*, 265. This points to the way in which the Neoplatonic 'great chain of being' is historicised in his thought. I have referred to Moltmann's temporalised Neoplatonism at the end of 2.2 above. While I see Moltmann as historicising the motif of descent and emanation in the differentiating direction of time and eschatologising the motif of return in the re-integrating direction of time, I do not find the latter appropriation of Neoplatonism in Bloch. Hence my claim that Moltmann has a very different ontology. For a good account of the structure of Bloch's thought which addresses the themes of inner and outer, subject and object (priority being given to the former in both cases), telos, recapitulation, and metempsychosis, see Capps, *Time Invades the Cathedral*, chap. 2 ("Ernst Bloch: Steward of Hopes, Dreams, Mysteries"). There is surprisingly little here that reminds me of the structure of Moltmann's thought.

[21] Cox, afterword in *The Secular City Debate*, 200.

exciting new epoch in theology could begin, one in which Ernst Bloch's work would be extraordinarily important."[22]

This enthusiasm for Bloch had much to do with Cox's belief that it was the future that could provide the secular world with a viable sense of transcendence.[23] Philosophically speaking, the difference between the two atheists, for Cox, was the difference between life and death. "Heidegger plumbs the caliginous depths of 'anxiety', 'care' and '*Sein zum Tode*' ['being unto death']," he noted, while Bloch's basic categories are " 'frontier', 'future', 'the New' and the '*Traum nach vorwarts*' "—which we might translate as the 'forward-pointing dream' or 'the dream we follow'.[24] In contrast with the *Sein zum Tode*, Cox implies, this way of being is a 'dreaming unto life'. Consequently, "Bloch presses the same difficult questions Heidegger raises but does so within an ontology that seeks to question and subvert the tight finitude of Heidegger's constricted human world."[25]

Bloch might have approved of this favourable comparison, though he would no doubt have posed it more sharply, having reserved some of his most withering criticisms for Heidegger.[26] How ironic it is, then, that Moltmann, whose then recent *Theologie der Hoffnung* Cox referred to as "stunning,"[27] would go on to develop a view of the future—a view of a future that "cometh"—that would bear far more similarity to Heidegger's *Zukunft* than Bloch's *futurum*.

In the final chapter of his seminal work *Being and Time*, Heidegger distances himself from the entire Western philosophical tradition "since Aristotle" by refusing to reduce time to something that we can 'tell', to something we can count or measure by looking at the hands of the clock or the position of the sun. 'Is that the time?!', we exclaim. 'It's time to go. It's getting dark already. The bus will be leaving any moment. I don't get paid for overtime. We'll have to find the time to finish this in the morning'. To answer the question of time by looking at our watch, for Heidegger, is to allow the "*full* essential structure of world-time" to become "levelled off and covered up" in an "ordinary" understanding in which time is reduced to a series of "nows" (including the "no-longer-now" and the "not-yet-now") that are like "Things

---

[22] Cox, afterword in *The Secular City Debate*, 202. His emphases.
[23] See Cox, afterword in *The Secular City Debate*, 198–99. In the final sentence on p. 203, Cox says that his critics, who were commenting on his *The Secular City* (New York: Macmillan, 1965), "have turned my face toward the future, where if man meets God again, that encounter must take place." Cf. Cox, "Ernst Bloch and 'The Pull of the Future'," 202–203: "With Bloch's help, we can be unremittingly concerned with the secular without sacrificing the transcendent. God is not above, or beneath us, or even just 'within' us. He is ahead."
[24] See *The Principle of Hope*, 3:1365–70 ("Forward dream, sobriety, enthusiasm and their unity"). We could also speak here of 'the dream we pursue'.
[25] Cox, afterword in *The Secular City Debate*, 200. His italics.
[26] See *Principle of Hope*, 1:110 and 1:145 and *Principle of Hope*, 3:1160–61.
[27] Cox, afterword in *The Secular City Debate*, 198.

... 'seen' ontologically within the horizon of the idea of presence-at-hand."[28] 'What is time?' and 'What is the time?' are conflated in a "metaphysics of presence"[29] which has been described by one Heidegger scholar as "the nadir of *inauthentic* temporality."[30]

Nevertheless, even this "ordinary," denatured, alienated view of time is 'revealing' in its own way. As Heidegger explains,

> Thrown and falling, Dasein [(the) human (manifestation of) being] is proximally and for the most part lost in that with which it concerns itself. In this lostness, however, Dasein's fleeing in the face of that authentic existence which has been characterised as "anticipatory resoluteness", has made itself known; and this is a fleeing which covers up. In this concernful fleeing lies a fleeing *in the face of* death—that is, a looking-away *from* the end of Being-in-the-world. This looking-away from it, is in itself a mode of that Being-*towards*-the-end which is ecstatically *futural*. The inauthentic temporality of everyday Dasein as it falls, must, as such a looking-away from finitude, fail to recognize authentic futurity and therewith temporality in general.[31]

So if I do not look away but face (the ever-present possibility of) my own death in "anticipatory resoluteness" (or in 'openness', if we understand "Entschlossenheit" here as 'Ent-schlossenheit', 'unclosedness'), if I am no longer (mis-)guided by "public time" from which I am only concerned to "snatch as much ['time'] as possible," but instead "grasp[] the finitude of [my] existence,"[32] what does authentic temporality look like? According to Heidegger,

---

[28] Martin Heidegger, *Being and Time*, trans. John Macquarrie and Edward Robinson (San Francisco: HarperCollins, 1962), div. 2, chap. 6, 473–75 [421–23]. His emphasis. The page numbers to the German edition here and in the citations below are placed in square brackets. I will restrict my comments to *Being and Time*, given its massive influence on modern theology, thus largely bracketing Heidegger's later thought. For an analysis that includes Heidegger's emphases in earlier and later works, see Richard Polt, "Being and Time," in *Martin Heidegger: Key Concepts*, ed. Bret W. Davis (Durham, UK: Acumen, 2010), 69–81.

[29] Although a phrase associated with contemporary philosophers who are both dependent on and critical of Heidegger (notably Derrida), the "metaphysics of presence" is used by some Heidegger interpreters to paraphrase his thought in precisely this context. See, e.g., Chanter, *Time, Death, and The Feminine*, xiv.

[30] Michael Inwood, "Time, Temporality and Timeliness," in *A Heidegger Dictionary*, by Michael Inwood (Oxford: Blackwell, 1999), 221. My emphasis.

[31] Heidegger, *Being and Time*, div. 2, chap. 6, 477 [424]. His emphases. For the proposal that Dasein is the set of human "activities and experiences [that] manifest a feel for what Being is," see John McCumber, *Time and Philosophy: A History of Continental Thought* (Montreal: McGill-Queen's University Press, 2011), 166. On "falling" and "resoluteness," see Hubert L. Dreyfus, *Being-in-the-World: A Commentary on Heidegger's* Being and Time, *Division 1* (Cambridge, MA: MIT Press, 1991), 313–22. On "resoluteness" see also the following note. On the "ecstatic[]," see n. 35 below.

[32] Heidegger, *Being and Time*, div. 2, chap. 6, 477 [424–25] read together with the "snatch[ing] . . . back" of div. 2, chap. 5, 435 [384]. For a good discussion of

Ecstatico-horizonal temporality temporalizes itself *primarily* in terms of the *future*....[33] [T]he future as ecstatically understood—the datable and significant 'then'—does not coincide with the ordinary conception of the 'future' in the sense of a pure "now" which has not yet come along but is only coming along....[34] The "now" is not pregnant with the "not-yet-now", but the Present arises from the future in the primordial ecstatical unity of the temporalizing of temporality.[35]

These are dense passages, the detailed exegesis of which lies beyond the present discussion. But what is clear is that in rejecting a view of time centred

---

"Entschlossenheit" and its connection to the "Augenblick" (or 'moment') of Kierkegaard, see Dreyfus, *Being-in-the-World*, 318–22. Perhaps there is a connection between Heidegger and Moltmann (and not just Kierkegaard and Moltmann) with respect to Moltmann's view of the moment as discussed in 3.5.2 and 3.5.3 above.

[33] Heidegger, *Being and Time*, div. 2, chap. 6, 479 [426]. His emphases. The alternative translation found in Martin Heidegger, *Being and Time*, trans. Joan Stambaugh, rev. ed. (Albany, NY: State University of New York Press, 2010), 405, has "*out of* [not "in terms of"] the *future*" here. First emphasis mine. In the Macquarrie and Robinson translation (which I will be citing unless otherwise stated), the passage continues,

In the way time is ordinarily understood, however, the basic phenomenon of time is seen in the '*now*', and indeed in that pure 'now' which has been shorn in its full structure—that which they call the 'Present'. One can gather from this that there is in principle no prospect that *in terms of this kind of 'now'* one can clarify the ecstatico-horizonal phenomenon of the *moment of vision* which belongs to temporality, or even that one can derive it thus. Correspondingly, the future....

His emphases. On "[e]cstatico-horizonal temporality," see n. 35 below. On authenticity and the authentic present (or "Present" in the above passage), see Dreyfus, *Being-in-the-World*, 322–28. On the authentic "temporalizing" of temporality, see n. 37 below.

[34] Heidegger, *Being and Time*, div. 2, chap. 6, 479 [427]. The passage continues, "And the concept of the past in the sense of the pure "now" which has passed away, is just as far from coinciding with the ecstatical "having-been"—the datable and significant 'on a former occasion'."

[35] Heidegger, *Being and Time*, div. 2, chap. 6, 479 [427]. The following commentary on Heidegger's terminology from Paul Gorner, *Heidegger's* Being and Time*: An Introduction* (Cambridge: Cambridge University Press, 2007), 169 is relevant here:

The temporality of Dasein as coming-towards-itself (future, *Zu-kunft*), coming-back-to-itself (past, having-been-ness, *Gewesenheit*), and enpresenting (present, *Gegen-wart, Gegenwärtigen*), in their essential interconnection, is *ecstatic* inasmuch as in its three dimensions it has the character of being *outside itself*. Each ecstasis is a kind of movement (*Entrückung*) outside itself. But this 'movement' outside itself, this ecstasis of temporality, is not a directionless movement... but has a 'whereto'... or 'whither'... which Heidegger calls the *horizon* or *horizonal schema* of the ecstasis. It is for this reason that he calls the original temporality of Dasein ecstatic-*horizonal* temporality.

His italics and emphases. Cf. Heidegger, *Being and Time*, div. 2, chap. 4, 416 [365].

in presence, Heidegger is giving (or is claiming to give[36]) a certain priority to the future,[37] which he distinguishes from the ontologically impoverished 'future-present' (to use Moltmann's terminology) that is characteristic of our "ordinary" conception. For Heidegger, because death is coming, our time—my time—will come. Even in the 'a-voidance' of our finitude, we reveal our being.

Heidegger's emphasis elsewhere in this work on *Zukunft* (future) as a coming rather than as something we simply make happen—a meaning highlighted by his hyphenated spelling of *Zu-kunft*—suggests a parallel of some kind with Moltmann's *adventus*. This is especially evident in the following passage in which Heidegger states,

> [Dasein's] letting-itself-*come-towards*-itself in that distinctive possibility which it puts up with, is the primordial phenomenon of the *future as coming towards* [*Zukommen*-lassen ist das ursprüngliche Phänomen der *Zu-kunft*].[38] If either authentic or inauthentic *Being-towards-death* belongs to Dasein's Being, then such Being-towards-death is possible only as something *futural* [als *zukünftiges*], in the sense that we have now indicated, and which we have still to define more closely. By the term 'futural', we do not here have in view a "now" which has *not yet* become 'actual' and which sometime *will be* for the first time. We have in view the coming [Kunft] in which Dasein, in its ownmost potentiality-for-Being, comes towards itself. Anticipation makes Dasein

---

[36] A number of Heidegger interpreters would claim that he does not really give priority to the future. Thus Chanter, in *Time, Death, and The Feminine*, xiv–xv, writes sympathetically,
> Levinas argues that Heidegger does not manage to overcome the traditional privilege of the present in his reinterpretation of time. He suggests that Heidegger's emphasis of Dasein's finitude does not escape the priority of the present, but remains caught up in it, since Heidegger's understanding of death is not radical enough. For Levinas, death is absolutely other. He claims that Heidegger's notion of being-toward-death amounts to a recuperation of the metaphysics of presence.

The point here in part would seem to be that for Heidegger, if I face my death, then Dasein is individuated authentically in the here and now—in the present. For Levinas, the true futurity and transcendence of my future death, a death I will not experience, is thus denied. Furthermore, it is the death of the other that is significant for Levinas. Here Moltmann would concur. See CoG, 96, cited in n. 53 below.

[37] Thus Sherover, in *The Human Experience of Time*, 519–47, entitles his selection's from Heidegger's *Being and Time* "The Priority of the Future," a phrase that is found in, e.g., *Being and Time*, div. 2, chap. 3, 378 [329]. Cf. Inwood, "Future," in *A Heidegger Dictionary*, 77–79. In a characteristically lucid essay, "The Flow of Time," in *The Philosophy of Time: A Collection of Essays*, ed. Richard M. Gale (New Jersey: Humanities Press, 1968), 355–77, William Barrett notes, on p. 366, that in *Being and Time*, "the future is the primary tense because man and his projects are in the foreground, and man temporalizes [cf. *Being and Time*, div. 2, chap. 6, 479 [426] cited above]—i.e. establishes himself meaningfully in time—out of his openness toward the future."

[38] The German and emphases in parentheses here are taken from 372n3 of the ET. Later parentheses are part of the main text of the ET.

authentically futural, and in such a way that the anticipation itself is possible only insofar as Dasein, *as being*, is always coming towards itself—that is to say, in so far as it is futural in its Being in general.[39]

The affinity with Moltmann is striking. It is certainly noteworthy that in one passage, Moltmann underlines the distinction between " 'the future' and 'the coming' " and between "extrapolation and anticipation"[40] by citing Heidegger's claim that the "calculat[ion] [of] ... what is destined" constitutes the "destruction of the future."[41] Also significant is that when Moltmann brings his discussion of "The Experience of History against the Horizon of its Future"[42] to a close with the words, "The primary phenomenon of primordial and authentic temporality is the future," he is quoting from *Being and Time*.[43]

Rather than seeing Moltmann's thought as derived from Heidegger (whom he cites fairly infrequently[44]), it is best to see the latter's philosophy and the existentialist phenomenology that he inspired as providing a clue to an intellectual context in which (and against which) Moltmann's thought has taken shape. Heidegger's phenomenological analysis of *Zu-kunft*, for example, may help us locate the philosophical milieu in which Moltmann is writing, a milieu

---

[39] Heidegger, *Being and Time*, div. 2, chap. 3, 372–73 [325]. Emphases from the ET.
[40] GC, 134. Part of this passage is cited in 2.4 above. Cf. 2.4n78 above.
[41] GC, 339–40n54, citing Heidegger, *Holzwege*, 5th ed. (Frankfurt: Klostermann, 1972), 301. This work, now available in English as: Martin Heidegger, *Off the Beaten Track*, ed. and trans. Julian Young and Kenneth Haynes (Cambridge: Cambridge University Press, 2002), was first published in 1950. For the relevant passage in the ET, see "Anaximander's Saying," in *Off the Beaten Track*, 246.
[42] This is the title to GC, chap. 5, sec. 5.1.
[43] GC, 130 citing *Being and Time*, div. 2, chap. 3, 378 [329]. Heidegger's original phrase is in italics.
[44] Moltmann's most sustained discussion of Heidegger occurs in TH, 255–58, a section (chap. 4, sec. 4e) that concludes by saying that Heidegger's anti-historicism constitutes a "losing sight of history as such." (Cf. EiT, 120–22 referred to below.) Citing Heidegger in CrG, 36, Moltmann comments positively in CrG, 76n16 on his understanding of Christian theology as a "theology of the cross" but rejects the idea of discipleship as the choosing of a "hero" in CrG, 61 and CrG, 78n48. CPS, 193–94 contains a brief, sympathetic discussion of Heidegger's view of anticipation. For significant references in GC, see nn. 40, 41, and 43 above. For criticism of Heidegger's anthropocentrism, see CoG, 300 and EiT, 120–22 where, contrary to Heidegger, Moltmann asserts, in EiT, 121, "Historical *Dasein* is *Dasein* in history, not just the historicity of *Dasein*." His italics. Here Moltmann would approve of Barrett's attempt, in "The Flow of Time, 376, to "use[] Heidegger against Heidegger" and thus free his thought from "any semblance of a subjective idealism."

In BP, 233, Moltmann refers to Daniel Louw's dissertation "written ... in Tübingen on Heidegger and myself." See Daniel Johannes Louw, "Toekoms tussen hoop en angs: 'n ondersoek na die funksie van die "ontologie van die nog-nie-syn" in die hedendaagse filosofie en teologie van die hoop, met besondere verwysing na die denke van Ernst Bloch en Jürgen Moltmann" (PhD diss., University of Stellenbosch, 1972). Normally (in line with its subtitle), this unpublished work in Afrikaans is cited as a study of Moltmann, Bloch, and the 'not-yet'.

very different from that which gives rise to Anglo-American analytic philosophies of time.[45] Similarly, Heidegger's analysis of the interwoven nature of the three "ecstaces" of temporality gives rise to an understanding of past, present, and future as "internally related"—a development that may be seen as pivotal for the literature with which Moltmann interacts concerning the modalisation of time.[46] The concept of philosophical milieu also helps us

---

[45] Thus Sherover's introduction to what he calls "The Structure of Experiential Time" in *The Human Experience of Time*, pt. 7 (437–65), provides us with an intellectual milieu within which Moltmann's approach to time can be readily appreciated. Cf. the post-Heideggerian reading/appropriation of Hegel's view of time (which consciously reads Hegel against the grain of his own thought) to be found in Hoffmeyer, *The Advent of Freedom: The Presence of the Future in Hegel's Logic*, also commented on in 4.1n115 above. This contains a number of striking similarities to Moltmann's view of time. It also contains a number of references to contemporary German theology.

[46] Heidegger, *Being and Time*, div. 2, chap. 3, 377 [329]. Cf. n. 35 above. On the interwovenness of the ecstates, see also Heidegger, *Being and Time*, div. 2, chap. 4, 401 [350]. On the parallel interwovenness of past, present, and future in Moltmann's modalisation of time, see 3.3 above. That the past, present, and future are "internally related" for Heidegger is how John Macquarrie aptly puts it in *Heidegger and Christianity* (London: SCM Press, 1994), 40, 43.

While Macquarrie's discussion is very helpful, his tendency to equate the ecstaces and the modes of time is an (understandable) oversimplification. Although the three ecstases, which underlie the three principal structures of Dasein's being (projection, thrownness, and concern), clearly correspond to the future, past, and present, respectively, they do not include (and must not be identified with) the everyday notion of time as a series of 'nows' (i.e., the future as not-yet-now, the past as no-longer-now, and the present as now)—a series that is easily accommodated within the modalisation of past, present, and future. That said, the 'nows' and the ecstases are related, for Heidegger, in that "ordinary" time, to use the terminology that runs through *Being and Time*, div. 2, chap. 6 (see, especially, 478–79 [426–27]), presupposes and is derived from ecstatic, "primordial" time (which Gorner, in his helpful discussion in *Heidegger's Being and Time*, chap. 8, retranslates as "original" time). There is thus a parallel between the titles to div. 1, chap. 6, sec. 44 (b): "The primordial phenomenon of truth [as disclosure] and the derivative character of the traditional [propositional] character of truth" and to div. 2, chap. 6: "Temporality . . . as the Source of the Ordinary Conception of Time."

While Moltmann's focus is on God and creation rather than on Dasein's existential coming-towards-itself, coming-back-to-itself, and letting-itself-be-encountered, Heidegger's distinction between ordinary and primordial/original time has some affinity with Moltmann's distinction between the phenomenal and transcendental levels of time, and thus between the phenomenal *futurum* and transcendental *adventus*, as discussed in 2.4 above. On the modalisation of time, which, in his understanding, can elucidate both our ordinary and eschatological temporal experience (whether authentic or not), Moltmann refers, in GC, 128, to the work of Georg Picht, A.M. Klaus Müller, Arthur Prior, Niklas Luhmann, Reinhart Koselleck, and Erich Jantsch. As a thinker in the analytic tradition, A.N. Prior is the exception that proves the rule here as is clear from his *Time and Modality* (Oxford: Clarendon Press, 1957). Moltmann cites his later, equally 'analytic' work *Past, Present and Future* (Oxford: Oxford University Press, 1967). On Picht as Heidegger's pupil, see n. 48 below.

explain some interesting similarities between Moltmann's view of time and that of one of Heidegger's contemporaries, the French phenomenologist Eugène Minkowski, even though the latter is (to the best of my knowledge) not cited in Moltmann's corpus.[47] As for more 'direct' influence, it should also be noted that Moltmann does refer positively to the work of Heidegger's pupil Georg Picht at a number of strategic points.[48]

But it is also fruitful to read Moltmann's thought as an *answer* to Heidegger in certain respects. If Moltmann would concur with seeing Heidegger's futurity as moving beyond the *futurum* of our dreams of mastery and progress, it is doubtful that he would see this coming future as truly eschatological, as more than (what I, in adapting his terminology, have termed) a historical *adventus*.[49] The being-towards-[my]-death authentically faced, anticipated, and understood

---

[47] See, in particular, Eugène Minkowski, *Lived Time: Phenomenological and Psychopathological Studies*, trans. Nancy Metzel (Evanston, IL: Northwestern University Press, 1970)—a work first published in French in 1927. Chapter 4, entitled "The Future," (79–129), includes a section (92–102) on "Desire and Hope" (these corresponding somewhat to "activity" and "expectation") followed by a discussion of "Prayer" (103–11). Near the end of the latter section, in *Lived Time*, 109, Minkowski writes,
> We say that hope surpasses expectation and goes further into the future; prayer goes even further, so far that it goes "to the limit.". . . In prayer I completely embrace the moving wave of becoming; I see it directed towards me as if coming from a powerful and luminous source.

Sherover, in *The Human Experience of Time*, 453, writes that for Minkowski,
> [T]here are two different ways in which the future enters into my horizon of life: the first is that activity which, indeed, 'pushes' toward the future and thereby helps to create it; its opposite is not passivity but expectation, which marks one's attitude as he merely lets the future come to him.

Cf. Minkowski's diagram in *Lived Time*, 90. This is a distinction between what I would call the foundational and transcendental directions of time (on which see 5.2 below). This corresponds to Moltmann's distinction between *futurum* and *adventus*.

[48] See TH, 41; CrG, 334 (and 340n35); CPS, 383n62; GC, 111, 129, 199 (and 347n24), 266 (and 353n44); WJC, 236 (and 371n34); and CoG, 26 (and 344n59), 133 (and 357n10), 260, 286, 287, 291 (and 379n83 also with reference to Heidegger). The Heidegger-Picht connection is also referred to in SW, 66 and 86. Cf. Georg Picht, "The God of the Philosophers," *Journal of the American Academy of Religion* 48, no. 1 (1980): 61–79 and Christopher Morse, *The Logic of Promise in Moltmann's Theology* (Philadelphia: Fortress Press, 1979), 55–57. For Moltmann's discussion of theologian Christian Link, an assistant to Picht at Heidelberg from 1969–76, see his "Schöpfung im Horizont der Zeit," *Evangelische Theologie* 52, no. 1 (1992): 86–92.

[49] See 2.4 above, especially with reference to my discussion of GC, 133. While the distinction between *futurum* and *adventus* in this context allows us to appreciate what Macquarrie, in *Heidegger and Christianity*, 36, calls Heidegger's "secularized and individualized eschatology," the fact that this is a "historical [rather than eschatological] *adventus*" can also help us appreciate why McCumber, in *Time and Philosophy*, 175, interprets Heidegger's conception of death as a quasi-*telos*. Cf. n. 53 below.

in an "existentiell manner"[50] is not the being-through-and-beyond-death of authentic hope. The vector of transience continues to eclipse God's future. The future of and for the entire cosmos is lost in the all-too-human futurity of Dasein.[51] Faith is overshadowed by fate, Hoffnung by Schicksal, eschatology by Geschichte/Geschick.[52] Despite the focus that finitude may bring to human existence here and now, Death, not Life, has the last word.[53]

---

[50] Heidegger, *Being and Time*, div. 2, chap. 6, 477 [425]. Cf. *Being and Time*, Intro., chap. 1, 33 [12]: "The question of existence never gets straightened out except through existing itself. The understanding of oneself that leads *along this way* we call '*existentiell*'." His emphases.

[51] On Moltmann's critique of Heidegger as anthropocentric, see the references cited at the end of n. 44 above. I am not commenting on the thought of the 'later' Heidegger in this brief section. Nevertheless, in my judgment, Heidegger's later explicit rejection of "humanism" (on which see Inwood, "Humanism," in *A Heidegger Dictionary*, 100–102), a humanism he never intended in *Being and Time*, still does not yield the 'cosmic' vision that Moltmann would desire. That said, the later Heidegger did claim that even in *Being and Time*, Being transcends Dasein. He also made it clear that Dasein was not a Sartrean individual. See the helpful discussion in George Pattison, *The Later Heidegger* (London: Routledge, 2000), 1–14.

[52] While it is certainly possible to read Heidegger's view of (individual) fate (Schicksal) as well as (communal) destiny (Geschick) as intended to identify positive realities akin to providence and calling that are not captured by "fate" in everyday English (cf. the discussions in Stephen Mulhall, *Heidegger and* Being and Time, 2nd ed. (London: Routledge, 2005), chap. 7 and Inwood, "Fate and Destiny," in *A Heidegger Dictionary*, 67–69), I am postulating that Moltmann, in the light of Christian hope, would not find a more positive reading of Heidegger sufficiently compelling. An important passage on "fate" (Schicksal) from *Being and Time*, div. 2, chap. 5, 435 [384] is cited and discussed in TH, 256.

[53] The focus and direction that our mortality may instill is central to Heidegger's claim that there is something "positive" for us in death as the "end" of Dasein (*Being and Time*, div. 2, chap. 1, 290 [246]). As McCumber, *Time and Philosophy*, 175, puts it:

> We have a future, are *essentially* futural beings, because we are going to die. And we live coherent lives, rather than merely drifting, for the same reason. Death, as the "end of Dasein", thus performs the same function that a *telos* does for Aristotle: it organizes our lives around our basic commitments, or at least provides the impetus for us to do so.

His emphasis and italics. While Moltmann need not deny the (half-)truth in such a "negative theory of time" (CoG, 292; he clearly alludes to Heidegger earlier in this paragraph on CoG, 291, referring to him explicitly in CoG, 379n83), the fundamental issue for a theology and life of hope is that "the teleology of creation is not its eschatology" (WJC, 303, cf. 2.5 above). Moltmann is also clearly responding to Heidegger's notion of human existence as being-towards-death in CoG, 96 (citing him in CoG, 353n85), where he notes, "in actual truth the death of others, the death of people we love, is the real experience of death we go through." He would agree with Levinas' assessment of Heidegger here. Cf. n. 36 above.

If, contrary to a Christian point of view, death rather than life has the last word in Heidegger, this is even more so with respect to the futurity emphasised by later existentialists such as John-Paul Sartre. See, e.g., Sartre's 1943 work, *Being and Nothingness: A Phenomenological Essay on Ontology*, trans. Hazel E. Barnes (1957;

Nevertheless, Heidegger's attempt to break with the view of time that he finds in the entire Western tradition read together with his (related) reversal of the Aristotelian priority given to actuality over possibility[54] suggest a significant affinity with Moltmann. Even within what Cox (with some justification) refers to as "the tight finitude of Heidegger's constricted human world," we may feel the "pull of the future."

To suggest that any contemporary German theologian's thought has been shaped by Heidegger and the issues he raises has a certain *prima facie* plausibility given his influence on Continental philosophy. The fact that Heidegger's recognised theological influence extends to the thinking of Moltmann's fellow 'theologian of hope' J-B Metz is also significant.[55] Although it falls beyond the scope of the present study, the possibility that Moltmann can be understood as (at least in effect if not in conscious intention) more thoroughly eschatologising certain themes in (the) Heidegger (of *Being and Time*)—themes that Heidegger himself has taken over from the history of theology[56]—is worthy of further investigation.

---

repr., New York: Washington Square Press, 1992), pt. 2, chap. 2, sec. 2, C, "The Future" (180–87).

[54] See *Being and Time*, div. 1, chap. 5, 183 [143–44],

    As a modal category of presence-at-hand, possibility signifies what is *not yet* actual and what is *not at any time* necessary. It characterizes the *merely* possible. Ontologically it is on a lower level than actuality and necessity. On the other hand, possibility as an *existentiale* is the most primordial and ultimate positive way in which Dasein is characterised ontologically.

His emphases. Cf. *Being and Time*, Intro., chap. 2, 63 [38], "Higher than actuality stands *possibility*." His emphasis. On the priority of possibility/potentiality over actuality in Moltmann, see 2.2 above together with CoG, 26, 286–87 (with reference to Picht and Bloch) and EiT, 32.

[55] This was noted in Capps, *Time Invades the Cathedral*, 94–95: "Johannes Metz's principal theological and philosophical mentors are Karl Rahner and Martin Heidegger." The numerous similarities between Metz and Moltmann are easy to see in Johann-Baptist Metz and Jürgen Moltmann, *Faith and the Future: Essays on Theology, Solidarity, and Modernity* (Maryknoll, NY: Orbis, 1995); and Johann-Baptist Metz and Jürgen Moltmann, *Meditations on the Passion: Two Meditations on Mark 8:31–38*, trans. Edmund Colledge (New York: Paulist Press, 1979).

[56] Heidegger's indebtedness to the history of theology is widely recognised. Thus Mulhall, *Heidegger and* Being and Time, chap. 5 (on *Being and Time*, div. 2, intro. and chaps. 1–2) is entitled "Theology Secularized." Cf. Stephen Mulhall, *Philosophical Myths of the Fall* (Princeton: Princeton University Press, 2005), chap. 2; John D. Caputo, "Heidegger and Theology," in *The Cambridge Companion to Heidegger*, ed. Charles B. Guignon, 2nd ed. (Cambridge: Cambridge University Press, 2006), 326–44; Ben Vedder, "Ontotheology and the Question of God(s)," in *Martin Heidegger: Key Concepts*, ed. Bret W. Davis (Durham, UK: Acumen, 2010), 219–30; and Bret W. Davis, "Heidegger on Christianity and Divinity: A Chronological Compendium," in *Martin Heidegger: Key Concepts*, ed. Bret W. Davis (Durham, UK: Acumen, 2010), 231–59. One example of Heidegger's indebtedness might be his view of our authentic 'powerlessness' as noted in relation to Moltmann in 6.5n166 below.

To find a more-than-suggestive point of contact with what is surely the central feature of Moltmann's understanding of time—the distinction between time's historical and eschatological directions—however, we need to look elsewhere (although we shall not be moving entirely beyond the milieu of existentialist phenomenology). The philosophy of time suggested by neo-Calvinist philosopher Hendrik Hart is, in my judgment, most promising in this respect.

5.2 Foundational and Transcendental Time in the Philosophy of Hendrik Hart

Change, movement, growth, development, and progress take place in a certain direction. The past must come before the future, before precedes after, and the future comes after the present. The temporal series displays an irreversible direction of past, present, future. Time [therefore] moves out of the past and into the future. . . .
[At the same time,] [e]vents are directed; and they are directed by anticipation. The directing is done by something toward which the process moves; for that very reason, however, this "something" is not really present. The anticipation of the future directs the present. . . . Time has an anticipatory qualifying direction as well as a retrocipatory founding direction. The latter direction is the existential foundation of all possibility, while the former directs the temporal process. They may be referred to as the founding and directing orders of time. They temporally found and direct the dynamic of reality.
Certain things must happen before or after others: seeding before harvesting, for example, and the hostages were freed after the Shah died. This is a matter of temporal priority determined by the order of reality, and experienced in the actuality of events. It is in the actuality of events that order and subjectivity [law and response] . . . are integrated in time. Events move within structural limits and in a certain direction, so they are directed and supported at the same time. As a result, a diversity of moments are pulled in time into a unity of direction. In time, that unity and diversity also become fully integrated, for then the order of unity is met in an actual integral unity of functioning. In this way unity and diversity are also temporal moments. The movement of all things, the genetic process of growth, the ontic structure of anticipated meaning—all of this activity is a phase of the temporal process being directed towards fullness, totality, and fulfilment. Everything that is real must start somewhere and have its foundation in something. But everything also goes somewhere and has a destiny. If we look at reality from the point of view of the future, then that future directs the present. Through anticipation, the future becomes a basis for the present direction of things.[57]

---

[57] Hendrik Hart, *Understanding Our World: An Integral Ontology* (Lanham, MD: University Press of America, 1984), 264–65. I have also explored Hart's position in "Foundational and Transcendental Time: An Essay," in *Philosophy as Responsibility: A Celebration of Hendrik Hart's Contribution to the Discipline*, ed. Ronald A. Kuipers and Janet Catherina Wesselius (Lanham, MD: University Press of America, 2002), 63–

These paragraphs comprise the greater part of a section entitled "Temporal direction" in Hendrik Hart's major work in systematic philosophy, *Understanding Our World: An Integral Ontology*. Here a distinction is made between two temporal orders which, in the language of an earlier version of this passage, are described as the "foundational" and "transcendental" directions of time.[58] Hart's claim that "Time moves out of the past and into the future," which is based on viewing existence in this first, foundational direction, seems unremarkable as it accords with the well-known linear view of time. But he also notes that "If we look at reality from the point of view of the future, then that future directs the present." To adapt his language, we might say that in this transcendental (or 'opening') direction, 'Time moves out of the future and into the past'. Like Moltmann's *adventus*, this future (which is associated with "fullness, totality, and fulfilment") is not to be understood in terms of an Aristotelian (or Blochian) entelechy. Indeed, Hart's distinction between the *foundational* and *transcendental* directions of time bears a striking resemblance to Moltmann's distinction between the *historical* and *eschatological* directions of time.

Before proceeding further, it will be helpful to place these suggestions within a wider context. Hart claims that he "owe[s] [his] view of time entirely to Herman Dooyeweerd,"[59] the Dutch philosopher and legal theorist who, paralleling Heidegger's attempt to speak of a fuller experience of temporality than one dominated by our time-keeping, developed a multi-dimensional, creation-wide view of (what he called) "cosmic time."[60] However, as I have argued elsewhere,[61] Hart has, with respect to the notion of the two temporal directions, made an original contribution by taking one of Dooyeweerd's *ontological* distinctions and exploring its implications for an understanding of the temporal process.[62]

---

79. As that essay is based on a draft version of this chapter, it, in part, parallels paragraphs in this present section.
[58] Hendrik Hart, "Draft for Proposed ICS Systematic Philosophy Syllabus," 2 vols. (Toronto: unpublished ms, 1976), 1:148.
[59] Hart, *Understanding Our World*, 414n6.
[60] There is a helpful discussion of time in L. Kalsbeek, *Contours of a Christian Philosophy: An Introduction to Herman Dooyeweerd's Thought*. A Supplement to the Collected Works of Herman Dooyeweerd, ser. C, vol. 2, ed. Bernard and Josina Zylstra (1975; repr., Lewiston, NY: Mellen, 2002), chap. 20. This work is probably the clearest single-author introduction to Dooyeweerd in English.
[61] See my "Foundational and Transcendental Time."
[62] In this respect, Dooyeweerd's original discussion of this distinction is very under-developed. Cf. the brief reference to "the twofold direction of time" and "the foundational and transcendental temporal direction" in Herman Dooyeweerd, *A New Critique of Theoretical Thought*, 4 vols., trans. David H. Freeman and William S. Young (Philadelphia: Presbyterian and Reformed, 1953–58), 2:191–92. There is at least one suggestive connection made between the "transcendental direction" and the eschatological consummation of history in *A New Critique*, 2:337. The following discussion will explore this while rejecting the link between eschatological and supra-temporal suggested in *A New Critique*, 1:33—a link Hart also rejects along with several

Dooyeweerd often uses 'temporal' terminology in order to elucidate his ontology or theory of general structures rather than to explore the nature of 'time' in the usual sense of the term.[63] It is interesting that a parallel with Heidegger can be drawn at this point.[64] Hart has taken the distinction between the foundational and transcendental directions of the modal order (an ontological order to be explored in 5.2.1 below) and 're-temporalised' it, thus developing the philosophy of time latent within Dooyeweerd's theorising about the order of creation.

After briefly exploring the 'temporal' nature of ontology as practised by Hart and Dooyeweerd in the context of analysing the foundational and transcendental directions of being, I will offer some suggestions on how a number of Hart's ontological distinctions might further open up the distinction he makes between the two directions of time. In this I will be making explicit what I take to be implicit in the paragraphs cited at the beginning of this section as read within *Understanding Our World* as a whole. Distinctions and connections to be explored include: (i) modes of being and modes of time, (ii) founding, qualifying, and guiding in relation to past, present, and future, (iii) expression and reference in relation to immanence and transcendence, and finally, the two directions of time in relation to (iv) creation and eschaton and (v) differentiation and integration. The aim is to bring Moltmann's view of time into conversation with Hart's revision of Dooyeweerd in a way that is meaningful for those familiar with one or more of these thinkers. The results are summarised in figure 7 in 5.3 below.

---

other key elements in Dooyeweerd's philosophy of time in Hendrik Hart, "Problems of Time: An Essay," in *The Idea of a Christian Philosophy: Essays in Honour of D.H.Th. Vollenhoven*, ed. K.A. Bril, H. Hart, and J. Klapwijk, special issue, *Philosophia Reformata* 38 (Toronto: Wedge, 1973), 30–42. For other ways in which this expansion of Hart's thinking represents a departure from Dooyeweerd, see n. 98 below.

[63] Thus C.T. McIntire in "Dooyeweerd's Philosophy of History," in *The Legacy of Herman Dooyeweerd: Reflections on Critical Philosophy in the Christian Tradition*, ed. C.T. McIntire (Lanham, MD: University Press of America, 1985), 87, sees his theory of "cosmic time" as, in certain respects, "a misnomer."

[64] Albert M. Wolters in "The Intellectual Milieu of Herman Dooyeweerd," in *The Legacy of Herman Dooyeweerd: Reflections on Critical Philosophy in the Christian Tradition*, ed. C.T. McIntire (Lanham, MD: University Press of America, 1985), 15 writes,

> [T]here is one point which may establish a connection between Heidegger and Dooyeweerd: the idea of cosmic time. Vincent Brümmer has shown that Dooyeweerd introduced his concept of time in the late 1920s, about the time he read Heidegger [he studied *Being and Time* intensively]. Dooyeweerd understood time as a kind of ontological principle of intermodal continuity bearing very little relation to what we call time in ordinary language. The same can be said for Heidegger's conception of time, which seems also to be a general ontological principle of continuity. This similarity merits further investigation and analysis.

5.2.1 Modes of Being/Time

The most basic distinction in Hart's ontology as articulated in this work is the distinction (/correlation) between the "world order" and the "ordered world."[65] Within the latter, Hart makes a further, three-fold distinction between "functors functioning in relationship," functions approximating to the properties, actions, and experiences of functors or entities.[66] Central to his ontology of functionality is the notion of a modal order, "modes" being understood as the irreducible kinds of functioning that we grasp in concepts.

As a follower of Dooyeweerd, Hart understands the various modes of our humanity as arranged in an ascending order of (kinds of) ontological complexity from the numerical up to the pistical.[67] Within this order, it is possible to analyse the typical ways in which lower or earlier modes have a "foundational" impact on the higher or later modes, while the latter open or qualify the former in the "transcendental" direction. The foundational role of the biotic mode-of-being, for example, is evident in the fact that we cannot pray and thus be people of faith if we do not breathe. The transcendental influence of faith on our analytic activities can be seen in our beliefs, without which we cannot think.

The modal order is not a great chain of being with the Divine at the top and godless matter at the bottom. Humans (who are active/receptive in all the modes or ways-of-being-in-the-world) vitally depend on trees (as biotic subjects-agents) for oxygen and thus for their future. Similarly, the rain forests depend for their future on humanity rejecting its misplaced faith in 'progress' and engaging in its shaping of creation's history in covenant with God and (thus) with all of God's creatures. God's blessing for life must thus be mediated foundationally and transcendentally throughout the cosmos.

The fact that influence and dependence can be detected in both the foundational and transcendental directions of the modal order has implications for the internal structure of the modes themselves. As Hart's discussion makes clear, modal irreducibility does not entail viewing the modes-of-being as akin

---

[65] In *Understanding Our World*, xxi, Hart writes, "In this book I consider the correlated pair of ordered world and world order to be the most fundamental relationship which philosophy needs to treat." Cf. *Understanding Our World*, 37. "World order" is understood as a creation order, a normative order for the world, while "ordered world" refers to the whole of existence in and as response to that order. Creation order is further explored in my "Foundational and Transcendental Time," 73–77 and in Nicholas Ansell, "For the Love of Wisdom: Scripture, Philosophy, and the Relativisation of Order," in *The Future of Creation Order*, ed. Gerrit Glas, Jeroen de Ridder, Govert Buijs, and Annette Mosher (Dordrecht: Springer, forthcoming).
[66] See Hart, *Understanding Our World*, 1.
[67] For Hart, the basic modes of existence are: the numeric, the spatial, the kinematic, the energetic, the biotic, the psychic, the formative, the symbolic, the analytic, the social, the economic, the juridical, the ethical, and the pistical. See *Understanding Our World*, 190–98. The "pistical" mode is the mode of faith. The main difference between Hart's modes of being and those of Dooyeweerd is that Hart does not understand history as a mode. See n. 98 below.

to the distinct layers of a wedding cake. The way in which higher modes depend on and respond to the lower in the foundational direction is evident in modal "retrocipations" within these higher modes of being. At the same time, the dependence and response of the lower or earlier kinds of functionality on and to the higher in the transcendental direction can be seen in modal "anticipations" within the lower.[68]

To use two of Hart's own examples, "aptitude" is a psychic retrocipatory "moment" within the techno-formative mode of functioning, while "verification" is an analytic anticipation of the certainty of faith.[69] In the former example, psychic sensitivity comes to a particular form of expression within "formative" functioning, which is centred on the means-end relationship. In the latter, analytic procedures must be understood with reference to our capacity for faith (understood as our trust/hope in what we take to be Ultimate).

In such abstract discussions, one does not expect to focus on individual cases or temporal processes except as ways of illustrating more permanent features of our world. Change, development, decay, the coming into being and passing away, all associated with time, elude our conceptual grasp as does individuality and singularity. While recognising that 'permanent' is also a temporal category, we may still grant that ontology is the study of being rather than becoming.

Nevertheless, a significant number of technical terms utilised by Hart and Dooyeweerd in their ontological investigations have temporal meanings that do not first and foremost denote the more constant, perduring features of our world. Among these we may include *anticipations*, *earlier* and *later* modes, modal *moments*, and functions of *destination*.[70] It is also possible to speak of the modes (or modalisation) of time,[71] '*mode*' itself being a temporal term (the Latin *modo*—meaning 'just now', as in 'outmoded' or 'modernity'—being the adverbial form of *modus*). Such language suggests a world on the move, a historical world.

Why does such language show up in the field of ontology? Hart's account suggests that epistemologically (and thus ontologically) speaking, looking at the world modally is the result of viewing it from the vantage point of one of its

---

[68] Similarly, Calvin G. Seerveld in "Dooyeweerd's Legacy for Aesthetics," in *The Legacy of Herman Dooyeweerd: Reflections on Critical Philosophy in the Christian Tradition*, ed. C.T. McIntire (Lanham, MD: University Press of America, 1985), 61 and 59 contrasts "Dooyeweerd's prism-refracted colors" with Nicolai Hartmann's "rungs of a ladder" by noting that "Dooyeweerd posits that these modes of meaning show both a mutual irreducibility and a veritably isotropic interpenetration of each other." Here, I refer to this as mutual dependence. Later in this section, I will distinguish between foundational 'dependence' and transcendental 'openness'. But here my emphasis is on the interpenetration and responsiveness occurring in both directions.
[69] See Hart, *Understanding Our World*, 195 and 194.
[70] A function of "destination" is a "qualifying" function as I will use that term. Thus an actual friendship is "qualified" by the ethical mode, given the fact that it is a relationship of loyalty, commitment, and (to use an old English word) "troth" (as in 'betrothal').
[71] See, e.g., CoG, 284.

modes, the analytic, as it is only from this perspective—from this kind of experience and knowledge—that the world is seen first and foremost as consisting of kinds of functors and functions.[72] Yet ontology is the study of all existence in terms of what may be analytically or conceptually grasped. Ontologists are not logicians. They are not engaged in the study of concepts, but in conceptual study. Our ontological investigations occupy a place in time from which we conceive of a world in time (or better: a temporal world).

Consequently, although much that we know of our world in non-theoretical experience becomes highly relativised within theory, time is never bracketed from our awareness but is experienced within rational-conceptual experience as (or in relationship to the) perduring. Transience, in as much as it comes into view, will tend to be related to what is stable and law-like. In this context, features of our largely non-conceptual awareness of the world's temporal character are not absent from our theoretical experience of the world but find their own theoretical (or conceptual) counterparts and expressions. Given the relativity—relatedness—of theory to all that we know (and to all the ways in which we come to know, to all our knowings), this is entirely legitimate, enhancing the chances of our ontologies being relevant to the rest of our knowledge/experience. One way in which the (largely and variously) dynamic nature of the 'world' of pre-theoretical experience shows up in the 'world'[73] of ontology is in the way any given irreducible kind of functioning may be seen to express and refer to "earlier" and/or "later" modes of being.[74]

If the temporal nature of many ontological categories used by followers of Dooyeweerd is to be expected and welcomed, it is appropriate to ask whether certain ontological distinctions that (in their own way) already reflect the dynamic character of our world might not be (re-)applied to our understanding of time. To that end, I will follow Hart in offering some examples to illustrate that the foundational-transcendental distinction first developed in ontology is extremely illuminating when applied to an analysis of temporal process. Some interesting points of connection between Hart and Moltmann will emerge in this context. This discussion will also prove fruitful for exploring the nature-grace relationship.

---

[72] See Hendrik Hart, "Dooyeweerd's *Gegenstand* theory of theory," in *The Legacy of Herman Dooyeweerd: Reflections on Critical Philosophy in the Christian Tradition*, ed. C.T. McIntire (Lanham, MD: University Press of America, 1985), 143–66.

[73] These two 'worlds' are of course the same world experienced in different ways.

[74] In this exposition, I have placed terms that function as technical terms in the philosophy of Dooyeweerd and his followers, such as "earlier" and "later," within full quotation marks, reserving single quotation marks for words (such as 'world') that I wish to otherwise highlight. In context, this terminology should make sense. Cf. Albert M. Wolters, "Glossary," in *The Legacy of Herman Dooyeweerd: Reflections on Critical Philosophy in the Christian Tradition*, ed. C.T. McIntire (Lanham, MD: University Press of America, 1985), 167–71, which is a condensed version of his glossary in L. Kalsbeek, *Contours of a Christian Philosophy*, 307–15.

While (arguably) time never travels backwards,[75] it may be viewed in two directions analogous to the two complementary perspectives from which we may analyse modal order. The three fundamental "modes" of time can be viewed in terms of their mutual influence from the foundational perspective of Past→ Present→ Future and from the transcendental perspective of Future→ Present→ Past (or Past ←Present ←Future).[76] In the first, the past is the basis upon which the present and future are built; in the second perspective, it is the future that orients present and past.[77]

In this context, it is worth recognising a distinction between the directions of (a) influence and (b) response (understood as either dependence or openness) within each of these two perspectives. Foundationally speaking, the past influences or shapes the present while both shape the future (represented above as "Past→ Present→ Future"). At the same time, the present is a foundational response to the past just as the future will be a response to both. Thus we may also represent the foundational direction, in which retrocipation or referring

---

[75] I sympathise with Ben Turnbull, the narrator of John Updike's novel *Towards the End of Time* (1997; repr., New York: Balantine, 1998), 202: "The arrow of time. Some scientists think its direction is reversible in quantum situations, and others think it would be reversible if the universe were as smooth at the end of time as it was in the beginning. I can't quite picture it myself." Cf. *Towards the End of Time*, 213–14

[76] In portraying foundational influence as 'Past→ Present→ Future' I am interpreting the arrow of time differently from Moltmann. But the difference is not as great as it looks. See figure 2 above and the explanation in 2.3 above.

[77] As I explain below, the future here orients the present via our 'anticipatings'. I do not intend to reify the future. Ultimately, it is the promises we trust that guide history.

As it need not be confined to human action and experience, influence or causation in the transcendental direction may be a fruitful way to (re-)conceive what the 'Intelligent Design' movement means by its central metaphor. In this light, the naturalism that this movement (rightly) resists recognises only the foundational direction. For a nuanced introduction, see William A. Dembski, *The Design Revolution: Answering the Toughest Questions about Intelligent Design* (Downers Grove, IL: InterVarsity Press, 2004). Especially relevant here is chap. 34, in which Dembski discusses the difference between a "process" (which is truly gap-less) and "creative innovation," both of which, he says, can be seen as concurrent in the origin and development of life. If one were to relate Dembski's (brief but insightful) argument here (in *The Design Revolution*, 249–52) to the two directions of time (and to the two directions of modal order), perhaps a truly integral, non-dualistic alternative to evolutionary naturalism could take shape. Put in the language of the framework I am advocating, Dembski comes close to saying that *newness*, at one and the same time, *emerges* (foundationally) and *arrives* or *comes into being* (transcendentally) (cf. the pregnant/expecting metaphor in 5.3 below). As such an approach allows for the simultaneous recognition of the 'ongoing' and the 'incoming', it could help the 'ID' paradigm escape (a) the confines of the mechanistic thinking that sympathetic critic, Steve Fuller, detects in his *Science vs Religion? Intelligent Design and the Problem of Evolution* (Cambridge: Polity, 2007), 28, 43, 56–58, and (b) the mechanist/vitalist problematics he identifies in *Dissent over Descent: Intelligent Design's Challenge to Darwinism* (Cambridge: Icon, 2008), 155–58, without watering down its critique of (what might be called) 'emergentistic' (and thus reductionistic) views of change and development.

back in time is of fundamental importance, as: Past ⇐Present ⇐Future. Similarly, in the transcendental direction in which our anticipation of the future is fundamental,[78] response (or openness) can be represented as: Past⇒ Present⇒ Future. The two-way nature of each perspective is set out below.

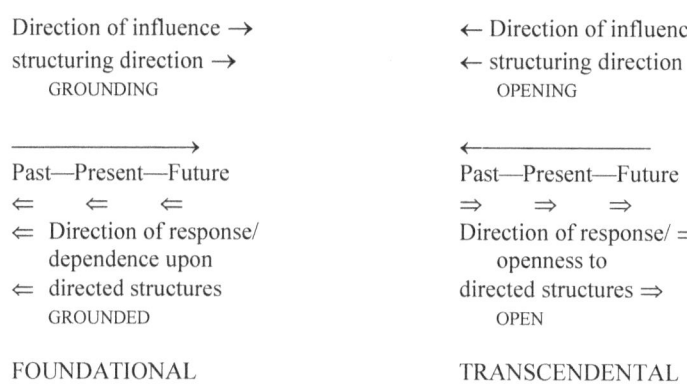

figure 6

To anticipate some theological claims that I will make presently, it should be noted that foundationally speaking, because the modes of any action, experience, or event refer back to earlier kinds of functioning, to the self as centre of intention, and ultimately to God as the foundation and origin of all existence (to God as Creator), the past is not an autonomous source of what comes afterwards as it cannot be considered apart from God as the origin and beginning of all becoming (except for the coming into being of evil). In the transcendental direction, God is the end and goal of history anticipated in the present by those who receive that future as a promise.[79]

---

[78] As I explain below, anticipation is related to the promises we trust. I speak of 'anticipation' here rather than 'expectation' as the latter term may connote hopes that are based on the past. 'Well, what did you expect?', we say to those who should have known better. 'Expectancy' however speaks more of hope than planning and prediction.
[79] To speak of God as origin (or Origin) and end (or End) means that God is made known in and via created origins and ends. The beginning and the fulfilment both reveal God. God is known through and revealed by creation-new creation, by the ongoing foundation supplied by the past and by the pull of the future. God works foundationally via the gifts s/he gives and transcendentally via the promises s/he makes. I do not mean to 'identify' God with creation (or time) ontologically but covenantally. Language for God ('origin', 'future') points to the creation/history 'in terms of' which God is known. There is no extra-creational language for God available to us. For the God of covenant, such (impossible) language is unnecessary (an issue I will return to in 8.3 below). Just as to call God 'Father' need not humanise God ontologically but simply confesses how God is really present in a particular (creaturely) way, thus meeting a particular cluster of

One of the many parallels that exists between modal and temporal order concerns the similarity between (a) the way the past currently founds the present and thus makes it possible, even as the present makes the past present (as what Moltmann would call the "present past"[80]) and (b) the way a modal aspect of a reality plays an indispensable foundational role in an act, event, or relationship even as the reality of which it is a dimension is qualified or characterised by a higher or later mode. In both instances, what is earlier is encapsulated by or taken up into a later reality without losing its own identity. Thus friendship finds an important foundation, basis, and impetus in emotional affinity but is qualified or characterised by the ethical mode of "troth." Thus attraction is taken up into fidelity. On the one hand, commitment and loyalty, while they may point us to the special nature of friendship, are not free-floating, with no roots in the earlier modes of existence. There is more to actual friendship than what characterises it. On the other hand, troth is not the 'icing on the cake' but characterises the whole, multi-modal relationship, including the ongoing emotional affinity that attracts people to one another in the first place. By analogy, the present must have its origins in the past. Consequently, there is more to what we rightly refer to and know as 'the present' than the present in a modal sense. But while we might say that the present has a past 'aspect', it is nevertheless a temporal reality that is wholly "qualified" or "characterised" by the present mode of time. The present *past* is the *present* past.

5.2.2 Founding, Qualifying, Guiding: Past, Present, Future

In Hart's terminology, the qualifying/founding dynamics of an event or relationship are called its x/y (read: "x over y") structure.[81] By analogy, the past can be seen as a "y" that is foundationally related to the "x" of the present. The transcendental side of this relationship—how the "x" of the present qualifies the "y" of the past—is evident if we analyse how our hopes for the future affect the way in which we allow the past to be expressed in the present.

Because all life is ultimately guided (= "G") by human faith (even if that is not faith in the true God), Hart claims that all acts, events, and relationships have a "G over (x over y)" structure.[82] A friendship, for example, is not only ontologically *founded* in a certain affinity and *qualified* by troth, but (along with the rest of life) is *guided* by faith. This raises the question of whether the temporal relationship between past, present, and future can be seen in terms of a "G over (x over y)" structure. Is it helpful, for example, to see the past as founding the present while the future guides the present?

---

human needs, so to call God "the goal of history" need not temporalise God. But this not an argument for divine atemporality either. Given my focus on God's creational presence, I wish to emphasise that the *God* of time is the God *of time*.

[80] See 3.3 above.

[81] See Hart, *Understanding Our World*, 445, s.v. "function."

[82] See Hart, *Understanding Our World*, 446, s.v. "guiding."

While there is a significant parallel between faith as a mode of being and the future as a mode of time, the temporal "G over (x over y)" structure that I would like to suggest should not be understood as a G/x/y in which the present (as an x) is guided exclusively by the future. It would also be a mistake to assume that either faith or the future can be understood from only a transcendental perspective. Our lives are not only (to be) guided *by* the future (transcendentally) but are (to be) guided *into* the future (foundationally). Faith, in other words, plays a role in both directions.[83] (Moltmann's preference for the transcendental direction in this context will be explored in 5.3 below).

To clarify matters, some comments on the special character of the faith mode are called for. The foundational spiritual direction of all existence comes to expression most fully in this mode-of-being, as it is in the limit-experience of faith-qualified knowing that we become conscious of the founding gift and call of (and for) life that comes from God and is mediated through all of the pre-fiduciary sides of our humanity. In the transcendental direction, faith refers us to the destiny towards which we are moving and thus receives ultimate guidance from the God (or god) in whom (/which) we place our hope. Faith can thus be referred to as a transcendental guiding function as well as being understood as that mode in which we experience life as foundational empowerment rooted in God. Foundationally, it may be helpful to speak of faith as religious *trust* (in the God of creation and thus the creation of God) while faith in a transcendental sense is religious *hope* (in the God beyond [present] creation and thus of the age to come). In faith, we connect with both our Origin and Destiny. To be founded on and oriented towards the God of past and future is to find present spiritual direction and guidance in and for our time.

If we examine the modes of time in terms of a "G over (x over y)" structure, therefore, we may say that just as friendship, for example, is simultaneously *founded* in a certain affinity, *qualified* by (that is developed and integrated) within troth, and *guided* by faith, so by analogy, human life is *founded* in (our orientation to) the *past*, *qualified* by the *present*, and *guided* by (our orientation to) the *future*. Bearing in mind the above discussion of the foundational and transcendental role of faith, this future must be understood in two senses. We are guided by our orientation to the future as (a) the space into which we present-ly seek to extend the gift we have received (the foundational future, or what Moltmann terms the future as *futurum*) and as (b) that which we receive as a promise yet to come (the transcendental future, corresponding to Moltmann's understanding of the future as *adventus*).[84]

---

[83] In other words, I will be arguing that the temporal "founding" and "directing" mentioned in the opening quotations to 5.2 above from Hendrik Hart's work are, in my terminology, both forms of 'guiding' (or 'directing').

[84] See 2.3–2.4 above. Given my argument at the end of 2.4 that Moltmann's *futurum-adventus* distinction is actually a distinction between phenomenal, historical becoming and transcendental, eschatological coming, or between the *historical* direction *of* time and the *eschatological* direction *for* time, then, to be more precise, we should say that (a) the foundational future (in Hart's and my sense) is a future of and for time that

Guidance ("G") is thus understood as occurring in both the transcendental and foundational directions. (Thus, where Hart speaks of the "founding and directing orders of time," in the passage cited at the beginning of 5.2, I would rather speak of time's 'founding' and 'opening' directions.) Guidance is thus mediated by both past and future and by both the "x" and the "y" of a temporal "x/y" structure. The present is thus (normatively speaking) the time in which the development (or differentiation) and integration of past and future, gift and promise, takes place. In extending the present to the future in a foundational sense and in opening the present to the future in a transcendental sense, we allow ourselves to be guided by the gift and promise of life that is experienced in faith.

5.2.3 Expression and Reference: Immanence and Transcendence
In the ontological analysis of modal order, it is helpful to make a distinction between foundational "expression" and transcendental "reference" because the normal connotations of "expression" are relevant to discussions of divine and creaturely *immanence* while "reference" is relevant to the topic of creaturely and divine *transcendence*.[85] To return to some previous examples, aptitude—a "techno-formative" retrocipation to the psychic mode—can be seen as the foundational "expression" of sensitivity 'immanent within' our formative capacity to relate means to ends. In verification—a transcendental analytic anticipation of faith—our analytic procedures must be understood with "reference" to a faith certainty that 'transcends' what can be fully known in conceptual experience or within "the logical space of reasons."[86] Another example is the distinction between a 'symbol' (such as a national flag or the Twin Towers of the World Trade Center) which, as such, incarnates and

---

corresponds to Moltmann's *futurum* and the future for time from which it flows, which I have termed 'historical *adventus*' (2.4 above) while (b) the transcendental future (again, following Hart's and my use of that term) is a future of and for time that corresponds to Moltmann's *novum* and the future for time from which it flows, which is Moltmann's eschatological *adventus*. In 5.3 below, I will argue that the transcendental future of and for existence, *contra* Moltmann, should not be given ontological priority over the foundational future.

[85] Dooyeweerd, it would seem, also tends to connect "expression" with his use of the term "meaning" while using "religion" to refer to "reference" to God. Cf. James H. Olthuis, "Dooyeweerd on Religion and Faith," in *The Legacy of Herman Dooyeweerd: Reflections on Critical Philosophy in the Christian Tradition*, ed. C.T. McIntire (Lanham, MD: University Press of America, 1985), 23.

[86] In other words, verification is impossible without reference to what we trust as certain. In the introduction to this chapter (including n. 3 above), I refer to this 'faith certainty' when discussing the "universalism of hope." The "logical space of reasons" is a phrase associated with, and coined by, the twentieth-century philosopher, Wilfrid Sellars.

expresses what it symbolises and a 'sign' or 'icon', which points or refers beyond itself to another reality.[87]

Distinguishing between foundational, immanent expression and transcendental, transcendent reference also proves fruitful when exploring the two directions of time. When time is viewed in the foundational direction, we may speak of the past paving the way for, and finding expression in, the present. At the same time, the present gives expression to the past. It is now the past *of the present*. For those alive today, the past is *our* past, right *now*. This past—or "present past" (to use Moltmann's terminology[88])—continues to exist as part of the present, as part of its foundational structure and direction. It has not 'been and gone' as if it has passed out of existence. In human development, we can see how the present is built on the foundation of the past. Thus various life stages are described as "epigenetic."[89] Yet these early stages are not just scaffolding that we must kick away once we reach the heights of adulthood. They live on within us. One example of the immanent, foundational expression of the past in the present can be seen in the way we speak of an adult's 'inner child'—a phrase frequently used in best-selling works of popular psychology. We may thus speak in this context of the present's 'inner past'.

Turning our attention to the transcendental direction, while ontological anticipations might be said to be "expressions" of the higher in the lower, it is far more helpful to describe them as "references" to the higher in the lower. Anticipations are evidence of an openness that refers us beyond an earlier mode to a fuller reality that transcends it. Anticipations highlight how relatively lower modes are receptive to a higher reality and oriented to it without 'embodying' or make it present 'within' themselves. The expression that they can give to what transcends them is thus far more limited than the expression that retrocipations give to more foundational realities. Thus the psychic functioning of a pet dog might anticipate or become sensitively open to some of our symbolic and conceptual distinctions without language *per se* ever coming to expression within its (psychic) life. When it responds to its name or to a phrase said in a familiar tone of voice, its behaviour can only be understood with reference to human symbols and concepts that it cannot fully internalise. It may respond to what we say but taking part in a conversation lies beyond its ability.

The difference between foundational, retrocipatory expression and transcendental, anticipatory reference finds additional support in an examination of the transcendental direction of time. In founding the present, the

---

[87] Here I am drawing in part on Paul Tillich's observation in *Dynamics of Faith* (New York: Harper and Row, 1957), 42, that "signs do not participate in the reality of that to which they point, while symbols do." In connecting symbols to the foundational direction and icons to the transcendental, I do not wish to deny that actual symbols and icons have meaning in both directions. I refer only to dominant characteristics.

[88] Cf. the discussion of the modalisation of time in 3.3 above.

[89] Erik Erikson made this term popular in the world of psychology, having borrowed it from embryologists. See, e.g., his *Identity and the Life-Cycle* (New York: International Universities Press, 1959).

past structures, directs, and finds expression in the present. At the same time, the present makes the past present in its own way. Transcendentally, however, the future that guides us via our anticipation of it is not expressed or made 'present' in the here and now in the same way. It remains transcendent rather than foundational, acting as a transcendent reference point (or point of orientation) beyond the present rather than coming to expression within it. Yet it has a real (transcendental) role to play in the here and now.

Perhaps we might express this by saying that the foundational future is a reality that '*is* (not yet)' while the transcendental future '*is not* (yet)'! Movement towards this latter future (unlike the future viewed in the foundational direction) is not a matter of the unfolding of nascent realities and presently existing structures. The "future present" that is coming is thus irreducible to the "present future" that is developing.[90] Here it seems that we need a philosophical distinction between reality (the real) and existence (what 'is'—a verbal form of being linked to the present). Existence does not exhaust what is real. The present (/presence) does not contain time in its fullness. The transcendental future is a reality that *transcends* existence. Yet as such it is still a 'creational'—or more strictly speaking '*new creational*'—reality. Transcendence, like immanence, is a feature of the world/time that God creates/brings to fulfilment.

Put another way, we can say that in the transcendental direction, the future that comes to us is known in anticipation with the result that the present is opened up to that future. Yet the future that helps to *make the present* is not *made present*, but always—*qua* future—transcends us. Transcendentally, in relation to the present, the future may be imminent but it is never immanent. If the foundational future is implicit or immanent within the potentiality of the present, the transcendental future is, to borrow a phrase from Moltmann, a "paradigm of transcendence."[91]

---

[90] For the distinction between "future present" and "present future" to function as an effective shorthand for my proposed distinction between the foundational and transcendental directions of time, it is important to remember that the main contrast is between (eschatological) *coming into* existence and (creational) *developing out of* prior existence. While I accept the modalisation of time discussed in 3.3 above, that is secondary here. Both my and Moltmann's understanding of the modalisation of time would not preclude speaking (in part) of a coming "present future" and a developing "future present." (Furthermore, for Moltmann, there is coming that is part of the non-eschatological coming-and-going of historical time. Hence my reference to his implicit notion of a 'historical *adventus*' in 2.4 above.)

[91] See Moltmann, "The Future as a New Paradigm of Transcendence," in FC, 1–17 (and the earlier translation, "The Future as New Paradigm of Transcendence," in RRF, 177–99). For the openness of modernity to this since Kant, see Jürgen Moltmann, *Theology Today: Two Contributions towards Making Theology Present*, trans. John Bowden (London: SCM Press, 1988), 77–78. Cf. 2.3n57 above. While Moltmann reserves all talk of transcendence in this context for the eschatological future in distinction from the "historical future," (see 2.1 and 2.3 above), I do not as I see *history* as having a

5.2.4 Creation and Eschaton

In knowing the coming future in hope, we are put in touch with a not-yet, a fullness that is not yet manifest, a fulfilment towards which we are moving, ultimately a time when God will be "all in all."[92] This eschatological horizon, which is closed down by evil, is opened up again in redemption. From this point of view, we can appreciate why both Dooyeweerd and Moltmann, following Augustine, speak of creation as "restless."[93] Because the connotations of this word are too negative,[94] however, it is preferable to speak of creation as 'on the move' in hope and anticipation. This lack of rest is not necessarily something fallen. It is part of the original eschatological dynamic of history.

In the foundational direction, in as much as we have lived (and continue to live) our lives in covenant with God, time, and history express/reveal/embody/make present who God is, who we truly are, and what the authentic nature of creation is (to be). In the transcendental direction, which occurs simultaneously, time and history—again in as much as we keep covenant—anticipate and thus refer beyond the present to a coming time characterised by divine and creaturely fullness and fulfilment. We may thus posit a distinction and correlation between (God in) 'what is to be' and (God in) 'what is to come'. To highlight the connections with the previous section, we may say that, in being guided from the 'inside-out', our lives are expressive of (our faith, understood as trust, in) the divine ground of be(com)ing, while, in being guided from the 'outside-in', our lives make sense with reference to (our faith, understood as hope, in) the divine, eschatological horizon of existence.

It is also helpful, therefore, to interpret the foundational direction of time as the '*creational*' direction in which we know God as the *Origin* out of which we move into the future (*futurum*). Similarly, the transcendental direction of time is the *eschatological* direction in which we know God as the *Destiny* that comes towards us as God's promises come to pass. Both directions are thus 'creational' in the more-than-foundational sense that they refer to the 'creation' in which we (are to) live. The eschatological direction, however, refers to the fulfilment of history and thus ultimately to the coming of what the Scriptures, in the midst of a history that has been closed down by sin and idolatry, call the 'new creation'. Thus in the transcendental direction, we do not move beyond creation/time to God (as Dooyeweerd seems to think[95]) any more than in the foundational direction. But we do move beyond the present (that is, the present

---

transcendental-*eschatological* (as well as a foundational-creational) direction. See 5.3 below.
[92] This is, of course, biblical language. See 1 Cor 15:28, for example.
[93] For Dooyeweerd, see *A New Critique*, 1:11. For Moltmann, see 3.2n68 above.
[94] Cf. Olthuis, "Dooyeweerd on Religion and Faith," 22.
[95] For a critique of Dooyeweerd's temporal-supratemporal distinction, see Olthuis, "Dooyeweerd on Religion and Faith," 32–34 and Peter J. Steen, *The Structure of Herman Dooyeweerd's Thought* (Toronto: Wedge, 1983), especially chap. 3.

creation), the transcendental direction referring us to both divine and 'creational' fullness.

The 'creational' and eschatological (or 'new creational') directions to our life each show God and creation to be in covenant, not in a competitive zero-sum relationship. The glory of creation is the glory of God—and vice versa. We have our existence ('creationally') from God and (eschatologically) unto God (cf. Rom 11:36), the Alpha and Omega. Simultaneously, creation (foundationally) expresses God and (transcendentally) refers to God. It has no other existence (or reality). Creation *is* meaning (as Dooyeweerd would say[96]); it does not *have* meaning. Or, to cite one of Dooyeweerd's most influential North American followers, H. Evan Runner, "Life is relig*ion*,"[97] not merely relig*ious*.

5.2.5 Differentiation and Integration

This way of understanding the 'creational' and eschatological nature of time can be fruitfully related to the correlation of differentiation and integration, interpreted as the relationship between diversified unity and unified diversity.[98]

---

[96] In Dooyeweerd's words from *A New Critique*, 1:4: "Meaning is the being of all that has been created and the nature even of our selfhood."

[97] See Henry Vander Goot, ed., *Life is Religion: Essays in Honor of H. Evan Runner* (St. Catherines, ON: Paideia, 1981). My emphasis. On Dooyeweerd's use of the term "religion," see n. 85 above.

[98] Here I am following Dooyeweerd's attempt to honour the simultaneous way in which history ought (normatively speaking) to manifest differentiation and integration. See his important 1958 essay, "The Criteria of Progressive and Reactionary Tendencies in History," in *Christian Philosophy and the Meaning of History*. The Collected Works of Herman Dooyeweerd, ser. B, vol. 1, ed. D.F.M. Strauss (Lewiston, NY: Mellen, 1996), 47–66. (Cf. Hart, *Understanding Our World*, 265–66.) But there are significant differences. Following McIntire, "Dooyeweerd's Philosophy of History," 89–96, I would reject Dooyeweerd's understanding of history as a modal reality in favour of a trans-modal view. Dooyeweerd's reductionist position (as I see it) was an (understandable) attempt to resist historicism. Perhaps it is this modal view of history that leads Dooyeweerd to see the two directions of time as more related to ontological questions concerning structural unity, diversity, and "coherence" (cf. *A New Critique*, 2:190–92) than to time and history in a fuller sense. (Cf. Hendrik Hart, "Reply to Respondents," in *An Ethos of Compassion and the Integrity of Creation*, ed. Brian J. Walsh, Hendrik Hart, and Robert E. VanderVennen (Lanham, MD: University Press of America, 1995), 120: "[T]ime in Dooyeweerd primarily means medium of diversity. In time, unity, which transcends time, breaks into (coherent) diversity.") Like McIntire ("Dooyeweerd's Philosophy of History," 97–106), I see far more potential for historical understanding in Dooyeweerd's notion of the "opening process" (in which "anticipations" play an important role). Yet when McIntire claims that Dooyeweerd's view of cultural development "cannot handle the future" (103), I suspect that this is the case. In my terminology, his discussion suggests that Dooyeweerd's reading of cultural history is overly 'foundationalistic'. His "anticipations" sound as if they are the unfoldings of a 'given' structure. Although, the transcendental-eschatological direction of time is not given its due, I would still maintain that the richness of Dooyeweerd's

Normatively speaking, looking at the human person in the 'creational', foundational direction, we can see the person as a *spiritual unity* that is expressed *as a bodily diversity*.[99] In this differentiating direction, our many (many-sided) actions can be seen to cohere when we see how they refer back to our present self as the centre of intention and origin of action. Looked at in the eschatological, transcendental direction, this present *diversity* of and within action(s) refers forward to the self that we are implicitly or explicitly promising to be by living the way we do. Our acts must thus be understood with reference to this transcendental *unity*. In making and keeping our promises, the differentiation, letting go, or *kenosis* of who we are that occurs as we give of ourselves in our actions is reintegrated as we make a covenant to which we bind ourselves, and thus move in time towards who we are to become.

The differentiation, unfolding, and expression of the gift of the past in the present (the foundational direction) is a process of 'dissemination' rooted in the "foundational command" (or original blessing/benediction) of Gen 1:31[100] in which we are called to actively forge continuities by preserving all that will serve life in the future. Such preservation must be understood as keeping our inheritance alive in history. The talent we have been given must be invested rather than 'safely' buried underground (cf. Matt 25:14–30). The continuity comes from realising (making real) the potential of what has already been entrusted to us. At the same time, this action must be coupled with a willingness to let go of the past. Being reactionary and becoming nostalgic in the extreme sense of 'living in the past' (rather than living *out of* the past) actually thwarts the genuine continuity that characterises a living tradition.

In the transcendental direction, change occurs not by unlocking already existing potential but by opening the present to a new future. Receiving the *pro/missio* of the future in hope should lead us not only to actively engage in

---

ontology (cf. his rejection of entelechy in *A New Critique*, 3:59–61) allows its reality to be glimpsed.

Johan van der Hoeven, in an important review of McIntire, ed., *The Legacy of Herman Dooyeweerd* in sec. 2 of his "Matters of Mission and Transmission: On the Progress of Ecumenical-Reformational Thought," *Philosophia Reformata* 52 (1987): 182–207, a review that is cautious towards and, in some places, critical of the revisions of Dooyeweerd suggested in this work (some of which I follow), notes (on p. 188) the prevalence given to Dooyeweerd's transcendental direction of time by J.P.A. Mekkes. This emphasis has, in turn, probably influenced Hart's revision of Dooyeweerd.

[99] 'Bodily' here means more than the organic 'body'. It means the self *in action* or the *experiencing* self. Cf. James H. Olthuis, "Be(com)ing: Humankind as Gift and Call," *Philosophia Reformata* 58 (1993): 153–72, especially 159–60, although I resist identifying the spirit/body distinction with a directional/foundational distinction. On "spirit" see Hart, *Understanding Our World*, 454, s.v. "Spirit, soul." Cf. his definition of "Body" on p. 440.

[100] This phrase is taken from Al Wolters, "The Foundational Command," in *Year of Jubilee, Cultural Mandate, Worldview*, ed. B. van der Walt. Study Pamphlet 382 (Potchefstroom: Institute for Reformational Studies, 1999), 27–34. (On whether this is a "command" per se, see n. 105 below.) The language of 'dissemination' also captures the theme of the 'seed' prominent in Genesis.

innovation (beyond mere development of past trends), but also to open ourselves to the risk and surprise of the unknown.

Although our letting go of the past and our letting be(come) of the future is often painful and frightening in a fallen world, time (unlike evil) need not be seen as a threat to the unity of the self for we can trust that in time and in God's grace, we may move out of and towards the mystery of who we are (to be).[101]

5.3 Comparison with Moltmann

The following summary of my understanding of the distinctives of the foundational and transcendental directions of time (in figure 7 below) seeks to highlight how the preceding discussion sheds light on Moltmann's position while also paving the way for an alternative. The inclusion of 'nature' and 'grace' categories in this context anticipates the following chapter. Briefly stated however, grace is understood as the simultaneous gift/promise of Life and call to Live, in response to which our true nature comes into being. This will be explored briefly later in this section.

Not only does the foundational and transcendental distinction find its counterpart in Moltmann's distinction between the historical and the eschatological directions,[102] but (with few exceptions[103]) the respective specific features listed in each column can also be found in Moltmann's work. Although the foundational direction does receive attention in his thought, anyone who is familiar with Moltmann's writings will immediately recognise that it is the features I have listed under the category of the transcendental direction of time that coincide with most of the distinctive emphases of his theology. Whether this indicates a depreciation of the foundational direction—which amounts to the eclipse of creation—is an issue to which I will return later in this section (and in chapter 6).

---

[101] This is an alternative to seeing the heart of our humanity as "supra-temporal" as Dooyeweerd does. Cf. n. 95 above.

[102] To clarify a central difference, though, I would not identify "history" with the foundational direction of time, but would wish to speak of history's creational-foundational and transcendental-eschatological directions.

[103] Exceptions include the more specifically ontological rather than cosmogonic features listed above. This has much to do with the fact that Moltmann tends not to focus on ontological questions. Meeks, in his *Origins of the Theology of Hope*, 105, goes as far as to say that Moltmann "attempts to develop a concept of history without an ontology." Some of the following distinctions are more implicit than explicit in Moltmann, such as the creational/eschatological distinction.

FOUNDATIONAL (or 'founding')	TRANSCENDENTAL (or 'opening')

Grace as:
  gift/call; *Auf/Gabe*
Direction of *influence*:
  Past→Present→Future
	Grace as:
	  promise/call; *Pro/Missio*
	Direction of *influence*:
	  Past←Present←Future

Nature as:
Direction of *response*:
  Past⇐Present⇐Future
	Nature as:
	Direction of *response*:
	  Past⇒Present⇒Future

memory	anticipation
gratitude	expectancy
dependence upon	openness to
faith as trust	faith as hope

(foundational) expression of:
  earlier in later/
  lower in higher
	(transcendental) reference of:
	  earlier to later/
	  lower to higher

differentiation of the gift of
  the past in the present and
  towards the future
	re-integration occurs in
	  the present through
	  commitment to promise

modal retrocipations	modal anticipations
immanence	transcendence
within	beyond
incarnational	iconic
symbol	sign
origin	destiny
continuity	change
already	not yet
of old	new
preservation	innovation
letting go of what was	openness to the risk/surprise of what is to come
redemption as re-storation	redemption as re-newal
creation as grounded	creation as open
roots	horizons
God as Ground of being	God as Fullness of being
God as: origin/beginning/source/alpha	God as: destiny/end/goal/omega
ontological priority of the past	ontological priority of the future
future as *futurum*	future as *adventus*

future as predictable
  on basis of the past/present
	future as unpredictable
	  on basis of the past/present

past as irretrievable (the past past)	remembered hope/ hopeful memory (past future)
God in creation	creation in God

CREATIONAL direction
  of time
	ESCHATOLOGICAL direction
	  of time

figure 7

The distinction between the foundational and transcendental (or 'creational' and eschatological) directions is not that between two 'realms' but concerns the whole of reality in the relation to the two directions of time, time (unlike space which is, for me, a mode of existence) being an all-embracing category. The distinction does not constitute a contradiction, in my view, but a fundamental correlation. To describe a mother(/-to-be) as 'pregnant' with a child and as 'expecting' a baby is to highlight two complementary perspectives on one temporal reality. The first describes a process that is full of potential, a gift that is coming to fruition. The second describes a time that is full of promise and that is coming closer and closer. In the first, the present at any given moment is built epigenetically upon the past. In the second, the present moves and expands as it is open(ed) to the pull of the future. Emergence and arrival thus occur together. There are not two futures: the transcendental and the foundational. Rather the future may be viewed in two directions. Neither direction has privileged status. There is no need to drive a wedge between the foundational and transcendental as the gift and promise of life both come from the same God. Both mediate God's grace. Consequently, as I will argue in 6.1 below, both gift and promise make salvation (including universal salvation) possible.

As there is, in my view, a contradiction between Moltmann's historical and eschatological directions of time, at least prior to the consummation, this point bears reiterating. It is important to affirm that God relates to us in the transcendental, eschatological direction as the coming divine 'fullness' of creation (1 Cor 15:28) even as God "is filling the universe in all its parts" (Eph 1:23, REB) or "fills all in all" (NRSV) in the 'creational', foundational direction—thus relating to us as ground and origin of present existence (without being the origin of evil).

A good case can be made for this claim biblically if we attend to intertextual echoes in the context of canonical themes.[104] Ephesians 1:23 comes from a passage that alludes to Ps 8 (see Eph 1:22a/Ps 8:6b [MT, 8:7]). The theme of human dominion central to that psalm therefore refers Paul's discussion of "fill[ing]" back to blessing of Gen 1:28 in which humanity as the image of God is authorised to fill and subdue the earth—a benediction that is often referred to as the 'cultural mandate', the calling to make history.[105] In Christ, Paul seems to be saying, this dominion is realised (and is now extended over the evil that did not exist in the beginning). The human "fill[ing]" of creation, when done in covenant with God, thus results in God "fill[ing]" the world with God's

---

[104] For a more detailed exploration along these lines, see my "Commentary: Genesis 1:12f., Daniel 2:35 and Ephesians 1:22f.," *Third Way* 25, no. 1 (February 2002): 24. Cf. also my "The Call of Wisdom/The Voice of The Serpent," 38–39 and 54–55.

[105] In addition to Wolters, "The Foundational Command," see Hans Walter Wolff, *Anthropology of the Old Testament*, trans. Margaret Kohl (London: SCM Press, 1974), chap. 18. *Contra* Wolters, the cultural 'mandate' in question—the calling to make history—is actually a blessing not a commandment (see Gen 1:28a), rooted in a jussive not an imperative (see Gen 1:26a). Hence my reference to benediction.

presence.¹⁰⁶ In the eschatological consummation (cf. 1 Cor 15:28), creation comes to its creaturely and divine 'fulfilment' when God is "all in all." Thus, the two directions of time are correlates. To anticipate the discussion of the next chapter, in being covenantally related to God in both directions, we (foundationally) receive life as *gift* (the grace of the already, the grace of/in the 'given') and are thus empowered to heed the *call* to live. Thus life is *Auf/Gabe*. At the same time, we also (transcendentally) anticipate life as promise/*promissio* (the grace of the not-yet) and are thus empowered to respond to our life (as) mission/*missio*. Thus life is *pro/missio*.¹⁰⁷

Implicit in this line of interpretation is the claim that God was not "all in all" in the beginning, even though the original creation may be affirmed as "very good" (Gen 1:31) nevertheless and nonetheless. God's filling of all things is tied to humanity filling the earth with God's presence. This means that there would always have been the need for an eschaton, an eschatological fulfilment of history.¹⁰⁸ As Emil Brunner has argued,

> The first thing is always what God wills as Creator; but—*even apart from our sin*—it is not the last. For he wills to lead the creation out beyond itself, into the perfecting of all things. God does not preserve the world simply in order to preserve it, but in order that he may perfect it.¹⁰⁹

By speaking this way, it is possible to imply that the original creation was 'imperfect' in the sense of being flawed. The eschatological perfecting of creation would thus be seen as overcoming an ontological deficiency—a position I would reject.¹¹⁰ But one might simply mean that God was not all in all in the beginning but will be all in all in the end. The latter claim—which is central to Moltmann's understanding¹¹¹—is one I would wish to affirm: aside

---

¹⁰⁶ There is thus more than a linguistic connection between the *plēroumenou* of Eph 1:23 and the *plērōsate* of the LXX (Septuagint) of Gen 1:28.

¹⁰⁷ On the *promissio-missio* distinction/correlation in Moltmann, see 6.3 below.

¹⁰⁸ In 6.6 below, I will suggest that multiple eschatological consummations may be a better way of looking at what God intended/intends. Cf. n. 121 below.

¹⁰⁹ Emil Brunner, *The Divine Imperative: A Study in Christian Ethics*, trans. Olive Wyon (1941; repr., Cambridge: Lutterworth Press, 2002), 214. My emphasis.

¹¹⁰ Whether Brunner's position implies an originally deficient, imperfect, flawed creation falls outside the scope of this study. Certainly a case could be made for this interpretation. Whether Moltmann's view of what he calls "the first, temporal and *imperfect* creation" (CoG, 91, my emphasis—a passage briefly discussed in 3.4 above) implies a 'low' view of the original creation is an important question. My comments later in this section will suggest that it does. But his view that God becomes all in all only in the eschaton does not necessarily imply an eclipse of creation.

¹¹¹ See CoG, 91:

> [T]he eternal creation will perfect creation in time. The grace of God which overcomes sin and the consequences of sin does not lead back to the creation of the beginning, but completes and perfects what that creation was made and destined for. It is true that God judged the first creation to be 'very good', but the new creation for glory is more.

from sin, we may speak of a movement within—and a movement of—the goodness of creation towards the consummation of history. Thus understood, goodness is itself a dynamic category and not a timeless norm or ideal.

Moltmann makes this point well with reference to the sabbath of Gen 1:

> The verdict on creation that it was 'very good' does not mean that it was in the Greek sense perfect and without any future; the Hebrew means that it was fitting, appropriate, corresponding to the Creator's will. The accounts of creation-in-the-beginning do not as yet talk about a creation in the glory of God. Only the sabbath of creation is more than 'very good'. It is 'hallowed', 'sanctified', and therefore points to creation's future glory. The sabbath is, as it were, the promise of future consummation built into the initial creation.[112]

In my view, this makes sense of why 'sabbath' in the biblical traditions is seen as having both 'creational' and 'redemptive' significance, even though 'creation' and 'salvation' are distinct motifs. In the two versions of the Decalogue, Exod 20:8–11 grounds sabbath in God's creation of the world, while Deut 5:12–15 emphasises the redemptive significance of the seventh day, thus anticipating the sabbatical idea of the Jubilee (Lev 25, Isa 61: 2, Luke 4:19) which looks towards healing from sin and injustice. Putting these understandings together, we might say that as an 'eschatological' day, the sabbath of Gen 1 points towards the *fulfilment* of *creation* and the call to make history given to humanity in Gen 1:26–28, while subsequent sabbaths also point towards the *fulfilment* of God's desire, given our sin, to bring *redemption* to that history so that God's creational-eschatological goal of becoming "all in all" might be realised. (We shall return to the sabbath as an ending that is also a new beginning in both creational and redemptive contexts in 6.6 below).

This point of contact with Moltmann allows us to resist—or certainly to relativise—a persistent criticism that has been made against him by some theologians in the Reformed (neo-Calvinist) tradition decisively influenced by Dutch statesman and theologian Abraham Kuyper.[113] In this Kuyperian

---

Cf. CoG, 264:
> What [hope] looks for is creation's final consummation. . . . This end does, no doubt, 'correspond' to the beginning inasmuch as the beginning is completed, and is not replaced by something different. But the end is much more than the beginning.

[112] CoG, 264. In GC, 5, Moltmann writes, "According to the biblical traditions, creation is aligned towards its *redemption* from the very beginning." My emphasis. This is a very different claim; one I will dispute later in this section.

[113] For the following 'Kuyperian' objections to Moltmann, see Bouma-Prediger, "Creation as the Home of God," 87–90 and *The Greening of Theology*, chaps. 4 and 7; Douglas J. Schuurman, *Creation, Eschaton, and Ethics: The Ethical Significance of the Creation-Eschaton Relation in the Thought of Emil Brunner and Jürgen Moltmann* (New York: Peter Lang, 1991), especially chap. 4: "The Creation-Eschaton Relation in Moltmann's Theology"; his earlier study "Creation, Eschaton, and Ethics: An Analysis of Theology and Ethics in Jürgen Moltmann," *Calvin Theological Journal* 22 (1987): 42–67; and Walsh, "Theology of Hope and the Doctrine of Creation," 60–69. I see my

tradition, redemption is often understood as 'restoration', whereas Moltmann prefers to speak of 'renewal'. From within this paradigm, Moltmann's eschatological emphasis is seen as implying a view of salvation that fails to affirm creation. Fears are expressed about what is seen as a radical discontinuity between Moltmann's *creatio nova* and the world that Gen 1:31 declares to be "very good." Moltmann, however, sees restorative views of redemption as too conservative to be expressive of biblical hope.[114]

Here we do not need to side with either Moltmann or his critics. If 'restoration' (in this context) highlights redemption in (/of) the foundational direction, 'renewal' highlights its transcendental counterpart: creation must be (re-)opened to its eschatological fulfilment 'beyond' what was implicit in the beginning. In my view, which attempts to give both directions of history—and thus of redemptive history—their due, history, to be healed, needs to be re-grounded in the gift of life *and* opened once again to the promise of the eschaton.

This 'third way' allows us to recognise (with Moltmann) that the 'Reformed' position in question fails to honour the transcendental horizon of history. We can also see why Moltmann, given his (one-sided) eschatological focus, sees (with some justification) a restorative understanding of redemption as advocating a backward-looking, history-denying *restitutio in integrum*.[115] Although the Reformed theologians in question claim that Moltmann's rejection of a *restitutio* does not apply to their own position in which God's healing is seen to embrace the fruits of human culture down the ages, history in this Reformed paradigm is still understood as the development of the potential that was given to creation in the beginning. Because the eschatological direction of time is minimised, so too is the eschatological re-direction of time in salvation. Consequently, the biblical drama is typically understood in terms

---

own thought as lying within the Kuyperian tradition, although my response to Moltmann is far more sympathetic. See nn. 116–17 below and 6.1n6 below.

[114] See Moltmann's discussion of the Reformed notion of *transformatio mundi* in CoG, 270–72 which indicates how he would respond to the specifically Kuyperian Reformed tradition. Despite Moltmann's often positive interaction with Dutch reformed theology (on which see Hendrikus Berkhof, "Moltmann zwischen zwei Niederländern," in *Gottes Zukunft—Zukunft der Welt: Festschrift für Jürgen Moltmann zum 60. Geburtstag*, ed. Hermann Deuser, Gerhard Marcel Martin, Konrad Stock, and Michael Welker (Munich: Chr. Kaiser Verlag, 1986), 469–80), it is significant that almost all of Moltmann's references to Kuyper are negative. See, for example, CPS, 43–44 and SL, 108.

[115] See 4.1 and 4.2 above. Among the texts cited there is WJC, 188, in which Moltmann states,

> Re-conciliation is a backward-looking act. It presupposes an unscathed world which was destroyed by human sin, and which reconciliation restores. Reconciliation is the negative of the negative, its purpose being to put into effect once more the original, positive condition: *restitutio in integrum*.

His italics. After citing Bultmann to exemplify this "old mythical pattern (primal condition—apostasy—return home)," he adds, "But the statement says nothing about the totally new thing which the resurrection has brought into the world."

of the motifs of creation, fall, and redemption, the latter theme being understood as the restoration of creation (specifically the reestablishment of a normative creation order).[116] The radical re-new-al of creation is reduced to purging the past and its *futurum* from evil. Moltmann, by contrast, holds to a vision of redemption as the healing and re-opening of the movement from creation to eschaton in which God becomes all in all. In a model in which both directions of time are valued, I suggest, the Kuyperian and Moltmannian emphases could be integrated.[117]

If speaking of redemption as a re-opening of history to its eschatological fulfilment and not just as a restoration of the primordial gifting and blessing of creation allows us to make contact with Moltmann's theology, it also calls for critical distance. Because, for Moltmann, it is the transcendental direction of time in which redemption is (most clearly) manifest, the historical and

---

[116] See the works cited in n. 113 above. H. Evan Runner's copy of RRF (which I now own) contains the following marginal note (in Runner's handwriting) that clearly exemplifies this view of redemption. Alongside Moltmann's claim, on RRF, 4, that we encounter the word "new" on "practically every page of the New Testament," which Moltmann argues is part of the "antithesis of "Old" and "New" Testaments," Runner responds: "But: Old & New Admin[istration] of a New Covenant. The 'Old' & 'New' of the Testaments is secondary to the New Direction of the Gospel *within the (old) Creation structure*. Redemption does save what went awry!" His underlining and my italics.

[117] One might say: 'we must see salvation as *restoring the original gift and blessing of life* and *re-opening the movement from creation to eschaton in which God becomes all in all*'. For the shift from a *futurum*-oriented view of eschatology to one that looks to integrate this with an *adventus* focus, the neo-Kuyperian interchange between Smith and Olthuis is instructive. See James K.A. Smith, "Determined Hope: A Phenomenology of Christian Expectation," in *The Future as God's Gift: Explorations in Christian Eschatology*, ed. David Fergusson and Marcel Sarot (Edinburgh: T. and T. Clark, 2000), 200–27; James H. Olthuis, "Unlike Any Other Hope: The Eschatological Structure of Hope," in *The Logic of Incarnation: James K.A. Smith's Critique of Postmodern Religion*, ed. Neal DeRoo and Brian Lightbody (Eugene, OR: Pickwick, 2009), 182–92; and James K.A. Smith. "Continuing the Conversation," in *The Logic of Incarnation: James K.A. Smith's Critique of Postmodern Religion*, ed. Neal DeRoo and Brian Lightbody (Eugene, OR: Pickwick, 2009), 203–22, especially 218–21.

The Reformed works cited in n. 113 above may also all be placed in the tradition of Kuyperian neo-Calvinism. It is interesting that that Abraham Kuyper's successor at the *Vrije Universiteit*, theologian Herman Bavinck, held to a far more eschatologically developed position with respect to creation and redemption. In this respect, I see my own position as more in the tradition of Bavinck than Kuyper. See Syd Hielema, "Herman Bavinck's Eschatological Understanding of Redemption" (ThD diss., Wycliffe College, Toronto School of Theology, 1998). It is significant that Hendrik Hart's input is appreciated in the preface. Hart's enthusiasm for the implications of this piece of work is evident in his "Notes on Dooyeweerd, Reason and Order," in *Contemporary Reflections on the Philosophy of Herman Dooyeweerd*. A Supplement to the Collected Works of Herman Dooyeweerd, ser. C, vol. 1, ed. D.F.M. Strauss and Michelle Botting (Lewiston, NY: Mellen, 2000), 129, where he notes Dooyeweerd's affinity to Kuyper at the expense of Bavinck. On Bavinck, see further 6.1n6 below.

eschatological directions are seen as in contradiction. Creation may be affirmed as "good" in Moltmann's theology but it is ultimately subsumed within the New Creation.[118] Evidence that the creational-foundational direction of history is depreciated includes the strong suggestion in Moltmann's writings that differentiation will come to an end (in an important sense at least) in the Age to Come. If it is possible to argue that in his eschatological vision there is to be ongoing differentiation of a kind that is simultaneously reintegrated once the transcendental conditions of time are transformed—and I have argued that this is his intention—,[119] nevertheless the fact that *transience* would seem to have no future in his theology[120] all but proves that the temporal finitude of God's creation is ultimately overcome and thus denigrated. Whatever the nuances of his position, Moltmann's eschatology cannot be construed as a celebration of the ongoing differentiation of history.[121]

I have already argued that the distinction between *creation* and *fall* is blurred in Moltmann's understanding of the historical, differentiating direction of time.[122] There is, I suggest, a correlative conflation in the direction of eschatological integration between *redemption* and *eschaton*. Thus Moltmann refers to the fulfilment of history, which was always part of God's intention even before or apart from sin, as "redemption." He writes,

> According to the biblical traditions, creation is aligned towards its *redemption* from the very beginning; for the creation of the world points forward to the sabbath, 'the feast of creation'.... On the sabbath the creation is *completed*.[123]

In a telling passage in *The Spirit of Life*, he writes in a similar vein,

> [I]n the coming of the Spirit of the resurrection of the dead and in the power of the new creation of all things, this world is revealed as a world of death which has failed to find God and itself. Transitory time and the mortality of all the living was hitherto held to be the 'natural' condition of created things, because there was no *alternative*; but this condition now emerges as sick. In the daybreak colours of their new creation, all things are revealed in their 'sickness unto

---

[118] Cf. the final paragraph of 4.4 above.
[119] See 3.6 in light of 2.5 above.
[120] See 3.2 above.
[121] In 6.6 below, I will argue that the ongoing differentiation of history in the eschaton is not incompatible with seeing creation reaching its destiny at the eschaton. The present creation's destiny, I will argue, is itself a new beginning.
[122] See 4.2 above.
[123] GC, 5–6. My emphases. (With reference to the following discussion of reconciliation and redemption, "redemption" in the German text in *GS*, 20 is "Erlösung"). Cf. GC, 277 and GC, 287–90 (a section entitled "The Feast of Redemption") where these connections are made repeatedly. In my view, creation is aligned towards its *consummation* from the very beginning; an idea I would distinguish from *redemption*. Given human sin, the movement to the eschatological consummation needs to be redeemed. The eschaton becomes the goal of *redemption*. In the beginning, however, the eschaton is the goal of *creation*.

death'. Once there is reason to hope for the world's *redemption*, that world ceases to be seen as natural and finite. It can now be perceived as an *unredeemed* world. Out of the general transience of things, *unredeemed* creation can be heard 'sighing and groaning' for its liberation.[124]

At first glance, it may look as if Moltmann is speaking about the way in which the resurrection highlights how our fallen world needs to be healed from the effects of our sin. But this is not the case. When Moltmann has such healing in mind, he usually speaks of "*reconciliation* [Versöhnung]."[125] If we bear in mind that transience and mortality are, for him, part of the fabric of creation from the beginning,[126] then it becomes clear that here Moltmann is speaking of an eschatological future for the present creation that transcends and contradicts[127] ordinary historical differentiation. In Moltmann's terminology, this is "*redemption* [Erlösung]."[128] Admittedly, in as much as this world,

---

[124] SL, 88. My emphases. (With reference to the following discussion of reconciliation and redemption, "redemption" and "unredeemed" in the German text in *DGL*, 100 are "Erlösung" and "unerlöste[n]").

[125] For references, see n. 128 below. My emphasis.

[126] See 3.2 and 3.4 above.

[127] As I understand the contours of Moltmann's position, although the eschatological direction opposes the historical in the present age, the eschaton sees the harmonisation of the two directions.

[128] See nn. 123 and 124 above. My emphasis. On the reconciliation/redemption distinction/correlation, see: TH, 58, 290; CrG, 186–87 [*DgG*, 174]:

[Christ's] sacrifice on the cross for the *reconciliation* [Versöhnung] of the world is the *immanent* dimension of his *eschatological* resurrection in the glory of the coming kingdom.... The *reconciling* [versöhnende] power of his suffering and death is the power of the resurrection. However, its purpose is not to make itself superfluous, but to become the basis for *new, redeemed* [erlöste] existence, which owes itself to the crucified Christ.

My emphases; GC, 12 [*GS*, 26]: "we have to distinguish between [the Spirit's] cosmic, ... reconciling [versöhnende] and ... redeeming [erlösende] indwelling"; GC, 244 [*GS*, 244]: "God's creation, reconciliation [Versöhnung] and redemption [Erlösung]"; WJC, 32 [*DWJC*, 49]:

What has already come into the world through the Christ who has come and is present, is the justification of the godless and the *reconciliation* [Versöhnung] of enemies. What has not yet come is the *redemption* [Erlösung] of the world, the overcoming of all enmity, the resurrection of the dead, and the new creation.

My emphases; WJC, 319; CoG, 104 [*DKG*, 125]: "So in Christ we are indeed already *reconciled* [versöhnt] with God, but we still live and die in an *unredeemed* [unerlösten] world, and together with this world look with longing for the new creation." My emphases; and EiT, 76: "we [should] distinguish the theology of *reconciliation* [Versöhnungstheologie] eschatologically from the theology of *redemption* [Erlösungstheologie] (because reconciliation is the anticipation of redemption, and redemption the completion of reconciliation)." My emphases.

On reconciliation, see CrG, 171, 182; WJC, 188 (as cited in n. 115 above), 284: "According to Paul, 'reconciliation' is the beginning of the new creation, not its final goal"; SL, 146; and EiT, 90, "From van Ruler I learnt that in his theology of

through sin, finds itself enclosed in transience rather than being able to live in the hope of the transience of transience, in as much as this world finds itself stuck in the historical direction *in itself*,[129] the dawning of the Age to Come, evident in the resurrection, signifies liberation from sin and thus signifies "redemption" in a conventional sense. But this coming "redemption" is (also) the eschatological fulfilment of history that God always intended (even aside from our sin). "Unredeemed"[130] means penultimate, unfinished, historical. That the world be "redeemed" was God's will from eternity.

The creation/fall and redemption/eschaton conflations in Moltmann's theology cohere well with (indeed they result from even as they give rise to) his (implicit) belief that the temptation that he sees built into the nature of history from the beginning must be eradicated prior to the consummation.[131] History's fulfilment, in this respect, liberates us from history's origin. The fact that temptation is 'ontologised' (built into the fabric of reality) in this way (even if sin, strictly speaking, may not be) seriously undermines the creation-affirming view of life (and salvation) to which the Scriptures call us.[132] But once

---

reconciliation Barth had neglected eschatology, just as Hegel, the philosopher of reconciliation, had also done in his time."

On redemption, in addition to GC, 5–6, 277, and 287–90, cited above, see GC, 94: "... the eschatological redemption of the whole creation through Christ"; GC, 228: "The perspective of eschatological glorification ... is whole, integral and all-embracing, because it is redemptive"; GC, 317: "Messianic belief in creation is a perception of the world and human beings in the messianic light of their redeeming future" (on the messianic incarnation as intended from the beginning in Moltmann's thought, see below); WJC, 292 (in a sympathetic summary of Teilhard): "The completion of creation in the divine unification is higher than the redemption of the world from its sins, and is redemption's goal"; SL, 9: "Redemption is the final new creation of all things out of their sin, transitoriness and mortality, for everlasting life, enduring continuance and eternal glory"; CoG, 29 (which connects images of redemption and consummation to the new creation); CoG, 40 (which sympathetically summarises Benjamin's distinction between "two contradictory orders of time: the secular order, with its striving for happiness within history, and the messianic order of redemption, which runs counter to that"); and CoG, 91 (in the context of the overcoming of death not sin).

Some of Moltmann's references to "redemption" (including some of those listed above) seem to include a reference to healing from sin even as they look ahead to the eschatological fulfilment of creation. It is possible that, for Moltmann, "reconciliation" and "redemption" are often terms that refer to what I would call "redemption" as the overcoming of evil in the foundational and transcendental directions respectively. For what seems to be a more traditional use of "redemption," see GC, 234; CoG, 265, and 273.

[129] On the significance of any phenomenon as 'in itself' cut off from the eschaton, see: on the past 'in itself', 3.3 (and 3.3n128) above; on death 'in itself', 3.4 (and 3.4nn153 and 178) above; and on differentiation 'in itself', 3.6 (and 3.6n270) above.

[130] CoG, 104 as cited in n. 128 above.

[131] See 4.2 above.

[132] For a detailed argument against reading the serpent of Gen 3:1 as a source of temptation within the good creation, see my "The Call of Wisdom/The Voice of The Serpent."

temptation is given that place, it is understandable that Moltmann would insist that it be annihilated with the coming of God's glory. Thus the choice of the language of *redemption*—with its connotations of healing and liberation—*for the fulfilment of history* (even apart from sin) is not accidental. The eschatological movement from the beginning is not simply a matter of creation coming to maturity or moving from one degree of glory to another for Moltmann (as it would be for me). Something must be overcome: the primordial Hell of the Godforsaken space.[133]

Because there is a need for redemption (healing) even prior to the creation of the first humans (and thus prior to sin), the incarnation becomes a necessity for Moltmann regardless of the Fall of Adam and Eve and their descendants. Thus he objects to the radical Anselmian view of Dutch Reformed theologian Arnold van Ruler in which "sin is 'the emergency' and Christ 'God's emergency measure' for its elimination" because this assumes that "at the end everything is once more just as good as it was at the beginning."[134] This beginning is clearly "just" not "good" enough. Not only sin, but its historical possibility (probability?, inevitability?) must be overcome.[135] More importantly, when Moltmann speaks of God in Christ kenotically entering into our finitude and our "situation of . . . sin *and God-forsakenness* as well,"[136] incarnation can be seen as the way in which the eternal love of God eliminates the primordial Godforsakenness of Hell itself. It is against this background, or foreground, that we should read Moltmann's claim that,

> [T]he Son of God did not become man simply because of the sin of men and women, but rather for the sake of perfecting creation. So 'the Son of God would have become man even if the human race had remained without sin'.[137]

There are other ways to affirm this last statement without postulating a radically flawed creation in need of perfection. One could, for example, see the incarnation of God as a calling God intended for all human beings in the beginning and thus interpret God incarnate in/as Jesus of Nazareth as a specific and special response to sin and its consequences while affirming God's incarnational intent—in/as humanity—apart from sin. This line of thought can also make sense of why, in the context of redemption, the New Testament often seems to speak of the incarnation of God in Christ being 'fleshed out' in the 'Body' of Christ. Thus the Church in Eph 1:23 (to extend our earlier discussion

---

[133] See 4.1 above.
[134] EiT, 90. Cf. TKG, 114–16 and WJC, 178.
[135] See TKG, 116.
[136] TKG, 119. My emphasis.
[137] TKG, 116. Cf. GC, 91 on the cross as the "consolidation of the universe" as cited in 4.3.1 above. In TKG, 116, Moltmann is answering a question (cf. TKG, 115) that is posed in the theological tradition. He continues, "That is how we should have to answer the question, if we wanted to embark on empty speculation." Despite the charge of speculation, Moltmann embarks on it nevertheless. Why is it "empty"? Perhaps because in his theology, human sin is, if not ontologically necessary, still historically inevitable.

of this passage) is said to be "the fullness of him who fills everything in every way" (NIV) or "who fills all in all" (NRSV).[138] Moltmann's approach, by contrast, requires a specific incarnation of God in Christ apart from sin so that the Godforsaken space may be filled. Even aside from sin, a descent into Hell was necessary for God to become all in all.

Given the way in which the distinction between creation and fall is blurred in Moltmann's thought, the historical and eschatological directions are inevitably opposed to each other, even though (even as) they are ultimately harmonised as the historical is taken up into the eschatological in the final redemption of all things. Rather than seeing a nature-grace correlation as existing in both directions of time (which I will suggest in the following

---

[138] Cf. John 1:13; 1 John 3:1–2; Rom 8:29; and 5.4 below. I have explored this kind of Christology in my *The Woman Will Overcome the Warrior*, 206–12. Ruether's own "Spirit Christology" moves in this direction to some extent. It is interesting that as a 'foundational direction' theologian (see *The Woman Will Overcome the Warrior*, 220–22), Ruether is open to the idea of ongoing historical incarnation, while Moltmann, as a 'transcendental direction' thinker resists this strongly (see e.g., CPS, 75 as cited in 3.3 above). That God will dwell in humanity as a whole seems clear from his idea of "cosmic incarnation" (see 3.1, cf. 2.4 and 2.5, above). But this is set in a strictly *eschatological* context. The same is true in GC, 218 where the distinction and correlation of the (penultimate) historical and (ultimate) eschatological directions is evident when Moltmann writes,

> [T]he human being has been created 'in the direction of' the image of God which Christ is—that is with the whole trend of his designation—so that the creation of human beings is open for the incarnation. Then the christology is understood as the fulfilment of the anthropology, and the anthropology becomes the preparation for the christology.

Also eschatological in focus (for "gather[ing]," as we saw in 2.5 above, is an eschatological notion for Moltmann) is the reworking of Rom 8:29 in GC, 242–43 where he writes,

> Only the Son [among the persons of the Trinity] becomes human, and embodies the image for which human beings are created. Christ is the only-begotten Son and, as the image of God the Father, is at the same time the first-born among many brothers and sisters. So as *imago Christi* human beings are gathered into his relationship of sonship, and in the brotherhood of Christ the Father of Jesus Christ becomes their Father also.

His italics. When speaking of historical incarnation, Moltmann's language is far more guarded. Thus in GC, 78, speaking of God's relationship to his "image on earth" (i.e., in the present age), he writes, "In a certain sense God enters into the creatures whom he has designated to be his image." Then, as he begins to look at the historical as a correlate of the eschatological, he continues,

> In the context of the messianic traditions about the likeness to God, we can at all events say that the creatures who are destined to be the image of God are also destined for the becoming human of the Son of God; and it is in this that they will find the fulfilment of their designation.

At this point, the *eschatological* context of a corporate view of incarnation becomes explicit: "The 'image of the invisible God' created in the beginning is destined to be 'the image of the Son of God *incarnate*'." My emphasis.

chapter), Moltmann tends to see the historical direction as 'nature' which eschatological 'grace' (or "glory" in his terminology) presupposes, completes, subsumes, ultimately relativises, and thus negates. This eclipse of creation is seen most clearly in the way in which temporal finitude has no ongoing future in Moltmann's vision.

To highlight how his theology fails to affirm the foundational direction of time in this respect, I will briefly sketch an alternative vision of the 'gift of transience' in 6.6 below. This vision suggests a very different eschatology as it flows out of an understanding of 'creational grace' (also to be discussed in the next chapter)—a reality whose absence more than any other, I will suggest, threatens to undermine the plausibility of Moltmann's vision of universal salvation.

5.4 Panentheism?

I will conclude this chapter on a more positive note, however. Having emphasised an eschatological-historical vision in which God might be seen as incarnate in humanity, which is a perspective that focuses on the foundational direction of time inasmuch as humanity is called to fill the earth with God's presence and inasmuch as the meaning of 'Christ' is historically differentiated in Christ's Body, I will now say something about God becoming "all in all" in the light of the transcendental direction.

In turning our attention from 'God in creation' to 'creation in God', I will highlight a point of contact with Moltmann that I believe can be biblically justified. First, however, some critical distance is necessary. The eclipse of creation in Moltmann's vision of the new creation has much to do with the way the world and its history are seen as being 'taken up' into God in the eschaton (even as God finally enters creation). Moltmann's eschatological 'panentheism' would seem to refer to a "redemption" or completion of history in which the primordial God-creation distinction is overcome.[139] When creation is 'taken up' into the glorified life of the Trinity, Moltmann's use of *Aufhebung* and its cognates in the pertinent passages suggests a 'sublation' or 'subsuming' of one reality to another.[140] In the eschaton, it would seem, creation will be denatured.

This is not what Moltmann intends. He writes,

> A mutual indwelling of the world in God and God in the world will come into being. For this, it is neither necessary for the world to dissolve into God, as pantheism says, nor for God to be dissolved in the world, as atheism maintains. God remains God, and the world remains creation. Through their mutual

---

[139] See CoG, 295 and 307 as cited in 3.1 above and CoG, 306–307, cited most fully in 4.3.3n241 above, and discussed in 4.1, 4.2, and especially at the end of 4.3 above.

[140] See in particular EiT, 40, cited in 2.5n131 above. For a discussion of *Aufhebung*, see 2.5 (including 2.5n155) above. For the 'taking up' of creation into God's life, see 2.5 above (including 2.5n131) and 3.1 above.

indwelling, they remain unmingled and undivided, for God lives in creation in a God-like way, and the world lives in God in a world-like way.[141]

This vision is a laudable one. Whether Moltmann's theology can sustain it, however, is another matter. As I have argued in the previous section, in his conception of time existing eschatologically within God's eternity, temporal finitude has no real future. Consequently, creation's promised "world-like" existence cannot, in my judgment, be realised.

Nevertheless, conceiving of the creation as being 'in' God is not necessarily incompatible with a creation-affirming theology. Certainly in the context of intra-creational relationships, it is meaningful to speak of a given reality as 'encapsulated' within another reality without implying that its nature is eclipsed or subsumed.[142] A friendship may be 'taken up' into a romance or life partnership, for example, while playing an ongoing, vital, foundational role within a relationship that is now of another kind. Similarly, a life partnership or marriage may give rise to and (for a time) be lived out within the wider, everyday context of a family. Naturally, this need not mean that partners leave being friends and lovers behind when they become parents and thus members of the same family. Indeed, everyone takes it for granted that partners who are no longer friends will become separated, if not legally then certainly emotionally. Put in more philosophical terms, a friendship that is 'taken up' into, or 'encapsulated' within, a life partnership (and, by extension, lived out, to some extent, within a family) is not like the engine of a car, a mere 'part'—albeit an indispensable one—within a greater 'whole'. Friendships are relationships that have their own value and integrity. Nevertheless and therefore, in the context of a marriage or life partnership, a friendship can be seen as a "y" in an "x over y" structure (to use the language of 5.2.2 above). At one and the same time, the "y" plays an ongoing foundational role, while the "x" transcendentally opens up the meaning and character of the original relationship to something new. The couple are (as we say) 'more than just good friends'.

If we can speak of one created reality or kind of relationship as existing within another while (in principle) maintaining its identity, can we not use such language to speak of the relationship between creation and God? Perhaps saying that creation exists 'within' God need not imply that creation is subsumed within a greater whole. Perhaps 'panentheistic' language may have its place, not as a total explanation or ultimate description of the God-world relationship but as a way of naming some of the contexts in which God's presence with us and for us may be experienced.

---

[141] CoG, 307.

[142] Here I allude to Dooyeweerd's notion of "enkapsis," which is articulated well in Hart, *Understanding Our World*, 218–21, where enkaptic relationships are distinguished from the part-whole relationships (cf. *Understanding Our World*, 211–18). I allude to the notion of enkapsis at the end of 5.2.1 above.

Moltmann tends to cite 1 Cor 15:28 in order to refer to biblical support for a "panentheistic" vision.[143] It is, however, his use of a Johannine passage on which I will comment here. Further to his claim that "The Creator becomes the *God who can become inhabited*," he writes,

> In John 17.21, in Jesus's high priestly prayer, we find precisely delineated the connection between the trinitarian indwellings of the divine persons and their shared openings of themselves to become the living space for created beings:
> That they may all be one,
> even as thou, Father, art in me and I in these,
> that they also may be in us.[144]

Moltmann cites this text in isolation and makes no further comments. When read within John's Gospel as a whole, however, this passage becomes even more supportive of the idea that creation will dwell in God.[145]

The claim that the Father is in Jesus even as Jesus is in the Father also occurs in John 10:38 and in John 14:10, 11, and 20. On close examination, this is not a "trinitarian" (or intra-divine) indwelling that is extended to a relationship between God and humanity only in John 17:21. This father-son language speaks of the God-creation relationship throughout.

It is most significant that when his Jewish opponents take offence at the idea that he is "God's Son" (John 10:36), Jesus, far from claiming that he is thereby fundamentally different from them, points out (in 10:34) that according to Scripture (Ps 82:6 specifically), human leaders may be referred to as "gods." In keeping with the fact that God's "son" in the Old Testament typically refers to Israel or Israel's representative king (see Ps 2:7), and in keeping with the notion found in Gen 5:3 that sonship reveals the dynamics of what it means to image God, Jesus' status as one who is in God as God is in him seems to be related to his *humanity*.

He also insists, much to the baffled annoyance of his opponents, that his claim to be "one" with the Father (10:30) is linked to the miracles he performs (10:32). These words occur between the intensely controversial healing of the blind man in John 9 and the even more revolutionary raising of Lazarus from the dead in John 11. If we think that such miracles set Jesus apart from us, we might assume that the 'oneness' with the Father that is expressed in these mighty acts of God makes him something we are not. Yet in John 14, where Jesus tells us that he is in the Father as the Father is in him three times, he says that his followers will do greater miracles than he has done (14:12). The connection with our humanity—a humanity uniquely yet supremely revealed in Jesus—remains.

---

[143] See, for example, TKG, 105 and SL, 212.
[144] CoG, 299. His emphasis. Cf. GC, 16, where he refers to John 10:30 and 14:11.
[145] For what follows, see my "Commentary: John 2:15–16, 18–19; 10:30–39 and 14:2a, 3," *Third Way* 26, no. 6 (Summer 2003): 15. I will be following the NRSV unless otherwise stated.

The idea that God is, in some sense, 'in' us is generally thought to be acceptable in contemporary Christianity, especially if we are speaking of the presence of God's Spirit rather than claiming that the Word may become "flesh" (to use the language of John 1:14) in us. The claim that we are 'in God' is, by contrast, relatively unfamiliar. But Jesus speaks in both of these ways. And when he does so, he is not simply speaking about himself. In John 17, the theme of Jesus being "one" with the Father returns when Jesus prays to the Father that his followers "may be one, as we are one" (17:22). Clearly 'oneness' here (and thus in John 10:30) is not about being the same kind of being ('God') but refers to two parties being of one heart and mind. In other words, this is the oneness of covenant as when man and woman are 'one' flesh—a union that is supposed to characterise their whole relationship. The oneness is so close that instead of the language of 'with', we have the language of 'with-in': "[A]s you, Father, are in me and I am in you," prays Jesus in v. 21, "may they also be in us."

When Jesus' followers are one with God and thus one with each other—one with each other and thus one with God—they are in the Father and the Son. To speak of God in creation and creation in God, therefore, is more biblical than is commonly realised. In Jesus and in his relationship to the Father, we may see ourselves. Indeed the prologue to John's Gospel, just before telling us that the Word that was with God and that was God in the beginning (1:1) "became flesh" (1:14), declares, in 1:12–13: "to all who received him, who believed in his name, he gave power to become children of God, who were born, not of blood or of [human decision] or of the will of man, but of God." Although traditional Christian thought tends to drive a wedge between God's "children" and God's "son" (vv. 12–14), these words should not be forgotten when, in the Greek of the next verse, we are told: "The Word became flesh and lived [literally tabernacled]" not only "*among* us" (NRSV, NIV, and most translations), but '*in* us' (*en hēmin*, 1:14).[146]

---

[146] Although I am still following the NRSV in this paragraph, the reference to "human decision" in 1:13 is taken from the NIV, which is to be preferred here. (Despite my misgivings about the NIV, expressed in 0.7n38 above, many contemporary translations, including the NIV, are particularly helpful at certain points.) The NRSV's reference to the will of the "flesh" at this point, though faithful to the Greek, obscures the positive, incarnational meaning of the "flesh" of v. 14 (although the fact that the Word enters into our willful human environment is part of its meaning). To pause to clarify this in the main text would risk muting the connection between the "children" of v. 12 and the "son" of v. 14.

As for the 'wedge' that has been driven between the "children" and the "son," some might point to the v. 14 itself. But here the reference to Jesus as God's "only" son (Greek, *monogenēs*), when read in the context of vv. 12–13, means 'firstborn' or 'favoured' as in Heb 11:17. In addition to John 3:16, 18, and 1 John 4:9, the same term occurs in John 1:18. If this is a reference to the "son" (preferring NRSV to NIV), the clear echo between this verse and the later description of the 'beloved'—not 'only'—disciple in 13:23 is instructive.

It is interesting that Jesus' words in John 10:25–38 are spoken in the Temple area (see vv. 22–23). Similarly, his words to the disciples in John 14 occur after he has told them that "[i]n my Father's house there are many dwelling places" (14:2)—the "Father's house," according to its only other occurrence in 2:16, being a clear reference to the Temple. When Jesus promises his followers, "if I go and prepare a place for you, I will come again and will take you to myself, so that where I am, there you may be also" in 14:3, the phrase "where I am" refers to the "place" in which he is dwelling or living as these words are uttered, prior to the resurrection. Read in context, this indicates that Jesus has replaced the Temple, a theme introduced in 2:19–20. He is the presence of God with his people, the one who dwells or 'tabernacles' with them according to the Greek of 1:14 (echoing Exod 33:7–11 and 40:34–38).

And this is where the idea of us being "in" God fits. As John puts it in Rev 21:22: "I saw no temple in the city, for its temple is the Lord God the Almighty and the Lamb." If we connect this with the way the Jerusalem Temple was structured to be a microcosm of the world and the meeting place between heaven and earth,[147] then the life of the Age to Come that has now begun is life lived in the covenant between the Father and the Son, or, in the language of the book of Revelation, in the covenant between the Almighty and the Lamb who together embrace the new heavens and the new earth. In this covenantal sense, therefore, our *dwelling in creation*[148] may be viewed as our *dwelling in God*.

For Paul, God will be "all in all" (1 Cor 15:28). Jesus is "the firstborn among many brothers" and sisters (Rom 8:29, NRSV margin and NIV). In John's eschatological vision,[149] we are in God as God is in us. The Word is to be made

---

[147] On this and biblical 'temple theology' in general, see Margaret Barker, *The Gate of Heaven: The History and Symbolism of the Temple in Jerusalem* (London: SPCK, 1991) and G.K. Beale, *The Temple and the Church's Mission: A Biblical Theology of the Dwelling Place of God* (Downers Grove, IL: InterVarsity Press, 2004), especially chap. 2. See also Crispin Fletcher-Louis, "Commentary: Mark 13:24ff and 30f," *Third Way* 21, no. 7 (September, 1998): 20 and Crispin Fletcher-Louis, "Commentary: Genesis 1:26 and Exodus 20:4f," *Third Way* 22, no. 9 (December 1999): 21.

[148] Jesus is not going to prepare a place for us 'in heaven' in John 14:3 as 'heaven' is normally understood. But "creation" here (as elsewhere) should be understood as 'heaven and earth', on which see 6.1.1 below.

[149] Here I refer to both the Gospel of John and to the book of Revelation. To see both as in some significant sense 'Johannine' does not rest on a particular theory of their authorship. On this latter issue, however, I am sympathetic to the common authorship that Stephen S. Smalley discerns in *Thunder and Love: John's Revelation and John's Community* (Milton Keynes, UK: Nelson Word, 1994) and that Luke Timothy Johnson is open to in his judicious discussion in *The Writings of the New Testament: An Interpretation*, 3rd ed. (Minneapolis, MN: Fortress Press, 2010), 461–63 and 512–15. In distinction from Smalley, however, I would follow Richard Bauckham, *The Testimony of the Beloved Disciple: Narrative, History, and Theology in the Gospel of John* (Grand Rapids, MI: Baker, 2007), in seeing the "John" in question as a disciple of Jesus who, though he was the beloved disciple, was nevertheless not one of the twelve. Although Bauckham does not go beyond saying that the John of the book of Revelation is a "Jewish Christian prophet," in *The Theology of the Book of Revelation* (Cambridge:

flesh in the sons and daughters of God. We do not simply live before God's presence, but within God's presence, within the "cosmic temple" that Moltmann finds in Rev 21[150] and that is present in Jesus in John 14:2–3.

All in all, Moltmann's citation of John 17:21 is appropriate. Covenantally speaking, God and creation will be 'one'. Theologians concerned to develop a biblical eschatology today, therefore, need not object to the mutual *perichoresis* of God and creation.[151] Within a creation-affirming eschatology, some form of 'panentheism' need not be out of place. For in the Father's house are many (in)dwellings.

Cambridge University Press, 1993), 2, I see no difficulty and much merit in identifying him with the John about whom Bauckham is so specific with respect to the Fourth Gospel.
[150] CoG, 308.
[151] Although I agree that making 'Being' dynamic (or amorous) does not get us out of the problems of Greek ontotheology, nevertheless with respect to *perichoresis*, my evaluation of Moltmann differs from the neo-Calvinist critique found in John W. Cooper, *Panentheism—The Other God of the Philosophers: From Plato to the Present* (Grand Rapids, MI: Baker, 2006), chap. 10, "Moltmann's Perichoretic Panentheism."

CHAPTER 6

The Nature of Grace

Moltmann's distinction between the historical and eschatological directions of time, I have been suggesting, is simultaneously insightful and misleading. In chapter 5, I argued that although this two-fold distinction goes a long way towards recognising and honouring time's foundational and transcendental directions, it also functions as a distinction between the conflated biblical themes of creation/fall and redemption/eschaton. As an alternative, I suggested that fall and redemption each occur in both temporal directions.

This critical comment is not intended to detract from what I see as Moltmann's genuine and important insight. As a way of distinguishing between creation and eschaton, Moltmann's philosophy of time is helpful in that he sees the historical movement towards the future-as-*futurum* as presupposed by, and brought to completion in, an eschaton in which God becomes all in all. In his view, teleological (or 'front loaded') models of time are theologically inadequate as there is a newness that enters history from the future as *adventus*. Consequently, because God is not all in all in the beginning—because the consummation of history (even apart from sin) cannot be construed as simply the outworking or differentiation of what is given with/in history's origin—, the redemption of time cannot be seen as (I would add: merely) the restoration of creation's primordial goodness.

At the same time, because the distinction between the creational and eschatological directions also functions for Moltmann as the distinction between fall and redemption, the consummation of history is (in effect) the simultaneous fulfilment, perfection, relativisation, and negation of time's foundational, differentiating direction. This leads to a paradoxical—and problematic—position in which the fulfilment of history would seem to entail the overcoming of history.

The present chapter will continue to explore this eclipse of creation by examining how Moltmann's philosophy of time shapes the way he relates 'nature' and 'grace'. The alternative model of time's foundational and transcendental directions offered in chapter 5, I will argue, is suggestive of a 'creational' grace (6.1) that is obscured by the structure of Moltmann's theology (6.3–6.5), his own explorations into the giftedness of life notwithstanding.

'Creational' grace, I will contend, is vital for any plausible universalist position, given the criteria discussed in 0.7, 1.5, and 5.0 above, because it makes it possible to 'envision'[1] a universal, human response to God's salvation that is neither (i) rooted in an unfallen essence or impulse within our nature (which minimises evil) nor (ii) dependent on the will of each and every human being autonomously choosing God's offer of Life rather than Death (which misconstrues the nature of freedom). 'Creational' grace (together with 'eschatological' grace) allows us to honour the 'covenantal' nature of the relationship between heaven and earth (6.1.1) and thus glimpse a 'covenantal universalism' in which 'nature' is not neutral towards God such that it must be 'overcome' to secure a salvation for all. It also provides us with an alternative to seeing 'nature' or the 'natural' as a 'realm' or principle that is 'good as far as it goes' before grace takes us beyond its limitations. In the covenantal relationship between God and creation, explored below, nature and grace are distinguished yet 'one'. In the light of 5.4 above, grace may be seen 'in' nature, while nature comes into its own only 'within' grace.

The aim of bringing Moltmann's theology into conversation with such an approach, and the aim of exploring the connections between Moltmann's position and the stance adopted by Karl Barth in his famous 'nature-grace' debate with Emil Brunner (in 6.2 below), is, in line with the 'dialogical' nature of the previous chapter, to deepen our analysis and evaluation of his thought. A central question is whether and to what extent Moltmann's universalism honours authentic human freedom. Towards the end of the chapter (in 6.6), I will address the broader, yet related, question of the extent to which Moltmann's eschatology affirms created finitude. Is transience the mark of an imperfect creation that will pass away? Or does temporal finitude speak to us of the giftedness of life, a giftedness that will have a future in God's future?

6.1 Creational Grace

Any position that would posit a truly free, universal response to God's grace has to ensure that its eschatological claims are not undermined by its understanding of human nature. In Reformed, or more specifically Calvinist, theologies, our humanity cannot be understood apart from the sovereignty of God, but is expressed in our willing and grateful subjection to divine Law. As God's sovereignty extends over the whole of life, this emphasis helps us avoid a spirituality modeled on a spurious split between sacred and secular. Consequently, such a Reformed understanding of the Will of the Sovereign helps us avoid a false polarity between Law and Gospel. While this is a helpful starting point, in my view, it is important to see grace as a far richer reality than our God-given ability to (once again) obey divine Law. Our receiving/working out of God's grace—a grace that can be understood foundationally as the gift and call of Life and transcendentally as the promise and call of Life—is far

---

[1] An argument that helps us 'envision' universal salvation is not a watertight argument. It simply helps make universal salvation thinkable.

more than (and often other than) subjection. In responding to (not just obeying) God's *grace* (which is more than God's will), we find our true *nature*. 'Nature' and 'grace' are two sides of the mystery of existence.

In figure 6 above, I distinguished between (i) influence and (ii) response—or between (i) direction (i.e., direction-giving) and (ii) structure—as two correlative 'sides' or movements within each of the two temporal directions. (Although there is the risk of terminological confusion, we could also think of these two sides as correlative dynamics or 'directions' within the foundational-creational and transcendental-eschatological directions of time.) If we view existence covenantally, then, normatively speaking, the former dynamic (influence, directing) can be identified as God's 'grace', which may be mediated by creation/time, while the latter (response, including resulting structures) can be understood in terms of the theological category of 'nature' as it is correlated with grace. Nature in responding to grace, becomes 'graced'. In the rediscovery and realisation of our true, 'graced nature', we participate in God's creative and redemptive work and mediate God's grace—the gift-promise/call of and to Life—to others.[2]

Our participation in the covenant is our participation in 'freedom'. In the mystery of grace, our life is our own as we are given the 'space' to respond and initiate in our own way. Yet this space is not neutral as it calls us to recover, maintain, deepen, and expand our relationship with God and creation from freedom to freedom (see Gal 5:1). Grace, therefore, not only evokes our response, but also elicits our covenantal initiative and innovation. In refusing to find our life in God, by contrast, we may choose *autonomy*, but, according to the Scriptures, we do not thereby choose Life or freedom (see Deut 30:15–16 and Jas 1:25 and 2:12). Authentic self-determination eludes us. As Karl Barth puts it:

> It is true that man's God-given freedom is choice, decision, act. But it is genuine choice; it is genuine decision and act in the right direction.
>
> It would be a strange freedom that would leave man neutral, able to choose, decide, and act rightly or wrongly! What kind of power would that be! Man becomes free and is free by choosing, deciding, and determining himself in accordance with the freedom of God.[3]

---

[2] The 'grace/graced nature' distinction that I am suggesting somewhat parallels the distinction, found in pre-Reformation theology, between "uncreated" and "created" grace. R. Kearsley in "Grace," in *New Dictionary of Theology,* ed. Sinclair B. Ferguson and David F. Wright (Leicester, UK: Inter-Varsity Press, 1988), 280, describes the former as "the gift of God himself which underlies all other kinds of grace in salvation" and the latter as "the effect or impact of uncreated grace upon the individual's own 'nature' or disposition."

[3] Karl Barth, "The Gift of Freedom: Foundation of Evangelical Ethics," in *The Humanity of God* (Atlanta, GA: John Knox Press, 1960), 76–77. This essay reveals a side of Barth's theology not (so) clearly visible in the earlier works on which we shall focus in 6.2 below. Cf. n. 52 below.

The Nature of Grace

In the model I am proposing, grace (in contrast to much Protestant theology in particular) is not only a category of redemption or salvation;[4] it must also be understood in its creational and eschatological dimensions as coming to us (respectively) in the foundational and transcendental directions of time. Grace is not simply God's gift/promise of forgiveness and simultaneous call to repentance and sanctification (redemptive grace); it is the creational gift/call and eschatological promise/call of/to Life itself. Furthermore, the dynamics of sin and temptation must also be understood in terms of these distinctions.

This understanding of what we might call the 'grace' of existence and the 'dis-grace' of evil, to borrow a term from Leonardo Boff, can be briefly set out as follows:

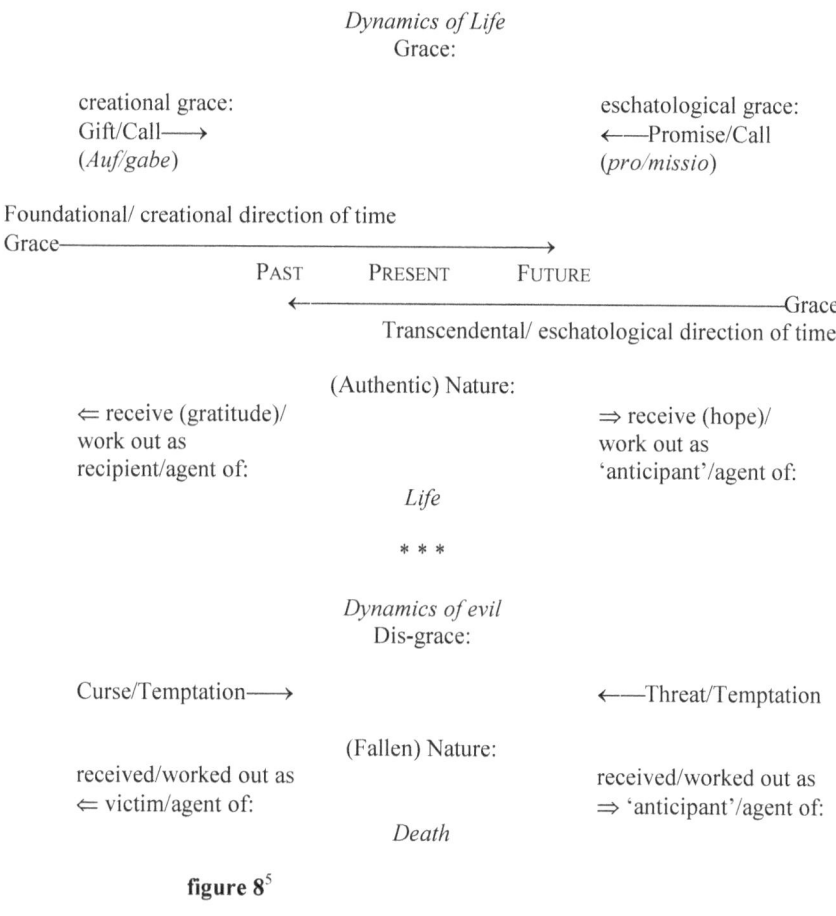

figure 8[5]

---

[4] See 4.2n60 above.

[5] For the language of "dis-grace" in the context of evil, cf. Boff, *Liberating Grace*, 4 et passim. As I do not explore an alternative view of the nature of evil in this study in any

In this model, redemptive grace *opposes* our fallen nature but *restores* and *renews* our authentic nature by enabling us to receive creational and eschatological grace. The goal of redemption is the healing of creation and the eschatological fulfilment of history. This allows for agreement with the Kuyperian tradition's insistence that grace 'restores' nature while making contact with those theologies that believe that grace 'completes', 'perfects', or even 'elevates' nature (understanding such 'completion' as eschatological

---

detail, a few comments are in order so as to clarify the implications of the model set out in figure 8.

In 1.3 above, I noted Moltmann's observation that the authors of *The Mystery of Salvation* had apparently abandoned the Anglican tradition in general and the theology of Augustine in particular in order to follow in the footsteps of Pelagius (who was, as Moltmann would have been well aware when he made the comparison, also from Britain). The contrast that Peter Brown has drawn, in his *Augustine of Hippo: A Biography* (London: Faber and Faber, 1967), 365–66, between the theological anthropologies of these two highly influential thinkers provides a helpful backdrop to my proposal here. He writes,

> The Pelagian man was essentially a separate individual: the man of Augustine is always about to be engulfed in vast, mysterious solidarities. For Pelagius, men had simply decided to imitate Adam, the first sinner: for Augustine, they received their basic weakness in the most intimate and irreversible manner possible; they were born into it by the mere fact of physical descent from this, the common father of the human race.

(Cf. his discussion of their respective views of sin and freedom on pp. 372–75.)

It is important that we are not distracted by Augustine's (infamous) view of original sin at this point. We do not need to believe that evil is passed on by *generation* to recognise that it is passed on by *generations*. Moltmann's view of evil (analysed in 4.2) certainly suggests that "vast, mysterious solidarities" are crucial to understanding the evils in which we are "engulfed." Furthermore, because he is clearly not a libertarian individualist, his theology would encourage us to recognise that no one does evil simply 'for the hell of it'.

This important, powerful, inter-individual, inter-generational context is implied in the notion that we are simultaneously victims and agents of sin, as expressed briefly in figure 8. For how this might relate to Adolf Hitler, often seen as the epitome of evil beyond redemption, see Alice Miller, "Adolf Hitler's Childhood: From Hidden to Manifest Horror," in *For Your Own Good: Hidden Cruelty in Child-rearing and the Roots of Violence*, trans. Hildegarde and Hunter Hannum, 2nd ed. (New York: Farrar, Straus, and Giroux, 1984), 142–97. Although Moltmann may not probe the social or inter-generational nature of our individual evils in his writings, there is an excellent, recent discussion of victim/agent dynamics in EoH, chap. 12.

Naturally, this has implications for my understanding of what constitutes a viable universalism. As agents of evil, we need to repent. As victims of evil, we need to be set free. As the gift precedes the call (a point that will be reiterated in the Conclusion in 8.4 below), and as curse precedes temptation (cf. n. 15 below), so in God's redemptive grace, liberation or setting free from our bondage to sin precedes, makes way for, and is extended by our repentance. It also follows that there is a social, intergenerational side not only to sin but to its overcoming. This will be explored in 7.2, 7.3, and 8.2–8.4 below. In grace in general, and in salvation in particular, we are "engulfed in"—or better, embraced by—"mysterious solidarities."

fulfilment not as adding a higher realm or transcending/correcting an original ontological imperfection).[6]

To clarify the contours of this perspective further, it will be helpful to revisit some familiar biblical themes. In particular it will be instructive to look at the

---

[6] See 4.2n62 above. For an interesting expression of the Kuyperian sensitivities to the nature-grace relationship in biblical studies, See Al Wolters, "Nature and Grace in the Interpretation of Proverbs 31:10–31," in *The Song of the Valiant Woman: Studies in the Interpretation of Proverbs 31:10–31* (Carlisle, UK: Paternoster, 2001), 15–29 (= *Calvin Theological Journal* 19 (1984): 153–66). Wolters explicitly cites Kuyper as exemplifying the 'grace restores nature' approach (25) and uses this phrase ("grace restores nature") three times of Herman Bavinck in his translator's preface to Jan Veenhof, *Nature and Grace in Herman Bavinck*, trans. Albert M. Wolters (Sioux Centre, IA: Dordt College Press, 2006), 1–2 (= Jan Veenhof, "Nature and Grace in Bavinck," trans. Al Wolters, *Pro Rege* 34, no. 4 (June 2006): 11. [Pagination from the *Pro Rege* version will be placed in square brackets after pagination from the Dordt College Press version, below]). The text that follows Wolters' preface is his translation of Jan Veenhof, *Revelatie en Inspiratie: De Openbarings en Schriftbeschouwing van Herman Bavinck in vergelijking met die der ethische theologie* (Amsterdam: Buijten en Schipperheijn, 1968), 345–65.

Despite Wolters' restorationist claims, in his own translation, Bavinck is cited as saying, "Grace *restores* nature *and* raises it to its highest *fulfillment*, but it does not add a new, heterogenous component to it" (25 [22]) and "There is a movement from creation through redemption to sanctification and glorification. The point of arrival *returns* to the point of departure, and is simultaneously a high point *elevated* high above the point of departure." (26 [22]). My emphases. (The first citation is translated from Herman Bavinck, *Gereformeerde Dogmatiek*, 4th ed. (Kampen: J.H. Kok, 1928–30), 3:582 [cf. *Sin and Salvation in Christ*, vol. 3 of *Reformed Dogmatics*, ed. John Bolt, trans. John Vriend (Grand Rapids, MI: Baker, 2006), 577]; the second is from Herman Bavinck, *Magnalia Dei: Onderwijzing in de Christelijke Religie, naar Gereformeerde Belijdenis* (1909; repr., Kampen: J.H. Kok, 1931), 128–29 [cf. *Our Reasonable Faith: A Survey of Christian Doctrine*, trans. Henry Zylstra (Grand Rapids, MI: Baker, 1977), 144]. See the discussion of Wolters' interpretation of Bavinck in Hielema, "Herman Bavinck's Eschatological Understanding of Redemption," 386–94 and 426n131. For Hielema's discussion of "elevation" in Bavinck, see 172–288.

Ironically, Walsh in "Theology of Hope and the Doctrine of Creation," 61–62 follows Wolters' misreading of Bavinck to oppose Bavinck's view of the nature-grace relationship to that of Moltmann. In my view, Bavinck represents a point of contact between Moltmann and the Kuyperian tradition worthy of further exploration. Hielema detected 'Bavinckian' tendencies in my own work (see "Herman Bavinck's Eschatological Understanding of Redemption," 356–58) long before I did. Cf. 5.3n117 above. For a discussion that parallels the present section yet with extended analysis of Bavinck's position, see Nicholas Ansell, "It's About Time: Opening Reformational Thought to the Eschaton," *Calvin Theological Journal* 47, no. 1 (April, 2012): 98–121. For a recent overview of Reformed, including Kuyperian, thinking about redemption from a South African perspective, see Ernst M. Conradie, *Saving the Earth? The Legacy of Reformed Views on "Re-creation"* (Münster: LIT Verlag, 2013), especially chaps. 3 and 7, on Bavinck and Moltmann, respectively.

relationship between heaven and earth in this (nature-grace) context, especially as this will also help us explore some connections with Moltmann's theology.[7]

6.1.1 Heaven and Earth: The Covenantal Dynamics of Existence

One of the merits of this model, I suggest, is that it enables us to reject all forms of dualism without falling into reductionism. Thus in accepting the biblical vision of the New Creation as our final destiny rather than the 'heaven' of much traditional Christian piety,[8] for example, there is still scope within this model to understand the nature of 'heaven' as the term is used throughout the Scriptures. The preceding discussion of the gift-promise and call of (and to) Life can help us see an alternative way of viewing heaven and earth that does not require us to see them in terms of a dichotomy or sliding scale between spirit and matter. At the same time the importance of 'heaven' within a creation-affirming spirituality may also be fully recognised.[9]

'Heaven' and 'earth' may still be distinguished within creation, but they are not to be seen as separate realms that interact or exist in parallel. In the Bible, the phrase "the heavens and the earth" is often a merism that evokes the extremes of sky and land in order to signify all that God has created (Gen 1:1; 2:1, 4; cf. Isa 65:17; Rev 21:1). Because of the daily dependence of nomadic and agricultural peoples on the rain (and the sun), however, 'the heavens' (as a part of creation) came to symbolise for Israel the way in which life was not autonomous or self-sustaining, but an ongoing gift-promise of God, to be received with gratitude and anticipated in hope. 'The heavens' thus spoke of the origin, source, and future of existence on 'earth'. This is central to the story of manna in the wilderness (Exod 16), for example.

'Earth' in this perspective is not a self-contained reality. The Promised Land that Israel is to enter and embrace as its home cannot be understood without reference to the dynamics of grace. The ground beneath our feet is not a basis for autonomy. It is not a possession. Once the Israelites think of this land as

---

[7] Thus Moltmann's approach to the topic to be explored in 6.1.1 (heaven and earth) will be addressed in 6.3 below.

[8] On what heaven is not, see the very helpful popular book by David Lawrence, *Heaven . . . It's Not the End of the World* (London: Scripture Union, 1995). I find the discussion in Terence E. Fretheim, *The Suffering of God: An Old Testament Perspective* (Philadelphia: Fortress Press, 1984), 37–39 and in various works by N.T. Wright such as, *New Heavens, New Earth: The Biblical Picture of Christian Hope* (Cambridge, UK: Grove, 1999) and *Surprised by Hope: Rethinking Heaven, the Resurrection, and the Mission of the Church* (New York: HarperOne, 2008) to be generally supportive of my proposal.

[9] The following discussion of heaven parallels my "Commentary: Colossians 3:1f.," *Third Way* 22, no. 1 (February 1999): 22. Biblical citations will be from the NRSV unless otherwise noted.

theirs by right—as no longer promised, as no longer a gift—either they cannot enter it, or (if they are already within its borders) they cannot keep it.[10]

The earth is not a temptation in this context, but is caught up in our idolatry.[11] Certainly it is not seen as evil 'matter' to be contrasted with heavenly spirit. In the Bible, evil is frequently symbolised not by the earth but by 'the sea' (e.g., Mic 7:19; Rev 21:1) as evil cannot be the 'ground' of true human existence.

Given this understanding, it makes sense that God should speak to his people and provide for them 'from heaven'. In some cases, 'heaven' and 'God' become almost synonymous, hence Matthew's use of the phrase "the Kingdom of heaven" where the other synoptics refer to the Kingdom of God. Yet even here, the point is that (the restoration/realisation of) God's reign over the earth is a gift and promise of God rather than an autonomous human achievement. The language of 'heaven' always speaks of the giftedness of creation and the promise of the future.

The gift and call of God, on the one hand, and the receiving and working out of that gift/call, on the other hand, thus became symbolised in the Bible by the relationship between heaven and earth.[12] The way the crops of the earth grew in response to the rain from the skies spoke to the Hebrews of God's covenant with creation. In the covenantal dynamics of life, our existence must be open to its Origin and Destiny. The earth can produce no fruit without receiving the rain of the heavens. Life flourishes in the correlation of nature and grace. Isaiah 45:8 expresses this understanding, in the context of redemption, as follows:

> "Shower, O heavens, from above,
>   and let the skies rain down righteousness;
> let the earth open, that salvation may spring up,
>   and let it cause righteousness to sprout up also;
>   I the Lord have created it."

Like Adam and Eve, therefore, we must continue to draw our very breath from beyond ourselves (Gen 2:7). Similarly, true authority cannot ground or legitimate itself, but must be received 'from above'. It is in this sense that Jesus' kingdom is "not of this world" (John 18:36, NIV) or "from this world" (NRSV). The fact that our citizenship is "in heaven" (Phil 3:20) means that the gift/call and promise/call of who we are, and are to be, lies beyond, or is not exhausted by, our response. We are to receive our fundamental orientation by

---

[10] See Walter Brueggemann, *The Land: Place as Gift, Promise, and Challenge in Biblical Faith*, 2nd ed. (Philadelphia: Fortress Press, 2002). Although Brueggemann's analysis is helpful, he often fails to integrate gift and call.

[11] *Contra* Brueggemann, *The Land*, chap. 4 and cf. the argument in my "The Call of Wisdom/The Voice of The Serpent."

[12] One can speak of promise/call here too. In what follows, I will tend to explore the gift/call as this is a dimension of the grace-nature relationship that Moltmann minimises (cf. 6.3 below).

fixing our eyes on what "cannot be seen" (2 Cor 4:18). Then, in the light of this empowering grace and blessing, we may live out or make visible the life we have been given and the life to which we are called. In touch with the very source of our being, we know that the gift of our life will not be revoked, but shall be fleshed-out anew on earth in the Resurrection (2 Cor 5:1–10).

Our vertical and horizontal metaphors for the spirituality of existence may thus be brought together. What we experience in the present, 'between' past and future, of the gift and promise of Life may be said to come from 'heaven'. Our very existence from beginning to end is given/promised to us from 'above'.[13]

Being open to heaven enables us to make God present in the world. God's Word and Spirit are to be made incarnate. God's will is to be done on earth as it is in heaven. In this perspective, it is not possible to be so heavenly minded that one is no earthly good. The folly of setting one's mind on "earthly things" that Paul opposes (Phil 3:19) has nothing to do with celebrating the gift of creation. It is the error of trying to find one's identity and purpose autonomously by grasping at the world as if it can be a possession. (This, and not the denigration of the 'body', is what Paul means by a life lived after the "flesh" rather than

---

[13] As we normally associate 'above' with 'transcendence', it might be thought that I am exploring heaven, or the gift and promise of and to Life, in terms of 'foundational transcendence' and 'transcendental transcendence' respectively. Actually, I see the foundational direction of heaven and of earth in terms of immanence and the transcendental direction of heaven and of earth in terms of transcendence. For the former, we might even coin the term *'prescendence'* or, if we also wish to allude to that which precedes, *'precendence'*.

It is a mistake, I believe, to see immanence ('prescendence') as something that we can conceptually grasp in a relatively straightforward manner while a healthy recognition of transcendence (alone) restores mystery to the world. This assumption seems to run through James K.A. Smith's otherwise helpful discussion of post-modern (critiques of) phenomenology, *Speech and Theology: Language and the Logic of Incarnation* (London: Routledge, 2002). There is far more to the gift/call of Life than we can understand. Even here we know more than we can tell. In addition to that which transcendently 'exceeds' our concepts (or ideas) there is that which immanently 'precedes' them, a 'depth' that cannot be grasped. Cf. n. 175 below.

This motif is alive and well in much feminist theology. On Rosemary Radford Ruether, see 5.3n138 above. See also Catherine Keller, "Pneumatic Nudges: The Theology of Moltmann, Feminism, and the Future," in *The Future of Theology: Essays in Honor of Jürgen Moltmann*, ed. Miroslav Volf, Carmen Krieg, and Thomas Kucharz (Grand Rapids, MI: Eerdmans, 1996), 142–53 and her more recent *Face of the Deep: A Theology of Becoming* (London: Routledge, 2003). To return to the symbolism of 'above', in this context, 'Heaven' in the Bible has nothing to do with a patriarchal preference for the Sky-Father over the Earth-Mother. If the Israelites had not been so dependent on the rains, the earth (in its depths) could easily have symbolised the giftedness of/to life. Cf. the 'well of life' theme in Gen 2:6 and throughout Genesis.

after the Spirit.[14]) In that way lies destruction (Phil 3:19). The secularism that would ignore heaven ends up losing the earth.

This perspective can also makes sense of why Paul can speak of Christians being 'in heaven' *during* their earthly lives (Eph 2:6). Heaven is a thoroughly creational category that highlights the spirituality of all of life and presupposes the earth as the theatre of God's glory. At the same time, it follows that evil is not simply an 'earthly' matter. Gift-promise and call find their counterparts in curse-threat and temptation (cf. figure 8 above).[15] The conflict that the Bible pictures as taking place 'in the heavens' (e.g., in Daniel and Revelation) has nothing to do with locating spiritual realities in another world beyond creation. Such language speaks of the fundamental or 'principial' conflict between God and the powers and principalities in which the very giftedness and future of life and the very meaning of our existence is at stake because humanity has given itself to idolatrous forces in which it hopes to find the 'heavenly' or foundational-transcendental source/goal of abundant life. When the forces of evil are opposed by Jesus and the martyrs, therefore, it follows that Satan will be thrown down from heaven (Luke 10:18; Rev 12:9, 10). Cut off from God's past and God's future, "his time is short" (Rev 12:12).

Within the covenantal dynamics of creation, angels need no longer be viewed as 'matterless spirits' but as bringers of the gift/promise of life together with the call of God from heaven to earth.[16] This is in keeping with the fact that 'angel' in Hebrew and Greek simply means messenger—a terms that signifies an office or calling rather than a specific kind of being. As the 'directional' nature of the divine gift and promise of existence can be mediated by creation,

---

[14] Rudolf Bultmann, who, in my view, so misunderstood the biblical portrayal of heaven and earth, nevertheless puts this well in his seminal essay "New Testament and Mythology," in *Kerygma and Myth: A Theological Debate*, by Rudolf Bultmann and Ernst Lohmeyer, Julius Schniewind, Helmut Thielicke, and Austin Farrer, ed. Hans Werner Bartsch (New York: Harper and Row, 1961), 1–44. He writes, "[W]hat does [Paul] mean by "flesh"? Not the bodily or physical side of human nature, but the sphere of visible, concrete, tangible, and measurable reality . . . . When a man chooses to live entirely in and for this sphere . . . , it assumes the shape of a "power"." (18). "The authentic life, on the other hand, would be a life based on unseen, intangible realities. Such a life means the abandonment of all self-contrived security. This is what the New Testament means by "life after the Spirit" or "life in faith". For this life we must have faith in *the grace of God*. It means faith that the unseen, intangible reality actually confronts us as love, opening up our future and signifying not death but life" (19, his emphasis).

[15] To open up the heavenly/earthly dimensions of evil is to open up the temporal meaning of evil. In the curse of evil, we find ourselves embedded in the evils of the past by which we are victimised and out of which, aside from God's grace, we act into the future. Curse leads to temptation which leads to sin by which the curse is extended to others. Cf. n. 5 above.

[16] The following discussion parallels my "Commentary: Luke 20:27–36," *Third Way* 22, no. 2 (March 1999): 22. Cf. n. 194 below.

this angelic calling is one that any of God's creatures (familiar or unfamiliar) may fulfil.[17]

This interpretation fits remarkably well with the biblical witness. In this light, the parallels that are drawn between the cherubim and the wings of the wind in Ps 18:10 and between the angels and the morning stars in Job 38:7 can be seen as examples of synonymous parallelism. This approach also sheds light on the reference to the winds as God's "angels" in Ps 104:4 (NIV margin, cf. Heb 1:7, NIV and NRSV); the typically human appearance of angels in the Old Testament; the fact that the Galatians welcomed Paul "as an angel of God" (Gal 4:14, NRSV *contra* NIV); the identification of what would appear to be church leaders as angels in the book of Revelation (2:1, 8, 12, 18; 3:1, 7, 14); the claim that Christians will one day judge angels in 1 Cor 6:3 (to be taken as a parallel to 6:2); and the intriguing similarity between the heavenly beings and the creatures of the earth in Ezek 1:4–10 and Rev 4:7.[18] In the light of these last two texts in particular, all of creation can be seen as involved in the struggle for liberation from the curse we have brought upon the world. All of God's creatures may play a vital 'angelic' role in revealing God's purposes, doing his will, and mediating the empowering energies of God's grace.

6.2 The Barth-Brunner Debate

So how could this nature-grace model in general, and this notion of 'creational' grace in particular, help someone who wants to make a case for universal salvation? Can important elements of such an approach be detected in Moltmann's writings, suggesting a way in which he could further strengthen the appeal and plausibility of his own position?

In 4.2 above, I suggested that, "Briefly formulated, 'nature' might be said to correspond to what is within our power while 'grace', by contrast, could be said to refer to what we need that is beyond our control (or beyond the power of creation). If 'nature' could thus be said to be our responsibility (in some sense), 'grace' would thus point to God's gifts and promises, to God's action rather than to our own." The most famous interchange on the issues surrounding this nature-grace relationship in modern theology is undoubtedly the Barth-Brunner debate, which took place just prior to the outbreak of the Second World War.[19]

---

[17] This perspective can also make sense of why the Bible may speak of 'angels' being involved in evil. But there is no compelling biblical evidence, in my opinion, for equating 'fallen' angels with demons. The latter call for a different interpretation, but this lies beyond the scope of the present discussion. For a rejection of this traditional identification, cf. Karl Barth, *Church Dogmatics* 3/3, ed. G.W. Bromiley and T.F. Torrance (Edinburgh: T. and T. Clark, 1961), 289–531, especially 519–31.

[18] On the angels of, e.g., Matt 13 as Roman soldiers, see 7.1 (including 7.1n36) below. On Hos 12:4 in relation to Gen 32, see 7.3 (including 7.3n139) below.

[19] The interchange that began as a pair of brochures in German in 1934 was published in English as, Karl Barth and Emil Brunner, *Natural Theology: Comprising "Nature and Grace" by Professor Dr. Emil Brunner and the Reply "No!" by Dr. Karl Barth*, trans. Peter Fraenkel (London: Geoffrey Bles, Centenary Press, 1946). The recent reissue

As this discussion brings many of the central issues to the fore very clearly, I will also offer some of my own suggestions against this background.

There is another reason why a brief examination of this debate is helpful here. In 5.1 above, I suggested that Moltmann can be interpreted as, philosophically speaking, working in a 'Heideggerian' milieu in which some of his ideas can be seen as answering Heidegger by radically 'eschatologising' some of his distinctions. Theologically speaking, I believe that Moltmann can be fruitfully understood as working in a Barthian milieu.[20] Indeed, some commentators have suggested that Moltmann has 'eschatologised' Barth's basic response to Brunner's proposed nature-grace model, an issue to which we will return in 6.5 below. That Barth also advocated universal salvation[21] makes a Barth/Moltmann comparison of additional interest.

It is noteworthy that, in addition to addressing grace in a redemptive sense, Emil Brunner also speaks of the *grace* of "*creation*" (and "preservation").[22] His handling of this category, however, is ultimately disappointing. True creational grace, I would argue, is a gift/call of and to Life in which God's Spirit/Word come(s) to us (via creation/history as Brunner rightly notes[23]) by virtue of our

---

(Eugene, OR: Wipf and Stock, 2002) has identical pagination. As my discussion of this important text is a means to an end—to shed light on the nature-grace relationship in Moltmann (see n. 52 below)—I will not engage the secondary literature in any detail, nor pursue the way Barth and Brunner reflected on this debate later in their respective careers. For an excellent discussion, see Trevor Hart, "The Capacity for Ambiguity: Revisiting the Barth-Brunner Debate," in his *Regarding Karl Barth: Toward a Reading of His Theology* (Downers Grove, IL: InterVarsity Press, 1999), 139–72.

[20] Cf. Moltmann's own self-description, in his foreword to *God, Hope, and History: Jürgen Moltmann and the Christian Concept of History*, by A.J. Conyers, vii, as a "nonconformist in that theological school to which I owe the most: the Barth school." Cf. his more recent comments in BP, chap. 4, 64–65, and 109–11. There is much to be said for seeing Moltmann's theology as answering Barth while remaining indebted to him. This certainly seems to be the case with Moltmann's doctrine of creation. Thus Walter Brueggemann in his editor's foreword to *From Creation to New Creation: Old Testament Perspectives*, by Bernhard W. Anderson (Minneapolis, MN: Fortress Press, 1994), viii, comments that *God in Creation* is a work in which Moltmann can be seen as "devoting a great deal of energy ... to moving beyond Barth ... even if in a Barthian posture." Similarly in the context of suggesting that it is fruitful to ask "how Moltmann's theology of creation continues the 'classical' Barthian *Heilsgeschichte* approach and how he transcends or even departs from it" in his *Creation—An Ecumenical Challenge? Reflections Issuing from a Study by the Institute for Ecumenical Research Strasbourg, France* (Macon, GA: Mercer University Press, 1989), 95 (his italics), Per Lønning notes on p. 99 that Moltmann "is somewhat weighed down by [the] Barthian ... suspicion about creation as givenness." This relates to my claim towards the end 6.4 below and in n. 112 below that for Moltmann there is a surplus of the Giver over the given but not a surplus of the gift over the given.

[21] This is sometimes contested. But Moltmann interprets Barth as a kind of universalist (see CoG, 248–49). For the purposes of this study, that is sufficient reason to treat him as such.

[22] See Brunner, "Nature and Grace," 20–21, 28, 30 and especially 51. My emphasis.

[23] See Brunner, "Nature and Grace," 9.

being human. From this, I suggest, it follows that to be *truly* human requires our response. Yet we frequently reject Life (in its various dimensions: biological, psychological, economic, etc.) in varying degrees. Brunner, by contrast, speaks as if all people respond positively but automatically. "Ordinances" of creation or preservation, he writes, "are created and maintained by instinct and reason. Even the believer, who by reason of his faith understands their ultimate sense better than the unbeliever, cannot but allow his instinct and his reason to function with regard to these ordinances . . . ."[24] Furthermore,

> [T]hrough the preserving grace of God they are known also to 'natural man' as ordinances that are necessary and somehow holy and are respected by him as such. For it is peculiar to the preserving grace of God that he does his preserving work both by nature acting unconsciously and by the reason of man.[25]

Earlier, he speaks of "divine ordinances of nature" that "do not belong to the realm of redemption, of the Church, but belong to the realm of divine preservation, in which natural impulse and reason are constituent factors."[26] This talk of two *realms* reveals a basic nature-grace dualism despite his insistence that both realms manifest God's will.[27]

---

[24] Brunner, "Nature and Grace," 30.
[25] Brunner, "Nature and Grace," 31.
[26] Brunner, "Nature and Grace," 30.
[27] This emphasis on God's will (in the singular) is expressed in the ET of the title of one of Brunner's most important works (cited in 5.3n109 above): *The Divine Imperative*. Yet the original German title, *Das Gebot und die Ordnungen*—'The Command and the Ordinances'—highlights Brunner's 'soft' (i.e., 'both-and') dualism of grace and nature (Christ and [almost Christ above] culture, cf. 4.2n62 above) that can be represented as follows:

Grace Church; realm of redemption	redemptive grace	leads to salvation; Gospel	special revelation, 'event' unmediated by time	*Gebot*/ command; personal; here and now	God's will requires response of faith
Nature world; realm of creation	creational/ preserving 'grace'	insufficient for salvation; law	general revelation, mediated by history	*Ordnungen*/ ordinances; impersonal; perduring	God's will works via human reason and instinct

This upper realm, taken on its own, provides a significant parallel—or 'point of contact'—with Barth and helps explain the earlier alliance. But as a 'grace against nature' thinker (despite also being a theologian who also sees grace as embracing nature), Barth cannot tolerate even the relative legitimacy given to the lower realm. This helps explain his charge of "compromise" in "No!," in 69, 72.

While Brunner speaks of all people in some sense knowing the ordinances of creation and preservation, he stresses that this is not sufficient for salvation.[28] But this awareness does, in its own way, make salvation possible. That this *partial* knowledge is still partial *knowledge* points simultaneously to our ongoing humanity,[29] the continuity of what he calls the "formal" image of God since the fall[30] (despite our loss of the "material" image[31]), our responsibility before God,[32] and our sense of sin, which presupposes knowledge of God prior to the experience of salvation.[33] All this means that there must be a point of contact between nature and grace located in the formal *imago Dei*.[34] Brunner reasons,

> The Word of God could not reach a man who had lost his consciousness of God entirely. A man without conscience cannot be struck by the call "Repent ye and believe the Gospel." What the natural man knows of God, of the law and of his own dependence upon God, may be very confused and distorted. But even so it is the necessary, indispensable point of contact for divine grace.[35]

This claim lies right at the heart of the Barth-Brunner dispute for Barth finds all talk of a point of contact dangerous, and is at pains to stress that even our consciousness of sin can only come about in the context of redemptive grace.[36]

Barth's reaction to the very idea that there is a realm of nature that is oriented to grace—summed up in the title of his response: *"Nein!"*—makes

---

[28] See Brunner, "Nature and Grace," 26, 27. He implies that he is unlike Calvin in this respect on p. 44.

The German for 'ordinance' is 'Ordnung', often translated 'order' (as in 'creation order'). This fits Brunner's usage well as he would seem to have a universal, a-temporal Law in mind in this context. Thus he says, "The whole arrangement of the world, with its fixity and the permanency of its being, is a manifestation of God" (49). Later he writes, "God has not simply put us into a "world," but into his creation, whose laws can be known in spite of sin, by those who know God in Jesus Christ" (52). He also speaks of "divinely appointed objective limits to our freedom and objective guides to the ordering of our society" (52) which the Holy Spirit teaches us to know truly "in accordance with the needs of the moment" (53). Given this theological/philosophical realism in the realm of nature (which is admittedly coupled with a more 'event' oriented view of revelation in the realm of grace/redemption), it is no surprise that Brunner accuses Barth of "theological nominalism" (54). But why not avoid this realist/nominalist dilemma by seeing creational grace as having both "order" (or universality) *and* individuality?

[29] See Brunner, "Nature and Grace," 32.
[30] See Brunner, "Nature and Grace," 23.
[31] See Brunner, "Nature and Grace," 24.
[32] See Brunner, "Nature and Grace," 31.
[33] See Brunner, "Nature and Grace," 32.
[34] See Brunner, "Nature and Grace," 31 and 56.
[35] Brunner, "Nature and Grace," 32–33.
[36] This is dealt with at some length in Karl Barth, *Church Dogmatics* 4/1, ed. G.W. Bromiley and T.F. Torrance (Edinburgh: T. and T. Clark, 1962), 358–413. For Barth's objections to the "point of contact" in "No!," see my following paragraph.

sense once we realise that 'nature' (and thus 'natural theology') for Barth always means autonomy from God, human effort, human control, self-justification, idolatry, and thus evil. Hence his talk of "the demon,"[37] "the serpent,"[38] the charge that Brunner is a "heretic,"[39] the reference to "the church of the antichrist,"[40] and the constant fear that natural theology of any kind gives ammunition to the "German Christians."[41]

The linking of the 'natural' to autonomous, god-less, all-too-human *control* can be found in his charge that natural theology usually deals with its data "as if one had [the subjects of grace and revelation] pocketed, as if one had knowledge of them below one instead of always behind and in front."[42] A point of contact between our nature and God's grace is impossible. Even our despair, prior to the impact of God's grace, is an expression of our autonomy.[43] Salvation depends on the total opposition between God's grace and human nature (autonomy). Thus, following Luther, he says, "If anyone is *incapable* of glorying in his *own power*, this is a sign of election."[44]

Barth stands firmly in the Calvinist tradition in opposing all forms of 'synergism' (co-operation between God and humans, grace and nature) with respect to salvation. Salvation is through divine grace and not human works. Brunner's appeal to the "sovereign, freely electing grace of God,"[45] says Barth, is incompatible with his appeal to "a 'capacity for revelation' in man, which is merely supported by grace."[46] We are drowning men who can neither swim nor cry out for help. We don't even contribute a few strokes when rescued.[47]

---

[37] Barth, "No!," 70.

[38] Barth, "No!," 76. Perhaps Barth is implying here that natural theology at/tempts to eat from the "tree of the knowledge of good and evil" of Gen 3.

[39] Barth, "No!," 90.

[40] Barth, "No!," 128.

[41] Barth, "No!," 99 and 105.

[42] Barth, "No!," 77.

[43] This is contrary to what even he might have thought when writing his famous Romans commentary (see Barth, "No!," 115). In "No!," 120, he writes,

> The world which I have cleared of gods is truly neither the kingdom of the living God nor even a preparation for it, but probably the worst of all forms of diabolism, by which I can oppose that kingdom. What has this grasping after the judgeship of the world in common with the obedience of Christ of 2 Corinthians x, 5? ["We demolish arguments and every pretension that sets itself up against the knowledge of God, and we take captive every thought to make it obedient to Christ" (NIV).] Where is every thought brought into captivity? Does it not triumph all the more in unmitigated hybris? Is there any form of pride worse than that of a certain type of Kierkegaardianism? Has there ever been a more explicit Prometheanism than that of the philosophy of an existence despairing of itself?

[44] Barth, "No!," 119. My emphases.

[45] Barth, "No!," 77.

[46] Barth, "No!," 79.

[47] See Barth, "No!," 79, 82, and 87.

So how do we respond to God's grace? What is the point of contact, that part in us that (fallen though we are) says Yes to God's Yes? How does nature respond to Grace? For Barth, these questions are wrong-headed. He writes, "The Holy Ghost ... does not stand in need of any point of contact but that which he himself creates."[48] God decides to save the drowning man. So how is it that we respond to salvation if, prior to salvation, we are unable to respond? The answer for Barth is that a miracle occurs.[49] "Man," he says, "is a being that has to be overcome by the Word and the Spirit of God . . . ."[50] Our role is like that of Mary in the virginal conception.[51] Roman Catholicism's (Barth would say synergistic) view of Mary's acceptance of her role in the incarnation is not what he has in mind. It is hard to escape the impression here that for Barth, we are symbolically (and stereotypically) 'female', passive, receptive, acted upon, overcome.[52] This is (to use Berkouwer's phrase) the "triumph of grace"[53] over nature/fallenness.

---

[48] Barth, "No!," 121.

[49] See Barth, "No!," 117, 121, and 124.

[50] Barth, "No!," 126.

[51] See Barth, "No!," 123–24. cf. 93.

[52] The correct way to interpret Barth's theology is (sometimes hotly) contested. I here only intend to offer a 'plausible' reading of "No!" (and not of Barth's later work, for example, although I will refer to his *The Epistle to the Romans* below as this is an earlier work) as a means to a particular end: the identification of some perennial nature-grace problematics for the purpose of shedding light on Moltmann's position. I am aware that some Barth interpreters see him affirming human agency. See for example, John Webster's important collection of essays, *Barth's Moral Theology: Human Action in Barth's Thought* (Edinburgh: T. and T. Clark, 1998). In 7.2 (including 7.2n107) below, I will cite Miroslav Volf's appeal to Barth's "robust" sense of human agency in the context of salvation. In my opinion, this becomes increasingly plausible, indeed probable, with Barth's later work, such as the essays found in *The Humanity of God*. This is especially the case with the 1956 essay "The Humanity of God" (which Clifford Green selects to open a section called "Barth Introduces his Theology" in his significantly titled anthology, *Karl Barth: Theologian of Freedom* (London: Collins, 1989), 46–66). It is perhaps even more the case with the 1953 essay, "The Gift of Freedom" (69–96 as cited in n. 3 above). That we might detect a creation-affirming or creation-embracing intent in Barth's early work also strikes me as plausible. The role of the divine 'Yes' in the pre-Barth/Brunner debate work *The Epistle to the Romans* (cited below) supports this. But is this an affirmation of human agency? With respect to "No!," surely the *structure* of his thought evident in his handling of the nature-grace relationship—not just the polemical tone and thus potentially one-sided nature of his essay—militates against any agency-affirming *spirit*! In this reading, I am focussing on the structural dimension of his (early) writing. Perhaps some of Barth's early writings in 'ethics' (some of which have only recently been published) witness to a continuity between the earlier and later Barth (see John Webster, "Introducing Barth," in *The Cambridge Companion to Karl Barth*, ed. John Webster (Cambridge: Cambridge University Press, 2000), 12–14) that might call for a different reading of "No!" But, to repeat my earlier point, a 'plausible' rather than 'definitive' reading is adequate for my present purpose. It could be said that I am more interested in the 'Barthian' character of Moltmann than the 'Barthian' character of Barth!

Supporters of Brunner might want to say that he is not appealing to some autonomous realm of *nature*, but to creational and preserving *grace* by means of which *God's will* comes to pass. Barth would not accept this. He claims that grace is not really in view in Brunner's lower realm. "[H]ow," he asks, "can Brunner maintain that a real knowledge of the true God, however imperfect it may be (and what knowledge of God is not imperfect?) does not bring salvation?"[54] This is, I believe, an excellent point that calls Brunner's whole position into question. 'Creational' *grace* must be connected to the gift of Life. In a fallen context in need of redemption, this gift of Life—originally given with creation—must be intimately connected to the offer of New Life. At the same time, creation and redemption need to be distinguished. I will elaborate on these points below.

A great strength of Barth's theology, I suggest, is his realisation that God's grace lies beyond all human power and control.[55] It is a gift that empowers. Our very existence is graced. Theology must contend with what Matthew Fox has called "Original Blessing."[56] Barth puts it well: "Creation is the work of the truly free, truly undeserved grace of the one true God, both as an act *and* in its continuance."[57]

The gift precedes our ability to respond. Our capacity to respond to the gift of Life is itself a gift of Life. We don't choose to be born. Our capacity to choose is itself born due to, thanks to, those who have helped bring us into existence. If we may speak here of the giving of others then such giving may be seen as mediating the giving of God. Gift precedes response. A response can embody/express the gift, can be gifted, can rest in something beyond, or prior to, itself. But the gift is beyond our control, grasp, understanding. It is never exhausted in our responses. Our 'being' precedes our 'doing'. Our 'being' is not an 'essence' within. The gift/call of who we are is prior to, more than, what we make of ourselves.

By the same token, we may say that within creation, life moves from heaven to earth. Adam and Eve are to receive the breath of life, God's breath, into their lives as their very lives (Gen 2:7). To attempt to possess the gift is to lose it. Autonomy is as foolish as holding one's breath, neither breathing in nor out, neither receiving nor letting go. True human flourishing occurs between

---

[53] See Berkouwer, *The Triumph of Grace in the Theology of Karl Barth* as cited above in 4.0n2, 4.2n77, and 4.4n249 above.

[54] Barth, "No!," 82.

[55] See, e.g., Barth, "No!," 117.

[56] See Matthew Fox, *Original Blessing: A Primer in Creation Spirituality Presented in Four Paths, Twenty-Six Themes, and Two Questions* (Santa Fe, NM: Bear, 1983).

[57] Barth, "No!," 83. His emphasis. Here Barth is agreeing with Brunner but in order to argue that there is no grace other than "the grace of Jesus Christ." Whether Barth's Christocentrism here effectively ignores creation in the name of redemption and providence remains an open question. Thus, although I cite Barth in the next couple of paragraphs, I am not claiming to follow him on his terms.

mystery and mystery, gift and promise, Origin and Destiny. This is the very spirituality of existence.[58]

The gift of New Life (salvation) makes the original blessing available once more. The *for-giving* of God's redemptive grace (mercy) is more than, but not less than, the *giving* of God's creational grace. We cannot choose to be saved anymore than we can choose our birth.[59] "Not even the starting-point of the way 'from death to life' . . . lies within the sphere of what is possible for us,"[60] as Barth observes, not because we are so terrible, but because Life can't be earned even by a sinless person. It isn't a possession or a reward. It's a gift and call to be received and worked out. The tragedy of our bondage to evil is that existence becomes a curse/threat that tempts us to overcome our fear through possession, control and/or abdication of our responsibility. Pride (Barth's constant target[61]) comes *after* a fall, a cover for our fear.[62] Given our fearful attempt at autonomy, the gift of Life/New Life eludes us. We trust nothing beyond our control. Thus we need God's grace to break through before we can take responsibility, face our sin, and be rid of our illusions.[63]

Where I differ from Barth and Brunner (for different reasons) is in believing that this grace unto salvation can be 'creational' and may be mediated by human beings outside of the Church and God's redemptive 'interventions'. Even in a fallen world, God is present in human life. Life, even basic existence, presupposes God's presence (just as evil makes God absent outside of redemption). Where the gift of life is honoured and received (in expressions and experiences of love and justice, for example), the human nature that develops in this context is graced. Graced nature 'naturally' responds to redemptive grace. Thus creational grace is not redemptive grace, but may be a grace 'unto' salvation. We should also add that in a fallen world, graced nature exists in degrees. The "point of contact" that it provides for redemptive grace is not a connection between nature and grace (typically understood) but between redemptive *grace* and creationally *graced* nature (that is nature that has been graced by creational grace).

Perhaps we need to be more optimistic *and* more pessimistic than either Brunner or Barth about this "point of contact." Assuming a grace-nature correlation for creation and for redemption ('nature' being the response-side in each context), we can postulate that for those who have responded most fully to creational grace and thus to the gift/call of Life that is *re*affirmed in redemptive

---

[58] In speaking of the 'spirituality of existence' here, I am evoking the biblical original blessing theme (cf. n. 56 above) and echoing Olthuis' appropriation of Dooyeweerd, as found in the section entitled "Spirituality of Creation" in Olthuis, "Dooyeweerd on Religion and Faith," 22–23.
[59] See Barth's comments on John 3:3 in "No!," 118.
[60] Barth, "No!," 118, citing John 5:24 and 1 John 3:14.
[61] See, for example, Barth, "No!," 120 as cited in n. 43 above.
[62] See James H. Olthuis, "The Covenanting Metaphor of the Christian Faith and the Self Psychology of Heinz Kohut," *Studies in Religion/Sciences Religieuses* 18, no. 3 (1989): 313–24.
[63] See Barth, "No!," 117.

grace, there is a 'natural' point of contact with redemption. (Brunner might accept that.) Here, the Gospel reaffirms and supplements what is already known. Prior to the explicit witness of the Gospel, salvation may even have been experienced already. But for those who have rejected Life in the extreme, the point of contact between creation and redemption lies on the 'grace' side rather than the (graced) 'nature' side, i.e., with God's gift/call to Life/New Life rather than with the response. (Barth might accept that.)[64]

How does this relate to universalism? In Barth's theology, God's embrace of all people in his grace is linked to his conviction that all of us are elected or predestined to salvation in Jesus Christ, there being no will of God outside of what is expressed in him. The double predestination of Calvin's "horrible decree" is thus rejected.[65] Moltmann, as we have seen in 4.3.1 above, is more than happy to follow Barth's Christocentrism in this respect. For Barth, God's electing 'Yes' (*grace*) rather than our belief or unbelief (*nature*) is what is decisive.[66] God's verdict of justification is creative, a *creatio ex nihilo*, bringing about a new creation that in no way emerges out of the old.[67] The " 'nevertheless' " of God's righteousness, justification, and forgiveness "contradicts every human logical 'consequently'."[68]

Nevertheless, Barth's universalism raises questions about the role of the *human* Yes/No. Is synergism replaced by a divine monergism in which we do nothing? Are we simply overpowered by God's sovereignty? Barth is convinced that God's Yes to us and our Yes to God—God's freedom and our freedom—go together. Again, the parallels with Moltmann (see 4.3.3 above) are intriguing. God, says Barth, "is the hidden home at the beginning and end of

---

[64] With this flexible approach, it may be possible to see each of the five nature-grace models referred to in 4.2n62 above as helpful in a given context.

[65] A good, succinct account of this can be found in the introduction to Green, ed., *Karl Barth: Theologian of Freedom*, 31. Cf. Bruce McCormack, "Grace and Being: The Role of God's Gracious Election in Karl Barth's Theological Ontology," in *The Cambridge Companion to Karl Barth*, ed. John Webster (Cambridge: Cambridge University Press, 2000), 92–110.

[66] See Green, ed., *Karl Barth: Theologian of Freedom*, 32. Cf. Moltmann's view of God's salvation being prior to and merely experienced in faith, for which see CoG, 245 (as cited in 1.4.2 and 4.3.3 above).

[67] As we shall see in 6.5 below, the new forms a "point of contact" with the old but the old does not form a "point of contact" with the new. In Karl Barth, *The Epistle to the Romans*, trans. Edwyn C. Hoskyns (Oxford: Oxford University Press, 1933), 102 we read:

> This declaration is creatio ex nihilo, creation out of nothing. Uttered by God from his tribunal, it is grounded in Him alone, and is without occasion or condition. Such creation is assuredly genuine creation, the creation of the divine righteousness in us and in the world. When God speaks, it is done. But the creation is a new creation; it is not a mere eruption, or extension, or unfolding, of that old 'creative evolution' of which we form a part, and shall remain a part, till our lives' end.

[68] Barth, *The Epistle to the Romans*, 93.

all our journeyings. Disloyalty to him is disloyalty to ourselves."[69] Elsewhere he writes, "When God has been deprived of his glory, men are also deprived of theirs."[70]

In Barth's position, God's Yes to creation embraces a humanity that cannot naturally say Yes to God. In grace, we respond to God's freedom and find our true freedom.[71] But how does that human response come about? On the one hand, to reply: 'in grace' seems to beg the question. If grace is something God 'does', how can this help us conceive of something humans do? On the other hand, Barth's sharp distinction between nature and grace would seem to suggest that any other answer than 'in grace' requires us to assert the existence of a human nature that can reach up to God in its own power and autonomy.

Perhaps this dilemma is not insoluble. A case for a 'covenantal' universalism can be made, I suggest, if we root the claim that 'all respond *to* God's grace *in* God's grace' in the conviction that we are created for Life and for God 'from the beginning'. Responding to God's creational grace is the warp and woof of our authentic nature. Redemption is the reaffirmation, liberation, and restoration of our true nature, rather than being a *creatio ex nihilo*. Our true nature is a gift/promise that responds to the gift/promise. In the context of grace, our true nature, we might say, 'comes into its own'. This is not autonomy or heteronomy. Our *response* to the gift/call of Life is *our* response, our *life*. This is freedom truly defined. Freedom is not 'doing what we want'. Freedom is not doing 'what God wants' instead of 'what we want'. Freedom is faithfully keeping covenant with the God of Life in the way we choose. A universal salvation that is non-coercive must, in my view, affirm the fact that we are made for God, made for Life, to respond to Life, to initiate Life, to live (and without God there is no life) by being who we are (who we are called to be). In this sense, salvation (including universal salvation) reveals our very nature.

Redemptive grace reaffirms and re-offers the gift of life. Graced nature 'naturally' responds by God's grace to God's grace. This is neither divine monergism nor syn-ergism (in the pejorative sense). Our working out of the gift-promise of life is covenantal. It is not a 'work' of the kind the reformers opposed. In covenant with God, our work is also God's work while remaining thoroughly our own (in a non-possessive, non-autonomous sense).[72] The biblical writers assume that covenant is not a 50/50 relationship. It is as if both sides somehow contribute 100%. Hence a text like Phil 2:12—"work out own your salvation with fear and trembling; for it is God who is at work in you, enabling you both to will and to work for his good pleasure"—does not fit our Calvinist or Arminian theologies. It is significant that Moltmann also eschews a zero-sum relationship between God and humanity in this context (see 1.4.2

---

[69] Barth, *The Epistle to the Romans*, 46.
[70] Barth, *The Epistle to the Romans*, 51.
[71] See the quotation from Barth, "The Gift of Freedom," 76–77 in 6.1 above.
[72] Cf. Brunner's explorations into the unity of gift and task and into the potential unity of divine and human agency in *The Divine Imperative*, 242–44.

above). God is the God of creation. Creation is the creation of God. To love God is to love life. It is to find and celebrate our freedom. Only with God may we be human.

Universal salvation (in the sense that I am advocating) therefore means that God and creation, grace and nature, heaven and earth will, in the covenantal sense, finally be 'one'. Some universalist positions sound as if human freedom is side-stepped or eclipsed in the triumph of salvation over sin, thus suggesting that nature is negated by grace. Other universalist positions sound as if their plausibility rests in God's ability to evoke a 'natural' impulse for the divine located deep within our humanity in a place (relatively) untouched by sin and evil. This implies that nature has a merely extrinsic relationship to grace and vice versa.[73] A theology of creational grace and creationally graced nature, however, suggests a truly covenantal alternative.

6.3 Creational Grace in Moltmann?

Can the category of creational grace, which is so central to the above discussion, be found in Moltmann's writings? I began my own explorations in 6.1.1 above by suggesting that a fresh approach to the relationship between heaven and earth would shed light on the dynamics of the nature-grace relationship. This is a useful starting-point in our evaluation of Moltmann in this respect, as the perspective offered above provides a significant point of contact with his theology, even as it serves to highlight an important difference.

In his affirmation of a "dual world," Moltmann also seeks to avoid both a reductionism that is insensitive to the spirituality of all existence while rejecting the dualistic conception of two realms.[74] Thus he sees Isa 45:8 in a very similar

---

[73] These two approaches might be seen as exemplified by Karl Barth and John Hick, respectively. Keith Randall Schmitt, in *Death and After-Life in the Theologies of Karl Barth and John Hick: A Comparative Study* (Amsterdam: Rodopi, 1985), 161, writes that in Barth, "God's grace is so overwhelming that there remains little, if anything, for man to do save affirm it." Later he comments, "[W]hile Barth places a special emphasis upon divine grace Hick is much more reserved and in a sense antithetical in this regard, this being a result of the emphasis Hick places on the natural predispositions of man."

[74] For the language of the "dual world," see GC, 158 as discussed in 4.2 above. In "Jesus and the Kingdom of God," *Asbury Theological Journal* 48, no. 1 (Spring 1993): 12, Moltmann expresses sentiments about this non-dualistic duality that are very similar to my own suggestions in 6.1.1 above. He writes,

> Those who want to understand [the Kingdom of God] as otherworldly always refer to Jesus' words "my kingship is not from this world" (John 18:36). In doing this they overlook the fact that this is a statement about the *origin* but not about the *location* of the Kingdom. Of course it is not "from" this world, but rather from God, otherwise it could not heal this sick world. . . .
>
> If it is the Kingdom of the creator God then it encompasses the entire creation, heaven and earth, the invisible and the visible sides of this world and is therefore otherworldly in heaven as well as worldly on earth. In the Lord's Prayer we pray for the coming of the Kingdom "on earth as in heaven," and mean with heaven the side of creation which already totally corresponds to God

light to that suggested above. " '[T]he open heaven'," he says, "means that the earth will be fruitful once more. . . . and life will be born."[75]

As discussed in 4.2, 'heaven' is identified with the creative potentialities for the earth, potentiality being "higher ontologically" than actuality for Moltmann just as the Advent future exceeds the modes of time.[76] Angels are seen in this context as "God's potencies in the realm of his potentialities."[77] Where I wish to speak of the empowering energies of *heaven* as God's gift/call of Creation and promise/call of the New Creation to which the *earth* is invited and empowered to respond (and speak of 'angels' as defined in the above discussion in this context[78]), Moltmann will also speak of (what I am calling) this 'grace-nature' relationship as a heaven-earth correlation. In his words,

> [I]n Christ the space of heaven and the region of the earth are to be united. . . . In the movement of God, his becoming human and his self-surrender on the cross, heaven too opens itself for the earth, and earth for heaven. Heaven and earth are clasped and gathered into a whole, and in the all-embracing peace of Christ arrive at their open communication with one another.[79]

In Moltmann's thought, the dwelling place of the Father—heaven—and of the Son—the earth—are united in the dwelling place of the Holy Spirit who manifests in the present the energy of the coming New Creation.[80] Does this mean that the 'grace' of heaven and the 'nature' of the earth are united in (the movement towards) the coming 'glory' of God as all in all? Only if, to recall material discussed in 4.2 above, we are referring to the relationship between the *coelum gratiae* and the earth in the eschatological redirection of time.[81] As I

> and with the earth the still disputed side of creation. We expect a new heaven and a new earth from the future of the Kingdom.

His emphases.

[75] GC, 171, where Moltmann refers explicitly to Isa 45:8 (on which see 6.1.1 above). Cf. CoG, 278.

[76] CoG, 287 as discussed in 2.3 above.

[77] GC, 163, cf. WJC 106. Moltman's view of angels is briefly discussed in 4.2 above.

[78] My understanding of angels offered in 6.1.1 above can incorporate the impersonal forces that Moltmann seems to have in mind.

[79] GC, 171.

[80] Moltmann says this explicitly in GC, 162. See also Celia Deane-Drummond, "Jürgen Moltmann on Heaven," in *The Unseen World: Christian Reflections on Angels, Demons and the Heavenly Realm*, ed. Anthony N.S. Lane (Carlisle, UK: Paternoster, 1996), 49–64.

[81] In 4.2 above, I focussed mainly on "the heaven of nature." Moltmann discusses "the heaven of grace" and "the heaven of glory" in GC, 169–75 and 181–84. In GC, 170, he writes,

> The *coelum gratiae* opens and is perceived in the movement of God towards the liberation and redemption of the world. The one side of this divine movement is the becoming human of the Son; the other side in his ascension into heaven. . . .

have suggested, *nature* (for Moltmann) is best understood as the foundational-differentiating direction of history, while *grace* marks the transition to the transcendental-integrating movement of the *glory* of the New Creation.[82] This (nature-grace-glory) distinction cuts across Moltmann's heaven-earth distinction.

Nature, grace, and glory can also be correlated with Moltmann's threefold distinctions between (i) creation, reconciliation, and redemption[83] and (ii) God's acts from *heaven* (that is the heaven of nature, grace, and glory respectively) of forming, encompassing, and redeeming the *earth*.[84] Grace (in Moltmann's terminology) may thus be related to the middle term of each of these triads. While for me, *heaven* (whether viewed in the creational or eschatological direction of time) is always related to (and is a way of naming) *grace* (be that creational, redemptive, or eschatological), for Moltmann, heaven in the historical direction of time is a heaven of *nature*.

There is, in other words, virtually no acknowledgment—certainly no explicit acknowledgment—of what I am calling 'creational grace' in Moltmann's theology, even when heaven is in view. (I say 'virtually' because a close examination of the nuances of Moltmann's thought—which will be offered below—will require that I qualify this statement to some extent). Although the archetypes for earthly realities that Moltmann locates in the *coelum naturae*—a perspective that calls to mind the 'creation order' of the Reformed (including the Kuyperian) tradition—might be related to the giftedness of life, his discussion of the evil energies of the heaven of nature, together with his use of the language of fallen angels in this context,[85] clearly signifies Moltmann's close association of heaven in the historical direction of time with the notion of curse rather than (or more than) with gift.

There is nothing wrong with being aware of the impact of evil on (and in) the foundational direction of time provided that time's transcendental direction is seen as equally in need of healing. But as the *curse* of life, in my understanding, finds its transcendental counterpart in the *threat* of the coming future (see figure 7 above), it is significant how hard it is to document references to this latter form of temptation and evil in Moltmann's corpus.[86] Similarly, fallen angels and the destructive energies of heaven are nowhere

---

The *coelum gloriae* opens and is perceived in the coming of the glory of the triune God. With the advent of God's glory, heaven and earth will be created anew. So final blessedness will be experienced 'in heaven as it is on earth'.

His italics. There is also some discussion of the *coelum gratiae* in 4.3.1 above, where the theme of opening, evident in the quotation above, is explored.

[82] See 4.2 above.
[83] See GC, 244 and other texts cited in 5.3n128 above.
[84] See GC, 166 as discussed in 4.2 above.
[85] See 4.2 above.
[86] It is extremely hard to find references to the *advent* (as opposed to the *futurum*) of evil in Moltmann's writings. An exception that proves the rule is GC, 133, which is discussed in 2.4 above as referring to what I there call (in adapting Moltmann's terminology) a "historical adventus."

The Nature of Grace 285

discussed in the context of the *coelum gratia* or *coelum gloriae*. Because, to reiterate an important point made in 5.3 above, creation and fall are often conflated in Moltmann's historical direction of time, grace is associated almost exclusively with the eschatological direction. Instead of seeing the foundational and transcendental directions of time as equally affected by evil and equally in need of redemption, Moltmann, I am suggesting, tends to equate the creational direction with fallenness while the eschatological direction is associated with redemption. The apparently inherent ambiguity of historical differentiation is what he, in his terminology, refers to as "nature."[87] Grace, by contrast, which is (predominantly) grace *for* but not *of* creation, is a manifestation of God's coming glory. His understanding of the nature of grace is consequently one-sided, weakening the case he makes for a universal salvation that can affirm covenantal freedom.

Another way in which this can be seen is by comparing the relative frequency with which the ideas of *pro/missio* and *Auf/Gabe* (or their equivalents) appear in Moltmann's writings. As may by now be predictable, the correlation of promise and mission is indeed common in his corpus, especially in *Theology of Hope*.[88] Thus we are told that,

> If the promise of the kingdom of God shows us a universal eschatological future horizon spanning all things—'that God may be all in all'—then ... the man of hope ... is compelled to ... guide all things towards their new being. ... The *pro-missio* of the kingdom is the ground of the *missio* of love to the world. ...[89] The *promissio* of the universal future leads of necessity to the universal *missio* of the Church to all nations.... The history of the future of Christ and the historic character of the witnesses and missionaries condition each other and stand in a correlation of *promissio* and *missio*.[90]

---

[87] In CoG, 91, he writes, "Theologically, we call 'nature' the state of creation which is no longer creation's original condition, and is not yet its final one." Cf. GC, 59. See the discussion in 4.2 above.

[88] In addition to TH, 224 and 225 cited below, see also TH, 44 (on the correlation of *promissio* and *fides*), 110 (on seeing revelation in terms of promise and mission), 120 ("Promise and command, the pointing of the goal and the pointing of the way, therefore belong immediately together."), 121 ("All the commandments are explications of the one commandment, to love God and to cleave to him (Deut. 6.5), and this one commandment is but the reverse side of the promise. It commands (*gebietet*) what the promise offers (*bietet*)," his italics), 145 (on law and promise being mutually exclusive), 161 ("call and promise"), 162 (cited in n. 92 below), 189 ("a mission that knows itself in the service of the promised future of this event"), 196 ("the horizon of promise and mission"), 202 ("mission and promise"), 203 ("the *missio* of Jesus becomes intelligible only by the *promissio*," his italics), 206 ("Man learns his human nature not from himself, but from the future to which the mission leads him."), and 289 ("The call and mission of the 'God of hope' "). References in later (i.e., post-TH) works include, CPS, 359 (the church's apostolicity as a "category of promise and commission"); GC, 227 (cited below); and EiT, 107 (on the *promissio/fides* correlation, cf. TH, 44).

[89] TH, 224. His italics.

[90] TH, 225. His italics.

The gift/call correlation, which is suggested in the fact that the German word for 'call' or 'task'—*Aufgabe*—contains the German word for 'gift'—*Gabe*—and which is common in part for this reason in German theological literature,[91] is, by contrast, only rarely invoked. When it does occur, Moltmann will often be at such pains to stress the theme of promise and call as well that the theme of *Auf/Gabe* receives virtually no development in its own right.[92] At times, the eschatological horizon so dominates the discussion that 'gift' becomes another word for promise, albeit an eschatological promise that has been given in and to the present age.[93]

The way in which the theme of *pro/missio* eclipses that of *Auf/Gabe* parallels the way in which the more general idea of 'promise' pervades Moltmann's writings while that of 'gift' is rare.[94] As I have argued that the

---

[91] See, for example, Brunner, *The Divine Imperative*, 242, especially 242n2.

[92] Thus in TH, 162, he writes,
> The imperative of the Pauline call to new obedience is . . . not to be understood merely as a summons to demonstrate the indicative of the new being in Christ, but it has also its eschatological presupposition in the future that has been promised and is to be expected . . . . Hence it ought not to be rendered merely by saying: 'Become what you are!', but emphatically also by saying: 'Become what you will be!'

[93] For example, in CPS, 339–40, once more using the distinction/correlation between indicative and imperative, Moltmann's states that,
> Because in Christ the church is one, it ought *to be* one. Those who receive its unity in Christ ought to seek its unity. The one people of the one kingdom ought to lay the foundations of unity among men. Because in Christ the church is holy, its members ought to fight sin and sanctify its life through righteousness. Because they are sanctified through the Spirit, they ought in obedience to sanctify all things for the new creation. Because in Christ it is open to the world, it ought to be catholic, testifying everywhere to the all-embracing kingdom.

His emphasis. If this sounds like a correlation of gift and call, then we must read Moltmann's words in the light of his earlier claim on p. 339 that "the church acquires her existence from Christ's messianic mission and the *eschatological gift* of the Spirit, then her characteristics are messianic predicates at the same time." My emphasis.

For the notion of given promise, see e.g., TH, 88 ("the promise in its givenness . . . not in its pastness") and 228 ("the promise that is given with the Christ event"). The eschatologising of the notion of gift can be seen in CPS, 34 ("the eschatological gift" of the Spirit which is the "power of futurity"), 205 ("the eschatological gift of the Holy Spirit" who is "the power of the divine future"); and TH, 326 ("The word of God is itself an eschatological gift. In it the hidden future of God for the world is already present."). TH, 206 is also typical. Here Moltmann writes, "[W]e have the divine righteousness always as a *gift* that is *pledged*, disputed and subject to testing, that is, we have it in terms of *promise* and *expectancy*." My emphases. Cf. his contrast in TH, 296 between the "gift entrusted to our charge" and the eschatologising of tradition that he goes on to propose.

[94] Thus, for example, Moltmann will say of the sabbath of Gen 1, in CoG, 264 (as cited in 5.3 above), that it is "the promise of future consummation built right into the initial creation," but he does not speak of sabbath as reflecting the gift of God's prior work in establishing life on earth. See 5.3 above. Cf. David Billings, "Natality or Advent:

latter notion is vital for constructing a viable universalism, we will pay special attention to some of the passages in which Moltmann does show sensitivity to the giftedness of life. There is also one place where he does explore the gift/call motif in a positive way that deserves our attention in this context.

Although there are very few references to the *Auf/Gabe* theme in his later works, it is interesting to note that as Moltmann attempts to articulate a more creation-affirming theology, his tendency to eschatologise the notion of gift makes way for a more balanced perspective.[95] But it is, significantly, only when Moltmann begins to develop a view of the Spirit in relation to God as Creator—and thus not just as the energy, or "eschatological gift,"[96] of the New Creation—that we find a relatively full discussion of gift and call. This occurs in the context of a discussion of sanctification, understood as a making holy of our creaturely life in the present age.

In *The Spirit of Life*, a work whose title reflects precisely this more creation-oriented role for the Spirit, Moltmann writes,

> Sanctification as *gift* leads to sanctification as *charge*. For whatever God declares to be holy ought to be kept holy by human beings: the sabbath, the people, created beings. God's community with us is the foundation and motive for our community with God. . . .[97]
>
> In the response of their lives to the life-giving word of God, believers are not merely the passive objects of divine sanctification. They are also the new determining subjects of the Gestalt or configuration of their own lives. . . . In this new life . . . [a]n inward holiness can grow. But it doesn't develop from the

---

Hannah Arendt and Jürgen Moltmann on Hope and Politics," in *The Future of Hope: Christian Tradition amid Modernity and Postmodernity*, ed. Miroslav Volf and William Katerberg (Grand Rapids, MI: Eerdmans, 2004), 125–45, in which it is proposed that Moltmann's eschatological focus needs to be supplemented by Arendt's notion of natality. This gets at (a dimension of) what I mean by life as gift being a necessary correlate to life as promise.

It is not too much of an exaggeration to say that the theme of promise (especially in relation to hope, revelation, time, anticipation, and eschaton) is present on virtually every page of Moltmann's major works in the background if not in the foreground. This makes documenting the presence of the general idea of promise almost redundant. For Moltmann's early trilogy, we are well served by Morse, *The Logic of Promise in Moltmann's Theology*. This idea is especially pervasive in TH. The fact that it is still vital to the way Moltmann approaches theology 35 years later is evident in EiT 32 (on time's arrow), 55 (on the Bible), 87–113 (a chapter that, obviously echoing Morse's work, is entitled "The Logic of Promise"), 88 (on the influence of the reformation on Moltmann in this context and on the idea of the "coming" kingdom), 95 (on the link between promise and personal identity), and 102–103 (on the contrast between promise and conception). On the important notion of the "surplus" of the promise, see 6.4 below. On the *promissio-missio* correlation, see n. 88 above.

[95] Thus in GC, 227, in the context of a discussion of sanctification, Moltmann writes, "[L]ikeness to God is both a gift and a charge, indicative and imperative. It is charge and hope, imperative and promise."

[96] CPS, 339 as cited in n. 93 above.

[97] SL, 174.

habit of good deeds. It springs from the goodness of the person who is loved by God and already sanctified. . . .[98]

[T]he works of the flesh are 'made' but the fruit of the Spirit 'grows'. We cannot make it, but we can let it grow in us. . . .[99]

Life in the Spirit is a life in the 'broad place where there is no cramping' (Job 36. 16). . . . We explore the depths of this space through the trust of the heart. We search out the length of this space through extravagant hope. We discover the breadth of this space through the torrents of love which we receive and give. God's Spirit encompasses us from all sides and wherever we are (Ps. 139). Christ's Spirit is our immanent power to live—God's Spirit is our transcendent space for living.[100]

Here gift and call, receiving and giving, God's work (in us) and our work (in God) are seen as 'one'. As Moltmann puts it,

> God is not merely a determining subject, over against [gegenübersteht] the world. He is also the wellspring from which all life comes; he is the tree that brings forth fruit; he is the light whose rays give light and warmth to everything.

This oneness is not just covenantal (as when we speak of a man and woman being 'one flesh'); it is ontological. The above metaphors, which Moltmann admits "are aptly described by the neo-Platonic term 'emanation'," in his understanding "leave the difference between Creator and creature behind, and show the torrent of energies flowing from God to human beings."[101] In this Spirit of Life we receive the gift of life and are empowered to live life to the full. The panentheism of the Age to Come, in which God the Creator comes to dwell in his creation as it dwells in him, may be experienced in the present in the Spirit of Life, which is Life in the Spirit.

I have said that the theme of 'creational grace'—that is the empowering gift/call, indeed the "*charge*,"[102] of Life—is 'virtually' absent in Moltmann's theology. But this is an exception that proves the rule as here, God's Spirit as the wellspring of existence is seen as Origin and Source rather than as the eschatological fullness to which we are drawn. As Moltmann's view of salvation may not succeed in answering concerns about the overpowering or

---

[98] SL, 175.
[99] SL, 176.
[100] SL, 178–79. My emphases.
[101] SL, 177 [*DGL*, 191].
[102] "charge," which I have italicised, and which is Moltmann's term in GC, 227, cited in n. 95 above, and in SL, 174, cited in the text above, is a wonderfully rich term here as in English it connotes (i) commandment/calling, (ii) care, and (iii) empowering energy. The term in the original German texts—*GS*, 232 and *DGL*, 189 respectively—is "Aufgabe," which does not convey this range of meaning, although Moltmann does highlight the Gabe-Aufgabe relationship in both passages. (Thus when Moltmann speaks of "the gift entrusted to our charge" in TH, 296 (cited in n. 93 above) he refers (in *TdH*, 273) to "dem anvertrauten Gut.")

eclipse of the human will that universalist positions typically evoke,[103] this strong hint of a role for the Spirit as empowering humanity to go for Life and not Death (in the covenantal sense of Deut 30:15–20) rather than as overcoming our nature in an eschatological "triumph of glory"[104] is very significant.

Recognition of the giftedness of life as theologically significant can be found in other places in Moltmann's more recent (more creation-affirming) writings. For example, in *God in Creation*, we find that just as the notion of 'gift' can be eschatologised in Moltmann's writings, so 'promise' may plausibly be viewed in the creational-foundational direction of time.[105] Thus Moltmann writes,

> It is theologically necessary to view created things as real promises of the kingdom; and it is equally necessary, conversely, to understand the kingdom of God as the fulfilment, not merely of the historical promises of the world, but of its natural promises as well.[106]

Similarly, later in the same work we read,

> The goal of this history is not a return to the paradisal primordial condition. Its goal is the revelation of the glory of God. It is true that this end 'corresponds' to the beginning in the sense that it represents the fulfilment of the real promise *implanted in creation itself*; but the new creation of heaven and earth in the kingdom of glory surpasses everything that can be told about creation in the beginning.

This reference to a "promise" that is "*implanted in creation itself* [die in der Schöpfung selbst angelegt ist]"[107] refers to a giftedness that distinguishes it from the "[p]romise" that "announces the coming of a not yet existing reality from the future of the truth," to cite *Theology of Hope*. Strictly speaking, Moltmann is not here denying his earlier insistence that what is disclosed "does not illuminate a future which is *always somehow inherent in reality* [die irgendwie immer schon der Wirklichkeit inhärent ist]."[108] But his emphasis on how the "*creation itself*" has been *invested with*—and in that sense *has*—"real promise" is striking.

The Spirit of Life, which is possibly Moltmann's most creation-affirming work, also highlights the gift—in my terminology the creational grace—of non-

---

[103] On the eclipse of human freedom, see the discussion in 4.3, 4.3.1, 4.3.3, and 4.4 above.
[104] See chap. 4 above, especially 4.2 and 4.4.
[105] I will qualify this claim to some extent in 6.5 below.
[106] GC, 63 as discussed in 6.5 above.
[107] GC, 207 [*GS*, 215]. My emphasis. "[A]ngelegt" here (from 'anlegen') could be translated as 'invested'.
[108] TH, 85 [*TdH*, 76]. My emphasis.

human as well as human existence. After quoting Silesius's saying "The rose flowers without a why,"[109] he writes,

> [A]s for the ultimate questions of life and existence, we shall never grasp why there *is* anything at all, and why we—we of all people—should exist. But if we have kept anything of the pristine awareness we had as children, we shall be able to marvel at the uniqueness of every moment, just as, when we were children—when we were born and woke to life—we were astonished because life itself was new and for-the-very-first-time.[110]

"[E]very mother and every child," he writes in *Experiences in Theology*, "knows that life is born and is a *gift*."[111]

That the gift is 'more than' or is 'deeper than' the given (in my language, that 'creational grace' is more than the 'graced nature' in which we experience the gift) is another important theme that Moltmann would seem to acknowledge.[112] The passage from *The Spirit of Life* cited above continues,

> Out of its fathomless source, life thrusts forward to expression, expression through living. That is why the deeper experiences of life remain uncompleted. We discover ourselves in them again and again, each time in a different way. This is the charm of re-membrance. We experience life with these experiences, and they travel with us.[113]

Here, we should note, memory is valued not as a way to reappropriate the eschatological hope that was experienced in the past[114] but for the way it mediates the foundational-historical gift and call of life itself.

The fathomless source of the gift of life is related, in Moltmann's understanding, to love. "True human life," he writes, "comes from love, is alive in love, and through loving makes something living of other life too." Reworking some familiar terms in theological anthropology, he continues,

> Our 'soul' is where our love is, and 'spirit' is the breath of the life that is loved and loving. Our question about life, consequently, is not whether our existence might possibly be immortal, and if so which part of it; the question is: will love

---

[109] SL, 22. (Here the saying is accidentally attributed to Rilke.) Cf, Moltmann's sympathetic quotation, in EiT, 90, of van Ruler as saying, "I smell a rose, and smell the kingdom of God." On the connection between these two sayings, see 8.4 below.
[110] SL, 22. His emphasis. In contrast to this celebration of the miracle of existence, see his discussion of when "life's gifts are grabbed and monopolized" in SL, 125.
[111] EiT, 148. My emphasis.
[112] In the discussion below, I suggest that he recognises the distinction between Giver and given more than the distinction between gift and given.
[113] SL, 22.
[114] See the discussion of the eschatological significance of memory and the past in 3.3 above.

endure, the love out of which we receive ourselves, and which makes us living when we ourselves offer it.[115]

Elsewhere, the source of life is related to the presence of the Spirit in us, which Moltmann understands as signifying a "relatedness that is immortal."[116] What endures death is thus not the immortal soul of traditional Christian theology nor Ernst Bloch's "kernel" of existence thought to be an "eternally creative wellspring" that "cannot die because it is not yet alive."[117] The source of (our) life lies in something far deeper than ourselves. Given God's covenant faithfulness to us and given his presence in us as the Spirit, that which endures is our "answerability [Verantwortlichkeit] to God" which "cannot have bounds set to it by death."[118]

In the concept of our "answerability," we move in my terminology from 'creational grace' to 'graced nature'. As "answerability" taken on its own sounds like a response to the call-side of the *Auf/Gabe*, this raises the question of whether our response to the gift-side, with its important themes of the divine gracing and empowering of our agency, is present in Moltmann's view of the resurrection to life beyond death. Here, far from being eclipsed by the life of the new creation, the 'creationally graced—and thus 'gift-ed'—nature' of human existence is boldly affirmed: "[T]hose whom God 'raises' at the end of time must 'rise' themselves. Their power from below corresponds to the power from above."[119]

Moltmann reiterates and develops this point by positing the following question:

> Is there an immanent power of this kind in 'the flesh' too which will raise it on that Day of God's? Is there anything in this vulnerable and mortal flesh which is immortal and can provide the energy for the regeneration of the flesh?[120]

In a response that draws on patristic reflections on 1 Cor 15:38, Moltmann relates this "power" and "energy" (which had earlier been intimately connected to the Spirit of Life[121]) to the theme of love once again. In one of the most striking passages in his entire corpus, he writes,

> In the image of the grain of wheat, this power is the power of surrender, the power to become seed in the earth. It is only out of this power that the plant grows. Put without metaphors, this means: the love which makes bodily life here

---

[115] CoG, 53.
[116] CoG, 72.
[117] CoG, 64.
[118] CoG, 74 [*DKG*, 92]. "Verantwortlichkeit" has strong connotations of responsibility, accountability, and liability. It does not indicate a general 'responsiveness'.
[119] WJC, 261.
[120] WJC, 261.
[121] Earlier in WJC, 261 he writes, "Life is energy, and the energies flow from the body. Are they not the energies of the creative Spirit of God?"

live is also the power which here ensouls bodily life. Life ensouled by the power of love becomes vulnerable and dies painfully. The hope for the resurrection of the flesh which lives and is ensouled through love sustains love through the wounds and the dying, and does not let up. The love which is the power of the 'sowing' here and the resurrection which is the power of the 'harvest' there are two sides of the same thing. What is there called the resurrection of the body is here called the love that ensouls the flesh. Love which here spends itself and surrenders itself in love, there rises up to glory. Love is therefore the immanent power of resurrection in the flesh. The resurrection is the transcendent perfecting of love.[122]

In Moltmann's vision, because 'nature' is 'graced' (so to speak) by its origins in the "fathomless source" of and unto life, creation may give birth to (the kingdom of) God.[123]

To sum up the preceding discussion, the Spirit of God—which in the model I am proposing is God as the Gift and Promise that is mediated by creation/time and always accompanied by the Call of the Word of God—is not exclusively identified by Moltmann with the promise of the New Creation and the transcendental movement of the present creation. Despite his emphasis on the eschatological redirection of time, the founding gift of/to life and the empowering energies of the Spirit of Life are themes that may be found in his more recent, more creation-affirming, writings. The creational energies of Love ensure that even our mortal flesh has a future in God's future.

Despite the positive features of this vision, questions remain. Whether Moltmann presents us with a one-sidedly *kenotic* view of our agency in relation to the Age to Come is an issue to which we shall return in 6.5 below. Whether Moltmann's acknowledgement of (what I am calling) 'creational grace' and 'graced nature' is sufficient to make a difference in his view of universal salvation is also something that remains to be seen. It is to this important question that we shall now turn.

---

[122] WJC, 262–63. For an early exploration of the significance of the biblical theme of sowing and reaping to our resurrection, see Jürgen Moltmann, "Hope beyond Time," trans. M. Douglas Meeks, *Duke Divinity School Review* 33, no. 2 (Spring 1968): 109–14, especially 113.

[123] This is precisely what Moltmann says. Speaking more cosmically in CoG, 279, he refers to a "potency . . . inherent in the earth" that is "a hidden presence of Christ." "If the divine Redeemer is himself present in this earth in hidden form," Moltmann concludes, "then the earth becomes the bearer or vehicle of his and our future." Thus Christoph Blumhardt is right: " 'Nature is the womb of God'." This is all in answer to a question Moltmann poses on CoG, 278: "[D]oes this temporal earth itself hold within it the promise of the new earth of eternal life?" Moltmann's early statement in TH, 226, that "this world 'cannot bear' the resurrection and the new world created by the resurrection" needs to be qualified in the light of his mature theology. But see also 6.5 below.

6.4 Eschatological Grace

Moltmann's basic response to the Barth-Brunner debate is not to open up the category of grace to include a creational presence of God in the gift and call of life, even if some resources for this line of thought might be detected in his writings (as explored in 6.3 above). Instead he prefers to approach the nature-grace question of the relationship between our and God's salvific will/power by speaking of nature, grace, and *glory* (as we have seen in 4.2 above).

Although it is certainly possible to understand "glory" in a creational-foundational sense—and postulate that the human task in/from the beginning was to reflect God's glory that shines in the darkness of Gen 1:3 so that the light might, in our shaping of history, fill all things in every way[124]—"glory" is almost always a transcendental-eschatological term for Moltmann.[125] And it is,

---

[124] This reading draws on the common biblical association between glory and light (see e.g., Exod 33:18 with Exod 34:29; 2 Cor 3:19; and Rev 21:23) and glory and image (see e.g., Ps 8:5 and 1 Cor 11:7). I am interpreting the light of Gen 1:3 that was created prior to the lights of Gen 1:14 as divine glory. Given the rule that the greater and lesser lights are given over the day and the night in Gen 1:16–18, it is also plausible to interpret the "Let *us* make [humanity] in our own image" of Gen 1:26 as addressed to a creation that includes the sun and moon. Imaging God (Gen 1:26–27) can then be seen as reflecting the divine glory. In the fall, the darkness gains the power to resist the light (cf. John 1:5).

It is interesting that Moltmann also connects the glory with the light of Gen 1:3 in TKG, 124. But he eschatologises what I take to be a creational theme. He writes,

The coming glory of God . . . already shines on the face of Christ, lighting up the hearts of men and women, as the light shone in the darkness on the first day of creation (II Cor. 4.6).

[125] See TH, 115 ("It is not that consummated history reveals God, but God's universal revelation in the coming of his fullness of his glory brings history to its consummation."), 131 ("Yahweh's coming glory"), 164 ("that glory of God" in relation to "the still outstanding eschaton"), 201 ("the coming revelation of the glory of God" and "the coming, promised glory of God"); CrG, 163 ("the coming God and his glory"), 167 ("God . . . will reveal himself in his glory only at the end of the old age and the beginning of the new"); CPS, 58 ("the eschatological statements about the coming, liberating glory of God can be proleptically transferred to Christ"), 59 ("This trinitarian history of glorification points beyond itself to the goal of the trinitarian history of God's dealings with the world. Here the thinking which directs its questions back to the origin is out of place"), 60 ("God . . . comes to his glory in the joy of redeemed creation"), 83 (creation's "consummation in glory"); TKG, 86 ("The Easter witnesses saw the crucified Jesus in the pre-reflection of God's coming glory on earth."), 88 ("the coming glory of the Father"), 124 (quoted in n. 124 above); GC, 229 ("the glory of the new creation"); WJC, 32 ("The love of God has become manifest through Christ. But the glory of God has not yet broken forth out of its hiddenness."), 191 ("this love is not yet the glory of God through which death itself will be annihilated"), 196 ("the grace which reaches us is the present form of God's glory"), 291 ("In nature's preservation and development, God already prepares the consummation of his creation, for his grace thrusts forward to the revelation of his glory."), 319 ("the eschatology of the glorification of God"); SL, 163 ("What is experienced here in the Spirit as God's love is only the beginning of what will be experienced then as God's glory. Sanctification is the beginning of glorification; glorification is the completion of sanctification."), 308 ("In

he thinks, with reference to this eschatological reality that nature and grace—together with all the questions surrounding their relationship—are to be understood.

This eschatological focus not only helps Moltmann escape the confines of the original Barth-Brunner debate,[126] it also leads him to reject the second part

---

'the transcendent origin' of salvation, we see the primordial, self-opening Trinity; in its eschatological consummation we find the Trinity resting in its glory.''); CoG, 318 (the glory of the New Jerusalem), 323–24 (the "glorification of God"), 336 ("The glory of God is not to be found . . . in his laborious self-realization by way of his self-emptying, but follows upon that on the eternal day of resurrection."); EiT, 57–58 (" 'Love' is . . . nothing less than the real presence of the living God in this world, just as, on the other hand, 'glory' will be his real presence in the world to come."), and 63 ("with the raising of Christ, the revelation of God's glory begins, the glory which overcomes the force of time, together with the power of death, and which will bring about the eternal creation."). See also the discussion of the "glorification" of the Trinity in 2.5 and in figure 4 in chap. 3 above and cf. "glory" in figure 5 in the light of chap. 4 above.

References to "glory" in a non-eschatological context are few. They include GC, 279 ("the world-less, eternal glory which precedes creation and out of which God creatively acts"); CoG, 296 (the "veiling of [God's] glory" in the *zimzum*) and 334 ("The resurrection glory corresponds to that primordial glory of the Son with the Father.")

[126] Moltmann's most extended engagement with the Barth-Brunner debate—or to be more precise: with the issue of 'natural theology' central to that debate—occurs in his most recent 'major' work, EiT, chap. 6 (especially 75–80). Here Barth's "doctrine of lights" (75) is of more interest to him than the original Barth-Brunner interchange (which features on pp. 77 and 80. The latter also receives comment in GC, xi.)

At the end of a section with the provocative title "Christian theology itself is the true natural theology," much of which is a sympathetic critique of Barth's mature reflections on this subject, he concludes (in EiT, 79), "[i] *After* the analogy of faith comes the analogy of essence, [ii] *after* the theology of the cross comes the theology of glory, [iii] *after* the theology of grace the theology of nature, and [iv] *after* the theology of nature natural theology." His emphases.

Let us briefly examine each of these four pairs in order in the light of the preceding discussion. *First*, the reference to the analogies of faith and essence deals with the relation of faith and reason, a classic grace-nature issue. In the former analogy, comments Moltmann, we arrive at knowledge in a movement from above (in the light of revelation as favoured by Barth) while the *analogia entis* moves from below (as stressed in classic natural theology with its 'apparent' starting point in reason's ability to prepare us for a knowledge that God in his grace brings to completion. I say 'apparent' because Moltmann points out in EiT, 78 that in the case of Aquinas, the " 'natural' preparation" offered for the Gospel is clearly shaped by Christian revelation. This is "a consciously Christian natural theology," it would seem, from which Barth's doctrine of lights hardly differs). Citing the ascent and descent of the angels on Jacob's ladder, Moltmann opts (in EiT, 78) for "a dialectical play of reciprocal knowing" further described as "the analogy of essence *in* the analogy of faith." His emphasis. In the *second* pairing, the theologies of cross and glory, Moltmann is referring to the way justification, in putting the sinner right with God, puts us "in a position to know the creaturely world in its accord and correspondence with God" (78–79). The *third* pairing, the theologies of grace and nature, covers the same ground for here Moltmann is expressing his conviction that "natural theology," in principle and in actual practice, is really "an

of the mediaeval formulation *"gratia non destruit, sed praesupponit et perfecit naturam"*[127] in favour of his own "three-term dialectic,"

> *gratia non perfecit, sed preparat naturam ad gloriam aeternam;*
> *gratia non est perfectio naturae, sed praeparatio messianic mundi ad regnum Dei.*[128]

Grace does not complete nature. It is "the coming glory" that "will complete both nature and grace, and [that] hence already determines the relationship between the two here and now." No longer petrified into an antithesis, nature and grace must be seen "in a forward perspective," and "as complementary aspects of a common process" or "messianic movement."[129]

---

advance radiance of the eschatological theology of glory" (76). Thus "nature" is being interpreted eschatologically as anticipating creation's fulfilment in God's kingdom. In the *fourth* and final pairing, Moltmann's envisions a "theology of nature," that is (presumably) a view of "nature" in that anticipatory sense as funding a "natural theology," by which he means a life-affirming public theology that deals with "the mystery of God's presence in all things" (80). (Here "natural" certainly includes "nature" in the sense of the non-human creation.)

This eschatologising of 'nature' and "natural theology" can be found in *Theology of Hope* written more than 35 years earlier. In TH, 282, he writes,

> A 'natural theology' of this kind, however, in which God is manifest and demonstrable to every man, is not the presupposition of Christian faith, but the future goal of Christian hope. This universal and immediate presence of God is not the source from which faith comes, but the end to which it is on the way. ...
> *Theologia naturalis* is at bottom *theologia viatorum*, and *theologia viatorum* will always concern itself with the future *theologia gloriae* in the form of fragmentary sketches.

His italics. In EiT, these "sketches" are possible because " 'Natural theology' understands the world sacramentally as the real presence and advance radiance of the coming kingdom" (73). It is "a fore-*shining* of revealed theology's eschatological horizon, the theology of glory" (72). His emphasis.

Although Moltmann describes natural theology as "at once a *recollection* of creation and an eschatological *hope* for creation" (my emphases) and stresses that "The Holy Spirit in its efficacies is the bridge between creation-in-the-beginning and creation's eternal goal" (73), the eschatological horizon looms larger than the creational. 'Nature' effectively means (in my terminology) *eschatologically graced nature*. Creational(ly) grace(d nature), apart from a passing reference to the Spirit's efficacies, does not seem to be in view. When Moltmann says that "All created things and all living beings then become in their existence *real promises* of their future in God's world to come" (73, his emphasis), that promise may (in part) have a foundational-creational meaning. His reference to GC, 60–65 in EiT, 73n96 (352n96), makes this plausible (though see 6.5 below). But overall the nature-grace relation is understood by relating both nature and grace to glory.

[127] GC, 7. His italics. 'Grace does not destroy, but presupposes and perfects nature.'
[128] GC, 8. His italics. 'Grace does not perfect, but prepares nature for eternal glory; grace is not the perfection of nature, but the messianic preparation of the world for the kingdom of God.'
[129] GC, 8–9.

Moltmann's distinction here between "grace" and "glory" parallels the distinction he makes elsewhere between salvation (or "reconciliation") and "redemption."[130] Reconciliation, he would say, does not bring creation to its fulfilment. Salvation does not bring creation to that eschatological perfection—to "redemption" in his terminology—in which its initial vulnerability to sin is onto/theologically[131] overcome.

"Glory" in Moltmann's terminology is thus a combination of 'eschatological grace' and 'redemptive grace' to use the terminology of my proposed alternative model. On the one hand, this 'grace' is an eschatological promise rather than a response to our sin; it is thus not 'redemptive' grace as that term is normally used. At the same time, as Moltmann has in mind a bringing to completion of both creation *and salvation* ("nature" and "grace" in his terminology here), "glory" is a form of 'redemptive' grace in both his and my use(s) of that term.

Is this eschatological grace in Moltmann's theology conceived of in such a way that universal salvation looks (at least relatively) plausible? More specifically, does he conceive of a response to that grace, thus avoiding the charge that his universalism is coercive? If, as I have argued in 4.2 above, there is no 'natural' impetus towards glory in the creational-historical direction for Moltmann, and if 'creationally graced nature' is a category that despite its apparent recognition in his more recent work nevertheless does not seem to play a significant role in his discussion of nature-grace issues in the context of salvation, does he (at least) propose an 'eschatologically graced nature' that honours human agency, specifically in the context of salvation? The answer to these questions appears to be a positive one.

"The surplus of grace over and above the forgiveness of sins and the reconciliation of sinners," writes Moltmann in *The Trinity and the Kingdom of God*, "represents *the power of the new creation* which consummates creation-in-the-beginning."[132] That this eschatological 'grace' (which, as we have seen, he elsewhere prefers to term "glory") is a power in history is an idea established in *Theology of Hope* where it is expressed in terms of the "divine promise" that "itself contains the power of its fulfilment in the faithfulness and might of the God who promises."[133] While Moltmann is emphatic that this promise does not "depend" on human obedience for its fulfilment,[134] but is "unconditional,"[135] its fulfilment is not unrelated to obedience. Put negatively, "the promise determines the existence of the recipient and all he does and

---

[130] See 5.3 (especially 5.3n128) above.

[131] On ontotheology, cf. 4.0n1 above. It is an appropriate term as "redemption" for Moltmann requires a transformation to both the structure of creation and the being of God.

[132] TKG, 116 as cited in 4.3.3 above. My emphasis.

[133] TH, 123. Cf. TH, 147, "Between this once-for-all validation of the promise [in the Christ event] and its fulfilment in the glory of God there stands only the dependability of God himself."

[134] See TH, 123, 145, and 147.

[135] TH, 147.

suffers. It is not that *vice versa* the fulfilling of the promise is determined by the existence and behaviour of the recipient."[136] Put more positively, "the commandments of the covenant" which are "nothing else but the ethical reverse of the promise itself," are " 'easy' to fulfil in the power that comes of hoping in God and waiting upon him."[137] Thus the power of eschatological grace in history is one that *empowers* human action.[138]

If the "unconditional" nature of the promise sounds as though the eschatological grace under discussion is "irresistible"—and Moltmann does indeed refer to grace in this way[139]—we should also take note of his many references to "prevenient" grace, which by definition is a grace that " 'comes before' a person's ability to repent and believe."[140] However this term is precisely understood in a given context, its use in theological literature always signifies a grace that does not eclipse our nature. While Moltmann's "prevenient" grace may often include the idea of a grace that (in a temporal sense) "comes before" the full realisation of God's glory,[141] human responsiveness is certainly honoured. "The justification of the sinner and prevenient grace come about when a person believes," writes Moltmann, before stressing that a person's "pure passivity of receiving" in this context is "a

---

[136] TH, 147. His italics.

[137] TH, 121.

[138] Cf. TH, 206, "Divine righteousness is not merely a gift that has been made manifest, but means also the power of the Giver which is at work in the life of the believer." This issue of the empowering nature of eschatological grace should be related to the discussion of *pro/missio* in 6.3 above and vice versa.

[139] See TH, 211 ("the promise which will be fulfilled in all and show itself in the very deadliness of death to be *irresistible*"); CrG, 129 ("the *unconditional* and free grace of God"), 176 ("the *unconditional* grace which makes righteous the unrighteous"), 275 ("the *unconditionality* and universality of God's community of Grace"), and 246 ("*indestructible* election"). My emphases.

[140] Kevin J. Vanhoozer, "Effectual Call or Causal Effect? Summons, Sovereignty and Supervenient Grace," *Tyndale Bulletin* 49, no. 2 (1998): 215–51 (reprinted in his *First Theology: God, Scripture and Hermeneutics* (Downers Grove, IL: InterVarsity Press; Leicester, UK: Apollos, 2002), 96–124). The quotation is from p. 223, where Vanhoozer especially links prevenient grace to non-reformed theologies in general and "free-will theism" in particular. Harvey, "Grace," 109, writes that prevenient grace is one of those forms of grace identified in Roman Catholic theology that "rest[s] on the view that G[race] is a supernatural power that, *without destroying the freedom of the will*, infuses the virtues of faith, hope, and charity into the soul, virtues that are rewarded with the final vision for which life is destined." My emphasis. Yarnold, "Grace," 245, notes, "Prevenient grace is God's grace anticipating any movement by man towards God."

[141] I suspect this is at least a connotation of the term in most of its occurrences. Certainly it seems clear in CPS, 230 where Moltmann says, "Infant baptism is not a token of prevenient grace; it is a sign of the prevenient faith of the parents." Cf. also his discussion of "prevenient notions" and concepts as "prevenient-anticipations" in EiT, 54. For other references to 'prevenience', see CrG, 105, 128, 130; CPS, 87, 230, 246, 248, 279; WJC, 89, 102, 103, 186, 337; SL, 152; and CoG, 105.

creative receptivity."[142] That Moltmann often speaks of the prevenience and unconditionality of grace in the same breath[143] testifies to his refusal to interpret the divine-human (grace-nature) encounter as a zero-sum relationship.[144] Monergism and synergism would both seem to be rejected.

If there is a "creative receptivity" of God's eschatological grace on our part, it follows that Moltmann recognises what I am calling 'eschatologically graced nature'. Certainly our nature in this context includes our capacity for *faith*, which is not our ability to contribute to our salvation, for Moltmann, but is the way in which we experience God's grace in the here and now.[145] By the same token, 'eschatologically graced nature' also describes our *hope* together with all those experiences and actions that, though they may be aimed at a planned *futurum* in time, are nevertheless reoriented in hope towards the *advent(us)* of God's coming Kingdom.[146]

No attempt to name the experience of eschatological grace in history is complete for Moltmann without reference to "liberation," which means far more than being set free from our sins or even finding freedom from the sins of others. The power of this eschatological grace in history—indeed we might speak here of the liberating nature of its power *over* history—is related to the

---

[142] CPS, 230. In CPS, 245 he even speaks of Christ's "open, prevenient invitation" in the Lord's Supper.

[143] See CrG, 130; CPS, 230, 246; WJC, 186, 337; and CoG, 105.

[144] Cf. CrG, 249, "In their struggle against each other, theism and atheism begin from the presupposition that God and man are fundamentally one being. Therefore what is ascribed to God must be taken from man and what is ascribed to man must have been taken from God" and CPS, 78, "The modern alternative, according to which either there is a God, in which case man cannot be free, or man is free, but then there cannot be a God, is not valid here." This brief discussion should be read in the light of 1.4.2 and the detailed discussion of "freedom" in 4.3.3 above and vice versa.

[145] See CoG, 245 as discussed in 1.4.2 and 4.3.3 above.

[146] For an example of the distinction between faith and hope in Moltmann (which corresponds somewhat to the distinction between trust and hope [as sides of faith] in figure 6 in 5.3 above), see the quotation at the end of this footnote. On the relation/distinction between our transcendent hopes and our immanent hopes, see 2.1 above. On *adventus* and *futurum*, see 2.3 above. On hope and planning, see HP, especially the title essay (178–99) and GC, 135. The centrality of a praxis-oriented and praxis-orienting hope in Moltmann's corpus was firmly established in TH. That centrality in still evident in EiT, pt. 2: "Hermeneutics of Hope" (86–179). The way hope should shape action is succinctly expressed towards the end of Moltmann's article "Hope," in *A New Dictionary of Christian Theology*, ed. Alan Richardson and John Bowden (London: SCM Press, 1983), 272,

> Just as faith ties a person to the crucified Christ, so hope opens up this faith to the all-embracing future of the risen Christ. In hope for the kingdom of God the Christian also experiences the contradiction between resurrection and life and a world of evil and death. Faith which opens itself to hope does not bring peace, but disquiet. In contrast to the reality we experience, love accepts the earth because it hopes for the new creation. Thus hope draws believers into the life of love and frees them for solidarity with the whole suffering creation.

fact that to experience liberation is to experience a "glory" that (in Moltmann's terminology) is more than "grace," a "redemption" that is more than "reconciliation," and the energies of an eschaton that, in its power to bring the world and its history to completion and perfection, is more than creation. In this light, writes Moltmann,

> [L]iberation ... hold[s] within itself the experience of an *added value* over against sin, an added value which excludes the next Fall after the restoration of creation. If where sin has increased grace 'abounds all the more' (Rom. 5.20), then this added value of grace is its power to end, not just actual sin, but even the possibility of sinning, not just actual death but even the being-able-to-die ....[147]

This "surplus" of eschatological grace, which "represents the power of the new creation,"[148] is related to the character of the promise that awakens and sustains hope. The fact that the promise contains a "surplus" beyond past, present, and future fulfilment is what keeps it alive in history as this is what keeps history alive to the coming kingdom.[149] In my understanding, this "surplus" points to the way grace 'funds' nature but can never be fully 'realised' by it such that the nature-grace distinction would become superfluous. Indeed, the distinction between heaven and earth continues into the New Creation (Rev 21:1).

I would like to argue that the way grace transcends (is not exhausted by) nature shows up not only in the "surplus" meaning that the promise (and *pro/missio*) has over its historical realisations but also in the "surplus" value of the gift (and *Auf/Gabe*) over the given. The "charge"[150] of/to Life is not exhausted, or 'dis-charged', in the way we live. The gift of who we are (to be) is not revoked even when we die. This is vital for understanding the power of creational grace in history. And in salvation. Yet this is not a theme that Moltmann explores. Consequently, the theme of creational grace is never developed in Moltmann's vision of universal salvation. That there is an appreciation for 'eschatologically graced nature' allows him to honour human agency to a certain extent. But a robust view of 'creationally graced nature', which could do so much to allay fears that our humanity is eclipsed in the "triumph of glory" (see my comments at the end of 4.4 above), is lacking.

Why do the hints that we find in Moltmann's writings on this theme (as explored in 6.3 above) never contribute to his case for universalism? This, I would contend, relates to the overall philosophical framework of his theology. I

---

[147] CoG, 263–64. His emphasis. Moltmann refers here to Augustine's movement from *posse non peccare* to *non posse peccare* as discussed in 4.3.3 and 4.4 above. For the distinction between grace and glory, and reconciliation and redemption for Moltmann, see 4.2 and 5.3n128 above.
[148] TKG, 116 as cited above.
[149] On promise as containing a surplus beyond historical fulfilment, see CPS, 24; GC, 286; WJC, 238; SL, 152; EiT, 91, 105, and 126. Cf. the discussion in 2.3 above.
[150] See n. 102 above.

would like to argue that the gift of creation (including the surplus of the gift over the given) and the promise of new creation (including its surplus value over its historical realisations) are ultimately two sides of grace that work together and that are of a piece in the realisation of salvation. If the gift/promise character of Life is honoured in our theologies, universal salvation, I suggest, becomes far more viable and imaginable. For Moltmann, however, the promise supersedes the gift/given as the latter is ultimately seen as deficient. He may say that the Spirit as source of life is "fathomless."[151] But the fact that we may speak of the "surplus" of the Giver over the given in his theology does not mean that we may speak of the surplus value of the gift, at least not as analogous to the surplus of the promise.

This is, I suggest, related to the *Neoplatonic* tendencies in Moltmann's cosmogony.[152] In the eschatological (re)direction of time, the surplus of grace can empower nature in its openness to the liberation of the new creation *endlessly*. In the historical direction, however, God's fullness is kenotically poured out into time, becoming more and more alienated from its divine Origin. This will only be overcome when God becomes all in all, when time is taken up into the divine life and when eternity enters time, thus eradicating the transience that marks the finitude of the divine energies in the present age. The "Great Chain of Being"[153] has been (as it were) turned on its side, the two-fold movement of emanation/*kenosis* and return/*theosis* becoming the movement towards creation's past and God's future respectively.[154]

Moltmann does speak of the Spirit of Life as a "wellspring"[155] from which life emanates (and is explicit about his adoption of Neoplatonic language in this context as we have seen in 6.3 above). That he is attempting to develop a creation-affirming theology that relates God to (what I am calling) the foundational-differentiating direction of time in an intimate way is clear. But this divine presence would ultimately seem to end in non-being as the divine energies dissipate. "Physis," writes Moltmann, "is Being that brings forth. But

---

[151] SL, 22 as cited in 6.3 above.

[152] On Moltmann's Neoplatonism, see 2.2, 3.6, especially 3.6n258, 4.2, and 6.3 above.

[153] The classic work remains Arthur O. Lovejoy, *The Great Chain of Being: A Study of the History of an Idea* (Cambridge, MA: Harvard University Press, 1948). Cf. chap. 9, "The Temporalizing of the Great Chain of Being." Much of this focuses on the recasting of the move up the Great Chain of Being as historical progress in modernity. I am highlighting the way Moltmann recasts the downward movement. My main objection to 'Great Chain of Being'-thinking (even in its temporalised form) concerns not only the way the Creator/creation distinction is blurred but also the way in which the Divine is located at only one end of the 'chain'.

[154] In this context, Sherover's comment in *The Human Experience of Time*, 33, that "Plotinus ... shift[ed] the Aristotelian focus on the past as the source of generation to the source of the future as the source of continuing fulfilments" is interesting. What Sherover notes as a shift that was "only suggested and left without development" in Plotinus has been developed within a Hegelianised, Neoplatonic cosmogony by Moltmann.

[155] SL, 177 as cited in 6.3 above.

that is only one side of her: If future (*futurum*) is her eternal process of becoming, past is her eternal process of dying."[156] What holds for the offspring of this "eternally fruitful womb of Being" would seem to hold for the energies that emanate from the wellspring of the Spirit of Life. The future as *futurum*, though it may come from the very Spirit of Life, has no surplus value that can overcome transience.

Nevertheless—and with Moltmann there is always a nevertheless—*futurum* and *adventus*, nature and grace, creation and eschaton, the historical and the eschatological, *kenosis* and *theosis* are not merely or finally opposites. Even the "process of dying," as we shall explore the next section ('God in history?'), is itself related to the coming of God's glory.

6.5 God in History?

My suggestion that the structure of Moltmann's thought prevents him from fully affirming God's presence in history finds support in the fact that God, in Moltmann's theology, does not fully (unambiguously) guide and energise human action and agency in the foundational direction of time. In this regard, it is worth examining once more the nature of human agency in the remarkable passage about our role in the resurrection quoted in 6.3 above. Here Moltmann states,

> In the image of the grain of wheat, this power is *the power of surrender*, the power to become seed in the earth. . . . The love which is the power of the 'sowing' here and the resurrection which is the power of the 'harvest' there are two sides of the same thing. What is there called the resurrection of the body is here called the love that ensouls the flesh. Love which here *spends itself and surrenders itself in love*, there rises up to glory. Love is therefore the immanent power of resurrection in the flesh. The resurrection is the transcendent perfecting of love.[157]

This is not the language of power in the usual sense, but the language of *kenosis*. Here, I suggest, we have what Moltmann elsewhere describes as the turning around of the storm of history (which includes Augustine's "storms of incoherent events"[158]) in the resurrection storm.[159] "Sowing" and "harvesting" parallel the contrast between *historical* "spreading out," "splitting up," "fanning out," and "unfurling" and *eschatological* "gathering," "uniting," and "glorifying" that we explored in 2.5 above. More specifically, our *historical* surrender is perfected in God's *eschatological* raising to new life. *Kenosis* thus (that is, in God's grace) leads to *theosis*.

---

[156] CoG, 25 as cited more fully in 2.4 above. His italics. The description of Physis as the "eternally fruitful womb of Being" is part of the same passage.
[157] WJC, 262–63. My emphases.
[158] Augustine, *Confessions*, 244 as cited in 2.2 above.
[159] See 2.1 and 3.6 above.

Moltmann does affirm human agency here in a context in which many theologians might be content to speak of what God alone will do. This is promising as it suggests that his vision of the Final Judgment will not exemplify the kind of monergistic, coercive, creation-eclipsing theology that some associate with universal salvation. Nevertheless, the gift/call of and to life of creational grace is being understood in this context in a valid yet restricted sense as the call to 'let go'. Our surrender is an 'act' performed in the hope that God will himself act by overturning history. Letting go of the life we have been given in the hope that God will not revoke the gift of who we are, in the hope that we shall be fleshed out anew in the Age to Come, is not what Moltmann seems to have in mind. I understand him as saying, by contrast, that in *surrender*, we experience the *gift* of our mortal lives coming to an *end*, *open* to the *promise* of the resurrection. The gift, in other words, makes way for the promise.[160]

Receiving, running with, and letting go of who we are (to be) in the *Auf/Gabe-pro/missio* of time, all the while trusting that God acts and will continue to act in us *historically* in this life and beyond, is, I propose, the very rhythm of Life in covenant with God. Gift and promise are two sides of the same coin, two ways of looking at history. Yet for Moltmann, creational gift and eschatological promise are opposed. For him, our resurrection, strictly speaking, does not (will not) occur *in* history (although it happens *to* history). This is why Moltmann makes the striking claim that "Christ's resurrection ... is not a historical event; it is an eschatological happening to the crucified Christ."[161]

Moltmann's reluctance or failure to unambiguously affirm that God acts in the foundational direction of time is not limited to his discussion of our death/resurrection. His view of the relation between God's presence and our power to shape history expressed elsewhere exemplifies his tendency to oppose eschatological grace to our historical nature. This opposition—which in my view exists because Moltmann has a weakened appreciation for the grace of creation—has not escaped the notice of his critics (though they do not use this terminology).

Let us consider a revealing essay, "Theology in the Project of the Modern World,"[162] in which Moltmann opens a section entitled "Hope for God without millenarianism" with the words,

> The God of the Bible, according to the book of promises and according to the book of the Gospel, is the God 'who is and who was and who is to come' (Rev.

---

[160] On 'making way' in this sense, see 2.4, 3.2, 4.1, and 5.1 above.

[161] CoG, 69. Cf. EiT, 108, "Christ's historical death and his eschatological resurrection certainly do not belong qualitatively on the same, single line." Peter C. Hodgson, in his *Jesus—Word and Presence: An Essay in Christology* (Philadelphia: Fortress Press), 238 (cf. 17), suggests that with respect to Moltmann's discussion of the resurrection in TH, "the terminological distinction between *historisch* and *geschichtlich* marks what we might call an "horizontal" dualism." His italics.

[162] Jürgen Moltmann, "Theology in the Project of the Modern World," 1–21.

1:4). That is to say, he will appear in his full divinity only in his coming kingdom.[163]

For any student of Moltmann, these are familiar words,[164] very much in line with the characteristically eschatological thrust of his theology from first to last (or rather, from last to first). But this emphasis has not always been enthusiastically received. Seven years earlier, for example, John Marsden had noted, "Moltmann makes great play of the biblical formula in the book of Revelation, which describes God as the one "who is and who was and who is to come," rather than simply "will be," yet he always ignores the first part of the affirmation!"[165] This commentator, a Christian socialist searching for a viable political theology, clearly wants to focus on the God who "is," the God whose guidance and presence we need in the here and now. This God is not merely present *to* history as the presence of the future. This is the God *of* history.

Read against this critical observation, it is interesting that in his next sentence, Moltmann states,

> The questions is: Where has God already come? Where are we so certain of his presence that we can live and act with the assurance of God and ourselves?

Here he seems to anticipate the charge that his emphasis on the Advent future of God undermines present Christian action in and for the world. It looks as if he is about to demonstrate that his theology can affirm the creational, foundational presence of God.

As we read on, however, what we find is the same kind of distinction that we observed in his discussion of the resurrection. He writes,

> The messianism of modern times said: "With God we will enter lordship over the earth, and with Christ we will judge the nations." This messianic dream became a nightmare for the people and an overcharge for the dreamers, ending in cold desperation. But *it is not in our dominion* that the coming God is present through his life-giving Spirit; it is in our *hope*. *It is not in our power* that the grace that raises us up is made perfect; it is in our *weakness*.[166]

---

[163] Moltmann, "Theology in the Project of the Modern World," 16.
[164] Moltmann cites Rev 1:4 to this effect frequently. See, e.g., CoG, 23 (as discussed in 2.3 above) and GC, 133. An early instance, which is cited by Marsden (cf. the following note), is Jürgen Moltmann, "Theology as Eschatology," in *The Future of Hope*, ed. F. Herzog (New York: Herder and Herder, 1970), 13.
[165] John Marsden, *Marxian and Christian Utopianism: Towards a Socialist Political Theology* (New York: Monthly Review Press, 1991), 157.
[166] Moltmann, "Theology in the Project of the Modern World," 16. My emphases. In the light of 5.1, the following passage from Heidegger, *Being and Time*, div.2, chap. 5, 436 [384] may be relevant:
> If Dasein, by anticipation, lets death become powerful in itself, then, as free for death, Dasein understands itself in its own *superior power*, the power of its finite freedom, so that in this freedom, which 'is' only in its having chosen to make such a choice, it can take over the *powerlessness* of abandonment to its having

The question of how we exercise power to promote justice in the here and now seems to be left unanswered. Hope is opposed to dominion. Weakness is valued instead of power.[167] God seems at best only indirectly related to the future that humanity might bring about in history.

It is at this point—i.e., with respect to the somewhat indirect and ambiguous way in which God seems to be related to history—that Moltmann's theology has often been judged and found wanting. Marsden, for example, writes,

> Moltmann's understanding of eschatology in terms of the arrival of the future rather than simply the extrapolation of the present does help express the element of transcendence in history. However, the language he uses suggests an unhelpful severing of the relation between past and future insofar as he understands transcendence as not bearing any relation to the immanent processes of history. Indeed so strong is his emphasis on the "novum," that he falls into a form of quasi-supernaturalism, in the sense that *the activity of God is presented in opposition to the workings of the created order*.[168]

While Marsden's critique cannot be accepted without reservation, the charge of "opposition" certainly makes sense of the sharp distinction Moltmann often draws between the historical and eschatological directions of time.[169] Is there no sense in which grace may be discerned in our historical power?, we may ask. Is the work of the life-giving Spirit opposed to our dominion in every

---

done so, and can thus come to have a clear vision for the accidents of the Situation that has been disclosed.
His emphases. For commentary, see Mulhall, *Heidegger and* Being and Time, 187 and Dreyfus, *Being-in-the-World: A Commentary on Heidegger's* Being and Time, *Division 1*, 318–19. Dreyfus' attention to the influence of Kierkegaard here is also significant.

[167] Here there would seem to be a point of contact between Moltmann and John D. Caputo, *The Weakness of God: A Theology of the Event* (Bloomington, IN: Indiana University Press, 2006). In my view, however we might go about rethinking omnipotence theologically, it is surely significant that Paul refers to "Christ *crucified*" as "Christ the *power* of God" in 1 Cor 1:22–24. Cf. n. 174 below.

[168] Marsden, *Marxian and Christian Utopianism*, 156. My emphasis. Marsden's concern about Moltmann's lack of affirmation of creation parallels the critical response of many theologians in the Kuyperian tradition. In fact Brian Walsh's neo-Kuyperian essay (see n. 6 above) is cited approvingly in *Marxian and Christian Utopianism*, 214n66 at this point in Marsden's assessment.

[169] For example, in CoG, 324, Moltmann prefaces his claim that "Ethical existence is gathered up and perfected in the aesthetic existence of doxology" by stating, "It is impossible to stress sufficiently the significance of the glorification of God for the inward and outward *liberation of men and women from the plans and purposes of their workaday world*." My emphasis. Cf. Jürgen Moltmann, "The Liberation of the Future and its Anticipations in History," in *God Will Be All in All: The Eschatology of Jürgen Moltmann*, ed. Richard Bauckham (Edinburgh: T. and T. Clark, 1999), 265–89, especially 280, where Moltmann writes, "Work allows people to exist in their own world; the sabbath rest leads them into God's creation again, and into his pleasure in them themselves." Does this not come perilously close to dualism? Certainly it is not hard to see how someone like Marsden might find this exasperating.

The Nature of Grace 305

way, shape, or form? Instead of romanticising weakness, should we not genuinely and faithfully exercise authentic power by empowering others? If Gen 1:26–28 calls us to make history, can we not trust that God will be active in that history and that history and eschatology should not be opposed to one another?

Convinced that he effectively ignores the God who is and who will be in the name of a God who is to come, Marsden observes,

> Moltmann rightly recognised that Weiss and Schweitzer have thrown down the fundamental challenge to twentieth-century theology. But like Barth, who also made eschatology his starting point, Moltmann ends up by abandoning a radical this-worldly perspective in terms of his perception of the Kingdom. To replace Barth's "Wholly Other" with the "Wholly Future" makes it no less a transcendent irrelevance.[170]

In the light of this second, damning comment, it is interesting that once more in the passage under investigation, Moltmann goes on to state that "we go a step beyond" the "typically millenarian" assumption that "God is like us—we are like God. We rule with God and God is on our side," when "we try to revere and perceive God as the *Wholly Other* (Karl Barth) in what is 'other' and strange (Emmanuel Levinas)."[171] In response to Marsden, this might be described as a stance of 'transcendent relevance'—a phrase that well captures Moltmann's own passion for a political theology and that exposes the rather blunt and unnuanced nature of Marsden's critique.[172]

---

[170] Marsden, *Marxian and Christian Utopianism*, 160. The parallel with Barth is also drawn in Langdon Gilkey, *Reaping the Whirlwind: A Christian Interpretation of History* (New York: The Seabury Press, 1976), 234. Marsden refers to Gilkey's critique as "seminal" (*Marxian and Christian Utopianism*, 214n70). For a helpful discussion of Barth's eschatology in relation to Moltmann, see Gerhard Sauter, "Why Is Karl Barth's Church Dogmatics Not a 'Theology of Hope'? Some Observations on Barth's Understanding of Eschatology," *Scottish Journal of Theology* 52, no. 4 (1999), 407–29.

[171] Moltmann, "Theology in the Project of the Modern World," 17–18. His emphasis.

[172] Cf. Meeks, *Origins of the Theology of Hope*, 153,

> The basic critical character of Moltmann's political theology is molded by the otherness of God which is not Wholly Other (*ganz anders*), but the Wholly Transforming (*der ganz Ändernde*). The Wholly Transforming One is the Father who suffers in the Son's cross "for us."

His italics. However, we should take note of Peter Hodgson's comment, in his *Jesus—Word and Presence*, 16–17nn36–37, that "*Ganz-Ändernde*" (which he cites with reference to [Meeks' translation of] Moltmann, "The Future as New Paradigm of Transcendence," in RRF, 190 [where the ET reproduces the German terms] and 199) is better translated as "wholly altering." (He is supported here by Margaret Kohl's translation of the slightly revised version of this essay, "The Future as a New Paradigm of Transcendence," in FC, 11 and 17.) Moltmann, Hodgson points out, does not adopt what H. Richard Niebuhr would have called a 'Christ transforms culture' position (cf. my discussion in 4.2n62 above) but "is closer to that of "Christ Against Culture" or "Christ and Culture in Paradox"." While this is an insightful observation, Moltmann's mature theology exhibits a far more complex Christ-culture or grace-nature relationship

But this does not mean that Marsden's concerns are groundless. Moltmann's welcome move in the direction of 'postmodern ethics'[173] only intensifies the questions we must put to him: Is God only present in what is beyond our control, in what challenges (or should challenge) our power?[174] Is

---

than this, in my judgment. At the end of 5.3 above, for example, I suggested that "Moltmann tends to see the historical direction as 'nature' which eschatological 'grace' (or "glory" in his terminology) presupposes, completes, subsumes, ultimately relativises, and thus negates." That said, Hodgson's judgment is not inaccurate with respect the (early) Moltmann on whom Meeks is commenting.

[173] On Levinas-influenced postmodern ethics as a quest for transcendence see my "Embracing the Thorny Way: Review of *The Postmodern God*, ed. Graham Ward (Oxford: Blackwell, 1997) and *Knowing Other-wise: Philosophy at the Threshold of Spirituality*, ed. James Olthuis (New York: Fordham University Press, 1997)," *Third Way* 21, no. 1 (February 1998): 26. An important work that is indebted to Levinas and resonates well with the post-metaphysical (rather than the ontotheological) side of Moltmann's theology is Richard Kearney, *The God Who May Be: A Hermeneutics of Religion* (Bloomington, IN: Indiana University Press, 2001). Sadly, there is only one reference to Moltmann in this work (see 123–24n29, cf. 28). Kearney's (over-) identification of Moltmann with process theology fails to capture the distinctive nature of the future in his thought. (What Moltmann said over forty years ago in his "Response to the Opening Presentations," in *Hope and the Future of Man*, ed. Ewert H. Cousins (Philadelphia: Fortress Press, 1972), 58—one of those presentations being by process theologian John Cobb—holds for his mature theology also: "I am not so much interested in Whitehead in regard to his process-thought and his "becoming God" with a primordial and consequent nature, though I like his phrase about God as "the great companion—the fellow-sufferer who understands".") The singular reference to Moltmann (342n33, cf. 334) in Merold Westphal's response piece, "The God Who Will Be: Hermeneutics and the God of Promise," *Faith and Philosophy* 20, no. 3 (July, 2003): 328–44 is also disappointing in this respect.

[174] José Miguez Bonino, in an early response in his *Doing Theology in a Revolutionary Situation* (Philadelphia: Fortress Press, 1975), 149, notes that despite Moltmann's reference to "the materializations of God's presence" that "no theology of liberation ... can do without" (cf. CrG, 337, although the ET is slightly different), Moltmann's concern to "avoid sacralizing a particular ideology or power structure" makes him retreat from such "materializations." Bonino does not want "materializations" that "run the risk of mystical identifications." But he does want theologians to identify "historical, analytical, and ideological mediations" between God's Kingdom and history. "There is no *divine* politics or economics," he writes. "But this means that we must resolutely use the best *human* politics and economics at our disposal." His emphases. But this seems to propose a non-sacralised yet *secular* view of historical reality as Theo Witvliet rightly discerns in *The Way of the Black Messiah: The Hermeneutical Challenge of Black Theology as a Theology of Liberation*, trans. John Bowden (London: SCM Press, 1987), 50. I would rather explore how the divine and human might be brought together. Does Jesus not show us a way of exercising authority in history that is radically different from the millenarianism that Moltmann is so right to reject? Is this not the way Paul sought to follow Jesus? For in deciding "to know nothing except Christ and him crucified" while teaching the triumphant Corinthians, the apostle claims that, in his own person, he effectively revealed "the Spirit's *power*" (1 Cor 2:2–5). Finding God in the Call of the

normativity or authenticity in history only to be sought in transcendence, in otherness, and in the eschatological redirection of history? Is the Gift and Call of life in all its fullness (including the gift of ourselves and not merely the call of the "other") not also suggestive of the way we are to make God present on earth? Moltmann's theology may honour God's relevant transcendence (and transcendent relevance), but what about God's immanent relevance?[175]

Ultimately, Moltmann's persistent tendency to see God's presence as an otherness we anticipate in hope rather than as the gift of life in the here and now that we may receive and even embody in gratitude is connected to his inability to affirm, unambiguously, that creation's present alienation from God lies in the cosmic impact of human sin and not in its ontological or temporal finitude. This has its roots in his view of creation taking place within God in the God-less space of the *nihil* (as discussed in 4.1 above). Prior to the annihilation of this Hell, God cannot be unambiguously revealed/incarnated in the foundational-creational direction not just because of the way our sin makes God absent (as I would argue) but because the world is founded on the withdrawal (*zimzum*) of God's presence.

Moltmann does want to speak of God in creation, but in his position, prior to the eschaton, God's inexhaustible fullness exists for the world only in a transcendental-eschatological sense. Creationally speaking, by contrast, divine plenitude as the wellspring of existence—what we might (for Moltmann) call God's exhaustible fullness—is kenotically poured out in time. This does provide a norm for human 'action' though hardly for the authority that Gen 1:26–28 would seem to envision. Divine *kenosis* is a model not for the shaping of history but for suffering, surrender, and hope in what is beyond our control.

And yet—and this is the paradox of the Christ event[176]—this self-surrender is what totally transforms history. "It was on the historical Golgotha that Christ triumphed," notes Moltmann, "not in the apocalyptic Armageddon. . . . It is on Golgotha that the coming God is present in history."[177] As Moltmann explains in *The Church in the Power of the Spirit*,

> If we trace the thought of the *sending* of the Son consistently to the end, we are bound to talk about God's vulnerability, suffering and pain, in view of Christ's

---

Other needs to play a role in the way we shape history. But this does not exhaust the Call of the Gift and Promise of Life. Cf. n. 167 above.

[175] Some might find it helpful to see God's immanent relevance in terms of God's transcendence in the foundational direction of time. To speak of God's (foundational) transcendence in this context has the merit of highlighting the fact that God is not exhausted in God's foundational-immanent presence. But I would still prefer to speak of the 'depths' of God's immanence, or of God's 'prescendence' in this context. Cf. n. 13 above.

[176] See the discussion in 4.3.1 above.

[177] Jürgen Moltmann, "Theology in the Project of Modernity," in *God for a Secular Society: The Public Relevance of Theology*, by Jürgen Moltmann, trans. Margaret Kohl (London: SCM Press, 1999), 18–19. (This essay is a later version of "Theology in the Project of the Modern World.")

passion, his death on the cross and his descent into hell. God experiences suffering, death and hell. *This is the way he experiences history.*

If we think in the direction of the *glorification*, then—in view of the resurrection, exaltation and perfection of Christ, and remembering the history of the Spirit—we must talk about God's joy . . . . *This is the way God creates history.*

God *experiences* history in order to *effect* history. He *goes out of himself* in order to *gather into himself.*[178]

Human hope and 'weakness' must be seen in this light, therefore. Our *kenosis* is the nature that grace prepares for the coming of God's glory. In our 'letting go', creation may 'make way' for the eschaton. In our surrender, the transience of the present age is finally revealed as the dawn of the Age to Come. Death and resurrection are thus two sides of the same coin.

Our dying or letting go might be seen as a dimension of our response to the gift of life made in the light of the promise of the life of the Age to Come. Does this mean that our surrender 'leads to' our new life? It is more accurate to say that, for Moltmann, the promise of new life empowers us to let go of our old life in hope. There is, in other words, a continuity between death and resurrection that is established eschatologically rather than historically. The surrender of life in hope is thus an eschatological response, an instance of our eschatologically graced nature being open to the coming of God's (and thus our) future as much as it is an act of historical *kenosis*. History, for Moltmann, does not *naturally* (and we might translate 'naturally' as 'historically') lead to the eschaton. In *grace*, however, the present age may be said to make way (or even pave the way) for the Age to Come.[179]

Given Marsden's description of Moltmann's opposition between transcendence and history as somewhat Barthian in character, it may be helpful to ask how Moltmann's position relates to the dynamics of the nature-grace relationship that come to the fore in the Barth-Brunner debate. In the foundational-creational direction, we might say, there is no "point of contact" between nature and grace for Moltmann. In this respect, he can be heard as eschatologising Karl Barth's "No!" to Emil Brunner. Thus Trevor Hart writes of Moltmann's theology,

> There is, then, a *contradiction* between that which characterizes the new creation and that which marks the old, between the promise and our experience of the present. This, we might note, is essentially the point which Barth was making in his notorious dispute with Emil Brunner over natural theology, albeit cast now in

---

[178] CPS, 63–64 as cited in 2.5 above (and also discussed in 2.6 and 4.3.1 above). My emphases.

[179] Cf. the comment near the end of 6.3 above, with references supplied in n. 123 above, that there is a sense in which even for Moltmann creation may be said to give birth to the kingdom of God.

terms of an eschatological framework.... There is no natural capacity for the new within the old.[180]

Moltmann signifies his agreement that there is an opposition between old and new in his theology whilst also qualifying Hart's analysis by entitling his response essay, "Hope and Reality: *Contradiction* and *Correspondence*." On the relationship between this world and the new creation, he writes,

> The continuity does not run from the old to the new, or from here to there, or from the past to the future; it runs from the new to the old, from there to here, and from the future to the past.[181]

Here, I suggest, Moltmann eschatologises Barth's claim that "The Holy Ghost ... does not stand in need of any point of contact but that which he himself creates."[182] In other words, he not only reinterprets Barth's "No!" to natural theology but also Barth's divine 'Yes' to creation, the embrace of nature by grace. There is no point of contact between nature and grace, but there is between grace and nature. The point of contact, "the continuity" or "correspondence" to use Moltmann's words, occurs in (or from) the eschatological direction of time.

In a truly history-affirming theology, continuity could (also) be affirmed in the foundational direction as the eschaton could be seen as the fulfilment of the Gift of creation. I have noted that Moltmann sometimes speaks of the creation as "promise" in precisely this way.[183] Creation, it seems, does not merely anticipate a future that is coming. It is itself a promise that will be fulfilled in glory. How does this fit with Moltmann's claim that the connection between this age and the next runs from the future to the past and from new to old? The

---

[180] Trevor Hart, "Imagination for the Kingdom of God? Hope, Promise, and the Transformative Power of an Imagined Future," in *God Will Be All in All: The Eschatology of Jürgen Moltmann*, ed. Richard Bauckham (Edinburgh: T. and T. Clark, 1999), 49–76. Quotation from p. 68. My emphasis. For Hart's interpretation of the Barth-Brunner debate, see his "The Capacity for Ambiguity: Revisiting the Barth-Brunner Debate," cited in n. 19 above. For a helpful account of the motif of contradiction in Moltmann's early work, see Jerry A. Irish, "Moltmann's Theology of Contradiction," *Theology Today* 32, no. 1 (July 1975): 21–31.

[181] Moltmann, "Hope and Reality: Contradiction and Correspondence," 77–85. My emphases added to the title. Quotation from p. 83. In the light of the passages cited in n. 123 above (cf. n. 179 above), I think that it is possible to stress the continuity in Moltmann's position more than Moltmann does himself here. Richard Bauckham and Trevor Hart in their discussion of this topic in *Hope against Hope: Christian Eschatology in Contemporary Context* (London: Darton, Longman, and Todd, 1999), refer with approval to Moltmann's claim in TH, 226 that the creation " 'cannot bear' " the new creation (cf. n. 123 above). With reference to Moltmann's mature thought, however, this needs to be relativised in my opinion.

[182] Barth, "No!," 121 as cited in 6.2 above.

[183] See the discussion of GC, 63 and GC, 207 in 6.3 above.

key to this question lies in yet another parallel that may be drawn between the theologies of Moltmann and Barth.

Moltmann's suggestion (discussed in 6.4 above) that we modify the second part of the mediaeval proposition "*gratia non destruit, sed praesupponit et perfecit naturam*," implies that he sees the first part of this formulation as essentially correct. It was Emil Brunner's claim, however, that Karl Barth's theology violated the proposition at precisely this point.[184] We do not need to decide between Barth and Brunner for the purposes of the present discussion. What we can say is that Barth is vulnerable to this kind of accusation (at least in his writings from this early period). For example, Edwyn Hoskyns translates Barth as claiming at one point in his *Epistle to the Romans*, that in being confronted by the righteousness of God, "We stand ... before an irresistible dissolution of the world of time and things and men, before a penetrating and ultimate KRISIS, before the supremacy of a negation by which all existence is rolled up."[185] It is this kind of language that Brunner probably has in mind.

The parallel with Moltmann becomes evident when we realise that negation is not God's last word to creation in Barth's theology as the "No!" is in the service of the divine 'Yes!'. Nature is paradoxically embraced by grace. Clifford Green's comments on the passage just cited are helpful in this respect. He notes,

> Here and elsewhere Hoskyns translates with "dissolution" Barth's *Aufhebung*. Hegel used this term, with its opposite popular meanings of destroy and preserve, in his dialectic. In Barth it means not only negation, dissolution, but also overcoming and transcending. Theologically Barth thinks of the logic of justification by grace, of the negation and affirmation of the gospel of cross and resurrection.[186]

Whether this invalidates Brunner's accusation, or whether it simply requires that he modify his critique is a question we can leave to one side. What is most interesting is that Moltmann uses the same double meaning in relation to his claim that creation "is the real promise of the kingdom of God" and as such

---

[184] Brunner makes this claim in "Nature and Grace," 21 (citing a slightly different wording: "*gratia non tollit naturam sed perficit*") and confronts this by stressing the restorative nature of redemption in pp. 33–35. Barth rejects this reading of his theology, while also asserting in "No!," 93, that the creation (or nature) is hardly to be seen as a motor car that can (i.e., that has the capacity to) be repaired.

[185] Barth, *The Epistle to the Romans*, 91, commenting on Rom 3:21, 22a.

[186] Green, ed., *Karl Barth: Theologian of Freedom*, 335n32. His italics. He continues, "cp. his discussion in CD 1/2, Par. 16, 'The Revelation of God as the *Aufhebung* of religion,' where the German word is misleading if translated simply as 'abolition.' " His italics. Brunner, of course, prior to his debate with Barth, would have read *The Epistle to the Romans* (the second edition of which had appeared more than ten years earlier in 1922) in German. But it is still understandable that such a nuance could be missed, or thought to be absent. (The German original of *Church Dogmatics* 1/2 was not published until 1938, but is still indicative of Barth's thought and terminology at the time of the Barth-Brunner debate.)

"belongs to the history of the kingdom."[187] Ironically, where attention to the meaning(s) of *Aufhebung* and its cognates makes Barth's opposition of nature and grace appear less damning, it makes Moltmann's apparently creation-affirming statements questionable.

Moltmann's language makes it sound as if the *futurum* of history and the *adventus* of the eschaton are ultimately the same future. It sounds as if the kingdom is the realisation of the Gift—the grace—of creation, thus implying a continuity from past to present, old to new. But the way grace affirms, fulfils, and perfects nature here involves negation.[188] Positively Moltmann writes, "The promise is *caught up and absorbed in its fulfilment* [wird . . . aufgehoben]." Yet he immediately adds, "when what has been promised is realised, the promise is *discarded* [abgetan]."[189]

"[A]t the end of this history," writes Moltmann, "the world as creation . . . is destined to be revealed in its eternal transfiguration."[190] Read in the light of the basic structure of Moltmann's theology, the gift of creation—"creation as the real promise of the kingdom"—may be seen as coming, or being brought, *to fulfilment* in glory in the *eschatological* direction even as creation as promise comes *to an end* in the *historical* direction. Creation is taken up into New Creation for evermore. Creation finally makes way for New Creation. The eternal transfiguration thus reveals an eschatological continuity between new and old and a historical discontinuity between old and new.

Creation, therefore, does and does not have a future. The nature-grace relationship in Moltmann's theology is as complex as it is paradoxical:

Gratia (non) destruit, sed praesupponit et perfecit naturam.

6.6 The Gift of Transience

The eclipse of creation in Moltmann's eschatology is most evident in the way the "eternal transfiguration" that permanently fills the primordial void also marks the final annihilation of transience.[191] As I have argued that Moltmann's

---

[187] GC, 63 as cited as discussed in 2.5 above.
[188] On fulfilment/negation, see 3.1 and 4.2 above.
[189] GC, 63 [*GS*, 77]. My emphases. See the fuller citation and discussion in 2.5 above.
[190] GC, 63.
[191] See 3.2 and 4.1 above. Miroslav Volf, in "After Moltmann: Reflections on the Future of Eschatology," in *God Will Be All in All: The Eschatology of Jürgen Moltmann*, ed. Richard Bauckham (Edinburgh: T. and T. Clark, 1999), 241n13, defends Moltmann from Catherine Keller's claim, in her *Apocalypse Now and Then: A Feminist Guide to the End of the World* (Boston: Beacon, 1996), 18, that Moltmann's eschatology advocates not only the end of injustice but the end of "finitude itself." With respect to temporal finitude, she certainly has a point (although Volf's reference to CoG, 265 does call for some nuancing here). The "eternal transfiguration [ewigen Verklärung]" (GC, 63 [*GS*, 77]) is compatible with " 'eternal time' [ewiger Zeit]" (GC, 213 [*GS*, 220], cf. 2.4, 3.1, 3.5.1) but not with ongoing transience. In the eternal time of the eschaton, there will be "change without transience [Veränderung ohne Vergehen]" according to GC, 213 [*GS*, 220], a passage cited in 3.1 and discussed in 3.2 above. Given the nuances of

view of grace is related to his philosophy of time, we shall draw this chapter to a close by asking whether a vision of creational grace can offer us an alternative vision of transience as a gift that has a real, ongoing future in the Age to Come.[192]

We should begin, I suggest, with the recognition that the *gift* and *promise* of life is the *call* to embrace our *finitude*. When Gen 2:7 tells us that God formed Adam from the dust and breathed into his nostrils, this does not mean that human beings are made up of two substances. The point is that our very existence is a gift/promise that comes to us from before ourselves and from beyond ourselves. In the act of breathing, we receive the breath of God and the Spirit of life. To grasp at our existence in autonomy is as foolish as holding our breath. 'In ourselves' we can have no more life than the dust (cf. Eccl 3:20). We must depend on and draw life from what is outside. But there is even more to our existence than receiving the gift of life and responding to the call to live. Because the gift is finite, because all gifts have limits that are themselves part of the gift, we must also let go. To live, we must not only be prepared to breathe in, but to breathe out, confident that the gift will be renewed.

Because the continuous change and changing continuity of our selves—the mystery of our identity—is not founded in a fixed essence deep within us nor in a realm beyond the ravages of time but in the gift and promise of who we are (to be), because the gift, promise, and calling of our existence from heaven can never be exhausted in our earthly response—including even the fleshing-out of our redeemed selves in the resurrection—, it follows that the letting go of our lives, the passing through of certain unrepeatable stages of life (at the right time), the dying and passing away that is an unavoidable characteristic of time, is not to be feared. This is part of the very dynamics of existence. Now and in the Age to Come.

History does not come to an end in the eschaton. Differentiation and integration—which are, normatively speaking, two sides of the same coin[193]—will continue. How might we imagine this? Here a biblical pattern may be

---

Moltmann's all-embracing eschatological monism, speaking of the "annihilation" of transience (as I do here) might be seen as overly negative. One might claim that Moltmann's vision of "change without transience" describes a state in which 'God's good gift of transience' is taken up into the fullness of time. Consequently transience is no longer "without" or 'outwith' (outside) the dynamic change of eternal life. It has a future 'within' change and 'as' change. This is a valid reading, in my view. But although it is conceived within a monistic vision, the "without" is still a negation. Temporal finitude, in losing its autonomy and independence from God, loses its identity 'with' God. The redemption *of* time is, in this respect, a redemption *from* time.

[192] Cf. Richard Bauckham's comment in his "Eschatology in *The Coming of God*," in *God Will Be All in All: The Eschatology of Jürgen Moltmann*, ed. Richard Bauckham (Edinburgh: T. and T. Clark, 1999), 12, "In assessing Moltmann's eschatology, it needs to be considered whether transience cannot be evaluated in a more discriminating way." See also his discussion in his later contribution to the same volume, "Time and Eternity," 155–226, especially 186. My re-evaluation of transience differs from his.

[193] Dooyeweerd stressed this in his philosophy of history. See 5.2.5n98 above.

instructive. If we read Gen 2 in the light of Gen 1:28, the four rivers flowing from the centre of Eden beyond the Garden (Gen 2:10–14) indicate that Adam and Eve and their descendants were called to take the Gift/Call of Life beyond Paradise to the ends of the earth in the course of history. *Eden* was thus established as a microcosm of and for the *creation* (a role taken over by the Promised Land in the unfolding of redemption[194]). When the present creation is finally purged of evil in the coming of God's Kingdom, I suggest, creation-as-the-earth may be seen as an Eden in relation to the creation-as-the-entire-(macro-)*cosmos*.[195]

With the dawn of the eschaton, history, in the full cosmic sense, will have barely begun. Paul speaks of us being transformed 'from glory to glory' (2 Cor 3:18[196]), suggesting an ongoing process. As I have already suggested in 6.4 above, this is intimately related to the human task of reflecting the glory of God that shines in the darkness of Gen 1:3 so that the light might, in our authentic shaping of history, fill all things in every way (cf. Gen 1:28; 1 Cor 15:28; and Eph 1:22–23).[197] Ultimately, therefore, "all things" may thus be taken as referring to the cosmos as a whole. If glory is itself a historical category, then so is fulfilment.[198] In this sense, we could speak of multiple eschata or, alternatively, we could picture the arrival of the eschaton, which marks the historical end of evil, as the coming of a New Creation that itself is eschatologically open. Because within the covenantal dynamics of life, there will still be a distinction between heaven and earth (cf. 6.1.1 above), there will continue to be more to the *gift* of life than the *given* and more to the *promise* of life than what may be fully *realised*.

I have already briefly reflected on the eschatological significance of sabbath in 5.3 above. One of the themes that connects sabbath as a creational and as a redemptive motif in the Scriptures is the way this 'day' consistently marks an ending that is itself a new beginning. God's sabbath rest in Gen 1 which brings God's initial work of creation to a close marks (a transition to) the beginning of

---

[194] In 9.4 below, I am in effect suggesting that the New Jerusalem of Rev 21–22 also plays this role as there is still a mission to the sinners and the nations beyond its gates (cf. 21:24 and 22:2).

[195] It would, I think, be facile to dismiss this as a science-fiction fantasy, because science fiction fantasies (facile or otherwise), together with the 'space race' of the 1960s, might be seen as reflecting a sense of calling in relation to a cosmos that is (as far as we know) uninhabited. What is the relation of this vast space to God's (and our) future? There is no reason why this cannot be a serious theological question.

My suggestion that there will be a cosmic outworking of the human task to fill the earth with God's glory (Gen 1:28), a task that, though it cannot be reduced to it, clearly includes reproduction, might seem at odds with Jesus's claim that we shall be "like the angels" with respect to marriage in the Age to Come. But see my "Commentary: Luke 20:27–36," 22 (in the light of 6.1.1 above).

[196] This is to translate the phrase literally.

[197] See n. 124 above.

[198] If we say that we lead a 'fulfilled' life, we do not mean that it can't change or get better. We most probably mean that life is 'fulfilling' in an ongoing way.

humanity's work as created co-creators, for example. Similarly, the sabbatical significance of Israel's exodus from Egypt in Deut 5:12–15 marks the end of slavery and the birth of a people. Likewise, the "year of the Lord's favour" (Isa 61:2 and Luke 4:19) signifies the end of exile and the beginning of the New Creation. The eschatological sabbath should, I suggest, be seen in the same light. Although the exegetical argument is my own, this is an idea close to Moltmann's heart. To cite the opening sentence to *The Coming of God*: "*In the end is the beginning.*"[199]

In a truly creation-affirming eschatology and in a truly eschatological view of creation, there is no need for transience to become a thing of the past when God's Kingdom arrives (and continues to arrive) in all its fullness.[200] Communally, individually, and globally, time will be experienced fully as it will be experienced without fear. The temporal differentiation of letting-go and the temporal integration of anticipating and remembering will be experienced together as the passing, coming, and abiding rhythms of the Spirit of life. The life of the Age to Come (contrary to Moltmann's predictions) can be envisioned as an age of "change *with* transience, time *with* the past, and [in this sense] life *with* death."[201] The hope of the New Creation of Heaven and Earth is that we will be so empowered to embrace our finitude and (thus) so embraced by the ongoing creational and eschatological grace of God that our transience need never come to an end.[202]

---

[199] CoG, ix. His emphasis. Cf. CoG, xi: "... I have deliberately avoided calling this book about Christian eschatology 'The Last Things' or 'The End of All Things', but have given it the title: *The Coming of God*. In God's creative future, the end will become the beginning, and the true creation is still to come and is ahead of us." His emphasis. Cf. Moltmann's more recent work, IEB.

Old Testament/Hebrew Bible scholars disagree about whether the phrase translated in the KJV as "These are the generations of the heavens and the earth . . . ." in Gen 2:4a is an *epilogue* to the opening account of creation, thus forming an *inclusio* with Gen 1:1 (thus e.g., J.P. Fokkelman, *Reading Biblical Narrative: An Introductory Guide*, trans. Ineke Smit (Louisville, KY: Westminster John Knox Press, 1999), 124) or an *introduction* to what the heavens and the earth bring forth in history (in line with the way the *toledoth* (begetting/generating) formula functions as a heading/introduction in every other occurrence in Genesis (5:1; 6:9; 10:1; 11:10; 11:27; 25:12; 36:1; and 37:2, as Fokkelman notes on 158–59). Given the close textual association between Gen 2:4a and the sabbath of the previous verse, it is worth considering whether this phrase functions as both an ending and beginning simultaneously.

[200] Thus I would resist Moltmann's attempt to affirm ongoing history without affirming ongoing transience in CoG, xi: "[W]hat is called the end of history is also simply the end of *temporal* history and the beginning of the *eternal* history of life." My emphases.

[201] See GC, 213 as cited in 3.1 above. The original contains a threefold "without" rather than my emphatic "with"!

[202] For a positive reading of the references to transience in Ecclesiastes, which are typically translated/interpreted negatively as references to vanity, see Jacques Ellul, *Reason for Being: A Meditation on Ecclesiastes*, trans. Joyce Main Hanks (Grand Rapids, MI: Eerdmans, 1990). Cf. Norbert Lohfink, *Qohelet*. Continental Commentary Series, trans. Sean McEvenue (Minneapolis, MN: Fortress Press, 2003).

CHAPTER 7

Doing Justice (According) to Scripture

A central aim of this study has been to ascertain whether the view of universal salvation that Moltmann has developed is sufficiently robust and nuanced to stimulate widespread interest and enjoy widespread respect not only within mainstream Protestant theology but also within the wider Christian community (0.7, 1.5, 4.3, and 5.0). Any formulation of universalism that could win such respect would be quite the achievement. The ease with which one can draw up a long list of Church councils that have condemned universal salvation and have declared those who advocate it to be 'anathema' illustrates its heterodox nature in the judgment of those who have wielded ecclesiastical power down the ages.[1] Today, it is fair to say that the many Christians who do not find this position objectionable nevertheless find it highly implausible. The hope that universal salvation could be widely considered a genuine Christian theological option seems incredible. Yet this study has been undertaken in the conviction that Moltmann's contribution to developing a viable universalism is such that this is at least not unthinkable.

In 1.5 above, I noted that the main reasons given for rejecting a universalist interpretation of salvation is that such a position invariably and inevitably undermines freedom, justice, and Scripture. In the light of such objections, Moltmann's understanding of both divine and human freedom has therefore been given considerable attention in the above discussion (see 1.4.2, 4.3, 4.3.1, 4.3.2, 4.3.3, 4.4, 6.3, and 6.4 above). Although we have made a preliminary investigation into Moltmann's attention to the issue of justice and the authority of Scripture (see 1.4.3 and 1.4.5 above), these topics require further examination and will be the focus of the present chapter. First we will explore some exegetical considerations with the aim of removing a central 'biblical' objection to Moltmann's proposals. Then we shall explore his vision of what the 'Final Judgment' actually is (as opposed to what it is not).

The 'dialogical' approach of previous chapters will also be employed in the present discussion. Given the strong connections in subject matter between this and chapter 1, it is fitting that, in 7.1 below, we should explore the New Testament scholarship of N.T. Wright as he was a major contributor to *The*

---

[1] For such listings, see Bauckham, "Universalism: A Historical Survey," 49–50; Morey, *Death and the Afterlife*, 233–34; and Walker, *The Decline of Hell*, 21–23.

Mystery of Salvation, the Anglican work examined at the beginning of this present study.[2] On the nature of the Final Judgment, in 7.2 below, we shall pay close attention to the work of Miroslav Volf, a former doctoral and postdoctoral student of Moltmann who has provided important commentary on his eschatology.[3] In our concluding section, 7.3, we shall bring the thinking of Moltmann and Volf on the 'social' or interpersonal dimension of the Final Judgment into conversation with some passages from the book of Genesis that do not usually feature in our discussions of eschatology. We shall take as a point of departure a contemporary reading of Isa 60 by neo-Kuyperian theologian Brian Walsh.[4]

To ask whether Moltmann's universalist position undermines or promotes a commitment to Justice and to Scripture is not to judge his theology by criteria that are extraneous to his own concerns. In the penultimate paragraph of an essay entitled "My Theological Career," he writes,

> If I were to attempt to sum up the outline of my theology in a few key phrases, I would have at the least to say that I am attempting to reflect on a theology which has:
> – a biblical foundation,
> – an eschatological orientation,
> – a political responsibility.[5]

Whether Moltmann's "eschatological orientation" eclipses or complements a 'creational grace' that would help his case for universal salvation has been central to the analysis of his philosophy of time in chapters 2 and 3 and to the discussion of the nature-grace relationship in chapters 4, 5, and 6. The issue of "political responsibility" will be discussed in 7.2 below where it will be related to Moltmann's vision of a Final Judgment in which "the executioners will not finally triumph over their victims" and in which "the victims will not triumph over their executioners."[6] But first we must turn our attention to the issue of "a biblical foundation."

7.1 A Biblical Foundation?

Given that any universalist understanding of salvation faces the considerable intellectual challenge of being simultaneously persuasive within the conflicting paradigms of Arminian and Calvinist theology (see 4.3 above), Moltmann's position has the distinct advantage of being rooted not in a theoretical argument so much as in a confessional claim: universal salvation is what the God who is

---

[2] See *The Mystery of Salvation*, as examined in 1.2 and 1.3 above.
[3] See Volf, "After Moltmann: Reflections on the Future of Eschatology."
[4] Walsh has also provided an important analysis of Moltmann's thinking. See Walsh, "Theology of Hope and the Doctrine of Creation," referred to in 0.7n37, 3.4n158, 5.3n113, 6.1n6, and 6.5n168 above and 8.3n27 below.
[5] Moltmann, "My Theological Career," in HTG, 182. Cf. 1.5n166 above.
[6] CrG, 178 as cited in 1.1 above.

revealed in Christ has promised to bring about. As a theology of—or as a theology centred in—the cross (see 1.4.1, 4.3.1, and 4.4), all questions of conceptual coherence are relativised—and as such related—to what is revealed to us in and through Christ's "descent into Hell" (as explored in 1.3, 1.4.1, 4.1, and 4.3.1). Whether (in some sense) God *has to* save all people is secondary; God is revealed as the God who *will* save all people. Whether we can *explain* how all might willingly respond to God's grace is not crucial; this is the future that is revealed to us. Christian theological reflection, Moltmann can claim, has no right to judge whether or not this revelation and this hope is acceptable. This is theology's true starting point.

In the light of this fundamental appeal to revelation, the question of a biblical foundation looms large. How can Moltmann's *Christocentric* vision of universal salvation deal with a *Christ* whose words form what is probably the main biblical *challenge* to his position, a *Christ* whose words would seem to *refute* the idea that Hell (whether annihilative or the source of ongoing torment) will itself be annihilated and will thus not be God's final word to anyone? Moltmann might be able to deal with other biblical objections to his universalism by appealing to a Christocentric reading of Scripture. But this hermeneutical strategy is double-edged as it undercuts any attempt to relativise Jesus' own preaching with reference to 'Hell'. Because this biblical material highlights a very significant, perhaps fatal, weak-point in Moltmann's position, it will be the focus of our attention.

Before we (re-)examine Moltmann's answer,[7] let us look at the texts in question. If we take the *New International Version* as our initial guide, we find fourteen specific references to "[H]ell," all of which are in the New Testament. This is one more than may be found in the *New Revised Standard Version*. If we focus on texts that are normally thought to have a 'final' judgment in view,[8]

---

[7] For an earlier examination, see 1.4.5 above.

[8] I have chosen the NIV in this section not only because it has more references to "hell" than translations that are more popular with scholars, such as the NRSV, but because it tends to reflect a conservative evangelical theology/eschatology that a successful universalism would have to address exegetically. Cf. 9.0n1 below. For some misgivings about the NIV as a translation in addition to what follows, cf. 0.7n38 above.

The three references to "hell" in which a 'final' judgment is not the focus are 2 Pet 2:4–9, which refers to a verbal form of *tartaros* (Tartarus); Luke 16:23, which refers to *hadēs* (Hades); and Jas 3:6, which refers to *géenna* (Gehenna).

The first of these, 2 Pet 2:4–9, is of no direct relevance to the final judgment of human beings. The thrust of this passage is that "the Lord is well able to rescue the good from their trials, and hold the wicked for their punishment until the Day of Judgment (v. 9, NJB)" (or more literally 'until a day of judgment'). (For arguments that an intermediate punishment is not to be inferred from the Greek as some translators have thought (cf. NIV), see Richard J. Bauckham, *Jude, 2 Peter*. Word Biblical Commentary 50 (Waco: Word, 1983), 253–54.). If his readers are "the good" or "the godly," the false teachers of v. 3 are "the wicked." That they will not be spared judgment is illustrated from the fate of three groups: the wicked at the Flood, those who perished in the destruction of Sodom and Gomorrah, and—in the verse that, according to translators,

eleven remain (as in the NRSV), seven to be found in Matthew's Gospel (Matt 5:22, 29, 30; 10:28; 18:9; 23:15, 33), the other four being parallel texts (three

---

contains the reference to "hell"—the angels whom "God did not spare . . . when they sinned, but sent them to hell, putting them in gloomy dungeons to be held for judgment" (v. 4, NIV). This alludes to the story of the Watchers, which was an intertestamental interpretation of Gen 6:1–4 found in 1 Enoch (a book which has influenced 2 Pet probably via Jude [see Bauckham, *Jude, 2 Peter*, 138–50]). At best, this reference in 2 Pet is to the temporary detention of non-human beings. "Hell" is a very poor translation of (the verbal form of) *tartaros* (*contra* NIV and NRSV), a word that is better rendered literally as 'thrown into Tartarus'. The NJB has "the underworld" here. The very similar passage in Jude 6 merely speaks of the angels being "under gloom" or "in darkness" (NIV).

The only time the NIV translates the Greek *hadēs* as "hell" is in Luke 16:23. For similar reasons to 2 Pet 2:4, this text is also quite irrelevant to the task at hand, despite its widespread use by defenders of hell-fire. When it occurs in the LXX, *hadēs* is "almost always" a translation of the Hebrew *Sheol* (see Joachim Jeremias, "*Hades*," in *The Theological Dictionary of the New Testament*, ed. Gerhard Kittel, trans. G. Bromiley (Grand Rapids, MI: Eerdmans, 1964), 1:146–49; cf. Richard Bauckham, "Hades, Hell," in *The Anchor Bible Dictionary*, ed. David Noel Freedman (New York: Doubleday, 1992), 3:14–15; and Bauckham, "Descent to the Underworld," in *The Anchor Bible Dictionary*, ed. David Noel Freedman (New York: Doubleday, 1992), 2:145–59). These connotations are carried into the New Testament, where the word means the grave, the abode of the dead, and the power of death. Matt 11:23 thus speaks of Capernaum following the fate of Sodom and Gomorrah by going down "to the depths" (NIV). Matt 16:18 says that the gates of Hades will not prevail against the Church. The keys of death and Hades are given to Christ in Rev 1:18 and eventually Hades is thrown into the lake of fire in Rev 20:14. The parable of Lazarus and the rich man in Luke 16: 19–31 presupposes familiarity with popular Jewish ideas about the 'intermediate state'. The veracity of these ideas is not the focus of the story (contrary to the way it has been used by those on either side of the everlasting punishment-annihilationism debate). The point of the parable is to issue a warning to the Pharisees "who loved money" (v. 14) and who are thus challenged to stop assuming that they and not the beggars are children of Abraham (vv. 22–23). In Abraham's words to the rich man, Jesus is calling them, here and now, to pay attention to what the Law and the Prophets are really saying (compare vv. 16–17 and v. 29). The implication is that, "even if someone rises from the dead" (v. 31), they will not repent. Neither Lazarus nor the rich man have undergone the Final Judgment. Bauckham, in "Hades, Hell," 14, notes that *hadēs* is "sometimes, but *misleadingly*, translated 'hell' in English versions of the NT." My emphasis. The NIV avoids making this error (found so frequently in the KJV) in all but this verse. Presumably, the traditional link between this passage and the fate of the unrepentant was thought to be well-founded. The NJB and the NRSV, however, wisely offer a transliteration. The revision of the NIV, *Today's New International Version* (TNIV), also has "Hades."

Finally, we come to Jas 3:6, where we read, "The tongue . . . is a fire, a world of evil among the parts of the body. It corrupts the whole person, sets the whole course of his life on fire, and is itself set on fire by [Gehenna]." The connection between Gehenna, evil, and fire will be discussed below. What distinguishes this text from the other references to Gehenna in the NT is that it is not linked to a coming judgment. Thus it too can be ignored for our purposes.

occurring in Mark 9:43–7 and one in Luke 12:5). All of these references to "[H]ell" are found on the lips of Jesus.

In the following listing, I have cited the NIV unless otherwise stated, substituting "[Gehenna]" (*géenna* being the Greek original) for "hell" for reasons that will be discussed below.

In Matt 5:22, having warned his listeners that they must surpass the righteousness of the Pharisees or else they "will certainly not enter the kingdom of heaven," (v. 20), Jesus says,

> ... anyone who is angry with his brother will be subject to judgment. Again, anyone who says to his brother, 'Raca' is answerable to the Sanhedrin. [Again], anyone who says, 'You fool!' will be in danger of the fire of [Gehenna].[9]

In Matt 5:29–30, which is part of the same discourse, Jesus warns his audience,

> If your right eye causes you to sin, gouge it out and throw it away. It is better for you to lose one part of your body than for your whole body to be thrown into [Gehenna]. And if your right hand causes you to sin, cut it off and throw it away. It is better for you to lose one part of your body than for your whole body to go into [Gehenna].

Mark 9:43–47, which parallels this passage, contains the three references to Gehenna found in that gospel. Differences in the Markan version include: (i) a threefold parallel between the hand (v. 43), the foot (v. 45), and the eye (v. 47); (ii) a contrast between "entering life" and "going into [Gehenna]" in the first example, "entering life" and being "thrown into [Gehenna]" in the second, and "entering the kingdom of God" and being "thrown into [Gehenna]" in the third; (iii) the addition of "into the unquenchable fire" after "into [Gehenna]" in v. 44; (iv) the description of Gehenna as a place where, in the language of Isa 66:24, "their worm does not die, and the fire is not put out" in v. 48 (and in vv. 44 and 46 in some manuscripts that the NIV, like the NRSV, doesn't follow); and (v) the additional saying in v. 49, "Everyone will be salted with fire."

In Matt 10:28, in the context of commissioning of the disciples to take the message of the kingdom to Israel, and warning them that this is a task that will provoke persecution (v. 22) and will not be complete before the coming of the Son of Man (v. 23), Jesus tells the twelve,

> Do not be afraid of those who kill the body but cannot kill the soul. Rather, be afraid of the [o]ne who can destroy both body and soul in [Gehenna].

The one occurrence of Gehenna in Luke is located in the parallel passage found in Luke 12:4–5, where just after a warning about the Pharisees (v. 1) and just before a reference to the Son of Man (v. 8), Jesus tells a crowd of many thousands,

---

[9] The second "Again" is my own, replacing the unwarranted "But" of the NIV that masks the parallelism. The TNIV has "And" here (cf. NRSV).

> ... do not be afraid of those who kill the body and after that can do no more. But I will show you whom you should fear: Fear him who, after the killing of the body, has power to throw you into [Gehenna].

Matt 18:9 repeats 5:29 but with the contrast that we find in Mark 9:45 between "entering life" and being "thrown into [Gehenna]," here expanded to "the fire of [Gehenna]." This parallels 18:8 in which those with two hands and two feet are "thrown into eternal fire" (*to pur to aiōnion*).

In Matt 23:15, in a long discourse in critique of Israel's leaders, Jesus says to the teachers of the law and the Pharisees, "you travel over land and see to win a single convert, and when he becomes one, you make him twice as much a son of [Gehenna] as you are." In v. 33, the same leaders, who have just been described as the descendants of those who murdered the prophets (v. 32), are asked, "How will you escape from being condemned to [Gehenna]?"

How does Moltmann interpret such material within his universalist paradigm? As we have seen in 1.4.5 above, he would seem to argue that these texts are "penultimate"[10] and thus do not reveal God's 'final' dealings with unrepentant sinners. The "temporal No" of judgment must be relativised by God's "etern[al] ... Yes" of "everlasting ... grace."[11] As he offers no exegetical arguments for such a conclusion, however, he is very vulnerable to the accusation that he is simply domesticating this material by relativising it within a theological schema. While his critics might concede that interpreting the passages in question within a prior framework is hard to avoid, the concern here is that he is imposing a theological schema onto the biblical givens in order to secure what is (to him) an acceptable conclusion. Put bluntly, the Scriptures—and the biblical Jesus of the gospels—are not being allowed any real authority over his theological framework.

---

[10] CoG, 242, as discussed in 1.4.2 above.

[11] CoG, 243 as cited and discussed in 4.3.2 above. In his foreword to Robert Thomas Cornelison, *The Christian Realism of Reinhold Niebuhr and the Political Theology of Jürgen Moltmann in Dialogue* (San Francisco: Mellen Research University Press, 1992), iv, Moltmann writes,

> Christian Realism emphasizes the transcendence of God and his JUDGMENT against this sinful world. This is indeed correct. But the judgment of God is always only a precursor of the *kingdom of God*, because, in a prophetic and apocalyptic sense, the justice of God in the world will become the foundation for the new world of God. The judgment of God is, in an eschatological sense, only temporary. The last word is: "See, I make all things new." (Revelation 21:5). The NO of God to injustice, sin, and death, serves, following a biblical interpretation, the YES of God to all creatures whom he has created out of love and therefore will also redeem. One who simply stops with the eschatological understanding of the judgment of God as *finis historiae*, stops too quickly. One needs to go a bit further in order to discover the *telos mundi* in the new creation of all things.

His emphases and italics. Despite this reference to "a biblical interpretation," as stated, this is a *theological* argument not an *exegetical* one.

Furthermore, many if not all of the Gehenna texts attributed to Jesus would seem to exemplify the "penal law of retaliation" that he finds so unworthy of the Gospel. Can the Christ of the Bible be at odds with Moltmann's "christological" approach to Scripture?[12] It would seem as though Moltmann has no alternative than to declare these words of Jesus to be inauthentic.[13] His options appear limited: either recalcitrant, particularist material is subsumed within a universalist paradigm that is imposed on the text, or else a canon within the canon is invoked in order to judge offensive sayings attributed to Jesus as being without authority. Whether Moltmann is happy to draw such conclusions is unclear. That others will see such conclusions as implicit in his writings to date seems unavoidable. As things stand, unless Moltmann can qualify what he has written, his lack of a persuasive biblical foundation for his position—a foundation that minimally cannot be read as being in opposition to the words of Jesus—renders his case for universal salvation radically implausible to much of Christendom (including many of its theologians).

In my opinion, what looks like an Achilles heel is not a fatal weakness as there are plausible *exegetical*, rather than *theological*, arguments that can be made in favour of a "penultimate" reading of the judgment these texts announce. Although the following line of interpretation is indicative of my own approach to the exegesis of the apocalyptic material found in the gospels and in other parts of the New Testament, these reflections are offered here to indicate one way in which Moltmann's argument might be supplemented.

To begin to understand the passages from the gospels, we need to explore what Gehenna might have meant to Jesus' followers and opponents. Lloyd Bailey argues that we can distinguish three ways the word is used in Jewish literature prior to and around the time of the New Testament: "as an ordinary

---

[12] On the "penal law of retaliation," see WJC, 337. See also 1.4.5 and 1.4.3 above and 7.2 below. For this in relation to Moltmann's "christological" view of biblical authority, see Moltmann, "The Liberation of the Future and its Anticipations in History," 272n13, where Moltmann says, with reference to contemporary "*Armageddon eschatology*." His emphasis.
> This dualistic apocalyptic about the final struggle between Christ and Antichrist can be detected in the biblical writings. But *is it Christian, in the christological sense of the word*? It seems to reflect Manichaean influence, rather than to be an expression of the hope founded on the raising of the crucified Christ.

My Emphasis. If one wishes to emphasise that "A christology of the way of Christ will always interpret his way in the light of his goal" (WJC, xv), then one might relativise the Jesus of the gospels, and his teaching, to his own "future" (WJC, xiv). But if the Jesus of the gospels *fails to anticipate* (our view of) Jesus' own future, this is surely a sign that we are no longer developing a *christologia viae*.

[13] To the best of my knowledge, he does not explicitly do this with any of the texts listed above. Although he sees the "penal law of retaliation" as 'apocalyptic' and sub-Christian in character (see the previous note), it is interesting that he provides a positive, yet decidedly non-apocalyptic, reading of Matt 24:1–14 in "The Return of Christ," in *The Gospel of Liberation*, by Jürgen Moltmann, trans. H. Wayne Pipkin (Waco, TX: Word, 1973), 105–12.

geographical location in Jerusalem; as an extraordinary place of punishment for the wicked, located in the area of Jerusalem; and as an otherworldly place of punishment for the wicked after death."[14] Exegesis has tended to assume that the third meaning (found in the rabbinic tradition) is present in the words of Jesus (or in the Evangelists' portrayal[s] of his teaching). I will argue that the second meaning is the one intended.

The earliest biblical references to Gehenna view it as a geographical place. It is simply the valley (of the son[s]) of Hinnom, or *gê hinnōm* (see Josh 15:8 and 18:16; cf. Neh 11:30). Modern geographers identify this either with the valley just east of the walls of ancient Jerusalem (the Wadi Kidron) or just to the west (the Wadi er-Rababi) or, finally, with the valley just to the south of the Old City (the Wadi en-Nar) where the other two valleys come together.[15]

In Jer 7:30–34, however, this valley is no longer a piece of real estate that anyone would want to own, having now become a place associated with judgment—imminent, historical judgment directed against Israel. Thus we read:

> The people of Judah have done evil in my eyes, declares the Lord. They have set up detestable idols in the house that bears my Name and have defiled it. They have built the high places of Topheth[16] in the Valley of Ben Hinnom to burn their sons and daughters in the fire—something I did not command, nor did it enter my mind. So beware, the days are coming, declares the Lord, when people will no longer call it Topheth or the Valley of Ben Hinnom, but the Valley of Slaughter, for they will bury the dead in Topheth until there is no more room. Then the carcasses of the people will become food for the birds of the air and the beasts of the earth, and there will be no one to frighten them away. I will bring an end to the sounds of joy and gladness and to the voices of bride and bridegroom in the towns of Judah and the streets of Jerusalem, for the land will become desolate.

---

[14] Lloyd R. Bailey, "Gehenna: The Topography of Hell," *Biblical Archaeologist* 49, no. 3 (September 1986): 187–91. Quotation from p. 187. The following discussion draws on much of this lucid article, except where I depart from his interpretation of NT material as stated. The third position he identifies can be found in the rabbinic tradition. As Bo Reicke, "Gehenna," in *The Oxford Companion to the Bible*, ed. Bruce M. Metzger and Michael D. Coogan (Oxford: Oxford University Press, 1993), 243, notes: "In the Mishnah and later rabbinic texts, the name Gehenna . . . has superseded the older terms for underworld (Sheol)."

[15] See Bailey, "Gehenna," 187–88. Cf. Stephen Von Wyrick, "Gehenna," in *Eerdmans Dictionary of the Bible*, ed. David Noel Freedman, Allen C. Myers, and Astrid B. Beck (Grand Rapids, MI: Eerdmans, 2000), 489 and Richard A. Spencer, "Hinnom, Valley of," in *Eerdmans Dictionary of the Bible*, ed. David Noel Freedman, Allen C. Myers, and Astrid B. Beck (Grand Rapids, MI: Eerdmans, 2000), 592.

[16] As noted by Brian P. Irwin, "Topheth," in *Eerdmans Bible Dictionary*, ed. David Noel Freedman, Myers, and Astrid B. Beck (Grand Rapids, MI: Eerdmans, 2000), 1321, Topheth was probably "at the lower end of the Hinnom valley close to the southern tip of the City of David." Its name may derive from the consonants of the Aramaic word for 'fireplace' combined with the vowels from the Hebrew word for 'shame'.

Similar language is used in Jer 19, where an imminent siege of Jerusalem is prophesied in response to Israel's idolatry. The references to burning sons and daughters in the fire (see Jer 7:31; 19:5; and 32:35) refer to atrocities associated with Judah's kings Ahaz and Manasseh (2 Kgs 16:2–3 and 21:1–6). That such sacrifices were practiced in the Valley of Hinnom is made explicit in 2 Kgs 23:10 and in the parallel accounts of the reigns of Ahaz and Manasseh found in 2 Chr 28:3 and 33:6.

The valley continues to be associated with idolatry and fire in the prophetic tradition, but now the fire is seen as coming from God. In Isa 30:33, God declares,

> Topheth has long been prepared; it has been made ready for the king [of Assyria; cf. v. 31].ts fire pit has been made deep and wide, with an abundance of fire and wood; the breath of the Lord, like a stream of burning sulfur, sets it ablaze.

In this imminent, historical judgment, we have fire and sulfur, or fire and brimstone, which hark back to the destruction of Sodom and Gomorrah (Gen 19:24) to reappear in the book of Revelation (see Rev 14:10; 19:20; 20:10; and 21:8).

The same valley is also intended as the location for the judgment described in the final verse of the book (which, as we have seen, is cited in Mark 9:48). Thus Isa 66:23–24 reads,

> "From one New Moon to another and from one Sabbath to another, all mankind will come and bow down before me," says the Lord. "And they will go out and look upon the dead bodies of those who rebelled against me; their worm will not die, nor will their fire be quenched, and they will be loathsome to all mankind."

During the rise and fall of Jewish nationalism—a period that includes the Maccabean revolt against the Seleucids (169–160 BCE), the Great War against Rome (66–70 CE), and the revolt of Bar Kokhba, also against Rome (132–136 CE)—it is not hard to see how these passages from Isaiah, taken together with the portrayal of God's judgment of the nations in Joel 3, could have fuelled the conviction that the dead bodies of Israel's enemies should and would be cast into this Gehenna.[17]

While a nationalistic agenda that would equate God's enemies with Israel's enemies is foreign to the prophetic tradition, it remains the case that for the Old Testament prophets, Gehenna is understood as the place where the wicked will be punished with fire in the "last days" (reading e.g., Isa 30 and 66 in the light of 2:2 [NIV]). But as this is an earthly place outside Jerusalem and as the "last days" are clearly understood as taking place within history, this is quite

---

[17] On the burning of the dead bodies of Israel's enemies in this valley, see Bailey, "Gehenna," 188 and Von Wyrick, "Gehenna," 489. While the valley in Joel 3:2, 12, 14 is symbolically rather than geographically named, its close vicinity to Jerusalem, as identified in 2:9 and 3:16, meant that it would have been associated, if not identified, with the Valley of Hinnom.

different from the view of Gehenna in later rabbinic literature in which the Valey of Hinnom has become an underworld or otherworldly realm that has been in existence since the creation. Such a place can indeed be identified with the 'Hell' of traditional Christian theology. The Gehenna of the Hebrew Bible and Christian Old Testament cannot.[18]

If we examine how and when this third, otherworldly or 'underworldly', usage of 'Gehenna' arose, a good case can be made for saying that it is anachronistic to attribute this meaning either to the historical Jesus or to the gospel writers. Before exploring this point further, however, I first want to propose that we see what happens to Jesus' use of Gehenna if we view it as in line with Old Testament prophetic (historical) usage—a possibility that is so obvious that it is remarkable that it has been so ignored by New Testament exegetes.

If the Gehenna of the gospels does continue the Old Testament tradition of imminent, this-worldly judgment, it is important to recognise that Jesus' words consistently contain an ironic, prophetic reversal. For whereas the passages from Isaiah and Joel, referred to above, see the valley as the place where *the nations* will be judged as "those who have rebelled against me," to cite God's words in Isa 66:24a, Jesus clearly sees the valley as the place where *Israel* will be judged. This confounding of a nationalistic misconstrual of the prophetic tradition is precisely the point of the citation of Isa 66:24b, the final words of the book of Isaiah, in Mark 9:47–48:

> And if your eye causes you to sin, pluck it out. It is better for you to enter the kingdom of God with one eye than to have two eyes and be thrown into [Gehenna], where " 'their worm will not die, nor will their fire be quenched'."

Here the repetition of "you" and "your," addressed to Jesus' Jewish contemporaries, confronts and reverses a certain way of hearing Isaiah's repetition of "their" worm and "their" fire. The echo of Isa 66:24 found in the Protestant Apocrypha in Judith 16:17 represents a more mainstream appropriation.

Furthermore, Jesus' reversal is in keeping with the role of Gehenna in the prophetic warning of Jeremiah, which is directed towards his own people. The probability that this connection is deliberate—the probability that Jesus is consciously standing in the tradition of Jeremiah—gains considerable support from a detailed study by Michael Knowles that demonstrates the presence of numerous themes and allusions to this particular prophetic book (and to subsequent traditions about its prophet) in Matthew—the gospel that contains seven out of the eleven references to Gehenna in the synoptics.[19]

---

[18] They can be *related*, as I will suggest later in this section, but not *identified*.
[19] See Michael Knowles, *Jeremiah in Matthew's Gospel: The Rejected-Prophet Motif in Matthaean Redaction*. Journal for the Study of the New Testament Supplement Series 68 (Sheffield, UK: Sheffield Academic Press, 1993).

If Jesus is to be understood as issuing prophetic warnings about a coming historical judgment against Israel, this strongly suggests that his words relate (at least primarily) to the destruction of Jerusalem by Rome one generation later in 70 CE. Given Jeremiah's clash with the leaders of his day for prophesying the destruction of the Holy City and its Temple at the hands of the Babylonians centuries earlier, this is further evidence for seeing parallels between the ministries of Jesus and this most controversial of prophets.

One reason why the connections between the warnings of Jeremiah and Jesus about a coming (historical) crisis have not been fully appreciated is (arguably) due to a widespread misreading of the apocalyptic language present in those passages where Jesus speaks of future events in terms of the coming of the Son of Man, the separation of the sheep and the goats, the throwing of the weeds into the fire, and the signs of the end of the age (see Mark 13; Matt 25:31–46; 13:36–43; and 24:1–25:30). This misunderstanding, which has been compounded by the tendency of most biblical scholars to sharply separate apocalyptic thought from the this-worldly concerns of the prophetic tradition, has led many to read Jesus' words about God's wrath in general and Gehenna in particular as being about the 'end of the world' and a subsequent divine judgment involving realities beyond human history such as heaven and hell (as traditionally conceived). In my view, by contrast, the fact that the Gehenna of the gospels has a more intensely 'apocalyptic' significance than the Gehenna of Jeremiah does not makes it any less historical. Indeed, as I shall suggest below, Jeremiah's portrayal of the fall of Jerusalem can itself be classified as (proto-) apocalyptic in character.

The distinction and the relation between prophetic and apocalyptic literature is a matter of ongoing debate. Stephen Travis notes that while some Old Testament scholars believe that apocalyptic thought developed out of prophecy (as opposed to parseeism, wisdom literature, or hellenism), they still differentiate apocalyptic from the prophetic tradition in crucial ways.[20] It is popular among such scholars to believe that while Second Isaiah introduced the distinctions between heaven and earth and between past age and future age that would become central in apocalyptic, his cosmic vision was still integrated within an affirmation of history. By contrast, his followers are believed to have shifted their attention to a supra-historical realm due to the oppression they suffered at the hands of those in political power. Travis cites P.D. Hanson as claiming that,

> [T]he apocalypticism of their symbolic universe was predicated upon the disintegration of the present order and the creation of a new cosmic order of blessedness for the elect. Responsibility to the political order which was a

---

[20] See Travis, *Christian Hope and the Future of Man*, 27–33. Much of the following account is based on chaps. 2 and 3 of this work which, though now an older study, sets out the issues very clearly. For my own way of defining apocalyptic, especially with reference to the book of Revelation, see the Appendix to the present study.

central characteristic of prophetic eschatology was abandoned in favour of a new super-mundane universe of meaning.[21]

While the greater political stability of the time of Ezra resulted in apocalyptic remaining temporarily dormant, political oppression under Antiochus IV Epiphanes is believed to have triggered it again in the book of Daniel and in the writings of the monks of Qumran.

Travis points out, against the views of those he is summarising, that the pessimistic view of history in apocalyptic literature was not so much a denigration of history *per se*, but was rooted in an empirical observation of what life was actually like in the exilic period after the fall of Jerusalem.[22] He also notes that far from inevitably leading to an apolitical stance, apocalyptic writings actually mobilised support for the rebellion of the Maccabees.[23] Nevertheless he still maintains that the distinction between prophetic and apocalyptic, whilst "overworked" is "useful" as a generalisation.[24] His acceptance of the claim that apocalyptic writings hold to a transcendent rather than historical eschatology can be seen in his comment that the ideas of resurrection and *post-mortem* judgment that they were responsible for introducing "were a significant affirmation that the meaning of human existence cannot be discovered entirely within life and history."[25]

If one posits some kind of continuity between this understanding of apocalyptic and Jesus' view of history (at least as portrayed by the gospel writers), one important consequence is that this tends to reinforce the widely held assumption that the texts about the 'parousia' were intended to refer to events at the end of time. Given that Jesus spoke of this 'coming' or 'arrival' as something that could be expected soon, this leads to the problem of "the delay of the parousia" first identified by Albert Schweitzer and Johannes Weiss. "To a great extent," writes Travis, this is the problem to which "every major twentieth-century interpretation of Jesus' eschatology has been a response."[26]

---

[21] P.D. Hanson, "Apocalypticism," in *Interpreter's Dictionary of the Bible: Supplementary Vol.*, ed. Keith R. Crim (Nashville, TN: Abingdon, 1976), 32 as cited in Travis, *Christian Hope*, 31. Cf. Karl Rahner's disparaging comments about apocalyptic in "The Hermeneutics of Eschatological Assertions," in *More Recent Writings*, vol. 4 of *Theological Investigations*, trans. Kevin Smyth (Baltimore, MD: Helicon; London: Darton, Longman and Todd, 1966), 323–46, especially 337.

[22] See Travis, *Christian Hope*, 37. Here he is drawing on the conclusion of Richard Bauckham's valuable essay "The Rise of Apocalyptic," *Themelios* 3, no. 2 (January 1978): 10–23.

[23] See Travis, *Christian Hope*, 38.

[24] Travis, *Christian Hope*, 35.

[25] Travis, *Christian Hope*, 40.

[26] Travis, *Christian Hope*, 19. Responses to the 'delay' include viewing it as: (i) a mistake that explains the origin of the Christian worldview; (ii) an error on a topic incidental to Jesus' message; (iii) a result of the Evangelists' failure to understand Jesus' realised eschatology; and (iv) evidence for the need to demythologise the New Testament. For these and other reactions see Travis, *Christian Hope*, 19–23. Moltmann

Travis' proposed solution, which parallels the response favoured by a number of evangelicals,[27] is to counter the charge that Jesus was in error by claiming that while he was indeed speaking of the end of history, he was doing so in a way that highlighted the immediate significance of that future event. Thus he writes,

> In the Bible, prophets repeatedly foretell God's acts of salvation and judgment in a way which suggests that the great day of fulfilment is imminent. In a literal and total sense, such prophecies remain unfulfilled. But they are affirming that each crisis, each blessing which follows the words of the prophet is a partial realization within history of the ultimate victory of God. Even if this ultimate victory, which we call the parousia, is delayed, the shadow of Christ's eschatological presence began already to fall in the period inaugurated by his ministry, death and resurrection. The imminence language of Jesus asserts that the age of the decisive fulfilment has already dawned, the kingdom of God is being manifested here and now, and the present manifestations guarantee God's ultimate triumph through Christ.[28]

This apologetic strategy has implications for the interpretation of Gehenna. If we grant that Jesus' language about the imminence of the parousia is similar to the way he speaks about the imminent danger of being thrown into Gehenna, and if we assume that both ideas belong closely together in his eschatology, then those who see the parousia as an event that, in its literal (or full) sense, has been 'delayed' are unlikely to entertain the idea that the warnings about Gehenna have already come to pass in the destruction of Jerusalem in 70 CE. The prophetic utterances of Jeremiah and the apocalyptic language of Jesus become split apart, the former referring to events in time, the latter to our destiny in eternity.[29] Two very different Gehennas are formed: Jeremiah's Valley of Slaughter and the Hell of Christian orthodoxy.

N.T. Wright's approach to these issues, which is strikingly different from that of fellow evangelical Stephen Travis, flows from his conviction that scholars have fundamentally misunderstood apocalyptic language.[30] It is as if a

---

sees the *parousia* in terms of an event that is still 'future', yet identifies that future with an *advent* future rather than a *futurum* in a linear view of time. See WJC, 327. The delay is thus not a failed prediction but a promise that has not yet come to pass. As Bauckham notes in "Time and Eternity," 180–82, this does not solve the 'problem' of the delay so much as reconceive it in terms of theodicy.

[27] See Travis, *Christian Hope*, 22–23.

[28] Travis, *Christian Hope*, 90.

[29] In this perspective, the only way Gehenna and the parousia can become imminent in any straightforward sense for all but earth's final generation is if these terms are understood as referring to what individuals will experience at death. This view has become very popular due to the de-eschatologisation of the biblical worldview, on which see below.

[30] See N.T. Wright, *The New Testament and the People of God*, vol. 1 of *Christian Origins and the Question of God* (London: SPCK; Philadelphia: Fortress Press, 1992), 280–99, on which the following summary is dependent.

future generation were to conclude that our way of referring to the fall of the Berlin wall as an 'earth-shattering event' was out of touch with reality because there was no mention of seismic activity on the Weather Channel. Any analogy has its limits. But Wright's basic point is that, properly understood, apocalyptic language is not rooted in flights of fancy, nor in attempts to either escape reality or grasp at the some kind of trans-historical—or "super-mundane"—level of meaning. Instead, its concern is with thoroughly historical events, which it describes in rich metaphors in order to invest them with their ultimate significance.[31]

Wright builds on the critique launched by George Caird (and by Marcus Borg, a fellow student of Caird) against Schweitzer's assumption that the Christian Jews of the first century were expecting the world to end with the 'parousia' or coming of the kingdom of God.[32] Claiming that this reflects a radical misreading of the Jewish worldview of that time, he writes,

> Sometimes, no doubt, extraordinary natural phenomena were both expected, witnessed and interpreted within a grid of belief which enabled some to see them as signs and portents. No doubt eclipses, earthquakes, meteorites and other natural phenomena were regarded as part of the way in which strange socio-political events announced themselves. The universe was, after all, regarded as an interconnected whole (which is not the same thing as a closed continuum). But the events, including the ones that were expected to come as the climax of YHWH's restoration of Israel, remained within (what we think of as) the this-worldly ambit. The "kingdom of God" has nothing to do with the world itself coming to an end. That makes no sense either of the basic Jewish worldview or of the texts in which the Jewish hope is expressed. It was after all the Stoics, not the first-century Jews, who characteristically believed that the world would be dissolved in fire.[33]

---

[31] For Hanson's reference to a "super-mundane universe of meaning," see n. 21 above. For Wright's focus on ultimate significance, see his *The New Testament and the People of God*, 282–83. This concern with the ultimate significance of real events pertains, in his view, whether the events are remembered or anticipated.

[32] Caird's position is especially accessible in *The Language and Imagery of the Bible*, chap. 14 ("The Language of Eschatology"). Cf. Marcus J. Borg, *Conflict, Holiness and Politics in the Teachings of Jesus* (1984; repr., Harrisburg, PA: Trinity Press International, 1998), chap. 8 ("Jesus and the Future"). Wright provides a substantial preface to the most recent edition of each of these works. An example of a significant study that ignores the Caird/Wright approach entirely is Vicky Balabanski, *Eschatology in the Making: Mark, Matthew and the Didache*. Society for New Testament Studies Monograph Series 97 (Cambridge: Cambridge University Press, 1997). Cf. also Alan E. Bernstein, *The Formation of Hell: Death and Retribution in the Ancient and Early Christian Worlds* (Ithaca, NY: Cornell University Press, 1993) and Martha Himmelfarb, *Tours of Hell: An Apocalyptic Form in Jewish and Christian Literature* (Philadelphia: University of Pennsylvania Press, 1983).

[33] Wright, *The New Testament and the People of God*, 285. Wright continues in parentheses,
> This has the amusing corollary that scholars have thought of such an explanation as a Jewish oddity which the church grew out of as it left Judaism behind,

The misconstrual of apocalyptic as akin to the acosmism of Gnosticism has come about because its *dualities* of the two ages, God and creation, and good and evil have been misread as implying an anthropological and cosmological *dualism*, and because its "hugely figurative" language has been interpreted literalistically.[34] Scholars have seen the end of the space-time universe when the writers of apocalyptic saw the end of the present world order, and drew on the kind of language needed to begin to do justice to the earth-shattering significance of such terrible (yet hopeful) events. In this respect they were no different from the thoroughly prophetic (and I would add: 'proto-apocalyptic') Jeremiah who had spoken of the coming destruction of Judah and the Temple in terms of the unmaking of creation (see Jer 4:23–28).[35] As the Jerusalem Temple represented creation as a whole, such cosmic language was entirely fitting.[36]

The way apocalyptic language has been misread is particularly striking in the case of the book of Daniel. Thus, in Wright's understanding, the "[S]on of [M]an" of Dan 7:13 (who later plays an important role in Jesus' apocalyptic discourses in, e.g., Mark 13:26) is not a heavenly being but a metaphor for Israel (compare Dan 7:14 with 7:18 and 7:27), seen as the new humanity that, like Adam in Gen 1, rules over the beasts, here associated with the pagan nations.[37] In addition to providing a coherent, compelling interpretation of the book in its original setting, Wright argues, this is most likely the way Daniel was read in the first century, with the fourth beast being identified as Rome.[38]

Turning our attention to the New Testament, the connection between Jesus and the Son of Man is to be understood, first and foremost, in terms of the gospel writers' portrayal of Jesus as embodying Israel's mission. Yet "the coming" of this Son of Man—a coming not to *earth* but to *YHWH's throne* thus signifying divine vindication, again as in the book of Daniel[39]—does not mark

---

whereas in fact it seems to be a pagan oddity that the church grew into as it left Judaism behind—and which, perhaps, some Jews moved towards as they despaired of the old national hope and turned towards inner or mystical hope instead.

[34] See Wright, *The New Testament and the People of God*, 297–99. Quotation from p. 299.

[35] See Wright, *The New Testament and the People of God*, 299. Cf. 333, including the quotation from E.P. Sanders.

[36] This point is well made in Crispin H.T. Fletcher-Louis, "The Destruction of the Temple and the Relativization of the Old Covenant: Mark 13:31 and Matthew 5:18," in *'The Reader Must Understand': Eschatology in Bible and Theology*, ed. K.E. Brower and M.W. Elliott (Leicester, UK: Apollos, 1997), 145–169. The same point, *pace* Fletcher-Louis, can be found in *The New Testament and the People of God*, 224 (via the quotation from Safrai). But it is not developed.

[37] See Wright, *The New Testament and the People of God*, 293–97.

[38] See Wright, *The New Testament and the People of God*, 304.

[39] See Wright, *The New Testament and the People of God*, 297 (summarising 291–97) and N.T. Wright, *Jesus and the Victory of God*, vol. 2 of *Christian Origins and the Question of God* (London: SPCK; Minneapolis, MN: Fortress Press, 1996), 360–65, especially 361 (which is much clearer on this point). This latter work has evoked a

the end of Roman occupation, contrary to the way Dan 7:13–14 would have been understood in the first century. Rather, the meaning of this event in Mark 13:26, taken within that chapter as a whole, points to the radical subversion of Jewish apocalyptic hopes in Jesus. As Wright puts it,

> The truth (from Mark's point of view) is so staggering, not least because of what is implied all through [his gospel], and eventually is stated plainly enough in chapter 13. The coming of the kingdom does not mean the great vindication of Jerusalem, the glorification of the Temple, the real return from exile envisaged by the prophets and their faithful readers. It means, rather, the desolation of Jerusalem, the destruction of the Temple, and the vindication of Jesus and his people. Jerusalem and its hierarchy have now taken on the roles of Babylon, Edom and Antiochus Epiphanes in this stark retelling of their story. They are the city whose fall spells the vindication of the true people of Israel's god. The prophecies of rescue from the tyrant have come true in and for Jesus and his people. When the city falls they must get out and run; this is their moment of rescue, salvation, vindication.[40]

A close study of the main Old Testament allusions in Mark 13, as set out below, shows that Wright's argument is extremely well grounded.[41]

---

response volume—Carey C. Newman, ed., *Jesus and the Restoration of Israel: A Critical Assessment of N.T. Wright's* Jesus and the Victory of God (Downers Grove, IL: InterVarsity Press, 1999)—which contains a number of discussions of Wright's view of NT apocalyptic to which Wright himself responds towards the end of the volume in "In Grateful Dialogue: A Response," 244–78.

[40] Wright, *The New Testament and the People of God*, 395–96, cf. 459–60. Wright consistently connects the vindication of Jesus and his followers with Jesus' resurrection and exaltation. See, e.g., *The New Testament and the People of God*, 461–62 as cited below. On resurrection as vindication (a connection that goes back to Dan 12:1–3), see N.T. Wright, *The Resurrection of the Son of God*, vol. 3 of *Christian Origins and the Question of God* (London: SPCK; Minneapolis, MN: Fortress Press, 2003), 408–11, a discussion that ends with the references to the destruction of the Temple in Mark 14:58 and John 2:19. On the latter, cf. 5.4 above.

[41] What follows expands on Wright, *The New Testament and the People of God*, 396n88. The undeniable connection that emerges between Jerusalem and Babylon here (cf. the quotation in n. 45 below) raises interesting questions about the interpretation of Babylon in the book of Revelation, which I explore in the Appendix.

Mark	OT Allusions	Verbal/Thematic Parallels
13:2	Jer 51:26	no stone left/mountain/Babylon
13:7	Jer 51:46	rumours of war/don't be afraid/Babylon
13:14a	Dan 9:27; 11:31; 12:11 (cf. 1 Macc 1:54)	abomination of desolation/ temple/ Antiochus IV Epiphanes
13:14–17	Jer 51:6, 45	flee Babylon
13:19	Dan 12:1	trouble as has never been/ deliverance of the faithful
13:24	Isa 13:10	sun darkened/Babylon
13:24–5	Isa 34:4	stars fall/Edom
13:26–27	Dan 7:13–14	the coming of the Son of Man/ vindication of the faithful
13:27	Deut 30:3–4; Zech 2:6	gathering/end of exile

figure 9

How then are we to understand "the Son of Man coming in clouds with great power and glory" (Mark 13:26)? In line with its Danielic usage, says Wright, this must be seen as the decisive, public vindication of the true Israel, now understood as Jesus. This suggests that the "parousia" (a word that may be translated as [royal] "presence" rather than "coming") needs to be reinterpreted. According to Wright,

> The most likely meaning for these particular "apocalyptic" texts within early Christianity ... is not the expectation of the *return* of Jesus, but the proclamation that he had already been vindicated, in his resurrection and exaltation, and that he would be further vindicated when the city which had opposed him, and over which he had pronounced his sternest warnings, would in turn be destroyed.[42]

The actual 'return' of Jesus is mentioned outside the gospels (in, e.g., Acts 1:10). And Wright does interpret 1 Thess 4:13–18 as closely paralleling 1 Cor 15:12–28 and thus looking beyond the imminent vindication of Jesus to the final vindication of his followers at the consummation of history, a two-part distinction that he believes is first worked through by Paul prior to 70 CE.[43] But once we distinguish between this 'return' from the 'coming to YHWH's throne' specified in the apocalyptic discourses of the gospels, we can see that there are no signs in early Christian writings of a worldview crisis due to the absence of

---

[42] Wright, *The New Testament and the People of God*, 461–62. His emphasis. The translation of "parousia" is discussed on p. 463 and in N.T. Wright, "The Future of Jesus," in *The Meaning of Jesus: Two Visions*, by N.T. Wright and Marcus Borg (London: SPCK; New York: HarperCollins, 1999), 201–202. Moltmann, with the vast majority of interpreters, sees the 'parousia' as Christ's return. See, for example, Moltmann, "The Return of Christ,"105–12.

[43] See Wright, "The Future of Jesus," 202–204.

the Second Coming. "[T]he old scholarly warhorse of the 'delay of the parousia'," says Wright, "has had its day at last, and can be put out to grass once and for all."[44] The vindication, 'coming', and parousia of the Son of Man occur in the events of 70 CE.

Once other elements of Jesus' apocalyptic warnings are located in the imminent future of his contemporaries, it becomes increasingly probable that 'Gehenna' is being used as a place of judgment near Jerusalem in line with the usage in the prophetic tradition. If Israel does not repent, Jesus warns, then they will share the same destiny as Jeremiah's contemporaries in the Valley of Slaughter. Like the Gentile enemies of the Maccabees, their corpses will be burned in Gehenna.[45] They will be the weeds that are pulled up and thrown into the fire (Matt 13:40). The "angels" sent by the Son of Man to perform this task (Matt 13:39ff.) symbolise none other than the Romans.[46]

When the Romans virtually razed Jerusalem to the ground, much of the city wall and many of its inhabitants literally ended up in the Valley of Hinnom.[47]

---

[44] Wright, *The New Testament and the People of God*, 462. For a similar approach to apocalyptic themes, worked out independently from Wright (though she later became his doctoral student), see Sylvia Keesmaat, "The Coming of the Son of Man in Luke-Acts" (MA thesis, McMaster University, 1990).

[45] Wright, in *The New Testament and the People of God*, does not offer this reinterpretation of Gehenna. David Collins (on the basis of a lecture series by Wright entitled "The Quest for the Historical Kingdom" delivered at the Institute for Christian Studies, Toronto, in 1989) was quick to extend Wright's analysis of apocalyptic in this direction (with special reference to Matthew's Gospel) in his fine paper "Hell and Tradition" (Toronto: Institute for Christian Studies, 1990) two years prior to the publication of Wright's first volume. That Wright accepts this extension of his exegesis is clear in his essay "Jerusalem in the New Testament," in *Jerusalem Past and Present in the Purposes of God*, ed. P.W.L. Walker, 2nd ed. (Carlisle, UK: Paternoster; Grand Rapids, MI: Baker, 1994), 53–77, where he writes on p. 63,

> [T]he sayings about [the] judgment [of Jerusalem] are normally either read as *post facto* rationalizations or spiritualized into threats of *post mortem* hellfire. They are neither. They are the solemn historical warnings, based on Jesus' understanding of himself and his vocation, that the system which now operates in Jerusalem is playing out the role of Babylon, and is ripe for the destruction predicted in the prophets. The beautiful city has indeed become the 'harlot'.

His italics. Cf. *Jesus and the Victory of God*, 183, 330–31, 336, and 454–55n47.

[46] This, of course, fits well with my discussion of angels in 6.1.1 above. For a view of the angels in Mark 13:27 that is also very compatible with my approach, see Wright, *Jesus and the Victory of God*, 363.

[47] See Collins, "Hell and Tradition," 20. For a first-century CE account, see Josephus, *The Jewish War*, bks. 5–7, including bk. 5, chap. 12, secs. 3–4. One contemporary translation, Josephus, *The Jewish War*, ed. E. Mary Smallwood, trans. G.A. Williamson, rev. ed (London: Penguin, 1981), 488, aptly places "Gehenna" on its map of Jerusalem in 70 CE. It is often claimed that Gehenna was the location of the city's garbage dump. If correct, this would reinforce the way in which Jerusalem was (in contemporary parlance) thoroughly 'trashed'. Bailey, "Gehenna," 188–89, disputes this identification as anachronistic on historical grounds, in distinction from all other articles that I have

In the destruction of Jerusalem and its Temple, the purging of Israel that Paul, in Rom 9–11, says the Old Testament had long anticipated,[48] finally takes place. Two men are walking up a hill. While one is left, the other is taken, not in the 'Rapture' of dispensationalist fundamentalism, but in judgment (Matt 24:40, cf. Luke 17:34–37). Those who have not cut off hand or foot to sever themselves from the spiritual direction of the rest of the nation, and those who fail to heed Jesus' words to flee to the mountains (rather than join the nationalistic resistance movement) in Mark 13:14, become the goats separated from the sheep (Matt 25:31). It is not the Gentiles who are judged but the descendants of Abraham.[49] For "many will come from the east and the west, and will take their places at the feast with Abraham, Isaac and Jacob in the kingdom of heaven. But the subjects of the kingdom will be thrown outside, into the darkness, where there will be weeping and gnashing of teeth" (Matt 8:11–12).

Stars fall from the sky and the sun is darkened (Mark 13:24), for this is truly the end of the old world order. The fire associated with Gehenna is "eternal" (Matt 18:8–9) in most translations (including the NIV and NRSV). But the Greek term—*aiōnios*—actually fits perfectly in this thoroughly temporal, historical context as it means 'belonging to the age to come'.[50] The fire of Gehenna is therefore not endless but eschatological, signifying the judgment that has and will bring the old age to an end. As a manifestation of the Final Judgment in which all evil will be totally eradicated to make way for the full arrival of the Age to Come,[51] this apocalyptic ending is also a beginning (cf. 6.6 above). The

---

consulted on the topic (although curiously Wright, *Jesus and the Victory of God*, 183n142 seems to cite Bailey against his own view).

[48] For an excellent discussion, see N.T. Wright, "Christ, the Law and the People of God," in *The Climax of the Covenant: Christ and the Law in Pauline Theology*, by N.T. Wright (Edinburgh: T. and T. Clark, 1991), 231–57.

[49] This way of expressing things particularly fits Mark 13. In the Appendix, I argue that the book of Revelation is also focussed on the 'apocalyptic' event of 70 CE. There, the judgment is first for Israel but also for the Gentile world as Jerusalem represents the Old World Order or Old Age. This way of thinking is also present in the reference to the nations in Matt 25:32. But the emphasis on Israel in Matt 8:11–12 (cited below) is clear.

[50] This translation allows us to maintain the inverse parallelism of Matt 25:46, while robbing traditionalists of their main 'proof text' against universalists and annihilationists. (Moltmann's attempt to deny the inverse parallelism by appealing to an eternal-temporal distinction, as discussed in 1.4.5 above, is thus unnecessary.)

This translation also helps us appreciate how the double reference to '*ôlām* in Dan 12:2 is being intertextually developed within (Matthew's account of) Jesus' teaching (cf. n. 55 below). Biblical terms traditionally thought to refer to the eternal or everlasting need to be translated in a contextually sensitive way. Overlooking this mars the discussion in Bernstein, *The Formation of Hell*, 232–33 despite his awareness that eternity is such a loaded term in Augustine's systematic control of the same biblical material in pp. 318–21. On Rev 20:10, see 9.3n61 below.

[51] That the imminent judgment involves the suffering of unrepentant Jews does not signify that the final, eschatological reality that is being manifest is God-imposed torment. The final defeat of evil, anticipated here, could be understood in terms of

'apocalypse' itself, which includes the fall of Jerusalem and its Temple (as I will suggest in the Appendix on the book of Revelation, below), is the transition between the two ages. The death-throes of the old world order are the birthpangs of the new creation.

This approach makes it quite unnecessary to interpret Gehenna as an infernal, otherworldly realm in which the wicked are destined to spend their *post-mortem* existence. Furthermore, there is evidence to suggest that this all-too-common reading is not only less plausible than the one I am suggesting, but is very dubious on historical grounds.

While there is a world of difference between the prophetic-historical understanding of the Valley of Hinnom (even in its apocalyptically intensified form in the gospels) and the use of the same place name to designate a hellish underworld, there is one point of connection that may help to explain the shift in meaning that Gehenna underwent. As Bailey points out, altars in the ancient world served to connect the realm of the worshipper with that of the deity. Thus Jacob erects an altar at Bethel believing on the basis of a dream that a "gate of heaven" is located there (Gen 28:17). Isaiah 57:5–6 refers to the worshippers of Molech as pouring out liquid offerings to him in valleys. Altars were sometimes connected to pipes that carried sacrificial blood to the deities believed to dwell beneath them. Thus since human sacrifices were made in the Valley of Hinnom, this would suggest that Gehenna was seen as (or associated with) the entrance to the underworld itself.[52]

If the presence of altars in the Valley of Slaughter to underworld deities helps explain how Gehenna came to refer to the underworld as a non-earthly realm, it is important to ask *when* this shift occurred. The issue here is not when did the Jews begin to refer to an underworld, but when did they start referring to an underworld as 'Gehenna'?

Bailey claims that the earliest references are found in the New Testament and in early rabbinic literature. The only New Testament text he cites is Matt 10:28, a passage that provides no contextual support for his position, but fits the interpretation I have suggested without difficulty. The rabbinic literature he refers to is from the Babylonian Talmud. Yet even the Mishnah, which forms the earliest part of this collection, was not compiled until the end of the second century CE. Admittedly, Bailey points to the usage of Gehenna for the underworld in sayings attributed to Rabbi Shammai, who lived around the time of Jesus, and to Rabbi Yohanan ben Zakkai, who lived in the first century CE. Yet it is arguably the case that such sayings reflect the later theologies of their

---

universalism, annihilationism, or traditional orthodoxy. This text alone cannot tell us which of these positions is in touch with the expectations of the biblical story (but see the Appendix on the book of Revelation). The main thrust of my argument here is that this exegetical approach removes what many would judge to be the main 'biblical' argument against universalism.

[52] See Bailey, "Gehenna," 189–90.

compilers and redactors rather than the outlook of those to whom they have been attributed.[53]

What Bailey fails to recognise, I contend, is that the only evidence we have for this third use of Gehenna comes from literature produced in Jewish circles after 70 CE.[54] The destruction of the Holy City and its Temple, the waning of

---

[53] As the Jewish scholar, Alan Segal points out in his *Paul the Convert: The Apostolate and Apostasy of Saul the Pharisee* (New Haven, CT: Yale University Press, 1990), xiv,

> Many fundamental rabbinic traditions can no longer be assumed to date from the time of Jesus, though they purport to be even more ancient. Although rabbinic Judaism claims the Pharisees as forebears, the differences between the rabbis and the Pharisees are great. The Pharisaic movement was but one among a variety of sects in the first century, and rabbinic Judaism matured with the publication of the Mishnah around 220 C.E. The Pharisaic traditions may have originated in the first two centuries or much earlier, as is often claimed. As in any oral literature, these traditions may have been altered in transmission, especially by rabbinic editors in the late second century. . . .

He goes on to speak of how the current understanding of the development of rabbinic tradition has "cast into serious doubt two centuries of Christian scholarship, which too blithely used the Mishnah and Talmud as the main source for understanding the Jewish opposition to Jesus" (xv). Cf. Doron Mendels, *The Rise and Fall of Jewish Nationalism: Jewish and Christian Ethnicity in Ancient Palestine* (Grand Rapids, MI: Eerdmans, 1992), 5. To this we should add that the change in eschatological outlook after 70 CE (discussed below) would make a recasting of earlier sayings about Gehenna not unlikely.

[54] At this point, I find a crucial lack of precision in much of the secondary literature. The projection of later texts back on to the gospels is especially evident in J. Lunde, "Heaven and Hell," in *Dictionary of Jesus and the Gospels*, ed. Joel B. Green, Scot McKnight, and I. Howard Marshall (Downers Grove, IL: InterVarsity Press, 1992), 309–11.

Of all the 'extra-biblical' or 'intertestamental' works thought to shed light on Gehenna in the NT, 1 Enoch and 4 Ezra are the most important both historically and theologically. The former is considered canonical in the Ethiopian Orthodox tradition, while the latter (preserved as chapters 3–14 of 2 Esdras [chapters 1–2 and 15–16 of the latter being Christian additions]) also has this status in the Russian Orthodox and Coptic traditions. (We should note that those who read it in the Vulgate Appendix knew a text that was actually missing 4 Ezra 7:36–140 (cf. Bruce W. Longnecker, *2 Esdras* (Sheffield, UK: Sheffield Academic Press, 1995), 110–12) and thus missing the reference to Gehenna, discussed in n. 55 below.) 1 Enoch, pertinent strata of which predate 70 CE by many centuries, will receive special attention here while 4 Ezra and other, later material will receive comment in the following note.

We may begin by observing that the geographical, prophetic interpretation of Gehenna makes good sense of the reference to the "cursed valley" in 1 Enoch 27:1–2 (thus Bailey, "Gehenna," 188 but *contra* Cheryl A. Kirk-Duggan, "Hell," in *Eerdmans Dictionary of the Bible*, ed. David Noel Freedman, Allen C. Myers and Astrid B. Beck (Grand Rapids, MI: Eerdmans, 2000), 572–73, which is misleading at this point). It is important to note that this valley is distinct from the underworld of 1 Enoch 22 (cf. George W.E. Nickelsburg, *1 Enoch 1: A Commentary on the Book of 1 Enoch, Chapters 1–36; 81–108*. Hermeneia (Minneapolis, MN: Fortress Press, 2001), 308 but *contra* D.S. Russell, *Divine Disclosure: An Introduction to Jewish Apocalyptic* (London: SCM Press, 1992), 98–99). Furthermore, the fact that the chapters that follow (1 Enoch 28–

nationalistic hopes, and the increasing vulnerability to a more otherworldly spirituality influenced by Hellenism, provide the perfect context, I suggest, for Jewish thinkers to start using Gehenna in this new sense.[55] Jerusalem,

---

36) lack "explicit eschatological material" but "fill out the comprehensive tour of the ends of the earth" begun in 1 Enoch 17, as John J. Collins notes in *The Apocalyptic Imagination: An Introduction to Jewish Apocalyptic Literature*, 2nd ed. (Grand Rapids, MI: Eerdmans, 1998), 55–56, should (*contra* Collins) come as no surprise, as this material, from what is usually considered the earliest (third century BCE) part of 1 Enoch, is in line with the geographically located portrayal of Gehenna in the OT prophetic tradition. I think that a good case can be made for discerning the same perspective when this valley is in view in later parts of 1 Enoch. See 1 Enoch 54:2 (cf. 53:1, 5 and the note on the displacement of 54:2 in George W.E. Nickelsburg and James C. VanderKam, *1 Enoch: A New Translation* (Minneapolis, MN: Fortress Press, 2004), 68) and 90:26 (where the valley, seen as an "abyss ... south of that house" [i.e. Jerusalem], is distinguished from the "abyss" of vv. 24–25, as noted by Nickelsburg, *1 Enoch 1*, 403–404). In my view, the distinction between Gehenna and Sheol maintained in the work of VanderKam and Nickelsburg is to be preferred over against the strong inclination to identify them in Marius Reiser, *Jesus and Judgment: The Eschatological Proclamation in Its Jewish Context* (Minneapolis, MN: Fortress Press, 1997), 66 (including 66n127) and 68.

[55] Before we get to the otherwordly impact of Hellenism on Jewish eschatology after 70 CE (on which cf. the end of the quotation from Wright in n. 33 above), we should pause to look at 4 Ezra 7:36 as an important transitional text requiring special comment. (For the inclusion of this Jewish apocalypse within 2 Esdras, which is Scripture in some Christian traditions, see n. 54 above. Textually, 4 Ezra = 2 Esdras 3–14.).

It is instructive to contrast my proposed way of situating and understanding the fall of Jerusalem as the apocalyptic transition between the two ages (cf. the Appendix on the book of Revelation, below) with the perspective of 4 Ezra, which sees the fall of Jerusalem as a punishment for Israel's sins that is unconnected to the transition between the old age and the new. In this Jewish apocalyptic work from the end of the first century CE (cf. "the thirtieth year after the destruction of the city" of 4 Ezra 3:1 [= 2 Esdras 3:1], NRSV), part of the answer to this most traumatic of events is that the future Messiah will judge Rome (11:38–46 and 12:31–33) and set free the remnant of Israel "making them joyful until the end comes, the day of judgment, of which I spoke to you at the beginning" (12:34). This time of joy would seem to be the four hundred years of 7:28, which precede the judgment described in 7:32–44.

Of all the texts that are seen as shedding light on the gospels in this respect, the reference to Gehenna in 4 Ezra 7:36 (= 2 Esdras 7:36) seems to be in a unique category. While Gehenna is still distinguished from Hades in contrast to the rabbinic literature (see 4:7–8 and 8:53), 4 Ezra (2 Esdras 3–14) does parallel the rabbinic tradition in seeing Gehenna as having been created before the world, as Reiser notes in *Jesus and Judgment*, 123 with reference to 7:70. And while there are echoes of the prophetic tradition's judgment of the nations here (see 7:37, cf. the discussion in Michael Edward Stone, *4 Ezra: A Commentary on the Book of Fourth Ezra*. Hermeneia (Minneapolis, MN: Fortress Press, 1990), 222 and cf. the later 5 Ezra 2:28–29 [= 2 Esdras 2:28–29]), this judgment is now seen as taking place after a resurrection in the transition between the present age and the age to come.

This is a significant departure from the OT, where the vision (rather than the developed belief, cf. John E. Goldingay, *Daniel*. Word Biblical Commentary 30 (Dallas,

surrounded as it was by a valley into which Israel expected her God to throw her pagan Roman enemies, was no longer the geographical-spiritual centre of their world. Thus the sayings of earlier rabbis about Gehenna were naturally reinterpreted to refer to a hellish underworld.[56]

The intense insecurity of the period between the accession of Marcus Aurelius (161 CE) and the conversion of Constantine to Christianity (312 CE) fuelled a widespread dualistic cosmology that would ensure that the Christians

---

TX: Word, 1989), 306–308) of postmortem, post-resurrection judgment/vindication, found only in Dan 12:2, is not explicitly associated with Gehenna. If we see 4 Ezra as developing an allusion to Gehenna that is *implicit* in Dan 12:2—based on a (plausible) linguistic connection between Dan 12:2 and Isa 66:24 established by the occurrence in only these passages of *dērā'ôn* (translated in the NIV as that which is "loathsome" or worthy of "contempt"), cf. Nickelsburg, *1 Enoch 1*, 319 and Goldingay, *Daniel*, 281, 308—then this is very different from the development of Dan 12:2 that we find in Matt 25:46, on which see n. 50 above within the argument of the present section.

In my judgment, therefore, 4 Ezra 7:36 marks an important transition between the OT and NT understanding of Gehenna, on the hand, and post-biblical conceptions of Hell, on the other. Other pre-Diaspora Jewish texts also from the first century CE (for current views of their dating and location, see Collins, *The Apocalyptic Imagination*) either give fleeting or confused attention to Gehenna (see 2 Baruch 59:10; Apocalypse of Abraham 15:6 [cf. the comments in James H. Charlesworth, ed., *Apocalyptic Literature and Testaments*, vol. 1 of *The Old Testament Pseudepigrapha* (New York: Doubleday, 1983), 686, 696]; and Testament of Moses 10:10 [cf. the rejection of R.H. Charles' textual emendation in *Apocalyptic Literature and Testaments*, 933]). By the time we get to the Sibylline Oracles 1:101–103; 2:293; and 4:106, later in the first century and written beyond the promised land, Gehenna and Tartarus have become synonymous (cf. the blending of Gehenna and Sheol in the rabbinic tradition in n. 14 above).

[56] To argue that the NT writers, notably the authors of the synoptic gospels, also adopted this later Jewish reinterpretation and attributed it to Jesus because they too were living after the events of 70 CE is unpersuasive, in my view. Even if (as is widely believed) Matthew and Luke were written anywhere up to twenty years after the fall of Jerusalem (Mark being frequently dated prior to this event), the impact of the destruction of the Temple on the this-worldly hopes of first century non-Christian Jews cannot be taken as a key to early (Jewish and Gentile) Christian eschatology as the future hopes of the Christian communities were not *centred* in the Jerusalem Temple.

It is also worth noting that, scholarly convention/consensus notwithstanding, a plausible case can be made for dating all of the synoptics prior to 70 CE. See John A.T. Robinson, *Redating the New Testament* (London: SCM Press, 1976), much of which remains pertinent. In my view, whenever the synoptics reached their final form, driving a wedge between the Gehenna of Matthew and the Gehenna of Luke (*contra* Chaim Milikowsky's article "Which Gehenna? Retribution and Eschatology in the Synoptic Gospels and in Early Jewish Texts," *New Testament Studies* 34 (1988): 238–49), or between the Gehenna of the gospels and the Gehenna of Jesus, the Jewish apocalyptic prophet, is unnecessary.

of that period would also identify Gehenna with 'Hell'.[57] The eclipse of hope in a resurrection on a New Earth coupled with belief in an immortal soul that would experience the bliss or torment it deserved at death, further reinforced the assumption, made again and again down the ages, that Jesus was talking of a *post-mortem* judgment for individuals.[58] When we also bear in mind the role that Hell played in the enforcement of social order and fidelity to the church,[59] we can see why this fiery underworld found such a secure place in the cosmologies of Western Christendom.

Insensitivity to the nature of apocalyptic language and widespread misinterpretation of first-century Jewish hopes have led scholars to believe that Jesus and his contemporaries were looking for an end not to the current world order, but to the world itself. This, together with the projection of later, 'hellenised' beliefs about Gehenna from the Mishnah back onto the New Testament, has ensured that biblical scholars, regardless of their not uncommon antipathy towards the orthodoxies of the Church, have (mis)read the New Testament in a similar way and have thus been impotent to challenge or correct popular misunderstandings at this point. All modern translations of the Bible simply perpetuate this most unfortunate error of judgment. Jesus, standing in the tradition of Jeremiah, did indeed warn his contemporaries of the dangers of being thrown into *Gehenna*. But 'Hell' is another story.[60]

---

[57] On this period, see E.R. Dodds, *Pagan and Christian in an Age of Anxiety: Some Aspects of Religious Experience from Marcus Aurelius to Constantine* (New York: W.W. Norton, 1965).

[58] On this shift away from biblical eschatology, see Rowell, *Hell and the Victorians*, 23, 28, and 42. See also the very full survey of early Christian understandings of resurrection in Wright, *The Resurrection of the Son of God*, 209–583

[59] See Rowell, *Hell and the Victorians*, 1 and Walker, *The Decline of Hell*, 4, 23–24, 69, and 82. Rowell (83n79), cites one anonymous nineteenth century critic of F.W. Farrar as saying,
> Once remove the restraints of religion, teach the poor that future punishment is a fable, and what will be left to hinder the bursting forth with savage yells of millions of ravening wolves, before whom the salt of the earth will be trodden underfoot, Church establishments dissolved, and baronial halls become piles of blackened ruin?

Walker (159–60) notes that even those who rejected eternal punishment still distinguished between a secret esoteric doctrine for themselves and a vulgar exoteric doctrine (i.e., the standard view) that was to be presented to the masses in order to maintain the social order.

[60] Rowell, in *Hell and the Victorians*, 145, cites Farrar from a letter to Troutbeck, a member of the translation committee for the Revised Version of the New Testament (of 1881), as saying,
> By retaining the word "Hell" [the other committee members] will invariably stereotype in the minds of the ignorant, many conceptions which probably every one of them would reject as false; if they use the word "Gehenna" *they use the word which our Lord Himself taught them to use*, and follow the example of the Evangelists. Dare they do otherwise? More perhaps than any of us can at present decide may hang on the issue of their decision.

In conclusion, I believe there are good grounds for saying that Moltmann's claim that the judgment referred to in the texts in question is "penultimate" can be defended as rooted in a sound intuition. But an exegetical argument such as the one offered above is vital if his position is ever to be considered plausible and worthy of discussion within the wider Christian community.

Given his *Christocentric* way of approaching Scripture, the claim that Moltmann's universalism is at odds with *Christ's* own teaching about 'Hell', if sustained, would undermine his entire position. That is why I have paid so much attention to it. It would be a mistake, however, to claim that 'the' central objection to universal salvation has now been removed as these texts, important though they may be, are always read within an overarching understanding of (a) the nature of God—specifically the relationship between God's love and God's wrath—and (b) the way in which God overcomes sin and evil. Overarching, non-universalist readings are not dependent on the synoptic apocalypse or on a particular interpretation of the words of Jesus. Therefore a fully adequate "biblical foundation" for universalism, which goes beyond the limits of the present study, would require paying attention not only to specific texts but to the overall shape and thrust of the biblical canon.

Exegesis, in other words, tends to operate within a wider biblical theology. To illustrate this point, let us consider an Old Testament example. Elaborating on his conviction that "it is possible to integrate ... the particularistic statements [of the Bible] into the universalistic statements," Moltmann states,

> Whenever I would preach about these texts of condemnation, I would preach ... with a view towards the condemnation and destruction sermon of the prophet Jonah. That is, I would preach particularism as self-destroying prophecy and would not be disappointed.[61]

There is much to commend Moltmann's reading. "Forty more days and Ninevah will be overturned," proclaimed Jonah (3:4b). Yet God, we are told, "did not bring upon them the destruction he had threatened" (3:10b). Although Jonah is not only "disappointed" but angry (4:1), God's mercy has the last word. Hence the moving words of 4:11 (the final verse of the book): "Nineveh has more than a hundred and twenty thousand people who cannot tell their right hand from their left, and many cattle as well. Should I not be concerned about that great city?" For Moltmann, this is, no doubt, evidence of the biblical fact that God "judges the sins of the world so as to save the world."[62]

But the selective nature of this reading—and what reading is not selective?—is also instructive. Many Christians, aware of the way Jesus himself refers to the story of Jonah in Matt 12:39–42 and Luke 11:29–32, will want to emphasise something that Moltmann seems to ignore completely: the *repentance* that comes between Jonah's "condemnation and destruction

---

Emphasis in Rowell. How right Farrar was!
[61] Moltmann et al., "Talk-back Session with Dr. Jürgen Moltmann," 41.
[62] CoG, 243 with reference to 1 Sam 2:6.

sermon" and God's mercy (see 3:7–9). "When God saw what they did and how they turned from their evil ways," we are told, "he had compassion . . ." (3:10a). What role does repentance play here? Is it a prerequisite for God's compassion (3:10)? Does it allow an already existing compassion to be made real in history? Or is it somehow the outworking of God's concern (4:11)?

The above rereading of the 'Gehenna' material notwithstanding, the integration of particularism into universalism (to use Moltmann's terminology) still raises many biblical concerns. The role of repentance in Moltmann's view of salvation (which has already been an issue in 4.3.3 above) will be addressed once again in the concluding chapter (in 8.1 and 8.3), together with his understanding of the relationship between God's love and God's wrath (in 8.2). Biblical support for his conviction that judgment is unto salvation will be explored with reference to the book of Revelation in the Appendix (in 9.5).

That said, I would like to suggest that some real progress has made in the above discussion towards developing a more robust biblical foundation for Moltmann's position. In challenging the claim that Jesus' preaching points to an eternal separation between the saved and the lost in this way, it becomes conceivable that those biblical passages that would seem to refer to universal salvation might finally receive the attention they deserve.

Moltmann refers to Eph 1:10; Col 1:20; Phil 2:10; 1 Cor 15; Rom 5:18, and 11:32 in this context.[63] In addition to 1 Tim 4:10, we may also add: John 3:17, 12:47; Heb 2:9; 1 Tim 2:6; Tit 2:11; 1 John 2:2; and John 12:32. This is a substantial body of material. If I were to outline my own case for universal salvation, then, in addition to exploring the "judgment unto salvation" theme of 9.5 throughout the biblical canon, I would certainly attend to these passages in some detail. In the present context, however, I must confine myself to pointing out that while there are standard ways of interpreting these passages in non-universalist ways, it is most interesting that with respect to the last seven, Calvinists have difficulty refuting the universalist implications of the first four, while Arminians have difficulty with the final three. When it comes to the task of detailed biblical exegesis, it is not just universalists who have their work cut out.

7.2 Doing Justice to the Final Judgment

In the previous section, I argued that the fire of Gehenna that we may now associate with the events of 70 CE should be interpreted as a manifestation of the eschatological judgment in which all evil will be totally eradicated, to make way for the full arrival of the new age. The fact that such a Final Judgment is necessary for inaugurating the new creation is assumed and asserted throughout Moltmann's corpus.[64] It is thus not to be "demythologize[d] . . . as an

---

[63] See CoG, 240–41.
[64] See TH, 129 (his sympathetic description of "a judgment that paves the way for something finally new . . . [which is] annihilation for the sake of greater perfection"); WJC, 155 ("the divine judgment out of which the kingdom of righteousness and justice

antiquated apocalyptic concept."⁶⁵ In this section, we will explore whether Moltmann's vision of its role in the renewal of all things is sensitive to the cry for justice that many fear will be undermined by a belief in universal salvation

It is probably fair to say that Moltmann's statements about what this Judgment *is* are less clear than his statements about what it is *not*. Certainly it is not to be visualised in "horrible visions of hell."⁶⁶ And he never tires of saying that it is not about retribution.⁶⁷ Final Judgment in that sense has been vicariously endured for us all by Christ.⁶⁸ Consequently God's judgment will be

---

proceeds"), 315 ("the meaning of this judgment ... is solely the victory of the divine righteousness that is to become the foundation of the new creation of all things"); CoG, 233 ("The whole cosmos .... will be newly created, having endured death and judgment"), 236–37 (which speaks of "the Last Judgment .... serv[ing] the revelation and establishment of God's righteousness and justice among all people and all things, so that God can build his 'new world' on lasting justice, and can therefore create for eternal peace"); and EiT, 109 ("The eschatological horizon .... is the new creation of all things which that judgment ["the 'Last Judgment' "] inaugurates.").

⁶⁵ WJC, 315.

⁶⁶ WJC, 315.

⁶⁷ In addition to 1.4.3 and 1.4.5 above, see TH, 193 (where his claim that "The place of the Torah shining in the light of the fullness of divine glory is taken by ... the judgment seat of Jesus Christ" would seem to imply a move beyond retribution), 211 (where the resurrection is described as "a conquest of judgment" presumably in this sense); CrG, 142 ("in the final judgment God replaces his sovereign righteousness by his law of grace. In this way, the future hope is free from visions of revenge and dreams of omnipotence on the part of the oppressed and the weak. ... God comes not to carry out just revenge upon the evil, but to justify by grace sinners .... This [is a] liberation from legalism, which was bound and is always bound to lead to retribution ..."), 171 (where this link between legalism and retribution is also present when Moltmann speaks of "the law of grace in the midst of judgment, and creative love in the midst of legalism"), 178 (on the contrast between the righteousness of God revealed in the resurrection of the crucified Christ and "the final triumph of the law"); WJC, 335–38 (on "The Apocalyptic Law of Retaliation" as discussed in 1.4.5 above and including the passage from WJC, 337–38 as discussed below), 378–79n2 (in critique of the Heidelberg Catechism); SL, 135 ("The crucified Christ has nothing to do with a God of retribution, or a divine judge presiding over a criminal court"); CoG, x (where he asks rhetorically, "Is the Last Judgment God's final solution for human history?"), 110 (against "the legalistic form of Daniel 12.2"), 114–15 (against all forms of "karma"), 117 ("the merciless law of karma"), 196 (against "legalistic, apocalyptic ideas of judgment"), and 250 ("it is not retaliatory justice").

⁶⁸ In addition to 1.4.1, 4.1, and 4.3.1 above, see CrG, 168 (cited in the following note); TKG, 82 (where he speaks of "The Father who sends his Son through all the abysses and hells of God-forsakenness, of the divine curse and final judgment"); WJC, 155 ("Golgotha .... is the anticipation of the divine judgment out of which the kingdom of righteousness and justice proceeds. What has already happened to Christ is representative of what will happen to everybody: it is a happening *pars pro toto*. Consequently he has suffered vicariously what threatens everyone," his italics), 224 ("Christ has vicariously anticipated the final judgment of God for all the Godless and the

a manifestation of God's grace[69] to be anticipated not in fear but in hope.[70] "[I]t is high time," writes Moltmann, "to discover *the gospel of God's judgment* and to awaken *joy in God's coming righteousness and justice*."[71]

What kind of justice evokes joy rather than fear? In *The Crucified God*, Moltmann draws a contrast between the proclamation of Jesus and that of John the Baptist by observing,

> Jesus broke through legalistic apocalyptic, because he proclaimed *justitia justificans* rather than *justitia distributiva* as the righteousness of the kingdom of God, and anticipated it in the law of grace among the unrighteous and those outside the law.[72]

In his more recent works, Moltmann repeatedly describes this as a "creative" justice.[73] Although it will "*restore* this ruined world and put everything to rights again,"[74] it brings a *new* creation into existence. It is thus "redemptive," in the sense discussed in 5.3 above, rather than (merely or primarily) restorative. As Moltmann puts it,

> This Judgment has to do with God and his creative justice, and is quite different from the forms our earthly justice takes. What we call the Last Judgment is nothing other than the universal revelation of Jesus Christ, and the

---

unjust"); and SL, 212–13 ("Evil, sin, suffering and damnation are 'in God': 'Thou who bearest the sins of the world . . . '.").

[69] See for example CrG, 168 ("The final judgment has already been made in his execution. Jesus' deliverance to men and their attitude to him are decisive for the final judgment. His forgiveness of sins is God's law of grace.") and 229 ("believers . . . sense in judgment [God's] coming grace").

[70] See TKG, 91; WJC, 315, and 322.

[71] CoG, 235 as cited in 1.4.3 above. His emphases.

[72] CrG, 177. His italics. Cf. WJC, 225: "If at the Last Judgment the crucified One himself is the judge, the justice that will prevail is his merciful and justifying righteousness, and none other."

[73] See SL, 129, "Nor is it the righteousness which establishes justice retributive justice, requiting good with good, and evil with evil (*iustitia distributiva*). It is a creative righteousness (*iustitia justificans*)." His italics. Cf. WJC, 335, where he states, "[T]he divine righteousness which is under discussion here has nothing to do with rewards and punishments. It is a righteousness that *creates* justice and puts people right, so it is a redemptive righteousness (Isa. 1.27)." My emphasis. Similarly in CoG, 236 he writes, "Can the righteousness which the Last Judgment serves be any righteousness other than the righteousness of God which *creates* justice and redeems, the righteousness to which the law and the prophets testify, and which the apostle Paul proclaimed in his gospel as justifying righteousness?" My emphasis. This point is made repeatedly in CoG, 250. Cf. the quotation below. Here we may detect another point of contact between Moltmann and Hendrik Hart. See the latter's "The Just Shall Live by Faith: Reformational Reflections on Public Justice and Racist Attitudes," *Christian Scholar's Review* 16, no. 3 (1987): 265–82 where he explores the social implications of the understanding of 'justice as mercy' to be found in Isa 30:18.

[74] CoG, 250. My emphasis.

consummation of his redemptive work. No expiatory penal code will be applied in the court of the crucified Christ. No punishments of eternal death will be imposed. The final spread of the divine righteousness that creates justice serves the eternal kingdom of God, not the final restoration of a divine world order that has been infringed. Judgment at the end is not an end at all; it is the beginning.[75]

Not only is this *justitia justificans* the culmination of justification[76] experienced in history by those who put their faith in God; it also confronts and transforms unbelievers. He writes,

> [O]n his day God will come forth from his hiddenness in history. He will lead those who are his to victory and *will pronounce judgment on his enemies*. He will judge Israel too, as Amos stresses. But at the end of it all he will fill the world with the radiance of his glory, so that *all will see him as he is, extol him, and become righteous in praise of God* (Isa. 35.10; 40.5).[77]

What exactly is the relationship between this judgment and this revelation that transforms God's enemies into the righteous?[78] If earlier in the same work, Moltmann can observe that "[t]he people to whom Christ 'appeared' [in history] were so overwhelmed that they apparently had no choice,"[79] can we conclude that this eschatological change of heart is 'automatic'? Does this "creative" justice have anything to do with the justice for which those who have suffered from the horrendous injustices of history long with all their hearts? Are their oppressors to be brought to justice or simply justified?

The answer to these important, interconnected questions is anything but clear not least because Moltmann does not give them sustained attention. In one of his fuller statements, he writes,

> Judgment is the side of the eternal kingdom that is turned towards history. In that Judgment all sins, every wickedness and every act of violence, the whole injustice of this murderous and suffering world, will be condemned and annihilated, because God's verdict effects what it pronounces. In the divine

---

[75] CoG, 250 (here using "redemptive" with a more traditional meaning). Moltmann continues in CoG, 251, "Its goal is the restoration of all things for the building up of God's eternal kingdom." This shows that, for Moltmann, "restoration" is a means to an end—or rather a means to a beginning.

[76] See SL, chap. 6 ("The Justification of Life") and Jürgen Moltmann, "Justification and New Creation," in *The Future of Creation*, by Jürgen Moltmann, trans. Margaret Kohl (London: SCM Press, 1979), 149–71.

[77] WJC, 322. My emphases. The same line of thought is implicit in CoG, 254 where he writes, "What Christ *accomplished* in his dying and rising is *proclaimed* to all human beings through his gospel and will be *revealed* to everyone and everything at his appearance." His emphases.

[78] Or (to borrow the words of CoG, 255): What is the relationship between "*God's Judgment*, which puts things to rights, and *God's kingdom*, which awakens to new life"? Moltmann's emphases. This question is explored below.

[79] WJC, 226.

Judgment all sinners, the wicked and the violent, the murderers and the children of Satan, the Devil and the fallen angels will be liberated and saved from their deadly perdition through transformation into their true, created being, because God remains true to himself, and does not give up what he has once created and affirmed, or allow it to be lost.[80]

Here we are presented with a juxtaposition of annihilation and transformation which presumably correspond to what Moltmann goes on to describe as the "two sides" of "[t]he eschatological doctrine about the restoration of all things": "*God's Judgment*, which puts things to rights, and *God's kingdom*, which awakens to new life." The same distinction is implied when Moltmann states, "It is a source of endlessly consoling joy to know, not just that the murderers will finally fail to triumph over their victims, but that they cannot in eternity even remain the murderers of their victims."[81] To focus on the "judgment" side of these two statements, we need to ask not only *how* God "puts things to rights" but more specifically how they are put right *between* oppressors and their victims.

Furthermore, is Moltmann's way of putting things likely to be a source of consolation or joy to the innocent victims of history? What is revealed in Christ's eschatological appearance is the "general pardon" of Good Friday.[82] "It is noticeable," writes Moltmann, "that Jesus forgives sins without any conditions—without confession and without any token of reparation. He does what according to Israelite ideas only the judge of the world can do at the Last Judgment: pardon the accused."[83] But does this mean that there is no place for "reparation"? If the Judgment inaugurates the new creation, can we not say that the grace of forgiveness makes way for the justice of reconciliation? Can we squeeze this meaning out of Moltmann's enigmatic statement "Transforming grace is God's punishment for sinners"[84] and give some real content to the "law" that Christ applies, the purpose of which Moltmann so briefly (and thus, for our present purposes, so inadequately) refers to as "rehabilitation [Resozialisierungsstrafrechtes]"?[85]

---

[80] CoG, 255 as cited in 1.4.3 above and (in part) in 8.3 below.
[81] CoG, 255. His emphases.
[82] CoG, 254.
[83] WJC, 115.
[84] "The Logic of Hell," 47 as discussed in 1.3 above. That preliminary discussion suggested that the answer is 'Yes'.
[85] WJC, 338 [*DWJC*, 363] as cited in 1.4 above. To translate the German "Resozialisierungsstrafrechtes" as a referennce to Christ's "law" of "rehabilitation" as found in the English version cited here, is accurate as far as it goes. But this does not fully capture the (potential) force of the German term. While "Resozialisierung-" suggests a 'resocialisation' or "rehabilitation" and while "-[R]echtes" refers to "law," the middle element, "[S]traf-," emphasises the 'penal' nature of the process. Indeed, 'Strafrecht' means 'criminal law'. The contrast in the English translation between Christ's "law" whose "purpose is rehabilitation" (WJC, 338) and the "ultimate" apocalyptic "law of retaliation" (WJC, 337) also referred to earlier as "the penal law of

"On the one hand," writes Moltmann, "we have apocalyptic Christianity, which subordinates the saving gospel of Jesus—viewed as God's last offer in history—to the ultimate law of retaliation in the Last Judgment. On the other hand we have Christian eschatology, which sees *Jesus* in the figure of the universal judge and expects that he will finally bring justice to those who have never received justice, and will make the unjust just."[86] There is no doubt where Moltmann's sympathies lie. The former may be "Christianity," but only the latter is truly "Christian." That the Jesus of his vision will "make the unjust just" is clearly evident. But can he, or does he, at one and the same time, affirm that this Jesus will "finally bring justice to those who have never received justice"? Or to ask a more pertinent question, does he anywhere move beyond mere affirmation (which we find in this passage) to spelling out what this might mean?

To begin to find an adequate answer, we will have to piece together various statements and hints that Moltmann has made. Although the fact that this is necessary points to a significant *lacuna* in his writings, the fact that such a piecing-together is possible points to the potential of his overall position to respond to criticisms that might otherwise render his project implausible to many.

There is one passage in particular that points to the justice that will be exercised in the Last Judgment in a way that should dispel the suspicion that Moltmann's universalism is permissive towards the oppressors of history. Taking issue with a proposal often associated with annihilationism, he writes,

> There is a modern evangelical idea about a *conditional immortality*, according to which no one finds a life after death without believing and unless God confers eternal life; all the rest simply remain dead. But I do not find this very helpful ..., because it excludes God's judgment. *Mass murderers might possibly welcome this solution, because they would then not have to answer before God's judgment for what they had done.*[87]

---

retaliation" (WJC, 337) is not unfair to Moltmann's intended meaning. (Much of the relevant passage is cited in 1.4 above.) But we should not overlook the fact that in the German text, this is a contrast between "Vergeltungs*straf*recht" and "Resozialisierungs*straf*echtes" (*DWJC*, 362–63, my emphases). The latter could fairly be translated as 'the penal law of rehabilitation' (provided its restorative nature, which is clearly indicated in the English translation in WJC, is not thereby minimised).

[86] WJC, 337–38. His emphasis.

[87] CoG, 109. Second emphasis mine. Cf. his comment in "A Conversation with Jürgen Moltmann," in *Faith: Conversations with Contemporary Theologians*, ed. Teofilo Cabestrero, trans. Donald D. Walsh (Maryknoll, NY: Orbis, 1980), 137, "Without liberation, without new justice, the church's message of reconciliation becomes "appeasement," as the English would say." Indeed! Cf. his brief yet forthright claim in Moltmann, *Creating a Just Future*, 36–37, "God is the judge of the murderers and the avenger of the victims. The nuclear catastrophe will not annihilate this apocalyptic horizon of the last judgment but will rather lead humankind directly into it." It is a shame that Moltmann has not been this forthright in his major writings.

There are thus solid grounds for concluding that Moltmann holds to a double-sided and double-edged conception of Final Salvation/Judgment from which the mass murderer is neither "excluded" nor "exempt." In Moltmann's words, "Davon ist niemand ausgenommen oder fregestellt . . . ."[88]

But the question of 'How?' remains.

In 1.6 above, I suggested that it might be fruitful to bring Moltmann's theology into dialogue with the vision of justice and reconciliation to be found in *St. Peter's Apocalypse*.[89] To bring these two horizons together, we shall first turn to the work of theologian, Miroslav Volf.

In the preface to his highly acclaimed *Exclusion and Embrace: A Theological Exploration of Identity, Otherness, and Reconciliation*, Volf reveals that this work had its origins in a question put to him as a Croatian by his former doctoral supervisor, Jürgen Moltmann: "But can you embrace a četnik?"[90] Volf's later essay "The Final Reconciliation: Reflections on a Social Dimension of the Eschatological Transition"[91] may be fruitfully read as an important and extended postscript to this work. And to this question.

Volf does not refer to *St. Peter's Apocalypse* in this essay. But he might have done, for like the author(s) of that second century work, he finds "profound eschatological insights"[92] in the vision of *post-mortem* reconciliation between victims and perpetrators put before us in Plato's *Phaedo*. Highlighting a "social dimension" (as his title puts it) to the Final Judgment that the theological tradition "has severely under-emphasized"[93] and that even contemporary theology has "inadequately addressed,"[94] Plato's "eschatological myth"[95] can help us recognise that,

> For the perpetrator to be released [from the Hell of the Acherusian lake], something needs to happen *between* the perpetrator and the victim, not just *in* each of them (for instance, repentance in the case of the perpetrator, or inner healing, in the case of the victim). . . . Though justice is indispensable, required also are the psychological and interpersonal phenomena of repentance and forgiveness, of a sense of guilt and the offer of mercy.[96]

---

[88] Moltmann, "Am Ende ist alles Gottes: Hat der Glaube an die Hölle ausgedient?," 543, as discussed and translated in 1.3 above.

[89] That is the St. Peter's Apocalypse as interpreted in the light of the Rainer fragment discussed in 1.6 above rather than in accordance with the extent Ethiopic text.

[90] Miroslav Volf, *Exclusion and Embrace: A Theological Exploration of Identity, Otherness, and Reconciliation* (Nashville, TN: Abingdon, 1996), 9. His italics. On Volf's work on Moltmann's eschatology, see n. 3 above. A četnik is a Serbian fighter.

[91] Volf's discussion of Jonathan Edwards in this important essay is referred to in 1.2n26 above.

[92] Volf, "The Final Reconciliation," 98.

[93] Volf, "The Final Reconciliation," 94.

[94] Volf, "The Final Reconciliation," 91.

[95] Volf, "The Final Reconciliation," 95.

[96] Volf, "The Final Reconciliation," 98. His emphases.

To incorporate this insight into a truly Christian theology, Volf insists that it be firmly placed within "an economy of grace,"[97] a grace "which does not negate justice but affirms it precisely in the act of transcending it."[98] Where Socrates' judges remain "on the sidelines,"[99] thus leaving the murderer and his victim to reconcile or not as the case may be, a Christian vision recognises a "third party" who would "in the precise function of a judge who suffered the victim's fate and was judged in the perpetrator's place, be at the very center of their reconciliation."[100]

Volf is clearly intent on emphasising and honouring both the human and divine sides of this "judgment of *grace*."[101] On the one hand, noting that the Last Judgment without its human appropriation is "unthinkable" as a transition to "the world of perfect love," he writes,

> The divine judgment will reach its goal when, by the power of the Spirit, all eschew attempts at self-justification, acknowledge their own sin in its full magnitude, experience liberation from guilt and the power of sin, and, finally, when each recognizes that all others have done precisely that—given up on self-justification, acknowledged their sin, and experienced liberation. Having recognized that others have changed—that they have been given their true identity by being freed from sin—one will no longer condemn others but offer them the grace of forgiveness. When that happens, each will see himself or herself and all others in relation to himself and herself as does Christ, the judge who was judged in their place and suffered their fate.[102]

On the other hand, although divine forgiveness cannot be a "substitute for inter-human forgiveness,"[103] he still finds it important to state that "the subject of the eschatological transition is God rather than human beings."[104] This emphasis, along with the claim that human reconciliation has already been accomplished *de jure* in Christ, is necessary, he thinks, to give certainty to the Final Judgment's outcome.[105] "[T]he will's turning to God and holding onto God," he writes, "is itself God's work."[106]

In order to avoid positing a view of this divine act in Christ in which human agency—and thus the social dimension of the eschatological transition—is eclipsed, Volf appeals to Barth's view that in Christ "we are awakened to our own truest being as life and act."[107] Thus, following Luther, he stresses that

---

[97] Volf, "The Final Reconciliation," 98.
[98] Volf, "The Final Reconciliation," 97.
[99] Volf, "The Final Reconciliation," 97.
[100] Volf, "The Final Reconciliation," 98.
[101] Volf, "The Final Reconciliation," 102. His emphasis.
[102] Volf, "The Final Reconciliation," 103.
[103] Volf, "The Final Reconciliation," 101.
[104] Volf, "The Final Reconciliation," 95 and 104 (where this identical statement occurs).
[105] See Volf, "The Final Reconciliation," 104. His italics.
[106] Volf, "The Final Reconciliation," 105.
[107] Volf, "The Final Reconciliation," 105n73, citing Barth's *Church Dogmatics* 4/1, 12. On Barth's "robust" view of human agency, as Volf puts it here, see also 6.2 above.

"God 'does not work in us without us'."[108] In that light, the essay as a whole is an attempt "to thematize more clearly the character and import of human participation as an inter-human activity within the overarching account of the eschatological transition accomplished by the power of the Spirit."[109] "Grace" is thus "the defining origin and sustaining power" of this "whole process," while "human participation" is "a fruit and indispensable medium of that grace that transforms sinful persons and their relationships."[110] The eschatological transition is therefore "a divine act toward human beings which is also a social event between them."[111]

Although it is clear from this essay that Volf is not a universalist[112]—in fact his comments on the restitution of all things in *Exclusion and Embrace* sympathetically yet critically address Moltmann's proposals to this end[113]—, it

---

[108] Volf, "The Final Reconciliation," 107.
[109] Volf, "The Final Reconciliation," 107.
[110] Volf, "The Final Reconciliation," 107–108.
[111] Volf, "The Final Reconciliation," 93.
[112] In "The Final Reconciliation," 103–104, Volf writes,
   For those, however, for whom the judgment day does not become the day of giving and receiving grace, it will become a day of wrath leading to a hellish world of indifference and hate. Seeking to justify themselves as Christ the judge reveals the truth about their lives, they will, in Matthean terms, seize their debtors "by the throat", demand payment, and, since it will not be forthcoming, condemn them "into the prison" until they do pay (Matt. 18:30). They will have thereby shown themselves as not having received divine grace and will therefore be "handed over" by God "to be tortured" until they pay their "entire debt" (Matt. 18:34). To refuse to show grace to the offender and to receive grace from the offended, is to have rejected God's judgment of grace.
[113] In *Exclusion and Embrace*, 299n7, Volf writes,
   In powerful passages about the restitution of all things, Jürgen Moltmann has proposed recently to consider God's judgment at the end of history an exercise in rectifying justice, parallel to the justification of the sinner in the middle of history ([CoG], 235–55). The result of God's judgment thus conceived fits well with our desire for the final triumph of God's love, but we should keep in mind that nothing could guarantee the achievement of this result without divine "violence." There is no need to postulate the existence of full self-immunized incarnations of evil to make plausible that, from the perspective of such a person, her transformation into a cheerful doer of what from God's perspective is good will involve violence.... We find this act of transformation tolerable and tend not to call it "violent" only because, as Christians, we share the perspective of the divine transformer and identify with the desired result. The only way to avoid divine violence towards those who refuse to be changed nonviolently is to stipulate in advance that no one will refuse to be changed by the lure of God's love. Though those who have been touched by God's love ought to hope for a universal nonrefusal, if they are not blind to the human condition they will be hesitant to count on it. Hence the possibility of final condemnation.
In the following footnote (299n8), Volf expresses his own "hope for a universal nonrefusal" by referring to CoG, 249 in which Moltmann discusses "open

is still fair to say that his argument could very easily be incorporated into a universalist framework. His serious attempt to integrate our mutual "justification" and embrace[114] within an eschatological Christ event that is a *judgment* of grace/judgment of *grace* is also more than capable of honouring the concerns of *St. Peter's Apocalypse*.

In my judgment, there is not only very little here with which Moltmann would disagree but much that he would embrace enthusiastically.[115] Volf effectively supplies what is in my view the 'missing piece' to Moltmann's vision of the Final Judgment. Moreover, there are strong indications that Volf sees Moltmann's thought as pointing in the direction that he is exploring. This is indicated in two important footnotes that frame his essay. In the first, having referred to a German burial service "in which a kind of post-mortem reconciliation between the deceased and their enemies is enacted in the form of a prayer,"[116] he notes that it was Moltmann who drew his attention to this

---

universalism." Volf does not use such terminology though, preferring to cite the saying, "I am not a universalist, but God may be." Interestingly, in "All Things New: Invited to God's Future," *Asbury Theological Journal* 48, no. 1 (Spring 1993): 36, Moltmann uses almost identical words of himself. But these must be read in context.

[114] Volf, "The Final Reconciliation," 93.

[115] Cf. Moltmann's brief yet clearly favourable reference to the social dimension of judgment and to Volf's "The Final Reconciliation" in IEB, 144 and 171n4 and the more sustained expression of the same line of thought in Jürgen Moltmann, "The Final Judgment: Sunrise of Christ's Liberating Justice," *Anglican Theological Review* 89, no. 4 (Fall 2007): 565–76, especially 572n2, which is reiterated in "Sun of Righteousness: The Gospel about Judgment and the New Creation of All Things," in SRA, 139 and 238n10. The main point of contention would be Volf's rejection of universal salvation. In addition to offering a different approach to Matt 18:23–35 (see EiT, 163–164), Moltmann's comments in CoG, 109 suffice to indicate the basic thrust of his probable reply. He writes,
> The Lausanne Covenant of evangelical theologians says: 'Those who reject Christ repudiate the joy of salvation and condemn themselves to eternal separation from God.' They will therefore not only be damned by God. They also damn themselves. Is this theologically conceivable? Can some people *damn themselves*, and others redeem themselves by accepting Christ? If this were so, God's decisions would be dependent on the will of human beings. God would be the auxiliary who executes the wishes of people who decide their fate for themselves. If I can damn myself, I am my own God and judge. Taken to a logical conclusion this is atheistic.

His emphasis. To speak of rejecting God's grace amounts to the same thing. How does this cohere with our salvation being accomplished *de jure* in Christ to be realised *de facto* as part of "an unfailing divine work" as he puts it in "The Final Reconciliation," 104? Moltmann might find this reliance on Barth's approach to reconciliation insufficiently eschatological. But he might still cite Volf's own words back to him by asking, Is not "the will's turning to God and holding onto God . . . itself God's work" ("The Final Reconciliation," 105)?

[116] Volf, "The Final Reconciliation," 91.

"custom."[117] In the second, after reiterating the inadequacy of a Final Judgment that focusses solely on individuals receiving their just deserts, he notes, "A recent notable eschatology which takes seriously social relations and stresses the primacy of grace in the eschatological transition is Moltmann's *The Coming of God*."[118]

As the present study should indicate, it is easy to document the primacy of grace in this work and in Moltmann's corpus as a whole. But an emphasis on the social, inter-personal dimension of the Final Judgment is virtually impossible to detect in the pages that Volf cites.[119] Perhaps he is reading what he knows of Moltmann's views from personal conversation[120] into the vague references to "reconciliation"[121] that appear in this the most detailed of Moltmann's portrayals of the Final Judgment.

The fact that the "final spread of the divine righteousness that creates justice" implies a social dimension to the "Restoration of All things"[122] can be inferred from the way Moltmann approaches the issue of justice and reconciliation in contexts other than that of the Final Judgment. This is evident, for example, in his understanding of the relevance of the Trinity for human relations. "The perichoretic at-oneness of the triune God," he writes, "corresponds to the experience of the community of Christ, the community which the Spirit unites through respect, affection and love."[123] The question raised in *The Church in the Power of the Spirit* as to whether and how "Christian fellowship" may "exist between the hangman and his victims"[124] would in his mature theologising ultimately be answered in this context. Volf sounds nowhere more 'Moltmannian' than in his penultimate sentence: "The final reconciliation is the eschatological side of the vision of social transformation contained in the movement of the Triune God toward sinful humanity to take them up into the circle of divine communal love."[125]

---

[117] See Volf, "The Final Reconciliation," 108n2. Although this does not seem to be a well-known "custom" in Germany, prayer for reconciliation with the enemies of the deceased was clearly present in the printed burial service for Ernst Käsemann, the relevant part of which is cited by Volf in this note.

[118] Volf, "The Final Reconciliation," 113n84. His italics. This follows the discussion on p. 107.

[119] He cites CoG, 250–55. But see CoG, 116–17 as discussed below.

[120] From my meeting with Professor Moltmann on September 23, 1998 in London, it became very clear to me that there was a social dimension to his thinking about the Final Judgment at that time. But documenting this from his writings was another matter.

[121] In CoG, 250, for example, Moltmann refers to "reconciliation without limits." That this might mean reconciliation between people and not simply with God is not specified.

[122] CoG, 250.

[123] TKG, 157–58.

[124] CPS, 346.

[125] Volf, "The Final Reconciliation," 108.

Eschatologically speaking, Moltmann's "social doctrine of the Trinity"[126] implies a social dimension to the Final Judgment.

---

[126] TKG, 19. With respect to his "social doctrine of the Trinity," one difficulty that Moltmann faces in making intra-trinitarian love a norm for human love, especially a love that would overcome profound alienation, is that love within the Trinity exemplifies a love for the same (and a love for otherness in what is the same) rather than a love for the fundamentally other. This problem is highlighted by Henry Jansen, *Relationality and the Concept of God* (Amsterdam: Rodopi, 1995), chap. 4 ("Jürgen Moltmann: God as Community"). In his "Moltmann's View of God's (Im)mutability: The God of the Philosophers and the God of the Bible," *Neue Zeitschrift für systematische Theologie und Religionsphilosophie* 36 (1994): 284–301, Jansen presents the problem succinctly (on p. 295) as follows:

> Moltmann understands the love of the Trinity as perfect in that the members of the Trinity are constantly engaged in a life of self-giving. This dynamic perfection is also the model for human society. But the love of the members of the Trinity is seen as analogical (*philia*) and the love of the Trinity for creation is seen as dialectical (*agape*) (love of like for unlike). To protect the unity of God, Moltmann must finally deny that the Trinity is constituted by alterity, in which case he must hold that there is one model for the Trinity *a se* and another for the Trinity *quoad nos*. This logical conclusion causes a rift in that the very unity of the immanent and economic Trinity which Moltmann has been so much at pains to elucidate. At the same time, it is difficult to see how the perfection of the Trinity can serve as an ideal for human society if dialectical love is superior, as it is in Moltmann's mind, to the analogical love that constitutes the Trinity, since the latter is not as such oriented towards that which is different from oneself. For Moltmann this finally constitutes a need for God, since love of like for like is not enough.

His italics. Jansen is certainly identifying some important issues here. But a number of comments are in order. Firstly, if we focus on the trinitarian history as taking place in both directions of time (see 2.5 above), it is perhaps possible to see how, *for Moltmann at least*, the distinction between the immanent and economic 'Trinit*ies*', between God *a se* and God *quoad nos*, need not undermine the unity of the immanent and economic 'Trinit*y*'. Secondly, Jansen's claim that for God the "love of like for like is not enough" and that this "constitutes a need for God" is one that Moltmann would seem to accept. God "expects and needs love" he says explicitly in TKG, 99 (as cited in 4.2n91 above). But, it seems to me, this is not a fundamental problem for Moltmann's position because he does not posit the immanent Trinity as "perfection"—at least not in the way Jansen would seem to imply. We must not ignore the theme of "Divine Eschatology" here (to cite the title of CoG, chap. 5)! Admittedly, Jansen is writing before the publication of *Das Kommen Gottes* (CoG). But as Moltmann states in TKG, 161,

> If it is the quintessence of doxology, then the doctrine of the immanent Trinity is part of eschatology as well. The economic Trinity completes and perfects itself to immanent Trinity when the history and experience of salvation are completed and perfected. When everything is 'in God' and 'God is all in all', then the economic Trinity is raised into and transcended in the immanent Trinity. What remains is the eternal praise of the triune God in his glory.

Clearly, this "glory" does not leave the immanent Trinity unchanged. It is its fulfilment, glorification, and 'perfection' also. This means that, for Moltmann, even the immanent Trinity does not function as a norm for human life in an atemporal sense. This is one of

How might this "final spread of the divine righteousness that creates justice" relate to Moltmann's apparent insistence that "Mass murderers ... have to answer before God's judgment for what they ha[ve] done"?[127] There is perhaps only one passage in *The Coming of God* that can be said to really begin to answer this concretely. Reflecting on the inadequacy of seeing our "earthly, fragmentary" lives being "broken off" to be "absorbed into a different, divine life" without resolution, Moltmann stresses our need to think of some kind of "on-going history after death with our lives as we have lived them." This brings him to a space close to Volf and not far from *St. Peter's Apocalypse*. Giving clear expression to his conviction that theological reflection be oriented to, and guided by, genuine pastoral concerns and authentic spiritual desires, he writes,

> Purifying fire, transmigration of souls, the soul's journey, an expiatory passage through the faults and omissions of this life are all images for this [ongoing history]. If we leave aside the external ecclesiastical and political motives that were often bound up with ideas of this kind, and look simply at what is meant, we could after all say: I shall again come back to my life, and in the light of God's grace and in the power of his mercy *put right what has gone awry*, finish what was begun, pick up what was neglected, *forgive the tresspasses* [sic], heal the hurts, and be permitted to gather up the moments of happiness and to transform mourning into joy.[128]

Finally, we can bring out the social dimension of this process of resolution and reconciliation (which in the above passage is still somewhat vulnerable to an individualistic interpretation) by examining a theme that is most fully developed in Moltmann's early work, *The Church in the Power of the Spirit*. Here Moltmann insists that the Christ who will judge us in the future is present in history in a special way in the poor and the humiliated. Reflecting on Matt 25: 31–46, Moltmann notes,

> [T]he Son of man, who is also the world's Judge, calls all men to their account, judging them according to what they have done to him in his hidden presence in the poor.... It is not that the wretched are the object of Christian love or the

---

the reasons why, in the text above, I say that "*Eschatologically speaking*, Moltmann's "social doctrine of the Trinity" implies a social dimension to the Final Judgment." My emphasis.

[127] CoG, 109 as cited above.

[128] CoG, 116–17. My emphases. ('Trespasses' has been misspelt in the ET.) On CoG, 118, He concludes this section (entitled, "The Future of the Spoiled Life: Some Personal Thoughts"), by saying,
> So I would think that eternal life gives the broken and the impaired and those whose lives have been destroyed space and time and strength to live the life which they were intended for, and for which they were born. I think this, not for selfish reasons, for the sake of my personal completion, and not morally, for the sake of some kind of purification; I think it for the sake of the justice which I believe is God's concern and his first option.

Cf. Moltmann's evaluation of purgatory in CoG, 106.

fulfilment of a moral duty; they are the latent presence of the coming Saviour and Judge of the world, the touchstone which determines salvation and damnation.[129]

This strongly indicates that for mass murderers to answer for what they have done and to put right what has gone awry, they must come before their victims. To come face to face with Christ is to come face to face with those in whom He is already present. In the final analysis, therefore, Moltmann's eschatology is not politically irresponsible.[130] As the theme of Christ's hidden presence can be documented in Moltmann's later writings also,[131] it is entirely legitimate to read these powerful words from *The Church in The Power of the Spirit* alongside his discussion of eschatological justice in *The Coming of God*, thus filling in what is otherwise a serious *lacuna* in his systematic reflections on the Final Judgment.

7.3 Justice and Mercy: Face to Face

This chapter has focussed on two areas in which Moltmann's reflections on the Final Judgment need to be supplemented (rather than contradicted) if his eschatology is to enjoy widespread interest and discussion: the biblical

---

[129] CPS, 126–27. Moltmann insists that the "least of the brethren" cannot be reduced to poor and persecuted Christians (126). Instead he speaks of "two brotherhoods of Christ, the professed and professing brotherhood which is the community of the exalted one; and the unknown and disowned brotherhood of the least of men with the humiliated Christ" (129). (For an earlier exploration of this "twofold" conception of "brotherhood," though one in which the theme of judgment is underdeveloped, see Moltmann's essay "The Cross and Civil Religion," in *Religion and Political Society*, by Jürgen Moltmann et al, trans. and ed. the Institute of Christian Thought (New York: Harper and Row, 1974), 43–44. Cf. his "Hope in the Struggle of the People," in *The Passion for Life: A Messianic Lifestyle*, by Jürgen Moltmann, trans. M. Douglas Meeks (Philadephia: Fortress Press, 1978), 104–105.) While noting that "The apocalyptic Christ, the poor, hungry, forsaken Judge, has generally remained outside the door of church and society" (129), he states that it is equally one-sided and thus distorted to "wait for the coming Lord as an apocalyptic angel of revenge on behalf of those who are oppressed on earth" (132). Anticipating the two-fold distinction-connection between judgment and new creation stressed in later works and explored above, he continues (in conclusion),
> The fellowship of Christ lives simultaneously in the presence of the exalted one and of the one who was humiliated. Because of that it expects from his appearance in glory the end of the history of suffering and the consummation of the history of liberation.

[130] On political responsibility as one of Moltmann's own criteria for theology, see the introduction to this chapter. My concern here has been with Moltmann's explicit view of Final Judgment not with his ethics. For a recent, passionate, and nuanced call to justice and mercy for perpetrators of evil that includes reparation, see EoH, chap. 12 ("Divine and Human Righteousness and Justice"). This fine discussion has very positive eschatological implications.

[131] See WJC, 100–102, 336; and EiT, 249, 295.

foundations of his universalist view of Hell and the issue of justice in his portrayal of a Final Judgment that paves the way for universal reconciliation. I will bring these two concerns together in this final section by offering some biblical reflections on the eschatological embrace of justice and mercy as anticipated in some important chapters in the book of Genesis. These thoughts are offered in support of the general thrust of Moltmann's understanding of God's "*justice of mercy*."[132]

The idea that there will be a "social dimension" to the Final Judgment involving a face to face encounter between oppressor and oppressed is rooted in Scripture.[133] Consider the following passage from Isa 60:14–16 in which Israel is told,

> The descendants of those who oppressed you shall come bending low to you,
>   and all who despised you shall bow down at your feet;
> they shall call you the City of the Lord,
>   the Zion of the Holy One of Israel.
>
> Whereas you have been forsaken and hated,
>   with no one passing through,
> I will make you majestic forever,
>   a joy from age to age.
> You shall suck the milk of nations,
>   you shall suck the breasts of kings;
> and you shall know that I, the Lord, am your Saviour
>   and your Redeemer, the Mighty One of Jacob.

Commenting on v. 14 in particular, Brian Walsh captures well the impact of this remarkable prophecy:

> Imagine that! Hitler on his knees before 6,000,000 Jews, Oliver North and Ronald Reagan on their knees before Nicaraguan peasants, [former] Prime Minister [P. W.] Botha before Nelson Mandela and Steve Biko, various Prime Ministers and Ministers of Native Affairs kneeling before the Dene, Inuit, Lubicon and Innu people of Canada, you and I before those we have oppressed.[134]

Indeed, the cry for justice calls for this kind of imagination! But if we read this and the surrounding verses in the light of the book of Genesis, facing and bowing down before those we have oppressed is also related to the miracle of reconciliation.

---

[132] WJC, 90. His emphasis.
[133] The following paragraphs parallel my "Commentary: Genesis 27:29, Isaiah 60:14–16 and Genesis 32:27–30," *Third Way* 25, no. 6 (August 2002): 16. I will be following the NRSV unless otherwise noted.
[134] Brian Walsh, *Who Turned Out the Lights? The Light of the Gospel in a Post-Enlightenment Culture: An Inaugural Lecture* (Toronto: Institute for Christian Studies, 1989), 18.

When Jacob is blessed by his father (while in the process of stealing the birthright from his brother Esau) in Gen 27:29, the prophecy uttered by Isaac begins with a remarkable parallel,

"Let peoples serve you,
    and nations bow down to you.
Be lord over your brothers,
    and may your mother's sons bow down to you.
Cursed be everyone who curses you,
    and blessed be everyone who blesses you!"

Here the relationship between brothers is seen as a microcosm of the relationship between Israel and the nations. This establishes a canonical, intertextual relationship[135] between Gen 27:29 and Isa 60:14–16.

To explore the full significance of the 'brothers as nations' motif, we need to see how the bowing down theme is worked out not only in the Jacob narratives but also in the story of Joseph. Given the way the blessings experienced by Jacob are passed on to his son in the prophecy of Gen 49:26, the parallel passing on that occurs with respect to the 'bowing down' theme may be seen as part of a narrative artistry that would have us recognise that this bowing down is not the underside of 'lordship' (27:29b), normally conceived, but is intimately related to both the receiving of blessing and, even more unexpectedly, the giving of blessing. The following discussion, therefore, will begin with the relationship between Joseph and his brothers. Then we shall return to Isaiah before finally looking at the remarkable way in which themes that are expanded in the Joseph narrative find their initial, concentrated depth-meaning in the relationship between Jacob (or 'Israel' as he is known after his struggle with God at the Jabbok) and Esau.

The underside of 'lordship' motif is introduced in Gen 37, where we are told that Joseph's brothers hate their father's favourite son not least because of the two dreams he has in which they are seen as bowing down to him (Gen 37:5–9). Years later, when they are forced to travel to Egypt for food, they fail to recognise the governor of the land as the brother they sold into slavery and bow down to him "with their faces to the ground" (Gen 42:6). Joseph then manipulates them into returning to Egypt a second time with Benjamin, whereupon they bow down to him again (Gen 43:26 and 28).

Yet finally, with weeping so extreme that even Pharaoh's household gets to hear about it (Gen 45:2), Joseph reveals himself to his brothers and kisses and weeps over each of them (45:15). The ones who oppressed Joseph and who are forced to bow down to him are thus forgiven, embraced, and blessed, being saved from starvation and being allowed to live in what the Pharaoh himself judges to be "the best part of the land" (Gen 47:6).

---

[135] For a defence of canonical and intertextual meaning, see my "The Call of Wisdom/The Voice of the Serpent: A Canonical Approach to the Tree of Knowledge."

Reading Isaiah's vision in the light of this story, we can see the *brothers* who come to Joseph as prefiguring the *nations* who will bow down to Israel. The counterpart to the miracle of reconciliation narrated in Gen 45–47 is seen in the promise that Israel will—to read Isa 60:16a literally (*contra* the NIV)—suck the breasts of Gentile kings. Israel and her enemies will be as close as a young child and its mother.

That such mother-child intimacy may be seen as mediating God's presence as a mother has already been expressed in Isa 49, in which there is a clear relationship between YHWH as nursing mother in vv. 14–15 and the Gentile queens who will nurse the children of Israel in 49:23a. Furthermore, Isa 60:16 is also thematically and verbally related to a remarkable passage in Isa 66, in which the poetic parallel and wordplay established between 'breasts' and 'glory' in v. 11 anticipate the close connection between Jerusalem as mother in vv. 11–12 and the explicitly divine, maternal promise of comfort found in v. 13.[136] There are thus complex relationships between the brothers/nations bowing down and *receiving* blessing (Gen 27:29; 45–47; 50:15–21) and between the nations bowing down and *mediating* or *giving* what must be seen as God's own blessing and comfort to Israel (Gen 27:29; Isa 60:14–16). This is the justice in store for "the descendants of those who have oppressed" Israel (Isa 60:14a), a justice beyond retribution and beyond restoration.

---

[136] The connection between Isa 66:11 and 60:16 is both thematic and verbal. If we modify the NRSV to bring out the poetic parallel, God's promise to Israel in Isa 66:11 reads:
   that you may nurse and be satisfied
      from her consoling breast [*šōd*];
   that you may drink deeply with delight
      from *the abundance of her glory* [*kevôd*].
In the verses that follow, the maternal nurture offered by Jerusalem is also revealed as the maternal nurture offered by YHWH. In 66:12, Jerusalem is portrayed as blessed by YHWH as she is seen as 'nursing from the overflowing glory [*kevôd*] of the nations' (this part of the verse is obscured in the NRSV but is clear in the NJB) as well as continuing to show maternal love to her own child. Then, in 66:13, YHWH's promises:
   As a mother comforts her child
      So I will comfort you;
   You shall be comforted in Jerusalem.
The connection to YHWH as mother links the 'glory' of vv. 11 and 12 to YHWH's glory in v. 18. It is unfortunate that, with the notable exception of the NKJV and NLT, the *šōd*/*kevôd* worldplay and parallel in v. 11, highlighted above, is not brought out in the English translations. This parallel is made possible by the unusual spelling/pointing of *šōd* (normally *šad*) which, apart from Job 24:9, occurs only here and in Isa 60:16—this being a passage in which *kevôd* (in addition to other terms for glory) is also prominent (see Isa 60:1, 2, and 13). This additional, verbal connection with Isa 66:11–13 is strong evidence that Isa 60:16 has divine depth and does not merely reflect the tendency of the empires of the ancient Near East to co-opt maternal imagery.

On the pervasive, biblical connection between glory and the female embodiment of the divine, see Nicholas Ansell, "Creational Man/Eschatological Woman: A Future for Theology." Inaugural address (Toronto: Institute for Christian Studies, 2006).

That this will be brought about by "the Mighty One of Jacob" (Isa 60:16) is significant as this phrase occurs elsewhere in the Hebrew Bible only in Isa 49:26, Ps 132:2–5, and Gen 49:24. This invites us to see further intertextual connections that we might otherwise miss, not least between Genesis and Isaiah. Within Isaiah itself, the fact this phrase is consistently associated with bowing down and breastfeeding not only underlines the continuities between Isa 49 and Isa 60, but also alerts us to the way the promise of Isa 49:23 ("kings shall be your foster fathers, and their queens your nursing mothers") has been radicalised in the striking imagery of Isa 60:16, even as the movement beyond retributive justice in the latter passage forms a redemptive contrast and response to the harsh judgment of Isa 49:26.

As for the relationship between Isaiah and Genesis, rich intertextual meaning is especially evident in the striking parallel between (a) the wordplay that connects 'breasts' and 'glory' in the Hebrew of the related Isa 66:11 (noted above) and (b) the triple wordplay that connects the "Almighty" with the blessings of 'breasts' and 'the heavens' in the Hebrew of Gen 49:25.[137] The

---

[137] Gen 49:25 in the NRSV (here slightly modified to bring out the plural of the heavens) reads:
  by the God of your father, who will help you
    by the Almighty [*šadday*] who will bless you
    with blessings of *the heavens* [*šāmayim*] above,
  blessings of the deep that lies beneath,
    blessing of the breasts [*šādayim*] and of the womb.
Nahum M. Sarnu, *Genesis*. JPS Torah Commentary (Philadelphia: Jewish Publication Society, 1991), 344, notes that the "sound-harmony" in Hebrew between "the deep" and "the womb" and between "heaven" and "breasts" is enhanced by the reversal of the "natural order" of womb and breast here (cf. Hos 9:14). (In other words, the poetry has a deliberate A, B, A', B' structure.) He also notes that there is "an obvious word play" between *šadday* and *šādayim*. The parallel with Isa 66:11 (see n. 136 above) is striking.

The relationship between Ps 132:2–5 and Gen 49:24 (together with the variant that replaces "Jacob" with "Israel" in Isa 1:24) noted by Leslie C. Allen, *Psalms 101–150*. Word Biblical Commentary 21, rev. ed. (Nashville, TN: Thomas Nelson, 2002), 270, though valid with respect to ark traditions, does not shed much light on "the Mighty One of Jacob" motif elsewhere. It is interesting, however, that due to its placement between Pss 131 and 133 within the Davidic 'songs of assent', the intense restlessness of Ps 132 that is set in motion by the unfulfilled Davidic "vow" to find a "resting place" for "the Mighty One of Jacob" (vv. 2 and 5) is related both to the 'unity among brothers' theme of Ps 133 and to the intimate image of the "weaned child with its mother" just a few verses before Ps 132:2 in Ps 131:2. As the Hebrew could be referring to a contented child (and contented soul, cf. the parallel with Ps 116:7) that is literally 'upon' its mother, perhaps this is a child that has just been breastfed. If "weaned" is intended here, the emphasis is on a child that is satisfied and not hungry. Maternal nurture—both human and divine—remains central to the image.

The close association of "the Mighty One of Jacob" with the maternal blessing of Gen 49:25, immediately after the first canonical appearance of the phrase in Gen 49:24, is thus arguably present in Ps 132 and clearly present in Isa 49 and Isa 60. It also fits with the repeated emphasis on blessing and mercy in Sir 51:12b.

relationship between Gen 27:29 and Isa 60:14–16, therefore, is supported and deepened by what we might call the (intratextual-intertextual) 'triangulation' that exists between Isa 60:16, Isa 66:11, and Gen 49:25.

This helps us better appreciate how Gen 49:25, as part of the prophetic blessing that Jacob passes on to his son in Gen 49:22–26, deepens and expands the prophetic blessing that Isaac utters to Jacob in Gen 27:29. Thus we are brought full circle to a consideration of how the theme of bowing down and reconciliation that journeys through the Joseph narrative and the book of Isaiah finds its initial expression and radical depth meaning in the life of Joseph's father.

At the end of his life, Jacob, now in Egypt, says to Joseph, "I did not expect to see your face" (Gen 48:11). Then it is Joseph who bows "with his face to the earth" (v. 12) before his father (with hands crossed) blesses his two sons. This connection between bowing, blessing, and face—indeed, the 'face of the other'[138]—refers back to what is, for Jacob, and for Israel, literally the most *defining* moment of his entire life. Having fled from Laban with Laban's two daughters and with his eleven sons (for Benjamin has yet to be born), Jacob must once again face Esau, from whom he fled years earlier after stealing his father's blessing. In fearfully preparing to cross the Jabbok, he wrestles with a *man* (as the text insists repeatedly in 32:24, 25, 26, 27, and 28 [cf. NIV]) who blesses him but who will not reveal his name. After being told by the man that he has struggled with *God*, Jacob, now renamed Israel, realises the ultimate meaning of this encounter: "For I have seen God face to face, and yet my life is preserved" (Gen 32:30).

When he finally meets Esau, we are told that he "bow[s] himself to the ground seven times" (Gen 33:3) and seeks to find favour in his eyes (vv. 8, 10, and 15) invoking the theme of blessing once again. It is remarkable not only that Esau runs to meet him, and that the two brothers are reconciled (here too with much kissing and weeping), but that Jacob says to the one he has wronged, "[T]ruly to see your face is like seeing the face of God—since you have received me with such favour" (Gen 33:10).

The name of the man at the Jabbok is thus revealed after all. Jacob—Israel—had been wrestling with God as Esau.[139] Israel, the man and thus the

---

[138] This phrase is common in discussions of 'postmodern ethics' as influenced by Emmanuel Levinas, whose work Moltmann shows appreciation for in his "Theology in the Project of the Modern World," 17–18, as noted in 6.5 above.

[139] This wrestling thus parallels, and forms an *inclusio* with, the wrestling of Jacob and Esau mentioned in Gen 25:22 (which also introduces the naming theme). These two wrestlings are placed in parallel in Hos 12:3 ("In the womb he tried to supplant his *brother*, and in his manhood he strove with *God*," my emphases), which thus supports my identification of the presence of (God as) Esau in Gen 32.

I take the wrestling of Gen. 32 as taking place in a vivid, revelatory dream. There is no modern dream/reality dualism here (cf. Gen 15:12–21), so the dream is implied in the Hebrew narrative rather than pointed out explicitly as would be the case in a modern narrative. Cf. Song of Songs 5:2–7 (which echoes 3:1–4). To an ancient reader/hearer, the fact that this encounter ended at daybreak (Gen 32:26) would be enough to indicate

people (cf. the two *brothers*/"[t]wo *nations*" prophecy of Gen 25:23), is blessed by God as Esau. In this defining moment in Israel's history—and in ours[140]—, divine and human forgiveness are two sides of the same coin.

In the Final Judgment, justice and mercy will embrace. In wrestling with God, we (will) wrestle with those we have oppressed. In facing God, we (will) face one another.[141]

---

this. Furthermore, it is no coincidence that at as soon as Jacob 'wakes up', on my reading, the narrative tells us: "Jacob looked up and there was Esau . . . (Gen 33:1, NIV which is stronger than the "saw Esau coming" of the NRSV).

Given the repeated emphasis on the "man" with whom Jacob wrestles in Gen 32:22–32, the reference to the "angel" with whom he wrestles in Hos 12:4 ("He strove with the angel and prevailed, he wept and sought his favor") coheres well with the discussion of 'angel' as a term that refers to an office in 6.1.1 above.

One aspect of Gen 32 that I do not touch on directly here is an important metaphor for Ton van Prooijen, *Limping but Blessed: Jurgen Moltmann's Search for a Liberating Anthropology* (Amsterdam: Rodopi, 2004).

[140] Here I am going beyond what would normally be considered to be 'exegesis' to highlight the significance of the text as it may be read within the Christian community. The following two sentences are also 'confessional' in this sense. Arguably (and here I am sure that Moltmann, Volf, and Walsh would agree), this way of doing or extending 'biblical theology' belongs in genuine theological discourse.

[141] Read carefully, Paul's imagery of the mirror in 1 Cor 13:12 implies that the face to face encounter with God includes facing ourselves. 2 Cor 3:18 (well translated by the NJB) also works with the mirror imagery in a more explicitly communal way. On the relationship between knowledge of God and knowledge of ourselves, cf. the opening chapter of John Calvin's *Institutes of the Christian Religion*, ed. John T. McNeill, trans. Ford Lewis Battles (Philadelphia: Westminster, 1960), 1:35–39.

CONCLUSION

Grace and *Spes*

"The rose flowers without a why."[1]
   (Angelus Silesius)

"I smell a rose, and smell the kingdom of God."[2]
   (Arnold van Ruler)

This engagement with the theme of universal salvation in Jürgen Moltmann's theology has sought to situate and thus interpret his vision of the annihilation of Hell within the overall structure and dynamics of his theocosmogony. In evaluating his position, I have paid close attention throughout to widespread concerns that universalist eschatologies typically and inevitably undermine human (and possibly divine) freedom, ignore justice for the oppressed, and seriously compromise biblical authority. I have also refocussed these concerns into a more positive question: can Moltmann's theology help us envision a truly 'covenantal' universalism?

In this concluding chapter, I will not attempt to summarise the preceding discussion—there is a separate summary provided at the end of this study—but will bring these investigations to a close by making some final comments on the strengths and weaknesses of Moltmann's proposals in the light of these objections. I will also offer some thoughts concerning the contribution I believe he has made towards a viable universalism that is worthy of further discussion, exploration, and development.

8.1 A Biblical Universalism?

On the whole, Moltmann's position can withstand the 'standard' criticisms of universal salvation well, in my judgment, especially if we take the liberty of supplementing his proposals in the light of his overall theology of hope. Given the fact that he does not address the nature of salvation and judgment in a

---

[1] Cited by Moltmann in SL, 22 (where it is accidentally attributed to Rainer Maria Rilke).
[2] Cited by Moltmann in EiT, 90.

thorough, systematic fashion (my portrayal of his thinking has had to draw on discussions that are scattered throughout his corpus), it is perhaps inevitable that there are some *lacunae*. In my view, these are not fatal. But they do call for further comment. There are also features of his thought that I believe require significant modification.

With respect to Scripture, I have argued (in 7.1 above) that an exegetical case can be made to support Moltmann's judgment about what is ultimate and penultimate with respect to the question of the single- or double-outcome of the Final Judgment. My own suggestions in the previous chapter, taken together with the Appendix on the book of Revelation, are hardly comprehensive. That would require a separate study.[3] But I believe the exegesis I have offered is sufficient to indicate that what we might call Moltmann's 'biblical intuitions' should not be quickly dismissed.

As things stand, however, Moltmann is vulnerable to the charge that he has simply imposed the 'template' (or structure) of his own theology upon the biblical writings, predictably subordinating apocalyptic material (which would, in his framework, refer to an ending in the penultimate, historical direction of time) to more universal-redemptive biblical voices (which reveal the ultimate, eschatological direction of time, in his view). In the process, Moltmann's Christocentrism notwithstanding, the pronouncements on 'Hell' attributed to Jesus in the gospels are more or less brushed aside. The (eschatological) 'monism' that characterises the structure of his thought (as analysed in chapters 2 and 3 and as portrayed in figures 4 and 5 above) makes his universalism look rather like a foregone conclusion, not least with respect to his handling of Scripture. For those committed to biblical authority who are persuaded that the Scriptures teach that there will be (or may be) some who, impenitent to the end, will be excluded (or will exclude themselves) from the life of the Age to Come, more rigorous, sustained exegesis would no doubt be required.

Mention of the 'impenitent' brings us to another issue, also noted in the last chapter, that will be of concern to many: Moltmann's inattention to the importance of human repentance in the biblical portrayal of salvation. I shall return to this topic when discussing the issue of freedom (in 8.3 below). But here I will comment on how this relates to what I take to be the increasingly universal view of salvation that develops in Scripture.

The idea that salvation may be experienced by those whose unmitigated evil effectively puts them outside the covenant altogether is found towards the end of the Old Testament period in the story of Manasseh, a king of Judah whose list of iniquities includes—significantly, given the nature of the present study— the sacrifice of "his son" in "the fire in the valley of the son of Hinnom" (2 Chr 33:6, NRSV). Manasseh's actions are described as utterly detestable in 2 Kgs 21, leading the people of Judah into evil worse than any of the nations God had judged and removed before them. Manasseh's idolatry is so extreme that it pulls the full weight of the curses of Deut 28:15–68 down upon the heads of the covenant community (see Jer 15:4, which explicitly connects the curse of Deut

---

[3] I hope to pursue this in the near future.

28:25 to Manasseh). But 2 Chr 33 also records his repentance, the restoration of his rule, and the reforms that, though briefly reversed by his son, are extended by his grandson, Josiah.

Manasseh's penitence, which moves YHWH to mercy, clearly made an impression on the Chronicler, without whom Manasseh would appear, at least to the eyes of history, as beyond redemption. (The material found in 2 Chr 33:12–13, 19, 23 is entirely absent in the earlier, parallel account in 2 Kgs 21:1–18. This has implications for how we might treat other biblical passages in which the extent of salvation seems limited.) No doubt the author of Chronicles saw in Manasseh not only the lowest point in Israel's history but also the beginning of that return, predicted in Deut 30:1–10, that would mark the end of Israel's exile. This miracle of grace, subsequently celebrated in the fifteen penitential verses of *The Prayer of Manasseh*,[4] is an important precursor to the New Testament portrayal of God's embrace of those 'sinners' who, in the judgment of Jesus' opponents, were (to be) excluded from the blessings of the covenant.[5]

Those of us who live within a generation of the holocausts of the last century may well appreciate how shocking it is that leaders like Manasseh who have subjected the innocent to the very fires of 'Hell' might find forgiveness. But this is indeed a biblical theme. And it is one that helps Moltmann's case. Nevertheless, the scandalously 'universal'[6] understanding of the scope of salvation that is foreshadowed in Deut 30: 1–10 and 2 Chr 33 and is developed in the New Testament (including Matt 1:10!) would seem to call for a soteriology that emphasises rather than downplays the role of repentance. This is the case whether our theologies understand this in Arminian, Calvinist, or other terms. To this we must return.

8.2 Final Justice, Final Judgment

As for Moltmann's understanding of the Final Judgment, especially in relation to the question of final justice for the oppressed, the necessary theological reflection is not so much missing as incomplete. There are certainly indications, mentioned in 7.2 above, that Moltmann would accept the way I have sought to supplement his own proposals with the help of Volf's understanding of the 'social dimension' of God's judgment. If Moltmann were to write an article specifically on the Final Judgment today, I am confident that this is precisely the pattern of thought that we would find. In my judgment, this would merely make explicit what is already implicit in his writings to date.

---

[4] Excluded from the LXX, this is preserved as an appendix to the Vulgate.
[5] See David Neale, *None but the Sinners: Religious Categories in Luke*. Journal for the Study of the New Testament Supplement Series 58 (Sheffield, UK: Sheffield Academic Press, 1991). Neale suggests that the historical Jesus knew *The Prayer of Manasseh*.
[6] On the increasingly 'universal' scope of salvation, which is supportive of (though it may be distinguished from) universal*ism*, see Vogels, *God's Universal Covenant*.

The 'social dimension' to the Final Judgment might also be fruitfully related to the challenge of exploring and developing a viable 'covenantal' universalism as Volf's reflections would urge us not to separate the covenant between God and humanity from the covenant(s) that should exist between us as human beings (within and across families, cultures, and generations). Our covenant (and God's covenant) with our non-human neighbours, and its role in a truly 'universal' view of Final Judgment (cf. Rev 4:7 briefly discussed in 6.1.1 above), sadly exceeds the scope of the present study. But it is far too important not to be mentioned.

There is one other fairly common set of concerns about universal salvation, also relevant to the topic of Final Judgment, that has so far received only a passing mention in the previous chapters (cf. 1.5 above). Moltmann expresses these reservations and objections by posing the following pertinent questions:

> If *universalism* is proclaimed, is the result not the light-minded recklessness that says: why should I believe, and bother to lead a good and righteous life, if I and everyone else are going to be redeemed in any case? If we preach the redemption of all human beings, does the proclamation not really annul itself? Why is it necessary to preach what is going to happen anyway?[7]

Moltmann's answer seems to be that preaching the good news of God's future enables those who receive this message to embrace the world and their own lives in hope. Faith for Moltmann, we may recall, is not something we must have or exercise in order to be saved. It is not the transition from damnation to salvation; it is the way in which we *experience* the vital, eschatological "turning point" of history.[8] Here, it seems to me, the "especially" of 1 Tim 4:9–10 puts it best:

> This is a trustworthy saying that deserves full acceptance (and for this we labor and strive), that we put our hope in the living God, who is the Savior of all men [women and children], and especially [Greek: *malista*] of those who believe (NIV, cf. NRSV: "the Savior of all people, especially of those who believe").

There is therefore all the incentive in the world to come to faith and to proclaim the gospel in word and deed. To preach what is "going to happen anyway," Moltmann might say, that is: to preach the future of Christ's descent into Hell, is to call those without faith and hope into that reality in the here and now. For Moltmann, it seems only natural that the universalism central to the radical Pietism of the Blumhardt movement (also much admired by Karl Barth) should have inspired both political activism and fervent evangelism.[9]

---

[7] CoG, 239. His emphasis.
[8] CoG, 245 as cited and discussed in 1.4.2, 3.6, 4.1 (including 4.1n11), 4.2 (including 4.2n110), 4.3.1, and 4.3.3 above.
[9] See CoG, 238–39. Cf. J. Steven O'Malley, "The Role of Pietism in the Theology of Jürgen Moltmann," *Asbury Theological Journal* 48, no. 1 (Spring 1993): 121–27. For Barth's appreciation of Johann Christoph Blumhardt, see Karl Barth, *Protestant*

Moltmann's universalism of the cross awakens not only faith and hope, but also love. The objections set out above in question form therefore do not constitute a *Christian* argument against universalism from Moltmann's point of view. In fact such fated indifference would seem to express the despair and inertia that he associates with original sin.[10]

In the context of developing a universalist view of the Final Judgment, however, a little more might be said about the incentive to lead "a good and righteous life." Here, it seems to me, the notion of 'intrinsic' as opposed to 'extrinsic' reward is most helpful. 'We are only in it for the money', we say, as we 'do' our job, fulfil our contract, and wait for the weekend. But those who find what we tellingly call 'rewarding' work have no need to separate means and ends in this way. Work has become vocation. Our reward lies in seeing the fruit of our labours, or, to put matters in an eschatological context, in seeing our work come to fruition in the Age to Come. Viewed in this light, Paul's image of the building that is tested by fire in 1 Cor 3:12–15 is revealing. Some, he says, may be saved though their work may not survive into the new age (v. 15). But love will last (1 Cor 13:8). (Here we might compare 2 Pet 3:15, which sees "justice" surviving the fire.)[11] Current prophecies will cease in the sense that they will have been fulfilled,[12] but our works of love, the fruit of our love, whether that love is parental, political, romantic, or artistic, will have an ongoing life into (and in) the Age to Come. Such a line of thought seems to me to be entirely compatible with Moltmann's theology. It also provides an intrinsic incentive for righteousness.

So far, I have been commenting on areas of Moltmann's eschatology that are not so much objectionable as incomplete. One line of thought that needs to be *modified* rather than supplemented if a truly viable universalism is to be developed, however, concerns the way Moltmann's claim that God's judgment makes way for God's forgiveness is grounded not only in his philosophy of time, in which something temporal and temporary must make way for (and thus serve and participate in) something eternal and final, but also in a certain (related) understanding of the Divine (nature). Moltmann's eschatological relativisation of judgment, such that a double-outcome becomes unthinkable, is rooted in the belief that Love is the central divine attribute. God's wrath is seen

---

Theology in the Nineteenth Century, trans. Brian Cozens and John Bowden (London: SCM Press, 1972), chap. 28. Cf. Sauter, "Why Is Karl Barth's Church Dogmatics Not a 'Theology of Hope'?."

[10] See TH, 22 where despair is seen as the reverse side of the original sin of pride.

[11] On the eschatological significance of 1 Cor 13, see see Wright, *The Resurrection of the Son of God*, 296. For a discussion of 2 Pet, see pp. 462–63. On the eschatological significance of 1 Cor 3, see pp. 284–85. Given the temple language of 3:16–17, it seems likely that Paul has the judgment of the Jerusalem Temple in mind (cf. 7.1 above).

[12] In itself, 1 Cor 13:8 does not mean that the prophetic anticipation of the future will no longer exist in the Age to Come. It is remarkable how we typically (over-)read eschatological discontinuity into such passages. Paul is simply relativising the current prophetic insights of the Corinthian church (which failed to realise that prophecy too can be an expression of love).

as a passing anger as it is really wounded love and thus an expression of the Love that God simply and ultimately *is* (see 4.4 cf. 1.4.4 and 4.3.2). If we are to avoid relativising, and thus minimising, the nature of evil, however, I believe we need to find a different approach.

There is a passage in *Theology of Hope* that is most helpful in this context. Elaborating on the idea that biblical, especially Old Testament, "expectations receive their content in the mind's eye from the contrary experiences that were endured under the absence and hiddenness of the God of promise," Moltmann writes,

> Yahweh's coming glory shows itself in overcoming the experienced judgment and turning it to blessing. If this were to be expressed in theological terms, we should have to say: it shows itself in the overcoming of God by God—of the judging, annihilating God by the saving, life-giving God, of the wrath of God by his goodness.[13]

There are certainly points of continuity here with how Moltmann expresses himself in his later works. But what stands out in this passage is the stress on the fundamental *tension* that evil creates within the divine life, a tension that necessitates (in his striking phrase) the "overcoming of God by God." There is more to God's wrath than wounded love here, it would seem.

That God should love humanity into being and that this love should become deeply wounded when we break the very covenant of existence is profoundly biblical. That this divine pain should be expressed in anger and jealousy is also very much a part of the story of God according to the Scriptures. God's wrath towards '(evil) *humanity*' might well be conceived as (and in) wounded love, I suggest. But what of God's attitude towards '(human) *evil*'? Here, surely, the language of wounded love reaches its limits. Here we have a divine *anger* that God's love does not 'lie behind' but struggles to *overcome*. (Thus, the contrast between Gen 6:5–7 and Gen 8:21–22, in my view, cannot be explained (and is certainly not narrated) as the beginning and end of a story in which wounded love finds its resolution.) This is related to the fact that *evil* must be overcome rather than assimilated or sublated. The various theological nuances of *Aufhebung* and its cognates (cf. 2.5, 5.4, and 6.5 above) are not what we need here, I suggest (although we do need nuances). A creation-affirming faith may want to insist that the energies and desires of sin (can) be redirected towards the God of Life, and rightly so. But when Moltmann's monism pushes him to speak of sins themselves and not just sinners being redeemed (see the discussion at the end of 4.2 above), the fact that we are redeemed *from* evil, that evil is not redeemed, seems to be overlooked.

Our view of *divine* love/wrath has implications for our view of *human* love/wrath. And this is relevant to the way we might picture the social dimension of our role in the Final Judgment. If justice and mercy are to finally embrace (cf. 1.1, 1.3, 1.6, 7.2, and 7.3 above), human anger must not be

---

[13] TH, 131 as cited in part in 4.4 above.

silenced but must be given its due. Once again, Moltmann's reflections, though characteristically insightful, strike me as incomplete.

Commenting on Jesus' prayer that God forgive those who are crucifying him (Luke 23:34), Moltmann writes,

> With this prayer of Christ the universal religion of revenge is overcome and the universal law of retaliation is annulled. In the name of the Crucified, from now on only forgiveness holds sway. Christianity that has the right to appeal to him is a religion of reconciliation. To forgive those who have wronged one is an act of highest sovereignty and great inner freedom. In forgiving and reconciling, the victims are superior to the perpetrators and free themselves from compulsion to evil deeds.[14]

Volf cites this passage in his *Exclusion and Embrace* to illustrate the contrast between what he calls "the creative 'injustice' of forgiveness" and the "aping injustice of revenge."[15] But unlike Moltmann, he also stresses the *legitimate* thirst for justice that our passion for revenge may reveal and conceal. "Strangely enough," he writes, it is "the imprecatory Psalms"—in which "torrents of rage have been allowed to flow freely, channelled only by the robust structure of a ritual prayer"—that "may point to a way out of the slavery to revenge and into the freedom of forgiveness."[16]

This brings to mind some wise words of one of the great contemporary commentators on the Psalms, Walter Brueggemann. Combining pastoral sensitivity with exegetical-theological insight, he writes,

> My hunch is that there is a way *beyond* the Psalms of vengeance, but it is a way *through* them and not *around* them. And that is so because of what in fact goes on with us. Willy-nilly, we are vengeful creatures. Thus these harsh psalms must be embraced as our own. Our rage and indignation must be fully *owned* and fully *expressed*. And then (only then) can our rage and indignation be *yielded* to the mercy of God. In taking this route through them, we take the route God 'himself' has gone.[17]

This is the way, I suggest, that the energies and desires—dare we say those 'just desires'?—that fuel the lust for revenge may be redirected to the God of justice and mercy.

But we are not only "vengeful" or violent. We are violated. These words also allow us to place the prayers of the martyrs (including those honoured in *St. Peter's Apocalypse*) within a covenantal context and process in which the pain they articulate can be given its due. While that pain should not be so absolutised that the process of grief and redemption becomes frozen, neither

---

[14] Jürgen Moltmann, "Christus oder Konstantin," *Publik-Forum* 24, no. 17 (1995): 29 as cited and translated in Volf, *Exclusion and Embrace*, 122.
[15] Volf, *Exclusion and Embrace*, 122.
[16] Volf, *Exclusion and Embrace*, 123.
[17] Walter Brueggemann, *Praying the Psalms* (Winona, MN: Saint Mary's Press, 1986), 79. His emphases.

should it be dismissed or minimised in the name of a 'compassion' that would distance itself from those who refuse to suffer—or 'suffer with'—in silence.

If we take this route towards what Volf (echoing Moltmann) calls the "freedom of forgiveness," then according to Brueggemann, we take the route God has taken. We participate in God's life as God participates in ours, Moltmann would say. But the God whose wrath is really 'only' wounded love cannot fully participate in our pain and wrath, I suggest. In participating in the "overcoming of God by God," however, we may find that the God who is beside 'himself' in the face of evil is thereby also beside us.

In seeking to develop a viable universalism today, it is good to be aware of the best features of theologies of universal salvation that have been developed in earlier centuries, especially when the universalisms in question do not conform to the position(s) anathematised by mainstream 'orthodoxy'. At the end of chapter 1, therefore, I drew attention to the fact that the 'social dimension' of the Final Judgment that we find in *St. Peter's Apocalypse* seems to have inspired one of the forms of universalism that Augustine attempts to exclude from his *City of God*.[18] Although, thanks to Augustine in a double sense, this has left barely a trace historically, this is just enough for us to say that arguments against universalism that only have the eschatology of Origen (or Schleiermacher or Hick) in mind do not necessarily constitute a refutation of universalism 'at its best' with respect to the issue of justice for the oppressed.

Similarly, if we have misgivings (as I do) about a universalism grounded in the absolute centrality of divine Love, then it is helpful to know that until the seventeenth century, universalism was a theological position that tended to see a conflict between the attributes of God, with love eventually winning the day. According to historian D.P. Walker, a shift occurs in the universalism proposed by Peter Sterry and Jeremiah White. What was "most unusual," indeed "exceptional" about the view of these men, both of whom were chaplains to Oliver Cromwell after the Civil War, was that they "removed the possib[ility] of any such [internal!] conflict by making love the supreme attribute, out of which all the others grow and to which they must conform."[19] Today this sounds as predictable as it is familiar. Historically, however, there are alternatives. If we want a universalism attentive to the utter outrage of innocent suffering, and surely this is vital for any conceivable universalism—indeed for any view of redemption—today, then I would suggest that divine love (and human love) is better conceived as coming to the fore in the "overcoming of God by God."

---

[18] See Bauckham, "Augustine, the 'Compassionate' Christians, and the Apocalypse of Peter."

[19] Walker, *The Decline of Hell*, 110. Cf. Louise Hickman, "Love Is All and God Is Love: Universalism in Peter Sterry (1613–1672) and Jeremiah White (1630–1707)," in *"All Shall Be Well": Explorations in Universal Salvation and Christian Theology from Origen to Moltmann*, ed. Gregory MacDonald (Eugene, OR: Cascade, 2011), 93–115.

8.3 From Autonomy to Freedom

Moltmann's understanding of the nature of human freedom, I suggest, constitutes his single, greatest contribution towards a 'covenantal' universalism. This in itself makes his universalist theology of hope worthy of widespread discussion and ongoing development in my judgment. Paradoxically, though, it is here that we also encounter the most problematic features of his theology. Furthermore, there are some basic issues of interpretation concerning repentance that still need to be resolved in this context.

First however I will offer some comments on the nature of *God's* freedom in the universalist theology that Moltmann proposes. Here I will contrast Moltmann's 'universalism of the cross', in which God's freedom and nature are revealed in Christ's descent into Hell, with what we might call his 'theocosmogony of the cross' in which the dynamics of Godforsakenness assume a very central role in his *zimzum* doctrine of creation. An examination of the conditions of possibility implied in this understanding of creation will lead us to an evaluation of Moltmann's view of human freedom.

As we have seen in 4.3.2 above, Moltmann's answer to the common objection and concern that universalist positions inevitably eclipse God's freedom is that God's will is not subordinate to some kind of Law that dictates that God 'must' save all people. Instead, salvation flows out of God's goodness. God thus communicates his love in his freedom. As God's nature is more basic than God's will in Moltmann's conception, there is still more than a hint that God cannot but love, even though Moltmann does work hard at integrating divine freedom and necessity within what I have referred to (at the end of 4.3.2) as the 'grace of the divine nature'. It would be fair to Moltmann's understanding, I propose, to say that in expressing his goodness, God is free but not autonomous.

In order to evaluate his position, it might be helpful to step back from the 'realist/voluntarist'[20] debate in order to reflect on a more basic question concerning our language for God. The fact that all the terms we might use for God are 'creatiomorphic' seems undeniable. So how can we use the language of creation for the God of creation? To claim that 'prior to' (or 'outside') the creation of the world, God might have a (divine) *nature* and/or might express 'his' (divine) *will* is seen as (relatively) unproblematic by a great many theologians (including Moltmann, it would seem). But this way of speaking implies that 'nature' and 'will' as *created* realities do not come into existence *ex nihilo* as they, in their own finite way, exemplify, reflect, or ontologically participate in, realities or qualities that 'already' exist in an infinite, divine way in God. Arguably, this kind of (analogical) God-talk (which dominates most

---

[20] Divine voluntarism is more commonly contrasted with intellectualism, but I refer to 'realism' as I need to indicate a broader view of God's nature than God's 'Mind'.

discussions in theology and philosophy of religion) compromises the biblical idea of creation. But is there an alternative?[21]

In the faith language of the Scriptures, we find a wide range of creatiomorphic terms used to identify God's *presence*. The concern of the biblical writers is not to describe a 'Being' who is 'beyond' creation but a divine 'being-with' experienced (as) 'within' the covenantal dynamics of existence. Thus in Jer 9:17–18, we read:

> This is what the Lord Almighty says:
> "Consider now! Call for the wailing women to come;
>   send for the most skillful of them.
> Let them come quickly and wail over us
>   til *our eyes* overflow with tears
>   and water streams from *our eyelids*."
> (NIV, my emphases)

In an analogical view, such language for God is problematic. Theologians and philosophers of religion regularly contemplate God's infinite justice, inscrutable plans, archetypal qualities, sexless gender, and even 'his' bodiless feelings. But God's eyelids and God's tears are another matter and the specificity of God's revelation in Jer 9 and elsewhere is typically made to die the death of a thousand qualifications as the power and intimacy of God's words are explained away or passed over.[22] In the view I am proposing,

---

[21] I say that the analogical view compromises *creatio ex nihilo* here because *creatio ex nihilo* is the best-known attempt to articulate the radical view of creation we find in the Bible. This has its own problems, limits, and ambiguities but it provides the quickest way for me to indicate what I have in mind in this context. Cf. n. 27 below.

For a rare critique of the analogical tradition, see Roy A. Clouser, "Is God Eternal?," *Poznan Studies in the Philosophy of the Sciences and the Humanities* 73 (2000): 273–300. Clouser finds support for his alternative in the Cappadocians, Luther, Calvin, and Barth. His proposal that God takes on created properties might be fruitfully expanded, in my view, by the correlative claim that creation is called to reveal (and thus make real) the very presence of God. (This emphasis also allows us to move beyond the transcendental-phenomenal distinction (or dualism) that Clouser takes over from Kant (via Dooyeweerd). For an earlier articulation of his position, see his "Religious Language: A New Look at an Old Problem," in *Rationality in the Calvinian Tradition*, ed. Hendrik Hart, Johan van der Hoeven, and Nicholas Wolterstorff (Lanham, MD: University Press of America, 1983), 385–407 and the earlier, substantially different "Religious Language: A New Look at an Old Problem" (Toronto: Institute for Christian Studies, 1980). A strength of the earliest paper is Clouser's emphasis on how Neoplatonic, great-chain-of-being thinking lies behind the analogy theory and (by implication) the approach of negative theology.

[22] Convinced that v. 18 cannot be God's own words, the NET translation inserts the phrase "I said, 'Indeed, let them . . . .' " to (in the words of its footnote) "help clarify" (!) that a different (non-divine) speaker in intended. But, as noted by Terrence E. Fretheim, *Jeremiah*. Smyth and Helwys Bible Commentary (Macon, GA: Smyth and Helwys, 2002), 162, "The use of the first person plural in vv. 17–18 in a divine oracle means that God is included among the 'us,' *both* as one who mourns and is mourned for." His

however, such language makes sense as a reference to God's creation-affirming presence. Put simply, the tears of the women are the very tears of God.

In such a covenantal, this-worldly context,[23] the only kind of context in which and to which our language may refer (and need refer), 'central' or 'privileged' metaphors for God change in (and with) time. God as warrior makes way for God as king. God as father makes way for God as friend. And/or vice versa. Sometimes God is our rock. Sometimes God is love. In our own time, by extension, God may be experienced as the origin of existence, the ground beneath our feet, or (in more abstract language) the foundational past. Then again, God may also be the promise of life and thus experienced as our future.

We may say these are all facets of the same God. But we still need central terms. In attempting to faithfully name how God is present, how God is with us, no single term 'must' be central for all time. That would not be in keeping with the dynamic nature of Scripture.[24] 1 John 4:8b, in which we are told "God is love" (NRSV, NIV), is not a timeless, theological proposition but a confessional

---

emphasis. What Fretheim says about the "us" should be extended to the "our," specifically "our eyes ... tears ... eyelids." Some advocates of an analogical view of God-talk (such as open theists [and probably Fretheim himself]) happily allow the attribution of feelings and emotions to God. But the temptation to effectively dismiss the Bible's use of bodily language for God is acute (whether this is admitted or not) for all who advocate the *analogia entis* approach. For example, Michael S. Horton in "Hellenistic or Hebrew? Open Theism and Reformed Theological Method," in *Beyond the Bounds: Open Theism and the Undermining of Biblical Christianity*, ed. John Piper, Justin Taylor, and Paul Kjoss Helseth (Wheaton, IL: Crossway, 2003), 219 writes,
> Some advocates of divine suffering verge on caricaturing their own position when they criticize the traditional view, as Moltmann does, as holding [in CrG, 222] that "[God] cannot weep, for he has no tears. ... Does Moltmann believe that God possesses tear ducts? Or is he being as anthropomorphic as the texts he cites for his position?

Here, 'anthropomorphic' means applicable to human experience but not to divine reality. My proposed covenantal/creatiomorphic approach to biblical God-talk sees this as a false dichotomy.

[23] By 'this-worldly context', I do not mean the closed universe of Modernity. Cf. the discussion of heaven and earth as sides of creation in 6.1.1 above. In developing a 'creational' or covenantal view of language for God, I am here extending some of the thoughts briefly expressed in 5.2.1n79 above.

[24] The fact that some changes in the 'central' metaphors for God in the Bible may be related to the progressive nature of revelation does not mean, in my view, that the central metaphors of the NT are now 'final'. The biblical canon is 'closed' in order to leave the story of God-with-creation, and creation-with-God, *open*. See the discussion in my *The Woman Will Overcome the Warrior*, 98–103. Furthermore, Scripture itself (in 1 Cor 15:28) looks forward to when God will be "all in all," which can only expand our legitimate metaphors for God. On the diverse metaphors for God in Scripture and the question of 'privileged' metaphors, see *The Woman Will Overcome the Warrior*, 255–62. Cf. the useful discussion in Fretheim, *The Suffering of God*, chaps. 2 and 3 and in Sallie McFague, *Models of God: Theology for an Ecological, Nuclear Age* (Philadelphia: Fortress Press, 1987).

truth that is itself *truly* on the *way* to *life* (cf. John 14:6). If we speak of God 'loving humanity into being' (as I have in the discussion above), this says that love is an absolutely central need that God meets, that 'I am loved therefore I am'. To confess that God 'loves us into existence' need not be a metaphysical, onto-theological claim about Love as a divine rather than created nature or intention. With respect to the God of Abraham, Isaac, and Jacob, the realist/voluntarist dilemma is misguided. Sometimes we may need to stress God's being. Sometimes God's will should have priority. It depends!

If this relativisation of our central terms for God sounds relativ*istic*, then it is important to note that however God is to be named, Jesus is our touchstone as God in flesh and blood.[25] Here Moltmann's Christocentrism puts a healthy check on his realism. Although he does claim, metaphysically and not merely covenantally, that 'God *is* Love' (see 4.3.2), he does not go on to deduce or infer that God 'must' do and be X, Y, and Z. The greatest strength of Moltmann's universalism is that it is a universalism of the cross rooted in (an understanding of) what God has done in Christ. Questions of (does it matter) whether God could have done otherwise than love us and save us become secondary to our responsibility as theologians to reflect on what God has actually done (see 4.4 in the light of 4.3.1).[26] For Moltmann, therefore, God's freedom is certainly not eclipsed but is, together with God's nature, God's love, and God's will, revealed in (the redemption of) history.

In this sense, Moltmann's 'universalism of the cross', whether we agree with it or not, is first and foremost not a 'theological' proposal; it is a claim about what is revealed to us by God in Jesus Christ. The biblical-confessional nature of this claim, however, is in sharp contrast to Moltmann's *zimzum* doctrine of creation and its placing of Hell in the primordial *nihil* (cf. 4.1 above). Here an interpretation of the dynamics of the cross (which is appropriate in the context of understanding salvation) seems to have been retrojected back into a 'pre-covenantal context' (or 'pre-context') in a way that utterly violates the biblical distinction between creation and fall, creation and

---

[25] Here I take Jesus to be 'God' in the sense of God in flesh and blood, God *incarnate*. Cf. the discussion of the Creator/creation distinction in this context in my *The Woman Will Overcome the Warrior*, 209–12 (in the light of 206–209), which attempts to argue that 'Jesus the man is not God ontologically; Jesus the man is God incarnationally'. Having made this basic distinction, I am happy to observe that incarnation is as 'ontic' and 'ontological' as anything else in creation.

[26] Of course Moltmann *interprets* this in a particular way. But the *speculative* nature of his thinking evident in other areas of theology—cf. Richard Bauckham's reference to "undisciplined speculation" in his otherwise sympathetic "Moltmann's Theology: An Overview" in his *The Theology of Jürgen Moltmann*, 25 and G.C. Berkouwer's comments on the way Moltmann (in CrG) transgresses boundaries and limits accorded a healthy respect by Barth in his *A Half Century of Theology: Movements and Motives*, trans. Lewis B. Smedes (Grand Rapids, MI: Eerdmans, 1977), 254–55—is strictly subordinate here to a very confessional response to Christ's death and resurrection. Cf. my comments in 4.4 above.

salvation (cf. 5.3 above).[27] Although I accept Moltmann's 'universalism of hope' (see 5.0 above, cf. 8.4 below) and greatly appreciate his 'universalism of the cross', his 'theocosmogony of the cross' is a very different story.

---

[27] One way to undermine what I am calling the biblical creation-fall distinction is to appeal to the kind of *Chaoskampf* reading of Gen 1 that remains popular with many (but not all) OT scholars. Elements of this approach may be detected in Moltmann, "Creation and Redemption," 119–34, especially 125: "As the creation narratives themselves indicate, creation at the beginning is out of chaos." In his discussion at this point (which anticipates his later *zimzum* model) there are strong intimations that the '*un*formed' creation of Gen 1:2, in his understanding, is seen as '*de*formed' and in need of redemption. See the critique and response in Walsh, "Theology of Hope and the Doctrine of Creation."

Bernhard W. Anderson's important work, *Creation versus Chaos: The Reinterpretation of Mythical Symbolism in the Bible* (1967; repr., Philadelphia: Fortress Press, 1987) substantially challenged the *Chaoskampf* reading of Gunkel and his followers over forty years ago by arguing that in the Hebrew Bible/OT, this ancient Near Eastern (ANE) motif is transformed into the historical conflict with Israel's enemies. It is most significant that Jon D. Levenson in his *Creation and the Persistence of Evil: The Jewish Drama of Divine Omnipotence* (San Francisco: Harper and Row, 1988), pt. 2 (53–127), despite his enthusiasm for the *Chaoskampf* motif, has such a hard time finding it in the message of Gen 1–2. That he manages to ignore Anderson's study is also remarkable (an oversight that is only exacerbated by Levenson's brief—and from the point of view of its central argument, incidental—reference to Anderson's *Creation versus Chaos* in the 1994 preface to the Princeton University Press reissue of *Creation and the Persistence of Evil*).

I accept the claim that Gen 1:1–2a should probably be translated, "When God began to create [the] heaven[s] and [the] earth—the earth being unformed and void . . . ." as in the NJPS translation (cf. NRSV). I take it that *creatio ex nihilo* is a later attempt (found in, e.g., 2 Macc 7:8) to articulate a biblical view of creation in a different context from that of the author of Gen 1. That said, its absence as an explicit theme in Gen 1 does not provide a biblical basis for postulating the presence of primordial, recalcitrant matter as found in Plato's *Timaeus* or in the scenarios proposed in contemporary process theology, *contra* David R. Griffin, "Creation Out of Chaos and the Problem of Evil," in *Encountering Evil: Live Options in Theodicy*, ed. Stephen T. Davis (Atlanta, GA: John Knox, 1981), 101–19, especially 101–102 and his extended discussion in "Creation out of Nothing, Creation out of Chaos, and the Problem of Evil," in *Encountering Evil: Live Options in Theodicy*, ed. Stephen T. Davis, rev. ed. (Louisville, KY: Westminster John Knox, 2001), 108–25, especially 108–14. By the same token, the identification or association of the waters of Gen 1:2 with "chaos" in *The Jewish Study Bible: Tanakh Translation*, eds. Adele Berlin and Marc Zvi Brettler (Oxford: Oxford University Press, 2004), 13, lacks evidence in Gen 1 itself, and thus begs the question of whether Gen 1 is following or breaking with the thinking found elsewhere in the ANE. In my judgment, the NJPS and NRSV translations of Gen 1:1–2a fit with my view of 'covenantal' language for God very well. The author simply begins by telling us how God began to make the creation inhabitable for the creatures of the earth.

Moltmann's denigration of creation can be subtle. On the final page of his succinct essay, "Is the World Coming to an End or Has Its Future Already Begun? Christian Eschatology, Modern Utopianism and Exterminism," trans. Margaret Kohl, in *The Future as God's Gift: Explorations in Christian Eschatology*, ed. David Fergusson and

This is one place, at least, where the charges of 'speculation' that are sometimes brought against Moltmann's theology are on target.[28] The problem here, from my point of view, is not with the 'internal' coherence (or incoherence) of his model. Given my account of language for God, I find his exploration into 'the God of the pre-covenant' almost impossible to justify or make sense of. To attempt to go beyond (God-with-)creation, to attempt to name God prior to (God-with-)creation, is to attempt to go 'beyond' and 'before' language 'in' language. Such an exercise ignores the created limits of our language in general and of our God-talk in particular.

But the violation of the creation/fall distinction (which leads to a failure to properly distinguish, and thus properly relate, creation and salvation) is just as problematic as the blurring of the Creator-creation distinction. Even in as much as it can be taken as a (relatively) non-speculative and thus legitimate investigation into the transcendental conditions of and for present existence (that is, even if we choose to equate the 'pre-conditions' of the *nihil* with the transcendental conditions that are located in the *coelum naturae*, as discussed in 4.2 above), Moltmann's analysis of the 'pre-space space' seems to me to reflect the realities and possibilities of a fallen world rather than "very good" creation of Gen 1:31 that is, prior to sin, historically on its way—with God—to glory. In my view, the 'space for' evil that Moltmann associates with the primordial *nihil* does not precede the fall, but opens up through our idolatry.[29] Consequently,

---

Marcel Sarot (Edinburgh: T. and T. Clark, 2000), 129–38, he speaks, with approval, of the way world history in the biblical traditions "*doesn't begin with the Fall*. . . . It begins with the primordial blessing of *temporal* creation, and ends with the blessedness of the creation which will be *eternal*." My emphases. His collapsing of what is, from my perspective, the vital, biblical distinction between creation and fall is, from his perspective, simply a recognition that, in the words of TKG, 51, "*suffering* . . . has roots [not only in "sin" but] in the limitations of created reality itself." My emphasis. (Cf. the helpful overview provided by Ernst M. Conradie, "In Search of a Vision of Hope for a New Century," *Journal of Religion and Society* 1 (1999): 1–24, especially 14, http://purl.org/JRS (accessed March 11, 2004).) Hence the shift, in the above quotation, from the "*temporal* creation" to the "*eternal*." Here I would insist that (structural and temporal) finitude need not lead to suffering (that is, the suffering we associate with curse/temptation in distinction from the struggle and challenge of life which we may receive as a gift/call), provided that the finitude in question characterises a world and a history that is in ongoing covenant with God. The initial neutrality and ambivalence of the original creation in Moltmann's conception is evident in his next sentence in TKG, 51: "If creation-in-the-beginning is open for the history of good *and* evil, then . . . ." His emphasis. In my view, by contrast, the fall autonomously creates the opening for evil. Cf. nn. 29, 38, and 73 below.

[28] See the comments of Bauckham and Berkouwer cited in n. 26 above.

[29] See my "The Call of Wisdom/The Voice of the Serpent," where I argue this point with respect to temptation. Cf. n. 38 and 8.4 (including 8.4n73) below. Also implicit in my argument in this essay is that the mystery of the (autonomous) origin of evil lies in the way that it creates the conditions for its own possibility. Cf. n. 27 above and nn. 38 and 73 below. Although I refer to a 'space for' evil "open[ing] up through our idolatry," this is not to be confused with the *expansion* of meaning and possibility associated with

Hell—that is, Gehenna—comes into existence as an apocalyptic reality within history (see 7.1). For Moltmann, however, the 'space' or opening for evil lies in the primordial, Godforsaken space that—quite apart from human sin—necessitates (at least some kind of) a 'descent into Hell' if God is to become all in all (4.1). This conflation of creation and fall in the very conditions that make life possible, itself conditions, structures, and, in my judgment, distorts his entire theocosmology/theocosmogony.

From this conflation, it follows that the cross has to be far more than the outworking of God's redemptive-salvific grace. Indeed, as we have seen (in 3.6 above), it is the very centre of temporal reality, the "turning point"[30] (3.6) that makes possible the eschatological (not just soteriological) reintegration of time and eternity, creation and God. It is only through the cross, it would seem, that creation's positive, eschatological possibilities can become eternal realities. It is only through the descent into Hell that history's negative, primordial possibilities can become eschatological impossibilities. Indeed, the cross (for Moltmann) is, from (before) the beginning, so constitutive of reality—created and divine—that it is said to be the "centre" of the Trinity and the "consolidation" of all things (4.3.1).[31]

---

eschatological newness. With respect to evil, I suggest, we should speak of change in terms of the *contraction* of true meaning and genuine possibility.

[30] See the references to this pivotal phrase in 3.6n259 above.

[31] For the "consolidation," see GC, 91 as cited in 4.3.1 above and discussed in 4.3.1n163 above. For the cross at the "centre" of the Trinity, see TKG, 83 as cited in 4.3.1. This passage continues, "Before the world was, the sacrifice was already in God. No Trinity is conceivable without the Lamb, without the sacrifice of love, without the crucified Son. For he is the slaughtered Lamb glorified in eternity." This is connected to the "image of 'the Lamb who was slain from the foundation of the world' (Rev 5.12)." Cf. the apt comment of Mackey cited in 4.3.1n162 above.

One might think, given the way in which Moltmann comments on Rev 13:8 in his "Antwort auf die Kritik an »Der gekreuzigte Gott«," in *Diskussion über Jürgen Moltmanns Buch »Der gekreuzigte Gott«*, ed. Michael Welker (Munich: Chr. Kaiser Verlag, 1979), 179 and in "The Christian Doctrine of the Trinity," in *Jewish Monotheism and Christian Trinitarian Doctrine*, by Pinchas Lapide and Jürgen Moltmann, trans. Leonard Swidler (Philadelphia: Fortress Press, 1981), 54, that it is only the divine *willingness* to suffer that is from before creation. Perhaps one might read TKG, 168 in this light. Here Moltmann writes,

[T]he Son's sacrifice of boundless love on Golgotha is from eternity already included in the exchange of the essential, the consubstantial love which constitutes the divine life of the Trinity. The fact that the Son dies on the cross, delivering himself up to death, is part of the eternal obedience which he renders to the Father in his whole being through the Spirit, whom he receives from the Father.

In TKG, 161, however, Moltmann speaks of "The pain of the cross [which] determines the inner life of the triune God from eternity to eternity." Kenneth Surin in his *Theology and the Problem of Evil* (Oxford: Blackwell, 1986), 131, is certainly right to ask whether Moltmann is not "ontologizing evil and suffering" here. (Cf. 4.2n112 above and n. 35 below on the apparent legitimising of the Fall). Bauckham's comment, in *Moltmann: Messianic Theology in the Making*, 109, is also to the point:

Grace and Spes 375

In my judgment, Moltmann's 'theocosmogony of the cross', which shapes not only his view of salvation but also his *zimzum* doctrine of creation, is, in the etymological sense, 'preposterous' (or rather 'postpreterous') as what is prior (Latin, *prae*) and what comes after (Latin, *posterus*) have been reversed. In terms of the narrative movement of Scripture, it is as if the (divine) birthpangs of the New Creation central to Isa 42:13–16 have been made to (take) precede(nce over) the 'biblical foundation' of Gen 1. What is truly primordial—the 'Let there be's' of Gen 1 that lead to blessing not curse, benediction not temptation; the 'making space for' creation in which there is

---

If this does not make evil necessary, then contingent evil not only affects God in the course of his trinitarian history (cf. FC 77), but essentially determines his inner life from eternity. This conclusion results from the temptation, which Moltmann from *The Crucified God* onwards seems unable to resist, to see the cross as the key to the doctrine of God, not only in the sense that it reveals God as the kind of love which is willing to suffer, but in the sense that the actual sufferings of the cross are essential to who God is. This attempt to take God's temporal experience as seriously as possible oddly ends by eternalising it.

His italics. (Bauckham's parenthetical reference is to Moltmann's "The Theology of the Cross Today," in *The Future of Creation*, by Jürgen Moltmann, trans. Margaret Kohl (London: SCM Press, 1979), 59–79.)

As the pain that is opened up by the Godforsaken Hell of the *zimzum* is finally resolved for Moltmann when God becomes all in all, the suffering that Moltmann locates in the Trinity before the foundation of the world is, strictly speaking, pre-temporal rather than eternal. But this pre-creational suffering necessitates a (presumably painful) 'descent into Hell' quite apart from and prior to the events of Golgotha (even though this takes place in the events of Golgotha). Thus the cross is vital not only for the sake of salvation from sin but also for the "consolidation" (GC, 91) of creation from the very beginning.

As for Moltmann's exegesis in TKG, 83 (as cited above and in 4.3.1), the Lamb "slain from the creation of the world [*apo katabolēs kosmou*]" (NIV) may appear in Rev 13:8, but not in 5:12. While Moltmann follows a traditional way of translating the former text, it seems likely that "from the creation [or foundation] of the world" does not modify the preceding phrase but rather the writing down of names. Thus the NRSV translates Rev 13:8 as referring to "everyone whose name has not been written from the foundation of the world in the book of life of the Lamb that was slaughtered." Cf. the identical phrase (*apo katabolēs kosmou*) in 17:8 where we hear of names that have not been "written in the book of life from the creation of the world" (NIV) or "from the foundation of the world" (NRSV). Cf. also the same phrase in Matt 25:34 and Heb 9:26. In the latter case, this phrase is translated as "since the creation/foundation of the world" (NIV and NRSV cf. Matt 25:34 [NIV]).

To take Rev 13:8 as effectively referring to 'before' rather than 'from' the creation of the world (as Moltmann does) might be the result of reading it together with the reference in 1 Pet 1:20 to the lamb who was chosen or destined "before the creation of the world [*pro katabolēs kosmous*]" (NIV and NRSV). (Cf. the same phrase in Eph 1:4 with respect to 'election'.) But, like Heb 9:26, 1 Pet 3:18 insists that the crucifixion takes place in history. Whatever the preposition, the thrust of all of these texts is that our historical salvation comes from, and thus has its sure foundation in, God. Moltmann's speculative midrash is, at best, unnecessary. For how such texts are not more primordial than Gen 1:1, and may thus be read in the light of Gen 1:3, see n. 32 below.

not the slightest hint of divine suffering—is not properly distinguished from the (annihilating) evil—and thus the Hell—that seeks to place itself at the beginning of all things.[32]

Thus far, we have been discussing the affirmation and eclipse of God's freedom in Moltmann's thinking. But the conflation of creation and fall in the 'pre-space space'—a 'creation/fall' that needs to be overcome, in Moltmann's vision, in and through the 'redemption of time'—also leads us to his understanding of *human* freedom. In my reading, what I take to be the respective strengths and weakness of his position correspond to the distinction he makes between freedom in the eschatological and in the historical directions of time. The central ambiguity in his position with respect to the nature of repentance is related to the transition between these two directions in the *coincidentia oppositorum*.

Put briefly, what is perhaps Moltmann's most important contribution is that he insists that true freedom should not be conceived of as autonomy but in terms of our participation in God's goodness. Nevertheless the deadly (I would say 'fallen') tendency towards autonomy that he rightly resists seems to be part of (his conception of) the very structure of reality in the historical direction of time from the beginning.

Moltmann's negative view of the historical direction comes to the fore in his claim that "The temporality of earthly creation does not reflect the presence of God—it reflects his absence."[33] This is rooted in his *zimzum* doctrine of creation because the primordial *nihil* is, simultaneously, a space for life and a space for sin (see 4.1). In its positive and negative potentiality, this 'pre-space space' is historical, pre-eschatological freedom. This is clear in the following passage from *The Coming of God* where Moltmann tells us,

> Through the space conceded by God, creation is given detachment from God and *freedom* of movement *over against* him. If God were omnipresent in the absolute sense, and manifested in his glory, there would be no earthly creation. In order to make himself endurable for his earthly creatures, God has to veil his

---

[32] The primordiality of Gen 1 is sometimes undermined by appeal to the 'before the creation/foundation of the world' passages discussed in n. 31 above. But in my view, such confessional (rather than theological) texts need not even imply a pre-creational 'plan' of salvation. Read *canonically* (thus allowing our biblical foundation to begin at the beginning of the biblical narrative), they assure us that the '*Let there be*' *of/to Life* of Gen 1:3 (and throughout Gen 1)—a 'Let there be' of/to Life that is *reaffirmed* in salvation—will come to its eschatological fulfilment. Furthermore, where the NIV refers to "creation," the NRSV, rightly in my view, consistently refers to the "foundation" of the world in the texts cited in n. 31 above. NT references to what is "before the foundation of the world" (1 Pet 1:20; Eph 1:4) refer, canonically, to before Gen 1:9–10 but not to before Gen 1:1! With respect to Eph 1:4, this allows us to see Israel's election to be the light to the Gentiles and the Church's election to be a light to the world (see the discussion of election in 4.3.1n142 above) as rooted in the universe-wide, pre-redemptive, creational-eschatological "let there be light" of Gen 1:3, which is the "let there be light" of God's glory (see 6.4 including 6.4n124 above).

[33] CoG, 284 as cited in 3.3 and 3.5.1 above.

glory, since 'he who looks upon God must die'. Remoteness from God and spatial distance from God result in the withdrawal of God's omnipresence and 'the veiling of his face'. They are part of the *grace of creation*, because they are conditions for the *liberty* of created beings. It is only for sinners, who cut themselves off from God, that they become the expression of God's anger towards them in their God-forsakenness. If God himself enters into his creation through his Christ and his Spirit, in order to live in it and to arrive in his rest, he will then *overcome* not only the God-forsakenness of sinners, but also *the distance and space of his creation itself*, which *resulted in isolation from God, and sin*; for redemption can only mean that with sin itself the *potentiality for sin* has also been surmounted; otherwise redemption would not be final.[34]

The original freedom of creation is thus ambivalent as this so-called "grace of creation" that makes life with God possible is also a potentiality, space, or freedom that "resulted in isolation from God" and thus "sin." This space, this freedom, must be eschatologically "overcome" in the *annihilatio nihili*, which includes the annihilation of Hell (see 4.1 above). It is most telling that Moltmann does not speak of creational freedom as our space to move *with* God in history but as our "freedom of movement *over against* God." This language of autonomy from God, made possible because God withdraws what would be an unendurable heteronomy, an overwhelming otherness, suggests that Moltmann is forced to see the fall into sin as an 'accident waiting to happen'.[35]

---

[34] CoG, 306–307, cited (with some key German phrases) in 4.3.3n241. My emphases. See also the discussion in 4.3.3, 4.1, and 4.2 above. The "over against" in this passage, indicated by "gegenüber" in *DKG*, 336 (cf. the "distanced contraposition [distanzierten Gegenüber]" of CoG, 307 [*DKG*, 337] and the eschatological resolution of CoG, 295 [*DKG*, 325], cited in 3.1 and in 3.1n18), brings to mind another passage from CoG, 236 [*DKG*, 263] (cited in 1.4.4 above) in which Moltmann asks with respect to the Final Judgment,

Does God, as their creator, go with all his created beings into life, death and resurrection—or does God as judge stand over against [gegenüber] those he has created, detached and uninvolved, to pardon or condemn?

[35] Cf. 4.2 above. For my resistance to this way of thinking and for an exploration of the creation/fall distinction, see my "The Call of Wisdom/The Voice of The Serpent."

With respect to the Fall as an 'accident waiting to happen' and with respect to the progression from creational autonomy to eschatological freedom, there are some interesting parallels between the implicit logic of Moltmann's position and the version of 'Open Theism' developed by Gregory A. Boyd in his *Satan and the Problem of Evil: Constructing a Trinitarian Warfare Theodicy* (Downers Grove, IL: InterVarsity Press, 2001), especially chaps. 2 and 6 respectively. What I here call the progression from 'creational autonomy' to 'eschatological freedom' is in Boyd's terminology (in 122n8) a process in which "libertarian freedom becomes compatibilistic freedom." Although I firmly reject the idea of creational autonomy, I am still happy to affirm progression. But I would suggest there is a progression from *creational* freedom *with* God to *eschatological* freedom *with/in* God. Cf. 4.4n247 above.

If, in the logic of Moltmann's *zimzum* model of creation, the Fall is an accident 'waiting to happen', then it is hard (if not impossible) to see how his position can avoid legitimating human evil (cf. 4.2n112 and n. 31 above)—even though this is something

All this flows from Moltmann's remarkably negative model of creation. As I noted in 4.2 above, Hell is the Creator-creation distinction negatively conceived. Given the primordial Godforsaken space, the process of creation, though originating in God's best intentions, paves the way for a road leading from the Hell of the *zimzum* to the hells of human history. To be truly free, we cannot return to this "grace of creation," we cannot move *out of* our origins as we face the future. We must move *beyond* the gift of life in hope.

While I have very serious problems with the eschatological eclipse of the gift of creation that characterises Moltmann's theology (as discussed in 6.3 and 6.4 and countered most explicitly in 6.6 above), ironically the fact that creational freedom is so closely (mis-)identified with autonomy by Moltmann means that with respect to God's coming future and the open existence that this awakens in us, he develops a decidedly non-autonomous view of freedom that is very insightful.

"Wer die Wahl hat, hat die Qual," notes Moltmann citing a German proverb.[36] 'The person who has to choose has the torment of choice'. We need not resist the truth of this, Moltmann thinks, because "It is not the right to choose that defines the reality of human freedom. It is the doing of the good."[37] His negative point, at least, is well taken. Even in a culture so enamoured with the idea of autonomy, we are still aware that merely having choice, merely being faced with an alternative, does not make us free, for we may be 'damned if we do and damned if we don't'. Furthermore, we know that increasing our options does not necessarily increase our freedom. Those who have acquired Hannibal Lector's taste for human flesh have acquired 'real' choices that do not exist for us.[38] Yet in exercising such choices, and in coming to have them, they have lost their humanity. Autonomy and freedom are not the same.

Nevertheless, if our freedom lies in the doing of the good, we might ask, do we not still have to *choose* the good? Moltmann might agree. It depends. At one point he observes that "the logic of hell [seen as self-damnation and thus

---

he would certainly resist. In his early essay, "The Theology of the Cross Today," in FC, 77, he states that "we cannot go beyond the fact of evil for which no reason can be given, since every reason would be tantamount to an excuse." This is echoed and reinforced in his foreword to *Pilgrimage of Love: Moltmann on the Trinity and Christian Life*, by Joy Ann McDougall (Oxford: Oxford University Press, 2005), xiv, where he writes:
> Auschwitz and the death-camps of Treblinka and Maidenek: you do not understand such experiences with God, and you do not understand without God, as Elie Wiesel once said. One does not even want to understand it, because one does not want to offer any explanation.

These wise words make it clear that the legitimation of evil that an explanation would provide (by allegedly shedding light on how evil 'fits' and thus 'belongs' within a wider context) is the last thing that Moltmann would want.

[36] TKG, 55 as cited in 4.3.3 above.
[37] Moltmann, "The Logic of Hell," 47.
[38] In this example, we may discern the way in which transcendental conditions are affected by evil. Cf. nn. 27 and 29 above and 8.4, including 8.4n73, below.

self-annihilation] is nothing other than the logic of human *free will*, in so far as this is identical with the *freedom of choice*."[39] This wording suggests that there is a distinction to be made between "will" and "choice" with respect to freedom that has been overlooked by advocates of the "logic of hell." Perhaps Moltmann would be happy to say that finding freedom is not *choosing* the good, as if it were an item on a menu, but doing the good *willingly*.

If this is a fair reading, this makes sense of why (and how) Moltmann can so emphasise God's patient desire for our "free response" to 'his' love.[40] This is not an *impartial choice for* God. It is *willing participation in* God's life. As we have seen in 4.3.3 above, in Moltmann's "trinitarian doctrine of freedom"[41] we experience the ever deepening, ever expanding freedom of being God's slaves, God's children, God's friends on the way to the "total" freedom of glory.[42] My only misgivings about Moltmann's understanding of freedom as the "simple, undivided joy in the good" is that he might have made this more explicitly covenantal by stressing that we are called to, and are free to, participate in "the good" in our own way. This is *our* participation. Though it is "simple" in that we are to have no divided loyalties, our 'response' to God, which in the biblical tradition includes the way in which we may participate in the very shaping of God's will for history,[43] is not only uncoerced but unpredictable, initiating, responsive, complex, surprising, *ours*.

But how, given the structure of Moltmann's theology, do we get from the autonomous freedom of creation and fall to the participatory freedom of glory? This has already been explored in 4.3.3 above in some detail. But here I will focus on the possible role of repentance (a topic we left unconcluded at the end of 8.1 above).

Again this will be an exercise in filling in the gaps in Moltmann's account. It seems to me that Moltmann's understanding of repentance must be related to the way redemption includes the restoration of the *potentia oboedientialis*.[44] As this creational potential was lost in sin, not least, I suggest, because in Moltmann's understanding its nature as *posse non peccare* is structurally so close to autonomy,[45] the restoration of this potential in itself does not inspire much confidence in the idea of universal repentance. But redemption, as we have seen (in 5.3 above), means more than recovering something that has been lost. In this case it must include bringing our potential for obedience to its eschatological fulfilment. We might ask therefore whether in repentance, we participate in the transformation of the will from *non posse non peccare* to *non*

---

[39] Moltmann, "The Logic of Hell," 44. My emphases.
[40] TKG, 119 as cited in 4.3.1 above.
[41] TKG, 212 as cited in 4.3.3 above.
[42] TKG, 222 as cited in 4.3.3 above.
[43] See the important, breakthrough discussion in Fretheim, *The Suffering of God*, chap. 10, with respect to the role of the prophets in the divine council.
[44] See EiT, 158 as cited in 4.3.3 above.
[45] See TKG, 55 as cited in 4.4.3 above.

posse peccare. This is the question of the point of contact between nature and grace, or (to use Moltmann's terms) between nature and glory in grace.

Given the structure of Moltmann's theology as I understand it, repentance must be related to the awakening of hope. This awakening is an act of grace but the hope is ours. "*[G]ratia non perfecit, sed preparat naturam ad gloriam aeternam,*" writes Moltmann.[46] In hope we let go. Our *kenosis* in this respect, as I have argued in 6.5 above, is the (human) nature that grace (i.e., the "eschatological grace" explored in 6.4) prepares for the coming of glory. For all to come to salvation, all will repent in hope.[47]

How might we be sure that this will happen, given the assumptions and overall structure of Moltmann's theology? Because hope is at the heart of our true, open humanity just as despair is at the heart of the self-enclosure of sin.[48] As so many die in despair, and as Moltmann does not seem to explore the possibility that the experience of death itself might awaken saving hope,[49] it follows that the Final Judgment is the context in which he believes this "Conversion to the Future"[50] will take place. "In the divine Judgment," writes Moltmann, "all sinners, the wicked and the violent, the murderers and the children of Satan ... will be liberated and saved from their deadly perdition through transformation into their true, created being."[51] Given his understanding of that "true, created being" as openness to God's future and given his claim that there are two sides to the restoration of all things—God's judgment "which puts things to rights" and God's kingdom "which awakens to new life"[52]—the revelation that saves us does not, in Barth's striking phrase, confront us "like a boxer's closed fist,"[53] but "awakens" our hope, repentance, and freedom.[54]

---

[46] GC, 8 as cited, translated, and discussed in 6.4 above. His italics.

[47] This final repentance can be inferred from the repentance emphasised in CPS, 80–81 and discussed briefly near the beginning of 4.3.3 above in the context of freedom.

[48] See TH, 19–26.

[49] Here I allude to the idea that 'Near Death Experiences' (NDEs) are often positive experiences of religious hope because in believing that we are finally dying, the fear of death, which blocks religious trust, is paradoxically relativised, thus allowing us to be open to our deepest hopes, and thus be open to God. Cf. Hendrik Hart, "Whither Reason and Religion?," in *Searching for Community in a Withering Tradition: Conversations between a Marxian Atheist and a Calvinian Christian,* by Kai Nielsen and Hendrik Hart (Lanham, MD: University Press of America, 1990), 148–235, especially 233–34. This seems very compatible with Moltmann's anthropology. For Moltmann's comments on how the fear of death shapes our world, see his "There Is Enough for Everyone: A Sermon Given at Ryerson United Church, Vancouver, February 26th, 1989," Occasional Paper no. 2 (Vancouver: Vancouver School of Theology, 1989), 7–9.

[50] CPS, 80. Here this phrase is not used in the context of Final Judgment, but I believe using it this way fills in a gap in his thinking in a way that is faithful to his thinking.

[51] CoG, 255 as cited in 1.4.3 above.

[52] CoG, 255 as cited in 1.4.3 above.

[53] Barth, *The Epistle to the Romans,* 259.

[54] On hope, repentance, and freedom as connected, see CPS, 80.

I opened chapter 2 with the following, enigmatic passage from *The Coming of God* in which Moltmann states,

> It is only if a qualitative difference is made between God and human beings that God's decision and human decision can be valued and respected. God's decision 'for us', and our decisions for faith or disbelief no more belong on the same level than do eternity and time. We should be measuring God and the human being by the same yardstick if we were to ask: what, and how much, does God do for the salvation of human beings, and what, and how much, must human beings do?[55]

Here, as I suggested in 2.6 and 4.3.1 above, Moltmann is combining an eschatological-historical distinction and a transcendental-phenomenal distinction with respect to the different "level[s]" occupied by the divine and human will. How does this relate to repentance?

Historically speaking, the differentiation, *kenosis*, and alienation of phenomenal time from its transcendental source, which is the differentiation of time from eternity, parallels the way the human will, 'given time' and in its autonomy, becomes caught in sin, thus losing its creational freedom. In itself, it has no (advent) future. It is history. Our will for the future (as *futurum*) and God's will to save are not on the same level. "[I]t is not in our dominion that the coming God is present through his life-giving Spirit. . . . It is not in our power that the grace that raises us up is made perfect."[56]

But "God did not create the world for transience and death. He created it for *his own* glory, and therefore for *its own* eternal life,"[57] says Moltmann against the time-eternity dualism of Augustine. This must mean that the human will is not created for autonomy. "[I]t is not in our dominion that the coming God is present through his life-giving Spirit; *it is in our hope*. It is not in our power that the grace that raises us up is made perfect; *it is in our weakness*."[58] The wreckage of history that *Angelus Novus* watches with horror is countered by the dawn of God's future that has caught the gaze of *The Angel of the Annunciation* (cf. 2.1 above). In the subjection of passing time to the coming fullness of time in the eschatological redirection of history, the human and divine will are no longer structurally opposed but may become 'one' in parallel with the structure of aeonic time (as suggested in 4.3.1 above). Repentance, in which we give up our "dominion" in hope, might thus be compared to that 'moment' in which time, like the sabbath, opens itself to eternity and begins to participate in the life of the Age to Come.

If what we might call God's transcendental will and our phenomenal wills may become aligned in the eschatological (re-)direction of time, does this mean that in Moltmann's vision of universal salvation, God and creation, grace and

---

[55] CoG, 245, also cited in 1.4.2, 2.0, and 4.3.1 above.
[56] Moltmann, "Theology in the Project of the Modern World," 16 as cited more fully in 6.5 above and more fully below.
[57] GC, 124 as cited in 2.2 above. My emphases.
[58] Moltmann, "Theology in the Project of the Modern World," 16. My emphases.

nature, heaven and earth will finally be 'one' in the 'covenantal' sense explored in 6.2 above?[59] Here we must answer with a Yes and a No.

The best case that can be made for claiming that all will willingly respond to God's grace in God's grace, I suggest, needs to be rooted in the conviction that we were created *not* with a "freedom of movement over against"[60] God but for movement *with* God in history 'from the beginning'. True creational freedom (not only the eschatological fulfilment of freedom) is thoroughly covenantal from first to last. Responding to God's creational-eschatological grace is the warp and woof of our authentic nature. Redemption is the reaffirmation, liberation, and restoration of that true nature that is itself a gift/promise that responds to the gift/promise, thereby extending God's grace to others. In the context of grace, our true nature truly 'comes into its own'. Our *response* to the gift/call of Life is *our* response, *our life*. This is not autonomy or heteronomy. This is freedom truly defined. A universal salvation that is non-coercive, in my view, should celebrate the fact that we are made for God, made for Life, to respond to Life, to live (and without God there is no life) by being who we are (who we are called to be). In this sense, (universal) salvation reveals our very nature.

Redemptive grace reaffirms and re-offers the gift and promise of life. Our graced nature 'naturally' responds in God's grace to God's grace. This is neither divine monergism nor syn-ergism (in the pejorative sense). In covenant with God, our work does not supplement God's work but *is* God's work while remaining thoroughly our own (in a non-possessive, non-autonomous, and thus authentic sense). It is, to use Moltmann's phrase, "on the same level" in the sense that the doing of God's will "on earth as it is in heaven" (Matt 6:10, NRSV and NIV) means that God's will comes to pass in (our sovereignty over) history. God is the God of creation. Creation is the creation of God. To love God is to love *life* in the sense of Deut 30:15–20. To *live* is to find, celebrate, and express our freedom. Only with God may we be(come) human and explore "our true, created being."[61]

In salvation, we are put in touch (once again) with the gift and promise of our own lives. We are thus able to find our identity as selves, our intimacy with others (not only other human beings), and, in and through all this, our relationship with God. As *victims* of evil, we are set free from the evils to which we have been subjected and are thereby empowered, as *agents* of evil, to repent before those we have victimised, thus furthering their journey into freedom. The 'social dimension' of sin becomes the 'social dimension' of

---

[59] This and the following two paragraphs closely follow suggestions put forward at the end of 6.2 above.

[60] CoG, 306 as cited above.

[61] CoG, 255 as cited above. In this thoroughly covenantal view of creation, we might speak of the human person as, from the beginning, *homo respondens*. Freedom is thus not autonomy and autonomy is not freedom. Cf. H.G. Geertsema, "*Homo Respondens*: On the Historical Nature of Human Reason," *Philosophia Reformata* 58 (1993): 120–52.

grace.⁶² One of the great comforts of a firm belief in universal salvation is that when we find forgiveness from God for sins committed against those with whom reconciliation is not possible in the present age, we may take God's forgiveness as a promise that the full (divine and human) forgiveness we desire will take place in the Age to Come.

One of the strengths of understanding salvation as putting us in touch with the gift and promise of and for our existence is that the 'point of contact' (to return to the issue central to the Barth-Brunner debate explored in 6.2) is seen as lying not in some part of our humanity that is somehow untouched by evil, but in and between God's redemptive grace and our (creationally and eschatologically) graced nature. Our 'point of contact' with each other, which cannot be separated from our relationship with God, may be seen in the same light.

Because Moltmann undervalues creational grace in his theology (as examined in 6.3 above), the 'point of contact' is minimised and thus the 'grounds' for our willing response are greatly reduced. His universalism is saved from being heteronomous, however, and thus remains 'covenantal', because of his affirmation of our eschatologically graced nature (discussed in 6.4). In the end, the human will does not become God's will by being subjected to the divine alchemy of the cross (the concern expressed at the end of 4.3.1 above). In salvation, God's will and our will become 'one' through our willing participation.

Admittedly, this last point is implicit in Moltmann's writings rather than explicitly stated. But it makes sense within his theology as a whole. In Moltmann's theological anthropology, we are, from the very beginning, made for God's future and thus called to hope.⁶³ For a covenantal, universal salvation

---

⁶² Cf. my comments on the victim/agent connection in my discussion of the dynamics of evil in 6.1n5 above.

⁶³ We might wonder if hope is thus a 'creational' category. This is not the most helpful way to describe Moltmann's position. Hope does not seem to be an innate capacity for him as it is for Ernst Bloch. It is interesting that in his short work *Man: Christian Anthropology in the Conflicts of the Present*, trans. John Sturdy (London: SPCK, 1974), Moltmann in his opening chapter ("What is man?"), stresses our dynamic, open, unfinished, restless character yet does not address hope until the last section of the book ("Life in hope") in the context of redemption. But/therefore for Moltmann, with this eschatological horizon in mind, we might still say that from the beginning we are 'made for hope'. That said, Moltmann's relative antipathy towards the foundational-creational direction clearly limits his willingness to see faith (not just an openness for hope) as truly constitutive of being human from the beginning. This antipathy comes to the fore with reference to the nature of faith in Moltmann's response to James Fowler in Jürgen Moltmann, "Response," in *Hope for the Church: Moltmann in Dialogue with Practical Theology*, by Jürgen Moltmann with M. Douglas Meeks, Rodney J. Hunter, James W. Fowler, and Noel L. Erskine, trans. Theodore Runyon (Nashville, TN: Abingdon, 1979), 133–34. Over against faith development (in the historical direction of time), he places wonder (in the eschatological direction of time). Given the structure of his anthropology, I suggest, he would, along with hope, relate the latter (but not the former) to the "eccentric positionality" suggested by Helmut Plessner, which Moltmann refers to with

to be plausible in his framework, for our 'yes' and for the divine 'Yes' to 'co-respond' and coincide, God must awaken that hope within us all and thus bring us to Life. Then we shall turn from our autonomy to participate in the freedom for which we were created.

8.4 *Spes* (within the Economy of Grace)

Reading Moltmann's theology in the light of Volf's suggestions explored in the previous chapter suggests that there is and will be a 'social dimension' to this awakening to hope. Moltmann's universalism not only explicitly involves a Final Judgment but calls for (as it points towards) a view of Final Judgment in which to face God is to face one another (cf. 7.3 in the light of 7.2 above). God's grace to us and our grace towards one another cannot be separated. 'Universal' salvation involves us all in a complex global, intergenerational web of relationships as those who repent, as those who cry out for justice, as those who confront and are confronted, as those who forgive as we are forgiven, and as those who are forgiven as we forgive. And let us not forget the groaning other-than-human creation of Rom 8:19–22! It is in such a context, I suggest, that God may best be envisaged as awakening in us all the hope for justice and mercy that is the hope of salvation.

Volf speaks here of participating in an "economy of grace."[64] "Economy" is not only a time-honoured theological term; the way its contemporary usage connotes a vast network of relationships makes it an especially appropriate word. That this is an economy not of exchange but of *grace* also calls for further comment.[65] For if all are to be saved in this model of Final Judgment, does this mean that we all *must* repent, *must* forgive? If we *must*, how can this be a manifestation of grace? And if this is *not* something we *must* do, how can we claim that this salvation will be *universal*?

Here it seems to me we encounter the way in which grace and freedom ultimately transcend the category of law, even the 'law of the home', to stretch the etymology of "economy."[66] Is it fair to say that innocent victims 'ought' to forgive their oppressors? When in forgiving our enemies we go beyond justice, beyond the call of 'duty', and give someone something that they cannot claim

---

approval in Jürgen Moltmann, "The Alienation and Liberation of Nature," in *On Nature*, ed. Leroy S. Rouner (Notre Dame: University of Notre Dame Press, 1984), 142.

[64] Volf, "The Final Reconciliation," 98 as cited in 7.2 above.

[65] This brings us close to some very interesting issues in postmodern philosophy, theology, and ethics. See John D. Caputo and Michael J. Scanlon, eds., *God, the Gift, and Postmodernism* (Bloomington, IN: Indiana University Press, 1999) and Stephen H. Webb, *The Gifting God: A Trinitarian Ethics of Excess* (Oxford: Oxford University Press, 1996).

[66] In Greek, *oikonomia* (the management of the household) is closely related to *oikonomos*.

is theirs by right, we may speak of being 'called' to forgive, perhaps.[67] But the language of 'ought' and 'must' breaks down.

What we ought to do, what God's Law demands, may be related to the 'call' implicit in the gift and promise of Life (cf. 6.1 and 6.1.1 above). In this light, law (including the Mosaic law) may be seen as a manifestation of grace. To posit a dualism between law and grace, law and gospel, law and freedom is uncalled for. But there is a distinction. There is a sense in which the gift precedes the call, *Gabe* comes before *Aufgabe* making our response possible. Similarly the *promissio* embraces, even as it empowers us to embrace, the *missio*. The Spirit in this sense, the Spirit as gift and promise, comes 'before' the Word (Gen 1:2–3).[68] "We love because he *first* loved us" (1 John 4:19, NRSV and NIV. Cf. John 15:9).

Love, which includes yet exceeds an economy of justice and obligation, is something in which we freely participate. When all is said and done, we do not love in the fullest sense of the word because we 'have' to, or because this is God's command or will in that sense. Love transcends obedience. "For the law," says John (in John 1:17) "was given through Moses; grace and truth came through Jesus Christ."[69]

"The rose flowers without a why" said Silesius. "I smell a rose, and smell the kingdom of God," exclaimed Arnold van Ruler.[70] Indeed, the kingdom of God flowers without a why. Universal salvation will not happen because it 'has' to. Our hope should not, need not, rest on what must necessarily be the case.

---

[67] For this kind of 'calling', we may wish to use the term 'supererogation'. Cf. John Macquarrie, "Supererogation, Works of," in *A New Dictionary of Christian Ethics*, ed. John Macquarrie and James Childress (London: SCM Press, 1986), 612.

[68] Cf. 6.1n5 above.

[69] This translation is from the NIV, which closely parallels the NRSV. Herman Ridderbos, in his *The Gospel of John: A Theological Commentary*, trans. John Vriend (Grand Rapids, MI: Eerdmans, 1997), 57–58 is right to point to the "grace and truth" of the law in Exod 33–34 here. But he still does not do justice to the contrast in my opinion. I have explored this further in "Life after the Law? Rethinking Truth in the Light of John's Gospel" (unpublished paper). I believe Moltmann would agree with my argument here, not least with respect to the way the dynamics of love transcend our sense of normativity. Although I would appeal to a different philosophy of time, I empathise with what he says in SL, 303 (most of which is also cited in 3.5.2 above):

> What corresponds in life to the trinitarian doxology in the divine liturgy is the perception of *the eternal moment*. I mean by this an awareness of the present which is so intense that it interrupts the flow of time and does away with transience. We call the moment in which life is as intensively experienced as this, *ecstasy*. It is a momentary awareness of eternity, not a permanent one. Although every moment in life can be ecstatically lived in just this way, it is only the crowning ecstasies which interrupt everyday life; and *we feel that these belong to a different category that our everyday standards cannot grasp or judge them*.

His emphases except for the last sentence.

[70] See nn. 1–2 above.

We may be sure that something *will* happen if we know that it *must*. But we may also be certain that something will happen if we trust the *promise* that it *will*. Universality and necessity are strongly connected in our experience. (This may explain why 'universalism' sounds to many like a totalising claim or dogma.[71]) What *must* happen is related to the present transcendental conditions for existence, which hold 'universally' within their sphere.[72] But do these hold for God's ultimate future? Whatever misgivings I may have about the Godforsaken nature of the primordial *nihil* (as discussed in 4.2 and commented on briefly in 8.3), when this is considered in relation to the eschatological *annihilatio nihili*, Moltmann's thoughts, though speculative, reveal a sound intuition: the fundamental space for life, the very conditions for existence, will be changed in the eschatological fulfilment of creation.[73] Moltmann, it seems, never tires of citing Rev 21:5a: "Behold, I make all things new."[74] Given the resurrection of Christ, he understands this radical renewal of creation to include the very limits of possibility.[75] Our sense of what *will* happen eschatologically

---

[71] Thus Rowell, in *Hell and the Victorians*, 88, says of no less a critic of the traditional view of Hell than F.D. Maurice (whose stance contributed to him losing his position at King's College, London in 1853),
> It would be wrong to describe Maurice as a universalist, for universalism states as a *dogmatic certainty* that all men will be eventually saved, and Maurice suspected *the certainty of [the] system*. There is no doubt, however, that his understanding of God led him to hope that all men would eventually be saved.

My emphases. Dogmatism and the (closed) system are correlates here, presumably, because for systems to work, certain things *must* happen.

For an example of the charge of determinism and dogmatism leveled at Moltmann, apparently due to the mistaken assumption that his universalism implies an appeal to what *must* happen, rather than to what *will* happen, see Ryan A. Neal, *Theology as Hope: On the Grounds and Implications of Jürgen Moltmann's Doctrine of Hope*. Princeton Theological Monograph Series 99 (Eugene, OR: Pickwick, 2008), 205–10. The same assumption seems to be at work in David H. McIlroy, *A Trinitarian Theology of Law: In Conversation with Jürgen Moltmann, Oliver O'Donovan, and Thomas Aquinas*. Paternoster Theological Monographs (Milton Keynes, UK: Paternoster, 2009), 53.

[72] See Hart, *Understanding Our World*, chap. 2.

[73] In my view, the present conditions for and possibilities of life, which have been affected by evil (unlike the gift of/for life), will certainly be transformed, changed, healed, while the primordial conditions will be opened up to their eschatological fulfilment. Moltmann does not seem to (sufficiently) recognise this distinction, thus reading the stance of autonomy that is the result of sin back into the primordial conditions for existence. Cf. nn. 27, 29, and 38 above.

[74] See Moltmann, "All Things New: Invited to God's Future" and "The Logic of Hell," 47. Following Moltmann, I have cited Rev 21:5a from the *Revised Standard Version*. In CoG, 296 he connects the end of the primordial space with Rev 20:11. But this too (for Moltmann) should be seen in the light of Rev 21:5a, which is, significantly, the first biblical text he cites in CoG (see CoG, xi).

[75] Thus from the beginning of his career as a theologian of hope, Moltmann rejects a 'correspondence theory of (eschatological) truth'. See Jürgen Moltmann, "The Revelation of God and the Question of Truth," in *Hope and Planning*, by Jürgen

is therefore best governed not by our present understanding of what can and must happen, or by what seems (un)likely given typical human behaviour, but by trusting God's *promises*.

Ernst Bloch believed that hope, translated into philosophy as it should be, becomes what he called "*docta spes*," 'hope that understands'.[76] Citing this phrase while echoing Anselm's famous "*Fides quaerens intellectum*" ('faith seeking understanding'), and most likely thinking of Anselm's "*Credo ut intelligam*" ('I have faith so that I may understand'), Moltmann concludes the Introduction to his *Theology of Hope* with the words,

> '*Spes quaerens intellectum*' is the first step towards eschatology, and where it is successful it becomes *docta spes*.[77]

Unless we have an especially intellectual, indeed rationalistic, view of hope, we will always be conscious of a distinction—or 'gap'—between what we know in hope and how we understand existence in the light of that hope, between our actual hopes and our conceptual, theological, doctrinal, grasp of and articulation of our hopes. Hope can never be fully expressed intellectually or conceptually without ceasing to be the hope that guides our intellectual endeavours in particular and our lives in general.

A universalist *theology*, therefore, cannot be expected to intellectually justify a universalism *of hope* (to return to a distinction I made in 5.0), but it may articulate that hope in a particular academic context in a way that others may find attractive. It may explore certain implications, address particular objections, search out connections within our wider web of beliefs that might prove illuminating, and thus awaken and give support to the hope that all might be saved. Or it might stimulate us to integrate a different set of hopes with (and within) a different kind of theology.

Moltmann, trans. Margaret Clarkson (London: SCM Press, 1971), 3–30, especially 15–17 and Jürgen Moltmann, "Resurrection as Hope," in *Religion, Revolution, and the Future*, by Jürgen Moltmann, trans. M. Douglas Meeks (New York: Charles Scribner's Sons, 1969), 42–62, especially 51. He expresses this eloquently in his response to Janet Martin Soskice in Jürgen Moltmann, "Response," in *Christ and Context: The Confrontation between Gospel and Culture*, ed. Hilary D. Regan and Alan J. Torrance with Antony Wood (Edinburgh: T. and T. Clark, 1993), 62,
> How is the truth in a world of lies revealed? Like the light in the darkness, so comes the truth of God into the world of lies and becomes the victim of violence and injustice. In the crucified Christ, God's truth meets us as a contradiction to the contradictions of this world. In Christ, the suffering truth of God looks at us.

To catch Moltmann's characteristic irony, the final sentence must be read in the light of the title of Soskice's essay, "The Truth Looks Different from Here."

[76] Bloch, *Man on His Own*, 91. His italics. Cf. Jürgen Moltmann, "Introduction," in *Man on His Own: Essays in the Philosophy of Religion*, by Ernst Bloch, trans. E.B. Ashton (New York: Herder and Herder, 1971), 20.

[77] TH, 36. His italics.

In my judgment, Moltmann's *spes quaerens intellectum* has provided us with a theological universalism that merits serious, widespread discussion. I believe that his biblical intuitions (though exegetically underdeveloped) are sound. I am also convinced that his reflections on justice point to an understanding of the Final Judgment that is most promising. His main contribution, however, lies in his very insightful view of freedom. It is certainly true that the structure of his theocosmogony leads to an eschatological eclipse of creation and that this undermines his ability to envision a covenantal universalism in the fullest sense. But his contribution towards the development of such a theology remains very significant indeed. I hope that the present study furthers the in-depth discussion that his vision and articulation of universal salvation so richly deserves.

"*In the end is the beginning*," writes Moltmann in the opening sentence of the preface to *The Coming of God*.[78] I wish to draw this concluding chapter to a close, therefore, with some reflections not on Moltmann's "*docta spes*," but on the hope that lies at the "beginning" of (his) theology, the hope beyond expectation, the hope against hope. The pre-*spes spes*. This is the hope in which we might say (with Anselm and Moltmann), '*Spero ut intelligam*'.

Moltmann's pre-theological universalism of hope, as we have seen (in 1.4.1, 4.1, 4.3.1), is rooted in his response to the 'descent into Hell' in which Christ enters our Godforsakenness as our brother. Moltmann's autobiographical reflections indicate that this is the Christ who awakened him to hope in God soon after the Second World War and who has remained beside him ever since.[79]

There is something about this experience of Christ's descent into Hell, this experience of hope, as Moltmann articulates it, that refuses to be limited. Its infinite depth implies infinite breadth. It has inherently universal significance. It is like reading Paul's words in 1 Cor 15:22, "For as all die in Adam, so all will be made alive in Christ" (NRSV cf. NIV), as an all-embracing promise that resonates with our deepest desires even as it opens our eyes and our hearts to a whole new world that reverberates with expectation.

---

[78] CoG, x as cited and discussed in 6.6 above. His emphasis.
[79] In addition to BP, especially pt. 1, see Jürgen Moltmann, *The Source of Life: The Holy Spirit and the Theology of Life*, trans. Margaret Kohl (London: SCM Press, 1997), chap. 1, especially 4–5 and Jürgen Moltmann, *Experiences of God*, trans. Margaret Kohl (London: SCM Press, 1980), chap. 1, especially 6–9. Cf. Moltmann, "My Theological Career," in HTG, 166; EiT, 3–4; Jürgen Moltmann, foreword to *Origins of the Theology of Hope*, by Douglas Meeks (Philadelphia: Fortress Press, 1974), x–xi; Jürgen Moltmann, foreword to *Moltmann: Messianic Theology in the Making*, by Richard Bauckham (Basingstoke: Marshall, Morgan and Scott, 1987), viii; Jürgen Moltmann, "Jürgen Moltmann," in *How I Have Changed: Reflections on Thirty Years of Theology*, ed. Jürgen Moltmann, trans. John Bowden (London: SCM Press, 1997), 13; and Moltmann et al., "Talk-back Session with Dr. Jürgen Moltmann," 45. Moltmann's account of Christ's Descent in Hell should be read in the light of these reflections.

After this, scholarly attempts to 'correct' Paul's grammar[80] or to point out that 'all' he is referring to is the (inclusive yet less than universal) salvation of both Jews and Gentiles,[81] or the universal scope of God's offer to save,[82] may strike us as strained, plausible, or convincing. But they are anti-climactic. The hope that has welled up within us dissipates. Life returns to 'normal'.

But if Christ has entered our Hell, we need not abandon hope. In faith, hope, and love, we may surely connect the *promise* of v. 22 to the *God*, the *'universal'* God, of v. 28. For those who "will be made alive" (v. 22)—the "*all*" in question, the "*all*" to whom this promise has been made—will find their life *in* the *God* who will be nothing less than "*all in all*."[83]

---

[80] See e.g., Kenneth Barker, ed., *The NIV Study Bible*, rev. ed. (Grand Rapids, MI: Zondervan, 2002), 1797. The text, which is translated in the NIV as, "For as in Adam all die, so in Christ all will be made alive," is read as saying: 'All who are in Adam die; all who are in Christ will be made alive'. I regard this as an example of evangelical *Sachkritik* (content criticism)! More subtle is the argument of Anthony C. Thiselton, *The First Epistle to the Corinthians*. The Greek Testament Commentary (Grand Rapids, MI: Eerdmans, 2000), 1222–29. Having translated 1 Cor 15:22 as "For just as all die in Adam, even so all will be brought to life in Christ" (1222) he concludes: "The stress is not on ["all"] but on ["in Adam"] and ["in Christ"], as that in which the respective experiences and destinies are *grounded*" (1229). His emphasis.

[81] See e.g., N.T. Wright, "Towards A Biblical View of Universalism," *Themelios* 4, no. 2 (January 1979): 54–58. In this early article, Wright clearly allows his exegesis of Romans to control his handling of 1 Cor 15:22–28 (see p. 56), thus subordinating v. 28 and v. 22 to 1 Cor 15:23.

[82] See Scott M. Lewis, *"So That God May Be All in All": The Apocalyptic Message of 1 Corinthians 15:12–34*. Tesi Gregoriana Serie Teologia 42 (Rome: Gregorian University Press, 1998), 153.

[83] Biblical scholars and theologians have paid significant attention to the question of whether Paul's theology can be described as 'universalist' as so many of the texts suggestive of universalism—cf. the passages listed at the end of 7.1—are from the Pauline corpus. Some of the relevant secondary literature that has not already been cited includes: M. Eugene Boring, "The Language of Universal Salvation in Paul," *Journal of Biblical Literature* 105, no. 2 (1986): 269–92; Judith M. Gundry-Volf, "Universalism," in *Dictionary of Paul and His Letters*, ed. G.F. Hawthorne, R.P. Martin, and D.G. Reid (Downers Grove, IL: InterVarsity Press, 1993), 956–61; I. Howard Marshall, "Does The New Testament Teach Universal Salvation?," in *Christ in Our Place: The Humanity of God in Christ for the Reconciliation of the World; Essays Presented to James Torrance*, ed. Trevor A. Hart and Daniel P. Thimell (Exeter, UK: Paternoster, 1989), 313–28; Thomas Talbott, "The New Testament and Universal Reconciliation," *Christian Scholar's Review* 21, no. 4 (June 1992): 376–94; and Larry Lacy, "Talbott on Paul as a Universalist," *Christian Scholar's Review* 21, no. 4 (June 1992): 395–407.

The scholarly discussions about the overall shape of Paul's 'theology' are important and I hope to pay attention to them in a future study on the topic of Hell and universal salvation. Here, however, I am exploring 1 Cor 15: 22–28 in terms of the dynamics of hope. This leads to a different kind of argument. The kerygmatic or confessional thrust of the biblical writings cannot be reduced to, and should not/cannot be contained within, (our accounts of) the 'theology' of the relevant author. We are, I suggest, biblically called to 'go beyond the Bible in the spirit (and thus in the Spirit) of the Bible', and thus

discern its future (as well as plumb its depths). Cf. James H. Olthuis, with Donald G. Bloesch, Clark H. Pinnock, and Gerrard T. Sheppard, *A Hermeneutics of Ultimacy: Peril or Promise?* (Lanham, MD: University Press of America, 1987) and Hendrik Hart, *Setting Our Sights by the Morning Star: Reflections on the Role of the Bible in Postmodern Times* (Toronto: Patmos Press, 1989). In this respect, these two works from the neo-Kuyperian tradition resonate with Moltmann's discussion in EiT, 134–50. His words on pp. 144–45 are worth citing here:
> In the perspective of the eschatological finality of the death and resurrection of Christ, scripture is *closed* and complete.... But in the perspective of the Pentecostal beginning of the eschatological experiences of the Spirit, scripture is *open*. The eschatological experience of the Spirit is itself *the future* of scripture. It is for this, and looking towards this, that what has been passed down has been told, written down, read and continually interpreted afresh. With this future 'the fulfilment of Scripture' in the kingdom of God begins. In this respect we have to understand 'what is written' in the great framework [better: unfinished Story] of God's economy of the Spirit. Nothing less than that should be meant by the demand for a 'spiritual interpretation of Scripture'. So seen theologically, *God the Spirit* is the real interpreter.

His emphases.

APPENDIX

Birthpangs of the New Creation

> For nation will rise against nation, and kingdom against kingdom; there will be earthquakes in various places; there will be famines. This is but the beginning of the birthpangs (Mark 13:8; cf. Jer 4:31; 6:24; 22:23).[1]

The following exploration extends some of the exegetical suggestions of 7.1 into the book of Revelation.[2] In addition to providing further support to N.T. Wright's approach to biblical apocalyptic, on which I am dependent in that chapter, the discussion below will suggest a way of interpreting the symbolic significance of Babylon (9.1) and the woman who gives birth (9.2) that will set the stage for an examination of three themes that are highly relevant to the present study: judgment and vindication (9.3), fire and brimstone (9.4), and judgment unto salvation (9.5).

Normally John's Apocalypse is thought to have been written in the last decade of the first century CE, when the Christian community is believed to have been suffering from (at least the threat of) another wave of persecution instigated and executed by the Roman empire. In this reading, the "Babylon" of Rev 14:8, 16:19, 17:5, and 18:2 is almost universally taken as a symbol for Rome. Moltmann's own exegesis reflects these assumptions.[3] Two noteworthy

---

[1] Here I am citing the NRSV. For the rest of this Appendix, unless otherwise stated, I will be citing the NIV because I am, in part, challenging the conservative evangelical theology/eschatology that can be discerned in this translation. For some comments on the NIV, see 0.7n38 and 7.1n8 above. In the quotations that begin the subsections below, I have placed references to any significant alternatives offered by the NRSV in parentheses.
[2] The five sections of 9.1–9.5 below consist of edited/expanded versions of five previously published short articles: "Commentary: Revelation 17:3," *Third Way* 22, no. 6 (July 1999): 22; "Commentary: Revelation 12:1–6," *Third Way* 22, no. 8 (October 1999): 23; "Commentary: Revelation 20:1–5," *Third Way* 23, no. 1 (March 2000): 22; "Commentary: Revelation 20:11–15," *Third Way* 23, no. 10 (December 2000): 20; "Commentary: Revelation 1:7," *Third Way* 24, no. 1 (February 2001): 22.
[3] See, e.g., CoG, 308–19.

monographs that pay special attention to Moltmann's theology in the light of the book of Revelation also concur with this consensus.[4]

The following exegesis is based on the conviction that Revelation is written during the Jewish War of 66–70 CE (although many elements of my proposed reading do not absolutely require this). In line with the pattern of Old Testament allusions that are present in Mark 13, as set out in figure 9 in 7.1 above, I will also argue that "Babylon" is a symbol for Jerusalem, not Rome (although the latter is symbolised in the second half of the book by "the beast").[5] Given the widespread assumption that John's Apocalypse confronts the depravity of the Roman empire by announcing the utter destruction of its capital city, interpreters are understandably resistant to suggestions that such a judgment should be transferred to Jerusalem, not least because of fears of anti-Semitism or anti-Judaism. But the 'utter destruction' reading is mistaken, I will argue. If it is handled with hermeneutical and ethical sensitivity, one of the merits of the Babylon-Jerusalem identification, not least for those open to universal salvation, is that it provides us with a way of seeing the 'judgment unto salvation' dynamic at work. In what follows, therefore, the opening and closing sections (9.1 and 9.5), on "Babylon" and "Judgment unto Salvation," respectively, will prove to be surprisingly interconnected.

Although a minority position, dating the book of Revelation to around the time of the Jewish War does have significant scholarly support.[6] There is little

---

[4] See Michael Gilbertson, *God and History in the Book of Revelation: New Testament Studies in Dialogue with Pannenberg and Moltmann*. Society for New Testament Studies Monograph Series 124 (Cambridge: Cambridge University Press, 2003), 57–61, including 57n42, (on dating), and 198 (on Babylon); and Poul F. Guttesen, *Leaning into the Future: The Kingdom of God in the Theology of Jürgen Moltmann and the Book of Revelation*. Princeton Theological Monograph Series 117 (Eugene, OR: Pickwick, 2009), 111–12, including 111–12n5 and 112n6, (on dating), and 201–202, including 201n93, (on Babylon).

[5] See also 7.1nn41 and 45. G.K. Beale, in *The Book of Revelation: A Commentary on the Greek Text*. The New International Greek Testament Commentary (Grand Rapids, MI: Eerdmans, 1999), 25, states: "there is not one example of "Babylon" ever being a symbolic name for Israel, either before or after 70 A.D. This does not mean such an identification is impossible, but the burden of proof rests on those maintaining the Babylon = Jerusalem identification." The OT allusions in Mark 13, as highlighted by N.T. Wright and summarized in figure 9 in 7.1 above, provide extremely compelling evidence for precisely this identification.

[6] Here we must include the work of Christopher Rowland, an expert in apocalyptic literature, and Stephen Smalley, a well-known scholar of the 'Johannine' corpus. See Christopher Rowland, *The Open Heaven: A Study of Apocalyptic in Judaism and Early Christianity* (London: SPCK, 1982) 403–13; *Revelation* (London: Epworth, 1993); Stephen S. Smalley, *The Revelation to John: A Commentary on the Greek Text of the Apocalypse* (Downers Gove, IL: InterVarsity Press, 2005), 2–3; *Thunder and Love*, 35–56. See also E. Earle Ellis, *The Making of the New Testament Documents* (Leiden: Brill, 2002), 208–37; and John W. Marshall, *Parables of War: Reading John's Jewish Apocalypse*. Studies in Christianity and Judaism 10 (Waterloo, ON: Wilfrid Laurier University Press, 2001), chaps. 8 and 9. It is also significant that when John A.T.

doubt that the identification of Babylon as Jerusalem is far more contentious.[7] Yet in recent years, some highly respected scholars have come to endorse this position.[8] Further evidence that the dominant consensus cannot simply be assumed may be found in the work of those who think that the choice between Rome and Jerusalem is a false either-or.[9] As space prohibits extensive

---

Robinson argued for this position over thirty-five years ago at a time when it had clearly fallen out of fashion with New Testament scholars, he was nevertheless able to cite the support of a number of classical historians. See Robinson, *Redating the New Testament*, 221–53, especially 225. For the popularity of a Neronic dating in nineteenth-century scholarship, see Arthur W. Wainwright, *Mysterious Apocalypse: Interpreting the Book of Revelation* (Nashville, TN: Abingdon, 1993), 118. It is also worth noting that although he favours a later dating, David E. Aune, in his detailed discussion in *Revelation 1–5*. Word Biblical Commentary 52A (Dallas, TX: Word, 1997), lvi–lxx, notes several factors that would favour a date around the time of 70 CE.

Although the identification of Babylon with Rome, the interpretation of the image of the beast as a reference to emperor worship, and the presence of the Nero *redivivus* myth, all point to a later date according to many interpreters, I challenge the exegesis on which these correlations rely in 9.1 and 9.2, including n. 44 (on Babylon), n. 22 (on the image of the beast), and n. 45 (on the Nero *redivivus* myth).

[7] N.T. Wright notes in his *Jesus and the Victory of God*, 358,

I have discovered that this suggestion arouses anger in some circles, which is not explained simply as annoyance at an exegetical peculiarity (plenty of those are to be found in the journals, but they merely arouse curiosity). What is at stake here, and for whom?

I have made my own suggestion as to what is behind this, above: no one wants the distain that has been directed at the Roman empire (an empire that no one is invested in defending) from being transferred to Jerusalem. But this calls for hermeneutical care, not the a priori closing down of exegetical possibilities.

[8] Perhaps the single most important recent work is that of the Italian scholar, Edmondo F. Lupieri, *A Commentary on the Apocalypse of John*, trans. Maria Poggi Johnson and Adam Kamesar (Grand Rapids, MI: Eerdmans, 2006). Special mention should also be made of Margaret Barker, *The Revelation of Jesus Christ* (Edinburgh: T. and T. Clark, 2000), 279–301; and *The Gate of Heaven*, 49–56; Alan James Beagley, *The 'Sitz im Leben' of the Apocalypse with Particular Reference to the Role of the Church's Enemies* (Berlin: de Gruyter, 1987); Eugenio Corsini, *The Apoclaypse: The Perennial Revelation of Jesus Christ*, ed. and trans. Francis J. Maloney. Good News Studies 5 (Wilmington, DE: Michael Glazier, 1983) 321–38; J. Massyngberde Ford, *Revelation: A New Translation with Introduction and Commentary*. Anchor Bible 38 (New York: Doubleday, 1975), especially 276–93; Bruce J. Malina, *On the Genre and Message of Revelation: Star Visions and Sky Journeys* (Peabody, MA: Hendrickson, 1995), especially 219–23. Here we may also include Wright, "Jerusalem in the New Testament," 71–72. Cf. 7.1n45 and also n. 7 above. But with respect to his more recent Rome-centred exegesis of Revelation, see n. 16 below.

While this approach to the interpretation of Babylon fits naturally with a dating to around the time of the Jewish War (thus e.g., Lupieri, *A Commentary on the Apocalypse of John*, 43–44, including 44n147), none of these authors insist on this as a prerequisite for their position.

[9] See Edith McEwan Humphrey, *The Ladies and the Cities: Transformation and Apocalyptic Identity in Joseph and Aseneth, 4 Ezra, the Apocalypse and the Shepherd of*

engagement with the voluminous secondary literature on these and other questions of introduction and exegesis, let me note that I have carried out this conversation elsewhere.[10] Here I will mention some of the distinctive features of the approach I am advocating.

My overall interpretation of Revelation suggests that central to 'apocalyptic' as a genre, certainly to biblical apocalyptic, is an understanding of the 'apocalypse' itself as the transition between the two ages. I believe that this adds some much needed specificity to current definitions.[11] This "[i]n the end is the beginning" perspective, to borrow a phrase from Moltmann,[12] finds support in the midpoint and general pattern of the chiastic structure offered in figure 10 at the end of this Appendix. Among the exegetical possibilities that this approach opens up are a new approach to the Millennium (9.3)[13] and a new way of viewing Rev 21 and 22 within an inaugurated eschatology (9.4).

Hermas. Journal for the Study of the Pseudepigrapha Series 17 (Sheffield, UK: Sheffield Academic Press, 1995), 115n97; G.K. Beale and Sean M. McDonough, "Revelation," in *Commentary on the New Testament Use of the Old Testament*, ed. G.K. Beale and D.A. Carson (Grand Rapids, MI: Baker, 2007), 1081–161, especially 1140, where, in their commentary on Rev 17:16, they state that " 'Babylon' refers both to the pagan world and apostate Israel and to the apostate church that cooperates with it"; and Beale, *The Book of Revelation*, 883–86

[10] I hope to publish this research under the title, *Birthpangs of the New Creation: Judgment unto Salvation in the Book of Revelation*

[11] The most commonly cited definition at present is that offered by scholars of the Society of Biblical Literature workgroup, under the leadership of John J. Collins:

'Apocalypse' is a genre of revelatory literature with a narrative framework, in which a revelation is mediated by an otherworldly being to a human recipient, disclosing a transcendent reality which is both temporal, insofar as it envisages eschatological salvation, and spatial insofar as it involves another, supernatural world.

John J. Collins, "Introduction: Towards the Morphology of a Genre," in *Apocalypse: The Morphology of a Genre*, ed. John J. Collins. *Semeia* 14 (Missoula, MT: Scholars Press, 1979), 1–20. Quotation from p. 9. Cf. John J. Collins, *Daniel: With an Introduction to Apocalyptic Literature* (Grand Rapids, MI: Eerdmans, 1984), 4. My focus on the transition between the two ages as one way to sharpen up this current definition finds support in Martinus C. de Boer, "Paul, Theologian of God's Apocalypse," *Interpretation* 56, no. 1 (2002): 21–33, especially 24.

[12] This appears in italics in CoG, x and is discussed in 6.6 (and in 8.4) above.

[13] As I have not referred to Moltmann's discussion of the Millennium in the preceding chapters, mention should be made of Richard Bauckham's helpful overview and response, "Must Christian Eschatology Be Millenarian? A Response to Jürgen Moltmann," in *'The Reader Must Understand': Eschatology in Bible and Theology*, ed. K.E. Brower and M.W. Elliott (Leicester, UK: Apollos, 1997), 263–77, an expanded version of which has appeared as, "The Millennium," in *God Will Be All in All: The Eschatology of Jürgen Moltmann*, ed. Richard Bauckham (Edinburgh: T. and T. Clark, 1999), 123–47. Cf. Moltmann's response, "The Hope of Israel and the Anabaptist Alternative," in *God Will Be All in All: The Eschatology of Jürgen Moltmann*, ed. Richard Bauckham (Edinburgh: T. and T. Clark, 1999), 149–54.

This reading of the transition between the two ages as an 'apocalyptic judgment unto salvation' that was imminent for John but that for us lies in the distant past, is also unusual. As this 'apocalypse' reveals that evil has no future in God's New Creation, it is entirely supportive of the idea of a still future eschatological or Final Judgment as explored in 7.2, 7.3, and 8.2 above. Rather than positing two judgments, however, the apocalyptic transition may be seen as a judgment unto salvation that comes to fulfilment when God is all in all.

Given this perspective, the damning or annihilating Final Judgment of much 'Christian' theology and imagination is a judgment we should put behind us (see Rev 15:1 and 16:17).[14] While a highly punitive and retributive understanding of judgment has found support in the book of Revelation down the ages, it is hoped that the following discussion will help us see John's words in a different light.

Even though the following is little more than a sketch of an alternative approach, I trust that the cumulative effect of the intertextual and intratextual connections has some force—especially when read in the light of chapter 7 above. We will begin *in media res* with the symbolic significance of Babylon in Rev 17 before turning to the (related) symbolism of the woman who gives birth in Rev 12. This image will give us some insight into the way John has structured his apocalypse to reflect his conviction that the death-throes of the old world order are also the birthpangs of the new creation.

9.1 Babylon

> Then the angel carried me away in the Spirit into a desert. There I saw a woman sitting on a scarlet beast that was covered with blasphemous names and had seven heads and ten horns (Rev 17:3).

In the chilling language of Rev 17:16, John is told: "The beast and the ten horns you saw [in Rev 17:3] will hate the prostitute. They will bring her to ruin and leave her naked; they will eat her flesh and burn her with fire." This woman is the "great city that rules over the kings of the earth" (v. 18). She is also called "the great prostitute" (v. 1), the "mother of prostitutes and abominations," and "Babylon the great" (v. 5). So who or what is Babylon? And why does it matter?

An important clue is that v. 16 deliberately makes use of the language of Ezek 23:25–34, which describes God's judgment on Israel's capital city for lusting after the nations. The Babylon of John's Apocalypse would thus seem to be Jerusalem. But although this Old Testament allusion is widely

---

[14] Rev 15:1: "I saw in heaven another great and marvelous sign: seven angels with the last seven plagues—last, because with them *God's wrath is complete*" (NIV, cf. NRSV: "which are the last, for with them *the wrath of God is ended*"). Rev 16:17: The seventh angel poured out his bowl into the air, and out of the temple came a loud voice from the throne, saying, *"It is done!"* My emphases. I will return to this point in 9.5 below.

acknowledged, the current scholarly consensus understands the harlot to be a symbol for Rome.[15]

This dominant interpretation is not without evidence. The seven heads on which the woman sits are also called seven hills in v. 9 (or "seven mountains," in the NRSV), thus bringing to mind the seven hills on which Rome was built.[16] Likewise, the reference to the many waters (vv. 1, 15) recalls the popular first-century depiction of the goddess *Roma* sitting on the seven hills above the waters of the Tiber.[17]

But if the *beast* on which the woman sits is indeed the Roman empire, its seven heads also symbolising its emperors, an excellent case can still be made for identifying the *woman* with Jerusalem. John does allude to a popular portrayal of Rome. But in doing so, he deliberately invests a familiar form with new content. As this ironic twist has been missed by the majority of interpreters, it bears closer examination.[18]

In Rev 13:4, the people ask: "Who is like the beast?" While this question can be read on more than one level, the shocking answer that is revealed a few chapters later is: Israel, represented by Jerusalem. Here, as elsewhere in the Apocalypse, Old Testament allusion is the key to intended meaning. The references in Rev 17 to adultery (v. 2), prostitution (vv. 1, 6), abominations (v. 5), and the humiliation the woman will soon suffer by being stripped naked (v. 16), are strong evidence that John has Jer 13:25–27 in mind, including what the prophet, in v. 27, calls Jerusalem's "detestable [i.e., idolatrous] acts *on the hills*."[19] According to John, the "city [set] *on a hill*" (Matt 5:14, cf. Isa 2:2–4

---

[15] See, e.g., Beale and McDonough, "Revelation," 1139. Particularly revealing is G.R. Beasley-Murray, *Revelation*. The New Century Bible Commentary, rev. ed. (Grand Rapids, MI: Eerdmans, 1978), 259–60. He writes, "The language takes up phrase by phrase Ezekiel's prophecy of the destruction of Jerusalem . . . . Such is the fate of the harlot city of God. If Jerusalem is so judged, how much more the city of the beast?"

[16] It is presumably the strength of the allusion to Rome in Rev 17:9 that has persuaded N.T. Wright to abandon the Jerusalem-Babylon connection that he had found in the gospels and was open to finding elsewhere (see n. 8 above) in his popular commentary, *Revelation for Everyone* (London: SPCK, 2011), 153 et passim. The following argument aims to show that this abandonment is as unnecessary as it is unfortunate.

[17] See David E. Aune, *Revelation 17–22*. Word Biblical Commentary 52C (Nashville, TN: Thomas Nelson, 1998), 919–28.

[18] The irony has also been missed by most interpreters who identify Babylon with Jerusalem. Apart from the exegesis of Corsini, *The Apocalypse*, 321–38, which is on the right lines, in my view, I do not find the works listed in n. 8 above to be convincing with respect to their various ways of exegeting Rev 17:9. As collusion with local elites was the way the Roman empire maintained its rule (cf. Christopher Kelly, *The Roman Empire: A Very Short Introduction* (Oxford: Oxford University Press, 2006), chap. 3, which is actually entitled, "Collusion"), it is surprising that his has been missed.

[19] Partly because they are not alert to the intertextual significance of the hills in Rev 17:9, Beale and McDonough do not discuss the presence of Jer 13 here. But they do recognize the influence of Jer 2–4 on Rev 17:16 in "Revelation," 1139. There is no doubt that John knows the book of Jeremiah well (even though John's use of the other major prophets, Isaiah and Ezekiel has received more scholarly attention). In addition to

and Mic 4:1-3) has become so idolatrous and so 'pagan' that she can be portrayed as Rome *upon the seven hills!*[20] The "great city" of Rev 11:8, which most commentators identify with Jerusalem, and the "great city" of 17:18 are one and the same.[21]

The harlot's resemblance to Rome here follows the Old Testament principle that humans become like the gods/idols they worship (cf. Ps 115:8). Several chapters before Rev 17, John has already told us, in Rev 13:8 and 13:12, that the "inhabitants of the earth [*hoi katoikountes epi tēs gēs*]"—a better translation might be: 'the inhabitants of the [promised] land'—will "worship" the beast. Furthermore, their question, "Who is like the beast?" not only flows out of their worship of both the beast and the dragon in 13:4, but is immediately followed by the words, "Who can make war against him?" In this way, John lets the inhabitants of the land reveal, in their own words, just how enamoured they have become with the militaristic spirit of the empire.[22]

Beale and McDonough, "Revelation," see the references to Jeremiah in Beale, *The Book of Revelation;* and G.K. Beale, *John's Use of the Old Testament in Revelation.* Journal for the Study of the New Testament Supplement Series 166 (Sheffield, UK: Sheffield Academic Press, 1988). See also nn. 24 and 77 below.

[20] Especially when read in parallel with "the light of the world" motif in Matt 5:14a, the city set on a hill in v. 14b is, in the words of Donald A. Hagner, *Matthew 1-13.* Word Biblical Commentary 33A (Nashville, TN: Thomas Nelson, 1993), 100, "a metaphor that has unavoidable associations with Jerusalem on Mount Zion." If "city [set] on a hill [*polis . . . epanō orous keimenē*]" was a well-known phrase, it is interesting that the verb also means to lie or recline, making the connection between 'set' and 'sat' (Matt 5:14 and Rev 17:3, 9) easy to make.

[21] My emphases. References to "the great city" occur in 11:8; 16:19; 17:18; 18:10, 16, 18, 19, 21. My proposed interpretation allows for the first occurrence in 11:18 to function as the key to the other occurrences.

[22] As discussed in 7.1, including 7.1n41, above, much of Jesus' teaching can be read as warning Israel away from precisely this path of self-destruction. It is unfortunate that the dominant paradigm has focused on the imperial cult rather than militarism here and elsewhere in the book. Phillip A. Harland, in his article, "Emperor Worship," in *The New Interpreter's Dictionary of the Bible,* ed. Katherine Doob Sakenfeld (Nashville, TN: Abingdon, 2007), 2:255-57, notes, on p. 256, "With the exception of John's Revelation (esp. Rev 13), there are no indisputable references to worship of the emperor in the NT." My own exegesis of Rev 13 (and 17) suggests that it is the spirit of militarism, rather than emperor worship *per se,* that is the main focus of attention.

This is not to deny the biblical critique of empire that pervades the New Testament. Neither is this to say that the imperial cult has nothing to do with the beast's blasphemies (13:1, 5, 6; 17:3) (though see Lupieri, *A Commentary on the Apocalypse of John,* 202, for the possible connection to Isa 52:5 and the (pseudo-) Jewish blasphemy of 2:9—which is where this theme first occurs). It is simply to state that the central issue in the idolatrous worship of the beast by the inhabitants of the land/earth involves the militaristic violence that is reflected in 13:4 and also 13:10 (on which see n. 24 below). Given the symbolism of the "kings" in Rev 17, if John wanted to draw attention here to emperor worship, would he not focus on worship offered by or to the *heads* of the beast? Even the description of the beast's own blasphemy in 13:6 (in distinction from the idolatry of the inhabitants of the land) points in a different direction.

With the benefit of hindsight, we may wonder whether it is in giving itself over to this spirit, to the point of declaring 'Holy War' on Rome (in 66 CE), that Israel's collusion with the empire, which is so graphically portrayed in Rev 17:3, and which would seem to have been a major source of persecution for the Jewish and Gentile Christian community,[23] reaches its dénouement, or self-defeating resolution, when the beast is provoked to turn on the woman and devour her in Rev 17:16.

Although, in my view, proposals that posit external, historical correlations should not drive textual interpretation—false extra-textual connections, coupled with flat exegesis, have closed down the interpretation of this book more than any other!—, they may confirm, or prompt us to further explore, possible internal connections, and thus potentially significant intra-textual webs of meaning that might otherwise remain unnoticed. In addition to opening up a fruitful correlation between Rev 17:3–16 and 13:4, so that we may now see the "inhabitants of the [land]" becoming "like the beast . . . [by] mak[ing] war against him," this particular suggestion also draws our attention to a contested verse a little later in the same chapter, in which Jesus' warning against nationalistic violence in Matt 26:52 would seem to find an echo in the words of

---

That the inhabitants of the land become like the empire they oppose because they give themselves to the same religious (idolatrous) spirit also best explains the context for and reference to the image, i.e., the imaging, of the beast from the sea that is promoted by the beast from the land/false prophet in Rev 13:14, 15. Cf. Rev 14:9, 11; 15:2; 16:2; 19:20; 20:4. The fact that the worship of the image is promoted by the *false prophet* (see 13:14 in the light of 19:20) presupposes a covenant(-breaking) context. That the false prophet is also described as the *beast from the land* (see 19:20 in the light of 13:14) suggests that the one who promotes the worship of the image of the first beast to the inhabitants of the land also images (is [in] the image of) the first beast. This helps explain Austin Farrer's observation, in his *The Revelation of St. John the Divine* (Oxford University Press, 1964), 157, where he notes:

> It is not clear from St. John's Greek whether it is the false prophet or the speaking image which causes either the executions of [Rev 13] verse 15 or the brandings of 16; nor does it make any difference, since the speaking image is but the mouthpiece of the false prophet.

On the remarkable recovery of the beast from the sea, which inspires its worship in 13:3, 4, 12, 14, see n. 45 below. On the "mark" of 13:16–17 as modeled on "the synagogal practice of forbidding all dealings with the excommunicate" *and* as reflecting the Roman policy of "the restriction of the right of commerce (*ius commercii*) to Roman citizens, or other privileged classes," see Farrer, *The Revelation of St. John the Divine*, 157. Collusion between anti-Christian Jews and the empire here would fit with Beagley's argument, cited in the following note.

[23] For the largely internal-textual argument that anti-Christian Jews were using their connections with Rome to persecute members of the (Jewish and Gentile) Christian community (cf. the book of Acts), see Beagley, *The 'Sitz im Leben' of the Apocalypse*, chap. 2, especially 31–36, where he roots his investigation in an analysis of the letters to the seven churches in Rev 2–3.

Rev 13:10: "If you kill with the sword, with the sword you must be killed" (NRSV *contra* NIV).[24]

As the identification of the woman and the beast of Rev 17:3, 9, 16 with (different aspects of) the Roman empire is so prevalent in contemporary scholarship, we should ponder John's imagery a little longer. One reason why we say 'a picture is worth a thousand words' is because a picture ('can you just draw me a map?') may provide much needed *clarity*. But graphic and verbal images may also be deliberately *suggestive*. Figuring out what kind of picture John has given us is key to discerning whether a given interpretation is too straightforward or too subtle.

One of the best ways of approaching John's graphic image of the harlot, Babylon, seated upon the beast, I suggest, is to view it as the first century equivalent of a satirical political cartoon. Here, by way of illustration, we may

---

[24] The NRSV of Rev 13:10 reads:
"If you are to be taken captive,
   into captivity you go;
if you kill [*apoktenei* or *apokteinei*] with the sword,
   with the sword you must be killed [*apoktanthēnai*].
Here is a call for the endurance and faith of the saints."
The NIV differs with respect to 13:10b ("If anyone is to be killed [*apoktanthēnai*] with the sword, with the sword he will be killed [*apoktanthēnai*]") because it follows the two passive infinitives of ms. A (codex Alexandrinus). Although this is often judged to be the harder, and thus superior, reading, this rests on the assumption that these words are addressed to persecuted believers rather than to those who worship the beast. Here, however, I am persuaded by the text critical as well as exegetical argument of Farrer, *The Revelation of St. John the Divine*, 154–55, who, in effect, sides with the NRSV over the NIV (though he is writing in the days of its precursor, the RSV). John, he says, begins, in Rev 13:10a, by echoing Jer 15:2 to convey the fate of those who are persecuting the faithful (an echo that, in itself, is often taken as support for the 'passive endurance' meaning assumed in codex A [and NIV]), despite the fact that Jer 15:2 is a judgment text). However, Farrer also thinks (again, rightly in my view) that in 13:10b, John modifies Jer 15:2 by means of an echo of Matt 26:52, with the result that the first verb of the original should be understood as active [*apoktenei* or *apokteinei*] not passive [*apoktanthēnai*]—contrary to codex A and Jer 15:2. Consequently, "the disparity between the two limbs of St. John's sentence [i.e., between 10a and 10b] has naturally confused the copyists"—a point that holds, I would add, quite apart from whether the copyists are aware of Jer 15:2 or not. My own further suggestion would be that codex A (wrongly) assumes that v. 10b is addressed to Christians and thus 'corrects' the "if you kill [*apoktenei* or *apokteinei*]" of the original on the further assumption that the addressees are being encouraged to endure suffering, rather than being warned against/judged for embracing the violence of the empire/ways of the beast.

In the light of this interpretation of Rev 13:10a and 10b, the difficult saying in Rev 13:10c—in Farrer's translation (cf. KJV, *contra* NRSV and NIV): "Here is the enduring and trusting of the saints"—may now be read as answering the cry of Rev 6:10. In Farrer's words, it means: "this is the vindication of their blood upon *the inhabitants of earth* [the land] for which they have trustfully waited." His italics. See also the detailed and largely supportive discussion of Louis A. Vos, *The Synoptic Traditions in the Apocalypse* (Kampen: J.H. Kok, 1965), 104–109.

recall a popular poster of the early 1980s that, at first glance, seemed to depict the well-known Hollywood scene of Scarlett O'Hara in the arms of Rhett Butler but that on closer inspection revealed Margaret Thatcher in the arms of Ronald Reagan! [25] To those who saw this as a poignant comment on the real dangers of nuclear deterrence and Anglo-American collusion, the mushroom cloud in the background gave new meaning to the phrase 'Gone with the Wind'!

By analogy, most New Testament scholars have assumed that John's subversive portrait must be a genuine movie poster because Ronald Reagan really was a famous Hollywood actor. The irony—which is often so central to prophetic critique—has been missed. Consequently John's visual statement about the shocking *similarity* between "the great city" and Rome has been mistaken for a straightforward case of *identity*. Thus, while interpreters have correctly observed that the cargoes listed in Rev 18:11–13 were available in Rome, they have failed to note that they were *also* imported by Jerusalem, mostly for use in the Temple.[26] Similarly, while they have been right to compare the clothing of the woman with that of the Roman emperors, they have often overlooked the fact that she is *also* adorned like the Temple and attired like a Jewish High Priest.[27] Viewed in this way, placing the "city [set/sat[28]] on a hill" on the seven hills is a lesson in spiritual and political geography that you won't find on the map. That's why it evokes and provokes "wisdom" (Rev 17:9).

If this discussion helps make my proposed interpretation of John's imagery more plausible, the polemical exposure of Jerusalem's covenantal infidelity, or harlotry, that it brings to light might lead some to worry about anti-Semitism or anti-Judaism. But Jewish *self*-critique (and John is certainly Jewish[29]) is standard fare in the Hebrew Bible when the prophets see their fellow Jews breaking the covenant. It is also evident in the Dead Sea Scrolls.[30]

Furthermore, John's critique is not only aimed at Jerusalem. In Rev 16:19a, when Babylon finally falls, we are told that "The *great city* split into three parts, and the *cities of the nations* collapsed." This reference to "the nations" presupposes the common Old Testament distinction between Jews and

---

[25] Designed by Bob Light and John Houston, the poster, entitled "Gone with the Wind," is viewable at the website maintained by the Center for the Study of Political Graphics: http://www.politicalgraphics.org/home.html
[26] See Beagley, *The 'Sitz im Leben' of the Apocalypse*, 108–10
[27] See Ford, *Revelation*, 278, 287–88; Beale, *The Book of Revelation*, 886.
[28] See n. 20 above.
[29] For a detailed argument that John was a Palestinian Jew, who was a refugee from the promised land due to the first Jewish revolt of 66–73 CE, see Aune, *Revelation 1–5*, xlix–l. I concur (cf. n. 45 below). For more specific thoughts about the identity of John, see 5.4n149 above.
[30] For an example from the Qumran scroll, 4QpNah, see n. 71 below. It is important that such 'covenantal critique' is not seen as simply the hallmark of so-called 'sectarian' Judaism, however. Such critique is deeply rooted in the Hebrew Bible.

Gentiles.[31] In the fall of "the great city" of Jerusalem, which has come to represent not only Israel but the whole world in its rebellion against God, "the cities of the nations" are also condemned.

The 'representative' character of the "great city" requires further comment with respect to its positive (and not only its negative) meaning if it is not to be misconstrued as yet another form of anti-Judaism. In the Old Testament, the promised land, centred in Jerusalem and the Temple, is often regarded as a microcosm of the entire creation. This is reflected in the Hebrew of Ezek 5:5 and 38:12, which refers to Jerusalem as 'the navel of the land/earth'. It also finds expression in the belief that the Jerusalem Temple represents both the world as a whole and the meeting point between heaven and earth. Consequently, it is against this fundamentally positive background that the fall of the First Temple in Jer 4:23–28 (as discussed in 7.1 above) is seen as the unmaking of creation.

It is the same awareness of the macrocosmic meaning of certain events, I suggest, that explains why the progression that moves from a tenth of the city collapsing, in Rev 11:13, to the entire city being split into three parts in 16:19a, is framed by a reference to the temporary protection of the Jerusalem Temple in Rev 11:1–2, on the one hand, and by a reference to the passing away of "the first heaven and the first earth" in Rev 21:1, on the other hand—the latter being almost identical to the way the fall of the Second Temple is described in Mark 13:31.[32] Given this microcosm-macrocosm understanding of history, therefore, it is not hard to see why the fall of the great city and the cities of the nations, which I have made central to my understanding of the structure of the book (16:19a in figure 10 below), are seen as two sides of the same coin.

An appreciation of this pattern, in which events in Israel may depict God's dealings with humanity as a whole, is particularly important for the way we interpret the themes of exodus, exile, and return that run through the Old Testament story and into the New Testament. Other nations evidently have their own exodus experiences, thanks to the grace of God (Amos 9:7). Similarly, if the Canaanites are to be driven, or "vomit[ed]," out of the promised land, then this could also happen to the Israelites (Lev 18:28). What this means, I suggest, is that the drama of Israel's return from exile is best seen

---

[31] David Aune, despite being an advocate of the Babylon-as-Rome interpretation, notes, in *Revelation 6–16*. Word Biblical Commentary 52B (Nashville, TN: Thomas Nelson, 1998), 901, "this phrase provides some support for those who regard the great city in v 19a as Jerusalem, since it is implicitly contrasted here in the phrase the "cities of the nations."

[32] This parallels how the fall of the Temple that is prophesied by Jesus in Mark 13:1–2, yet seemingly ignored in what follows, is apocalyptically described in Mark 13:30–31: "Truly I tell you, this generation will not pass away until all these things have taken place. Heaven and earth will pass away, but my words will not pass away" (NRSV). See Fletcher-Louis, "The Destruction of the Temple and the Relativization of the Old Covenant: Mark 13:31 and Matthew 5:18." That the Temple has been destroyed in the events prior to Rev 21:1 also fits with the claim that the covenant between God and the Lamb constitutes the Temple of the New Creation in Rev 21:22.

as a revelation and an enactment of what God intends to bring about for the other peoples of the world. A transformation with respect to the microcosm brings about a change in the conditions of possibility for the macrocosm. Thus central to Israel's election for the sake of the nations—here a correct translation of Exod 19:5–6 is pivotal[33]—is the understanding that the promised land is that place where evil will be brought to a head so that the entire world can return from the exile that began with Adam and Eve's departure from Eden in Gen 3:23–24.[34]

This macrocosm-microcosm thinking, I take it, is why the phrase that is normally translated as "the inhabitants of the earth" can, in each of its ten occurrences in the book of Revelation also be understood to refer to 'the people of the [promised] land'.[35] In John's Jewish self-critique, Israel's failings are not ethnic, Semitic, or Jewish. They reveal the human condition.

But it is the human condition at that point in world history when God's commitment to confronting the problem of sin and alienation is coming to a head. If we are open to the possibility that John's words were first read and heard at the time of the Jewish War, therefore, then the truth as John sees it, the truth that he wants the churches of Rev 2–3 (and beyond) to face, is that although Jerusalem and Rome may appear to be mortal enemies, they are spiritually one. In that sense, Rev 17:3 parallels Luke 23:12 as it was in colluding to crucify Jesus that "Herod and Pilate became friends with each other" (NRSV). It is in this light, I suggest, that John's subversive picture of the great city of Jerusalem, mounted on her horny love beast and drunk on the blood of the saints, should be understood.

9.2 Birthing

> A great and wondrous sign appeared in heaven: a woman clothed with the sun, with the moon under her feet and a crown of twelve stars on her head. She was pregnant and cried out in pain as she was about to give birth. Then another sign appeared in heaven: an enormous red dragon with seven heads and ten horns and seven crowns on his heads. His tail swept a third of the stars out of the sky and flung them to the earth. The dragon stood in front of the woman who was about to give birth, so that he might devour her child the moment it was born. She gave birth to a son, a male child, who will rule all the nations with an iron scepter.

---

[33] For the translation of Exod 19:5b–6a as: 'Because the whole earth is mine, you shall be for me a priestly kingdom and a holy nation' (*contra* NIV and NRSV but correctly translated in EiT 97), see my "Commentary: Exodus 19:5–6," *Third Way* 25, no. 9 (November 2002): 22. This 'for the sake of the nations' understanding of what it means to be priestly and holy is reiterated in the 'light to the Gentiles' meaning of the suffering servant in Isa 49:6.

[34] For a discussion of Rom 9–11 in this context, see Wright, "Christ, the Law and the People of God."

[35] The ten occurrences are: 3:10 (NRSV, obscured in NIV); 6:10; 8:13; 11:10 (twice); 13:8; 13:12 (variant word order); 13:14; 17:2; and 17:8. Cf. Rev 1:7, discussed in 9.5 below.

And ["But," NRSV] her child was snatched up to God and to his throne. The woman fled into the desert to a place prepared for her by God, where she might be taken care of for 1,260 days (Rev 12:1–6).

When John first sees the harlot in Rev 17:6, he tells us, "I was greatly astonished." To understand why, it will be instructive to go back to the vision that opens Rev 12. Here, drawing on the imagery of Joseph's dream (Gen 37:9) and alluding to Israel's struggle to birth blessing and salvation for the nations (Isa 26:17–18),[36] John presents us in with a picture of a pregnant woman crying out in pain. But who is she? And who is her child?

Usually the male child is identified as Christ. But "son" is also a common biblical term for Israel (as in Exod 4:22–23; Deut 8:5; Isa 1:2; Jer 31:20; Hos 11:1; and Matt 2:15), not only for the king or Messiah who represents her (as in Psalm 2). This is why Zion's birthing of a community of salvation in Isa 66:7–8—a passage that Fekkes has argued lies behind Rev 12:5–6—may be described as the birth of "a son" (v. 7b).[37]

As it would be unlikely, perhaps unthinkable, for a New Testament author to summarise Jesus's life from birth to ascension whilst ignoring the crucifixion (contrast Rev 5:5–13), the "son" or "male child" whose 'delivery' (in a double

---

[36] See Jan Fekkes, *Isaiah and Prophetic Traditions in the Book of Revelation: Visionary Antecedents and their Development*. Journal for the Study of the New Testament Supplement Series 93 (Sheffield, UK: JSOT Press, 1994), 181–83 and Beale and McDonough, "Revelation," 1122–23. The Hebrew of Isa 26:18b is subject to divergent translations (here we may contrast the NRSV, REB, and NJPS, on the one hand, with the NIV and NJB, on the other). But Brevard S. Childs, in *Isaiah*. Old Testament Library (Louisville, KY: Westminster John Knox, 2001), 191, no doubt conscious of the relevance of Isa 25:1–12, including v. 6, captures the wider horizon of the nations well. Commenting on the apparent false pregnancy of Isa 26:17–18 and the exclamation that "we have brought no deliverance [NIV: salvation] to the earth," he notes, "All the divine promises of the new age and of Israel's transforming of the world have not been realized."

[37] See Fekkes, *Isaiah and Prophetic Traditions in the Book of Revelation*, 183–85. His view that Rev 12:2–5 combines an allusion to Isa 26:17–18 (see n. 36 above) with an allusion to Isa 66:7–8 is exactly right in my view. The NRSV translation of Isa 66:7–8 reads:
Before she was in labor
  she gave birth;
before her pain came upon her
  she delivered a son.
Who has heard of such a thing?
  Who has seen such things?
Shall a land be born in one day?
  Shall a nation be delivered in one moment?
Yet as soon as Zion was in labor
  she delivered her children.
My emphases. Cf. Milton S. Terry, *Biblical Apocalyptics: A Study of the Most Notable Revelations of God and of Christ* (1898; repr., Grand Rapids, MI: Baker, 1988), 384.

sense) is described here is best understood as the Jewish Christian community, elsewhere described as the 144,000 (Rev 7:4; 14:1, 3), a symbol that clearly alludes to the twelve tribes and thus to the twelve stars of Rev 12:1. The mother is Israel, represented by Jerusalem (cf. Paul's language in Gal 4:26).

If this identification of mother and child is correct,[38] then the "child" is crucial to God's purposes because it is the faithful witness of the 144,000 that will lead to the salvation of the multitude that is drawn from every tribe and tongue (see Rev 7:4–9 and 14:1–6). In John's expanding image, the child that has been kept safe within the womb of Israel until the time of leaving (cf. the protection given to the 144,000 in Rev 7:4) is thus the 'firstfruit' (Rev 14:4)[39] of the multitude.

The promise that the child "will rule all the nations with an iron scepter" (12:5) is taken from Ps 2:9 where it originally referred to Israel's king as the YHWH's anointed.[40] Because this language is used of Jesus later in Rev 19:15, we might think he is the child after all. But earlier in the book, exactly the same promise is given to those in Thyatira who do not commit adultery with Jezebel (Rev 2:26–27). While the NRSV is not wrong to understand the promise of v. 26 as given to "everyone who conquers and continues to do my works to the end," the NIV better helps us see the connection with Rev 12:1–5 due to the way it sticks to the collective singular of the Greek: "To him who overcomes . . . 'He will rule them with an iron scepter' . . . . I will also give him the Morning Star" (Rev 2:26–28). Also in keeping with this pattern is the fact that John, in Rev 14:1, places the 144,000 on Mount Zion—where God installs his "son" in Ps 2:6. Finally, we may note that the male child of Rev 12:5 is snatched up to "God's throne," which is where we find the 144,000 in Rev 14:3.

---

[38] As this identification is unusual, it is worth noting there are significant problems with the standard interpretations here. For example, even though Aune clearly supports a messianic understanding of the child, and even though he seems to support the identification of the child's mother with Israel (see *Revelation 6–16*, 682), he nevertheless admits on p. 688, "If the woman of 12:1 represents Israel, the problem is that there is no OT passage that personifies Israel as a mother and also speaks of her bearing a child messiah." Also problematic is that he cannot sustain the Israel reading (he thinks the mother would appear to represent the Christian community by 12:6, and clearly does so in Rev 14 [see *Revelation 6–16*, 691 and 707]—a shift that raises questions about the messianic interpretation of the child). On linguistic problems with seeing Rev 12:5 as a reference to the Ascension, see Ford, *Revelation*, 200. If the mother is Israel (represented by Jerusalem) and if the child is the 144,000, however, these problems disappear.

[39] Although it is invariably (and not incorrectly) translated as "first fruits" (NRSV) or "firstfruits" (NIV), *aparchē* is a collective singular that is worth retaining (as 'firstfruit'), given my collective interpretation of the "child" of Rev 12:1.

[40] In a book in which the Lion of Judah turns out to be a Lamb that has been slaughtered (Rev 5:5–6), we should not be too surprised by the parallel here between the child ruling the nations with a rod of iron (Rev 12:5) and the 144,000 bringing blessing and salvation to the nations (Rev 7:4–9 and 14:1–6). This is not the result of spiritualising (de-materialisng, de-naturing) power or rule but revealing its true nature as power-for, empowerment, and thus blessing.

The birth of the child in Rev 12 is therefore not a flashback but the climax of a process that John has been describing for many chapters. The breaking of the seven seals (Rev 6:1–8:1a) and the blasting of the seven trumpets (Rev 8:7–11:15), which are separated by a 'pregnant pause' of "about half an hour" in 8:1b, are suggestive of the phases of dilation and expulsion that lead up to the moment of childbirth/delivery (see figure 10 below).

After the child escapes the 'midwife from hell' (contrast Exod 1:15–21), the dragon turns its anger on the mother (Rev 12:13). When she flees, it then makes war against the rest of her offspring (Rev 12:17), which we may identify with other (Jewish and Gentile) Christian communities outside Jerusalem and the land of Israel, including the seven churches of Rev 2–3.

While John's imagery has clear Old Testament echoes, it also has several dimensions of meaning that must be carefully discerned. Although the woman's flight to the desert (Rev 12:6, 14) may be understood as an 'exodus' experience (to be explored in 9.5 below), it is also important to note that she is not carried by an eagle as Israel was in Deut 32:11. The fact that the wings of Rev 12:14 are her own is ominous as this prompts the reader (at least subconsciously) to recall the first beast of Daniel's vision (Dan 7:4), and thus associate the woman with Babylon.[41]

The next time we see the woman, in Rev 17:3, she is still in the desert but is now described as a harlot (17:1, 5).[42] The woman clothed with the sun, the mother who gives birth in 12:1–5, is now the "mother of prostitutes" of 17:5. No wonder John is astonished (17:6)! As in Ps 106 and Ezek 20:10–26, the wilderness has become the place of rebellion (though see 9.5 below on the redemptive significance of 12:14). She is also the "great city" (17:18). In 11:8, where we first encounter this phrase,[43] Jerusalem, where the "Lord was crucified," is called "Sodom" and "Egypt" due to its violation of the stranger and its persecution of God's people (see Isa 1:10). In Rev 17:5, this same city is called "Babylon."

---

[41] The fact that the eagle was also a common symbol for Rome, not least because of the standard carried into war by the Roman armies, coheres well with the woman's relationship to the empire, as explored in 9.1 above.

[42] This identification is rightly made by Lupieri, *A Commentary on the Apocalypse of John*, 252–53, who notes that otherwise, the woman of Rev 12 simply disappears from the narrative. Albertus Pieters, *Studies in the Revelation of St. John* (Grand Rapids, MI: Eerdmans, 1954), 250–54, notes that identifying the two women was common for those who interpreted the harlot of Rev 17 as the apostate church. As an advocate of 'preterism' in the Reformed tradition, Pieters was rightly looking to anchor the text in the first century CE. Unfortunately, as it does not seem to have occurred to him that Jerusalem could be the referent, he saw the choice as being between the church and Rome (see pp. 246–61) and opted for the latter. He seems unaware of earlier preterists who, despite misidentifying the woman of Rev 12, did make the Babylon-Jerusalem connection, such as J. Stuart Russell, *The Parousia: The New Testament Doctrine of Our Lord's Second Coming* (1887; repr., Grand Rapids, MI: Baker, 1999) and Terry, *Biblical Apocalyptics*.

[43] See n. 21 above.

Why this particular symbol? It is true that once Jerusalem is destroyed by Titus in 70 CE, Jews and Christians begin referring to Rome as 'Babylon' thereby associating the empire with the power that destroyed the Temple built by Solomon.[44] But if Nero, who was the sixth in a line of emperors that began with Julius Caesar, is to be identified as the sixth and thus current king of Rev 17:10, then John is writing before his death in 68 CE.[45] "Babylon" thus refers

---

[44] For an example from a Jewish work from around 100 CE that was also treasured by Christians (cf. 7.1nn54–55 above), see 4 Ezra 3. In its introduction to the book of Revelation, *The HarperCollins Study Bible: New Revised Standard Version*, ed. Harold W. Attridge, rev. ed. (San Francisco, CA: HarperCollins, 2006), 2087, notes, "the evidence suggests that Jews used this code name only *after* the Romans destroyed Jerusalem in 70." Its emphasis. However, in a clear demonstration of the circular logic that dogs both the correct dating of Revelation and the correct identification of Babylon, this is cited as an argument for a date for the book in the late first century. Cf. Beale, *The Book of Revelation*, 18–19, 25.

[45] In distinction from the more common 'early' date of 68–70 CE favoured by, e.g., Ellis, *The Making of the New Testament Documents*, 208–37, I would posit a date of around 66–68 CE for the writing of the book of Revelation. Cf. n. 29 above. Seeing Nero as the sixth king is based on a well-attested, traditional way of counting the emperors that can be found in Dio Chrysostom, *Discourses* 34:7; Josephus, *Antiquities* 18:32; and *Sibylline Oracles* 5:12–51, as noted in Attridge, ed., *The HarperCollins Study Bible*, 2107, where the main alternative ways of counting the emperors are set out.

Nero can also be convincingly identified with the "666" of Rev 13:18. For an excellent, very full discussion, see Richard Bauckham, "Nero and the Beast," in *The Climax of Prophecy: Studies on the Book of Revelation*, by Richard Bauckham (Edinburgh: T. and T. Clark, 1993), 384–452. For another possible dimension of meaning, see n. 54 below.

Scholars who accept this Nero-666 identification but who date Revelation after his death (whether they accept a date around 70 CE or closer to 100 CE) typically see the "eighth" king of Rev 17:11 as the Nero of the 'Nero *redivivus*' myth/legend (thus Bauckham, "Nero and the Beast," 407–31). In itself the *redivivus* myth, if present in Revelation, does not rule out an early dating as it began to circulate prior to 70 CE, fuelling (or at least being fuelled by) the presence of a Nero impostor in 69 CE. Cf. Kenneth L. Gentry, *Before Jerusalem Fell: Dating the Book of Revelation* (Tyler, TX: Institute for Christian Economics, 1989), 74–77. Furthermore, one could propose that as the beast of 17:11 is "an eighth but it belongs to the seven" (NRSV) or is "one of the seven" (NJB), we should see Nero as the eighth and as the sixth emperor. On the other hand, we must reckon with the argument that the myth itself, and thus, presumably, any reference to it in Revelation, presupposes Nero's death, thus ruling him out as the current, 'sixth' emperor. This would count against my way of correlating Nero with a straightforward way of reading the list of emperors.

Although there is force to this argument, there is considerable merit to Gentry's suggestion, in *Before Jerusalem Fell*, 315–16, that the reference to the 'eighth king' primarily indicates the renewal of the Roman empire (a renewal that is easily associated with Vespasian who assumed power in 69 CE). In this view, because 'seven' is the number of completion, 'eight' should be seen as pointing to a renewal or (pseudo-) resurrection of the 'seven'. To become fully persuasive however, such a position—with its focus on the beast rather than on one of its heads/kings—must deal with the wording of 17:11 in which the beast "that was and is not" (NRSV) is (if we translate literally) said

not to Rome (which is consistently portrayed as the beast, recalling the four beasts of Dan 7[46]) but, in line with its dominant Old Testament meaning,

---

to be: 'itself an eight and of the seven', i.e., 'an eighth and [*one*] *of the seven*' (cf. NJB, REB, and NET).

Here, I suggest, we may follow a suggestion put forward by Farrer (in a work that assumes a later date and thus does not share Gentry's apologetic concerns). Farrer's proposal, in *The Revelation of St. John the Divine*, 185, is that Rev 17:11 refers to the beast as "both an eighth and one (*i.e. the first*) of the seven." My emphasis. Here he is reading the Greek of 17:11 (*autos ogdoos estin kai ek tōn hepta:* 'itself an eighth and [*one*] *of the seven*') as referring back to Rev 13:3, in which it is said of the beast, "[o]ne of its heads seemed to have received a death-blow, but its mortal wound had been healed" (NRSV). With respect to Rev 13:3, Farrer correctly assumes (though he would have done well to explain this to the reader) that the number "[o]ne," in the phrase translated as "[o]ne of its heads," may be understood as an ordinal number rather than as a cardinal number (this is also noted by Aune, *Revelation 6–16*, 736. Cf. Farrer, *The Revelation of St. John the Divine*, 153, where he also notes (again rather briefly) the reference to 'one of the seals/the first seal' in Rev 6:1a, on which the NRSV and the NIV diverge with respect to the ordinal/cardinal distinction). Thus, to adapt the NRSV's translation of Rev 13:3, this means: 'The first of its heads seemed to have received a death-blow, but its [i.e., the beast's] mortal wound had been healed'. Read in the light of 13:3, therefore, the beast in 17:11 is, in Farrer's words, "both an eighth and one (*i.e. the first*) of the seven."

We do not have to adopt Farrer's (forced) argument that Nero is the first and eighth emperor. He is simply the sixth and current king of 17:10. As for the remarkable recovery, the focus is not on the head per se; it is the healing of the *beast's* mortal wound that is emphasised (on the second "its" of 13:3 as belonging to the beast, see Aune, *Revelation 6–16*, 736). This focus is borne out in the wording of Rev 13:12, 14. This means that the reference to the eighth head being the first of the seven in 17:11 is less a reference to a 'Julius Caesar *redivivus*' (so to speak) than to a *hydra-like* renewal of the (seven-headed, now eight-headed) *empire*. It is this apparent invincibility that inspires the inhabitants of the land to embrace the spirit of militarism, on which see 9.1, including 9.1n22, above.

John, in my view, anticipates such a renewal, given his awareness of what this means for God's purposes and promises with respect to the fall of the great city (which he anticipates, in part, because of the words of Jesus that we know from Mark 13—a text that many mainstream scholars [rightly] date to before 70 CE). That no one has been able to find anything like a close (let alone one-to-one) correlation between the seven or eight kings of Rev 17:9–11 and the year of the four emperors (69 CE: Galba, Otho, Vitellius, Vespasian)—which would surely have left more of a mark on the specifics of the text—suggests to me that John is not interpreting after the fact here. This supports my proposal that he is writing (just) before Nero's death. Cf. Lupieri, *A Commentary on the Apocalypse of John*, 44n147.

The interrelationship between the historical correlations scholars that think they see and the exegesis of the passages that are the textual side of such proposed correlations is complex. What is most important, methodologically, is that the former do not drive the latter. In my view, there is nothing in the book of Revelation itself that *demands* the presence of the Nero *redivivus* myth.

[46] The description of the beast in Rev 13:2 indicates a composite of the four beasts of Dan 7.

signifies the place of captivity and exile.[47] The naming and thus exposure of Jerusalem as "Babylon," a revelation that is first made to the 144,000 in 14:8 prior to the judgment of the "great city" in 16:19a, means: It is time to leave!

This 'exilic' interpretation of Babylon's significance fits the way John alludes to certain well-known Old Testament passages. In Rev 18:4, a voice from heaven says, "Come out of her, my people," recalling not only the summons to escape in Jer 51:45 but also the great prophecies of Isa 48:20, 49:9, and 52:11 in which the return from exile is described as a second exodus.[48] It is this 'first exodus-second exodus' connection that explains why the "Egypt" of 11:8 and the "Babylon" of 17:5 are both symbols for the same city.

Although she is the mother who has given birth to them, it is imperative that the (Jewish and Gentile) members of the Christian community do not become paralysed by the tragedy of the fall of Jerusalem. Here John would have seen the significance of Jesus' words that are included in Luke's version of the 'synoptic apocalypse': "When you see Jerusalem being surrounded by armies, you will know that its desolation is near.... When these things begin to take place, stand up and lift up your heads, because your redemption is drawing near" (Luke 21:20, 28). Remarkably, it is the judgment of the "holy city" (Rev 11:2) that marks the end of the exile.

One of Moltmann's most insightful biblical intuitions, in my view (see 1.4.5 and 7.1 above), concerns his conviction that God's judgment or justice is not to be seen as an absolute, or as an end in itself, but is related to—in the sense of being in the service of—the New Creation. Although Moltmann does not work this through exegetically, such a perspective can help us see that the apocalyptic judgment centred on Israel's capital in Rev 16–20 has become necessary if the light of God's glory is to reach the Gentiles—this also being an Old Testament pattern found, *inter alia*, in Isaiah, a book that John clearly knows very well (see the birthing imagery in Isa 26:17–18, as cited above, in the context of the blessing of the nations in Isa 25, and the judgment of Jerusalem in Isa 27).[49] By the end of the book of Revelation, the great vision of Isa 60, in which the "kings of the earth" will walk by the light of a (re)new(ed) Jerusalem and will return the blessing by bringing the glory of the nations to the city, is fulfilled (see Rev 21:24–26, echoing Isa 60:3, 5, 11). But in the earlier chapters, this eschatological horizon is closed down due to the way

---

[47] Babylon as place of exile seems to be the referent in 1 Pet 5:13 as "Babylon" seems to refer to the location of both Peter's community and the sister church he is writing to. This symbol at the end of the letter thus forms an *inclusio* with the reference to the "exiles of the Dispersion" in 1 Pet 1:1 (NRSV).

[48] See, e.g., the reference to Exod 17 in Isa 48:21, to Exod 15:1–18 in Isa 51:10, and the recalling of the initial exile to Egypt of Gen 46–47 in Isa 52:4. Cf. the excursus on Exodus typology in John D.W. Watts, *Isaiah 34–66*. Word Biblical Commentary 25, rev. ed. (Nashville, TN: Thomas Nelson, 2005), 609–10.

[49] See also n. 36 above. I think it likely that Isa 27:10–11 refers to Jerusalem and thus echoes Isa 1:7–9, even though the focus is on the hope of Isa 27:7–9. The main point here, though, is that John's way of thinking about Jerusalem has OT precedent.

"[t]he great city," which is identified with the woman John sees in Rev 17:3, "rules over the kings of the earth" (17:18).

For those interpreters who subscribe to the dominant interpretation of Babylon, there is little mystery as to the nature and extent of this rule. According to Beasley-Murray, if we read Rev 17:18 together with the reference to "the city of the seven hills" in Rev 17:9, then "there was one city only in the first century to which the description could refer, namely Rome, whose rule reached virtually to the limit of the world of western and mid-orient man."[50]

If, by contrast, Jerusalem is the "great city," we can best discern the nature of her rule not by looking for the rather 'obvious' (and thus unrevealing) correlations that are a characteristic of the dominant paradigm, but by a careful probing of intertextual allusions. Key here is the fact that the phrase, "the kings of the earth," which we find in Rev 17:18, is used in Ps 2:2 for those hostile rulers that are called to respect God's anointed son (this being a reference to the Davidic king that is understood messianically elsewhere in the New Testament, including Rev 1:5[51]). It is most interesting that Acts 4:25–27, in a context of persecution, cites Psalm 2 and identifies "the kings of the earth" not only with Pilate and the Gentiles but also with Herod and the people of Israel. This should caution us against too narrow an identification. But read in this light, John's meaning in Rev 17:18 would seem to be that true Davidic authority is being usurped with the result that even those Gentile "kings" who are persecuting the community of the Messiah are following Jerusalem's lead.

Like "the kings of the earth," the nature of the 'rule' of the "great city" in this context is also best discerned intertextually. Here, it is instructive to note that the gold and precious stones with which the harlot is dressed (Rev 17:4; 18:16) do not only have Temple connotations,[52] but are associated with (the powerful figure of) Wisdom (Prov 3:14–15; 8:10–11, 19)[53] by which (or with whom) "kings reign" and "rulers rule" (Prov 8:15–16, NRSV). Wise rule in Israel was not separated from the 'light to the Gentiles' motif but was seen, in the paradigmatic reign of Solomon, to spread not only to the ends of Israel but to the ends of the earth (see 1 Kgs 3:9, 12, 28; 4:29–34; 5:7; 10:1–13, 24). But in the spirit of Prov 9:13–18, which describes the deadly seductions of folly not Wisdom, the Jerusalem of Rev 17:18, who, in her own eyes, "rule[s] as a queen" in Rev 18:7, is leading "the kings of the earth" astray.[54] The wine that is

---

[50] Beasley-Murray, *Revelation*, 256 and 261.
[51] Thus Beale and McDonough, "Revelation," 1089, though they emphasise the influence of Ps 89 (88 MT) here. They also find the presence of Ps 2 in Rev 2:26–28 (see pp. 1095–96) and in Rev 19:15, 19 (see p. 1144). Cf. the discussion of 9.2 above. In addition to Rev 1:5, the intertextual relationship between Ps 2 and Rev 19:15, 19 specifically relates to the "kings of the earth."
[52] See 9.1, including 9.1nn26–27, above.
[53] Cf. the purple and fine linen of Rev 17:4 and 18:16 and the clothing of the woman who embodies wisdom in Prov 31:22.
[54] Although the "666" of Rev 13:18 can be convincingly identified with Nero, on which see n. 45 above, there may also be an allusion to the 666 talents of gold paid to Solomon in 1 Kgs 10:14 (and 2 Chr 7:13), thus providing a telling connection between the (i)

offered as part of the feast that Wisdom has prepared (Prov 9:2, 5) has, for the nations, as well as for the "inhabitants of the [land]," been replaced by "the maddening wine of her adulteries" (Rev 14:8; 18:3; cf. Rev 17:2).[55]

When the "great city" falls, therefore, this will signify God's judgment not only of Israel but of the entire world (see Rev 16:19a). At the same time, as we shall see, the purpose of this judgment is liberation: not only for the nations, and for the "kings of the earth" who reappear in Rev 21, but also for "the city [God] loves" (Rev 20:9).

'wisdom', (ii) merchants, (iii) Jerusalem, and (iv) Temple of 1 Kgs 9–11 and the (i) "wisdom" of Rev 13:18, (ii) the merchants of 18:3, 11, 15, and 23, (iii) the "Babylon" of 18:2, 21 (cf. 14:8 and 16:19a) over which the merchants lament in 18:15, 23, and (iv) the Temple of 11:1–2. This raises the question of whether John would have seen the account of the 666 talents as part of the fruit of Solomon's wisdom (cf. the wisdom-prosperity connection of 1 Kgs 10:7) or as anticipating the critique of Solomon that becomes overt in 1 Kgs 11 but that may also be discerned earlier.

Where and when one locates the 'fall' of Solomon in 1 Kings is an interesting question in its own right. Duane L. Christensen, in his *Deuteronomy 1:1–21:9*. Word Biblical Commentary 6A, 2nd ed. (Nashville, TN: Thomas Nelson, 2001), 381, notes that the warning that the king of Israel not amass horses, wives, and gold and silver is the structural centre of the "law of the king" in Deut 17:16–17, which is itself the structural centre of Deuteronomy as a whole. He also notes (pp. 382, 384) that the narrative of 1 Kgs 10–11 portrays Solomon violating this law in all three respects. Although Christensen does not specify, a very good case can be made for seeing the positive account of Solomon's wisdom (as blessing to the nations) coming to an end at 1 Kgs 10:13 ("Meanwhile King Solomon gave to the queen of Sheba every desire that she expressed, as well as what he gave her out of Solomon's royal bounty. Then she returned to her own land, with her servants"), with the 'fall' beginning in 1 Kgs 10:14: "The weight of gold that came to Solomon in one year was six hundred sixty-six talents of gold" (NRSV).

I judge it as highly likely that John read 1 Kgs in the light of Deut 17 in this way. The integrated cluster of allusions (noted above) is not a coincidence. The relevance of 1 Kgs 9–11 to his focus on Temple, wisdom/folly, and the militaristic spirit of the empire, is striking. The warning against multiple foreign wives in 1 Kgs 11:2 presupposes the positive association between women and wisdom, even as it sees wisdom becoming folly. That Solomon built chariot cities (1 Kgs 10:26) and was involved in international horse and chariot trading (1 Kgs 10:28-29) illustrates the fact that horses were seen as military, rather than agricultural, instruments (a theme that shows up again in relation to Jezebel, on whom see n. 77 below). Finally, John would have been acutely aware that such idolatry on the part of Solomon, or his first-century CE successors, could only lead to the destruction of the Temple, as 1 Kgs 9:6–9 made clear.

[55] The NRSV understands the wine of Rev 14:8 and 18:3, which is drunk by "the nations," as "the wine of the wrath of her fornication." In Rev 17:2, where a shorter phrase occurs, it is the "inhabitants of the [land]" who become drunk on "the wine of [her] fornication" (or "the wine of her adulteries" in the NIV). In the background here is the conviction that the wine offered by Wisdom is the fruit of living in covenant with God (Prov 3:10). Those who reject the way of wisdom, by contrast, "eat the bread of wickedness, and drink the wine of violence" (Prov 4:17).

9.3 Judgment and Vindication

And I saw an angel coming down out of heaven, having the key to the Abyss and holding in his hand a great chain. He seized the dragon, that ancient serpent, who is the devil, or Satan, and bound him for a thousand years. He threw him into the Abyss, and locked and sealed it over, to keep him from deceiving the nations anymore until the thousand years were ended. After that, he must be set free for a short time.

I saw thrones on which were seated those who had been given authority to judge. And I saw the souls of those who had been beheaded because of their testimony for Jesus and because of the word of God. They had not worshipped the beast or his image and had not received his mark on their foreheads or their hands. They came to life and reigned with Christ a thousand years. (The rest of the dead did not come to life until the thousand years were ended.) This is the first resurrection. Blessed and holy are those who have part in the first resurrection. The second death has no power over them, but they will be priests of God and of Christ and will reign with him for a thousand years (Rev 20:1–6).

The main reason that Rev 20:1–6 has received so much attention down the ages is that it is the only passage in the Bible to mention the Millennium. To see how it fits into John's vision, however, we need to see it as a commentary on 16:19a, where we read the now familiar words, "The great city split into three parts, and the cities of the nations collapsed." Significantly, this statement occurs at the centre of the chiastic structure to the book of Revelation proposed in figure 10 below.

Up to this point, John has told his story diachronically. But now he will spend several chapters exploring five different layers of meaning to this central event. While these are set out one after the other for the sake of clarity, they all happen at the same time. For the complete picture, we must imagine them together as if they were five acetates placed one on top of the other on an overhead projector. Viewed in this way, John's discussion of the Millennium can be seen in a new light.

'Layer one' (16:19b–19:4) highlights how the destruction of Jerusalem (which will take place in 70 CE) constitutes the judgment of the 'Holy City' for sins past as well as present. Hence this section begins: "God remembered . . . ." In 18:5 we read, "her sins are piled up to heaven, and God has remembered her crimes," while in 18:24, John tells us: "In her was found the blood of prophets and of the saints, and of all who have been killed on the earth" (or [promised] land). This text, which has clear parallels with Matt 23:29–39 (and Luke 11:47–51),[56] is not only referring to the murder of (Jewish and/or Gentile) Christians. As promised (6:10), the blood of God's servants down the ages will finally be avenged (see 19:2).

'Layer two' (19:5–21) highlights how the fall of Jerusalem marks the judgment of the beast, John's image for the Roman empire, and the false

---

[56] See the discussion in Vos, *The Synoptic Traditions in the Apocalypse*, 162–63.

prophet, a symbol for the Jewish leaders who have encouraged the persecution of Christians (see 2:9 and 3:9) through their collusion with Rome.[57]

In 'layer three' (20:1–6), we are told that Satan is bound for 1000 years so that he cannot deceive "the [Gentile] nations" (20:3). As a result, Jerusalem is destroyed as the beast and its horns (Rome and her allies) turn on the harlot (Jerusalem), as described in 17:16.

The vindication of the martyrs is also central to the Millennium. A key to interpreting its significance, I suggest, lies in seeing the 1000—or 10 x 100—years in which the saints "reign" with Christ (20:3–4) as occurring at the same time as the 10 x 1 hour period of authority given to the ten kings (17:12). These figures highlight the qualitative difference between these two simultaneous reigns. The Millennium is the 'Day of the Lord' (cf. 2 Pet 3:8). The destruction of Jerusalem—about a thousand years after the completion of the First Temple (and the royal palace) in the reign of Solomon—is viewed as the enthronement/vindication of those who have been betrayed by the City of David.

The language of "first resurrection" promised to these saints (20:5–6) reflects the close connection between the raising of the dead and the vindication of faithful Israel in Dan 12:3. "First" here means the first stage of a resurrection that will be completed beyond the actual limits of John's vision.

'Layer four' (20:7–10) focusses on the judgment of "Satan" and the Gentiles he has marshalled for his purposes. This "gathering" is referred to in 20:8 by means of a pun (*sunagagein*) on the word for 'synagogue' (*sunagōgē*),[58] thus forming a non-Jewish counterpart to the "synagogue of Satan" first mentioned in 2:9. (Cf. the chiastic structure of figure 10, which also sees the central themes of the seven letters as foreshadowing the main sections of the book.[59])

Because John keeps changing his perspective rather than his subject matter, it is no surprise to find that this same "gathering" (though without the reference to "Satan") also appears in 16:14–16, where the sacking of Jerusalem is referred to as the battle of Armageddon, literally 'Mount Megiddo'. Here John is deliberately combining an allusion to 'Mount Carmel', where false prophets were destroyed by fire in 1 Kgs 18:19–40, with a reference to 'Megiddo' on the plain, where King Josiah was mortally injured, having refused God's warning

---

[57] On the false prophet, see n. 22 above. On the collusion with the empire, see the reference to Beagley's discussion in n. 23 above.

[58] For the *sylagōgōn* (from *sylagōgein*, to take captive) of Col 2:8 as a polemic 'synagogue' pun, see N.T. Wright, *The Epistles of Paul to the Colossians and to Philemon: An Introduction and Commentary*. Tyndale New Testament Commentaries (Leicester, UK: Inter-Varsity Press, 1986), 100.

[59] Another example of this foreshadowing, set out in figure 10 below, involves the way "Jezebel" in the letter to Thyatira (Rev 2:18–29) is thematically connected to Rev 14:6–16:18. I comment on this further in n. 77 below.

not to fight in 2 Chr 35.20–24.⁶⁰ The futile and misguided nature of Israel's 'holy war' is thus underlined.

Central to 'layer four' is the Old Testament pattern in which nations used by God to judge Israel are themselves punished for daring to attack his covenant people (see Deut 32:25–27 and Isa 10:5–19). This is why idolatrous Jerusalem is called "the camp of God's people, the city he loves" in 20:9 (or "the camp of the saints and the beloved city" [NRSV]). Thus John shows us how the Gentile attack on the "great city" is not only the result of the binding of Satan (20:2) but (at the same time) also betrays his characteristic deception (20:7) for which he is finally judged in 20:10, the last verse of 'layer four'.⁶¹

---

⁶⁰ See the discussion in Beale and McDonough, "Revelation," 1136–37.

⁶¹ In line with the translation of *aiōnios* discussed in 7.1 (cf. 9.4 below), I take the torment of Satan in 20:10 that is described as "*eis tous aiōnan tōn aiōnōn*" (poorly translated as for "for ever and ever" by the NIV cf. NRSV) to mean 'until the full arrival of the Age to Come'.

As all universalist eschatologies since the time of Origen have had to face the challenge of the 'salvation of the devil' question (thought by many to be a *reductio ad absurdum* of the position), let me mention my earlier discussion, in "The Call of Wisdom/The Voice of the Serpent," 54–57, in which I argue that we may speak of there being a future for the serpent, even though—or precisely because—there is no future for 'the Satan'.

In "A Response to the Responses," in *The Politics of Discipleship and Discipleship in Politics: Jürgen Moltmann Lectures in Dialogue with Mennonite Scholars*, by Jürgen Moltmann et al, ed. Willard M. Swartley (Eugene, OR: Cascade, 2006), 119–31, Moltmann makes the surprising comment on 127,

> According to Paul, in the end God will destroy "all rulers, principalities and powers" because he will destroy death (1 Cor 15:24–26). Yet according to Ephesians 1:21 the exalted Christ apparently subjugates these powers, so that they must serve him. I find it difficult to reconcile these two statements about the powers. Because of this, I have followed 1 Corinthians.

(Cf. WJC, 285–86 as discussed in 3.4n164 above.) I take it that the powers *as powers* will be destroyed, i.e., will be no more, while the powers as fellow servants with Christ will be restored to their true nature and thus set free. Similarly, the Satan *qua* the Accuser (Rev 12:10) will be destroyed, while the wise serpent of Gen 3 (cf. Prov 30:19) will be healed. As the figures of Leviathan and Behemoth, both creatures of God in Job 41:1 and 40:15, lie behind the beast from the sea and the beast from the land in Rev 13:1 and 13:11, the same principle holds here too. Rome as empire will be destroyed in order to be set free in its true nature. Cf. n. 78 below. This is in deep agreement with what Moltmann writes in CoG, 255, as cited in 1.4.3 above and as discussed in 8.3 above:

> In that Judgment all sins, every wickedness and every act of violence, the whole injustice of this murderous and suffering world, will be condemned and annihilated, because God's verdict effects what it pronounces. In the divine Judgment all sinners, the wicked and the violent, the murderers and the children of Satan, the Devil and the fallen angels will be liberated and saved from their deadly perdition through transformation into their true, created being, because God remains true to himself, and does not give up what he has once created and affirmed, or allow it to be lost.

Although the fall of Jerusalem/Babylon is approached from so many angles as befits a highly complex and significant event, one thing is crystal clear: God's 'upside-down' sovereignty over history. While the evil forces that enact God's judgment are only briefly victorious for 10 x 1 hour before themselves being subjected to violence and destruction, those who lay down their lives for Christ's sake are, in their 1000 year reign, unambiguously vindicated.

9.4 Fire and Brimstone

> Then I saw a great white throne and him who was seated on it. Earth and sky fled from his presence, and there was no place for them. And I saw the dead, great and small, standing before the throne, and books were opened. Another book was opened, which is the book of life. The dead were judged according to what they had done as recorded in the books. The sea gave up the dead that were in it, and death and Hades gave up the dead that were in them, and each person was judged according to what he had done. Then death and Hades were thrown into the lake of fire. The lake of fire is the second death. If anyone's name was not found written in the book of life, he was thrown into the lake of fire (Rev 20:11–15).

'Layer five', or the fifth and final synchronic layer, is 20:11–15.[62] Here, I suggest, the fall of the "great city" of 16:19a, which has been identified with Sodom, Egypt, and Babylon (see 11:8; 16:19; 17:18; 18:10, 16, 18, 19, 21), thus calling to mind the patriarchal, Mosaic, and exilic eras, is portrayed as a judgment that is passed on the entire Old World Order. In this truly apocalyptic event, God reveals that the evil that has been committed on the earth throughout history has absolutely no future and thus no place in his New Creation. Invariably seen as a Final Judgment yet to come, this event occurred, and this judgment was passed, almost two thousand years ago.

If we remain attentive to Old Testament allusions, this portrayal of the judgment of the dead represents John's version of Dan 12:1b–2, where God declares: "There will be a time of distress such as has not happened from the beginning of nations until then. But at that time your people—everyone whose name is found in the book—will be delivered. Multitudes who sleep in the dust of the earth will awake: some to everlasting life, others to shame and everlasting contempt."[63] As noted in 7.1 above, when this text was translated

---

[62] J. Webb Mealy, in his study *After the Thousand Years: Resurrection and Judgment in Revelation 20*. Journal for the Study of the New Testament Supplement Series 70 (Sheffield, UK: JSOT Press, 1992), is particularly interested in what I have identified as layers four and five (Rev 20:1–6 and 20:7–10). Although he opts for a sequential approach, he recognises the plausibility of a parallel understanding on p. 179. To clarify further, however, in my approach, the layers are not parallel/alternate accounts of each other but synchronic layers that disclose different aspects of the apocalyptic transition (or different dimensions to the event described in Rev 16:19a).

[63] See the discussion of the 'opening of the books/names in the book' motif of Dan 7:10

into Greek for the Septuagint, "everlasting" was rendered as *aiōnios*, a word usually taken to mean 'eternal' but better understood as a literal reference to 'the age (to come)'. For John, that age was now arriving. The death-throes of the Old World Order marked the birthpangs of the New Creation.

Surprisingly perhaps, the motif of 'fire' and 'sulfur' (or fire and brimstone in older translations) that is represented in 20:14–15 by the threefold reference to the "lake of fire"—this being a shortened form of the "lake" of "fire" and "sulfur" referred to in 'layers' two and four (19:20; 20:10; cf. 21:8; see also 9:17–18 and 14:10)—supports this 'historical' interpretation of the judgment of the dead. While associated by generations of artists with an underworld strikingly reminiscent of pagan mythologies, John's "lake of fire" imagery originally comes from the destruction of Sodom (Gen 19:24–28), a city symbolically identified with Jerusalem in Rev 11:8.[64] In this context, John also alludes to the presence and development of this fire and sulfur motif in the Gehenna tradition (as exemplified by Isa 30:33)—the prophetic-historical significance of which has been explored in relation to the events of 70 CE in 7.1 above.[65]

This 'first-century' reading sheds new light on Rev 21–22 as portraying what was for John the imminent dawn of the New Age. Although often obscured by translations (the NRSV is superior to the NIV here), it is interesting that what he sees and describes in the present (such as the foundations of the New Jerusalem) will soon be historically established while the events placed in the future tense (such as the conquest of death) lie at the culmination of the new era that he sees coming into existence.

This perspective accounts for why the 'second' resurrection (implied in 20:5–6) is not part of John's vision. His focus on the near future also explains why the city is so empty and why the faithful to whom John is writing may enter it "soon" (22:7, 12, 20). More traditional readings would lead us to expect the sinners to be in the lake of fire at the end. Yet here we simply find them

---

and 12:1–2 in relation to Rev 20:12 in Beale and McDonough, "Revelation," 1150. On my reading, those whose names are in the book of life are safe from the macrocosmic-apocalyptic judgment that falls on Jerusalem in 70 CE. Those whose names are not safe must undergo the 'judgment unto salvation' (see 9.5 below).

[64] While Beale and McDonough, "Revelation," 1115, do list Gen 19:24, 28, together with Deut 29:23; 2 Sam 22:9; Isa 34:9–10; and Ezek 38:22 in their brief discussion of Rev 9:17, their discussion of Rev 20 is non-existent in this respect. Fekkes, *Isaiah and Prophetic Traditions in the Book of Revelation*, 207, notes the connection between Rev 19:20; 20:10, 14, 15; 21:8 and Isa 34:9–10, also noting that the latter text is "dependent on the Sodom model." Priority should be given to Gen 19 as the canonical starting point for this motif. The presence of Sodom in Rev 11:8 underlines this with respect to its meaning in Rev 20.

[65] On Isa 30:33, see 7.1 above. It is hard, if not impossible, to believe that this text would not come to mind for John when writing Rev 20:10–15. It is surprising that it is not discussed in either Beale and McDonough, "Revelation," or Fekkes, *Isaiah and Prophetic Traditions in the Book of Revelation*. It is noted in the helpful discussion of Farrer, *The Revelation of St. John the Divine*, 201.

outside the city (22:15). Even this exclusion must be read in light of the fact that there is still a mission to the nations (21:24; 22:2).

The final chapters of Revelation certainly have implications for how God will finally judge and redeem history because they show us how God *has* judged history. John's vision reveals that because sin has no future in God's world, idolaters are excluded from the city. Yet even this provides no ammunition for those who want to preach 'hellfire and damnation' as "On no day will [the] gates [of the New Jerusalem] ever be shut" (21:25 cf. 3:8). In God's grace, history, like the city that has come down from heaven, remains open. That is why (and that is because) evil does not have a hope in hell.[66]

9.5 Judgment unto Salvation

> Look, he is coming with the clouds,
>   and every eye will see him,
> even those who pierced him;
>   and all the peoples of the earth will mourn because of him.
> So shall it be! Amen (Rev 1:7).

Thus far, John's vision of the "great city" has been almost entirely negative. My claim that John sees in "Babylon" a Jerusalem that has become so 'pagan' that it can be portrayed as mounted on the seven hills of Rome and representing the whole world's alienation from and hostility to God must be read as an example of the kind of no-holds-barred Jewish self-critique that is deeply rooted in the Hebrew Bible/Old Testament and that was not uncommon in the first century. But even if the book of Revelation is seen as Jewish prophetic-apocalyptic literature, and thus not a 'Christian' critique of 'Jewish' infidelity,[67] we may still ask whether Israel has any future in John's vision. Must we not demand this in the light of the horrors of the holocaust?

Rev 1:7 (cited above), from the beginning of Revelation, provides an important and hopeful clue. Firstly, in line with Zech 12:10, which John is quoting, the "peoples of the earth" are best rendered as 'the tribes of the (promised) land' (although they may well represent the "earth" as a whole).[68] Secondly, as in Zech 12:12–13, their "mourning" is an act of repentance (compare John 19:34, 37). This suggests that Israel may be facing a judgment unto salvation.

If we look closely, this theme can be found in later chapters. In Rev 11:13, for example, after a tenth of the Holy City collapses, we are told that the

---

[66] Cf. my "Hell: The Nemesis of Hope?," which appears as an afterword to the aptly entitled *Her Gates Will Never Be Shut: Hope, Hell, and the New Jerusalem*, by Bradley Jersak.
[67] That the book of Revelation should not be seen as a 'Christian' work in that sense is a helpful emphasis in Marshall, *Parables of War*.
[68] Cf. the ten references to the 'inhabitants of the earth/land' listed in n. 35 above.

survivors "gave glory to the God of heaven." When the commentary provided by the *NIV Study Bible* tells us that this is "not an act of repentance but the terrified realization that Christ . . . is the Lord of all,"[69] it could hardly be more mistaken.

This "giv[ing] glory" must be read in the light of 14:7 where, just before the fall of Babylon (Jerusalem), an angel exhorts those who live in the (promised) land, as representatives of all the peoples of the earth, "Fear God and give him glory, because the hour of his judgment has come. Worship him . . . ." This view of judgment as a 'call to conversion' is also evident in the words of the song of the Lamb (15:4), sung just before the seven bowls of God's wrath are poured out: "Who will not fear you, O Lord, and bring glory to your name? For you alone are holy. All nations will come and worship before you, for your righteous acts have been revealed."

This confession of faith finds its answer in 21:24 when we are told that the nations will walk by the light of the New Jerusalem "and the kings of the earth will bring their splendour into it." Surely this includes the glory of Israel, past, present, and future, for on the gates of the City, John tells us in 21:12, "were written ["*are* inscribed" in the NRSV, my emphasis] the names of the twelve tribes of Israel."

This reading suggests that the wrath of Rev 6–20 should be read in the light of the redemption so evident in Rev 21–22. It bears repeating that when the New Age, in which we now live, finally dawns in John's vision, we find sinners not burning or annihilated in the lake of fire, as some might expect, but outside a city whose gates are always open (21:25–27; 22:15).

That God will have mercy on Israel is also suggested by a number of deliberate allusions that John makes to Hosea 2. In this chapter, the Israelites are told to plead with their mother, Israel (v. 2 cf. Rev 12:1–2), who, in her promiscuity, has tellingly decked herself out with jewels (v. 13 cf. Rev 17:4). God no longer considers her his wife (v. 2). Neither will YHWH show love to her children because, as "children of whoredom (NRSV)," they share her promiscuous ways (v. 4 cf. Rev 17:5). Instead of continuing to clothe her, she will be stripped naked and exposed before her lovers (vv. 3, 10 cf. Rev 17:16).

Nevertheless, judgment makes way for compassion. YHWH does not divorce Israel but decides to win her back by speaking to her tenderly in the desert into which he has led her (v. 14), a theme echoed in Rev 12:6, 14.[70] Tragically, in this case the wilderness becomes a place of rebellion (as in Ps 106 and Ezek 20:10–26) for the next time we see the woman in the desert is in 17:3, by which time she has become the harlot known as Babylon (as argued in 9.2 above). But YHWH's intention was that this would be "a place prepared for her by God, where she might be taken care of" (12:14).

The description of the "great city" as a harlot points, in Old Testament fashion, to the breaking of the covenant.[71] That such infidelity would bring

---

[69] See Barker, ed., *The NIV Study Bible*, 1978.
[70] The last of these allusions is noted in Beale and McDonough, "Revelation," 1124.
[71] The covenantal background to Old Testament references to harlotry is so widespread,

God's wrath upon Israel is nowhere clearer than in Lev 26, which speaks four times of a sevenfold judgment to come (vv. 18, 21, 24, and 28). This 4 × 7 structure is deliberately employed in the book of Revelation. We are familiar with the punishments introduced by the seven seals (5:1–9; 6:1–8:1a), trumpets (8:2–11:15), and bowls (16:1–17; 17:1; 21:9). Less well-known is the series of judgments heralded by the seven thunders (10:3). What is remarkable is that they are sealed up before they can take place (10:4). The full covenant wrath envisioned in Lev 26 is thus never unleashed.

The beginning of Rev 1:7 cites Dan 7:13. This "coming with the clouds" does not refer to Christ's 'second coming' (a phrase unknown in the Bible) but to a coming from earth to God (cf. the discussion of the parousia in 7.1 above). The "son of man" (1:13, for Dan 7:13 a reference to Israel) would thus be publicly vindicated. Christ (and his followers) will be shown to be worthy to share God's throne.[72] John sees Jesus' earthly ministry being vindicated here not by the tribes of the land being publicly humiliated as they face the Messiah they have crucified, but by their repentance and thus by their graced participation in their own liberation (cf. 8.3 above).

While I have placed this exploration of Rev 1:7 at the end of my discussion, an early discernment of its 'judgment unto salvation' significance can, naturally, set the tone for the way the book of Revelation is read from the beginning. The same goes, surprisingly perhaps, for the second half of the book with respect to the intertextual connotations of "Babylon." Although the title with which it is introduced in Rev 14:8, "Babylon the Great," is attributed to Nebuchadnezzar in Dan 4:30 (LXX),[73] its name, for the reader who approaches the text canonically, goes all the way back to Gen 10:10 and 11:1–9. Here "Babel"—the Akkadian form of Babylon—is the name for an empire that hears

---

that interpreters who identify the harlot with Rome are forced to invoke the two non-Israelite uses of this metaphor: for Tyre (Isa 23:15–18) and for Nineveh (Nahum 3:4). In the case of Tyre, the fact that she will dedicate her merchandise and wages to YHWH (Isa 23:18) signals a healing of the covenant she contracted with Israel together with a hoped-for restoration of her role in the building of the First Temple (see 1 Kgs 5–7; 1 Chr 14:1). As for Nahum 3:4, Ford, *Revelation*, 284, notes that this text is applied to Jerusalem in the relevant Qumran scroll (4QpNah). Here we might compare the way Old Testament allusions to Edom are applied to Jerusalem in Mark 13, on which see figure 9 in 7.1 above. It is not hard to believe that echoes of the judgment of Tyre-as-a-harlot in Isa 23:17, which Fekkes finds in Rev 17:2a; 18:3b, 9b, as detailed in his *Isaiah and Prophetic Traditions in the Book of Revelation*, 211–12, have been applied in the same way. Furthermore, the fact that Israel's idolatrous Queen Jezebel (whose strong connection to the harlotry theme in the book of Revelation is discussed in n. 77 below) was the daughter of King Ethbaal of Tyre and Sidon would only reinforce this. Even if we leave aside Tyre's once-positive role in Israel's history (which we should not, as the analogies with Edom are intriguing), a 'pagan' description of Jerusalem is far easier to explain than a 'covenantal' description of Rome!

[72] This coming with the clouds (to God's throne)—this public vindication—is echoed in the "I am coming soon" of Rev 22:7, 12, 20.

[73] As noted by Beale and McDonough, "Revelation," 1132.

God's blessing/benediction to fill the earth (Gen 1:28) as a curse (Gen 11:4). In being "scattered ... over the face of the whole earth" by God's judgment in Gen 11:9, however, history is not cursed but put back on track—this being the paradigmatic expression of the judgment unto salvation motif that flows out of God's promise never to destroy the world in Gen 9:11.[74]

What holds for the Babel/Babylon of Genesis also holds for the Babylon of Revelation. If we insist that the dominant approach to John's Apocalypse is right in its identification of Babylon with the Roman empire, then we cannot say this as there is no evidence of any future for this city beyond its demise in Rev 16–18.[75] Such a view would give biblical support to an annihilative, double-outcome view of judgment. But if Babylon is Jerusalem, as I have been arguing, then although the judgment upon, and annihilation of, its idolatrous nature is final—in the words of Rev 18:21, "the great city of Babylon will be thrown down, never to be found again"—nevertheless, what we might call its true creational-eschatological nature is revealed in the Jerusalem that comes from heaven to earth in Rev 21:2 (cf Gal 4:26).[76]

This is not an 'out with the old, in with the new' rupture (see Rev 21:5, cited below), but the redemption of the "great city"—an eschatological event that has truly universal(ist) implications.[77] Because, in the macrocosm-

---

[74] See the helpful discussion in Richard S. Briggs, "The Book of Genesis," in *A Theological Introduction to the Pentateuch: Interpreting the Torah as Christian Scripture*, ed. Richard S. Briggs and Joel N. Lohr (Grand Rapids, MI: Baker, 2012), 19–50, especially 37–49.

[75] While my focus here is on a future for Israel/Jerusalem, it also follows that there is no evidence visible from within the dominant paradigm for a judgment unto salvation for either Jerusalem or Rome. On the latter, given my proposed alternative, see n. 78 below.

[76] The notion of a true or authentic nature would be associated with heaven according to the discussion of 6.1.1 above. In Rev 3:12 and 21:2, she is the "new" Jerusalem; in Rev 21:10, she is simply "the holy city Jerusalem" (NRSV). In all three references, she is coming down from the heavens.

[77] At this point, some comments are in order about Jezebel, whose death in 2 Kgs 9 is alluded to in the fall of Babylon in Rev 18:21. In 9.4 above, I referred to the way themes central to the seven letters to the churches in Rev 2–3 foreshadow the way John has structured the Apocalypse. One example of such foreshadowing, set out in figure 10, involves the way "Jezebel" in the letter to Thyatira (Rev 2:18–29) is thematically connected to Rev 14:6–16:18 (and, by extension, to its structural counterpart in 16:19–19:4).

Some of the factors that connect Jezebel to Babylon include her description as a harlot (2 Kgs 9:22; Rev 17:1, 15–16; 19:2), her murder of the prophets (1 Kgs 18:4; Rev 18:4), and the fact that she is a queen (Rev 18:7). The description of her self-adornment just prior to her death in 2 Kgs 9:30 seems to be strongly echoed in Jer 4:30 (cf. Ezek 23:40). To this picture, Jer 4:30 adds the elements of scarlet and gold that parallel the scarlet and gold of the harlot's appearance in Rev 17:4 and 18:16. Cf. Beale, *The Book of Revelation*, 884. (For the often overlooked allusions to the Jezebel narrative of 2 Kgs 9 in Jer 4:30—which, in turn, is part of an extended passage (Jer 2–4) concerning the fall of Jerusalem that, according to Beale and McDonough, "Revelation," 1139, lies behind Rev 17—see Cornelis Vanderwaal, *Hal Lindsey and Biblical Prophecy*, trans.

microcosm thinking of Scripture, the "great city" and the "cities of the nations" (Rev 16:19a) are so connected, it follows that in the eschatological Jerusalem that heralds the dawn of the New Creation, all nations may recognise and may find their own future and thus their own return from exile.[78]

One of the saddest images in the book of Jeremiah of the judgment that will soon fall on Israel is found in Jer 7:34, at the end of the central Gehenna passage (Jer 7:30–34) cited in 7.1 above. Here God says, "And I will bring to an end the sound of mirth and gladness, the voice of the bride and bridegroom in the cities of Judah and in the streets of Jerusalem; for the land shall become a waste." This dark promise is reiterated in Jer 16:9 and 25:10 before it is emphatically reversed in the return from exile passage in Jer 33:11.

In the book of Revelation, this 'silencing of the sound of bride and bridegroom' motif is clearly cited in Rev 18:23 where it is said to Jerusalem as Babylon, the place of exile, that "the voice of bridegroom and bride will be

---

Theodore Plantinga (St. Catherines, ON: Paideia Press, 1978), 132–35.)

Jezebel's death in 2 Kgs 9:31–37 is one of the most violent and debasing in the whole of Scripture. Like Babylon in Rev 18:21, she is "thrown down [cf. 2 Kgs 9:33: "So they threw her down"] and will be found no more" (NRSV). That her flesh is devoured by dogs in 2 Kgs 9:36 is the closest precursor to the way the beast and the ten horns devour the flesh of the harlot in Rev 17:16. A royal burial is impossible because, in the words of 2 Kgs 9:37, her corpse ends up "like dung on the field" (NRSV).

In 2 Kgs 9:36, we may discern a grim irony as dogs in Canaanite mythology were seen as healers as well as guides to the afterlife. If we couple this with the fact that "[h]er remaining body parts [see 2 Kgs 9:35]—her head, the palms of her hands, and her feet—correspond to the symbolic appendages the Canaanite goddess Anath liked to wear as symbols of her power," then, as Deborah A. Appler puts it, in "Jezebel," in *The New Interpreter's Dictionary of the Bible,* ed. Katherine Doob Sakenfeld (Nashville, TN: Abingdon, 2008), 3:313–14, "In essence, [she] is portrayed as being destroyed by the very gods who should protect her." Given that horses were the military machines of the day (see n. 54 above), the fact that she is trampled underfoot by the horses of her own kingdom as soon as she hits the ground, may also be seen an indictment of her idolatrous faith.

So what are we to make of the intertextual presence of Jezebel's death in the book of Revelation? In my view, a moralising hermeneutic that would see her death as a cautionary tale—as exemplifying the self-destructive, dehumanising *telos* of idolatry—does not go far enough. The overall thrust of my approach to the book of Revelation is that if the Jezebel narrative foreshadows, and is included in, the judgment of the great city then we may also see her as included in the salvation of the great city (Rev 21–22). Cf. nn. 61 and 78 above.

The text does not 'force' this conclusion on us. Its universalist meaning both calls for and finds fulfilment in our hope—the fruit of which is assurance (Heb 11:1, cf. 0.5, 5.0, and 8.4 above). In the way we read Scripture, we participate in its message of grace. Cf. Moltmann's comments on what he calls " 'the fulfilment of Scripture'," cited in 8.4n83 above.

[78] On my reading, this includes Rome. The narrative of Nebuchadnezzar in Dan 4 shows that like the healing and return from (self-imposed) exile of this paradigmatic emperor (who becomes like a wild animal), the liberation/redemption of any empire involves the eradication of its idolatrous and dehumanising—i.e., bestial—nature. Cf. n. 61 above.

heard in you no more" (NRSV) before this negation is itself negated in the ultimate return from exile heralded by the marriage of Jerusalem and the Lamb.

In John's vision, the bride is not said to be the church (as human) in relation to Christ (as divine)—a misunderstanding that results from imposing a certain reading of Paul's imagery onto John—but is a city from heaven that represents God's divine presence in the coming together, or marriage, of heaven and earth.[79] In saying that the temple of the city "is the Lord God the Almighty and the Lamb" (Rev 21:22), John means that the life of the New Creation is found in the meeting of heaven and earth revealed in the covenant between God and the Lamb. Thus humanity will dwell in God as God dwells in us (see 5.4 above).

The clear parallel that is evident in the wording of Rev 21:9 ("Then one of the seven angels who had the seven bowls full of the seven last plagues came and said to me, "Come, I will show you the bride, the wife of the Lamb") and Rev 17:1 ("Then one of the seven angels who had the seven bowls came and said to me, "Come, I will show you the judgment of the great [harlot]," NRSV) is usually seen as signifying the utter contrast between the holy city of Jerusalem and the unholy city of Rome.[80] But it is only when we can discern Jerusalem in the symbols of Sodom, Egypt, and Babylon *and* in the symbol of "the holy city ... coming down out of heaven from God" that we can grasp, and hold on to, what "See, I am making all things new" (Rev 21:5) really means.[81]

This relationship between Rev 17:1 and 21:9—a relationship of radical redemption that sees judgment as serving, and coming to an end in, renewal— also sheds new light on Rev 15:1: "I saw in heaven another great and marvelous sign: seven angels with the last seven plagues—last, because with them *God's wrath is complete*" (NIV); last because "with them *the wrath of God is ended*" (NRSV, my emphases).

The judgment of the book of Revelation, which, Rev 15:1 declares, we are called to put behind us, is indeed a judgment unto salvation. The "wrath of God ... revealed from heaven," to use the language of Rom 1:18, is not what we might expect. Contrary to standard ways of reading the Apocalypse, John's perspective is well summed up in the remarkable words of Rom 11:32, where Paul, soon after declaring that "all Israel will be saved" (v. 26), writes,

---

[79] Cf. the close connection between the heavens and the female presence of God in Gen 49:25, as discussed in 7.3, including 7.3n137, above.

[80] See, for example, Richard Bauckham, *The Theology of the Book of Revelation*, 131–32.

[81] Rev 21:5 should give interpreters pause for thought as it is in sharp contrast to the 'out with the old [i.e. Rome], in with the new [i.e. Jerusalem]' framework that we impose on Rev 21–22. For the importance of Rev 21:5 to Moltmann, see 8.4, including 8.4n74, above.

"God has bound all men [and women] over to disobedience [and its consequences] so that he may have mercy on them all" (NIV).[82]

It is in this light, and in this hope, that we may hear the words of Rev 1:7 cited above: "So shall it be! Amen."

---

[82] Moltmann cites Rom 11:32 in the "Postscript about the Universal Theology of Grace and the Particularist Theology of Faith and the Universal Glorification of God" at the end of "Sun of Righteousness: The Gospel about Judgment and the New Creation of All Things," in SRA, 148, contrasting its "theocentric universalism" with the non-universalist "anthropocentric dualism" that he finds in the synoptic apocalypse and the book of Revelation. He is quite candid about needing to choose between them. Cf. 1.4.5n159 above. Whatever we think of 'canon within the canon' judgments (in distinction from judgments about what constitutes the dynamic centre to the canon), universalist theologies that (in effect) argue against (Jesus' words in) Mark 13 and the book of Revelation have little, if any, chance of convincing large segments of the Christian community. But there is a world of difference between choosing between Rom 1:18 and 11:32 and reading the former in the light of the latter (as Moltmann rightly does). A central aim of this 'apocalyptic appendix' (cf. TH, 15!) has been to suggest that the choice between the book of Revelation and Rom 11:32 is unnecessary. Mark 13:8, Rom 8:22, and Rev 12:2 are united in their witness to the birthpangs of the new creation!

A PROLOGUE: **1:1–8**

    B VISION of Son of Man amid the seven churches, leading to the *seven* letters: **1:9–3:22** [first letter (Ephesus) foreshadows letters two to seven]

        C THRONE VISION, which will lead to JUDGMENT of the Living: **4:1–11**

            D (i) The PRAISE/VINDICATION of the Lamb who was slain: **5:1–14** immediately followed by:
(ii) *DILATION*: The *First* Wave of judgment for the SYNAGOGUE OF SATAN, climaxing in the protection of the 144,000; blessing of the multitude: **6:1–7:17** (the *seven* seals begin: 6:1) [second letter (Smyrna): the "synagogue of Satan", endurance, vindication]

                E *EXPULSION/DELIVERY*: The *Second* Wave of judgment, leading to the rise of the BEAST and FALSE PROPHET, climaxing in the new song of the 144,000: **8:1–14:5**. Pregnant pause: 8:1 (the *seven* trumpets begin: 8:7; the *seven* thunders cancelled: 10:4). Birth: 12:5 [third letter (Pergamum): Balak/Balaam (false king/prophet)]

                    F *JEZEBEL AND HER LOVERS*: The *Third* Wave of judgment against BABYLON and her (Jewish and Gentile) subjects: **14:6–16:18** (the *seven* chalices/bowls begin: 15:1) [fourth letter (Thyatira): Jezebel and her lovers]

                        X Central Climax:*"The GREAT CITY split into three parts, and the CITIES OF THE NATIONS collapsed"*: **16:19a**

                    F' *First* Synchronic Layer: The judgment of BABYLON and her children for sins past/present, climaxing in the rejoicing of the multitude: **16:19b–19:4** [fifth letter (Sardis): remember]

                E' *Second* Synchronic Layer: The judgment of the BEAST and FALSE PROPHET: **19:5–21**

            D' (i) *Third* Synchronic Layer: VINDICATION/PRAISE of the Martyrs: **20:1–6** 'immediately' followed by:
(ii) *Fourth* Synchronic Layer: The judgment of SATAN and his (Gentile) "SYNAGOGUE" [pun in v. 8]: **20:7–10** [sixth letter (Philadelphia): "synagogue of Satan," endurance, vindication]

        C' *Fifth* Synchronic Layer: THRONE VISION leading to JUDGMENT of the Dead: **20:11–15**

    B' VISION of the New Jerusalem, bride from heaven for the Lamb: **21:1–22:5**

A' EPILOGUE: **22:6–21** [seventh letter (Laodicea): repentance, cf. Rev 22: 12–17]

figure 10: PROPOSED CHIASTIC STRUCTURE OF REVELATION

SUMMARY

The Annihilation of Hell:
Universal Salvation and the Redemption of Time
in the Eschatology of Jürgen Moltmann

Overview

This study is an engagement with the theme of universal salvation as viewed within the overall structure of Moltmann's theology, eschatology, and theocosmogony. Consonant with Moltmann's understanding, the main title, *The Annihilation of Hell*, refers to the *overcoming* of Hell as our eschatological hopes are realised, whilst at the same time alluding to Hell's own *annihilative power* in history—a power with which hope must contend. For Moltmann, Hell is the *nemesis* of hope. Yet hope clings to the certainty that God in Christ has *embraced* all things, even death and Hell, so that creation may participate in the divine Life of the Age to Come.

In Moltmann's highly 'original' and 'originary' interpretation, Hell has its beginning in the *nihil* that precedes God's active creating of all things, a *nihil* that God 'makes way for' within Godself. A positive way of describing Hell's redemptive 'an-nihil-ation', effected through Christ's descent into the Abyss, is to speak of God becoming 'all in all'. Universal salvation is thus related to negation and fulfilment: to the annihilation of primordial Godforsakenness and to the consummation of history.

In the annihilation of Hell as a possibility, and not just as an actuality, the relationship between God and creation, and thus the structure of reality itself, is fundamentally transformed. The *redemption of time* in this context (and thus in the subtitle to this study) refers not merely to the restoration of a goodness that existed in the past but to an eschatological fulfilment in which creation's future is opened to, and embraced by, God's coming future. Paying attention to 'redemption', as Moltmann uses this term, allows us to examine how salvation takes place within the distinction and relationship that he establishes between creation and eschaton. The redemption of *time*, in particular, including its need for transformation from the very beginning, is taken as a key to the structure of Moltmann's 'theocosmogony', the contours and dynamics of which exemplify what I call a 'contradictory/harmony monism' that is at once insightful and problematic.

Summary

A central way in which Moltmann's eschatology is evaluated is by examining whether the structure of his theology allows him to affirm a truly 'covenantal' universalism and thus avoid the polarisation many theologies (unwittingly) posit between divine heteronomy and human autonomy. Is universal salvation, as Moltmann envisions it, the affirmation of creation (understanding 'of' here as both a 'subjective' and 'objective' genitive)? Can Moltmann offer us a universalism that is biblically faithful? Or is his view of Final Judgment insensitive to the cry for justice?

It is the claim of this study that, despite the soteriological implications of Moltmann's highly negative and problematic doctrine of creation, universal salvation, as interpreted within his eschatological theology of the cross, resonates with the faith, hope, and love of the Gospel. This sympathetic critique, in entering into close dialogue with Moltmann's creative proposals, also offers an alternative universalism animated by a different philosophy of time that is far more attuned to 'creational grace' and to the gift of transience.

Synopsis

"[T]here is no one so lost that the eternal love cannot return—as long as hope shows something green." "Abandon every hope, who enter here." The Introduction to this study ("Inferno e Speranza") is framed by a juxtaposing of these two quotations from Dante. Despite the fact that Moltmann only pays sustained attention to universal salvation and Final Judgment in his more recent works, it is suggested that an *opposition* between Hell and Hope nevertheless animates Moltmann's entire corpus and thus calls out for eschatological *resolution*. These dynamics lead to a discussion of 'contradictory/harmony monism' as a possible key to the structure of Moltmann's overall theology.

Chapter 1 ("To Hell and Back") is a microcosm of the study as a whole in that it opens and closes with an exploration of the relationship between judgment and mercy, justice and reconciliation. Moltmann's critical review of *The Mystery of Salvation*, its affinity to his theology notwithstanding, serves to introduce Moltmann's own distinctive approach to universal salvation. The important issue of whether universalism necessitates the eclipse of human freedom is brought to the fore in this context, as is the 'Descent into Hell' motif that is central to Moltmann's Christocentric perspective (a motif that is reflected in the chapter title). Moltmann's understanding of authentic freedom, true justice, the nature of God (in particular, the relationship between God's love and God's wrath), and his approach to Scripture—all to be explored in further detail in later chapters—are introduced in order to give a preliminary indication of his overall position. The most widespread objections to universal salvation are also raised to provide a context within which Moltmann's universalism may be evaluated.

Moltmann's enigmatic statement that the *divine* decision to save and the *human* decision for or against faith do not exist on the same "level"—a distinction that he relates to the contrast between eternity and time—introduces chapter 2 ("The Reversal of Time in the Future of God"). In this (and the following) chapter, Moltmann's philosophy of time is taken to provide the key to the highly complex and nuanced structure and dynamism of his theology, not least his understanding of the relationship between the human and the divine—or nature and grace—in salvation. Of special interest here are the two 'directions' of time which Moltmann refers to as the historical and the eschatological, the latter being the anticipation within present history of the "redemption of time" mentioned in the title of chapter 3 (and in the overall title to this study). The relationship between the future as *futurum* and as *adventus*—here analysed as a relationship between phenomenal, historical becoming and transcendental, eschatological coming—is viewed as central to Moltmann's understanding of the nature-grace distinction/correlation.

While chapter 2 focusses on the present, historical opposition between the two directions of time, chapter 3 ("The Redemption of Time in the Presence of God") is concerned with their eschatological reintegration, or with what I call the 'coincidence of opposites' in and through which the God-world relationship is transformed. The way in which this "redemption" constitutes the simultaneous negation and fulfilment of temporal existence is explored with an eye to evaluating whether Moltmann's eschatology in general, and his universalism in particular, lead to an 'eclipse' of creation. Because Moltmann hopes and predicts that redeemed time will be characterised by "change without transience, time without the past, and life without death," transience, the past, and death are each examined in detail to see if Moltmann's eschatology is more affirmative of temporal finitude than it at first appears. The results are at best paradoxical. For Moltmann, it seems, we have to say that there is "no hope (but) for transience." Moltmann's eschatological monism, and the way its negation of creation differs from that of dualism, is given special attention at the end of this chapter.

Having thus explored the overall philosophical structure of Moltmann's thought, chapter 4 ("The Triumph of Glory") opens by placing his unique conception of Hell within his 'theocosmogony'. A discussion of the way he understands the nature-grace relationship (for him the relationship between nature, grace, and glory) is evaluated with reference to the differing emphases and concerns of Arminian and Calvinist views of salvation. Whether Moltmann's universalism might be able to satisfy the requirements of these two different theological paradigms is pursued by means of a description of his universalism of the cross, his discussion of the nature and will of God, and his conception of freedom. A preliminary response to Moltmann's universalism is offered at the close of this chapter. Here I come to the conclusion that although Moltmann's soteriology can respond well to standard Calvinist and Arminian objections, and thus could potentially win the respect of more mainstream Protestant theologians (and others), the "triumph of glory" theme in the end means that grace is eschatologised while creation is 'denatured'.

Chapters 5, 6, and 7 seek to deepen the analysis of the previous chapters by bringing Moltmann's thought into dialogue with the philosophical or theological proposals of other contemporary thinkers. Chapter 5 ("Between Creation and Eschaton: The Foundational and Transcendental Directions of

Time") extends the explorations of chapters 2 and 3 by bringing Moltmann's work into conversation with the philosophy of time proposed by neo-Calvinist philosopher Hendrik Hart. Chapter 6 ("The Nature of Grace") builds on the nature-grace material of chapter 4 by reading Moltmann in the light of the famous Barth-Brunner debate. Chapter 7 ("Doing Justice (According) to Scripture") returns to some concerns first raised in chapter 1 about the biblical foundations of Moltmann's position and the sensitivity (or insensitivity) of universalist theologies to the cry of the oppressed for justice in the Final Judgment. These exegetical and ethical concerns are pursued with the help of proposals that have been made by New Testament scholar, N.T. Wright and theologian, Miroslav Volf.

A comparison of my elaboration of Hart's philosophy of time with my interpretation of Moltmann's philosophy of time, offered in chapter 5, leads to the conclusion that although Moltmann is right to distinguish creation and eschaton and to maintain that God is not 'all in all' in the beginning, he nevertheless conflates creation and fall, on the one hand, and redemption and eschaton, on the other hand. This leads him to posit not only a correlation between the foundational and transcendental (or founding and opening) directions of time, but also a contradiction between them—a contradiction that is negotiated by the cross as a theocosmogonic "turning-point" through which the direction of time is redemptively reversed (as examined in chapter 4). The reality of 'creational grace', understood as the gift and call of and to Life in the foundational direction (as explored in chapter 6) is thereby minimised thus restricting the 'covenantal' potential of Moltmann's soteriology. At the same time, I point out that Moltmann's affirmation of eschatological grace, which is coupled with a one-sidedly *kenotic* view of our creationally graced nature, does allow for some affirmation of human agency in the dynamics of salvation.

The concluding chapter ("Grace and *Spes*") suggests that Moltmann's biblical intuitions are sound with respect to universal salvation, even if his proposals need further exegetical support (such as along the lines suggested in chapter 7). Similarly, his view of justice with respect to the Final Judgment is suggestive of the social view explored in that chapter, but also needs further development. In the longest (and perhaps most important) section of the concluding chapter, I suggest that Moltmann's most valuable contribution to a viable universalism lies in his development of a vibrant, non-autonomous view of eschatological freedom. At the same time, I point out that his view of creational freedom, which is overcome in the triumph of glory, is rooted in his highly problematic *zimzum* doctrine of creation in which the primordial *nihil*, as the space for autonomy, is nothing less that the creator-creation distinction itself, negatively conceived. Freedom of movement *with* God in covenant from the beginning is thus misconstrued as "freedom of movement *over against* God." It therefore follows that in Moltmann's eschatology, grace (for him the 'glory' that goes beyond the 'grace' of the cross) presupposes, completes, subsumes, fulfils, and negates nature: *Gratia (non) destruit, sed presupponit et perfectit naturam.*

If Moltmann's theocosmogony of the cross is deeply problematic as it undermines the goodness of creation from (before) the beginning, his universalism of the cross, heard as an articulation of hope, is persuasive and compelling. Rooted in God's promises revealed in and through Christ's descent into Hell, Moltmann's eschatological vision does not look forward to a universal salvation that *must* take place, but to a universal salvation that *will* take place.

Finally the Appendix ("Birthpangs of the New Creation") extends the exegetical concerns and proposals of the previous chapters into the book of Revelation. In this way, the biblical case for universalism finds support in its understanding of the transition between the two ages as a 'judgment unto salvation'. As Paul, himself an apocalyptic thinker, puts it in Rom 11:32: "God has bound all [people] over to disobedience so that he may have mercy on them all."

Bibliography

Works by Jürgen Moltmann

Moltmann's Works Cited in This Monograph

A Broad Place: An Autobiography. Translated by Margaret Kohl. Minneapolis, MN: Fortress Press, 2008. [= BP]
"A Conversation with Jürgen Moltmann." Interview by Teofilo Cabestrero. In *Faith: Conversations with Contemporary Theologians*, edited by Teofilo Cabestrero, translated by Donald D. Walsh, 121–38. Maryknoll, NY: Orbis, 1980.
"A Response to the Responses." In *The Politics of Discipleship and Discipleship in Politics: Jürgen Moltmann Lectures in Dialogue with Mennonite Scholars*, by Jürgen Moltmann et al, edited by Willard M. Swartley, 119–31. Eugene, OR: Cascade, 2006.
"All Things New: Invited to God's Future." *Asbury Theological Journal* 48, no. 1 (Spring 1993): 29–38.
"Am Ende ist alles Gottes: Hat der Glaube an die Hölle ausgedient?" *Evangelische Kommentare* 29 (September 1996): 542–43.
"Antwort auf die Kritik an »Der gekreuzigte Gott«." In *Diskussion über Jürgen Moltmanns Buch »Der gekreuzigte Gott«*, edited by Michael Welker, 165–90. Munich: Chr. Kaiser Verlag, 1979.
"Antwort auf die Kritik der »Theologie der Hoffnung«." In *Diskussion über die »Theologie der Hoffnung« von Jürgen Moltmann*, edited by Wolf-Dieter Marsh, 201–38. Munich: Chr. Kaiser Verlag, 1967.
"Can Christian Eschatology Become Post-Modern? Response to Miroslav Volf." In *God Will Be All in All: The Eschatology of Jürgen Moltmann*, edited by Richard Bauckham, 259–64. Edinburgh: T. and T. Clark, 1999.
"Christ in Cosmic Context." In *Christ and Context: The Confrontation between Gospel and Culture*, edited by Hilary D. Regan and Alan J. Torrance with Antony Wood, 180–91. Edinburgh: T. and T. Clark, 1993.
"Christus oder Konstantin." *Publik-Forum* 24, no. 17 (1995): 18–29.
Creating a Just Future: The Politics of Peace and the Ethics of Creation in a Threatened World. Translated by John Bowden. London: SCM Press, 1989.
"Creation and Redemption." In *Creation, Christ and Culture: Studies in Honour of T.F. Torrance*, edited by Richard W.A. McKinney, 119–34. Edinburgh: T. and T. Clark, 1976.
"Cross, Theology of the." In *A New Dictionary of Christian Theology*, edited by Alan Richardson and John Bowden, 135–37. London: SCM Press, 1983.
Das Kommen Gottes: Christliche Eschatologie. Gütersloh: Chr. Kaiser Verlagshaus, 1995. [= DKG]
"Der 'eschatologische Augenblick': Gedanken zu Zeit und Ewigkeit in eschatologischer Hinsicht." In *Vernunft des Glaubens: wissenschaftliche Theologie und kirchliche*

Lehre. Festschrift zum 60. Geburstag von Wolfhart Pannenberg, edited by John Rohls and Gunther Wenz, 578–89. Gottingen: Vandenhoeck and Ruprecht, 1988.
Der Geist des Lebens: Eine ganzheitliche Pneumatologie. Munich: Chr. Kaiser Verlag, 1991. [= *DGL*]
Der gekreuzigte Gott: Das Kreuz Christi als Grund und Kritik christlicher Theologie. Munich: Chr. Kaiser Verlag, 1972. [= *DgG*]
Der Weg Jesu Christi: Christologie in messianischen Dimensionen. Munich: Chr. Kaiser Verlag, 1989. [= *DWJC*]
"Descent into Hell." Translated by M. Douglas Meeks. *Duke Divinity School Review* 33, no. 2 (Spring 1968): 115–19.
Erfahrungen theologischen Denkens: Wege und Formen christlicher Theologie. Gütersloh: Chr. Kaiser Verlag/Gütersloher Verlaghaus, 2000. [= *EtD*]
"Ernst Bloch and Hope without Faith." In *The Experiment Hope*, by Jürgen Moltmann, translated by M. Douglas Meeks, 30–43. Philadelphia: Fortress Press, 1975.
Ethics of Hope. Translated by Margaret Kohl. Minneapolis, MN: Fortress Press, 2012. [= EoH]
Experiences in Theology: Ways and Forms of Christian Theology. Translated by Margaret Kohl. London: SCM Press, 2000. [= EiT]
Experiences of God. Translated by Margaret Kohl. London: SCM Press, 1980.
Foreword to *God, Hope, and History: Jürgen Moltmann and the Christian Concept of History*, by A.J. Conyers, vii–ix. Macon, GA: Mercer Press, 1988.
Foreword to *God's History in the Theology of Jürgen Moltmann*, by Siu-Kwong Tang, 11–13. Bern: Peter Lang, 1996.
Foreword to *Moltmann: Messianic Theology in the Making*, by Richard Bauckham, vii–x. Basingstoke, UK: Marshall, Morgan and Scott, 1987.
Foreword to *Origins of the Theology of Hope*, by M. Douglas Meeks, ix–xii. Philadelphia: Fortress Press, 1974.
Foreword to *Pilgrimage of Love: Moltmann on the Trinity and Christian Life*, by Joy Ann McDougall, xi–xiv. Oxford: Oxford University Press, 2005.
Foreword to *The Christian Realism of Reinhold Niebuhr and the Political Theology of Jürgen Moltmann in Dialogue*, by Robert Thomas Cornelison, i–v. San Francisco: Mellen Research University Press, 1992.
Foreword to *The Trinity, Creation and Pastoral Ministry: Imaging the Perichoretic God*, by Graham Buxton, xiii–xiv. Paternoster Theological Monographs. Milton Keynes, UK: Paternoster, 2005.
Foreword to *Time Invades the Cathedral: Tensions in the School of Hope*, by Walter H. Capps, xi–xv. Philadelphia: Fortress Press, 1972.
"Gerechtigkeit für Opfer und Täter." In *In der Geschichte des dreieinigen Gottes: Beiträge zur trinitarischen Theologie*, by Jürgen Moltmann, 74–89. Munich: Chr. Kaiser Verlag, 1991.
God for a Secular Society: The Public Relevance of Theology. Translated by Margaret Kohl. London: SCM Press, 1999.
God in Creation: An Ecological Doctrine of Creation. Translated by Margaret Kohl. London: SCM Press, 1985. [= GC]
"God's Kingdom as the Meaning of Life and of the World." Translated by Theo Weston. In *Why Did God Make Me?*, edited by Hans Küng and Jürgen Moltmann. *Concilium* 117 (August 1977): 97–103. New York: Seabury Press, 1978.
Gott in der Schöpfung: Ökologische Schöpfungslehre. Munich: Chr. Kaiser Verlag, 1985. [= *GS*]
History and the Triune God. Translated by John Bowden. London: SCM Press, 1991. [= HTG]

"Hope." In *A New Dictionary of Christian Theology*, edited by Alan Richardson and John Bowden, 272. London: SCM Press, 1983.

"Hope and Confidence: A Conversation with Ernst Bloch." In *Religion, Revolution and the Future*, by Jürgen Moltmann, translated by M. Douglas Meeks, 149–76. New York: Charles Scribner's Sons, 1969.

Hope and Planning. Translated by Margaret Clarkson. London: SCM Press, 1971. [= HP]

"Hope and Planning." In *Hope and Planning*, by Jürgen Moltmann, translated by Margaret Clarkson, 178–99. London: SCM Press, 1971.

"Hope and Reality: Contradiction and Correspondence; Response to Trevor Hart." In *God Will Be All in All: The Eschatology of Jürgen Moltmann*, edited by Richard Bauckham, 77–85. Edinburgh: T. and T. Clark, 1999.

"Hope beyond Time." Translated by M. Douglas Meeks. *Duke Divinity School Review* 33, no. 2 (Spring 1968): 109–14.

"Hope in the Struggle of the People." In *The Passion for Life: A Messianic Lifestyle*, by Jürgen Moltmann, translated by M. Douglas Meeks, 95–112. Philadelphia: Fortress Press, 1978.

Im Gespräch mit Ernst Bloch: Eine theologische Wegbegleitung. Kaiser Traktate 18. Munich: Chr. Kaiser Verlag, 1976.

In der Geschichte des dreieinigen Gottes: Beiträge zur trinitarischen Theologie. Munich: Chr. Kaiser Verlag, 1991. [= *IGG*]

"In the End, All Is God's: Is Belief in Hell Obsolete?" Translated by Paul F.M. Zahl. *Sewanee Theological Review* 40 (Easter 1997): 232–34.

In the End—the Beginning: The Life of Hope. Translated by Margaret Kohl. Minneapolis, MN: Fortress Press, 2004. [= IEB]

"Introduction." In *Man on His Own: Essays in the Philosophy of Religion*, by Ernst Bloch, translated by E.B. Ashton, 19–29. New York: Herder and Herder, 1971.

"Introduction to the 'Theology of Hope'." In *The Experiment Hope*, by Jürgen Moltmann, translated by M. Douglas Meeks, 44–59. Philadelphia: Fortress Press, 1975.

"Is the World Coming to an End or Has Its Future Already Begun? Christian Eschatology, Modern Utopianism and Exterminism." Translated by Margaret Kohl. In *The Future as God's Gift: Explorations in Christian Eschatology*, edited by David Fergusson and Marcel Sarot, 129–38. Edinburgh: T. and T. Clark, 2000.

"Jesus and the Kingdom of God." *Asbury Theological Journal* 48, no. 1 (Spring 1993): 5–17.

Jesus Christ for Today's World. Translated by Margaret Kohl. London: SCM Press, 1994.

"Jürgen Moltmann." In *How I Have Changed: Reflections on Thirty Years of Theology*, edited by Jürgen Moltmann, translated by John Bowden, 13–21. London: SCM Press, 1997.

"Justice for Victims and Perpetrators." In *History and the Triune God*, by Jürgen Moltmann, translated by John Bowden, 44–56. London: SCM Press, 1991.

"Justification and New Creation." In *The Future of Creation*, by Jürgen Moltmann, translated by Margaret Kohl, 149–71. London: SCM Press, 1979.

Kirche in der Kraft des Geistes: Ein Beitrag zur messianischen Ekklesiologie. Munich: Chr. Kaiser Verlag, 1975. [= *KKG*]

"Luther's Doctrine of the Two Kingdoms and its Use Today." In *On Human Dignity: Political Theology and Ethics*, by Jürgen Moltmann, translated by M. Douglas Meeks, 61–77. Philadelphia: Fortress Press, 1984.

Man: Christian Anthropology in the Conflicts of the Present. Translated by John Sturdy. London: SPCK, 1974.

"Methods in Eschatology." In *The Future of Creation*, by Jürgen Moltmann, translated by Margaret Kohl, 41–48. London: SCM Press, 1979.

"My Theological Career." In *History and the Triune God: Contributions to Trinitarian Theology*, by Jürgen Moltmann, translated by John Bowden, 165–82. London: SCM Press, 1991.

On Human Dignity: Political Theology and Ethics. Translated by M. Douglas Meeks. Philadelphia: Fortress Press, 1984.

"Perseverance." In *A New Dictionary of Christian Theology*, edited by Alan Richardson and John Bowden, 441–42. London: SCM Press, 1983.

Prädestination und Perseveranz: Geschicte und Bedeutung der reformierten Lehre 'de perseverantia sanctorum'. Neukirchen: Neuchirchener Verlag, 1961.

Preface to the paperback edition of *God in Creation: An Ecological Doctrine of Creation*, by Jürgen Moltmann, translated by Margaret Kohl, xi–xii. 1985. Reprint, Minneapolis, MN: Fortress Press, 1993.

Preface to the paperback edition of *The Trinity and the Kingdom*, by Jürgen Moltmann, translated by Margaret Kohl, vii–ix. 1981. Reprint, Minneapolis, MN: Fortress Press, 1993.

"Progress and Abyss: Remembering the Future of the Modern World." In *2000 Years and Beyond: Faith, Identity and the 'Common Era'*, edited by Paul Gifford, 16–34. London: Routledge, 2003.

"Progress and Abyss: Remembering the Future of the Modern World." *Review and Expositor* 97, no. 3 (Summer 2000): 301–14.

"Progress and Abyss: Remembrances of the Future of the Modern World." In *The Future of Hope: Christian Tradition amid Modernity and Postmodernity*, edited by Miroslav Volf and William Katerberg, 3–26. Grand Rapids, MI: Eerdmans, 2004.

Religion, Revolution, and the Future. Translated by M. Douglas Meeks. New York: Charles Scribner's Sons, 1969. [= RRF]

"Replying To Alan J. Torrance and Gustavo Gutiérrez." In *Christ and Context: The Confrontation between Gospel and Culture*, edited by Hilary D. Regan and Alan J. Torrance with Antony Wood, 205–209. Edinburgh: T. and T. Clark, 1993.

"Response." In *Christ and Context: The Confrontation between Gospel and Culture*, edited by Hilary D. Regan and Alan J. Torrance with Antony Wood, 60–62. Edinburgh: T. and T. Clark, 1993.

"Response." In *Hope for the Church: Moltmann in Dialogue with Practical Theology*, by Jürgen Moltmann with M. Douglas Meeks, Rodney J. Hunter, James W. Fowler, and Noel L. Erskine, translated by Theodore Runyon, 128–36. Nashville, TN: Abingdon, 1979.

"Response to the Opening Presentations." In *Hope and the Future of Man*, edited by Ewert H. Cousins, 55–59. Philadelphia: Fortress Press, 1972.

"Resurrection as Hope." In *Religion, Revolution, and the Future*, by Jürgen Moltmann, translated by M. Douglas Meeks, 42–62. New York: Charles Scribner's Sons, 1969.

"Schöpfung im Horizont der Zeit." *Evangelische Theologie* 52, no. 1 (1992): 86–92.

Science and Wisdom. Translated by Margaret Kohl. Minneapolis, MN: Fortress Press, 2003. [= SW]

Sun of Righteousness, Arise! God's Future for Humanity and the Earth. Translated by Margaret Kohl. Minneapolis, MN: Fortress Press, 2010. [= SRA]

"Sun of Righteousness: The Gospel about Judgment and the New Creation of All Things." In *Sun of Righteousness, Arise! God's Future for Humanity and the Earth*,

by Jürgen Moltmann, translated by Margaret Kohl, 127–48. Minneapolis, MN: Fortress Press, 2010.
"The Alienation and Liberation of Nature." In *On Nature*, edited by Leroy S. Rouner, 133–44. Notre Dame: University of Notre Dame Press, 1984.
"The Beginning of Time in God's Presence." In *The End of Time? The Provocation of Talking about God*, by Joseph Cardinal Ratzinger, Johann Baptist Metz, Jürgen Moltmann, and Eveline Goodman-Thau, edited by Tiemo Rainer Peters and Claus Urban, translated by J. Matthew Ashley, 54–64. New York: Paulist Press, 2004.
"The Bible, the Exegete and the Theologian: Response to Richard Bauckham." In *God Will Be All in All: The Eschatology of Jürgen Moltmann*, edited by Richard Bauckham, 227–32. Edinburgh: T. and T. Clark, 1999.
"The Christian Doctrine of the Trinity." In *Jewish Monotheism and Christian Trinitarian Doctrine*, by Pinchas Lapide and Jürgen Moltmann, translated by Leonard Swidler, 45–57. Philadelphia: Fortress Press, 1981.
The Church in the Power of the Spirit: A Contribution to Messianic Ecclesiology. Translated by Margaret Kohl. London: SCM Press, 1977. [= CPS]
The Coming of God: Christian Eschatology. Translated by Margaret Kohl. London: SCM Press, 1996. [= CoG]
"The Cross and Civil Religion." In *Religion and Political Society*, by Jürgen Moltmann and Herbert W. Richardson, Johann Baptist Metz, Willi Oelmüller, and M. Darrol Bryant, edited and translated by the Institute of Christian Thought, 14–47. New York: Harper and Row, 1974.
The Crucified God: The Cross of Christ as the Foundation and Criticism of Christian Theology. Translated by R.A. Wilson and John Bowden. London: SCM Press, 1974. [= CrG]
"The End of Everything Is God: Has Belief in Hell Had Its Day?" Translated by John Bowden. *Expository Times* 108 (June 1997): 263–64.
The Experiment Hope. Translated by M. Douglas Meeks. Philadelphia: Fortress Press, 1975.
"The Final Judgment: Sunrise of Christ's Liberating Justice." *Anglican Theological Review* 89, no. 4 (Fall 2007): 565–76.
"The First Liberated Men in Creation." In *Theology and Joy*, by Jürgen Moltmann, translated by R. Ulrich, 26–90. London: SCM Press, 1973.
"The Future as a New Paradigm of Transcendence." In *The Future of Creation*, by Jürgen Moltmann, translated by Margaret Kohl, 1–17. London: SCM Press, 1979.
"The Future as New Paradigm of Transcendence." In *Religion, Revolution and the Future*, by Jürgen Moltmann, translated by M. Douglas Meeks, 177–99. New York: Charles Scribner's Sons, 1969.
The Future of Creation. Translated by Margaret Kohl. London: SCM Press, 1979. [= FC]
The Gospel of Liberation. Translated by H. Wayne Pipkin. Waco, TX: Word, 1973.
"The Hope of Israel and the Anabaptist Alternative." In *God Will Be All in All: The Eschatology of Jürgen Moltmann*, edited by Richard Bauckham, 149–54. Edinburgh: T. and T. Clark, 1999.
"The Liberation of the Future and Its Anticipations in History." In *God Will Be All in All: The Eschatology of Jürgen Moltmann*, edited by Richard Bauckham, 265–89. Edinburgh: T. and T. Clark, 1999.
"The Logic of Hell." In *God Will Be All in All: The Eschatology of Jürgen Moltmann*, edited by Richard Bauckham, 43–47. Edinburgh: T. and T. Clark, 1999.

"The Lordship of Christ and Human Society." In *Two Studies in the Theology of Bonhoeffer*, by Jürgen Moltmann and Jürgen Weissbach, translated by Reginald H. Fuller and Ilse Fuller, 19–94. New York: Charles Scribner's Sons, 1967.

"The Lutheran Doctrine of the Two Kingdoms and its Use Today." In *The Politics of Discipleship and Discipleship in Politics: Jürgen Moltmann Lectures in Dialogue with Mennonite Scholars*, by Jürgen Moltmann et al, edited by Willard M. Swartley, 3–18. Eugene, OR: Cascade, 2006.

The Passion for Life: A Messianic Lifestyle. Translated by M. Douglas Meeks. Philadelphia: Fortress Press, 1978.

"The Passion of Christ and the Suffering of God." *Asbury Theological Journal* 48, no. 1 (Spring 1993): 19–28

"The Presence of God's Future: The Risen Christ." *Anglican Theological Review* 89, no. 4 (Fall 2007): 577–88.

"The Return of Christ." In *The Gospel of Liberation*, by Jürgen Moltmann, translated by H. Wayne Pipkin, 105–12. Waco, TX: Word, 1973.

"The Revelation of God and the Question of Truth." In *Hope and Planning*, by Jürgen Moltmann, translated by Margaret Clarkson, 3–30. London: SCM Press, 1971.

"The 'Rose in the Cross of the Present': Towards an Understanding of the Church in Modern Society." In *Hope and Planning*, by Jürgen Moltmann, translated by Margaret Clarkson, 130–54. London: SCM Press, 1971.

The Source of Life: The Holy Spirit and the Theology of Life. Translated by Margaret Kohl. London: SCM Press, 1997.

The Spirit of Life: A Universal Affirmation. Translated by Margaret Kohl. London: SCM Press, 1992. [= SL]

"The Theology of the Cross Today." In *The Future of Creation*, by Jürgen Moltmann, translated by Margaret Kohl, 59–79. London: SCM Press, 1979.

The Trinity and the Kingdom of God: The Doctrine of God. Translated by Margaret Kohl. London: SCM Press, 1980. [= TKG]

The Way of Jesus Christ: Christology in Messianic Dimensions. Translated by Margaret Kohl. London: SCM Press, 1990. [= WJC]

"The World in God or God in the World? Response to Richard Bauckham." In *God Will Be All in All: The Eschatology of Jürgen Moltmann*, edited by Richard Bauckham, 35–41. Edinburgh: T. and T. Clark 1999.

"Theodicy." In *A New Dictionary of Christian Theology*, edited by Alan Richardson and John Bowden, 564–66. London: SCM Press, 1983.

"*Theologia Reformata et Semper Reformanda*." In *Toward the Future of Reformed Theology: Tasks, Topics, Traditions*, edited by David Willis and Michael Welker, 120–35. Grand Rapids, MI: Eerdmans, 1999.

Theologie der Hoffnung: Untersuchungen zur Begründung und zu den Konsequenzen einer christlichen Eschatologie. Beiträge zur evangelischen Theologie. Theologische Abhandlungen, herausgegeben von E. Wolf. Band 38. 8th ed. Munich: Chr. Kaiser Verlag, 1969. [= *TdH*]

Theology and Joy. Translated by R. Ulrich. London: SCM Press, 1973.

"Theology as Eschatology." In *The Future of Hope*, edited by Frederick Herzog, 1–50. New York: Herder and Herder, 1970.

"Theology in the Project of Modernity." In *God for a Secular Society: The Public Relevance of Theology*, by Jürgen Moltmann, translated by Margaret Kohl, 5–23. London: SCM Press, 1999.

"Theology in the Project of the Modern World." In *A Passion for God's Reign: Theology, Christian Learning, and the Christian Self*, by Jürgen Moltmann,

Nicholas Wolterstorff, and Ellen T. Charry, edited by Miroslav Volf, 1–21. Grand Rapids, MI: Eerdmans, 1998.

Theology of Hope: On the Ground and the Implications of a Christian Eschatology. Translated by James Leitch. London: SCM Press, 1967. [= TH]

Theology Today: Two Contributions towards Making Theology Present. Translated by John Bowden. London: SCM Press, 1988

"There Is Enough for Everyone: A Sermon Given at Ryerson United Church, Vancouver, February 26th, 1989." Occasional Paper no. 2, 1–11. Vancouver: Vancouver School of Theology, 1989.

"Trends in Eschatology." In *The Future of Creation*, by Jürgen Moltann, translated by Margaret Kohl, 18–40. London: SCM Press, 1979.

Trinität und Reich Gottes: Zur Gotteslehre. Munich: Chr. Kaiser Verlag, 1980. [= TRG]

"Verschränkte Zeiten der Geschichte: Notwendige Differenzierungen und Begrenzungen des Geschichtsbegriffs." *Evangelische Theologie* 44 (1984): 213–27.

"Will All Be Saved, or Only a Few? A Dialogue between Faith and Grace." Translated by Margaret Kohl. In *Theology as Conversation: The Significance of Dialogue in Historical and Contemporary Theology; A Festscrift for Daniel L. Migliore*, edited by Bruce L. McCormack and Kimlyn J. Bender, 235–40. Grand Rapids, MI: Eerdmans, 2009.

ed. *How I Have Changed: Reflections on Thirty Years of Theology.* Translated by John Bowden. London: SCM Press, 1997.

et al. "Talk-back Session with Dr. Jürgen Moltmann." *Asbury Theological Journal* 48, no. 1 (Spring 1993): 39–47.

et al. *The End of Time? The Provocation of Talking about God.* Edited by Tiemo Rainer Peters and Claus Urban. Translated by J. Matthew Ashley. New York: Paulist Press, 2004

et al. *The Politics of Discipleship and Discipleship in Politics: Jürgen Moltmann Lectures in Dialogue with Mennonite Scholars.* Edited by Willard M. Swartley. Eugene, OR: Cascade, 2006.

and Ernst Bloch and Wolf-Dieter Marsch. "Gespräch über die Kategorie Novum." In *Im Gespräch mit Ernst Bloch: Eine theologische Wegbegleitung*, by Jürgen Moltmann, 55–62. Kaiser Traktate 18. Munich: Chr. Kaiser Verlag, 1976.

and Pinchas Lapide. *Jewish Monotheism and Christian Trinitarian Doctrine.* Translated by Leonard Swidler. Philadelphia: Fortress Press, 1981.

and M. Douglas Meeks, Rodney J. Hunter, James W. Fowler, and Noel L. Erskine. *Hope for the Church: Moltmann in Dialogue with Practical Theology.* Translated by Theodore Runyon. Nashville, TN: Abingdon, 1979.

and Johann-Baptist Metz. *Faith and the Future: Essays on Theology, Solidarity, and Modernity.* With an Introduction by Francis Schüssler Fiorenza. Maryknoll, NY: Orbis, 1995.

and Johann-Baptist Metz. *Meditations on the Passion: Two Meditations on Mark 8:31–38.* Translated by Edmund Colledge. New York: Paulist Press, 1979.

and Herbert W. Richardson, Johann Baptist Metz, Willi Oelmüller, and M. Darrol Bryant. *Religion and Political Society.* Edited and translated by the Institute of Christian Thought. New York: Harper and Row, 1974.

and Jürgen Weissbach. *Two Studies in the Theology of Bonhoeffer.* Translated by Reginald H. Fuller and Ilse Fuller. New York: Charles Scribner's Sons, 1967.

and Nicholas Wolterstorff, and Ellen T. Charry. *A Passion for God's Reign: Theology, Christian Learning, and the Christian Self.* Edited by Miroslav Volf. Grand Rapids, MI: Eerdmans, 1998.

Moltmann's Works Consulted but Not Cited

"Antwort." In *Worauf wir hoffen: Das Kommen Gottes und der Weg Jesu Christi*. Mit einer Antwort von Jürgen Moltmann, by Bertold Klappert, 139–56. Munich: Chr. Kaiser Verlag, 1997.

"Christianity and the Values of the Western World." Lecture, St. Paul's Cathedral, London, September 23, 1998.

"Christianity on the Threshold of the Third Millennium—What to Preserve and What to Leave Behind." Lecture, St. Paul's Cathedral, London, September 23, 1998.

"God Is Unselfish Love." Translated by Marianne M. Martin. In *The Emptying God: A Buddhist-Jewish-Christian Conversation*, edited by John B. Cobb and Christopher Ives, 116–24. Maryknoll, NY: Orbis, 1990.

"Hope and the Biomedical Future of Man." In *Hope and the Future of Man*, edited by Ewert H. Cousins, 89–105. Philadelphia: Fortress Press, 1972.

"Is 'Pluralistic Theology' Useful for the Dialogue of World Religions?" In *Christian Uniqueness Reconsidered*, edited by Gavin D'Costa, 149–56. Maryknoll, NY: Orbis, 1990.

"Nought for Your Comfort." *Third Way* 22, no. 9 (December 1999): 22–24.

"Pentecost and the Theology of Life." In *Pentecostal Movements as an Ecumenical Challenge*, edited by Jürgen Moltmann and Karl-Joseph Kuschel, 123–34. *Concilium* 1996, no. 3; Maryknoll, NY: Orbis, 1996.

The Power of the Powerless. Translated by Margaret Kohl. London: SCM Press, 1983.

"The Revolution of Freedom: The Christian and Marxist Struggle." Translated by M. Douglas Meeks. In *Openings for Marxist-Christian Dialogue*, edited by Thomas W. Ogletree, 47–71. Nashville, TN: Abingdon, 1968.

"Theology in Germany Today." In *Observations on "The Spiritual Situation of the Age"*, edited by Jürgen Habermas, translated by Andrew Buchwalter, 181–205. Cambridge, MA: MIT Press, 1984.

"Three Lectures on the Theology of Hope." Translated by M. Douglas Meeks. *Kalamazoo College Review* (Special issue, 1970): 1–24.

"Towards the Next Step in the Dialogue." In *The Future of Hope*, edited by Frederick Herzog, 154–64. New York: Herder and Herder, 1970.

"What Has Happened to Our Utopias? 1968 and 1989: Response to Timothy Gorringe." In *God Will Be All in All: The Eschatology of Jürgen Moltmann*, edited by Richard Bauckham, 115–21. Edinburgh: T. and T. Clark, 1999.

and Elisabeth Moltmann-Wendel. *God—His and Hers*. Translated by John Bowden. New York: Crossroad, 1991.

and Elisabeth Moltmann-Wendel. *Humanity in God*. New York: Pilgrim Press, 1983.

and Elisabeth Moltmann–Wendel. *Passion for God: Theology in Two Voices*. Louisville, KY: Westminster John Knox Press, 2003.

and Elisabeth Moltmann-Wendel et al. *Love: The Foundation of Hope; The Theology of Jürgen Moltmann and Elisabeth Moltmann-Wendel*. Edited by Frederic B. Burnham, Charles S. McCoy, and M. Douglas Meeks. San Francisco: Harper and Row, 1988.

Works That Significantly Engage Jürgen Moltmann's Writings

Works on Moltmann Cited in This Monograph

Ansell, Nicholas. "Its About Time: Opening Reformational Thought to the Eschaton," *Calvin Theological Journal* 47, no. 1 (April, 2012): 98–121.

———. "The Annihilation of Hell and the Perfection of Freedom: Universal Salvation in the Theology of Jürgen Moltmann (1926–)." In *"All Shall Be Well": Explorations in Universal Salvation and Christian Theology from Origen to Moltmann*, edited by Gregory MacDonald, 417–39. Eugene, OR: Cascade, 2011.

Bauckham, Richard. "Eschatology in *The Coming of God*." In *God Will Be All in All: The Eschatology of Jürgen Moltmann*, edited by Richard Bauckham, 1–34. Edinburgh: T. and T. Clark, 1999.

———. *Moltmann: Messianic Theology in the Making*. Basingstoke, UK: Marshall, Morgan, and Scott, 1987.

———. "Must Christian Eschatology Be Millenarian? A Response to Jürgen Moltmann." In *'The Reader Must Understand': Eschatology in Bible and Theology*, edited by K.E. Brower and M.W. Elliott, 263–77. Leicester, UK: Apollos, 1997.

———. "The Millennium." In *God Will Be All in All: The Eschatology of Jürgen Moltmann*, edited by Richard Bauckham, 123–47. Edinburgh: T. and T. Clark, 1999.

———. *The Theology of Jürgen Moltmann*. Edinburgh: T. and T. Clark, 1995.

———. "Time and Eternity." In *God Will Be All in All: The Eschatology of Jürgen Moltmann*, edited by Richard Bauckham, 155–226. Edinburgh: T. and T. Clark, 1999.

———, ed. *God Will Be All in All: The Eschatology of Jürgen Moltmann*. Edinburgh: T. and T. Clark, 1999.

———, and Trevor Hart. *Hope against Hope: Christian Eschatology in Contemporary Context*. London: Darton, Longman, and Todd, 1999.

———, and Trevor Hart. "The Shape of Time." In *The Future as God's Gift: Explorations in Christian Eschatology*, edited by David Fergusson and Marcel Sarot, 41–72. Edinburgh: T. and T. Clark, 2000.

Beck, T. David. *The Holy Spirit and the Renewal of All Things: Pneumatology in Paul and Jürgen Moltmann*. Princeton Theological Monograph Series 67. Eugene, OR: Pickwick, 2007.

Berkhof, Hendrikus. "Moltmann zwischen zwei Niederländern." In *Gottes Zukunft—Zukunft der Welt: Festschrift für Jürgen Moltmann zum 60. Geburtstag*, edited by Hermann Deuser, Gerhard Marcel Martin, Konrad Stock, and Michael Welker, 469–80. Munich: Chr. Kaiser Verlag, 1986.

Billings, David. "Natality or Advent: Hannah Arendt and Jürgen Moltmann on Hope and Politics." In *The Future of Hope: Christian Tradition amid Modernity and Postmodernity*, edited by Miroslav Volf and William Katerberg, 125–45. Grand Rapids, MI: Eerdmans, 2004.

Bonzo, J. Matthew. *Indwelling the Forsaken Other: The Trinitarian Ethics of Jürgen Moltmann*. Eugene, OR: Pickwick, 2009.

Bouma-Prediger, Steven. "Creation as the Home of God: The Doctrine of Creation in the Theology of Jürgen Moltmann." *Calvin Theological Journal* 32 (1997): 72–90.

———. *The Greening of Theology: The Ecological Models of Rosemary Radford Ruether, Joseph Sittler, and Jürgen Moltmann*. Atlanta, GA: Scholars Press, 1995.

Buxton, Graham. *The Trinity, Creation and Pastoral Ministry: Imaging the Perichoretic God*. Paternoster Theological Monographs. Milton Keynes, UK: Paternoster, 2005.

Capps, Walter H. *Time Invades the Cathedral: Tensions in the School of Hope*. Philadelphia: Fortress Press, 1972.

Chester, Tim. *Mission and the Coming of God: Eschatology, the Trinity and Mission in the Theology of Jürgen Moltmann and Contemporary Evangelicalism*. Paternoster Theological Monographs. Milton Keynes, UK: Paternoster, 2006.

Conradie, Ernst M. "In Search of a Vision of Hope for a New Century." *Journal of Religion and Society* 1 (1999): 1–24. http://purl.org/JRS (accessed March 11, 2004).

―――. *Saving the Earth? The Legacy of Reformed Views on "Re-creation"*. Münster: LIT Verlag, 2013.
Constas, Nicholas. "Eschatology and Christology: Moltmann and the Greek Fathers." In *God's Life in Trinity*, edited by Miroslav Volf and Michael Welker, 191–99. Minneapolis, MN: Fortress Press, 2006.
Conyers, A.J. *God, Hope, and History: Jürgen Moltmann and the Christian Concept of History*. Macon, GA: Mercer Press, 1988.
Cooper, John W. *Panentheism—The Other God of the Philosophers: From Plato to the Present*. Grand Rapids, MI: Baker, 2006.
Deane-Drummond, Celia. "Jürgen Moltmann on Heaven." In *The Unseen World: Christian Reflections on Angels, Demons and the Heavenly Realm*, edited by Anthony N.S. Lane, 49–64. Carlisle, UK: Paternoster, 1996.
―――. "Towards a Green Theology through Analysis of the Ecological Motif in Jürgen Moltmann's Doctrine of Creation." PhD diss., University of Manchester, 1992.
Deuser, Hermann, Gerhard Marcel Martin, Konrad Stock, and Michael Welker, eds. *Gottes Zukunft—Zukunft der Welt: Festschrift für Jürgen Moltmann zum 60. Geburtstag*. Munich: Chr. Kaiser Verlag, 1986.
Fergusson, David, and Marcel Sarot, eds. *The Future as God's Gift: Explorations in Christian Eschatology*. Edinburgh: T. and T. Clark, 2000.
Fiddes, Paul S. *The Promised End: Eschatology in Theology and Literature*. Oxford: Blackwell, 2000.
Geertsema, H.G. *Van boven naar voren: Wijsgerige achtergrondnen en problem van het theologische denken over geschiedenis bij Jürgen Moltmann*. Kampen: J.H. Kok, 1980.
Gilbertson, Michael. *God and History in the Book of Revelation: New Testament Studies in Dialogue with Pannenberg and Moltmann*. Society for New Testament Studies Monograph Series 124. Cambridge: Cambridge University Press, 2003.
Gilkey, Langdon. *Reaping the Whirlwind: A Christian Interpretation of History*. New York: Seabury Press, 1976.
Guttesen, Poul F. *Leaning into the Future: The Kingdom of God in the Theology of Jürgen Moltmann and the Book of Revelation*. Princeton Theological Monograph Series 117. Eugene, OR: Pickwick, 2009.
Hart, Trevor. "Imagination for the Kingdom of God? Hope, Promise, and the Transformative Power of an Imagined Future." In *God Will Be All in All: The Eschatology of Jürgen Moltmann*, edited by Richard Bauckham, 49–76. Edinburgh: T. and T. Clark, 1999.
Herzog, Frederick, ed. *The Future of Hope*. New York: Herder and Herder, 1970.
Highfield, Ron. "Divine Self-Limitation in the Theology of Jürgen Moltmann: A Critical Appraisal." *Christian Scholar's Review* 32, no. 1 (Fall, 2002): 49–71.
Hill, William J. "The Trinity as Event of the Cross: Jürgen Moltmann." In *The Three-Personed God: The Trinity as a Mystery of Salvation*, by William J. Hill, 166–75. Washington, DC: Catholic University of America Press, 1982.
Hodgson, Peter C. *Jesus—Word and Presence: An Essay in Christology*. Philadelphia: Fortress Press, 1971.
Irish, Jerry A. "Moltmann's Theology of Contradiction." *Theology Today* 32, no. 1 (July 1975): 21–31.
Jansen, Henry. "Moltmann's View of God's (Im)mutability: The God of the Philosophers and the God of the Bible." *Neue Zeitschrift für systematische Theologie und Religionsphilosophie* 36 (1994): 284–301.
―――. *Relationality and the Concept of God*. Amsterdam: Rodopi, 1995.

Kehl, Medard. " 'Bis du kommst in Herrlichkeit . . .': Neurre theologische Deutungen der 'Parousie Jesu'." In *Hoffnung über den Tod hinaus: Antworten auf Fragen der Eschatologie*, edited by Joseph Pfammater and Eduard Christen, 95–137. Zürich: Benziger Verlag, 1990.

Keller, Catherine. "Pneumatic Nudges: The Theology of Moltmann, Feminism, and the Future." In *The Future of Theology: Essays in Honor of Jürgen Moltmann*, edited by Miroslav Volf, Carmen Krieg, and Thomas Kucharz, 142–53. Grand Rapids, MI: Eerdmans, 1996.

Lønning, Per. *Creation—An Ecumenical Challenge? Reflections Issuing from a Study by the Institute for Ecumenical Research Strasbourg, France*. Macon, GA: Mercer University Press, 1989.

Louw, Daniel Johannes. "Toekoms tussen hoop en angs: 'n ondersoek na die funksie van die "ontologie van die nog-nie-syn" in die hedendaagse filosofie en teologie van die hoop, met besondere verwysing na die denke van Ernst Bloch en Jürgen Moltmann." PhD diss., University of Stellenbosch, 1972.

Mackey, James P. *The Christian Experience of God as Trinity*. London: SCM Press, 1983.

Marsden, John. "Eschatology and Politics: Jürgen Moltmann's Political Theology." In *Marxian and Christian Utopianism: Towards a Socialist Political Theology*, by John Marsden, 141–61. New York: Monthly Review Press, 1991.

Marsh, Wolf-Dieter, ed. *Diskussion über die »Theologie der Hoffnung« von Jürgen Moltmann*. Munich: Chr. Kaiser Verlag, 1967.

McDougall, Joy Ann. *Pilgrimage of Love: Moltmann on the Trinity and Christian Life*. Oxford: Oxford University Press, 2005.

McIlroy, David H. *A Trinitarian Theology of Law: In Conversation with Jürgen Moltmann, Oliver O'Donovan, and Thomas Aquinas*. Paternoster Theological Monographs. Milton Keynes, UK: Paternoster, 2009.

Meeks, M. Douglas. *Origins of the Theology of Hope*. Philadelphia: Fortress Press, 1974.

Miguez Bonino, José. *Doing Theology in a Revolutionary Situation*. Philadelphia: Fortress Press, 1975.

Morse, Christopher. *The Logic of Promise in Moltmann's Theology*. Philadelphia: Fortress Press, 1979.

Müller-Fahrenholz, Geiko. *The Kingdom and the Power: The Theology of Jürgen Moltmann*. Translated by John Bowden. London: SCM Press, 2000.

Neal, Ryan A. *Theology as Hope: On the Grounds and Implications of Jürgen Moltmann's Doctrine of Hope*. Princeton Theological Monograph Series 99. Eugene, OR: Pickwick, 2008.

O'Donnell, John J. *Trinity and Temporality: The Christian Doctrine of God in the Light of Process Theology and the Theology of Hope*. Oxford: Oxford University Press, 1983.

O'Malley, Steven. "The Role of Pietism in the Theology of Jürgen Moltmann." *Asbury Theological Journal* 48, no. 1 (Spring 1993): 121–27.

Otto, Randall E. *The God of Hope: The Trinitarian Vision of Jürgen Moltmann*. Lanham, MD: University Press of America, 1991.

Plathow, Michael. "Zeit und Ewigkeit: Ein Thema der christlichen Vorsehungslehre heute." *Neue Zeitschrift für systematische Theologie und Religionsphilosophie* 26, no. 2 (1984): 95–115.

Polkinghorne, John. *The God of Hope and the End of the World*. New Haven, CT: Yale University Press, 2002.

Primavesi, Anne V. "The Cross and the Rose: The Interaction of Lutheran Paradox and Hegelian Dialectic Exemplified in the Theology of Jürgen Moltmann." PhD diss., Heythrop College, University of London, 1987.
Prooijen, Ton van. *Limping but Blessed: Jurgen Moltmann's Search for a Liberating Anthropology*. Amsterdam: Rodopi, 2004.
Schuurman, Douglas J. "Creation, Eschaton, and Ethics: An Analysis of Theology and Ethics in Jürgen Moltmann." *Calvin Theological Journal* 22 (1987): 42–67.
———. *Creation, Eschaton, and Ethics: The Ethical Significance of the Creation-Eschaton Relation in the Thought of Emil Brunner and Jürgen Moltmann*. New York: Peter Lang, 1991.
Surin, Kenneth. *Theology and the Problem of Evil*. Oxford: Blackwell, 1986.
Tang, Siu-Kwong. *God's History in the Theology of Jürgen Moltmann*. Bern: Peter Lang, 1996.
Torrance, Alan J. "*Creatio ex Nihilo* and the Spatio-Temporal Dimensions, with Special Reference to Jürgen Moltmann and D.C. Williams." In *The Doctrine of Creation: Essays in Dogmatics, History and Philosophy*, edited by Colin E. Gunton, 83–103. Edinburgh: T. and T. Clark, 1997.
———. "Response to Jürgen Moltmann." In *Christ and Context: The Confrontation between Gospel and Culture*, edited by Hilary D. Regan and Alan J. Torrance with Antony Wood, 192–200. Edinburgh: T. and T. Clark, 1993.
Van den Brom, Luco J. "Eschatology and Time: Reversal of Time Direction?" In *The Future as God's Gift: Explorations in Christian Eschatology*, edited by David Fergusson and Marcel Sarot, 159–67. Edinburgh: T. and T. Clark, 2000.
———. "Eschatology and Time: Which Relationship?" In *Christian Hope in Context 1*. Studies in Reformed Theology 4, edited by A. van Egmond and D. van Keulen, 144–62. Zoetermeer: Uitgeverij Meinema, 2001.
Volf, Miroslav. "After Moltmann: Reflections on the Future of Eschatology." In *God Will Be All in All: The Eschatology of Jürgen Moltmann*, edited by Richard Bauckham, 233–57. Edinburgh: T. and T. Clark, 1999.
———, Carmen Krieg, and Thomas Kucharz, eds. *The Future of Theology: Essays in Honor of Jürgen Moltmann*. Grand Rapids, MI: Eerdmans, 1996.
Walsh, Brian J. "Theology of Hope and the Doctrine of Creation: An Appraisal of Jürgen Moltmann." *Evangelical Quarterly* 59, no. 1 (January, 1987): 53–76.
Welker, Michael, ed. *Diskussion über Jürgen Moltmanns Buch »Der gekreuzigte Gott«*. Munich: Chr. Kaiser Verlag, 1979.
Williams, Stephen N. *Jürgen Moltmann: A Critical Introduction*. Leicester, UK: Religious and Theological Studies Fellowship, 1987.
———. "Jürgen Moltmann: A Critical Introduction." In *Getting Your Bearings: Engaging with Contemporary Theologians*, edited by Philip Duce and Daniel Strange, 75–124. Leicester, UK: Apollos, 2003.
Witvliet, Theo. *The Way of the Black Messiah: The Hermeneutical Challenge of Black Theology as a Theology of Liberation*. Translated by John Bowden. London: SCM Press, 1987.

Works on Moltmann Consulted but Not Cited

Ansell, Nicholas. Review of *A Passion for God's Reign: Theology, Christian Learning, and the Christian Self*, by Jürgen Moltmann, Nicholas Wolterstorff, and Ellen T. Charry. Edited by Miroslav Volf. Grand Rapids, MI: Eerdmans, 1998. *Third Way* 21, no. 6 (July/August 1998): 29.

———. Review of *God for a Secular Society: The Public Relevance of Theology*, by Jürgen Moltmann. Translated by Margaret Kohl. London: SCM Press, 1999. *Third Way* 22, no. 3 (April 1999): 27.

———. Review of *God Will Be All in All: The Eschatology of Jürgen Moltmann*, edited by Richard Bauckham. Edinburgh: T. and T. Clark, 1999. *European Journal of Theology* 9, no. 2 (2000): 198–200.

———. Review of *The Coming of God: Christian Eschatology, by Jürgen Moltmann*. Translated by Margaret Kohl. London: SCM Press, 1996. *Themelios* 24, no. 2 (February 1999): 75–76.

Bergmann, Sigurd. *Creation Set Free: The Spirit as Liberator of Nature*. Translated by Douglas Stott. Grand Rapids, MI: Eerdmans, 2005.

Bratten, C.E. "Toward a Theology of Hope." In *New Theology No. 5*, edited by Martin E. Marty and Dean G. Peerman, 90–111. New York: Macmillan, 1968.

Capps, Walter H. *Hope against Hope: Moltmann to Merton in One Theological Decade*. Philadelphia: Fortress Press, 1976.

Carter, Dee. "Concepts of Atonement in Jürgen Moltmann's Theology." Paper presented at the Joint Post-Graduate Day Conference, University of Bristol, November 2, 1996.

Chopp, Rebecca S. "Jürgen Moltmann: The Language of God as the Language of Suffering." In *The Praxis of Suffering: An Interpretation of Liberation and Political Theologies*, by Rebecca S. Chopp, 100–17. Maryknoll, NY: Orbis, 1986.

Cornelison, Robert Thomas. *The Christian Realism of Reinhold Niebuhr and the Political Theology of Jürgen Moltmann in Dialogue*. San Francisco: Mellen Research University Press, 1992.

Cox, Harvey. "The Problem of Continuity." In *The Future of Hope*, edited by Frederick Herzog, 72–80. New York: Herder and Herder, 1970.

Dabney, D.L. "The Advent of the Spirit: The Turn to Pneumatology in the Theology of Jürgen Moltmann." *Asbury Theological Journal* 48 (Spring 1993): 81–108.

Dorrien, Gary J. "Jürgen Moltmann and the Dialectics of Hope." In *Reconstructing the Common Good: Theology and the Social Order*, by Gary J. Dorrien, 77–100. Maryknoll, NY: Orbis, 1990.

Doyle, Robert C. *Eschatology and the Shape of Christian Belief*. Carlisle, UK: Paternoster, 1999.

French, William C. "Returning to Creation: Moltmann's Eschatology Naturalized." *Journal of Religion* 68, no. 1 (January 1988): 78–86.

Genovesi, Vincent J. *Expectant Creativity: The Action of Hope in Christian Ethics*. Washington, DC: University Press of America, 1982.

Gilkey, Langdon. "The Universal and Immediate Presence of God." In *The Future of Hope*, edited by Frederick Herzog, 81–109. New York: Herder and Herder, 1970.

Gorringe, Timothy. "Eschatology and Political Radicalism: The Example of Karl Barth and Jürgen Moltmann." In *God Will Be All in All: The Eschatology of Jürgen Moltmann*, edited by Richard Bauckham, 87–114. Edinburgh: T. and T. Clark, 1999.

Gutiérrez, Gustavo. "Response to Jürgen Moltmann." In *Christ and Context: The Confrontation between Gospel and Culture*, edited by Hilary D. Regan and Alan J. Torrance with Antony Wood, 201–204. Edinburgh: T. and T. Clark, 1993.

Harvey, Van A. "Secularism, Responsible Belief, and the 'Theology of Hope'." In *The Future of Hope*, edited by Frederick Herzog, 126–53. New York: Herder and Herder, 1970.

Herzog, Frederick. "Towards the Waiting God." In *The Future of Hope*, edited by Frederick Herzog, 51–71. New York: Herder and Herder, 1970.

Ising, Dieter, with Günter Geisthardt, and Adelbert Schloz. *Bibliographie Jürgen Moltmann*. Munich: Chr. Kaiser Verlag, 1987.
Klappert, Bertold. *Worauf wir hoffen: Das Kommen Gottes und der Weg Jesu Christi. Mit einer Antwort von Jürgen Moltmann*. Munich: Chr. Kaiser Verlag, 1997.
Macleod, Donald. "The Christology of Jürgen Moltmann." *Themelios* 24, no. 2 (February 1999): 35–47.
MacQuarrie, John. *Christian Hope*. London: Mowbrays, 1978.
———. "Eschatology and Time." In *The Future of Hope*, edited by Frederick Herzog, 110–25. New York: Herder and Herder, 1970.
———. "Theologies of Hope: A Critical Examination." In *Thinking about God*, by John MacQuarrie, 221–32. London: SCM Press, 1975.
McGrath, Alister E. *The Making of Modern German Christology: 1750–1990*. 2nd ed. Leicester, UK: Apollos, 1994.
McWilliams, Warren. *The Passion of God: Creative Suffering in Contemporary Protestant Theology*. Macon, GA: Mercer University Press, 1985.
Mooney, Christopher F. "Response to Jürgen Moltmann." In *Hope and the Future of Man*, edited by Ewert H. Cousins, 105–109. Philadelphia: Fortress Press, 1972.
Ogden, Schubert M. "Response to Jürgen Moltmann." In *Hope and the Future of Man*, edited by Ewert H. Cousins, 109–16. Philadelphia: Fortress Press, 1972.
Otto, Randall E. "God and History in Jürgen Moltmann." *Journal of the Evangelical Theological Society* 35, no. 3 (September 1992): 375–88.
Polkinghorne, John. "Jürgen Moltmann's Engagement with the Natural Sciences." In *God's Life in Trinity*, edited by Miroslav Volf and Michael Welker, 61–70. Minneapolis, MN: Fortress Press, 2006.
Rasmusson, Arne. *The Church as Polis: From Political Theology to Theological Politics as Exemplified by Jürgen Moltmann and Stanley Hauerwas*. Notre Dame, IN: University of Notre Dame Press, 1995.
Ricoeur, Paul. "Freedom in the Light of Hope." In *Essays on Biblical Interpretation*, by Paul Ricoeur, edited by Lewis S. Mudge, 155–82. Philadelphia: Fortress Press, 1980.
Runia, Klaas. *The Present-Day Christological Debate*. Leicester, UK: Inter-Varsity Press, 1984.
Schweitzer, Don. "The Consistency of Jürgen Moltmann's Theology." *Studies in Religion/Sciences Religieuses* 22, no. 2 (1993): 197–208.
Sykes, S.W. "Life after Death: The Christian Doctrine of Heaven." In *Creation, Christ and Culture: Studies in Honour of T.F. Torrance*, edited by Richard W. A. McKinney, 250–71. Edinburgh: T. and T. Clark, 1976.
Wakefield, James L. *Jürgen Moltmann: A Research Bibliography*. ATLA Bibliography Series 47. Lanham, MD: Scarecrow Press, 2002.
Williams, Stephen N. "The Problem with Moltmann." *European Journal of Theology* 5, no. 2 (1996): 157–67.
Willis, W. Warte, Jr. *Theism, Atheism and the Doctrine of God: The Trinitarian Theologies of Karl Barth and Jürgen Moltmann in Response to Protest Atheism*. Atlanta, GA: Scholars Press, 1987.
Wood, L.W. "From Barth's Trinitarian Christology to Moltmann's Trinitarian Pneumatology." *Asbury Theological Journal* 48, no. 1 (Spring 1993): 49–80.
Wright, Nigel Goring. *Disavowing Constantine: Mission, Church and the Social Order in the Theologies of John Howard Yoder and Jürgen Moltmann*. Paternoster Theological Monographs. Carlisle, UK: Paternoster, 2000.

Yoo, Tae Wha. *The Spirit of Liberation: Jürgen Moltmann's Trinitarian Pneumatology*. Studies in Reformed Theology, Supplements 2. Zoetermeer: Uitgeverij Meinema, 2004.
Young, Norman. *Creator, Creation and Faith*. Philadelphia: Westminster Press, 1976.

Other Works Cited

Achtner, Wolfgang, Stefan Kunz, and Thomas Walter. *Dimensions of Time: The Structures of the Time of God, of the World, and of Humans*. Grand Rapids, MI: Eerdmans, 2002.
Alfeyev, Hilarion. *Christ the Conqueror of Hell: The Descent into Hades from an Orthodox Perspective*. Crestwood, NY: St. Vladimir's Seminary Press, 2009.
Allen, Leslie C. *Psalms 101–150*. Word Biblical Commentary 21. Rev. ed. Nashville, TN: Thomas Nelson, 2002.
Almond, Philip C. *Heaven and Hell in Enlightenment England*. Cambridge: Cambridge University Press, 1994.
Amis, Martin. *Time's Arrow: Or the Nature of the Offence*. London: Penguin, 1991.
Anderson, Bernhard W. *Creation versus Chaos: The Reinterpretation of Mythical Symbolism in the Bible*. 1967. Reprint, Philadelphia: Fortress Press, 1987.
———. *From Creation to New Creation: Old Testament Perspectives*. Minneapolis, MN: Fortress Press, 1994.
Ansell, Nicholas. *Birthpangs of the New Creation: Judgment unto Salvation in the Book of Revelation*. Unpublished ms.
———. "Commentary: Colossians 3:1f." *Third Way* 22, no. 1 (February 1999): 22.
———. "Commentary: Exodus 19:5–6." *Third Way* 25, no. 9 (November 2002): 22.
———. "Commentary: Genesis 1:12f., Daniel 2:35 and Ephesians 1:22f." *Third Way* 25, no. 1 (February 2002): 24.
———. "Commentary: Genesis 27:29, Isaiah 60:14–16 and Genesis 32:27–30." *Third Way* 25, no. 6 (August 2002): 16.
———. "Commentary: Luke 20:27–36." *Third Way* 22, no. 2 (March 1999): 22.
———. "Commentary: John 2:15–16, 18–19; 10:30–39 and 14:2a–3." *Third Way* 26, no. 6 (Summer 2003): 15.
———. "Commentary: Revelation 1:7." *Third Way* 24, no. 1 (February 2001): 22.
———. "Commentary: Revelation 12:1–6." *Third Way* 22, no. 8 (October 1999): 23.
———. "Commentary: Revelation 17:3." *Third Way* 22, no. 6 (July 1999): 22.
———. "Commentary: Revelation 20:1–5." *Third Way* 23, no. 1 (March 2000): 22.
———. "Commentary: Revelation 20:11–15." *Third Way* 23, no. 10 (December 2000): 20.
———. "Creational Man/Eschatological Woman: A Future for Theology." Inaugural address. Toronto: Institute for Christian Studies, 2006.
———. "Embracing the Thorny Way." Review of *The Postmodern God*, edited by Graham Ward. Oxford: Blackwell, 1997 and *Knowing Other-wise: Philosophy at the Threshold of Spirituality*, edited by James Olthuis. New York: Fordham University Press, 1997. *Third Way* 21, no. 1 (February 1998): 26.
———. "For the Love of Wisdom: Scripture, Philosophy, and the Relativisation of Order." In *The Future of Creation Order*, edited by Gerrit Glas, Jeroen de Ridder, Govert Buijs, and Annette Mosher. Dordrecht: Springer, forthcoming.
———. "Foundational and Transcendental Time: An Essay." In *Philosophy as Responsibility: A Celebration of Hendrik Hart's Contribution to the Discipline*,

edited by Ronald A. Kuipers and Janet Catherina Wesselius, 63–79. Lanham, MD: University Press of America, 2002.

———. "Hell: The Nemesis of Hope?" In *Her Gates Will Never Be Shut: Hope, Hell, and the New Jerusalem*, by Bradley Jersak, 191–210. Eugene, OR: Wipf and Stock, 2009.

———. "Life after the Law? Rethinking Truth in the Light of John's Gospel." Unpublished paper.

———. "The Call of Wisdom/The Voice of The Serpent: Towards a Canonical Approach to the Tree of Knowledge." *Christian Scholar's Review* 31, no. 1 (Fall 2001): 31–57.

———. *The Woman Will Overcome the Warrior: A Dialogue with the Christian/Feminist Theology of Rosemary Radford Ruether*. Lanham, MD: University Press of America, 1994.

Appler, Deborah A. "Jezebel." In *The New Interpreter's Dictionary of the Bible*. Vol. 3, edited by Katherine Doob Sakenfeld, 313–14. Nashville, TN: Abingdon, 2008.

Attridge, Harold W., ed. *The HarperCollins Study Bible: New Revised Standard Version*. Rev. ed. San Francisco, CA: HarperCollins, 2006.

Augustine. *Confessions*. Edited and translated by Henry Chadwick. Oxford: Oxford University Press, 1991.

Aune, David E. *Revelation 1–5*. Word Biblical Commentary 52A. Dallas, TX: Word, 1997.

———. *Revelation 6–16*. Word Biblical Commentary 52B. Nashville, TN: Thomas Nelson, 1998.

———. *Revelation 17–22*. Word Biblical Commentary 52C. Nashville, TN: Thomas Nelson, 1998.

Bailey, Lloyd R. "Gehenna: The Topography of Hell." *Biblical Archaeologist* 49, no. 3 (September 1986): 187–91.

Balabanski, Vicky. *Eschatology in the Making: Mark, Matthew and the Didache*. Society for New Testament Studies Monograph Series 97. Cambridge: Cambridge University Press, 1997.

Balthasar, Hans Urs von. *Dare We Hope "That All Men Be Saved"? With a Short Discourse on Hell*. Translated by David Kipp and Lothar Krauth. San Francisco: Ignatius, 1988.

Barker, Kenneth L., ed. *The NIV Study Bible*. Rev. ed. Grand Rapids, MI: Zondervan, 2002.

Barker, Margaret. *The Gate of Heaven: The History and Symbolism of the Temple in Jerusalem*. London: SPCK, 1991.

———. *The Revelation of Jesus Christ*. Edinburgh: T. and T. Clark, 2000.

Barrett, William. "The Flow of Time." In *The Philosophy of Time: A Collection of Essays*, edited by Richard Gale, 355–77. New Jersey: Humanities Press, 1968.

Barth, Karl. *Church Dogmatics* 1/2. Edited by G.W. Bromiley and T.F. Torrance. Edinburgh: T. and T. Clark, 1956.

———. *Church Dogmatics* 2/1. Edited by G.W. Bromiley and T.F. Torrance. Edinburgh: T. and T. Clark, 1957.

———. *Church Dogmatics* 2/2. Edited by G.W. Bromiley and T.F. Torrance. Edinburgh: T. and T. Clark, 1957.

———. *Church Dogmatics* 3/3. Edited by G.W. Bromiley and T.F. Torrance. Edinburgh: T. and T. Clark, 1961.

———. *Church Dogmatics* 4/1. Edited by G.W. Bromiley and T.F. Torrance. Edinburgh: T. and T. Clark, 1962.

―――. *Letters 1961–1968*. Edited by Jürgen Fangmeier and Hinrich Stoevesandt. Translated by G.W. Bromiley. Grand Rapids, MI: Eerdmans, 1981.

―――. "No! Answer to Emil Brunner." In *Natural Theology*, by Karl Barth and Emil Brunner. Translated by Peter Fraenkel, 65–128. London: Geoffrey Bless, Centenary Press, 1948.

―――. *Protestant Theology in the Nineteenth Century*. Translated by Brian Cozens and John Bowden. London: SCM Press, 1972.

―――. *The Epistle to the Romans*. Translated by Edwyn C. Hoskyns. London: Oxford University Press, 1933.

―――. "The Gift of Freedom: Foundation of Evangelical Ethics." Translated by Thomas Wieser. In *The Humanity of God*, by Karl Barth, 69–96. Atlanta, GA: John Knox Press, 1960.

―――. "The Humanity of God." Translated by John Newton Thomas. In *The Humanity of God*, by Karl Barth, 37–65. Atlanta, GA: John Knox Press, 1960.

――― and Emil Brunner. *Natural Theology: Comprising "Nature and Grace" by Professor Dr. Emil Brunner and the Reply "No!" by Dr. Karl Barth*. Translated by Peter Fraenkel. London: Geoffrey Bless, Centenary Press, 1948.

Bauckham, Richard. "Augustine, the 'Compassionate' Christians, and the Apocalypse of Peter." In *The Fate of the Dead: Studies on the Jewish and Christian Apocalypses*, by Richard Bauckham, 149–159. Leiden: Brill, 1998.

―――. "Descent to the Underworld." In *The Anchor Bible Dictionary*. Vol. 2, edited by David Noel Freedman, 145–59. New York: Doubleday, 1992.

―――. *God and the Crisis of Freedom: Biblical and Contemporary Perspectives*. Louisville, KY: Westminster John Knox Press, 2002.

―――. "Hades, Hell." In *The Anchor Bible Dictionary*. Vol. 3, edited by David Noel Freedman, 14–15. New York: Doubleday, 1992.

―――. *Jude, 2 Peter*. Word Biblical Commentary 50. Waco: Word, 1983.

―――. "Nero and the Beast." In *The Climax of Prophecy: Studies on the Book of Revelation*, by Richard Bauckham, 384–452. Edinburgh: T. and T. Clark, 1993.

―――. "The Apocalypse of Peter: A Jewish Christian Apocalypse from the Time of Bar Kokhba." In *The Fate of the Dead: Studies on the Jewish and Christian Apocalypses*, by Richard Bauckham, 160–258. Leiden: Brill, 1998.

―――. *The Climax of Prophecy: Studies on the Book of Revelation*. Edinburgh: T. and T. Clark, 1993.

―――. "The Conflict of Justice and Mercy: Attitudes to the Damned in Apocalyptic Literature." In *The Fate of the Dead: Studies on the Jewish and Christian Apocalypses*, by Richard Bauckham, 132–48. Leiden: Brill, 1998.

―――. *The Fate of the Dead: Studies on the Jewish and Christian Apocalypses*. Leiden: Brill, 1998.

―――. "The Rise of Apocalyptic." *Themelios* 3, no. 2 (January 1978): 10–23.

―――. *The Testimony of the Beloved Disciple: Narrative, History, and Theology in the Gospel of John*. Grand Rapids, MI: Baker, 2007.

―――. *The Theology of the Book of Revelation*. Cambridge: Cambridge University Press, 1993.

―――. "Universalism: A Historical Survey." *Themelios* 4, no. 2 (January 1979): 48–54.

Bavinck, Herman. *Gereformeerde Dogmatiek*. 4 vols. 4th ed. Kampen: J.H. Kok, 1928–30.

―――. *Magnalia Dei: Onderwijzing in de Christelijke Religie, naar Gereformeerde Belijdenis*. 1909. Reprint, Kampen: J.H. Kok, 1931.

―――. *Our Reasonable Faith: A Survey of Christian Doctrine*. Translated by Henry Zylstra. Grand Rapids, MI: Baker, 1977.
―――. *Sin and Salvation in Christ*. Vol. 3 of *Reformed Dogmatics*. Edited by John Bolt. Translated by John Vriend. Grand Rapids, MI: Baker, 2006.
Beagley, Alan James. *The 'Sitz im Leben' of the Apocalypse with Particular Reference to the Role of the Church's Enemies*. Berlin: Walter de Gruyter, 1987.
Beale, G.K. *John's Use of the Old Testament in Revelation*. Journal for the Study of the New Testament Supplement Series 166. Sheffield, UK: Sheffield Academic Press, 1988.
―――. *The Book of Revelation: A Commentary on the Greek Text*. The New International Greek Testament Commentary. Grand Rapids, MI: Eerdmans, 1999.
―――. *The Temple and the Church's Mission: A Biblical Theology of the Dwelling Place of God*. Downers Grove, IL: InterVarsity Press, 2004.
――― and Sean M. McDonough. "Revelation." In *Commentary on the New Testament Use of the Old Testament*, edited by G.K. Beale and D.A. Carson, 1081–161. Grand Rapids, MI: Baker, 2007.
Beasley-Murray, G.R. *Revelation*. The New Century Bible Commentary. Rev. ed. Grand Rapids, MI: Eerdmans, 1978.
Bell, Rob. *Love Wins: A Book About Heaven, Hell, and the Fate of Every Person Who Ever Lived*. New York: HarperOne, 2011.
Benjamin, Andrew. *Present Hope: Philosophy, Architecture, Judaism*. London: Routledge, 1997.
Benjamin, Walter. *Illuminations*. Edited by Hannah Arendt. Translated by Harry Zohn. New York: Schocken, 1968.
Berkouwer, G.C. *A Half Century of Theology: Movements and Motives*. Translated by Lewis B. Smedes. Grand Rapids, MI: Eerdmans, 1977.
―――. *Divine Election*. Translated by Hugo Bekker. Grand Rapids, MI: Eerdmans, 1960.
―――. *Faith and Justification*. Translated by Lewis B. Smedes. Grand Rapids, MI: Eerdmans, 1954.
―――. *The Triumph of Grace in the Theology of Karl Barth*. Translated by Harry R. Boer. Grand: Rapids, MI: Eerdmans, 1956.
Berlin, Adele, and Marc Zvi Brettler, eds. *The Jewish Study Bible: Tanakh Translation*. Oxford: Oxford University Press, 2004.
Bernstein, Alan E. *The Formation of Hell: Death and Retribution in the Ancient and Early Christian Worlds*. Ithaca, NY: Cornell University Press, 1993.
Bloch, Ernst. *Atheism in Christianity: The Religion of the Exodus and the Kingdom*. Translated by J.T. Swann. New York: Herder and Herder, 1972.
―――. *Avicenna und die Aristotelische Linke*. Frankfurt: Suhrkamp Verlag, 1963.
―――. *Das Prinzip Hoffnung*. 3 vols. Frankfurt am Main: Suhrkamp Verlag, 1954–1959.
―――. *Man on His Own: Essays in the Philosophy of Religion*. Translated by E.B. Ashton. New York: Herder and Herder, 1971.
―――. *The Principle of Hope*. 3 vols. Translated by Neville Plaice, Stephen Plaice, and Paul Knight. Cambridge, MA: MIT Press, 1986.
Boettner, Loraine. *The Reformed Doctrine of Predestination*. 1932. Reprint, Phillipsburg, NJ: Presbyterian and Reformed, 1980.
Boff, Leonardo. *Liberating Grace*. Translated by John Dury. Maryknoll, NY: Orbis, 1979.

Bonda, Jan. *The One Purpose of God: An Answer to the Doctrine of Eternal Punishment*. Translated by Reinder Bruinsma. 1993. Reprint, Grand Rapids, MI: Eerdmans, 1998.

Borg, Marcus J. *Conflict, Holiness and Politics in the Teachings of Jesus*. 1984. Reprint, Harrisburg, PA: Trinity Press International, 1998.

Boring, M. Eugene. "The Language of Universal Salvation in Paul." *Journal of Biblical Literature* 105, no. 2 (1986): 269–92.

Bouma-Prediger, Steven. "Bonhoeffer and Berkouwer on the World, Humans, and Sin: Two Models of Ontology and Anthropology." MPhil thesis, Institute for Christian Studies, Toronto, 1984.

Boyd, Gregory A. *Satan and the Problem of Evil: Constructing a Trinitarian Warfare Theodicy*. Downers Grove, IL: InterVarsity Press, 2001.

———, and Paul R. Eddy. *Across the Spectrum: Understanding Issues in Evangelical Theology*. Grand Rapids, MI: Baker, 2002.

Bratt, James D., ed. *Abraham Kuyper: A Centennial Reader*. Grand Rapids, MI: Eerdmans, 1998.

Briggs, Richard S. "The Book of Genesis." In *A Theological Introduction to the Pentateuch: Interpreting the Torah as Christian Scripture*, edited by Richard S. Briggs and Joel N. Lohr, 19–50. Grand Rapids, MI: Baker, 2012.

Bril, Kornelis A. *Vollenhoven's Problem-Historical Method: Introduction and Explorations*. Edited by John H. Kok. Translated by Ralph W. Vunderink. Sioux Center, IA: Dordt College Press, 2005.

Brower, K.E., and M.W. Elliott, eds. *'The Reader Must Understand': Eschatology in Bible and Theology*. Leicester, UK: Apollos, 1997.

Bruce, F.F. *The Canon of Scripture*. Downers Grove, IL: InterVarsity Press, 1988.

Brueggemann, Walter. Editor's foreword to *From Creation to New Creation: Old Testament Perspectives*, by Bernhard W. Anderson, vii–x. Minneapolis, MN: Fortress Press, 1994.

———. *Praying the Psalms*. Winona, MN: Saint Mary's Press, 1986.

———. *The Land: Place as Gift, Promise, and Challenge in Biblical Faith*. 2nd ed. Philadelphia: Fortress Press, 2002.

Brunner, Emil. *Eternal Hope*. Translated by Harold Knight. London: Lutterworth Press, 1954.

———. "Nature and Grace: A Contribution to the Discussion with Karl Barth." In *Natural Theology*, by Karl Barth and Emil Brunner. Translated by Peter Fraenkel, 15–64. London: Geoffrey Bless, Centenary Press, 1948.

———. *The Divine Imperative: A Study in Christian Ethics*. Translated by Olive Wyon. 1941. Reprint, Cambridge: Lutterworth Press, 2002.

Buchholz, Dennis D. *Your Eyes Will Be Opened: A Study of the Greek (Ethiopic) Apocalypse of Peter*. SBL Dissertation Series 97. Atlanta, GA: Scholars Press, 1988.

Bultmann, Rudolf. "New Testament and Mythology." In *Kerygma and Myth: A Theological Debate*, by Rudolf Bultmann and Ernst Lohmeyer, Julius Schniewind, Helmut Thielicke, and Austin Farrer, edited by Hans Werner Bartsch, 1–44. New York: Harper and Row, 1961.

Bush, George. *Anastasis: Or, the Doctrine of the Resurrection of the Body, Rationally and Scripturally Considered*. New York: Wiley and Putnam, 1845.

Caird, G.B. *The Language and Imagery of the Bible*. With a New Introduction by N.T. Wright. 1980. Reprint, Grand Rapids, MI: Eerdmans, 1997.

Calvin, John. *Institutes of the Christian Religion*. Vol. 1. Edited by John T. McNeill. Translated by Ford Lewis Battles. Philadelphia: Westminster Press, 1960.

Cameron, Nigel M. de S., ed. *Universalism and the Doctrine of Hell: Papers Presented at the Fourth Edinburgh Conference in Christian Dogmatics*. Carlisle, UK: Paternoster; Grand Rapids, MI: Baker, 1992.
Caputo, John D. "Heidegger and Theology." In *The Cambridge Companion to Heidegger*, edited by Charles B. Guignon, 326–44. 2nd ed. Cambridge: Cambridge University Press, 2006.
———. *On Religion*. London: Routledge, 2001.
———. "The Chance of Love: A Response to Olthuis." In *Cross* and Khôra: *Deconstruction and Christianity in the Work of John D. Caputo*, edited by Marko Zlomislić and Neal DeRoo, 187–96. Eugene, OR: Pickwick, 2011.
———. *The Prayers and Tears of Jacques Derrida: Religion without Religion*. Bloomington, IN: Indiana University Press, 1997.
———. *The Weakness of God: A Theology of the Event*. Bloomington, IN: Indiana University Press, 2006.
———, ed. *Deconstruction in a Nutshell: A Conversation with Jacques Derrida*. New York: Fordham University Press, 1997.
———. and Michael J. Scanlon, eds. *God, the Gift, and Postmodernism*. Bloomington, IN: Indiana University Press, 1999.
Chanter, Tina. *Time, Death, and the Feminine: Levinas with Heidegger*. Stanford, CA: Stanford University Press, 2001.
Charlesworth, James H., ed. *Apocalyptic Literature and Testaments*. Vol. 1 of *The Old Testament Pseudepigrapha*. New York: Doubleday, 1983.
Childs, Brevard S. *Isaiah*. Old Testament Library. Louisville, KY: Westminster John Knox Press, 2001.
Christensen, Duane L. *Deuteronomy 1:1–21:9*. Word Biblical Commentary 6A. 2nd ed. Nashville, TN: Thomas Nelson, 2001.
Clouser, Roy A. "Is God Eternal?" *Poznan Studies in the Philosophy of the Sciences and the Humanities* 73 (2000): 273–300
———. "Religious Language: A New Look at an Old Problem." In *Rationality in the Calvinian Tradition*, edited by Hendrik Hart, Johan van der Hoeven, and Nicholas Wolterstorff, 385–407. Lanham, MD: University Press of America, 1983.
———. "Religious Language: A New Look at an Old Problem." Toronto: Institute for Christian Studies, 1980.
Collins, David. "Hell and Tradition." Toronto: Institute for Christian Studies, 1990.
Collins, John J. *Daniel: With an Introduction to Apocalyptic Literature*. Grand Rapids, MI: Eerdmans, 1984.
———. "Introduction: Towards the Morphology of a Genre." In *Apocalypse: The Morphology of a Genre*, edited by John J. Collins, 1–20. Semeia 14. Missoula, MT: Scholars Press, 1979.
———. *The Apocalyptic Imagination: An Introduction to Jewish Apocalyptic Literature*. 2nd ed. Grand Rapids, MI: Eerdmans, 1998.
Corsini, Eugenio. *The Apoclaypse: The Perennial Revelation of Jesus Christ*. Edited and translated by Francis J. Maloney. Good News Studies 5. Wilmington, DE: Michael Glazier, 1983.
Cox, Harvey. "Afterword." In *The Secular City Debate*, edited by Daniel Callahan, 179–203. New York: Macmillan, 1966.
———. "Ernst Bloch and 'the Pull of the Future'." In *New Theology No. 5*, edited by Martin E. Marty and Dean G. Peerman, 191–203. New York: Macmillan, 1968.
———. Foreword to *Man on His Own: Essays in the Philosophy of Religion*, by Ernst Bloch, translated by E.B. Ashton, 7–18. New York: Herder and Herder, 1971.
———. *The Secular City*. New York: Macmillan, 1965.

Crockett, William. "The Metaphorical View." In *Four Views on Hell*, edited by William Crockett, 43–88. Grand Rapids, MI: Zondervan, 1992.

———, ed. *Four Views on Hell*. Grand Rapids, MI: Zondervan, 1992.

Cromartie, Michael, ed. *A Preserving Grace: Protestants, Catholics, and Natural Law*. Washington, DC: Ethics and Public Policy Center; Grand Rapids, MI: Eerdmans, 1997.

Dainton, Barry. *Time and Space*. Montreal: McGill-Queen's University Press, 2001.

Dante. *The Divine Comedy of Dante Alighieri: Inferno*. Translated by Allen Mandelbaum. Berkeley: University of California Press, 1981.

———. *The Divine Comedy of Dante Alighieri: Purgatorio*. Translated by Allen Mandelbaum. Berkeley: University of California Press, 1982.

Davis, Bret W. "Heidegger on Christianity and Divinity: A Chronological Compendium." In *Martin Heidegger: Key Concepts*, edited by Bret W. Davis, 231–59. Durham, UK: Acumen, 2010.

De Boer, Martinus C. "Paul, Theologian of God's Apocalypse." *Interpretation* 56, no. 1 (2002): 21–33.

Dembski, William A. *The Design Revolution: Answering the Toughest Questions about Intelligent Design*. Downers Grove, IL: InterVarsity Press, 2004.

Derrida, Jacques. "How To Avoid Speaking: Denials." Translated by Ken Frieden. In *Derrida and Negative Theology*, edited by Harold Coward and Toby Foshay, 73–142. Albany, NY: State University of New York Press, 1992.

———. "Khôra." Translated by Ian McLeod. In *On the Name*, by Jacques Derrida, edited by Thomas Dutoit, 87–127. Stanford, CA: Stanford University Press, 1995.

Deursen, Arie Theodorus van. *The Distinctive Character of the Free University of Amsterdam, 1880–2005: A Commemorative History*. Translated by Herbert Donald Morton. Grand Rapids, MI: Eerdmans, 2008.

Dixon, Larry. *The Other Side of the Good News: Confronting the Contemporary Challenges to Jesus' Teaching on Hell*. Wheaton: IL: Bridgepoint, 1992.

Dodds, E.R. *Pagan and Christian in an Age of Anxiety: Some Aspects of Religious Experience from Marcus Aurelius to Constantine*. New York: W.W. Norton, 1965.

Dooyeweerd, Herman. *A New Critique of Theoretical Thought*. 4 vols. Translated by David H. Freeman and William S. Young. Philadelphia: Presbyterian and Reformed, 1953–58.

———. "Cornelius Van Til and the Transcendental Critique of Theoretical Thought." In *Jerusalem and Athens: Critical Discussions on the Philosophy and Apologetics of Cornelius Van Til*, edited by E.R. Geehan, 74–89. Phillipsburg, NJ: Presbyterian and Reformed, 1980.

———. *Roots of Western Culture: Pagan, Secular, and Christian Options*. Edited by Mark Vander Vennen and Bernard Zylstra. Translated by John Kraay. Toronto: Wedge, 1979.

———. "The Criteria of Progressive and Reactionary Tendencies in History." In *Christian Philosophy and the Meaning of History*. The Collected Works of Herman Dooyeweerd. Series B, Vol. 1, edited by D.F.M. Strauss, 47–66. Lewiston, NY: Edwin Mellen Press, 1996.

Dreyfus, Hubert L. *Being-In-The-World: A Commentary on Heidegger's* Being and Time, *Division 1*. Cambridge, MA: MIT Press, 1991.

Dudiak, Jeffrey. "Barth's Doctrine of Nothingness: Creational and Theological Reflections." Toronto: Institute for Christian Studies, 1986.

Duffy, Stephen J. *The Graced Horizon: Nature and Grace in Modern Catholic Thought*. Collegeville, MN: Liturgical Press, 1992.

Edwards, David L., with John Stott. *Essentials: A Liberal-Evangelical Dialogue*. London: Hodder and Stoughton, 1988.
Edwards, Jonathan. *Sinners in the Hands of an Angry God*. Phillipsburg, NJ: Presbyterian and Reformed, 1992.
Eliade, Mircea. *From Gautama Buddha to the Triumph of Christianity*. Vol. 2 of *A History of Religious Ideas*. Translated by Willard R. Trask. Chicago: University of Chicago Press, 1982.
———. *From Muhammad to the Age of Reforms*. Vol. 3 of *A History of Religious Ideas*. Translated by Alf Hiltebeitel and Diane Apostolos-Cappadona. Chicago: University of Chicago Press, 1985.
———. *The Forge and the Crucible: The Origins and Structures of Alchemy*. Translated by Stephen Corrin. 2nd ed. Chicago: University of Chicago Press, 1978.
Ellis, E. Earle. "New Testament Teaching on Hell." In *'The Reader Must Understand': Eschatology in Bible and Theology*, edited by K.E. Brower and M.W. Elliott, 199–219. Leicester, UK: Apollos, 1997.
———. *The Making of the New Testament Documents*. Leiden: Brill, 2002.
Ellul, Jacques. *Reason For Being: A Meditation on Ecclesiastes*. Translated by Joyce Main Hanks. Grand Rapids, MI: Eerdmans, 1990.
Erikson, Erik. *Identity and the Life-Cycle*. New York: International Universities Press, 1959.
Farrar, Frederic W. *Eternal Hope: Five Sermons*. London: Macmillan, 1883.
Farrer, Austin. *The Revelation of St. John the Divine*. Oxford University Press, 1964.
Fekkes, Jan. *Isaiah and Prophetic Traditions in the Book of Revelation: Visionary Antecedents and their Development*. Journal for the Study of the New Testament Supplement Series 93. Sheffield, UK: JSOT Press, 1994.
Fletcher-Louis, Crispin H.T. "Commentary: Genesis 1:26 and Exodus 20:4f." *Third Way* 22, no. 9 (December 1999): 21.
———. "Commentary: Mark 13:24ff and 30f." *Third Way* 21, no. 7 (September, 1998): 20.
———. "The Destruction of the Temple and the Relativization of the Old Covenant: Mark 13:31 and Matthew 5:18." In *'The Reader Must Understand': Eschatology in Bible and Theology*, edited by K.E. Brower and M.W. Elliott, 145–69. Leicester, UK: Apollos, 1997.
Fokkelman, J.P. *Reading Biblical Narrative: An Introductory Guide*. Translated by Ineke Smit. Louisville, KY: Westminster John Knox Press, 1999.
Ford, J. Massyngberde. *Revelation: A New Translation with Introduction and Commentary*. The Anchor Bible 38. New York: Doubleday, 1975.
Fox, Matthew. *Original Blessing: A Primer in Creation Spirituality Presented in Four Paths, Twenty-Six Themes, and Two Questions*. Santa Fe, New Mexico: Bear, 1983.
Frame, John M. "Infralapsarianism." In *The Westminster Handbook to Reformed Theology*, edited by Donald K. McKim, 121–22. Louisville, KY: Westminster John Knox Press, 2001.
Fraser, J.T. *Of Time, Passion, and Knowledge: Reflections on the Strategy of Existence*. 2nd ed. Princeton, NJ: Princeton University Press, 1990.
———, ed. *The Voices of Time: A Cooperative Survey of Man's Views of Time as Expressed by the Sciences and by the Humanities*. 2nd ed. Amherst, MA: University of Massachusetts Press, 1981.
Fretheim, Terence E. *Jeremiah*. Smyth and Helwys Bible Commentary. Macon, GA: Smyth and Helwys, 2002.
———. *The Suffering of God: An Old Testament Perspective*. Philadelphia: Fortress Press, 1984.

Fudge, Edward William, and Robert A. Peterson. *Two Views of Hell: A Biblical and Theological Dialogue*. Downers Grove, IL: InterVarsity Press, 2000.

Fuller, Steve. *Dissent over Descent: Intelligent Design's Challenge to Darwinism*. Cambridge: Icon, 2008.

———. *Science vs Religion? Intelligent Design and the Problem of Evolution*. Cambridge: Polity, 2007.

Gadamer, Hans-Georg. *Hegel's Dialectic: Five Hermeneutical Studies*. Translated by P. Christopher. New Haven, CT: Yale University Press, 1976.

Gale, Richard M., ed. *The Philosophy of Time: A Collection of Essays*. 1968. Reprint, New Jersey: Humanities Press, 1978.

Gallagher, Joseph. *To Hell and Back with Dante: A Modern Reader's Guide to The Divine Comedy*. Liguori, MO: Triumph, 1996.

Ganssle, Gregory E., ed. *God and Time: Four Views*. Downers Grove, IL: InterVarsity Press, 2001.

Gardiner, Eileen, ed. *Visions of Heaven and Hell before Dante*. New York: Italica Press, 1989.

Geertsema, H. G. "*Homo Respondens*: On the Historical Nature of Human Reason." *Philosophia Reformata* 58 (1993): 120–52.

Gell, Alfred. *The Anthropology of Time: Cultural Construction of Temporal Maps and Images*. Oxford: Berg, 1992.

Gentry, Kenneth L. *Before Jerusalem Fell: Dating the Book of Revelation*. Tyler, TX: Institute for Christian Economics, 1989.

Gerstner, John H. *Heaven and Hell: Jonathan Edwards on the Afterlife*. Legionier Ministries and Grand Rapids, MI: Baker, 1991.

———. *Repent or Perish (with a Special Reference to the Conservative Attack on Hell)*. Ligionier, PA: Soli Deo Gloria, 1990.

Goldingay, John E. *Daniel*. Word Biblical Commentary 30. Dallas, TX: Word, 1989).

Gorner, Paul. *Heidegger's* Being and Time*: An Introduction*. Cambridge: Cambridge University Press, 2007.

Gorringe, Timothy. *God's Just Vengeance: Crime, Violence and the Rhetoric of Salvation*. Cambridge: Cambridge University Press, 1996.

Gray, Tony. "The Nature of Hell: Reflections on the Debate between Conditionalism and the Traditional View of Hell." In *'The Reader Must Understand': Eschatology in Bible and Theology*, edited by K.E. Brower and M.W. Elliott, 231–41. Leicester, UK: Apollos, 1997.

Green, Clifford, ed. *Karl Barth: Theologian of Freedom*. London: Collins, 1989.

Griffin, David R. "Creation Out of Chaos and the Problem of Evil." In *Encountering Evil: Live Options in Theodicy*, edited by Stephen T. Davis, 101–19, Atlanta, GA: John Knox Press, 1981.

———. "Creation Out of Nothing, Creation Out of Chaos, and the Problem of Evil." In *Encountering Evil: Live Options in Theodicy*, edited by Stephen T. Davis, 108–25. Rev. ed. Louisville, KY: Westminster John Knox Press, 2001.

Gundry-Volf, Judith M. "Universalism." In *Dictionary of Paul and His Letters*, edited by G.F. Hawthorne, R.P. Martin, and D.G. Reid, 956–61. Downers Grove, IL: InterVarsity Press, 1993.

Gunn, J. Alexander. *The Problem of Time: An Historical and Critical Study*. London: George Allen and Unwin, 1929.

Hagner, Donald A. *Matthew 1–13*. Word Biblical Commentary 33A. Nashville, TN: Thomas Nelson, 1993.

Hall, Christopher A., and John Sanders, *Does God Have a Future? A Debate on Divine Providence*. Grand Rapids, MI: Baker, 2003.

——— . "Does God Know Your Next Move? Part One." *Christianity Today* 45, no. 7 (May 21, 2001): 38–45.

——— . "Does God Know Your Next Move? Part Two." *Christianity Today* 45, no. 8 (June 11, 2001): 50–56.

Hall, Lindsay. *Swinburne's Hell and Hick's Universalism: Are We Free to Reject God?* Aldershot, UK: Ashgate, 2003.

Hanson, P.D. "Apocalypticism." In *Interpreter's Dictionary of the Bible*. Supplementary vol., edited by G. Buttrick, 28–34. Nashville, TN: Abingdon, 1976.

Harland, Phillip A. "Emperor Worship." In *The New Interpreter's Dictionary of the Bible*. Vol. 2, edited by Katherine Doob Sakenfeld, 255–57. Nashville, TN: Abingdon, 2007.

Harmon, Kendall S. "The Case against Conditionalism: A Response to Edward William Fudge." In *Universalism and the Doctrine of Hell: Papers Presented at the Fourth Edinburgh Conference in Christian Dogmatics*, edited by Nigel M. de S. Cameron, 193–224. Carlisle, UK: Paternoster; Grand Rapids, MI: Baker, 1992.

Harris, Errol E. *The Reality of Time*. Albany, NY: State University of New York Press, 1988.

Hart, Hendrik. "Dooyeweerd's Gegenstand Theory of Theory." In *The Legacy of Herman Dooyeweerd: Reflections on Critical Philosophy in the Christian Tradition*, edited by C.T. McIntire, 143–66. Lanham, MD: University Press of America, 1985.

——— . "Draft for Proposed ICS Systematic Philosophy Syllabus." 2 vols. Unpublished ms., Toronto, June 1976.

——— . "Notes on Dooyeweerd, Reason and Order." In *Contemporary Reflections on the Philosophy of Herman Dooyeweerd*. A Supplement to the Collected Works of Herman Dooyeweerd. Series C, Vol. 1, edited by D.F.M. Strauss and Michelle Botting, 125–46. Lewiston, NY: The Edwin Mellen Press, 2000.

——— . "Problems of Time: An Essay." In *The Idea of a Christian Philosophy: Essays in Honour of D.H.Th. Vollenhoven*, edited by K.A. Bril, H. Hart, and J. Klapwijk, 30–42. Special issue, *Philosophia Reformata* 38. Toronto: Wedge, 1973.

——— . *Setting Our Sights by the Morning Star: Reflections on the Role of the Bible in Post-modern Times*. Toronto: Patmos Press, 1989.

——— . "Reply to Respondents." In *An Ethos of Compassion and the Integrity of Creation*, edited by Brian J. Walsh, Hendrik Hart, and Robert E. VanderVennen, 115–28. Lanham, MD: University Press of America, 1995.

——— . "The Just Shall Live by Faith: Reformational Reflections on Public Justice and Racist Attitudes." *Christian Scholar's Review* 16, no. 3 (1987): 265–82.

——— . *Understanding Our World: An Integral Ontology*. Lanham, MD: University Press of America, 1984.

——— . "Whither Reason and Religion?" In *Searching for Community in a Withering Tradition: Conversations between a Marxian Atheist and a Calvinian Christian*, by Kai Nielsen and Hendrik Hart, 148–235. Lanham, MD: University Press of America, 1990.

Hart, Trevor. "The Capacity for Ambiguity: Revisiting the Barth-Brunner Debate." In *Regarding Karl Barth: Toward a Reading of His Theology*, by Trevor Hart, 139–72. Downers Grove, IL: InterVarsity Press, 1999.

——— . "Universalism: Two Distinct Types." In *Universalism and the Doctrine of Hell: Papers Presented at the Fourth Edinburgh Conference in Christian Dogmatics*, edited by Nigel M. de S. Cameron, 1–34. Carlisle, UK: Paternoster; Grand Rapids, MI: Baker, 1992.

Harvey, Van A. *A Handbook of Theological Terms*. New York: Macmillan, 1964.

Hasker, William. *God, Time, and Knowledge*. Ithaca, NY: Cornell University Press, 1989.
Hayes, Zachary J. "The Purgatorial View." In *Four Views on Hell*, edited by William Crockett, 91–118. Grand Rapids, MI: Zondervan, 1992.
Head, Peter M. "The Duration of Divine Judgment in the New Testament." In *'The Reader Must Understand': Eschatology in Bible and Theology*, edited by K.E. Brower and M.W. Elliott, 221–27. Leicester, UK: Apollos, 1997.
Hegel, G.W.F. *Lectures on the Philosophy of Religion: The Lectures of 1827*. Edited by Peter C. Hodgson. Translated by R.F. Brown, P.C. Hodgson, and J.M. Stewart, with H.S. Harris. Berkeley: University of California Press, 1988.
Heidegger, Martin. "Anaximander's Saying." In *Off the Beaten Track*, by Martin Heidegger, Edited and translated by Julian Young and Kenneth Haynes, 242–81. Cambridge: Cambridge University Press, 2002.
———. *Being and Time*. Translated by John Macquarrie and Edward Robinson. San Francisco: HarperCollins, 1962.
———. *Being and Time*. Translated by Joan Stambaugh. Rev. ed. Albany, NY: State University of New York Press, 2010.
———. *Holzwege*. 1950. Reprint, Frankfurt: Klostermann, 1972.
Hick, John. *Death and Eternal Life*. London: Collins, 1976.
Hickman, Louise. "Love Is All and God Is Love: Universalism in Peter Sterry (1613–1672) and Jeremiah White (1630–1707)." In *"All Shall Be Well": Explorations in Universal Salvation and Christian Theology from Origen to Moltmann*, edited by Gregory MacDonald, 93–115. Eugene, OR: Cascade, 2011.
Hielema, Syd. "Herman Bavinck's Eschatological Understanding of Redemption." ThD diss., Wycliffe College, Toronto School of Theology, 1998.
Hilborn, David, ed. *The Nature of Hell*: A Report by the Evangelical Alliance's Commission on Unity and Truth among Evangelicals (ACUTE). Carlisle, UK: Acute/Paternoster, 2000.
Himmelfarb, Martha. *Tours of Hell: An Apocalyptic Form in Jewish and Christian Literature*. Philadelphia: University of Pennsylvania Press, 1983.
Hoffmeyer, John F. *The Advent of Freedom: The Presence of the Future in Hegel's Logic*. Cranbury, NJ: Associated University Presses, 1994.
Holtrop, Philip C. "Decree(s) of God." In *The Westminster Handbook to Reformed Theology*, edited by Donald K. McKim, 54–56. Louisville, KY: Westminster John Knox Press, 2001.
Horton, Michael S. *For Calvinism*. Grand Rapids, MI: Zondervan, 2011.
———. "Hellenistic or Hebrew? Open Theism and Reformed Theological Method." In *Beyond the Bounds: Open Theism and the Undermining of Biblical Christianity*, edited by John Piper, Justin Taylor, and Paul Kjoss Helseth, 201–34. Wheaton, IL: Crossway, 2003.
Humphrey, Edith McEwan. *The Ladies and the Cities: Transformation and Apocalyptic Identity in Joseph and Aseneth, 4 Ezra, the Apocalypse and the Shepherd of Hermas*. Journal for the Study of the Pseudepigrapha Series 17. Sheffield, UK: Sheffield Academic Press, 1995.
Inwood, Michael. *A Heidegger Dictionary*. Oxford: Blackwell, 1999.
Irwin, Brian P. "Topheth." In *Eerdmans Bible Dictionary*, edited by David Noel Freedman, Allen C. Myers, and Astrid B. Beck, 1321. Grand Rapids, MI: Eerdmans, 2000.
Jeremias, Joachim. "Hades." In *The Theological Dictionary of the New Testament*. Vol. 1, edited by Gerhard Kittel, translated by G. Bromiley, 146–49. Grand Rapids, MI: Eerdmans, 1964.

Jersak, Bradley. *Her Gates Will Never Be Shut: Hope, Hell, and the New Jerusalem.* Eugene, OR: Wipf and Stock, 2009.
Jewett, Paul K. *Election and Predestination.* Grand Rapids, MI: Eerdmans, 1985.
Johnson, Elizabeth A. *She Who Is: The Mystery of God in Feminist Theological Discourse.* New York: Crossroad, 1997.
Johnson, Luke Timothy. *The Writings of the New Testament: An Interpretation.* 3rd ed. Minneapolis, MN: Fortress Press, 2010.
Jones, L. Gregory. *Embodying Forgiveness: A Theological Analysis.* Grand Rapids, MI: Eerdmans, 1995.
Josephus. *The Jewish War.* Edited by E. Mary Smallwood. Translated by G.A. Williamson. Rev. ed. London: Penguin, 1981.
Kalsbeek, L. *Contours of a Christian Philosophy: An Introduction to Herman Dooyeweerd's Thought.* A Supplement to the Collected Works of Herman Dooyeweerd. Series C, Vol. 2. Edited by Bernard and Josina Zylstra. 1975. Reprint, Lewiston, NY: The Edwin Mellen Press, 2002.
Kearney, Richard. *The God Who May Be: A Hermeneutics of Religion.* Bloomington, IN: Indiana University Press, 2001.
Kearsley, R. "Grace." In *New Dictionary of Theology*, edited by Sinclair B. Ferguson and David F. Wright, 280. Leicester, UK: Inter-Varsity Press, 1988.
Keesmaat, Sylvia. "The Coming of the Son of Man in Luke-Acts." MA thesis, McMaster University, 1990.
Keller, Catherine. *Apocalypse Now and Then: A Feminist Guide to the End of the World.* Boston: Beacon, 1996.
———. *Face of the Deep: A Theology of Becoming.* London: Routledge, 2003.
Kelly, Christopher. *The Roman Empire: A Very Short Introduction.* Oxford: Oxford University Press, 2006.
Kern, Stephen. *The Culture of Time and Space 1880–1918.* Cambridge, MA: Harvard University Press, 1983.
Kierkegaard, Søren. *Kierkegaard's The Concept of Dread.* Edited and translated by Walter Lowrie. 1944. Reprint, Princeton: Princeton University Press, 1957.
Kirk-Duggan, Cheryl A. "Hell." In *Eerdmans Dictionary of the Bible*, edited by David Noel Freedman, Allen C. Myers, and Astrid B. Beck, 572–73. Grand Rapids, MI: Eerdmans, 2000.
Klapwijk, Jacob. "Antithesis and Common Grace." In *Bringing into Captivity Every Thought:* Capita Selecta *in the History of Christian Evaluations of Non-Christian Philosophy*, edited by Jacob Klapwijk, Sander Griffioen, and Gerben Groenwoud, 169–90. Lanham, MD: University Press of America, 1991.
Klempa, William. "Supralapsarianism." In *The Westminster Handbook to Reformed Theology*, edited by Donald K. McKim, 214–15. Louisville, KY: Westminster John Knox Press, 2001.
Knowles, Michael. *Jeremiah in Matthew's Gospel: The Rejected-Prophet Motif in Matthaean Redaction.* Journal for the Study of the New Testament Supplement Series 68. Sheffield, UK: Sheffield Academic Press, 1993.
Knusden, Robert D. "Progressive and Regressive Tendencies in Christian Apologetics." In *Jerusalem and Athens: Critical Discussions on the Philosophy and Apologetics of Cornelius Van Til*, edited by E.R. Geehan, 275–98. Phillipsburg, NJ: Presbyterian and Reformed, 1980.
Kuyper, Abraham. *De Gemeene Gratie.* 3 vols. Amsterdam: Hoveker and Wormster, 1902–1905.
Kvanvig, Jonathan L. *The Problem of Hell.* Oxford: Oxford University Press, 1993.

Lacy, Larry. "Talbott on Paul as a Universalist." *Christian Scholar's Review* 21, no. 4 (June 1992): 395–407.
Lake, Donald M. "He Died for All: The Universal Dimensions of the Atonement." In *Grace Unlimited*, edited by Clark H. Pinnock, 31–50. Minneapolis, MN: Bethany, 1975.
Lawrence, David. *Heaven . . . It's Not the End of the World*. London: Scripture Union, 1995.
Le Poidevin, Robin, and Murray MacBeth, eds. *The Philosophy of Time*. Oxford: Oxford University Press, 1993.
Levenson, Jon D. *Creation and the Persistence of Evil: The Jewish Drama of Divine Omnipotence*. San Francisco: Harper and Row, 1988.
Lewis, Scott M. *"So That God May Be All in All": The Apocalyptic Message of 1 Corinthians 15:12–34*. Tesi Gregoriana Serie Teologia 42. Rome: Gregorian University Press, 1998.
Lieb, Irwin C. *Past, Present, and Future: A Philosophical Essay about Time*. Urbana, IL: University of Illinois Press, 1991.
Lohfink, Norman. *Qohelet*. Continental Commentary Series. Translated by Sean McEvenue. Minneapolis, MN: Fortress Press, 2003.
Longnecker, Bruce W. *2 Esdras*. Sheffield, UK: Sheffield Academic Press, 1995.
Lovejoy, Arthur O. *The Great Chain of Being: A Study of the History of an Idea*. Cambridge, MA: Harvard University Press, 1948.
Lucas, J.R. *The Future: An Essay on God, Temporality and Truth*. Oxford: Blackwell, 1981.
Lunde, J. "Heaven and Hell." In *Dictionary of Jesus and the Gospels*, edited by Joel B. Green, Scot McKnight, and I. Howard Marshall, 309–11. Downers Grove, IL: InterVarsity Press, 1992.
Lupieri, Edmondo F. *A Commentary on the Apocalypse of John*. Translated by Maria Poggi Johnson and Adam Kamesar. Grand Rapids, MI: Eerdmans, 2006.
MacDonald, Gregory. *The Evangelical Universalist*. Eugene, OR: Cascade, 2006.
———, ed. *"All Shall Be Well": Explorations in Universal Salvation and Christian Theology from Origen to Moltmann*. Eugene, OR: Cascade, 2011.
Macquarrie, John. *Heidegger and Christianity*. London: SCM Press, 1994.
———. "Supererogation, Works of." In *A New Dictionary of Christian Ethics*, edited by John Macquarrie and James Childress, 612. London: SCM Press, 1986.
Malina, Bruce J. *On the Genre and Message of Revelation: Star Visions and Sky Journeys*. Peabody, MA: Hendrickson, 1995.
Marshall, Christopher D. *Beyond Retribution: A New Testament Vision for Justice, Crime, and Punishment*. Grand Rapids, MI: Eerdmans, 2001.
Marshall, I. Howard. "Does the New Testament Teach Universal Salvation?" In *Christ in Our Place: The Humanity of God in Christ for the Reconciliation of the World; Essays Presented to James Torrance*, edited by Trevor A. Hart and Daniel P. Thimell, 313–28. Exeter, UK: Paternoster, 1989.
———. "Universal Grace and Atonement in the Pastoral Epistles." In *The Grace of God and the Will of Man*, edited by Clark H. Pinnock, 51–69. 1989. Reprint, Minneapolis, MN: Bethany, 1995.
Marshall, John W. *Parables of War: Reading John's Jewish Apocalypse*. Studies in Christianity and Judaism 10. Waterloo, ON: Wilfrid Laurier University Press, 2001.
McCormack, Bruce. "Grace and Being: The Role of God's Gracious Election in Karl Barth's Theological Ontology." In *The Cambridge Companion to Karl Barth*, edited by John Webster, 92–110. Cambridge: Cambridge University Press, 2000.
McCready, Stuart, ed. *The Discovery of Time*. Naperville, IL: Sourcebooks, 2001.

McCumber, John. *Time and Philosophy: A History of Continental Thought*. Montreal: McGill-Queen's University Press, 2011.
McFague, Sallie. *Models of God: Theology for an Ecological, Nuclear Age*. Philadelphia: Fortress Press, 1987.
McInerney, Peter K. *Time and Experience*. Philadelphia: Temple University Press, 1991.
McIntire, C.T. "Dooyeweerd's Philosophy of History." In *The Legacy of Herman Dooyeweerd: Reflections on Critical Philosophy in the Christian Tradition*, edited by C.T. McIntire, 81–117. Lanham, MD: University Press of America, 1985.
———, ed. *The Legacy of Herman Dooyeweerd: Reflections on Critical Philosophy in the Christian Tradition*. Lanham, MD: University Press of America, 1985.
McKinney, Richard W.A., ed. *Creation, Christ and Culture: Studies in Honour of T.F. Torrance*. Edinburgh: T. and T. Clark, 1976.
Mealy, J. Webb. *After the Thousand Years: Resurrection and Judgment in Revelation 20*. Journal for the Study of the New Testament Supplement Series 70. Sheffield, UK: JSOT Press, 1992.
Mellor, D.H. *Real Time 2*. London: Routledge, 1998.
Mendels, Doron. *The Rise and Fall of Jewish Nationalism: Jewish and Christian Ethnicity in Ancient Palestine*. Grand Rapids, MI: Eerdmans, 1992.
Miethe, Terry L. "The Universal Power of the Atonement." In *The Grace of God and the Will of Man*, edited by Clark H. Pinnock, 71–96. 1989. Reprint, Minneapolis, MN: Bethany, 1995.
Milikowsky, Chaim. "Which Gehenna? Retribution and Eschatology in the Synoptic Gospels and in Early Jewish Texts." *New Testament Studies* 34 (1988): 238–49.
Miller, Alice. "Adolf Hitler's Childhood: From Hidden to Manifest Horror." In *For Your Own Good: Hidden Cruelty in Child-rearing and the Roots of Violence*, by Alice Miller, translated by Hildegarde and Hunter Hannum, 142–97. 2nd ed. New York: Farrar, Straus and Giroux, 1984.
Minkowski, Eugène. *Lived Time: Phenomenological and Psychopathological Studies*. Translated by Nancy Metzel. Evanston, IL: Northwestern University Press, 1970.
Moltmann-Wendel, Elisabeth. *Autobiography*. Translated by John Bowden. London: SCM Press, 1997.
Morey, Robert A. *Death and the Afterlife*. Minneapolis, MN: Bethany, 1984.
Mosès, Stéphane. *The Angel of History: Rosenzweig, Benjamin, Scholem*. Translated by Barbara Harshav. Stanford, CA: Stanford University Press, 2009.
Mulhall, Stephen. *Heidegger and* Being and Time. 2nd ed. London: Routledge, 2005.
Muller, Richard A. *Christ and the Decree: Christology and Predestination in Reformed Theology from Calvin to Perkins*. Grand Rapids, MI: Baker, 1988.
———. "Freedom." In *The Westminster Handbook to Reformed Theology*, edited by Donald K. McKim, 87–89. Louisville, KY: Westminster John Knox Press, 2001.
———. *God, Creation, and Providence in the Thought of Jacob Arminius: Sources and Directions of Scholastic Protestantism in the Era of Early Orthodoxy*. Grand Rapids, MI: Baker, 1991.
Neale, David. *None But the Sinners: Religious Categories in Luke*. Journal for the Study of the New Testament Supplement Series 58. Sheffield, UK: Sheffield Academic Press, 1991.
Neville, Robert Cummings. *Eternity and Time's Flow*. Albany, NY: State University of New York Press, 1993.
Newman, Carey C., ed. *Jesus and the Restoration of Israel: A Critical Assessment of N.T. Wright's* Jesus and the Victory of God. Downers Grove, IL: InterVarsity Press, 1999.

Nickelsburg, George W.E. *1 Enoch 1: A Commentary on the Book of 1 Enoch, Chapters 1–36; 81–108*. Hermeneia. Minneapolis, MN: Fortress Press, 2001.

———, and James C. VanderKam, *1 Enoch: A New Translation*. Minneapolis, MN: Fortress Press, 2004.

Niebuhr, H. Richard. *Christ and Culture*. New York: Harper and Row, 1951.

Nietzsche, Friedrich. *On the Genealogy of Morals*. In *Basic Writing of Nietzsche*. Edited and translated by Walter Kaufmann, 437–599. New York: The Modern Library, 2000.

Oden, Thomas C. *The Transforming Power of Grace*. Nashville, TN: Abingdon, 1993.

Olson, Roger E. *Against Calvinism*. Grand Rapids, MI: Zondervan, 2011.

———. *Arminian Theology: Myths and Realities*. Downers Grove, IL: InterVarsity Press, 2006.

Olthuis, James H. "Be(com)ing: Humankind as Gift and Call." *Philosophia Reformata* 58 (1993): 153–72.

———. "Dooyeweerd on Religion and Faith." In *The Legacy of Herman Dooyeweerd: Reflections on Critical Philosophy in the Christian Tradition*, edited by C.T. McIntire, 21–40. Lanham, MD: University Press of America, 1985.

———. "God as True Infinite: Concerns about Pannenberg's *Systematic Theology*, Vol. 1." *Calvin Theological Journal* 27, no. 2 (November, 1992): 318–25.

———. "Models of Humanity in Theology and Psychology." Toronto: Institute for Christian Studies, 1978.

———. "Must the Church Become Secular?" In *Out of Concern for the Church: Five Essays*, by John A. Olthuis et al, 105–25. Toronto: Wedge, 1970.

———. "Testing the Heart of *Khôra*: Anonymous or Amorous?" In *Cross and Khôra: Deconstruction and Christianity in the Work of John D. Caputo*, edited by Marko Zlomislić and Neal DeRoo, 174–86. Eugene, OR: Pickwick, 2011.

———. "The Covenanting Metaphor of the Christian Faith and the Self Psychology of Heinz Kohut." *Studies in Religion/Sciences Religieuses* 18 (1989): 313–24.

———. "The Test of *Khôra*: Grâce à Dieu." In *Religion With/out Religion: The Prayers and Tears of John D. Caputo*, edited by James H. Olthuis, 110–19. London: Routledge, 2002.

———. "Unlike Any Other Hope: The Eschatological Structure of Hope." In *The Logic of Incarnation: James K.A. Smith's Critique of Postmodern Religion*, edited by Neal DeRoo and Brian Lightbody, 182–92. Eugene, OR: Pickwick, 2009.

———, with Donald G. Bloesch, Clark H. Pinnock, and Gerrard T. Sheppard. *A Hermeneutics of Ultimacy: Peril or Promise?* Lanham, MD: University Press of America, 1987.

Packer, James I. "Free Will." In *The Westminster Handbook to Reformed Theology*, edited by Donald K. McKim, 86–87. Louisville, KY: Westminster John Knox Press, 2001.

———. "Introductory Essay." In *The Death of Death in the Death of Christ*, by John Owen, 1–25. 1648. Reprint, Edinburgh: The Banner of Truth Trust, 1959.

Pannenberg, Wolfhart. "Appearance as the Arrival of the Future." In *New Theology No. 5*, edited by Martin E. Marty and Dean G. Peerman, 112–29. New York: Macmillan, 1968.

———. *Systematic Theology*. Vol. 3. Translated by Geoffrey Bromiley. Grand Rapids, MI: Eerdmans; Edinburgh: T. and T. Clark, 1998.

Parry, Robin A., and Christopher H. Partridge, eds. *Universal Salvation? The Current Debate*. Carlisle, UK: Paternoster, 2003.

Pattison, George. *The Later Heidegger*. London: Routledge, 2000.

Picht, Georg. "The God of the Philosophers." *Journal of the American Academy of Religion* 48, no. 1 (1980): 61–79.
Pieters, Albertus. *Studies in the Revelation of St. John*. Grand Rapids, MI: Eerdmans, 1954.
Pinnock, Clark H., ed. *Grace Unlimited*. Minneapolis, MN: Bethany, 1975.
———, ed. *The Grace of God and the Will of Man*. 1989. Reprint, Minneapolis, MN: Bethany, 1995.
——— et al. *The Openness of God: A Biblical Challenge to the Traditional Understanding of God*. Downers Grove, IL: InterVarsity Press, 1994.
Piper, John, Justin Taylor, and Paul Kjoss Helseth, eds. *Beyond the Bounds: Open Theism and the Undermining of Biblical Christianity*. Wheaton, IL: Crossway, 2003.
Polt, Richard. "Being and Time." In *Martin Heidegger: Key Concepts*, edited by Bret W. Davis, 69–81. Durham, UK: Acumen, 2010.
Powys, David J. *'Hell': A Hard Look at a Hard Question; The Fate of the Unrighteous in New Testament Thought*. Paternoster Biblical and Theological Monographs. Carlisle, UK: Paternoster, 1998.
Prior, A.N. *Past, Present and Future*. Oxford: Oxford University Press, 1967.
———. *Time and Modality*. Oxford: Clarendon Press, 1957.
Punt, Neal. *Unconditional Good News: Towards an Understanding of Biblical Universalism*. Grand Rapids, MI: Eerdmans, 1980.
Rahner, Karl. "The Hermeneutics of Eschatological Assertions." In *More Recent Writings*. Vol. 4 of *Theological Investigations*, by Karl Rahner. Translated by Kevin Smyth, 323–46. Baltimore, MD: Helicon Press; London: Darton, Longman and Todd, 1966.
Rand, Richard, ed. *Futures of Jacques Derrida*. Stanford, CA: Stanford University Press, 2001.
Reeves, Marjorie. *Joachim of Fiore and the Prophetic Future: A Medieval Study in Historical Thinking*. Rev. ed. Stroud, UK: Sutton, 1999.
Reicke, Bo. "Gehenna." In *The Oxford Companion to the Bible*, edited by Bruce M. Metzger and Michael D. Coogan, 243. Oxford: Oxford University Press, 1993.
Reiser, Marius. *Jesus and Judgment: The Eschatological Proclamation in Its Jewish Context*. Minneapolis, MN: Fortress Press, 1997.
Ricoeur, Paul. *Time and Narrative*. 3 vols. Translated by Kathleen Mclaughlin/Blamey and David Pellauer. Chicago and London: The University of Chicago Press, 1984–88.
Ridderbos, Herman. *The Gospel of John: A Theological Commentary*. Translated by John Vriend. Grand Rapids, MI: Eerdmans, 1997.
Robinson, John A.T. *In the End, God: A Study of the Christian Doctrine of the Last Things*. 2nd ed. London: Fontana, 1968.
———. *In the End, God . . . : A Study of the Christian Doctrine of the Last Things*, edited by Robin Parry, with an Introduction by Trevor Hart. Eugene, OR: Cascade, 2011.
———. *Redating the New Testament*. London: SCM Press, 1976.
Rose, Gillian. "Walter Benjamin—Out of the Sources of Modern Judaism." In *The Actuality of Walter Benjamin*, edited by Laura Marcus and Lynda Nead, 85–117. London: Lawrence and Wishart, 1998.
Rosenzweig, Franz. *The Star of Redemption*. Translated by William W. Hallo. Notre Dame, IN: Notre Dame Press, 1985.
Rowell, Geoffrey. *Hell and the Victorians: A Study of the Nineteenth Century Theological Controversies Concerning Eternal Punishment and the Future Life*. Oxford: Clarendon Press, 1974.

Rowland, Christopher. *Revelation*. London: Epworth, 1993.
———. *The Open Heaven: A Study of Apocalyptic in Judaism and Early Christianity*. London: SPCK, 1982.
Ruether, Rosemary Radford. *Gaia and God: An Ecofeminist Theology of Earth Healing*. San Francisco: HarperCollins, 1992.
Russell, D.S. *Divine Disclosure: An Introduction to Jewish Apocalyptic*. London: SCM Press, 1992.
Russell, J. Stuart. *The Parousia: The New Testament Doctrine of Our Lord's Second Coming*. 1887. Reprint, Grand Rapids, MI: Baker, 1999.
Sanders, John A. "Historical Considerations." In *The Openness of God: A Biblical Challenge to the Traditional Understanding of God*, by Clark Pinnock et al, 59–100. Downers Grove, IL: InterVarsity Press, 1994.
———. *No Other Name: An Investigation into the Destiny of the Unevangelized*. Grand Rapids, MI: Eerdmans, 1992.
Sarnu, Nahum M. *Genesis*. JPS Torah Commentary. Philadelphia: Jewish Publication Society, 1991.
Sartre, John-Paul. *Being and Nothingness: A Phenomenological Essay on Ontology*. Translated by Hazel E. Barnes. 1957. Reprint, New York: Washington Square Press, 1992.
Sauter, Gerhard. "The Concept and Task of Eschatology—Theological and Philosophical Reflections," *Scottish Journal of Theology* 41, no. 4 (1988): 499–515.
———. "Why Is Karl Barth's Church Dogmatics Not a 'Theology of Hope'? Some Observations on Barth's Understanding of Eschatology." *Scottish Journal of Theology* 52, no. 4 (1999): 407–29.
Sayers, Dorothy L. *Introductory Papers on Dante*. New York: Harper and Brothers, 1954.
Schleiermacher, Friedrich. *The Christian Faith*. Edited by H.R. Mackintosh and J.S. Stewart. Edinburgh: T. and T. Clark, 1928.
Schmitt, Keith Randall. *Death and After-Life in the Theologies of Karl Barth and John Hick: A Comparative Study*. Amsterdam: Rodopi, 1985.
Scholem, Gershom. *Alchemy and Kabbalah*. Translated by Klaus Ottmann. Putnam, CT: Spring, 2006.
———. *Kabbalah*. New York: Times, 1974.
———. *Major Trends in Jewish Mysticism*. 3rd rev. ed. New York: Schocken, 1961.
Seerveld, Calvin G. "Biblical Wisdom underneath Vollenhoven's Categories for Philosophical Historiography." In *The Idea of a Christian Philosophy: Essays in Honour of D.H.Th. Vollenhoven*, edited by K.A. Bril, H. Hart, and J. Klapwijk, 127–43. Special issue, *Philosophia Reformata* 38. Toronto: Wedge, 1973.
———. "Dooyeweerd's Legacy for Aesthetics." In *The Legacy of Herman Dooyeweerd: Reflections on Critical Philosophy in the Christian Tradition*, edited by C.T. McIntire, 41–79. Lanham, MD: University Press of America, 1985.
———. "The Pedagogical Strength of a Christian Methodology in Philosophical Historiography." In *Social Theory and Practice: Philosophical Essays in Honour of Prof. J.A.L. Taljaard*, edited by H. Conradie et al. Special issue, *Koers* 40, nos. 4–6 (1975): 269–313.
Segal, Alan. *Paul the Convert: The Apostolate and Apostasy of Saul the Pharisee*. New Haven, CT: Yale University Press, 1990.
Sherover, Charles M. *The Human Experience of Time: The Development of its Philosophic Meaning*. New York: New York University Press, 1975.
Smalley, Stephen S. *The Revelation to John: A Commentary on the Greek Text of the Apocalypse*. Downers Gove, IL: InterVarsity Press, 2005.

———. *Thunder and Love: John's Revelation and John's Community*. Milton Keynes, UK: Nelson Word, 1994.
Smith, James K.A. "Continuing the Conversation." In *The Logic of Incarnation: James K.A. Smith's Critique of Postmodern Religion*, edited by Neal DeRoo and Brian Lightbody, 203–22. Eugene, OR: Pickwick, 2009.
———. "Determined Hope: A Phenomenology of Christian Expectation." In *The Future as God's Gift: Explorations in Christian Eschatology*, edited by David Fergusson and Marcel Sarot, 200–27. Edinburgh: T. and T. Clark, 2000.
———. *Speech and Theology: Language and the Logic of Incarnation*. London: Routledge, 2002.
Smith, Quentin, and L. Nathan Oaklander. *Time, Change and Freedom: An Introduction to Metaphysics*. London: Routledge, 1995.
Smith, Wilfred Cantwell. *Faith and Belief*. Princeton, NJ: Princeton University Press, 1979.
Spencer, Richard A. "Hinnom, Valley of." In *Eerdmans Dictionary of the Bible*, edited by David Noel Freedman, Allen C. Myers, and Astrid B. Beck, 592. Grand Rapids, MI: Eerdmans, 2000.
"St. Peter's Apocalypse." In *Visions of Heaven and Hell before Dante*, edited by Eileen Gardiner, 1–12. New York: Italica Press, 1989.
Steen, Peter J. *The Structure of Herman Dooyeweerd's Thought*. Toronto: Wedge, 1983.
Stinson, Charles. "On the Time and Eternity 'Link'." *Religious Studies* 13 (March 1977): 49–62.
Stone, Michael Edward. *4 Ezra: A Commentary on the Book of Fourth Ezra*. Hermeneia. Minneapolis, MN: Fortress Press, 1990.
Talbott, Thomas. "The New Testament and Universal Reconciliation." *Christian Scholar's Review* 21, no. 4 (June 1992): 376–94.
Terry, Milton S. *Biblical Apocalyptics: A Study of the Most Notable Revelations of God and of Christ*. 1898. Reprint, Grand Rapids, MI: Baker, 1988.
The Mystery of Salvation: The Story of God's Gift; A Report by the Doctrine Commission of the General Synod of the Church of England. London: Church House, 1995.
Thiselton, Anthony C. *The First Epistle to the Corinthians*. The Greek Testament Commentary. Grand Rapids, MI: Eerdmans, 2000.
Tillich, Paul. *Dynamics of Faith*. New York: Harper and Row, 1957.
Tollefson, Terry Ray. "Paul Tillich: His Anthropology as Key to the Structure of his Thought." MPhil thesis, Institute for Christian Studies, Toronto, 1977.
Travis, Stephen H. *Christian Hope and the Future of Man*. Leicester, UK: Inter-Varsity Press, 1980.
Turetzky, Philip. *Time*. London: Routledge, 1998.
Turner, Alice K. *The History of Hell*. New York: Harcourt Brace, 1993.
Tutu, Desmond. *No Future without Forgiveness*. London: Rider, 1999.
Updike, John. *Towards the End of Time*. 1997. Reprint, New York: Balantine, 1998.
Valk, John. "The Concept of *Coincidentia Oppositorum* in the Thought of Mircea Eliade." MPhil thesis, Institute for Christian Studies, Toronto, 1979.
———. "The Concept of *Coincidentia Oppositorum* in the Thought of Mircea Eliade." In *Mircea Eliade: A Critical Reader*, edited by Bryan Rennie, 176–85. London: Equinox, 2006.
Van der Hoeven, Johan. "Matters of Mission and Transmission: On the Progress of Ecumenical-Reformational Thought." *Philosophia Reformata* 52 (1987): 182–207.
Vander Goot, Henry, ed. *Life Is Religion: Essays in Honor of H. Evan Runner*. St. Catherines, ON. Paideia Press, 1981.

Vanderwaal, Cornelis. *Hal Lindsey and Biblical Prophecy*. Translated by Theodore Plantinga. St. Catherines, ON: Paideia Press, 1978.
Vanhoozer, Kevin J. "Effectual Call or Causal Effect? Summons, Sovereignty and Supervenient Grace." In *First Theology: God, Scripture and Hermeneutics*, by Kevin J. Vanhoozer, 96–124. Downers Grove, IL: InterVarsity Press; Leicester, UK: Apollos, 2002.
———. "Effectual Call or Causal Effect? Summons, Sovereignty and Supervenient Grace." *Tyndale Bulletin* 49, no. 2 (1998): 215–51.
Vedder, Ben. "Ontotheology and the Question of God(s)." In *Martin Heidegger: Key Concepts*, edited by Bret W. Davis, 219–30. Durham, UK: Acumen, 2010.
Veenhof, Jan. "Nature and Grace in Bavinck." Translated by Al Wolters. *Pro Rege* 34, no. 4 (June 2006): 11–31.
———. *Nature and Grace in Herman Bavinck*. Translated by Albert M. Wolters. Sioux Centre, IA: Dordt College Press, 2006.
———. *Revelatie en Inspiratie: De Openbarings en Schriftbeschouwing van Herman Bavinck in vergelijking met die der ethische theologie*. Amsterdam: Buijten en Schipperheijn, 1968.
Vogels, Walter. *God's Universal Covenant: A Biblical Study*. Ottawa: University of Ottawa Press, 1986.
Volf, Miroslav. *Exclusion and Embrace: A Theological Exploration of Identity, Otherness, and Reconciliation*. Nashville, TN: Abingdon, 1996.
———. "The Final Reconciliation: Reflections on a Social Dimension of the Eschatological Transition." *Modern Theology* 16, no. 1 (January, 2000): 91–113
Vollenhoven, D.H.Th. "De Consequent Probleemhistorische Methode." *Philosophia Reformata* 26 (1961): 1–34.
———. *The Problem-Historical Method and the History of Philosophy*. Edited by Kornelis A. Bril. Translated by John de Kievit et al. Amstelveen: De Zaak Haes, 2005.
Von Wyrick, Stephen. "Gehenna." In *Eerdmans Dictionary of the Bible*, edited by David Noel Freedman, Allen C. Myers, and Astrid B. Beck, 489. Grand Rapids, MI: Eerdmans, 2000.
Vos, Louis A. *The Synoptic Traditions in the Apocalypse*. Kampen: J.H. Kok, 1965.
Vroom, Hendrik. "From Antithesis to Encounter and Dialogue: Changes in Reformational Epistemology." In *Philosophy as Responsibility: A Celebration of Hendrik Hart's Contribution to the Discipline*, edited by Ronald A. Kuipers and Janet Catherina Wesselius, 27–41. Lanham, MD: University Press of America, 2002.
Wainwright, Arthur W. *Mysterious Apocalypse: Interpreting the Book of Revelation*. Nashville, TN: Abingdon, 1993.
Walker, D.P. *The Decline of Hell: Seventeenth-Century Discussions of Eternal Torment*. London: Routledge and Kegan Paul, 1964.
Wallace, Dewey D., Jr. "Predestination." In *The Westminster Handbook to Reformed Theology*, edited by Donald K. McKim, 180–82. Louisville, KY: Westminster John Knox Press, 2001.
Walls, Jerry L. *Hell: The Logic of Damnation*. Notre Dame, IN: University of Notre Dame Press, 1992.
Walsh, Brian J. "A Critical Review of Pannenberg's *Anthropology in Theological Perspective*." *Christian Scholar's Review* 15, no. 3 (1986): 247–59.
———. "Futurity and Creation: Explorations in the Eschatological Theology of Wolfhart Pannenberg." MPhil thesis, Institute for Christian Studies, Toronto, 1979.

———. "Pannenberg's Eschatological Ontology." *Christian Scholar's Review* 11, no. 3 (1982): 229–49.

———. *Who Turned Out the Lights? The Light of the Gospel in a Post-Enlightenment Culture: An Inaugural Lecture*. Toronto: Institute for Christian Studies, 1989.

Watson, Philip S. *The Concept of Grace: Essays on the Way of Divine Love in Human Life*. London: Epworth, 1959.

Watts, John D.W. *Isaiah 34–66*, Word Biblical Commentary 25. Rev. ed. Nashville, TN: Thomas Nelson, 2005.

Webb, Stephen H. *The Gifting God: A Trinitarian Ethics of Excess*. Oxford: Oxford University Press, 1996.

Webster, John. *Barth's Moral Theology: Human Action in Barth's Thought*. Edinburgh: T. and T. Clark, 1998.

———. "Introducing Barth." In *The Cambridge Companion to Karl Barth*, edited by John Webster, 1–16. Cambridge: Cambridge University Press, 2000.

———, ed. *The Cambridge Companion to Karl Barth*. Cambridge: Cambridge University Press, 2000.

Wenham, John W. "The Case for Conditional Immortality." In *Universalism and the Doctrine of Hell: Papers Presented at the Fourth Edinburgh Conference in Christian Dogmatics*, edited by Nigel M. de S. Cameron, 161–91. Carlisle, UK: Paternoster; Grand Rapids, MI: Baker, 1992.

Westphal, Merold. "The God Who Will Be: Hermeneutics and the God of Promise." *Faith and Philosophy* 20, no. 3 (July, 2003): 328–44.

Whitrow, G.J. *The Natural Philosophy of Time*. 2nd ed. Oxford: Clarendon Press, 1980.

———. *Time in History: Views of Time from Prehistory to the Present Day*. Oxford: Oxford University Press, 1989.

Wolff, Hans Walter. *Anthropology of the Old Testament*. Translated by Margaret Kohl. London: SCM Press, 1974.

Wolters, Albert M. "Christianity and the Classics: A Typology of Attitudes." In *Christianity and the Classics: The Acceptance of a Heritage*, edited by Wendy E. Helleman, 189–203. Lanham, MD: University Press of America, 1990.

———. "Glossary." In *Contours of a Christian Philosophy: An Introduction to Herman Dooyeweerd's Thought*. A Supplement to the Collected Works of Herman Dooyeweerd. Series C, Vol. 2, by L. Kalsbeek, edited by Bernard and Josina Zylstra, 307–15. 1975. Reprint, Lewiston, NY: The Edwin Mellen Press, 2002.

———. "Glossary." In *The Legacy of Herman Dooyeweerd: Reflections on Critical Philosophy in the Christian Tradition*, edited by C.T. McIntire, 167–71. Lanham, MD: University Press of America, 1985.

———. "Nature and Grace in the Interpretation of Proverbs 31:10-31." *Calvin Theological Journal* 19 (1984): 153–66.

———. "Nature and Grace in the Interpretation of Proverbs 31:10-31." In *The Song of the Valiant Woman: Studies in the Interpretation of Proverbs 31:10-31*, by Albert M. Wolters, 15–29. Carlisle, UK: Paternoster, 2001.

———. "On Vollenhoven's Problem-Historical Method." In *Hearing and Doing: Philosophical Essays Dedicated to H. Evan Runner*, edited by John Kraay and Anthony Tol, 231–62. Toronto: Wedge, 1979.

———. "'Partners of the Deity': A Covenantal Reading of 2 Peter 1:4." *Calvin Theological Journal* 25 (April 1990): 28–44.

———. "The Foundational Command." In *Year of Jubilee, Cultural Mandate, Worldview*, edited by B. van der Walt, 27–34. Study Pamphlet 382. Potchefstroom: Institute for Reformational Studies, 1999.

———. "The Intellectual Milieu of Herman Dooyeweerd." In *The Legacy of Herman Dooyeweerd: Reflections on Critical Philosophy in the Christian Tradition*, edited by C.T. McIntire, 1–19. Lanham, MD: University Press of America, 1985.

———. Translator's preface to "Nature and Grace in Bavinck," by Jan Veenhof, translated by Al Wolters. *Pro Rege* 34, no. 4 (June 2006): 11.

———. Translator's preface to *Nature and Grace in Herman Bavinck*, by Jan Veenhof, translated by Albert M. Wolters, 1–2. Sioux Centre, IA: Dordt College Press, 2006.

Wood, David. *The Deconstruction of Time*. 1989. Reprint, Evanston, IL: Northwestern University Press, 2001.

Wright, N.T. "Christ, the Law and the People of God." In *The Climax of the Covenant: Christ and the Law in Pauline Theology*, by N.T. Wright, 231–57. Edinburgh: T. and T. Clark, 1991.

———. "In Grateful Dialogue: A Response." In *Jesus and the Restoration of Israel: A Critical Assessment of N.T. Wright's* Jesus and the Victory of God, edited by Carey C. Newman, 244–278. Downers Grove, IL: InterVarsity Press, 1999.

———. "Jerusalem in the New Testament." In *Jerusalem Past and Present in the Purposes of God*, edited by P.W.L. Walker, 53–77. 2nd ed. Carlisle, UK: Paternoster; Grand Rapids, MI: Baker, 1994.

———. *Jesus and the Victory of God*. Vol. 2 of *Christian Origins and the Question of God*. London: SPCK; Minneapolis, MN: Fortress Press, 1996.

———. *New Heavens, New Earth: The Biblical Picture of Christian Hope*. Cambridge, UK: Grove, 1999.

———. *Revelation for Everyone*. London: SPCK, 2011.

———. *Surprised by Hope: Rethinking Heaven, the Resurrection, and the Mission of the Church*. New York: HarperOne, 2008.

———. *The Epistles of Paul to the Colossians and to Philemon: An Introduction and Commentary*. Tyndale New Testament Commentaries. Leicester, UK: Inter-Varsity Press, 1986.

———. "The Future of Jesus." In *The Meaning of Jesus: Two Visions*, by N.T. Wright and Marcus Borg, 197–204. London: SPCK; New York: HarperCollins, 1999.

———. *The New Testament and the People of God*. Vol. 1 of *Christian Origins and the Question of God*. London: SPCK; Philadelphia: Fortress Press, 1992.

———. *The Resurrection of the Son of God*. Vol. 3 of *Christian Origins and the Question of God*. London: SPCK; Minneapolis, MN: Fortress Press, 2003.

———. "Towards a Biblical View of Universalism." *Themelios* 4, no. 2 (January 1979): 54–58.

Yarnold, E.J. "Grace." In *A New Dictionary of Christian Theology*, edited by Alan Richardson and John Bowden, 244–55. London: SCM Press, 1983.

Zuidema, S.U. "Common Grace and Christian Action in Abraham Kuyper." Translated by Harry Van Dyke. In *Communication and Confrontation: A Philosophical Appraisal and Critique of Modern Society and Contemporary Thought*, by S.U. Zuidema, 52–105. Assen: VanGorcum; Kampen: J.H. Kok, 1972.

———. "The Structure of Karl Barth's Doctrine of Creation." Translated by Art Helleman. In *Communication and Confrontation: A Philosophical Appraisal and Critique of Modern Society and Contemporary Thought*, by S.U. Zuidema, 309–28. Assen: VanGorcum; Kampen: J.H. Kok, 1972.

Author Index

Achtner, Wolfgang. 214.
Alfeyev, Hilarion. 40.
Allen, Leslie C. 357.
Almond, Philip C. 23.
Amis, Martin. 68.
Anderson, Bernhard W. 372.
Ansell, Nicholas. 24, 25, 88, 171, 194, 228, 229, 231, 246, 253, 255, 258, 267, 268, 269, 271, 306, 313, 354, 355, 356, 370, 371, 391, 394, 416.
Appler, Deborah A. 420.
Augustine. 22, 52, 59–64, 105, 109, 111, 124, 167, 173, 266, 299, 301, 338, 367.
Aune, David E. 393. 396, 400, 401, 404, 407.
Bauckham, Richard. 15, 17, 18, 19, 20, 22, 23, 51, 52, 56, 66, 68, 101, 134, 135, 169, 186,187, 189, 200, 216, 260, 261, 309, 312, 315, 317, 318, 326, 327, 367, 371, 373, 374, 375, 394, 406, 421.
Bailey, Lloyd R. 322–23, 332–35.
Balabanski, Vicky. 328.
Balthasar, Hans Urs von. 39.
Barker, Margaret. 260, 393.
Barrett, William. 222–23.
Barth, Karl. 3, 6, 37, 42, 76, 94, 136, 145, 147, 149, 150, 155, 160, 169, 182, 253, 264, 272–82, 294, 305, 309, 310, 347, 349, 363, 364, 369, 371, 380, 427.
Bavinck, Herman. 8, 250, 267.
Beagley, Alan James. 393, 398, 400, 412.
Beale, G.K. 260, 392, 394, 396, 397, 400, 403, 406, 409, 413, 415, 417, 418, 419.
Beasley-Murray, G.R. 396, 409.
Beck, T. David. 40.
Bell, Rob. 24.
Benjamin, Andrew. 214.
Benjamin, Walter. 55–57, 214, 215, 253.
Berkhof, Hendrikus. 77, 179, 249.
Berkouwer, G.C. 145, 160, 174, 208, 278, 371, 373.
Bernstein, Alan E. 328, 333.

Billings, David. 286, 287.
Bloch, Ernst. 65, 70, 76, 78, 114, 118, 120, 128, 134, 138, 185, 213–19, 223, 227, 383, 387.
Boettner, Loraine. 177, 178, 179.
Boff, Leonardo. 155, 173, 174, 265.
Bonda, Jan. 179.
Bonzo, J. Matthew. 11.
Borg, Marcus J. 328.
Boring, M. Eugene. 389.
Bouma-Prediger, Steven. 11, 93, 94, 248.
Boyd, Gregory A. 173, 377.
Briggs, Richard S. 419.
Bril, Kornelis A. 9.
Bruce, F.F. 17, 21.
Brueggemann, Walter. 269, 273, 366.
Brunner, Emil. 6, 78, 155, 247, 272–82, 286, 294, 309, 310, 427.
Buchholz, Dennis D. 17, 19, 51, 52.
Bultmann, Rudolf. 136, 249, 271.
Bush, George. 2, 3.
Buxton, Graham. 103.
Caird, G.B. 2, 3, 328.
Calvin, John. 30, 31, 36, 37, 177, 179, 275, 359, 369.
Capps, Walter H. 215, 218, 227.
Caputo, John D. 149, 214, 304, 384.
Chanter, Tina. 214, 220, 222, 227.
Charlesworth, James H. 337.
Chester, Tim. 40.
Childs, Brevard S. 403.
Christensen, Duane L. 410.
Clouser, Roy A. 369.
Collins, David. 332.
Collins, John J. 336, 337, 394.
Conradie, Ernst M. 267, 373.
Constas, Nicholas. 40.
Conyers, A.J. 189, 200.
Cooper, John W. 261.
Corsini, Eugenio. 393, 396.
Cox, Harvey. 215, 217–19, 227.
Crockett, William. 22, 25.
Cromartie, Michael. 154.
Dainton, Barry. 213.
Dante. 1, 2, 4, 16, 21, 32, 425.
Davis, Bret W. 227.
Deane-Drummond, Celia. 148, 283.

De Boer, Martinus C. 394.
Dembski, William A. 234.
Derrida, Jacques. 149, 214, 220.
Deursen, Arie Theodorus van. 8.
Dixon, Larry. 30.
Dodds, E.R. 338.
Dooyeweerd, Herman. 8, 9, 157, 229–233, 238, 241–44, 279, 312, 369.
Dreyfus, Hubert L. 220, 221, 304.
Dudiak, Jeffrey. 149.
Duffy, Stephen J. 155.
Edwards, David L. 24.
Edwards, Jonathan. 21, 22, 346.
Eddy, Paul R. 377.
Eliade, Mircea. 169, 186.
Ellis, E. Earle. 25, 392, 406.
Ellul, Jacques. 314.
Erikson, Erik. 239.
Farrar, Frederic W. 7, 23, 338–39.
Farrer, Austin. 398, 399, 407, 415.
Fekkes, Jan. 403, 415, 418.
Fiddes, Paul S. 146, 147, 167, 177, 178, 179, 190, 196, 203.
Fletcher-Louis, Crispin H.T. 260, 329, 401.
Fokkelman, J.P. 314.
Ford, J. Massyngberde. 393, 400, 404, 418.
Fox, Matthew. 278.
Frame, John M. 181.
Fraser, J.T. 213.
Fretheim, Terence E. 268, 369, 370, 379.
Fudge, Edward William. 25.
Fuller, Steve. 234.
Gadamer, Hans-Georg. 169.
Gale, Richard M. 213.
Gallagher, Joseph. 16.
Ganssle, Gregory E. 213.
Gardiner, Eileen. 16, 17, 18, 21.
Geertsema, H.G. 64, 382.
Gell, Alfred. 213.
Gentry, Kenneth L. 406, 407.
Gerstner, John H. 21, 22.
Gilbertson, Michael. 392.
Gilkey, Langdon. 305.
Goldingay, John E. 336, 337.
Gorner, Paul. 221, 224.
Gorringe, Timothy. 53.
Gray, Tony. 25.
Green, Clifford. 277, 280, 310.

Griffin, David R. 372.
Gundry-Volf, Judith M. 389.
Guttesen, Poul F. 392.
Gunn, J. Alexander. 213.
Hagner, Donald A. 397.
Hall, Christopher A. 176.
Hall, Lindsay. 203, 208.
Hanson, P.D. 326, 328.
Harland, Phillip A. 397.
Harmon, Kendall S. 25.
Harris, Errol E. 213.
Hart, Hendrik. 6, 228–44, 250, 257, 342, 380, 386, 390, 427.
Hart, Trevor. 15, 41, 48, 273, 309.
Harvey, Van A. 155, 173, 180, 297.
Hasker, William. 213.
Hayes, Zachary J. 155, 173.
Head, Peter M. 25.
Hegel, G.W.F. 94, 167, 168, 169, 171, 187, 204, 224, 253, 300.
Heidegger, Martin. 77, 206, 214, 218–27, 230, 273, 303, 304.
Hick, John. 178, 182.
Hickman, Louise. 367.
Hielema, Syd. 250, 267.
Highfield, Ron. 166, 203, 204.
Hilborn, David. 7, 26.
Hill, William J. 169, 187.
Himmelfarb, Martha. 328.
Hodgson, Peter C. 302, 305.
Hoffmeyer, John F. 169, 224.
Holtrop, Philip C. 181.
Horton, Michael S. 173–4, 177, 370.
Humphrey, Edith McEwan. 393–94.
Inwood, Michael. 220, 222, 226.
Irish, Jerry A. 309.
Irwin, Brian P. 322.
Jansen, Henry. 351.
Jeremias, Joachim. 318.
Jersak, Bradley. 7, 416.
Jewett, Paul K. 42, 173, 174, 178, 182.
Johnson, Elizabeth A. 153.
Johnson, Luke Timothy. 260.
Jones, L. Gregory. 53.
Josephus. 332, 406
Kalsbeek, L. 229, 233.
Kearney, Richard. 306.
Kearsley, R. 264.
Keesmaat, Sylvia. 332.
Kehl, Medard. 134.
Keller, Catherine. 270, 311.

Kern, Stephen. 213.
Kierkegaard, Søren. 70, 75, 105, 136, 142, 221, 276, 304.
Kirk-Duggan, Cheryl A. 335.
Klapwijk, Jacob. 154.
Klempa, William. 181.
Knowles, Michael. 324.
Knusden, Robert D. 8, 9.
Kunz, Stefan. 214.
Kuyper, Abraham. 154, 211, 248–49, 250, 267, 304.
Kvanvig, Jonathan L. 30.
Lacy, Larry. 389.
Lake, Donald M. 176.
Lawrence, David. 268.
Le Poidevin, Robin. 213.
Levenson, Jon D. 372.
Lewis, Scott M. 389.
Lieb, Irwin C. 213.
Lohfink, Norman. 314.
Longnecker, Bruce W. 335.
Lønning, Per. 273.
Louw, Daniel Johannes. 223.
Lovejoy, Arthur O. 300.
Lucas, J.R. 213.
Lunde, J. 335.
Lupieri, Edmondo F. 393, 397, 405, 407.
MacBeth, Murray. 213.
MacDonald, Gregory. 7.
Mackey, James P. 187, 374.
Macquarrie, John. 224, 225, 385.
Malina, Bruce J. 393.
Marsden, John. 303–305.
Marshall, Christopher D. 53.
Marshall, I. Howard. 176, 389.
Marshall, John W. 392, 416.
McCormack, Bruce. 280.
McCready, Stuart. 213.
McCumber, John. 220, 225, 226.
McDonough, Sean M. 392, 394, 396, 397, 400, 403, 406, 409, 413, 415, 417, 418, 419.
McDougall, Joy Ann. 16.
McFague, Sallie. 370.
McIlroy, David H. 386.
McInerney, Peter K. 213.
McIntire, C.T. 230, 242.
Mealy, J. Webb. 414.
Meeks, M. Douglas. 169, 216–18, 244.
Mellor, D.H. 213.

Mendels, Doron. 335.
Miethe, Terry L. 176.
Miguez Bonino, José. 306.
Milikowsky, Chaim. 337.
Miller, Alice. 266.
Minkowski, Eugène. 214, 225.
Moltmann, Jürgen. xiii–xiv, 1–9, 11–16, 19–20, 26–50, 53, 54–99, 100–44, 145–55, 157–72, 177–209, 210–19, 222–30, 236, 237, 239, 240, 241, 244–58, 261, 262–63, 266, 268, 272, 273, 280, 281, 282–312, 314, 315–17, 320–21, 339–46, 348–54, 360–390, 391, 392, 394, 408, 413, 420–22, 424–28.
Moltmann-Wendel, Elisabeth. 152.
Morey, Robert A. 23, 24.
Morse, Christopher. 225, 287.
Mosès, Stéphane. 56.
Mulhall, Stephen. 226, 227, 304.
Muller, Richard A. 42, 174.
Müller-Fahrenholz, Geiko. 76, 216.
Neal, Ryan A. 386.
Neale, David. 362.
Neville, Robert Cummings. 213.
Nickelsburg, George W.E. 335, 336, 337.
Niebuhr, H. Richard. 156, 305.
Nietzsche, Friedrich. 22.
Oaklander, L. Nathan. 213.
Oden, Thomas C. 155, 172, 173, 176.
O'Donnell, John J. 92.
Olson, Roger E. 174.
Olthuis, James H. 9–12, 59, 106, 149, 156, 157, 238, 241, 243, 250, 279, 306, 390.
O'Malley, Steven. 363.
Otto, Randall E. 8–9.
Packer, James I. 42, 175, 177, 195.
Pannenberg, Wolfhart. 11, 37, 204, 216.
Parry, Robin A. 7.
Partridge, Christopher H. 7.
Pattison, George. 226.
Peterson, Robert A. 25.
Picht, Georg. 225.
Pieters, Albertus. 405.
Pinnock, Clark H. 174, 176.
Plathow, Michael. 101.
Polkinghorne, John. 131.
Polt, Richard. 220.
Powys, David J. 25.

Prior, A.N. 224.
Primavesi, Anne V. 169.
Prooijen, Ton van. 359.
Punt, Neal. 175, 179.
Rahner, Karl. 326.
Rand, Richard. 214.
Reeves, Marjorie. 214.
Reicke, Bo. 322.
Reiser, Marius. 336.
Ricoeur, Paul. 213–14.
Ridderbos, Herman. 385.
Robinson, John A.T. 41, 178, 337, 392–93.
Rose, Gillian. 57.
Rosenzweig, Franz. 56, 92, 138, 214, 215.
Rowell, Geoffrey. 23, 27, 338, 339, 386.
Rowland, Christopher. 392.
Ruether, Rosemary Radford. 88, 255, 270.
Russell, D.S. 335.
Russell, J. Stuart. 405.
Sanders, John A. 174, 175, 176, 204.
Sarnu, Nahum M. 357.
Sartre, John-Paul. 226–27.
Sauter, Gerhard. 3, 305, 364.
Sayers, Dorothy L. 16.
Schleiermacher, Friedrich. 23, 24, 36, 367.
Schmitt, Keith Randall. 282.
Scholem, Gershom. 56, 148, 150, 185–86, 214.
Schuurman, Douglas J. 246.
Seerveld, Calvin G. 9, 58–59, 169, 232.
Segal, Alan. 335.
Sherover, Charles M. 214, 222, 224, 225.
Smalley, Stephen S. 260, 392.
Smith, James K.A. 211, 250.
Smith, Quentin. 213.
Smith, Wilfred Cantwell. 211.
Spencer, Richard A. 322.
Steen, Peter J. 241.
Stone, Michael Edward. 336.
Stott, John. 24–25.
Surin, Kenneth. 374.
Talbott, Thomas. 389.
Tang, Siu-Kwong. 69.
Terry, Milton S. 403, 405.

Thiselton, Anthony C. 389.
Tillich, Paul. 11, 58, 239.
Tollefson, Terry Ray. 11.
Torrance, Alan J. 69.
Travis, Stephen H. 48, 325–27.
Turetzky, Philip. 213, 214.
Turner, Alice K. 52.
Tutu, Desmond. 53.
Updike, John. 234.
Valk, John. 169, 186.
Van den Brom, Luco J. 131–32.
Van der Hoeven, Johan. 243.
VanderKam, James C. 336.
Vanderwaal, Cornelis. 419–20.
Vanhoozer, Kevin J. 297.
Vedder, Ben. 227.
Veenhof, Jan. 8, 179, 267.
Vogels, Walter. 180, 362.
Volf, Miroslav. 6, 22, 277, 311, 316, 346–50, 427.
Vollenhoven, D.H.Th. 8–12, 59, 123.
Von Wyrick, Stephen. 322, 323.
Vos, Louis A. 399, 411.
Vroom, Hendrik. 211.
Wainwright, Arthur W. 393.
Walker, D.P. 7, 22, 23, 315, 338, 367.
Wallace, Dewey D., Jr. 181.
Walls, Jerry L. 30.
Walsh, Brian J. 11, 13, 123, 248, 267, 304, 316, 354, 372.
Walter, Thomas. 214.
Watson, Philip S. 155.
Watts, John D.W. 408.
Webb, Stephen H. 384.
Webster, John. 277.
Wenham, John W. 25.
Westphal, Merold. 306.
Whitrow, G.J. 213.
Williams, Stephen N. 180.
Witvliet, Theo. 306.
Wolff, Hans Walter. 246.
Wolters, Albert M. 8, 89, 156, 230, 233, 243, 246, 267.
Wood, David. 214.
Wright, N.T. 6, 27, 268, 315, 327–33, 336, 338, 364, 389, 391, 392, 393, 396, 402, 412, 427.
Yarnold, E.J. 155.
Zuidema, S.U.149, 154.

www.ingramcontent.com/pod-product-compliance
Lightning Source LLC
Chambersburg PA
CBHW021231300426
44111CB00007B/497